West's Paralegal Today

THE LEGAL Team AT WORK

THE ESSENTIALS

West's Paralegal Today

Today THE LEGAL Team AT WORK

THE ESSENTIALS

Roger LeRoy Miller
School of Law
University of Miami

Mary S. Urisko
Madonna University, Michigan
Assistant Professor, Paralegal Program

WEST PUBLISHING

an International Thomson Publishing company I(T)P®

Albany • Bonn • Boston • Cincinnati • Detroit • London • Madrid
Melbourne • Mexico City • Minneapolis/St. Paul • New York • Pacific Grove
Paris • San Francisco • Singapore • Tokyo • Toronto • Washington

NOTICE TO THE READER

Copy Editor: Beverly Peavler
Composition: Parkwood Composition Service
Index: Bob Marsh
Cover Photographs: *Top left:* © Ed Malitsky, Liaison International. *Top right:* © PBJ Pictures, Liaison International. *Lower left:* © Larry Williams, Masterfile. *Lower right:* © J.A. Kraulis, Masterfile.
Credits and Acknowledgments: Photo credits and acknowledgments appear following the index

Delmar Staff

Publisher: Susan Simpfenderfer
Acquisitions Editor: Elizabeth Hannan
Developmental Editor: Rhonda Kreshover

Production Editor: Carolyn Miller
Production Manager: Wendy A. Troeger
Marketing Manager: Katherine M. Slezak

COPYRIGHT © 1995
By West Publishing
an imprint of Delmar Publishers
a division of International Thomson Publishing

The ITP logo is a trademark under license.

Printed in the United States of America

For more information, contact:

Delmar Publishers
3 Columbia Circle, Box 15015
Albany, New York 12212-5015

International Thomson Publishing–Europe
Berkshire House
168-173 High Holborn
London, WC1V7AA
England

Thomas Nelson Australia
102 Dodds Street
South Melbourne, 3205
Victoria, Australia

Nelson Canada
1120 Birchmount Road
Scarborough, Ontario
Canada M1K 5G4

International Thomson Editores
Campos Eliseos 385, Piso 7
Col Polanco
11560 Mexico D F Mexico

International Thomson Publishing GmbH
Königswinterer Strasse 418
53227 Bonn
Germany

International Thomson Publishing–Asia
221 Henderson Road
#05-10 Henderson Building
Singapore 0315

International Thomson Publishing–Japan
Hirakawacho Kyowa Building, 3F
2-2-1 Hirakawacho
Chiyoda-ku, Tokyo 102 Japan

2 3 4 5 6 7 8 9 10   XXX   03   02   01   00   99   98   97

Library of Congress Cataloging-in-Publication Data
Miller, Roger LeRoy.
    West's paralegal today: the essentials—the legal team at work /
Roger LeRoy Miller, Mary S. Urisko.
        p.   cm.
    Includes index.
ISBN   0–314–04595–3 (soft : acid-free paper)
    1. Legal assistants—United States.   I. Urisko, Mary S. II. Title.
KF320.L4M55 1995
340' .023'73—dc20
                                                    94–37656
                                                      CIP

DEDICATION

To Adi Erber,
who will forever be in front
of me on Christmas Ridge.
From your lifelong student,
RLM

To my mother,
for convincing me that I should write a textbook
and who, along with my father,
gave me the support that I needed to complete it.
MSU

The West Paralegal Series

Your options keep growing with West Publishing.

Each year our list continues to offer you more options for every course, new or existing, and on-the-job reference materials. We now have over 140 titles from which to choose.

We are pleased to offer books in the following subject areas:

Administrative Law	Family Law
Alternative Dispute Resolution	Federal Taxation
Bankruptcy	Intellectual Property
Business Organizations/Corporations	Introduction to Law
Civil Litigation and Procedure	Introduction to Paralegalism
CLA Exam Preparation	Law Office Management
Client Accounting	Law Office Procedures
Computer in the Law Office	Legal Research, Writing, and Analysis
Constitutional Law	Legal Terminology
Contract Law	Paralegal Employment
Criminal Law and Procedure	Real Estate Law
Document Preparation	Reference Materials
Environmental Law	Torts and Personal Injury Law
Ethics	Will, Trusts, and Estate Administration

You will find unparalleled, practical teaching support.

Each text is enhanced by instructor and student supplements to ensure the best learning experience possible to prepare for this field. We also offer custom publishing and other benefits such as West's Student Achievement Award. In addition, our sales representatives are ready to provide you with needed and dependable service.

We want to hear from you.

The most important factor in improving the quality of our paralegal texts and teaching packages is active feedback from educators in the field. If you have a question, concern, or observation about any of our materials or you have written a proposal or manuscript, we want to hear from you. Please do not hesitate to contact your local representative or write us at the following address:

West Paralegal Series, 3 Columbia Circle, P.O. Box 15015, Albany, NY 12212-5015.

For additional information point your browser to
http://www.westpub.com/Educate and **http://www.delmar.com**

West Publishing — *Your Paralegal Publisher*
an imprint of Delmar Publishers

an International Thomson Publishing company I T P

CONTENTS IN BRIEF

CONTENTS

CHAPTER 2
Careers in the Legal Community   29

CHAPTER 3
Regulation and Ethical Responsibilities 59

CHAPTER 4
Working in a Law Office   99

CHAPTER 5
The American Legal System   135

CHAPTER 6
The Civil Litigation Process   169

CHAPTER 7
Conducting Interviews and Investigations   215

DEVELOPING PARALEGAL SKILLS:
**Accessing Government
Information   244**

TODAY'S PROFESSIONAL
PARALEGAL:
Locating a Witness   249

CHAPTER 8
Computers and the Legal Profession   255

ETHICAL CONCERN:
Accuracy in Data Entry   256

THE LEGAL TEAM AT WORK:
**Communications Systems and
Teamwork   261**

CHAPTER 9
Legal Research, Analysis, and Writing   293

FEATURED GUEST:
E. J. Yera—Ten Tips for Effective Legal Research   302

DEVELOPING PARALEGAL SKILLS:
Understanding Case Citations   308

ETHICAL CONCERN:
Citing Sources   309

DEVELOPING PARALEGAL SKILLS:
Researching the U.S.C.A.   316

PARALEGAL PROFILE:
Diane Soroko   319

ETHICAL CONCERN:
The Importance of Finding Current Law   322

ETHICAL CONCERN:
"Confidential" Correspondence   323

DEVELOPING PARALEGAL SKILLS:
Writing to Clients   325

TODAY'S PROFESSIONAL PARALEGAL:
Mapping Out a Research Strategy   332

PREFACE

One of the fastest-growing occupations in America today is that of the paralegal, or legal assistant. It seems fitting, then, that you and your students should have a new textbook that reflects the excitement surrounding paralegal studies today. *West's Paralegal Today: The Essentials*, we believe, imparts this excitement to your students. They will find paralegal studies accessible and interesting. This book is modern, colorful, and visually attractive, which encourages learning. We are certain that you and your students will find this text extremely effective.

West's Paralegal Today makes the paralegal field come alive for the student. We use real-world examples, present numerous boxed-in features, and support the text with the most extensive supplements package ever offered for an introductory paralegal textbook. We have even developed a special series of teaching videos that show paralegals dealing with on-the-job situations.

West Publishing Company has been providing authoritative materials to the entire legal field for over 120 years. *West's Paralegal Today* draws on the expertise of a company that has had a long history of encouraging excellence in legal education.

All of the basic areas of paralegal studies are covered in *West's Paralegal Today*, including careers, ethics and regulation, law-office procedures, civil litigation, legal interviewing and investigation, the use of computers in legal work, and legal research and writing. In addition, there are a number of key features, which we describe below.

THE MOST MODERN AND UP-TO-DATE TEXT AVAILABLE

We have attempted to make sure that *West's Paralegal Today* is the most modern and up-to-date text available in today's marketplace. Specifically, your students will find the latest information, forms, documents, charts, and diagrams relating to currently required legal procedures.

For example, in the chapter on civil litigation, your students will read about the new requirements concerning service of process and discovery in federal court cases under the 1993 revision of the Federal Rules of Civil Procedure. We include illustrations of the new federal forms for waiver of service as well. Additionally, all information with respect to ethics and regulation reflects the most current laws, ethical guidelines, ethical opinions, and court rulings concerning this important aspect of paralegal practice.

A PRACTICAL, REALISTIC APPROACH

There sometimes exists an enormous gulf between classroom learning and on-the-job realities. We have tried to bridge this gulf in *West's Paralegal Today* by offering a text that is full of practical advice and "hands-on" activities. Exercises at the end of each chapter provide opportunities for your students to apply the concepts and skills discussed in the chapter. Many of the book's other key features, which you will read about below, were designed specifically to give your students a glimpse of the types of situations and demands that they may encounter on the job as professional paralegals. A special appendix at the end of the text (Appendix A) contains practical advice and tips for how to learn legal concepts and procedures, advice and tips that your students can also apply later, on the job.

West's Paralegal Today also realistically portrays paralegal working environments and on-the-job challenges. Ethical dimensions of the practice of law frame paralegals' work experiences to a significant extent. Because of this, we have made a special effort to show how seemingly abstract ethical rules affect the day-to-day tasks performed by attorneys and paralegals in the legal workplace.

KEY FEATURES

Every chapter in this text has the following special features, which are set apart and used both to instruct and to pique the interest of your paralegal students.

Developing Paralegal Skills

These boxed-in features present hypothetical examples of paralegals at work to help your students develop crucial paralegal skills. Some examples are the following:

- Conducting a Title Examination (Chapter 2).
- Erecting an Ethical Wall (Chapter 3).
- Federal Court Rules—Creating a Complaint Checklist (Chapter 6).
- The Tape-recorded Interview (Chapter 7).

Ethical Concerns

Every chapter presents, in the page margins, three or more *Ethical Concerns*. These features typically take a student into a hypothetical situation that clearly presents an ethical problem. When possible, students are told what they should and should not do in particular situations being discussed. Some examples are the following:

- Saying "If I were you . . . " and the UPL (Chapter 3).
- Communicating with Jurors (Chapter 6).
- Confidentiality and Interviews (Chapter 7).
- The Importance of Finding Current Law (Chapter 9).

The Legal Team at Work

These features stress the growing importance of the team approach to legal representation today. They illustrate how attorneys, paralegals, and other staff members work as a team to serve most effectively the needs of clients. Some examples are the following:

- Paralegal Education and the Concept of Teamwork (Chapter 1).
- Holding the Client's Many Hands (Chapter 4).
- In the Courtroom (Chapter 6).
- Humanizing Legal Practice (Chapter 7).

Featured-guest Articles

Each chapter has a contributed article written by an educator or an expert in the field. These articles offer your students practical tips for some aspect of paralegal work relating to the topic covered in the chapter. Some examples are the following:

- "Paralegal Career Planning and Development," by Denise Templeton, president and chief executive officer of Templeton & Associates, a legal-support services firm, and one of the founders of the Minnesota Association of Legal Assistants, the American Association for Paralegal Education, and the National Federation of Paralegal Associations (Chapter 2).
- "Ten Tips on Ethics and the Paralegal," by Michael A. Pener, instructor at Johnson County Community College, Overland Park, Kansas (Chapter 3).
- "Ten Tips for Drafting Interrogatories," by James W. H. McCord, director of paralegal programs at Eastern Kentucky University, Richmond, Kentucky (Chapter 6).
- "Keeping Current on Computer Technology," by Jan Richmond, instructor at St. Louis Community College, St. Louis, Missouri (Chapter 8).

Paralegal Profiles

Every chapter has a profile of a paralegal who is currently working in a specific area of law. These profiles open with a short biography of the paralegal and then present the paralegal's own answers to questions asked by the interviewer. The paralegal tells of his or her greatest challenges on the job, gives suggestions on what he or she thinks students should concentrate on when studying to become a paralegal, and offers tips for being a successful paralegal in his or her line of work. This feature gives your students insights into various legal specialties and the diversity of paralegal working environments.

Today's Professional Paralegal

Near the end of every chapter we have included a feature entitled *Today's Professional Paralegal*. This important feature exposes your students to situations that they are likely to encounter on the job and offers guidance on how certain types of problems can be resolved. Some examples are the following:

- Managing Conflict (Chapter 4).
- Arbitrating Commercial Contracts (Chapter 5).
- Drafting *Voir Dire* Questions Like a Pro (Chapter 6).
- Mapping Out a Research Strategy (Chapter 9).

OTHER SPECIAL PEDAGOGICAL FEATURES

We have included in *West's Paralegal Today* a number of additional pedagogical features, including those discussed below.

Chapter Objectives

Every chapter opens with five or six chapter objectives. Your students will know immediately what is expected of them as they read each chapter.

Chapter Outlines

In every chapter, just following the *Chapter Objectives*, a *Chapter Outline* lists both the first-level and second-level headings within the chapter. These outlines allow you and your students to tell at a glance what topics are covered in the chapters.

Vocabulary and Margin Definitions

Legal terminology is often a major challenge to beginning paralegal students. We have used an important pedagogical device—margin definitions—to help your students understand legal terms. Whenever an important term is introduced, it is done so in boldface type and defined. In addition, the term is listed and defined in the margin of the page, alongside the paragraph in which the boldfaced term appears.

At the end of each chapter, all terms that have been boldfaced within the chapter are listed in alphabetical order in a section called *Key Terms and Concepts*. The page on which the term is defined is given after each term. Your students can briefly examine this list to make sure that they understand all of the important terms introduced in the chapter. If they do not understand a term completely, they can immediately refer to the page number given and review the term.

All boldfaced terms are again listed and defined in the *Glossary* at the end of the text. Spanish equivalents to many important legal terms in English are given in Appendix I.

Exhibits and Forms

When appropriate, we present exhibits illustrating important forms or concepts relating to paralegal work. Many exhibits are filled in with hypothetical data. Approximately seventy exhibits and forms are included in *West's Paralegal Today*. They include those listed below:

- A Sample Retainer Agreement (Chapter 4).
- A Sample Complaint (Chapter 6).
- An Investigation Plan (Chapter 7).
- A Sample Court Case (a special *fold-out exhibit* in Chapter 9).

CHAPTER-ENDING MATERIALS FOR REVIEW AND STUDY

Every chapter contains numerous chapter-ending pedagogical materials. These materials are designed to provide a wide variety of assignments for your students. The chapter-ending pedagogy begins with the *Key Terms and Concepts*, which we have already mentioned. Next are the following materials.

Chapter Summary

Every chapter ends with a *Chapter Summary*—a series of numbered paragraphs that summarize the major points made in the chapter. These summaries can be used by students to review and test their knowledge of the topics covered in the chapter.

Questions for Review

In every chapter, following the *Chapter Summary*, are ten relatively straightforward questions for review. These questions are designed to test the student's knowledge of the basic concepts discussed in the chapter.

Ethical Questions

Because of the importance of ethical issues in paralegal training, we have also included at the end of each chapter two to four ethical questions. Each question presents a hypothetical situation, which is followed by one or two questions about what the paralegal should do to solve the dilemma.

Practice Questions and Assignments

The "hands-on" approach to learning paralegal skills is emphasized in the practice questions and assignments. There are two to four of these questions and assignments at the end of each chapter. A particular situation is presented, and the student is asked to actually carry out an assignment.

APPENDICES

To make this text a reference source for your students, we have included the appendices listed below:

A   Mastering *West's Paralegal Today:* How to Study Legal Concepts and Procedures.
B   The NALA Code of Ethics and Professional Responsibility.
C   The NALA Model Standards and Guidelines for the Utilization of Legal Assistants.
D   The NFPA Model Code of Ethics and Professional Responsibility.
E   The ABA Model Standards and Guidelines for the Utilization of Legal Assistants.
F   Paralegal Associations.

G   Information on the NALA's Certified Legal Assistant (CLA) and Certified Legal Assistant Specialist (CLAS) Examinations.
H   The Constitution of the United States.
I   Spanish Equivalents for Important Legal Terms in English.

SUPPLEMENTAL TEACHING/LEARNING MATERIALS

West's Paralegal Today is accompanied by what is arguably the largest number of teaching and learning supplements available for any text of its kind. We understand that instructors face a difficult task in finding the time necessary to teach the materials that they wish to cover during each term. In conjunction with a number of our colleagues, we have developed supplementary teaching materials that we believe are the best available today. Each component of the supplements package is described below.

Instructor's Manual

Written by text co-author Mary Urisko, the *Instructor's Manual* includes the following:

- Sample course syllabi.
- Chapter/lecture outlines.
- Teaching suggestions.
- Lists of supplemental materials.
- Answers to text exercises and questions.
- Suggested teaching uses for videos.
- Transparency masters.
- Handouts.

Computerized Instructor's Manual

For those instructors who wish to modify the *Instructor's Manual* by adding their own notes or who wish to print out some of the class-enrichment materials, we provide a fully computerized version of the *Instructor's Manual*. You may order the manual in any popular format.

Study Guide

Prepared by Kathleen Reed and Bradene Moore of the University of Toledo, the *Study Guide* provides the following:

- Chapter objectives are presented in a checklist form so that students can review systematically the areas they have studied and determine which areas need more attention.
- Chapter outlines provide succinct, easy-to-read summaries of the chapters and help students review the material. Study suggestions are included within the outlines, including tips on how to remember key information.
- Review questions in true-false, fill-in-the-blank, and multiple-choice formats provide students with an extensive review of the terminology and concepts presented in each chapter of the text. There are between thirty and fifty review questions for each chapter.

- Additional practice questions, questions for critical analysis, and ethical questions reinforce the concepts presented in the chapters.

Three-ring Binder

This binder holds all of the printed supplements that accompany the text.

Test Bank

Text co-author Mary Urisko has developed an extensive test bank that contains approximately fifty questions per chapter in multiple-choice and essay formats.

Computerized Test Bank

The test bank is available on the latest version of WESTEST, a highly acclaimed computerized testing system. WESTEST is offered for IBM PCs and compatible microcomputers or the Macintosh family of microcomputers. WESTEST allows instructors to do the following:

- Add or edit questions, instructions, and answers.
- Select questions by previewing the question on the screen.
- Let the system select questions randomly.
- Select questions by question number.
- View summaries of the test or test-bank chapters.
- Set up the page layout for exams.
- Print exams in a variety of formats.

Transparency Acetates

Transparency acetates covering many important exhibits are available free to adopters.

State-specific Supplements

State-specific supplements are available for California, Florida, New York, and Texas. These supplements are keyed to each chapter in the text and point out state-specific information when it differs from the text's discussion. For example, Chapter 7 of the supplement provides a detailed description of the state court system.

West's Law Finder

West's Law Finder is a brief (seventy-seven-page) pamphlet that describes various legal-research sources and how they can be used. Classroom quantities are available.

Sample Pages, Third Edition

This 225-page, soft-cover pamphlet introduces all of West's legal-research materials. The accompanying *Instructor's Manual* gives ideas for effectively using the material in the classroom. Classroom quantities are available.

Citation-at-a-Glance

This handy reference card provides a quick, portable reference to the basic rules of citation for the most commonly cited legal sources, including judicial opinions, statutes, and secondary sources, such as legal encyclopedias and legal periodicals. *Citation-at-a-Glance* uses the rules set forth in *A Uniform System of Citation*, Fifteenth Edition (1991). A free copy of this valuable supplement is included with every student text.

Guide to *Shepard's Citations*

How to Shepardize: Your Guide to Complete Legal Research through Shepard's Citations—1993 WESTLAW Edition is a sixty-four-page pamphlet that helps students understand the research technique of Shepardizing case citations. The pamphlet is available in classroom quantities (one copy for each student who purchases a new text).

Strategies for Paralegal Educators

Strategies and Tips for Paralegal Educators, a pamphlet by Anita Tebbe of Johnson County Community College, provides teaching strategies specifically designed for paralegal educators. It concentrates on how to teach and is organized in three parts: the WHO of paralegal education—students and teachers; the WHAT of paralegal education—goals and objectives; and the HOW of paralegal education—methods of instruction, methods of evaluation, and other aspects of teaching. A copy of this pamphlet is available to each adopter. Quantities for distribution to their adjunct instructors are available for purchase at a minimal price. A coupon in the pamphlet provides ordering information.

Handbook of Selected Court Cases

A booklet entitled *Handbook of Selected Court Cases Relating to Paralegal Issues* presents excerpts from twenty court opinions relating to paralegal issues, such as the unauthorized practice of law, paralegal compensation, and conflict of interest. The cases have been pulled from court decisions reported by West Publishing Company's WESTLAW Division. Each case excerpt is preceded by a full citation to the case and an introduction, in our own words, to the paralegal issue being addressed by the court and the court's decision on the issue. The ninety-six-page booklet is available for students on the instructor's request.

Data Disk

Forms needed to complete selected end-of-chapter practice questions and projects are provided on a data disk. Exercises that can be completed using the data disk are marked in the text with the following logo:

WESTLAW

West's on-line computerized legal-research system offers students "hands-on" experience with a system commonly used in law offices. Qualified adopters can receive ten free hours of WESTLAW. WESTLAW can be accessed with Macintosh and IBM PCs and compatibles. A modem is required.

WESTMATE Tutorial

This interactive tutorial guides students through the process of accessing legal resources on WESTLAW by using WESTMATE, the special software that West has created for that purpose. There are two versions of the tutorial, one for DOS and one for Windows.

LEGAL CLERK® Software

The LEGAL CLERK Research Software System simulates computerized legal-research programs commonly used in the law office. This interactive software package lets users search and review actual court decisions in three areas: Contracts; UCC/Article 2—Sales; and Legal Environment. LEGAL CLERK runs on IBM PCs and compatibles and comes with a free annual site license, plus an instructor's resource manual and a student user's guide that can be purchased by students.

Video Library

West is proud to present an extensive video library for use in the classroom. This library includes the following videotapes:

- **The Making of a Case**. This videotape, which is narrated by Richard Dysart, star of "L.A. Law," introduces the student to the meaning and importance of case law. It explains how cases are published and, in the process, provides an introduction to significant aspects of our legal system.
- **West's Legal Research Videos**. These videos teach the basis and rationale for legal research. The videos cover the three types of legal research tools—Primary Tools, Secondary Tools, and Finding Tools—as well as law reporters, digests, computer assistance, statutes, special searches, and CD-ROM libraries.
- **I Never Said I Was a Lawyer**. This videotape, which was produced by the Colorado Bar Association Committee on Legal Assistants, uses a variety of scenarios to inspire discussion and give students experience dealing with ethical dilemmas.
- **Drama of the Law II: Paralegal Issues**. This video series of five separate dramatizations is intended to stimulate classroom discussion about various issues and problems faced by paralegals on the job today. An *Instructor's Manual* is available.
- **Arguments to the United States Supreme Court**. In this video, accomplished lawyers, professors, and judges play various roles as the case *Federal Trade Commission v. The American United Tobacco Company* is argued before a mock United States Supreme Court. The arguments center on the question: Should commercial speech be protected as free speech? One of the

mock United States Supreme Court justices is Stephen G. Breyer, who has since been appointed to the Supreme Court.

- **Business Litigation**. This videotape, which was produced by the American Bar Association, is designed to show the various parts of a trial. Various segments have been taken from a mock trial to illustrate the actions that take place during a trial. The case involves a lost shipment of computer parts. The parties in this case are business firms. The plaintiff, BMI, is suing the defendant, Minicom, for breach of contract.
- **Trial Techniques: A Products Liability Case**. This video, which was produced by the American Bar Association, is designed to show the types of arguments used by plaintiffs and defendants in product-liability lawsuits. Various segments have been taken from a mock trial to illustrate these arguments. The specific case involves Mr. Lockette (the plaintiff) who is suing the World-Wide Motorcycle Company (the defendant) for injuries he sustained in a motorcycle accident. The plaintiff claims that the defendant defectively manufactured the motorcycle by failing to install a crash bar on the motorcycle as part of its standard equipment.
- **Selected Role-playing Exercises**. This video shows individuals acting out a variety of role-playing exercises involving paralegal, attorney, and client roles, as well as others.

ACKNOWLEDGMENTS

Numerous careful and conscientious individuals have helped us in this undertaking. We particularly wish to thank the paralegal educators listed below. In their reviews of the manuscript for *West's Paralegal Today,* these professionals offered us penetrating criticisms, comments, and suggestions for improving the text. While we haven't been able to follow each request, each of the reviewers will see that many of his or her suggestions have been taken to heart.

Laura Barnard
Lakeland Community College, Ohio

Jeptha Clemens
Northwest Mississippi Community College

Donna Hamblin Donathan
Marshall University Community College, Ohio

Susan Howery
Davenport College, Michigan

Wendy Edson
Hilbert College, New York

Pamela Faller
College of the Sequoias, California

Gary Glascom
Cedar Crest College, Pennsylvania

Dolores Grissom
Samford Community College, Alabama

Jean A. Hellman
Loyola University, Chicago

Marlene L. Hoover
El Camino College, California

Jane Kaplan
New York City Technical College, New York

Jennifer Allen Labosky
Davidson County Community College, North Carolina

Dora J. Lew
California State University, Hayward

Mary Hatfield Lowe
Westark Community College, Arizona

Gerald A. Loy
Broome Community College, New York

Linda Mort
Kellogg Community College, Michigan

H. Margaret Nickerson
William Woods College, Missouri

Martha Nielsen
University of California, San Diego

Elizabeth L. Nobis
Lansing Community College, Michigan

Joy D. O'Donnell
Pima Community College, Arizona

Francis D. Polk
Ocean County College, New Jersey

Ruth-Ellen Post
Rivier College, New Hampshire

Elizabeth Raulerson
Indian River Community College, Florida

Kathleen Mercer Reed
University of Toledo, Ohio

Lynn Retzak
Lakeshore Technical Institute, Wisconsin

Evelyn L. Riyhani
University of California, Irvine

Melanie A. P. Rowand
California State University, Hayward

Vitonio F. San Juan
University of La Verne, California

Susan F. Schulz
Southern Career Institute, Florida

A special thanks is due to the following paralegal educators, our featured guests in *West's Paralegal Today,* for enhancing the quality of our book with their tips and illuminating insights into paralegal practice:

Andrea Nager Chasen
Private Law Practice

Wendy B. Edson
Hilbert College, New York

James W. H. McCord
Eastern Kentucky University, Kentucky

Michael A. Pener
Johnson County Community College, Kansas

Kathleen Mercer Reed
University of Toledo's Community and Technical College, Ohio

Jan Richmond
St. Louis Community College, Missouri

Melanie A. P. Rowand
California State University, Hayward

Denise Templeton
President and chief executive officer of Templeton & Associates

E. J. Yera
Holmes Regional Medical Center, Florida

Additionally, we would like to extend our gratitude to those on-the-job paralegals who agreed to appear in the *Paralegal Profiles* of *West's Paralegal Today.*

We are also indebted to the following individuals, whose efforts contributed significantly to the quality of *West's Paralegal Today:* Roger Meiners, Jefferson Weaver, Darin Zenov, and Laura Valade, for their research assistance; Jennifer Sparks, for her many helpful comments and criticisms; and Elizabeth Cameron, for her numerous insights into the daily workings of the law office and the paralegal's role in legal work, as well as samples of forms used in the litigation and settlement processes. We also wish to thank Lavina Leed Miller and Barbara Curtiss for their editorial and proofreading assistance, and Marie-Christine Louiseau and Elliot Simon for their proofreading assistance. We are also grateful to Suzanne Jasin for her valuable assistance on this project, as well as to Beverly Peavler, whose expert copy-editing skills will not go unnoticed. Additionally, we extend our thanks to Richard F. X. Urisko for his guidance in regard to federal court litigation and the 1993 amendments to the Federal Rules of Civil Procedure, Jennifer Wanty Coté for her endless knowledge of the paralegal field and paralegal ethics, and Barbara Habermas for her editorial assistance.

In preparing *West's Paralegal Today*, we were the beneficiaries of the expertise brought to the project by an incredibly skilled and dedicated editorial, production, and printing and manufacturing team at West Publishing Company. Our editor, Elizabeth Hannan, successfully guided the project through each phase and put together a supplements package that is without parallel in the teaching and learning of paralegal skills. Patty Bryant, the developmental editor, was also incredibly helpful in putting together the *West's Paralegal Today* teaching/learning package. Additionally, we sincerely appreciate the efforts of our project editor, Bill Stryker, who designed what we feel is the most visually attractive paralegal text on the market, and Beth Kennedy, the production supervisor on the project. Finally, we particularly wish to thank our editor in chief, Clyde Perlee, Jr., whose expert supervision and guidance during each stage of the project kept us all on track.

We know that we are not perfect. If you or your students have suggestions on how we can improve this book, write to us. That way, we can make *West's Paralegal Today: The Essentials* an even better book in the future. We promise to answer every single letter that we receive.

Roger LeRoy Miller
Mary S. Urisko

West's Paralegal Today

THE LEGAL Team AT WORK

THE Essentials

TODAY'S PROFESSIONAL PARALEGAL

Chapter Objectives

After completing this chapter, you will know:

- What a paralegal is and does.
- How and why the paralegal profession developed.
- The professional organizations that exist for paralegals and the benefits of membership in them.
- The education and training available to paralegals.
- The skills that are useful for a paralegal to have.
- Some important personal attributes of the professional paralegal.

Chapter Outline

Introduction

The paralegal profession was first recognized as a profession in 1968 by the **American Bar Association (ABA),** a voluntary national association of attorneys (lawyers). In that year, the ABA formed the Special Committee on Lay Assistants for Lawyers. During the early 1970s, the committee met to study and discuss how lawyers could most effectively use nonlawyers in their practices. The paralegal profession continued to grow throughout the 1970s and 1980s, and it is now one of the fastest-growing occupations in the United States. You will read more about paralegal employment statistics, including paralegal salaries, in Chapter 2.

For the individual who seeks interesting and challenging work, the paralegal profession offers many opportunities. Paralegals deal with real people and real problems. Even when the paralegal is in a library doing legal research, the real world is not too far away. When locating and analyzing court cases, the paralegal will find that each case tells a story of its own, involving specific people and circumstances. Through their legal work, paralegals learn much about human nature, the law, and how the law applies to real-life problems.

Some of the most frequently asked questions concerning the paralegal profession are the following: What is a paralegal? What is the difference between a paralegal and a legal assistant? What do paralegals do? You will learn the answers to these questions in this chapter. You will also read about the evolution of the paralegal profession, paralegal education, and the kinds of skills and personal qualities that will help you become a successful paralegal.

What Is a Paralegal?

American Bar Association (ABA)
A voluntary national association of attorneys. The ABA plays an active role in developing educational and ethical standards for attorneys and in pursuing improvements in the administration of justice.

Generally, a **paralegal,** or a **legal assistant,** is a person sufficiently trained in law and legal procedures to assist attorneys in the delivery of legal services to the public. More specifically, the ABA's Standing Committee on Ethics and Responsibility defines a *legal assistant* as follows:

Paralegal (or Legal Assistant)
A person sufficiently trained or experienced in the law and legal procedures to assist, under an attorney's supervision, in the performance of substantive legal work that would otherwise be performed by an attorney. Often referred to as a legal assistant.

> The terms legal assistant and paralegal are used interchangeably, which means persons who, although not members of the legal profession, are qualified through education, training, or work experience, who are employed or retained by a lawyer, law office, governmental agency, or other entity in a capacity or function which involves the performance, under the direction and supervision of an attorney, of specifically delegated substantive legal work, which work, for the most part, requires a sufficient knowledge of legal concepts such that, absent that legal assistant, the attorney would perform the task.[1]

---

1. The ABA's definition is very similar to the definitions created by two of the largest national paralegal associations, the National Association of Legal Assistants (NALA) and the National Federation of Paralegal Associations (NFPA). These two organizations will be discussed shortly.

Several elements in the ABA's definition merit attention. First, the ABA states that the terms *legal assistant* and *paralegal* are used interchangeably. In this book, we follow this practice and use the terms synonymously.

Second, the ABA's definition states that a legal assistant may be qualified through "education, training, or work experience." The emphasis is on the ability to perform specified tasks, regardless of whether that ability was acquired through education or on-the-job experience. The definition acknowledges the fact that persons can acquire, through on-the-job training and experience, the knowledge and skills necessary to perform paralegal tasks. In fact, the first paralegals—and the founders of many paralegal associations—were highly qualified and skilled legal secretaries.

Third, the phrase "under the direction and supervision of an attorney" is a key element in the definition of a legal assistant. Legal assistants, or paralegals, are not attorneys; they are attorneys' assistants. Although paralegals perform work that traditionally has been performed only by attorneys, they do so under attorneys' supervision—that is, the ultimate responsibility for paralegal work falls on attorneys. Moreover, there are certain types of legal work that paralegals by law may not undertake. For example, a paralegal may not give legal advice, set legal fees, or (with rare exceptions) represent a client in court. (You will read more about what tasks paralegals may and may not perform in Chapter 3.)

Finally, the definition emphasizes that attorneys delegate "substantive legal work" to paralegals, legal work that, "absent the legal assistant," attorneys themselves would handle. This is an important element in the definition of a paralegal because it indicates that although paralegals are not attorneys, they do the kinds of work traditionally undertaken only by attorneys.

WHAT DO PARALEGALS DO?

Throughout this book, you will read about the different ways in which paralegals assist attorneys, and it would be impossible to list them all in this brief space. The following list is thus just a sampling of some of the types of tasks that paralegals typically perform.

• *Draft legal documents*—such as legal correspondence, documents to be filed with the courts, and interoffice memoranda.
• *Calendar and track important deadlines*—such as the dates when certain documents must be filed with the court.
• *Assist attorneys in preparing for trial*—by preparing exhibits, documents, and trial notebooks that the attorney will need to have on hand at trial. Some paralegals also assist attorneys during trials.
• *Interview clients and witnesses*—to gather relevant facts and information about a lawsuit, for example.
• *Conduct legal investigations*—to gather facts about a case by interviewing clients and witnesses and obtaining relevant records (such as medical records or the police report of an accident).
• *Organize and maintain client files*—or (as is often the situation) supervise the organization and maintenance of client files.
• *Conduct legal research*—to find, analyze, and summarize court decisions, statutes, or regulations applicable to a client's case.

ETHICAL CONCERN

Paralegal Expertise and Legal Advice

Paralegals often become very knowledgeable in a specific area of the law. If you specialize in environmental law, for example, you will become very knowledgeable about environmental claims. In working with a client on a matter involving an environmental agency, you might therefore be tempted to advise the client on which type of action would be most favorable to the client. Never do so. As will be discussed in detail in Chapter 3, only attorneys may give legal advice, and paralegals who give legal advice risk penalties for the unauthorized practice of law. Whatever legal advice is given to the client must come either directly from the attorney or, if from you, must reflect exactly (or nearly exactly) what the attorney said with no embellishment on your part. After consulting with your supervising attorney, for example, you can say to the client that Mr. X (the attorney) "advises that you do all that you can to settle the claim as soon as possible."

LAW CLERK

In the context of law-office work, a law student who works as an apprentice, during the summer or part-time during the school year, with an attorney or law firm to gain practical legal experience.

ASSOCIATE ATTORNEY

An attorney who is hired by a law firm as an employee and who has no ownership rights in the firm.

The specific kinds of tasks that paralegals perform vary, of course, from office to office. If you work in a one-attorney office, for example, you will probably not have much secretarial or clerical assistance. In other words, your job might overlap to some extent with that of the legal secretary. Your tasks might range from conducting sophisticated legal research and investigations to photocopying documents to answering the telephone while the secretary is out to lunch.

If you work in a larger law firm, you will have more support staff (secretaries, file clerks, and others) to whom you can delegate work. Your work might also be more specialized. Instead of working on a number of cases relating to different areas of the law, you might concentrate solely on certain types of cases. If you work in a law firm's real-estate department, for example, you will deal only with legal matters relating to that area of the law. In the next chapter, you will read about the variety of environments in which paralegals work.

ORIGINS OF THE PARALEGAL PROFESSION

The paralegal profession initially developed in response to the need for a legal professional to fill a position somewhere between that of an attorney and that of a legal secretary. To some extent, law clerks fill this need. A **law clerk** is a law student who gains practical experience in the law by working for a law firm. Law clerks are often hired on a temporary basis (for the summer, for example, when they are not attending school, or to assist on a specific project).[2]

The problem faced by law firms is that if they need permanent, full-time legal assistance, hiring a law student on a temporary or part-time basis will not fill this need. Another option is, of course, to hire a law-school graduate as an **associate attorney** (a hired attorney who, unlike a partner in a partnership, has no ownership rights in a firm) on a full-time basis, but this might be too great an expense for the firm's budget to bear.

Competent and experienced legal secretaries began to fill the need faced by many law firms to have full-time assistance at a lower cost. The first paralegals were legal secretaries who had become, through on-the-job experience, extremely competent and skilled in legal procedures. They learned how to do legal research and investigation, draft documents to be filed with the court, and perform other tasks that today's paralegals are trained to undertake. Eventually, legal assistants succeeded in defining themselves as a distinct professional group within the field of law. Paralegal professional associations and paralegal education programs further advanced the professional status of paralegals. Today, individuals who want to become legal assistants can enter a paralegal program and receive specialized training.

---

2. The term *law clerk* is also used to designate an attorney who does legal research and writing for a judge or a justice.

PARALEGAL ASSOCIATIONS AND PROFESSIONAL GROWTH

One feature that distinguishes a profession from other occupations is that the members of a profession form professional associations for the following purposes:

• To establish a forum (place) in which issues relating to their profession can be discussed, experiences can be shared, and communication networks can be established.
• To establish guidelines to regulate their activities, such as ethical codes of conduct.
• To determine the level of skills or educational preparation necessary to the type of work performed by the members of the profession.
• To establish or sponsor educational programs to train potential professional practitioners or provide continuing education for those members who are already practicing their profession.

The evolution of the *paralegal profession* is thus directly related to the formation of paralegal associations. The earliest paralegal associations were formed at the state and local levels. The formation of national paralegal associations in the mid-1970s significantly furthered the professional interests and goals of paralegals.

State and Local Paralegal Associations

By the early 1970s, there were numerous local paralegal associations. If you look at Appendix F at the end of this book, you will see that today every state has a paralegal association, and several states have many regional or local organizations within their borders. Practicing paralegals typically belong to their local (and/or state) paralegal association, as well as one of the national paralegal associations discussed below. Most **state bar associations**—associations of attorneys at the state level—also allow paralegals to become associate members of their organizations.

National Paralegal Associations

The **National Federation of Paralegal Associations (NFPA)**, which was founded in 1974, was created to represent paralegals at U.S. Senate hearings that were considering the question of whether paralegals should be regulated. NFPA represented the few local paralegal organizations that existed in 1974. As of 1994, its membership consisted of fifty-nine paralegal associations from around the country, reaching over 17,000 legal assistants. The member associations of NFPA are referred to as affiliated associations, or **affiliates,** of NFPA.

The **National Association of Legal Assistants (NALA)** was formed in 1975. Unlike NFPA, NALA has individual members. As of 1994, NALA had 3,751 individual members and 85 affiliated associations, reaching over 15,000 legal assistants nationwide. While both NALA and NFPA encourage the growth of the profession, they differ on the direction that the profession should take, as you will learn in Chapter 3.

STATE BAR ASSOCIATION
An association of attorneys within a state. Membership in the state bar association is mandatory in over two-thirds of the states—that is, before an attorney can practice law in a state, he or she must be admitted to that state's bar association.

NATIONAL FEDERATION OF PARALEGAL ASSOCIATIONS (NFPA)
One of the two largest national paralegal associations in the United States; formed in 1974. NFPA is actively involved in paralegal professional developments.

AFFILIATE
An entity that is connected (affiliated) with another entity. State and local branches of national or regional paralegal associations are often referred to as affiliates.

NATIONAL ASSOCIATION OF LEGAL ASSISTANTS (NALA)
One of the two largest national paralegal associations in the United States; formed in 1975. NALA offers a certification program for paralegals and is actively involved in paralegal professional developments.

Ethics and the Effective Utilization of Paralegals

As you will read in Chapter 3, the ethical codes and guidelines regulating attorneys urge attorneys to use paralegals effectively—because the effective use of paralegals in legal representation benefits the public by providing quality legal services at lower cost. Paralegal ethical codes and guidelines also reflect this commitment. As a paralegal, you will share in this ethical responsibility. What can you do to promote the effective use of paralegal services? One thing you can do is to join a paralegal association and work together with other association members toward this goal. Another thing you can do is to encourage your supervising attorney to delegate substantive work to you. For example, you might volunteer to take on certain tasks so that you can display your competence. Some attorneys do not yet realize how many tasks paralegals can competently perform and how beneficial it is for them (freeing up their time for other work and lowering clients' bills) to delegate substantive work to paralegals.

POSTBACCALAUREATE CERTIFICATE
A postgraduate certificate awarded by a college or university to an individual who, having already completed a bachelor's degree program, successfully completes a paralegal program of study.

As the profession grew, other national professional organizations were formed. Professional Legal Assistants, Inc. (PLA), was chartered in 1985. Other national paralegal professional associations include the Legal Assistant Management Association, the American Paralegal Association, and the National Association for Independent Paralegals. The names and addresses of some of these paralegal associations, as well as state associations, are given in Appendix F.

Benefits of Professional Membership

As a paralegal, you will find that membership in a paralegal association presents numerous benefits. Among other things, membership offers the following kinds of opportunities:

• To meet and network with others in your profession.
• To receive professional publications that keep you up to date on the latest issues in the profession.
• To continue your training and education through seminars, workshops, and other programs.
• To participate in meetings to develop policy relating to current issues affecting the paralegal profession.
• To indicate to potential employers that you are active in professional affiliations—a plus for the paralegal job candidate.

PARALEGAL EDUCATION

No law (as yet) requires paralegals to meet specific educational requirements. The paralegal will find, though, that the job market demands a certain amount of education and training. You will have difficulty finding employment as a paralegal without having completed a paralegal training course or without having obtained a degree in the field. Depending on your educational background and experience, you can spend anywhere from several months to several years obtaining a paralegal certificate or a degree.

Educational Options

Educational options for paralegals include certificate programs and degree programs. These programs are available through colleges and universities, community colleges, business schools, and trade schools.

Certificate Programs.   Many paralegals choose the certificate program. Depending on the student's educational background, certificate programs can take up to eighteen months to complete. A student who already has a bachelor's degree can attend a program offered through a college or university. Normally, this type of program takes one year to complete. The certificate that is awarded to the student who successfully completes this type of program is referred to as a **postbaccalaureate certificate,** or postgraduate certificate.

Another option is to attend a certificate program offered by a private, for-profit business school, trade school, or college. Typically, this type of program requires a high school diploma for admission. The length of time to complete such a program ranges from three to eighteen months. After the program is completed, the student receives a **paralegal certificate.**

Degree Programs.   Degree options include an associate's degree or a bachelor's degree. The **associate's degree** is a two-year degree, which normally is obtained from a two-year community college. The degree requirements are typically split evenly between general education courses (such as English, math, science, history, and social sciences) and law courses. A total of approximately 60 semester hours is required to complete an associate's degree.

A **bachelor's degree** requires the completion of about 120 semester hours. From 50 to 60 of these hours are spent in general education courses similar to those required for the associate's degree. In addition, students take courses in their major area—legal-assistant studies—and often select a minor field. Minors that complement a legal-assistant major include computer-information systems, business administration, communications, and public administration. These minors are helpful because they provide paralegals with useful skills and information relating to computer technology, business firms, and government agencies. Certain minors, particularly minors in environmental studies and computer-information systems, help to boost the legal assistant's marketability in today's job market, which increasingly requires knowledge and skills in these areas. Additionally, paralegals who combine a bachelor's degree in a field such as nursing with a paralegal certificate are highly sought after.

Curriculum—A Procedural Focus

A legal assistant's education includes the study of both substantive law and procedural law. **Substantive law** includes all laws that define, describe, regulate, and create legal rights and obligations. For example, a law prohibiting employment discrimination on the basis of age falls into the category of substantive law. **Procedural law** establishes the methods of enforcing the rights established by substantive law. Questions about what documents need to be filed to begin a lawsuit, when the documents should be filed, which court will hear the case, which witnesses will be called, and so on are all questions of procedural law. In brief, substantive law defines our legal rights and obligations; procedural law specifies what methods, or procedures, must be employed to enforce those rights and obligations.

Although paralegal students study both substantive law and procedural law, the emphasis is on procedural law. Law students, in contrast, focus mostly on substantive law. A law student might, for example, take a semester-long course in bankruptcy law. During that semester, the law student would study closely the substantive law governing bankruptcy—federal bankruptcy laws and court decisions interpreting those laws. A paralegal student might also take a semester-long course in bankruptcy. The paralegal student would study the general rules relating to bankruptcy, but the emphasis would be on bankruptcy forms and procedures. For example, the paralegal would learn

PARALEGAL CERTIFICATE
A certificate awarded to an individual with a high school diploma or its equivalent who has successfully completed a paralegal program of study at a private, for-profit business school or trade school.

ASSOCIATE'S DEGREE
An academic degree signifying the completion of a two-year course of study, normally at a community college.

BACHELOR'S DEGREE
An academic degree signifying the completion of a four-year course of study at a college or university.

SUBSTANTIVE LAW
Law that defines the rights and duties of individuals with respect to each other, as opposed to procedural law, which defines the manner in which these rights and duties may be enforced.

PROCEDURAL LAW
Rules that define the manner in which the rights and duties of individuals may be enforced.

which forms should be used for which types of bankruptcy proceedings, how to draft those forms, when the forms should be submitted to the bankruptcy court, and generally what procedures apply to specific types of bankruptcy actions.

The reason for the difference in the education of attorneys and paralegals has to do with their professional work. Attorneys are taught to analyze and solve legal problems so that they can advise clients on substantive legal matters. Legal assistants, in contrast, are trained in procedures so that they can assist in implementing attorneys' solutions to legal problems.

The ABA's Role in Paralegal Education

The ABA has played an active role in paralegal educational programs since the early 1970s. By 1973, the ABA had drafted and formally adopted a set of educational standards for paralegal training programs. Programs that meet these standards and that are approved by the ABA are usually referred to as **ABA-approved programs.** Today, the ABA approval commission consists of members of the ABA as well as representatives from NALA, NFPA, and the American Association for Paralegal Education, an association formed by paralegal educators and educational institutions. Of the paralegal education programs in existence today (over 650), the ABA has approved nearly 200. Paralegal schools are not required to be ABA-approved. ABA approval is a voluntary process that gives extra credentials to those schools that successfully apply for it.

Certification

Certification involves recognition by a private professional group or a state agency that an individual has met specified standards of proficiency. Note that certification, as used here, is not the same as receiving a paralegal certificate. A paralegal certificate means that the paralegal has successfully completed a specific course of studies. A *certified paralegal,* in contrast, is one who has demonstrated his or her knowledge and competence in the field by taking and passing an examination administered by a private professional group or a state agency.

A certification program for paralegals offered by NALA is the **Certified Legal Assistant (CLA)** Certification Program. Paralegals who wish to become certified by NALA may apply to take the CLA exam. In addition to the CLA exam, NALA offers exams for those who wish to become certified by NALA as specialists in certain areas of practice. To become a **Certified Legal Assistant Specialist (CLAS),** a legal assistant must demonstrate special competence in a particular field. Appendix G offers further information on NALA certification procedures and requirements.

Many states are now considering the development of state-administered or statewide voluntary certification programs, and some states are beginning to implement such programs. In 1994, for example, the Texas Bar Association Board of Legal Specialization established a voluntary certification program that permits paralegals in Texas to become certified as specialists in the following three areas: civil-trial law, personal-injury law, and family law. To

ABA-APPROVED PROGRAM
A legal or paralegal educational program that satisfies the standards for paralegal training set forth by the American Bar Association.

CERTIFICATION
Formal recognition by a private group or state agency that an individual has satisfied the group's standards of proficiency, knowledge, and competence; ordinarily accomplished through the taking of an examination.

CERTIFIED LEGAL ASSISTANT (CLA)
A legal assistant whose legal competency has been certified by the National Association of Legal Assistants (NALA) following an examination that tests the legal assistant's knowledge and skills.

CERTIFIED LEGAL ASSISTANT SPECIALIST (CLAS)
A legal assistant whose competency in a legal specialty has been certified by the National Association of Legal Assistants (NALA) following an examination of the legal assistant's knowledge and skills in the specialty area.

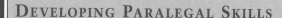

DEVELOPING PARALEGAL SKILLS

Preparing for the CLA Exam

Rita Barron received her postbaccalaureate paralegal certificate over a year ago. She has been working as a legal assistant since graduation. Rita plans to take the Certified Legal Assistant (CLA) exam in four months and has decided to talk to Jill Sanderson, a CLA who works in the same office as Rita, about the exam. Rita wants to ask Jill if she has any suggestions on how Rita could best prepare for it.

Rita arranges to have lunch with Jill the next day. Rita asks Jill how she prepared for the CLA exam. "Well," says Jill, "I formed a study group with several other paralegals who were preparing for the exam. It was great. We divided up the work among ourselves. We met once a week, and each member of the group shared with the other members his or her assignment for that week. For example, I remember that one week, I had to prepare a thorough outline of all of the procedures involved in a real-estate closing. I made copies of the outline for everyone in the group. Our joint efforts paid off: we all passed the exam with flying colors."

FORMING A STUDY GROUP

Inspired by Jill's study-group approach, Rita contacted several former classmates who were also planning to take the exam. They agreed to form a study group and then devised a plan for dividing among themselves the substantive-law subjects, such as bankruptcy law and real-estate law, that they had to cover. Each member was to prepare an outline on one of the subjects for the others. The group would review and discuss the outlines the following week, when they met. They would also ask each other questions and take some practice tests.

Rita brought copies of her outline of bankruptcy law to the next meeting, passed them out to the other members, and received their outlines in return. She was disappointed to see that two of the group's five members, Leslie and Eric, had not put in much time or effort.

EVALUATING THE STUDY GROUP

On her way home, Rita reevaluates the study group. She knows that she is committed to taking and passing the CLA exam, but she feels that not all of the other members of the study group are as serious about it as she is. She decides to talk to Jill again.

When Rita mentions the problem to Jill, Jill says, "You know, I should have warned you about this kind of problem. A study group can be great, but unless everybody knows exactly what they are supposed to do and puts in the effort, it won't work. You need to make sure that assignments are clear. At the end of each meeting, each person should clearly state, in his or her own words, what exactly that person will work on during the week. If you realize that you've got weak study-group members, drop out of the group. Otherwise, you'll end up teaching them more than they teach you. Unless you have a good study group, you might try another alternative: pay the money and take a professional review course. If you don't want to spend the money on a review course, you could try a self-study course, using your own notes or a CLA review book."

THE LEGAL TEAM AT WORK
Paralegal Education and the Concept of Teamwork

Throughout this book, you will encounter such terms and phrases as *teamwork, team effort,* and *team player.* Additionally, in a number of chapters, you will see features, such as this one, that emphasize the teamwork approach to legal representation. Law-office professionals have always worked as a team in the sense that the attorneys and support personnel all worked on behalf of clients. Today's law firms, however, increasingly recognize that effective teamwork means more than simply a joint effort. It also means allocating the workload in such a way that the expertise of the attorney, the paralegal, and others on the team is used *effectively.*

If an attorney delegated only secretarial tasks to his or her paralegal, that paralegal's training and skills would be underutilized. Similarly, if an attorney drafted routine legal documents rather than delegating the work to a paralegal capable of doing that work, the attorney would not be effectively using his or her own time. In the team approach to legal representation, the paralegal assists with the procedural aspects of a case while the attorney concentrates on those tasks that require an extensive knowledge of substantive law (or that can be undertaken legally only by an attorney).

For example, when a client goes to a law firm for advice on whether or how to incorporate a business, the attorney advises the client on the advantages and disadvantages of incorporation in view of the client's particular business situation, lets the client know what the attorney's assistance will cost, and so on. If the client decides to incorporate, the paralegal will assist in drafting the necessary documents, filing the documents with the relevant state office, and carrying out other tasks associated with the incorporation process. The lawyer and the legal assistant thus combine their efforts to function as a legal team.

---

become certified paralegal specialists in these areas, paralegals must meet minimum standards for certification.

In July 1994, the California Alliance of Paralegal Associations (CAPA) and NALA formally agreed to develop and administer a voluntary statewide certification program for paralegals in California. Under the 1995 pilot-tested program, California paralegals may become certified in several specialty areas, including the following: civil litigation, corporate law, real-estate law, probate and estate-planning law, and environmental law. The CAPA will work closely with NALA in implementing the program, and to qualify for the California certification examination, a paralegal must be certified by NALA as a CLA. Other states are also implementing statewide voluntary certification programs. The Louisiana State Paralegal Association, for example, developed a voluntary certification program for paralegals in that state.

PARALEGAL SKILLS

Paralegals need and use a variety of skills on the job. Depending on your personality traits, some skills will be easier than others for you to learn. For example, if you tend to be an organized person, you will have little difficul-

ty in acquiring and applying the organizational skills required of the paralegal. Throughout this book, you will read in detail about the specific skills
that you will need in your work as a paralegal. Here, we describe the general types of skills that paralegal work requires.

Organizational Skills

Being a well-organized person is a plus for a legal assistant. Law offices are
busy places. There are many phone calls to be answered and returned, witnesses to get to court and on the witness stand on time, documents to be
filed, and checklists and procedures to be followed. If you are able to organize files, create procedures and checklists, and keep things running smoothly, you will be doing a great service to the legal team and to clients.

If organization comes naturally to you, you are ahead of the game. If not,
now is the time to learn and practice organizational skills. You will find
plenty of opportunities to do this as a paralegal student—by organizing your
notebooks, devising an efficient tracking system for homework assignments,
creating a study or work schedule and following it, and so on. Other suggestions for organizing your time and work, both as a student and as a paralegal
on the job, are included in Appendix A at the end of this book.

You will also find in any university or public library an abundance of
books that offer guidelines on how to organize efficiently your work, your
use of time, and your life generally.

Analytical Skills

Legal assistants also need analytical skills, especially when engaging in tasks
relating to trials, legal investigations, legal research and writing, and certain
other assignments. Analysis is usually defined as the separation of a whole
into its parts. Legal professionals need to be able to take complex theories
and fact patterns and break them down into smaller, more easily understandable components. As you will read in Chapter 9, an important aspect of
legal research and writing involves analysis. Analysis is used to decipher the
meaning of the law as set forth in the decisions handed down by the courts
and in statutes passed by legislatures.

Analysis also involves, to some extent, the ability to synthesize—or put
together—facts and legal concepts in such a way that they form a single unit,
or "picture." For example, if you are conducting a legal investigation, you
will uncover numerous facts and opinions about a certain event, such as an
automobile accident. You will learn how the client believed the accident
occurred, how any available witnesses described it, and what facts are indicated or implied by medical records or police reports. As a paralegal, you will
want to discern how the facts and opinions you have gathered fit together
into patterns or sequences. Further, you will want to discern how the facts
fit into the legal strategy that your supervising attorney plans to pursue.

Computer Skills

In today's law office, computer skills are essential. At a minimum, you
should have experience with word processing—generating and revising documents using a computer. Although computers have reduced the need for

excellent typing skills, the ability to type rapidly and accurately is still a plus for the legal assistant. If you work for a small law firm, as many entry-level paralegals do, you will probably not have much secretarial or clerical assistance. Even if you work for a larger firm and have such assistance, you will still draft and revise numerous documents yourself.

Advances in computer technology continue to affect dramatically how business firms, including law firms, conduct their operations. Large law firms today are using sophisticated computer equipment and software to handle tasks ranging from document control to client billing procedures. Although smaller law firms are not always so extensively computerized, increasingly they are also investing in computer systems and legal software to reduce the time costs involved in legal work and to compete with larger firms. In Chapter 8, you will read in greater detail about computers and how they are used in the legal profession. Many experienced paralegals say that if they were paralegal students today, they would devote more time to studying computer technology and learning computer skills.

Interpersonal Skills

The ability to communicate and interact effectively with other people is an important asset for the paralegal. Paralegals work closely with their supervising attorneys, and the ability to cultivate a positive working relationship helps to get the work done more efficiently. Paralegals also work with legal secretaries and other support staff in the law office, with attorneys and paralegals from other firms, with court personnel, and with numerous other people. Paralegals frequently interview clients and witnesses. As you will read in Chapter 7, if you can relate well to the person whom you are interviewing, your chances of obtaining useful information from that person are increased.

There may be times when you will have to deal with clients who are experiencing difficulties in their lives, such as divorce or the death of a loved one. These people will need to be handled with sensitivity, tact, understanding, and courtesy. There will also be times when you will have to deal with people in your office who are under a great deal of stress or who for some other reason are demanding and less than courteous to you. You will need to know how to respond to these people in ways that promote positive working relationships. You will read more about these important "people skills" in Chapter 4 and other chapters in this text.

Communication Skills

Good communication skills are critical when working in the legal area. In fact, it is sometimes said that the legal profession is a "communications profession" because effective legal representation depends to a great extent on how well a legal professional can communicate with clients, witnesses, court judges and juries, opposing attorneys, and others. Poor communication can damage a case, destroy a client relationship, and harm the legal professional's reputation. Good communication, in contrast, wins cases, clients, and sometimes promotions.

Communication skills include reading and analytical skills, speaking skills, listening skills, and writing skills. We look briefly at each of these skills here.

Reading Skills.   Reading skills involve more than just being able to decipher the meaning of written letters and words. Reading skills also involve understanding the *meaning* of a sentence, paragraph, section, or page. As a legal professional, you will need to be able to read and understand many different types of written materials, including statutes and court decisions. You will therefore need to become familiar with legal terminology and concepts so that you understand the meaning of these legal writings. You will also need to develop the ability to read documents *carefully* so that you do not miss important distinctions—such as the difference in meaning that can result from the use of "and" instead of "or."

Oral Communication.   Paralegals must also be able to speak well. In addition to using good grammar, legal assistants need to be precise and clear in communicating ideas or facts to others. For example, when you discuss facts learned in an investigation with your supervising attorney, your oral report must communicate exactly what you found, or it could mislead the attorney. A miscommunication in this context could have serious consequences if it led the attorney to take an action detrimental to the client's interests. Oral communication also has a nonverbal dimension—that is, we communicate our thoughts and feelings through gestures, facial expressions, and other "body language" as well as through words. You will read more about both verbal and nonverbal forms of communication in Chapter 4.

Listening Skills.   Good listening skills are extremely important in the context of paralegal work. Paralegals must follow instructions meticulously. To understand the instructions that you receive, you must listen carefully. Asking follow-up questions will help you to clarify anything that you do not understand. Also, repeating the instructions will not only ensure that you understand them but also give the attorney a chance to add anything that he or she may have forgotten to tell you initially. Listening skills are particularly important in the interviewing context. In Chapter 7, you will read in greater detail about different types of listening skills and techniques that will help you conduct effective interviews with clients or witnesses.

Writing Skills.   Finally, it is important for paralegals to have excellent writing skills. Legal assistants draft letters, memoranda, and a variety of legal documents. Letters to clients, witnesses, court clerks, and others must be clear and well organized and must follow the rules of grammar and punctuation. Legal documents must also be free of errors. Lawyers are generally scrupulously attentive to detail in their work, and they expect legal assistants to be equally so. Remember, you represent your supervising attorney when you write. You will learn more about writing skills in Chapter 9.

PERSONAL ATTRIBUTES OF THE PROFESSIONAL PARALEGAL

There are many different attributes that help paralegals succeed in their careers. The paralegal who is responsible, reliable, committed to hard work, objective, ethical, and generally considerate of others will have an easy time meeting the challenges presented by his or her work. These attributes define

DEVELOPING PARALEGAL SKILLS

Working under the Supervision of a Lawyer

Carl Coates works as a legal assistant. Today, his supervising attorney, Geraldine Mallon, has asked him to come into her office to talk about an offer to purchase real estate that she wants him to prepare. The purchase offer is to be prepared for a client named Joseph Morgenstern. Geraldine currently handles all of the legal matters for Morgenstern's business. Now that he is about to purchase his dream home, Morgenstern wants the contract, if accepted, by the seller, to be "water tight."

THE ASSIGNMENT

Carl enters Geraldine's office. She asks him to have a seat at the nearby conference table and hands him a file. It contains some handwritten notes, a copy of a real-estate listing describing the property, and a standard purchase-offer form. They review the details of the offer that Morgenstern wants to make on the house. Carl indicates that although he studied real-estate transactions as part of his paralegal program, he has had no on-the-job experience with them.

Geraldine instructs him carefully in the details of the offer. Morgenstern wants to offer $250,000 for the house. He wants to put down $10,000 as *earnest money* (a deposit toward the purchase price of real estate to indicate that the offer is made seriously). This money will go toward his down payment at the *closing* (the final step in the purchase and sale of real estate). He also wants to specify in his offer that the kitchen appliances, all of the light fixtures, including the dining room chandelier, and all of the window treatments will be included in the sale of the home. The sale would be conditioned on two events: First, the house must pass a building inspection to Morgenstern's satisfaction. Second, Morgenstern must be able to obtain financing from a lending institution for the purchase.

PREPARING THE FIRST DRAFT OF THE PURCHASE OFFER

Geraldine then instructs Carl to use the purchase-offer form that is on one of the diskettes in the diskette "forms file"—model forms that can be loaded

an individual's personality and character, and they are also important in paralegal practice.

Responsibility and Reliability

The paralegal must be responsible and reliable. The practice of law involves helping people with their legal problems. A paralegal's mistake, such as missing a deadline for filing a certain document with the court, could cause a client to lose his or her legal rights (and possibly cause a lawsuit to be brought against the attorney).

Attorneys frequently mention how they *rely* on their paralegals to perform certain tasks for them. The responsible paralegal is reliable. He or she completes tasks accurately and on time. Paralegals often mention how

---

DEVELOPING PARALEGAL SKILLS, Continued

onto the computer and modified as necessary to customize them for a particular client's preferences. Geraldine feels that it will adequately protect Morgenstern's interests. Carl is to prepare the offer by copying the form from the diskette onto his computer's hard drive and then filling in all of the information that they have discussed, as well as the property description and any other information that the form requires. Carl understands the assignment and goes to his office to prepare the offer.

He begins by keying into the computerized form the real-estate listing, which gives a legal description of the property. He inserts the legal description in the appropriate section of the offer. He continues to the next section and inserts the amount being offered, the amount of earnest money to be deposited, and the two conditions. Carl continues to type in information until the purchase offer is completed.

REVIEWING AND REVISING THE PURCHASE OFFER

Carl then takes the offer to Geraldine for her review. She asks him to sit down, and they review the offer together. Carl has prepared it correctly, and Geraldine compliments him on his accurate work. While Carl is in Geraldine's office, Morgenstern calls. He tells Geraldine that he also wants to offer to buy the bar stools in the kitchen, which match the countertop perfectly. He will offer the seller $700 for the bar stools. Carl will now have to revise the offer to reflect this change.

Carl returns to his office to make the changes on the form, which is easy to do on the computer. He simply opens the document and inserts the information on Morgenstern's offer in the appropriate place on the form. Carl prints out a copy of the revised offer and gives it to Geraldine for her review. She approves Carl's insertion and asks him to call Morgenstern to let him know that the offer is ready for his signature.

Carl is pleased with his work. He knows that the next time he assists Geraldine in drafting an offer to purchase real estate, he will be more confident in his ability to draft the offer accurately.

---

important trust is to efficient teamwork in the legal office. Each team member must be able to trust the other members of the legal team to do their share of the work—or the team effort fails.

Commitment

Being committed to your work and the goals of the legal team is important, too. Many tasks can take hours, days, weeks, or even months to perform, and you must be committed to giving your best effort until the job is completed. Commitment to your work involves persistence.

For example, if you are trying to track down heirs to a will and you are having difficulty locating them, you must try everything possible to find them before you give up the search. You will need to review county birth and

FEATURED GUEST: WENDY B. EDSON

Ten Tips for Effective Communication

Biographical Note

Wendy B. Edson received her master's degree in library science (M.L.S.) from the University of Rhode Island and served as law librarian at the Buffalo, New York, firm of Phillips, Lytle, Hitchcock, Blaine and Huber. In 1978, she joined the legal-assistant faculty at Hilbert College, in Hamburg, New York, and helped to develop an ABA-approved bachelor's program in 1992. She teaches paralegalism and legal ethics, legal research, law and literature, and volunteerism. She also developed and coordinates the internship program. Edson reviews and publishes on the topics of paralegal education, legal research, and community service. She has lectured to legal professionals on legal research, teaching skills, internships, and community service.

Words! They are the building blocks of human communication. How we deliver and receive words can inspire or discourage, fascinate or repel. But how do we become skilled at maneuvering the *two-way* traffic of interpersonal communication? As in driving, we need to follow the "rules of the road." The rules of the road in regard to communication traffic are embodied in the following ten tips.

① Establish Communication Equality. Communication equality does not require that individuals hold equal status in an office or organization but requires that each party believe in *equal rights* to speak and listen. Observe someone whom you consider to be a good communicator. You will note that he or she demonstrates equality by actively listening and responding appropriately to whoever is speaking. Problems in the employment context often reflect communication ailments rooted in inequality. A firm belief in communication equality, despite job titles, will help to create a cooperative, productive working environment.

② Plan for Time and Space. Effective communication requires

time. Imagine your reaction to a request to work overtime if your supervising attorney took thirty seconds to order you to do the work versus taking two minutes to explain the reason for the request and listening to your response. In the first situation, the attorney saved one and a half minutes but scored "zero" in terms of communication skills. In today's rushed world, it is easy to overlook the importance of communication skills in morale building and creating a cooperative, efficient work force.

Effective communicators are aware of how the physical environment in which a conversation takes place can affect the communication process. Communication is always enhanced when the parties have reasonable privacy and are not continually interrupted. Another important factor is physical comfort. Choosing an inappropriate time and place for communication denies the importance of the matters being discussed and may send the wrong messages to both the speaker and the listener.

③ Set the Agenda. Skilled communicators prepare an *agenda*—whether written or mental—of matters to be discussed in order of their

priority. Frequently, both parties bring their respective agendas to a discussion, which means that priorities may need to be negotiated. A subordinate who brings up the topic of desired vacation time when the supervisor is preoccupied with a major project clearly demonstrates that his or her priorities are different from those of the supervisor.

Successful communication requires that the parties first negotiate a *common agenda*—that is, determine jointly the agenda for a particular discussion or meeting and what topics should take priority. Then, the topics can be dealt with one by one, in terms of their relative importance, to the satisfaction of both parties. *Agenda awareness* prevents parties from jumping from topic to topic without successfully resolving anything.

④ Fine-tune Your Speaking Skills. Observe an individual whom you consider to be a good speaker, whether before a group of persons or on a one-on-one basis. What skills does that individual demonstrate? Effective speakers work hard to express thoughts clearly; sometimes, they refer to notes or lists to refresh their memories. Skilled speakers also try to

FEATURED GUEST, Continued

communicate accurately and to talk about matters that they know will interest their listeners. They cultivate *communication empathy*—the sincere effort to put themselves in their listener's shoes. As you speak to others, pause occasionally and ask yourself: "Would I enjoy listening to what I am saying and how I am saying it?"

5   Cultivate Listening Skills. Listening is not just refraining from speaking while another person is talking but an *active* process—the other half of the communication partnership. An active listener does not interrupt the speaker. If you sense that the speaker is engaging in a monologue, responsive behavior—including body language, attentiveness, and appropriate remarks—can steer the conversation back to a dialogue without cutting off the speaker.

An active listener realizes that listening is an investment in effective communication. By truly responding to what is being said, rather than regarding listening time as insignificant or time to plan his or her own remarks, the skilled listener establishes a bond of trust with the speaker. Active listeners avoid preconceived ideas about topics being discussed and assume that they do not know all the answers.

6   Watch for Body Language. Body language is nonverbal communication that reflects our emotional state. Physical positions, such as leaning forward or away from the speaker while listening, can reinforce or negate our spoken responses. Body attitudes, whether relaxed (comfortable posture, leaning forward, uncrossed arms and legs, relaxed neck and shoulders) or tense

(stiff posture, backing away, crossed arms and legs, stiff neck and shoulders) vividly illustrate our response before we utter a word. Eye contact is one of the most important tools in the body-language toolkit for communication. Interviewers, social workers, and police officers—as well as most other people—commonly interpret steady and responsive eye contact to mean sincerity on the part of the speaker or listener.

7   Put Note Taking in Perspective. Overinvolvement in note taking detracts from the communication process because opportunities to listen actively, speak responsively, and be sensitive to body language are reduced. The speaker may ramble while the listener records the ramblings in extensive notes.

When it is necessary to take notes, it is helpful to establish some rapport with the speaker or listener before launching the note-taking process. Alternatively, follow-up notes can be a workable solution to the problem. The note taker can devote the interview time to communication and, after the interview, record his or her general impressions of the interview and identify specific issues that need to be discussed further.

8   Recognize the Role of Criticism. *Constructive criticism* focuses on specific actions or behaviors rather than personalities. It is objective rather than subjective. Criticism that is stated calmly and objectively ("There are not enough measurements on the Ferris scale drawing") is much more palatable for the person being criticized than is criticism in the form of a personal attack ("You did a terrible job"). By placing

> **"EYE CONTACT IS ONE OF THE MOST IMPORTANT TOOLS IN THE BODY-LANGUAGE TOOLKIT FOR COMMUNICATION."**

emphasis on actions instead of personalities, the parties can more easily work toward a satisfactory solution. If both the critic and the person being criticized can remain calm and can separate actions from personalities, then criticism will usually produce the desired result and *mutual* satisfaction.

9   Aim for Satisfactory Closure. Closure means "wrapping up" the communication. Successful communicators know that handling closure properly can leave a participant with a good feeling even if the solution was not exactly what he or she initially desired. Summarizing the discussion and checking for agreement or a need for further discussion will encourage all participants to follow the tenth tip.

10   Commit to Communicate. Excellent speakers and listeners have positive, self-confident attitudes that problems can be solved if the "rules of the road" are followed. Skilled communicators cultivate open minds, self-knowledge, and the ability to tolerate differences and empathize with others. They are committed to exercising their rights and responsibilities as speakers and listeners in the communication process.

marriage records to try to locate them through their siblings and spouses. If that does not work, you will need to contact state agencies, such as the motor vehicle department, to try to obtain addresses from their driver's licenses or vehicle-registration records. You might also have to advertise in newspapers. Being diligent in your search means that you keep going until you have exhausted virtually every possible information source.

Objectivity

Another personal attribute of professional behavior is objectivity. To the extent that personal emotions or biases interfere with the goal of serving the client's interest, the paralegal must set these emotions or biases aside. For example, your sympathy for a client's plight should not prevent you from acknowledging factual evidence that is harmful to the client's position.

Lawyers and paralegals sometimes find themselves working on behalf of clients whom, for one reason or another, they dislike or do not respect. You may dislike having to deal with one of your firm's overly aggressive business clients, for example, or with a criminal defendant charged with spousal abuse, which is extremely offensive to you. But these feelings should not affect the quality of the services rendered. The job of the attorney and the paralegal is to see that the client's interests are not harmed by their personal views or assumptions.

The Ability to Keep Confidences

One of the requirements of being a paralegal is the ability to keep client information confidential. The word *requirement* is used here because being able to keep confidences is not just a desirable attribute in a paralegal, but a mandatory one. As you will read in Chapter 3, attorneys are ethically and legally obligated to keep all information relating to the representation of a client strictly confidential unless the client consents to the disclosure of the information.[3] The attorney may share this information only with people who are also working on behalf of the client and who therefore need to know the information. Paralegals share in this duty imposed on all attorneys. If a paralegal reveals confidential client information to anyone outside the group working on the client's case, the lawyer (and the paralegal) may face legal consequences (including being sued by the client) if the client suffers harm as a result of the paralegal's actions.

Keeping client information confidential means that you, as a paralegal, cannot divulge such information even to your spouse, family members, or closest friends. You should not talk about a client's case in hallways, elevators, or other areas in which others may overhear your conversation. Keeping work-related information confidential is an important part of being a responsible and reliable paralegal.

---

3. Exceptions to the confidentiality rule are made in certain circumstances, as will be discussed in Chapter 3.

PARALEGAL PROFILE

Bankruptcy Specialist

GARY BRYER, a paralegal who specializes in the area of bankruptcy, works for the large Philadelphia law firm of Dechert, Price & Rhoads. Bryer's educational background includes two years of college at the Philadelphia Community College, where he studied journalism. He received his paralegal certificate from the Philadelphia Institute for Paralegal Training in May 1988. Since then, Bryer has been employed by several law firms, working solely in the area of bankruptcy and creditors' rights. Bryer is an active participant in the Philadelphia Association of Paralegals (PAP). In 1992, he was elected to the PAP's board of directors, and he has chaired or co-chaired PAP committees on bankruptcy and banking. He has taught paralegal classes (on a part-time basis) for local paralegal programs. He has also authored a series of articles on consumer bankruptcy and six articles exploring the topic of paralegal job searching.

What do you like best about your work?

"The thing I like best is drafting documents and pleadings. I also enjoy investigative work and training other paralegals. The field of bankruptcy is very fast paced, detailed, and focused on deadlines. Bankruptcy work is team oriented, although each team member enjoys a great deal of autonomy as well. I relish both the pressure and the independence."

What is the greatest challenge that you face in your area of work?

"The most challenging aspect of my job is coordinating a project from start to finish. Coordinating a project includes interacting with in-house services, as well as contracting with outside services. Just filing an ordinary complaint or motion with the court includes coordinating the efforts of numerous individuals—the responsible attorney and other attorneys working on the case, secretaries, document copiers, mail clerks, and delivery or courier services. Each project requires significant oversight. It can be difficult to work for eight to ten attorneys, each of whom has a separate agenda, and still meet deadlines."

What advice do you have for would-be paralegals in your area of work?

"My advice for those paralegals is to have a clear understanding that they support attorneys in the practice of law. They also need to know that paralegal work is important. Paralegals exist because they can provide substantive legal services at a lower cost than attorneys' services. Paralegals need to consciously determine what types of tasks they might enjoy day in and day out. There are many paralegals who don't like the fast-paced and pressured life of a bankruptcy paralegal. Some paralegals prefer transactional work, such as filling in forms or preparing tax returns. The area of law in which you work should reflect your personality and temperament. An entry-level position allows you the time to get to know the everyday basic duties, and later there will be many opportunities to take on further responsibilities. A paralegal can never be too completely prepared for a task. Finally, paralegals must learn to delegate and accept responsibility."

> **"THE AREA OF LAW IN WHICH YOU WORK SHOULD REFLECT YOUR PERSONALITY AND TEMPERAMENT."**

What are some tips for success as a paralegal in your area of work?

"A tip for success as a bankruptcy paralegal would be to learn the rules of the court system with which you work and keep abreast of the law. Another tip for success is to become actively involved in your field. Paralegals who are professionally active and involved eventually move into the better-paying and more responsible positions. Another tip is to complete every task that you work on efficiently and conscientiously—no matter how mundane the task may be. Most importantly, if you are flexible, thorough, and accommodating, you will be a welcome addition to any department or firm."

TODAY'S PROFESSIONAL PARALEGAL

A Winning Combination

Steven Latham is a legal assistant in the law offices of Melinda T. Oakwood. Melinda is a sole practitioner, which means that she owns her practice and practices alone. She shares office space with several other attorneys in an office building, however. Her practice is a general law practice, and she handles a variety of legal matters, including divorces, wills, real-estate matters, and personal-injury lawsuits.

Steven has worked for Melinda for seven years; it was his first job after graduating from a legal-assistant program. He is given a great deal of responsibility because he has shown Melinda that he is responsible and reliable in handling the work that she assigns to him. His work is always turned in on time, and it is always accurate.

LEARNING ON THE JOB

If Steven has questions, he always asks Melinda. When Steven first started working for Melinda, she told him that the only "stupid question" was the one that was not asked. She also told him that he should spend more time on assignments to be sure that they were thoroughly and accurately performed rather than rushing through projects and increasing the risk of inaccuracies. "It does me no good to spend time reviewing work that I have to give back to you to correct. I'd rather have it right the first time," Melinda told him. Steven had a strong sense of commitment, so he always saw a project through, even if it seemed to take forever.

Steven was also very lucky to have a supervising attorney who liked to teach him how to perform new assignments. Melinda had been a teacher for ten years before she went to law school. When Steven had a new type of document to prepare, for example, Melinda would give him a sample of the document and very good instructions. When Steven had to prepare the same document for a different case, Melinda would explain the differences between the first and second assignments and why the differences mattered, from a legal perspective.

IMPROVING PARALEGAL SKILLS

Melinda was also lucky to have Steven as her paralegal. He had many personal attributes that helped him on the job. He learned quickly and performed his work competently and efficiently. He also paid great attention to detail, unlike the paralegal that Melinda had had before Steven, who would send out letters and fail to include the documents that should have accompanied the letters. Melinda could also always count on Steven to keep client information confidential. That was especially important in the small town in which they lived and worked.

Steven already had good computer, organizational, and analytical skills when Melinda hired him. He did need to work at improving his communication skills, however, particularly his listening skills. Over time, he learned to listen carefully to Melinda's instructions and directions and to question her when he was not exactly certain of them.

THE RESULT: A WINNING LEGAL TEAM

Eventually, Melinda and Steven developed a solid working relationship. It took time for Steven to develop some of the skills that he needed, but Melinda was patient and a good teacher. It also took time to develop a trusting relationship in which Melinda could confidently delegate significant assignments to Steven, knowing that he would complete them accurately and on time. Now Steven and Melinda work efficiently and productively together. They like and rely on each other and enjoy their work. Theirs is a winning combination of talents and skills.

Other Attributes

Other attributes of the professional paralegal include accuracy, efficiency, attentiveness to detail, discretion, diplomacy, and the ability to work under pressure. Each of these attributes is considered to be appropriate in a law office because it enhances the firm's ability to serve the client's needs most effectively.

When deadlines are nearing and the pace of office work becomes somewhat frantic, it may be difficult to meet the challenge of acting professionally. For example, you may have to complete a brief (a document filed with a court to support an attorney's argument) by noon. It is 11 A.M., and you still have a considerable portion of the brief to complete. When the pressure is on, it is important to remain calm and focus on completing your task quickly and accurately to ensure quality work.

THE FUTURE OF THE PROFESSION

Since its beginnings over twenty-five years ago, the paralegal profession has been in a state of constant change, and by all indications, it will continue to undergo change during the 1990s and beyond. Legal services are costly, and the public is demanding access to more affordable legal services. This means that the role of the paralegal in delivering lower-cost legal services will most likely continue to expand. According to the U.S. Department of Labor's Bureau of Labor Statistics, paralegal employment is expected to grow much faster than the average for all occupations through the year 2005.[4]

By the early 1990s, many state bar associations had created special sections for legal assistants. Admission to state bar associations added greater recognition to the contribution made by legal assistants to the legal profession. Paralegal associations, state bar associations, state legislatures, the American Bar Association, and other groups are now debating whether some or all paralegals should be licensed by the state to work as paralegals. You will read more about this pressing issue confronting the paralegal profession in Chapter 3.

In brief, the paralegal profession is a dynamic, changing, and growing field within the legal arena. Although legal assistants initially worked only in the law-firm context, today's job opportunities for paralegals include working for corporations, government agencies, and other organizations—as you will learn in the following chapter. Those who enter the profession today will find not only a variety of career options but also the opportunity to help chart the course that the profession will take in the future.

---

4. *Occupational Outlook Handbook,* 1994–95 ed. (Washington, D.C.: Government Printing Office, 1994), p. 232.

KEY TERMS AND CONCEPTS

ABA-approved program 10	bachelor's degree 9	law clerk 6
affiliate 7	certification 10	legal assistant 4
American Bar Association (ABA) 4	Certified Legal Assistant (CLA) 10	National Association of Legal Assistants (NALA) 7
associate attorney 6	Certified Legal Assistant Specialist (CLAS) 10	National Federation of Paralegal Associations (NFPA) 7
associate's degree 9		

paralegal   4

paralegal certificate   9

postbaccalaureate certificate   8

procedural law   9

state bar association   7

substantive law   9

CHAPTER SUMMARY

1. The professional status of paralegals was first acknowledged by the American Bar Association in 1968. Since then, the paralegal profession has continued to grow, and it is now one of the fastest-growing occupations in the United States.

2. Many legal professionals use the terms *paralegal* and *legal assistant* interchangeably. A paralegal, or a legal assistant, can be defined as a person sufficiently trained in law and legal procedures to assist attorneys in the delivery of legal services to the public. Paralegal expertise may be attained through on-the-job experience or through paralegal training programs. Paralegals are not attorneys but attorneys' assistants. Attorneys supervise paralegal work and assume ultimate responsibility for it. Paralegals perform many of the tasks involved in legal representation that have traditionally been handled by attorneys. Certain tasks, however (such as giving legal advice, setting fees for legal services, and representing clients in court), can only be handled by attorneys.

3. Typical tasks performed by paralegals include drafting legal documents, calendaring and tracking important deadlines, assisting attorneys in trial preparations and at trial, interviewing clients and witnesses, organizing and maintaining client files, conducting legal investigations, and conducting legal research.

4. The first paralegals were legal secretaries who, through on-the-job experience, developed the skills and expertise now taught in paralegal training programs. The paralegal profession evolved rapidly because paralegals filled the growing need for lower-cost, permanent, and competent legal assistance.

5. The formation of paralegal associations was a significant step in the growth of the paralegal profession. By the early 1970s, numerous local paralegal organizations were in existence. By the mid-1970s, the National Federation of Paralegal Associations (NFPA) and the National Association of Legal Assistants (NALA)—the two leading national paralegal associations—had been formed. Paralegal professional associations provide a forum in which professional issues can be discussed, establish guidelines to regulate professional conduct, determine skill levels and educational requirements, and possibly establish or sponsor educational programs. Professional membership provides the following opportunities for paralegals: to meet and network with others in the profession, to receive publications issued by paralegal associations, to engage in continuing legal education, to participate in planning relating to current and future developments in the profession, and to indicate to potential employers an involvement in paralegal professional development.

6. Paralegal educational options include certificate programs and degree programs. A person who has a bachelor's degree can receive a postbaccalaureate certificate by completing a program offered by a college or university, which usually takes one year. Paralegal certificates can be obtained through programs of varying lengths, offered by business schools, trade schools, and other for-profit occupational training centers. Degree options include an associate's degree and a bachelor's degree. The curriculum in paralegal programs emphasizes procedural law, while the curriculum in law schools emphasizes substantive law. The training of paralegals and attorneys thus is complementary, which enhances the effectiveness of attorney-paralegal teamwork in legal representation.

7. The American Bar Association has played an active role in paralegal education programs since the early 1970s. Paralegal programs that meet standards established by the ABA (currently, nearly one-third of all paralegal programs) are called ABA-approved programs.

8. Certification involves recognition by a private professional group or a state agency that a person has met specified standards of proficiency. The National Association of Legal Assistants (NALA) has developed a certification program for paralegals. The possibility of state certification programs is being discussed in most states. By 1994, the state of Texas had adopted a voluntary certification program, and the California Alliance of Paralegal Associations agreed with NALA to develop a voluntary statewide certification program for paralegals in California.

9. Paralegals need to have a variety of skills. It is especially important for paralegals to have good organizational, analytical, computer, interpersonal, and communication skills.

10. Certain personal attributes are also important in paralegal practice. These attributes include responsibility, reliability, commitment to hard work, objectivity, the ability to keep confidences, accuracy, efficiency, attentiveness to detail, discretion, diplomacy, and the ability to work under pressure.

QUESTIONS FOR REVIEW

1. When and by which organization was the paralegal profession first recognized as a profession?

2. What is a paralegal? What are some of the key elements in the ABA's definition of a legal assistant? Is there any difference between a paralegal and a legal assistant?

3. What kinds of tasks do paralegals perform?

4. Why did the paralegal profession evolve? What needs within the legal profession do paralegals meet?

5. Name the two largest national paralegal associations in the United States. When and why were they formed? What are the benefits of belonging to a paralegal association?

6. What type of educational programs and training are available to paralegals? Must a person meet specific educational requirements to work as a paralegal?

7. How does the paralegal's education and training differ from the education and training of an attorney? What is the particular expertise of the paralegal?

8. What does *certification* mean? What is a CLA? What is a CLAS?

9. List and describe the skills that are useful in paralegal practice. Do you have these skills?

10. List and describe some of the personal attributes of a professional paralegal. Do you feel that persons who do not have these attributes can cultivate them? If so, how?

ETHICAL QUESTIONS

1. Carla Seegen is an experienced legal assistant who is also a licensed realtor. She sold real estate for eight years before becoming a paralegal. Carla works in a small law firm and has recently been assigned to work for Mike McAllister, who is a new attorney and the son of one of the firm's founding partners, John McAllister. Mike is asked to handle a real-estate closing for the firm's biggest client. Mike is unfamiliar with the client's business. Furthermore, he studied property law only briefly in law school and has no experience in real-estate transactions. Carla soon learns of Mike's lack of knowledge and experience because he does not ask her to draft the appropriate documents and undertake the kinds of tasks that are necessary for the closing. Whenever she mentions these things to Mike, however, or offers to show him what must be done, Mike becomes annoyed. Carla likes her job and knows that if she continues to annoy Mike, she may be fired. At the same time, she is concerned about the client's welfare and legal protection. Should she talk to one of the partners about the problem? Should she discuss the issue with John McAllister, Mike's father? How would you handle the situation?

2. Paula Abrams works for a law firm in a small, midwestern community. Her husband works as a sales representative for Benedetto Home Stores, a large home-supply store in the community. One day, Sal Benedetto consults with Paula's supervising attorney about the possibility of entering bankruptcy proceedings. Apparently, Benedetto Home Stores is facing a financial crisis, and Sal sees bankruptcy as the only solution. Paula's husband, Joseph, has worked for Benedetto for ten years, earns a good income, and

has a good benefits package. Their combined incomes support them, their three children, and Paula's mother. Paula wants to tell Joseph about the apparently impending bankruptcy of Benedetto Home Stores so that he can begin to look for another job as soon as possible. Paula knows that she has an ethical responsibility to keep this client information strictly confidential. Yet she also feels that she has an ethical responsibility to her family. Should Paula tell Joseph? What would you do if you were Paula?

PRACTICE QUESTIONS AND ASSIGNMENTS

1. Which of the following tasks might legal assistants do?

     a. Draft legal documents.

     b. Try cases in court.

     c. Calendar important deadlines.

     d. Give legal advice.

     f. Set legal fees.

     g. Interview clients and witnesses.

     h. Perform legal investigations.

2. Refer to Appendix F at the end of this book and find the answers to the following questions:

     a. Is there an affiliate of the National Association of Legal Assistants or the National Federation of Paralegal Associations in your city?

     b. Where is the nearest affiliate of either of these organizations located?

2

CAREERS IN THE LEGAL COMMUNITY

Chapter Objectives

After completing this chapter, you will know:

- What types of firms and organizations hire paralegals.
- Some areas of law in which paralegals specialize.
- What paralegals can expect to earn.
- How paralegals are compensated for overtime work.
- How to prepare a career plan and pursue it.

Chapter Outline

INTRODUCTION

As a paralegal, you will enjoy a broad spectrum of employment opportunities. In the past two decades, attorneys have begun to realize how the use of paralegals in the law office can help them achieve the goal of providing quality legal services at lower cost to clients. Paralegals perform a number of tasks that in the past only attorneys handled. By turning over these tasks to paralegals, whose hourly fees are lower than those of attorneys, law firms can represent more clients, and clients pay less for their services.

The fact that you are entering a growth profession presents further opportunities. As mentioned in Chapter 1, the first paralegals were legal secretaries who had acquired, through experience, the necessary skills and abilities to assist attorneys in substantive legal work within the law-firm environment. As the paralegal profession developed, so did opportunities for paralegals in other employment settings. Corporations began to realize how paralegals could be used effectively in their legal departments. Government agencies created positions for paralegals. Banks, insurance companies, and other types of firms and institutions began to hire paralegals to assist with work that required legal training. Today, most paralegals continue to work for law firms, as will be discussed shortly, but they are increasingly assuming greater responsibilities as attorneys realize the benefits of delegating substantive legal work to paralegals.

This chapter provides a point of departure for your career planning. In the pages that follow, you will read about where paralegals work, some special areas of paralegal practice, and how paralegals are compensated. You will also learn about the essential steps involved in planning for a successful career.

WHERE PARALEGALS WORK

Paralegal employers fall into three broad categories: law firms, corporations and other business organizations, and government agencies. This section describes the general characteristics of each of these three basic types of working environments.

Law Firms

When paralegals first established themselves within the legal community in the 1960s, they assisted lawyers in a law-firm setting. Today, as indicated in Exhibit 2.1, law firms continue to hire more paralegals than do any other organizations.

Law firms vary in size from the small, one-attorney office to the huge "megafirm" with hundreds of attorneys. As you can see in Exhibit 2.2 on page 32, the majority of paralegals working for law firms are employed by firms

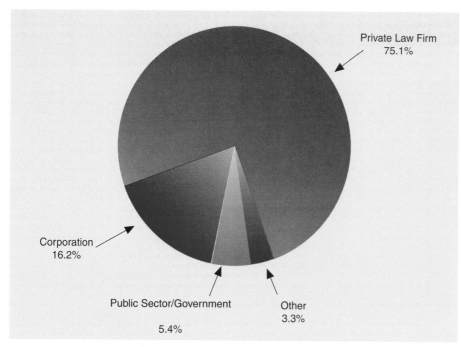

Source: Carol Milano, "Salary Survey Results," *Legal Assistant Today,* May/June 1993, p. 58.

EXHIBIT 2.1
Where Paralegals Work

having fewer than twenty attorneys, and 32.7 percent are employed by firms having four or fewer attorneys.[1]

Working for a Small Firm.   Many paralegals begin their careers working for small law practices, such as one-attorney firms or firms with just a few attorneys. To some extent, this is because of the greater number of small law firms, relative to large law firms. It may also be due to geographic location. For example, a paralegal who lives in a relatively rural environment, such as a small community, may find that his or her only option is to work for a small legal practice.

Working for a small firm offers many advantages to the beginning paralegal, and you should be aware of them. If the firm is a general law practice, you will have the opportunity to gain experience in many different areas of the law. You will be able to learn whether you enjoy working in one area (such as family law) more than another area (such as personal-injury law) in the event that you later decide to specialize. Some paralegals also prefer the often more personal and less formal environment of the small law office, as

---

1. One of the difficulties in describing law-firm environments is that the terms *small law firm* and *large law firm* mean different things to different people. In a large metropolitan city, for example, a firm with fifteen attorneys might qualify as a small law firm. In a smaller, more rural community, however, a firm with fifteen attorneys would be considered a very large law firm. In this text, we refer to law firms with fifteen or fewer attorneys as small law firms and firms with over fifteen attorneys as large firms.

EXHIBIT 2.2
Paralegal Employment in
Various Sizes of Law Firms

NUMBER OF ATTORNEYS IN FIRM	PERCENTAGE OF ALL LAW FIRM PARALEGALS EMPLOYED BY FIRM
0–4	32.7%
5–9	14.4%
10–19	16.3%
20–29	7.6%
30–75	18.4%
Over 75	10.6%

Source: Carol Milano, "Salary Survey Results," Legal Assistant Today, May/June 1993, p. 58.

well as the variety of tasks and greater flexibility that often characterize the small office.

A characteristic of small firms that may prove challenging to you has to do with compensation. Small firms pay, on average, lower salaries than larger firms do. As Exhibit 2.3 indicates, paralegal income is closely related to firm size. Generally, the larger the firm, the higher the paralegal salaries. Small firms also find it hard to afford the employee benefits packages, including insurance and pension plans, that large firms often provide for their employees.

Paralegals who work for small firms may also have less support staff to assist them. This means that if you work in a small law office, your job may involve a substantial amount of secretarial or clerical work.

Working for a Large Firm.   In contrast to the (typically) more casual environment of the small law office, larger law firms usually are more formal. If you work for a larger firm, your responsibilities will probably be limited to specific types of tasks and more well defined. For example, you may work for a department that handles (or for an attorney who handles) only certain types of cases, such as real-estate transactions. Office procedures and employment policies will also be more clearly defined and may be set forth in a written employment manual.

The advantages of the large firm include greater opportunities for promotions and career advancement, higher salaries and better benefits packages (typically), more support staff for paralegals, and (often) more sophisticated computer technology and greater access to research resources.

You may view certain characteristics of large law firms as either advantages or disadvantages, depending on your personality and preferences. For example, if you prefer the more specialized work and more formal working environment of the large law firm, then you will view these characteristics as advantages. If you prefer to handle a greater variety of tasks and enjoy the more personal, informal atmosphere of the small law office, then you might view the specialization and formality of the large law firm as disadvantages.

EXHIBIT 2.3
Paralegal Compensation

BY FIRM SIZE		BY TYPE OF EMPLOYER	
Number of Attorneys in Firm	Average Paralegal Salary	Employer	Salary
0–4	$28,411	Private law firm	$30,581
5–9	$30,251	Corporation	$34,915
10–19	$32,177	Public Sector/	
20–29	$33,312	Government	$29,241
30–75	$33,218	Other	$27,877
Over 75	$36,809		

BY YEARS OF EXPERIENCE		BY LOCATION OF FIRM	
Years of Experience	Salary	Location	Salary
0–2	$24,549	Metropolitan	$32,999
3–5	$27,644	Urban	$30,023
6–10	$32,983	Rural	$26,043
11–15	$33,989		
Over 15	$38,909		

BY AREA OF PRACTICE			
Area of Practice	Salary	Area of Practice	Salary
Administrative/Legislative	$32,478	Family Law	$26,238
Banking and Finance	$47,767	Intellectual Property	$38,219
Bankruptcy	$30,444	Litigation—Defense	$37,683
Corporate Law	$35,861	Litigation—Plaintiff	$30,112
Criminal Law	$26,871	Personal Injury	$27,873
Employment and Labor	$34,249	Real Estate	$31,815
Environmental	$29,141	Workers' Compensation	$26,195
Estate and Probate	$30,382	Other	$33,516

Source: Authors' estimates based on data reported in Carol Milano, "Salary Survey Results," *Legal Assistant Today*, May/June 1993, p. 48ff., and Bureau of Labor Statistics, *Monthly Labor Review*, various issues.

Corporations and Other Business Organizations

Over the past three decades, as mentioned earlier, paralegals have been given opportunities to work in business environments outside of law firms. Many of these businesses (such as insurance companies and banks) engage in activities that are highly regulated by government. Others (such as title insurance companies and law-book publishers) are in some way related to the practice of law.

An increasing number of paralegals work for corporate legal departments. Most major corporations hire in-house attorneys to handle corporate legal affairs. Some extremely large corporations have hundreds of attorneys on their payrolls. Paralegals who work for corporations ordinarily work under the supervision of in-house attorneys and assist them in such tasks as the following:

• Scheduling corporate meetings; drafting meeting notices, agendas, and minutes; and assembling documents necessary for meetings.

DEVELOPING PARALEGAL SKILLS

Contracts Administrator

 Martha Parnell, a legal assistant, works as a contracts administrator for the Best Engines Corporation. Martha's job is to take calls from buyers who want to negotiate contracts with Best Engines. The corporation uses preprinted forms containing provisions that Best Engines prefers to have in its contracts, terms that are advantageous to Best Engines. Some customers, however, buy large quantities of engines to use in factories, to pump oil from oil wells, or to pump oil through pipelines. These customers usually want to negotiate contracts that are less favorable to the seller (Best Engines) and that provide the buyer with more rights.

Martha's telephone rings. One of the company's sales representatives is on the line. He has a customer's attorney on hold who wants to negotiate the indemnity provision. The indemnity provision in the preprinted contract form requires the buyer to pay Best Engines for any losses arising under or resulting from the contract.

DEALING WITH A CUSTOMER'S REQUEST

The sales representative wants to know if Martha has time now for a conference call with the customer's attorney. Martha hesitates because she is in the middle of preparing another contract. The sales representative prods her. He tells her that this company is a major oil company that wants to purchase over $15 million worth of engines to use in a pipeline-expansion project. Martha agrees to talk to the attorney now.

The sale representative conferences the oil company's attorney into the call and introduces him to Martha. The oil company's attorney wants the indemnity provision reversed, so that Best Engines would be obligated to reimburse the oil company for any losses. He asks Martha if this could be accomplished. Martha tells him that Best Engines does not usually negotiate the indemnity provision, but because the oil company wants to make a sub-

---

• Preparing case files, drafting documents, and doing other work related to lawsuits in which the corporation is involved.
• Collecting and interpreting technical information for corporate reports to a regulatory agency (such as the Environmental Protection Agency).
• Drafting documents necessary to register for patent, trademark, or copyright protection for a corporate product.
• Researching laws and regulations that might affect corporate actions or policies.
• Preparing and reviewing corporate contracts.
• Working with outside counsel.

As noted in Exhibit 2.1, 16.2 percent of paralegals are now working in corporate or other business environments. On average, paralegals working for corporations receive higher salaries than those working for law firms, as indicated in Exhibit 2.3. Paralegals who work for corporations normally work more regular hours and experience less stress than paralegals who work for

---

DEVELOPING PARALEGAL SKILLS, Continued

stantial purchase, she will look into it. She asks him if the oil company would be willing to accept any other variations of the indemnity provision, such as splitting the indemnity or leaving it out entirely, so that state law would govern the issue. The attorney tells Martha that the oil company might agree to either of these possibilities.

CONSULTING WITH THE SUPERVISING ATTORNEY

Martha walks down the hall to her supervising attorney's office. She talks to the attorney, Joyce Ross, about modifying the indemnity provision. Joyce tells Martha that they will have to discuss it with the general counsel (the attorney who heads the corporate legal department) and get back to the customer's attorney later. Joyce picks up the phone and calls the general counsel's office. He is in the office but has just taken another call. His secretary asks Joyce what her call relates to, and Joyce explains the situation. The general counsel's secretary arranges a time for Joyce and Martha to meet with him.

MEETING WITH THE GENERAL COUNSEL

Later that day, Joyce and Martha go to the general counsel's office for the meeting. They sit down in his office, and Joyce explains the situation. The general counsel asks Martha several questions about the oil company's position on the indemnity provision. Would the oil company agree to eliminate the indemnity provision and rely on state law? Would the oil company be willing to split the indemnity? Would the indemnity provision be limited to certain types of losses, or would all losses, including personal injuries, be included?

   After Martha answers his questions, the general counsel tells Joyce and Martha that he will have to consult with both the vice president of marketing and the president of Best Engines and that he will call Martha as soon as he can to let her know the corporation's decision.

---

law firms. For example, unlike in law firms, in the corporate environment paralegals are not required to generate a specific number of "billable hours" per year (hours billed to clients for paralegal services performed—discussed in Chapter 4) because there are no clients to bill—the corporation is the client.

Government Agencies

A small but growing number of paralegals (around 5.4 percent) are employed by the government. Most paralegals who work for the government work for administrative agencies, such as the Environmental Protection Agency and the Social Security Administration. Paralegals who work for government agencies may be engaged in administrative appeals work (administrative agencies are discussed in Chapter 5), general or specialized legal research, the examination of documents (such as loan applications), and many other types of tasks.

Paralegals who work for government agencies normally work regular working hours, tend to work fewer total hours per year (have more vacation time) than paralegals in other environments, and, like paralegals who work for corporations, do not have to worry about billable hours. Additionally, paralegals who work for the government usually enjoy comprehensive employment benefits. Salaries, however, are on average lower than those offered by traditional law firms and other employers in the private sector, as indicated in Exhibit 2.3.

Paralegal Specialties

While many paralegals work for small firms that offer a wide range of legal services, other paralegals have found it useful and satisfying to specialize in one area of law. There are numerous opportunities for the paralegal who wishes to concentrate his or her efforts on a particular area and become a specialist. Here we discuss just a few of these specialty areas.

Litigation Assistance

LITIGATION
The process of working a lawsuit through the court system.

LITIGATION PARALEGALS
Paralegals who specialize in assisting attorneys in the litigation process.

PLAINTIFF
A party who initiates a lawsuit.

DEFENDANT
A party against whom a lawsuit is brought.

Working a lawsuit through the court system is called **litigation.** Paralegals who specialize in assisting attorneys in the litigation process are called **litigation paralegals.** Litigation paralegals work in general law practices, small litigation firms, litigation departments of larger law firms, or corporate legal departments. Litigation paralegals often specialize in a certain type of litigation, such as personal-injury litigation (discussed below) or product-liability cases (which involve injuries caused by defective products). Some litigation paralegals may also work primarily on behalf of **plaintiffs** (those who bring lawsuits) or on behalf of **defendants** (those against whom lawsuits are brought). Lawyers in a personal-injury practice, for example, often represent plaintiffs. Lawyers in a criminal-law practice represent criminal defendants—those accused of crimes.

You will read in detail about litigation procedures and the important role played by paralegals in the ligitation process in Chapter 6. We indicate below just a sampling of the kinds of work that a paralegal might perform during the litigation process:

• Interview a client to obtain detailed information about a case.
• Locate and interview witnesses.
• Contact relevant medical personnel and institutions, employers, or other sources of factual information relating to a case.
• Prepare documents to initiate (or defend against) a lawsuit and file them with the court, draft interrogatories (written questions to be answered under oath by the opposing party), attend depositions (recorded question-and-answer sessions in which an attorney questions a party or a witness), and summarize deposition transcripts.
• Prepare exhibits for trial, arrange to have all needed equipment and supplies in the courtroom at the time of the trial, create a trial notebook for the attorney to refer to during the trial, and prepare the client and witnesses for trial.
• Assist at trial and in any posttrial procedures, such as those required for appealing the case to a higher court.

Personal-injury Law

Much litigation involves claims brought by persons who have been injured in automobile accidents or other incidents as a result of the negligence of others. **Negligence** is a **tort**, or civil wrong, and someone who has been injured as a result of another's negligence is entitled under tort law to obtain compensation from the wrongdoer.

Paralegals who specialize in the area of personal-injury litigation often work for law firms that concentrate their efforts on personal-injury litigation. Personal-injury paralegals are also hired by insurance companies to investigate claims. Defendants in personal-injury cases are typically insured by automobile or other insurance, and a defendant's insurance company will therefore have an interest in the outcome of the litigation.

A paralegal working on a personal-injury case would typically perform the following types of tasks:

• Interview a client (plaintiff) to obtain details about an accident and the injuries sustained by the client.
• Interview witnesses to the accident to gather as much information about the accident as possible.
• Obtain medical reports from physicians and hospitals describing the plaintiff's injuries.
• Obtain employment data to verify the amount of lost wages that should be claimed as **damages**—if the client's current or future employment is affected by the injury.
• Obtain a copy of the police report, and, if necessary, consult with police officers and investigators who worked on the case.
• Generally, provide litigation assistance.

Criminal Law

Law is sometimes classified into the two categories of civil law and criminal law. **Civil law** is concerned with the duties that exist between persons or between citizens and their governments, excluding the duty not to commit crimes. Contract law, for example, is part of civil law. The whole body of *tort law,* which has to do with the infringement by one person of the legally recognized rights of another, is an area of civil law.

Criminal law, in contrast, is concerned with wrongs committed against the public as a whole. Criminal acts are prohibited by federal, state, or local statutes. In a criminal case, the government seeks to impose a penalty on a person who has committed a crime. In a civil case, one party tries to make the other party comply with a duty or pay for the damage caused by the failure to so comply.

A person accused of a crime is prosecuted by a *public prosecutor.* Public prosecutors (such as district attorneys) are government officials and are paid by the government. Accused persons may be defended by private attorneys or, if they cannot afford to hire counsel, by *public defenders*—attorneys paid for by the state to ensure that criminal defendants are not deprived of their constitutional right to counsel.

Paralegals who specialize in the area of criminal law may work for public prosecutors, public defenders, or criminal-defense attorneys. Criminal litigation

NEGLIGENCE
The failure to exercise the standard of care that a reasonable person would exercise in similar circumstances; in legal practice, the failure to fulfill professional duties.

TORT
A civil wrong, other than a breach of contract; a breach of a legally imposed duty.

DAMAGES
Money sought as a remedy for a civil wrong, such as a breach of contract or a tortious act.

CIVIL LAW
The branch of law dealing with the definition and enforcement of all private or public rights, as opposed to criminal matters.

CRIMINAL LAW
The branch of law that governs and defines those actions that are crimes and that subjects persons convicted of crimes to punishment imposed by the government.

is similar to civil litigation in many respects, and the kinds of work performed by litigation paralegals (described earlier) also apply in the criminal-law context. In addition to providing general litigation assistance, a paralegal working in the area of criminal law might perform the following tasks:

• As a public prosecutor's legal assistant, draft search warrants, which authorize law-enforcement officers to search a person or place.
• As a public prosecutor's legal assistant, draft arrest warrants, which authorize law-enforcement officers to arrest and take into custody a criminal suspect.
• As a defense attorney's legal assistant, assist a criminal defendant in making arrangements to post bail (so that the defendant can be released from custody until further proceedings are held).
• As a public prosecutor's legal assistant, act as a liaison between the police department and the public prosecutor's office.
• Generally, help to make sure that a criminal defendant's constitutional rights are not violated by any action undertaken by police officers or attorneys handling the case.

Corporate Law

CORPORATE LAW
Law that governs the formation, financing, merger and acquisition, and termination of corporations, as well as the rights and duties of those who own and run the corporation.

Corporate law consists of the laws that govern the formation, financing, merger and acquisition, and termination of corporations, as well as the rights and duties of those who own and run the corporation.

Paralegals who specialize in corporate law may work for a corporation, in its legal department, or for a law firm that specializes in corporate law. The demand for paralegals who are experienced in the area of corporate law is expanding. If you refer back to Exhibit 2.3 on paralegal compensation, you will see that paralegals specializing in this area also receive, on average, higher salaries or wages than paralegals in most other specialty areas.

Here are just a few of the tasks that a paralegal working in the area of corporate law might be asked to undertake:

• Prepare articles of incorporation and file them with the appropriate state office (usually the secretary of state's office).
• Draft corporate bylaws (rules that govern the internal affairs of the corporation).
• Prepare minutes of corporate meetings and maintain a minutes binder.
• Draft shareholder proposals.
• Review or prepare documents relating to the sale of corporate securities (stocks and bonds); assist a supervising attorney in making sure that federal and state requirements relating to the sale of corporate securities are met.
• Assist with legal work relating to corporate mergers and acquisitions, such as researching a corporation's financial status.
• File papers necessary to terminate a corporation's legal existence.

BANKRUPTCY LAW
The body of federal law that governs bankrupcy proceedings. The twin goals of bankruptcy law are (1) to protect a debtor by giving him or her a fresh start, free from creditors' claims; and (2) to ensure that creditors who are competing for a debtor's assets are treated fairly.

Bankruptcy Law

Bankruptcy law is a body of law that allows debtors to obtain relief from their debts. Bankruptcy law is federal law, and bankruptcy proceedings take place in federal courts (see the discussion of the federal court system in Chapter 5).

DEVELOPING PARALEGAL SKILLS
Obtaining a Police Report

 Maria Sanchez works as a paralegal in a one-attorney office. The attorney, Bob Billings, has just finished a meeting with a client who was arrested and charged with drunk driving and involuntary manslaughter. Bob will be defending the client, Jim Hannon, at the preliminary hearing.

Bob calls Maria into his office. He asks her to go to the police station to pick up a copy of the police report for the accident. He tells her the date of the accident was August 11, 1995, and that it occurred on Square Lake Road in Livingston, Minnesota. She will need to go to the Livingston Police Department. Bob also gives Maria the names of the parties involved in the accident and Hannon's driver's license number. Maria will need all of this information to obtain a copy of the police report. Additionally, Bob gives her a check, drawn on the law firm's account and made payable to the City of Livingston, in the amount of ten dollars to pay for the police report.

Maria drives to the police station. She enters the building and approaches the front desk. "May I help you?" asks the officer sitting at the front desk. "Yes. Where can I obtain a copy of the police report for a car accident?" asks Maria. "Did the accident occur in Livingston, and did the Livingston police respond?" asks the officer. "It happened here, and I believe that the Livingston police were at the scene," answers Maria. "Then fill out this form and I will get the report for you," instructs the officer.

Maria fills out the form and returns it to the officer. The officer keys the information into her computer and then prints out a copy of the police report. The officer hands the copy to Maria and takes her check. Maria thanks the officer and returns to the office.

The twin goals of bankruptcy law are (1) to protect a debtor by giving him or her a fresh start, free from creditors' claims; and (2) to ensure that creditors who are competing for a debtor's assets are treated fairly. Bankruptcy law provides for several types of relief, and both individuals and business firms may petition for bankruptcy.

Both large and small law firms practice bankruptcy law. A corporation undergoing bankruptcy proceedings (often in the form of a "reorganization," as provided for under bankruptcy law) may hire, on a temporary basis, a paralegal experienced in bankruptcy law to assist in the process. If you are working on behalf of a debtor who seeks bankruptcy relief, you might perform the following types of tasks:

• Interview the debtor (which may be an individual or a corporate representative) to obtain information relating to the debtor's income, debts, and assets.
• Review creditors' claims and verify their validity.
• Prepare the necessary documents for submission to the bankruptcy court.
• Attend bankruptcy proceedings.
• Assist in defending the debtor against any legal actions concerning the bankruptcy proceedings.

ETHICAL CONCERN

Confidentiality and Administrative Practice

Paralegals who deal with administrative agencies must remember at all times to keep client information confidential. Suppose that you are working on behalf of a client who is trying to obtain disability benefits. In pursuing the client's claim, you deal with a number of employees of the relevant state agency. One day, a person who states that he is working for the agency calls and asks you to send him information on your client's financial position (income, property holdings, and other assets) and gives you his fax number. You fax him this confidential information and then continue with your work on another case. What if the person who requested the information is not an employee of the agency after all but someone who, for any number of reasons, wants to learn of the client's financial condition? This can and does happen. To avoid breaching the duty of confidentiality, you should always verify that anyone requesting information has a right to obtain it. Generally, you should not transmit confidential information by fax.

WORKERS' COMPENSATION STATUTES
State laws establishing an administrative procedure for compensating workers for injuries that arise in the course of their employment.

Employment and Labor Law

Laws governing employment relationships are referred to collectively as *employment and labor law*. Employment and labor law includes laws governing health and safety in the workplace, labor unions and union-management relations, employment discrimination, wrongful employment termination, pension plans, retirement and disability income (Social Security), employee privacy rights (to a limited extent), the minimum wage that must be paid, and overtime wages.

Paralegals who are experienced in one or more of these areas of employment and labor law may work for law firms, corporations and other business entities, or government agencies. Often, paralegals specialize in just one area of employment law. For example, many paralegals work in the area of workers' compensation. Under state **workers' compensation statutes,** employees who are injured on the job are compensated from state funds (obtained by taxes paid by employers). Paralegals working in this area of employment law assist persons injured on the job in obtaining compensation from the state workers' compensation board. Some government agencies, including many state workers' compensation boards, allow paralegals to represent clients before agency hearings, which are conducted by agencies to settle disputes, or in negotiations with the agencies.

Numerous other areas of employment and labor law are regulated by administrative agencies, and paralegals working in those areas need to be familiar with the relevant agency's requirements and procedures. Here are just a few agencies that are involved in regulating the workplace and with which employment-law paralegals should be familiar:

- *National Labor Relations Board (NLRB)*—A federal agency that implements federal laws governing union organizational activities, union elections, and labor-management relations generally.
- *Occupational Safety and Health Administration (OSHA)*—A federal agency that implements federal laws governing safety in the workplace. OSHA establishes safety standards that employers must follow. State agencies also establish safety and health standards.
- *Equal Employment Opportunity Commission (EEOC)*—A federal agency that administers and enforces federal laws prohibiting employment discrimination on the basis of race, color, national origin, gender, religion, age, or disability. In most cases, before an employee can sue an employer for discrimination in violation of these federal laws, the employee must comply with EEOC procedures for handling such complaints. Only if the EEOC does not satisfactorily settle the claim may the employee file suit.
- *Labor Management Services Administration (LMSA)*—A federal agency that implements the provisions of the federal Employee Retirement Income Security Act (ERISA), which imposes certain requirements on employers in regard to pension funds.

Paralegals working in the area of employment and labor law often have extensive contact with these and other administrative agencies. If you work as a paralegal in the law-firm or corporate environment, you might undertake the following types of tasks, each of which may involve rules and procedures established by government agencies:

- Conduct research on labor law to determine how the law applies to a labor-management contract or dispute.
- Draft a contract setting forth the terms of a labor-management agreement.
- Assist in informal negotiations to settle a dispute between an employee and an employer or between a labor union and a firm's managers.
- Assist in formal dispute-settlement proceedings before one of the previously mentioned government agencies.
- Inform a client of the procedures involved in submitting a claim of employment discrimination to the EEOC and assist the client in preparing the necessary documents.
- Prepare the documents needed to initiate (or defend against) a lawsuit for employment discrimination in violation of federal or state law and generally assist in the litigation process.
- Contact and work with the state workers' compensation board on behalf of a client who is seeking compensation for injuries incurred during the course of employment.
- Draft employment policies to make sure that a business client (or a corporate employer) complies with federal and state laws prohibiting employment discrimination.
- Assist a business client (or a corporate employer) in benefits planning to ensure compliance with the requirements of ERISA and any other laws regulating employee benefits, such as health, life, or disability insurance.

Estate Planning and Probate Administration

Estate planning and probate administration both have to do with the transfer of an owner's property, or *estate*, on the owner's death. Through **estate planning,** the owner decides, *before* death, how his or her property will be transferred to others. The owner may make a **will,** for example, to designate the persons to whom his or her property shall be transferred. The formal requirements for a valid will are set forth in state statutes, and because these requirements may differ from state to state, paralegals working in this area should be familiar with their state's law governing wills. If the property passes by will, depending on the size of the estate and other factors, the genuineness of the will may have to be proved **(probated)** in **probate court** (a county or other court that handles probate procedures). Probate administration thus involves the procedures relating to the transfer of property *after* the owner's death.

The process of probate may take many months and, in some cases, more than a year. The *personal representative* (a person named in the will to handle the affairs of the deceased after his or her death) or an *administrator* (a person appointed by the court if no personal representative is named in the will) satisfies all obligations (pays debts, taxes, etc.) of the deceased. The personal representative or administrator also arranges to have the deceased's property distributed among the heirs in accordance with the will's provisions. Because the probate process can be time consuming, many people arrange to have at least some of their property transferred in ways other than by will.

One estate-planning possibility involves the establishment of a **trust,** a legal arrangement in which the property owner transfers legal title to his or

ESTATE PLANNING
Making arrangements, during a person's lifetime, for the transfer of that person's property or obligations to others on the person's death. Estate planning often involves executing a will, establishing a trust fund, or taking out a life-insurance policy to provide for others, such as a spouse or children, on one's death.

WILL
A document directing what is to be done with the maker's property upon his or her death.

PROBATE
The process of "proving" the validity of a will and ensuring that the instructions in a valid will are carried out.

PROBATE COURT
A court that probates wills; usually a county court.

TRUST
An arrangement in which title to property is held by one person (a trustee) for the benefit of another (a beneficiary).

Serving the Interests of Bereaved Clients

One of the hardest events to cope with is the loss of a loved one, yet it is precisely at this time that bereaved persons must also cope with funeral arrangements and legal formalities. These formalities may include checking with an attorney, locating a will if one was made, tending to the decedent's financial affairs, and so on. Undertaking these activities can be costly, and financial needs may cause further stress. These are factors that paralegals should keep in mind when dealing with clients during the probate process. Probate proceedings always take time, but the amount of time may be reduced by the paralegal who files the necessary forms in a timely fashion and follows up on the status of the proceedings to make sure that there are no unnecessary delays. Your kind or sympathetic words may be appreciated by a bereaved client; but you can best serve his or her interests by doing your job efficiently and responsibly and by undertaking any action you can to speed up the probate process.

INTELLECTUAL PROPERTY
Property that consists of the products of individuals' minds—products that result from intellectual, creative processes. Copyrights, patents, and trademarks are examples of intellectual property.

her property to a *trustee.* The trustee (which may be a relative or trusted friend of the property owner, an attorney, a law firm, or a banking institution) has a duty imposed by law to hold the property for the use or benefit of another (the *beneficiary* of the trust). A trust created during the owner's life is called a living trust. A trust provided for in a will comes into existence on the owner's death. Estate planning often involves life insurance. A person who wants to provide for a spouse and children after his or her death, for example, may obtain a life-insurance policy listing the spouse and children as beneficiaries. On the death of the insured person, the beneficiaries receive the amount specified in the policy.

Paralegals who specialize in the area of estate planning and probate frequently work for law firms, but they may also be employed by other firms or agencies, such as banks, as well as by probate courts. If you work in this area, these are some of the tasks that you might perform:

• Interview clients to obtain information relating to their assets, how and to whom they want to transfer their property on death, and what arrangements they want to have made for the guardianship of minor children.
• Draft wills and other documents required to set up a trust fund.
• Make sure that all procedural requirements are met during the probate process—that the proper documents are submitted to the court in a timely fashion, for example.
• Gather information relating to the debts and assets of the deceased, and assist in settling all financial and other obligations of the deceased.
• Locate heirs, if necessary.
• Explain probate procedures to family members or other heirs of the deceased and keep them informed of the status of the proceedings.

Intellectual-property Law

Intellectual property consists of the products of individuals' minds—products that result from intellectual, creative processes. Those who create intellectual property acquire certain rights over the use of that property, and these rights are protected by law. Literary and artistic works are protected by *copyright law. Trademark law* protects business firms' distinctive marks or mottos. Inventions are protected by *patent law.*

Although it is an abstract term for an abstract concept, intellectual property is nonetheless wholly familiar to virtually everyone. The book you are reading is copyrighted. Undoubtedly, the personal computer you use is trademarked and patented. The software you use on that computer might be copyrighted. The primary benefit of intellectual-property rights to the owner is that he or she controls the commercial use of the property. The owner, for example, may sell the intellectual-property rights to another, may collect royalties on the use of the property (such as a popular song) by others, and may prevent all but one publisher from reproducing the property (such as a novel).

Many law firms (or special departments of large law firms) specialize in intellectual-property law, such as patent law, while other firms provide a spectrum of legal services to their clients, of which intellectual-property law is only a part. Corporate legal departments may be responsible for registering copyrights, patents, or trademarks with the federal government.[2] Paralegal specialists in the area of intellectual property frequently undertake the following kinds of work:

• Interview clients who want to register for copyright, trademark, or patent protection of certain intellectual property, such as a new computer program, a product name, or an invention.
• Conduct research to find out whether someone has already applied for patent or trademark protection of an invention or product that the firm's client (or a corporate employer) wants to develop or register.
• Draft the documents that are necessary to apply for patent, trademark, or copyright protection.
• Draft contracts that provide for another's authorized use of a copyrighted, patented, or trademarked product.
• Assist in litigation resulting from the unlawful use of copyrighted, trademarked, or patented intellectual property.

Environmental Law

Environmental law consists of all laws that have been created to protect the environment. Environmental law involves the regulation of air and water pollution, natural-resource management, endangered-species protection, hazardous-waste disposal and the clean-up of hazardous-waste sites, pesticide control, and nuclear-power regulation.

ENVIRONMENTAL LAW
All state and federal laws or regulations enacted or issued to protect the environment and preserve environmental resources.

Employers of paralegal specialists in environmental law include administrative agencies (such as the federal Environmental Protection Agency, the state's natural-resource department, and the local zoning board), environmental-law departments of large law firms, law firms that specialize in environmental law, and corporations. Corporations with legal departments often employ environmental specialists. For example, a corporation may employ a paralegal as an *environmental coordinator* to assist the corporation in proper compliance with environmental regulations.

Here are some of the types of tasks that paralegal specialists in the area of environmental law frequently perform:

• Coordinate a corporate employer's environmental programs and policies and ensure that the corporation is complying properly with environmental regulations.
• Obtain permits from local, state, or federal environmental agencies to use land in certain ways (such as clearing trees or filling wetlands).
• Prepare forms and documents relating to the disposal of hazardous waste created by a corporate client's (or corporate employer's) manufacturing plants.
• Assist in litigation or other legal actions relating to violations of environmental laws. Paralegals play an important role in coordinating different

---

2. Copyrights are registered with the U.S. Copyright Office, Library of Congress, Washington, DC 20559. Patents and trademarks are registered with the Patent and Trademark Office, U.S. Department of Commerce, Washington, DC 20231.

aspects of the litigation (which may involve multiple violators) and in managing case files, which are often voluminous.

• Attend conferences with administrative-agency personnel or hearings conducted by an agency to assist in the settlement of a dispute.

• As an environmental agency employee, investigate and process claims of violations and assist in settling claims.

Real-estate Law

Real estate, or *real property,* consists of land and all things permanently attached to the land, such as houses, buildings, and trees and foliage. Because of the value of real estate (for most people, a home is their most expensive purchase), attorneys frequently assist persons or business firms that buy or sell real property to make sure that nothing important is overlooked. Paralegals who specialize in the area of real estate may find employment in a number of environments, including small law firms that specialize in real-estate transactions, real-estate departments in large law firms, corporations or other business firms that frequently buy or sell real property, banking institutions (which finance real-estate purchases), title companies, or real-estate agencies. Here we list just a few of the tasks that paralegals working in the area of real-estate might perform:

• Interview clients who want to buy or sell real property.
• Draft contracts for the sale of real estate.
• Conduct *title* examinations. (The title to real property represents the right to own and possess the property, and title examinations are conducted to see if there are any defects in the title.)
• Review title abstracts, which summarize the ownership history of real property.
• Draft mortgage agreements.
• Provide information to banking institutions involved in financing clients' real-estate purchases.
• Prepare *deeds* (a deed is a written document that transfers title from one person to another).
• Make sure that property transfers are recorded in the appropriate public office (usually the county register of deeds office).
• Schedule *closings* (the closing is the final step in the purchase of real estate).
• Attend closings (when permitted by state law to do so).

Family Law

Family law, as the term implies, deals with family matters, such as marriage, divorce, alimony, child support, and child custody. Family law is governed primarily by state statutes. If you specialize in this area, you will need to become familiar with your state's requirements concerning marriage and divorce procedures, child support, and related issues.

As a family-law specialist, you might work for a small family-law practice, a family-law department in a large law firm, or with a state or local agency, such as a community services agency, that assists persons who need

---

ETHICAL CONCERN

Questions about Child Custody

Divorcing clients frequently ask whether they can take their children out of the state while the mediation or divorce proceedings are under way. For example, suppose that Kerry Lynn, a paralegal, receives a call from a client who wants to know if it would be all right to take her children to her mother's home in another state over the weekend. Kerry tells the client that there is no problem with that. Normally, there would be no problem, but what Kerry doesn't know is that in this case, just two days ago, the court ordered that the children could not leave the state. The client, relying on Kerry's answer, violates the order. Kerry has both given legal advice to a client (which only attorneys may do) and has caused the client to suffer adverse legal consequences as a result of that advice. In your work as a paralegal, you may face similar questions from divorcing parents. You should always let the client know that as a paralegal, you cannot give legal advice, which you would be doing if you answered such questions.

REAL ESTATE
Land and things permanently attached to the land, such as houses, buildings, and trees and foliage.

FAMILY LAW
Law relating to family matters, such as marriage, divorce, child support, and child custody.

PARALEGAL PROFILE

Real-estate and Litigation Paralegal

DORA LEW received her bachelor of arts and master of arts degrees in Spanish language and literature from the University of California, Berkeley. After teaching Spanish for three years at that university and then two years at a private high school for girls, Lew became a secretary for a real-estate company, which immediately recognized her talents and gave her more responsibility. The company also put her through a master of business administration (MBA) program in international business at Armstrong University. Lew now works as a real-estate paralegal at the law firm of Landels, Ripley and Diamond.

What do you like best about your work?

"I enjoy the field of real estate because I am able to bring in all of my experience from the past to my current position. While working for Brobeck, Phlager and Harrison, I became the senior paralegal specializing in multimillion-dollar real-estate closings and related tasks. That experience helps me in my present job. I find I am able to utilize my experiences as a teacher, my experience in real estate, business, and the law. I have even used my Spanish in many situations when doing *pro bono* work. I also like the independence I have in my position."

What is the greatest challenge that you face in your area of work?

"I find that the most challenging aspect of my work is satisfying the twin goals of cost-efficiency and the generation of a superior work product. To meet these goals, it is important to "get it right" the first or second time. During the 1980s, clients called the attorneys to explain what they needed done, and then the attorneys would assign the work to paralegals. Now, clients are so cost-conscious that they often call me directly to skip a step. Of course, I run any client requests by the attorney, who may do some of the necessary work."

What advice do you have for would-be paralegals in your area of work?

"My advice is to be as detail-oriented as possible and to be the best you can be in all things that you do. Bringing to your position all experiences that you have had will add to your value as a paralegal. I would also advise paralegal students to get work experience. Without work experience, students can't get an idea of office culture and environment, which are important aspects of a job. When you start a job, for example, you're expected to know certain procedures, such as how to request supplies and fill out time sheets. Although you might have read about these procedures, you can only truly learn them through actual work experience."

> "BRINGING TO YOUR POSITION ALL EXPERIENCES THAT YOU HAVE HAD WILL ADD TO YOUR VALUE AS A PARALEGAL."

What are some tips for success as a paralegal in your area of work?

"Anticipation is the biggest tip I can give to a paralegal who hopes to be successful. If you anticipate your supervising attorney's needs, the problems that may arise in a case, and so on, you're always prepared to deal with the case more efficiently and effectively."

help with family-related problems. As a paralegal working in the area of family law, you might perform such tasks as the following:

• Interview a divorcing client to obtain information relating to the couple's assets and liabilities.
• Research state laws governing child custody and assist in making child-custody arrangements for a divorcing couple.

Conducting a Title Examination

 Kim Murphy is a paralegal working for the real-estate law firm of Clark & Clark. Today Kim is going to the Winston County Register of Deeds office to examine the title to the Spartan Shopping Center located in Winston County. One of Clark & Clark's clients is negotiating a sale of the shopping center, and Kim's supervising attorney must prepare an "abstract of title," which is a history of who owned the property, when past transfers were made, and other significant events. The abstract will be used to assure the buyer that he or she will receive good, clear, and marketable title to the property.

Kim arrives at the county offices. She takes the elevator to the third floor, where the Register of Deeds office is located. Kim approaches the counter, and a clerk asks her, "What do you need today?" Kim recognizes the clerk, Sam McGrath, who has worked there for as long as Kim has worked for Clark & Clark. He often assists Kim and is very helpful.

"Sam, I need the title records for the Spartan Shopping Center, located at 611 Harris Road, Dunham Township, Winston County," responds Kim. "Okay. I'll be right back with them for you, Kim," says Sam. He goes to a wall full of filing cabinets, opens a drawer, and looks for the title records of the Spartan Shopping Center.

EXAMINING OWNERSHIP RECORDS

Kim looks in a book on the counter, called the *Liber*, in which all of the deeds that are filed with the county are recorded. She locates the Spartan Shopping Center and then takes the *Liber* to a nearby table. She begins to read the ownership history of the property.

Sam brings the file folder containing copies of the deeds to Kim's table. She begins to read through each document. Kim looks at the copies to see if

• Draft a settlement agreement.
• Prepare the necessary documents to be filed with the court in a divorce suit and assist in the litigation process.
• Prepare a client for divorce proceedings.
• Assist a client—particularly a spouse who has never handled household financial affairs—in financial planning.

PARALEGAL COMPENSATION

What do paralegals earn? This is an important question for anyone contemplating a career as a paralegal. You can get some idea of what paralegals make, on average, from paralegal compensation surveys. Following a discussion of these surveys, we look at some other components of paralegal compensation, including job benefits and how paralegals are compensated for overtime work.

DEVELOPING PARALEGAL SKILLS, Continued

each one contains the same description of the property—to ensure that the entire parcel of land was conveyed (transferred) with each sale. Kim sees that it was. Kim also checks to make sure that the seller of the Spartan Shopping Center is the owner of the property.

CHECKING FOR LIENS

Next Kim looks for any *liens* (rights of creditors against the property for the payment of debts) that might have been filed against the property. Kim notes the mortgage lien, which is normal and expected. Typically, when the purchase of real property is financed by a mortgage loan, the lending institution places a lien on the property until the buyer has made all payments due under the terms of the loan contract. She also notes that the Internal Revenue Service (IRS) has placed a tax lien on the property. A tax lien means that the current owner is behind in the payment of taxes and that the IRS may *foreclose on* (take temporary ownership of) the shopping center, sell it, and use the proceeds to pay the overdue taxes. Any remaining proceeds will be returned to the shopping center's owner. If someone buys the shopping center and the IRS forecloses on it, the buyer could lose some, and perhaps all, of the money that he or she paid for the property.

THE CONSEQUENCES OF THE TAX LIEN FOR THE CLIENT

Kim realizes that the tax lien will make the property unsellable. Once the abstract is prepared, the buyer's attorney will learn about the lien and warn the buyer not to purchase the property because of the obvious risk. This tax lien must be resolved before Clark & Clark's client can sell the property.

Kim makes a copy of the tax-lien documents and then continues to review the file. When she has finished reviewing it, she returns it to Sam, thanks him for his help, and returns to the office to inform her supervising attorney of the tax lien.

Compensation Surveys

If you refer back to Exhibit 2.3, you can see that paralegal income is affected by a number of factors. We have already mentioned how the average income of paralegals is affected by firm size (smaller or larger) and the type of employer (law firm, corporation, or government). Other income-determining factors include years of experience working as a paralegal, as well as the area of practice. Note that the average salary of a paralegal working in the area of corporate law is $35,861, approximately $9,623 more than that of a paralegal working in the area of family law. Average salaries are also affected by location. The average salary for paralegals who work in metropolitan areas (major cities) is approximately $6,956 more than that of paralegals working in rural areas (small communities).

Exhibit 2.3 indicates *national* averages. To have a clearer picture of what your potential future income will be, you need to look at the average paralegal income in the state where you live or plan to work. As you can see in Exhibit 2.4 on page 49, paralegals working in Alaska earn, on average, over $23,590 more than paralegals working in Wyoming.

Keep in mind that salary statistics do not tell the whole story. Although paralegals earn more in California than in a midwestern state such as Nebraska (as shown in Exhibit 2.4), the cost of living is higher in California than in Nebraska. This means that your real income—the amount of goods and services that you can purchase with your income—may, in fact, be the same in both states despite the differences in salary. Salary statistics also do not reveal another important component of compensation—job benefits.

Job Benefits

Part of your total compensation package as an employee will consist of various job benefits. These benefits may include paid holidays, sick leave, group insurance coverage (life, disability, medical, dental), pension plans, and possibly others. Benefits packages vary from firm to firm. For example, one employer may pay the entire premium for your life and health insurance, while another employer may require you to contribute part of the cost of the insurance. Usually, the larger the firm, the greater the value of the benefits package.

● **When evaluating any job offer, you need to consider the benefits that you will receive and what these benefits are worth to you.**

Exhibit 2.5 on page 50 lists some of the factors you should ask or consider when evaluating a job offer.

Salaries versus Hourly Wages

Most paralegals (about 85 percent)[3] are salaried employees. In other words, they receive a specified annual salary regardless of the number of hours they actually work. Other paralegals are paid an hourly wage rate for every hour worked. Paralegals are frequently asked to work overtime, and how they are compensated for overtime work usually depends on whether they are salaried employees or are paid hourly wages. Many firms compensate their salaried paralegals for overtime work through year-end **bonuses,** which are special payments made to employees in recognition of their devotion to the firm and the high quality of their work. Some firms allow salaried employees to take compensatory time off work (for example, an hour off work for every hour worked beyond usual working hours). Employees who are paid an hourly wage rate are normally paid overtime wages.

BONUS
An end-of-the-year payment to a salaried employee in appreciation for that employee's overtime work, work quality, diligence, or dedication to the firm.

Federal Law and Overtime Pay

A major issue in the paralegal profession in regard to compensation has to do with overtime pay. Some paralegals who receive year-end bonuses question whether their bonuses sufficiently compensate them for the amount of overtime they have worked. The debate over overtime pay is complicated by the fact that the Fair Labor Standards Act (Wage-Hour Law) of 1938 requires employers to pay employees **overtime wages**—one and a half times their normal hourly rate for all hours worked beyond forty hours per week.

OVERTIME WAGES
Wages paid to workers who are paid an hourly wage rate to compensate them for overtime work (hours worked beyond forty hours per week). Under federal law, overtime wages are at least one and a half times the regular hourly wage rate.

---

3. Carol Milano, "Salary Survey Results," *Legal Assistant Today*, May/June 1993, p. 48; Bureau of Labor Statistics, *Monthly Labor Review*; and authors' estimates.

EXHIBIT 2.4
Paralegal Compensation by State

STATE	AVERAGE SALARY	STATE	AVERAGE SALARY
Alabama	$33,942	Montana	$22,896
Alaska	$41,583	Nebraska	$24,187
Arizona	$40,167	Nevada	$32,911
Arkansas	$36,254	New Hampshire	$30,186
California	$37,001	New Jersey	$28,224
Colorado	$28,156	New Mexico	$27,666
Connecticut	$34,069	New York	$35,714
Delaware	$48,145	North Carolina	$27,265
District of Columbia	$30,471	North Dakota	$25,166
Florida	$29,472	Ohio	$29,119
Georgia	$31,876	Oklahoma	$28,772
Hawaii	$31,890	Oregon	$32,150
Idaho	$22,365	Pennsylvania	$27,137
Illinois	$32,014	Rhode Island	$28,408
Indiana	$25,208	South Carolina	$24,941
Iowa	$26,567	South Dakota	$28,908
Kansas	$32,795	Tennessee	$31,239
Kentucky	$26,451	Texas	$33,181
Louisiana	$28,728	Utah	$25,469
Maine	$35,113	Vermont	$24,752
Maryland	$27,090	Virginia	$28,001
Massachusetts	$24,607	Washington	$31,693
Michigan	$29,305	West Virginia	(not available)
Minnesota	$32,641	Wisconsin	$28,120
Mississippi	$26,407	Wyoming	$17,993
Missouri	$29,996		

Source: Authors' estimates based on data reported in Carol Milano, "Salary Survey Results," *Legal Assistant Today*, May/June 1993, p. 48ff., and Bureau of Labor Statistics, *Monthly Labor Review*, various issues.

The act exempts certain types of employees from this overtime-pay requirement, however. *Exempt employees* include those who qualify under the terms of the act as holding "administrative," "executive," or "professional" positions.

The issue, then, is whether paralegals are exempt or nonexempt employees under the Fair Labor Standards Act. If they are exempt, they need not be paid an hourly overtime rate. If they are nonexempt, by law they must be paid overtime wages. Many firms argue that their paralegals are professionals and thus exempt from the act. Other firms, fearing possible liability for unfair labor practices, are beginning to pay overtime wages to their paralegals. Paralegals seem to be split fairly evenly on the issue. A poll taken in 1993 by the National Federation of Paralegal Associations indicated that 51 percent of paralegals supported exempt status and 49 percent preferred to be nonexempt employees (and thus receive overtime wages).

In early 1994, a federal court addressed this issue for the first time. The case arose when twenty-three paralegals who worked for Page & Addison, a law firm in Dallas, Texas, sought $40,000 in back wages for overtime hours that they had worked. The Department of Labor, which enforces the Fair Labor Standards Act, had concluded that the paralegals were nonexempt employees and thus subject to the act's overtime provisions. The federal court, however, disagreed, finding that paralegals could be classified as exempt (or professional) employees because they perform important work

EXHIBIT 2.5
What Is the Job Worth to You?

BENEFITS
What benefits are included? Will the benefits package include medical insurance? Life insurance? Disability insurance? Dental insurance? What portion, if any, of the insurance premium will be deducted from your wages? Is there an employee pension plan? How many paid vacation days will you have? Will the firm cover your paralegal association fees? Will the firm assist you in tuition and other costs associated with continuing paralegal education? Will the firm assist in day-care arrangements and/or costs? Will you have access to a company automobile? Does the firm help with parking expenses (important in major cities)?

CAREER OPPORTUNITIES
Does the position offer you opportunities for advancement? You may be willing to accept a lower salary now if you know that it will increase as you move up the career ladder.

COMPENSATION
Will you receive an annual salary or be paid by the hour? If you will receive an annual salary, will you receive annual bonuses? How are bonuses determined? Is the salary negotiable? (In some large firms and in government agencies, it may not be.)

COMPETITION
How stiff is the competition for this job? If you really want the job and are competing with numerous other candidates for the position, you might want to accept a lower salary just to land the job.

JOB DESCRIPTION
What are the paralegal's duties within the organization? Do you have sufficient training and experience to handle these duties? Are you underqualified or overqualified for the job? Will your skills as a paralegal be utilized effectively? How hard will you be expected to work? How much overtime work will likely be required? How stressful will the job be?

JOB FLEXIBILITY
How flexible are the working hours? If you work eight hours overtime one week, can you take a (paid) day off the following week? Can you take time off during periods when the workload is less?

LOCATION
Do you want to live in this community? What is the cost of living in this area? Remember, a $40,000 salary in New York City, where housing and taxes are very expensive, may not give you as much *real* income as a $25,000 salary in a smaller, mid-sized community in the Midwest.

PERMANENCE
Is the job a permanent or temporary position? Usually, hourly rates for temporary assistance are higher than for permanent employees.

TRAVEL
Will you be required to travel? If so, how often or extensively? How will travel expenses be handled? Will you pay them up front and then be reimbursed by the employer?

and exercise discretion and independent judgment.[4] Although the court decision in the *Page & Addison* case is significant, it does not mean that all paralegals will be classified as exempt employees. Very likely, the Department of Labor and courts hearing future cases, should cases arise, will evaluate the claims relating to overtime pay on a case-by-case basis and take into consideration the specific types of tasks undertaken by the paralegals involved.

PLANNING YOUR CAREER

Career planning involves essentially three steps. The first step is defining your long-term goals. The second step involves adjusting your long-term

---

4. *U.S. Department of Labor v. Page & Addison, P.C.*, U.S. District Court, Dallas, Texas, No. 91-2655, March 15, 1994.

goals to meet the realities of the job market. A third step is reevaluating your career after you have had some on-the-job experience as a paralegal.

Defining Your Long-term Goals

From the outset, you will want to define, as clearly as possible, your career goals, and this requires some personal reflection and self-assessment. What are you looking for in a career? Why do you want to become a paralegal? Is income the most important factor? Is job satisfaction (doing the kind of work you like) the most important factor? Is the environment in which you work the most important factor? What profession could best utilize your special talents or skills? Asking yourself these and other broad questions about your personal preferences and values will help you define more clearly your overall professional goals.

Do not be surprised to find that your long-term goals change over time. As you gain more experience as a paralegal and your life circumstances change, you may decide that your former long-term goals are no longer as satisfying. Also, at the outset of your career, you cannot know what opportunities might present themselves in the future. Career planning is an ongoing challenge for paralegals, just as it is for all persons. Throughout your career as a paralegal, you will probably meet other paralegals who have made career changes. Many paralegals, for example, decided to become paralegals after several years of working in another profession, such as nursing, business administration, or accounting. Changes within the profession, your own experiences, and new opportunities constantly affect the career choices before you. The realities you face during your career may play a significant role in modifying your long-term goals.

Short-term Goals and Job Realities

Long-term goals are just that—goals that we hope to achieve over the long run. It may take many years or even a lifetime to attain certain long-term goals that we set for ourselves. Short-term goals are the steps that we take to realize our long-term goals. As an entry-level paralegal, one of your short-term goals is simply to find a job.

Ideally, you will find a job that provides you with a salary commensurate with your training and abilities, a level of responsibility that is comfortable (or challenging) for you, and excellent job benefits. The realities of the job market are not always what we would wish them to be, however. You should be prepared for the possibility that you might not find the "right" employer or the "perfect" job for you when you first start your job search. You may be lucky from the outset, but then again, it may take several attempts before you find the employer and the job that best suits your needs, skills, and talents. Remember, though, that even if you do not find the perfect job at the outset, you can gain valuable skills and experience in *any* job environment—skills and experience that can help you achieve long-term goals in the future.

Reevaluating Your Career

Once you have gained experience working as a paralegal, you can undertake the third step in career planning: reevaluation. Assume that you have worked

FEATURED GUEST: DENISE TEMPLETON

Paralegal Career Planning and Development

Biographical Note

Denise Templeton is the president and chief executive officer of Templeton & Associates, a legal support services firm based in Minneapolis, Minnesota. She has been involved with the paralegal profession since she graduated from the Institute for Paralegal Training in Philadelphia in 1972. Her professional career has included work as a legal assistant in both the public and private sectors, as well as seven years as the director of the legal-assistant program at the University of Minnesota. In 1985, she founded the Minnesota Legal Assistant Institute, a private postsecondary certificate program. Templeton is also a founder of the Minnesota Association of Legal Assistants, the American Association for Paralegal Education, and the National Federation of Paralegal Associations (NFPA). She is currently on the NFPA Advisory Council.

In the early 1970s, the paralegal field was just beginning to be officially recognized, and its parameters were undefined. The larger law firms and corporate legal departments were the first to grasp the concept that legal assistants could free busy attorneys by taking over the more routine legal tasks. This enabled law firms to get more work done in the same amount of time and at a constant level of quality. Because paralegals were a less expensive resource than attorneys, clients were able to pay less for legal services without sacrificing quality.

Then, as now, the majority of paralegals were employed in the litigation area [relating to lawsuits]. Over time, more specialty areas have opened up, and today's paralegal can be involved in anything from real estate to environmental law. Many opportunities are available now, and many more will be

created in the future. People are entering the paralegal field in greater numbers each year. The successful legal assistant knows the importance of adopting a career-development strategy. My strategy includes six basic components: (1) self-awareness, (2) knowledge of the field, (3) openness to opportunity, (4) professional development, (5) support systems, and (6) periodic review.

SELF-AWARENESS

Self-awareness involves creating a vision. You must envision what you want and expect from a paralegal career based on your knowledge of yourself and what is important to you in your work. As you develop your career path, think about where you want to start and where you want to be in the long run. There are many possibilities in terms of both work environments and types of work. As a beginner, you may

seek a large, structured office and a position that is clearly defined. One of the larger law firms or a corporate legal department may provide you with this framework. You may, however, sense that a smaller, less structured environment would be more comfortable for you. Your duties may be more varied. In any event, analyze your previous experience and prioritize your goals. Decide which goal is most important for you.

KNOWLEDGE OF THE FIELD

In tandem with self-assessment, consider the realities of the paralegal field itself. Again, because of the many options available in terms of legal specialties and work environments, the paralegal field can accommodate many types of people.

Some areas of law require more intensity, time, and dedication than others. If you are already juggling the demands of a job and a family,

for a long enough period (two to four years, for example) to have acquired experience in certain types of paralegal work. At this point, you should reevaluate your career goals and reassess your abilities based on your accumulated experience.

Career Advancement. Paralegals who want to advance in their careers normally have two options: (1) being promoted or transferring to another depart-

FEATURED GUEST, Continued

for example, overtime may be a serious problem. Talk to people working in the area that interests you. Learn about the advantages and disadvantages of working in that area. The more you learn about that area, the more accurate and complete will be your picture of what to expect and how the position fits in with your vision.

OPENNESS TO OPPORTUNITY

By keeping an open mind and being aware of changing interests, you will be able to create new opportunities for yourself and take advantage of opportunities that arise as your career develops. Even if you have already created your vision of the ideal paralegal career path, stay open to possibilities that may present themselves. If you are trained in probate practice (which deals with the transfer of property on a person's death), for example, you may find that real estate is a compatible specialty. By making your interest in real-estate practice known to your supervisor, you demonstrate a willingness to expand your legal knowledge. Ultimately, you may work for a corporation in its real-estate management or development division. The idea of cross-training becomes increasingly more acceptable as firms develop a more flexible work force. When the economy takes a turn for the worse, those who have multiple skills can be reassigned rather than laid off.

PROFESSIONAL DEVELOPMENT

Closely aligned with openness to opportunity is staying aware of developments in your profession. Developing and maintaining professional contacts and reading paralegal publications regularly are great ways to keep up with trends in your field. This knowledge can help you decide when and how to make turns in your career path. Also, the critical skill of networking plays an important role for any professional, including the paralegal. From the beginning, keep a current list of the people you meet and the area in which they work. Become an active member of your local paralegal association. If there is no paralegal association in your community, then start one. Read the periodicals published by national paralegal associations and bar associations, and read materials that will keep you up to date on what is happening locally and nationally with paralegals. Ask paralegals and attorneys what they read, and attend continuing-education seminars to expand your knowledge base.

SUPPORT SYSTEMS

The value of having people give you encouragement and constructive criticism cannot be overstated. When you share ideas and concerns with others involved in your work, you will have a more balanced perspective on your work. Balance is an important ingredient in life.

> **"TODAY'S PARALEGAL CAN BE INVOLVED IN ANYTHING FROM REAL ESTATE TO ENVIRONMENTAL LAW."**

When you are working in an intense, deadline-oriented atmosphere, balance can be painfully elusive. That is why having friends and participating in activities both inside and outside the legal profession is important to your well-being. Promise yourself that you will take regular vacations with family and friends and keep yourself healthy, happy, and productive.

PERIODIC REVIEW

Remember, change is the only constant in life. Many opportunities exist now that were not possible when the paralegal field was new. Many new opportunities will arise in the future. By taking the time periodically to take stock of your own changing needs and desires, as well as the evolution of the field, you can decide which career step to take next and when to take it. For those paralegals who take charge of their own destinies, there are many ways to grow and prosper as legal professionals.

ment within the firm or (2) moving to another firm—and perhaps another specialty.

Larger firms often provide career paths for their paralegal employees. Moving from the entry-level position of *legal-assistant clerk* to the position of *legal-assistant manager,* for example, may be one career track within a large law firm. A career track with a state government agency might begin at a *legal-technician* level and advance to a *legal-specialist* level.

TODAY'S PROFESSIONAL PARALEGAL

Witness Coordination

Barbara Lyons works as a paralegal for a busy litigation firm. Today she is assisting with a medical-malpractice trial. Susan Weiss, the attorney for whom Barbara works, has asked Barbara to coordinate Susan's witnesses. It is 8:30 A.M., and Barbara and Susan are waiting in the courtroom for Dr. Max Brennan, the first witness that Susan will call today.

PLANNING A WITNESS'S ARRIVAL TIME

While they are waiting, Susan fills Barbara in on how the trial went yesterday and what she expects to happen today. Susan tells Barbara that she expects Dr. Brennan to be on the stand testifying from 9 A.M. until at least the lunch break. Then she expects that he will be cross-examined for an hour or two after lunch. Susan wants Barbara to have the next witness, Laura Lang, at the courthouse and ready to testify by 11 A.M., though, in the event that Dr. Brennan is excused earlier than expected.

Barbara had previously arranged with the witness to arrive at the courthouse by 11 A.M. but is concerned that Lang will not be on time. Even though Barbara met with Lang two times to review her testimony and prepare her for the trial experience, she was always late. Barbara tells this to Susan. Susan tells Barbara to go out into the hallway at 9 A.M. and call Lang. "Tell her that things are moving along more quickly than planned and to be here at ten o'clock. That should help to make sure that she will be here by eleven."

A WITNESS IS DELAYED

It is 8:35 A.M., and Dr. Brennan has not yet arrived. Susan asks Barbara to go out to the hallway and call him, first in his car and then his office, to find out where he is. Barbara opens her trial notebook to the witness section. Dr. Brennan's page is first because he is the first witness scheduled to appear. She locates the number for his car phone, jots it down on a scrap of paper, and leaves the courtroom. As she starts dialing Dr. Brennan's number, she sees him walk out of the elevator. Barbara puts the phone back and greets Dr. Brennan. "Sorry I'm running late, but I had an emergency this morning and I had to stop by the hospital before I came here," explains Dr. Brennan.

"I'm just glad to see you!" exclaims Barbara. "Let's go into the courtroom. You are the first witness, and Susan wants to see you," instructs Barbara. Barbara and Dr. Brennan enter the courtroom. Susan and Dr. Brennan talk briefly before the judge enters the courtroom. The court is called to order, and the trial resumes. Barbara sits at the counsel table while Susan questions Dr. Brennan on the stand. At 9:00 A.M., Barbara leaves the courtroom and calls Laura Lang.

TAKING PRECAUTIONS—ARRANGING FOR A WITNESS TO ARRIVE EARLY

Lang answers the phone. "Hello Ms. Lang. It's Barbara Lyons from Smith, White & White. Susan Weiss asked me to call you and tell you that the trial is moving faster than we anticipated. Susan would like you to be here at ten o'clock instead of eleven, if that's possible," advises Barbara. "Oh. Well, I suppose I can be there by then," responds Lang. "Do you remember how to get here?" asks Barbara. "Yes, I have the directions," answers Lang. "Good. I'll see you soon then, at ten o'clock," says Barbara. She returns to the courtroom.

At 9:55 A.M., Barbara leaves the courtroom again to wait in the hallway for Laura Lang. By 10:15 A.M., Lang has still not arrived. Barbara opens the courtroom door to listen. The testimony is going faster than Susan had anticipated, and Barbara can tell that Susan will probably be ready to put Lang on the stand in another thirty minutes or so. Barbara closes the courtroom door. She goes to the pay phone and dials Lang's telephone number. There is no answer. "I hope that she is on her way," thinks Barbara.

A TIMELY ARRIVAL

Now it is 10:45 A.M., and Lang is still not there. Barbara opens the courtroom door again and can tell that there is only about five minutes left in Dr. Brennan's testimony. She dials Lang's number again. No answer. Barbara continues to wait in the hallway, and a few minutes later, Lang appears. Barbara breathes a sigh of relief. She opens the courtroom door, catches Susan's eye, and nods her head.

Creating Opportunities.   Smaller firms, in contrast, usually have no prede-termined career path or opportunities for promotion and career advance-ment. If you are the only paralegal in a small law firm, there will be no spec-ified career path within the firm for you to follow. If you find yourself in this situation, you might consider staying with the firm and creating your own position or career ladder. Moving up the ladder is often a matter of bringing in someone new to assist you with your paralegal responsibilities. Are you prevented from taking on more complicated tasks (which you are capable of performing) because of your heavy workload, much of which could be han-dled by a paralegal with less experience? Suggest a plan to your employer that shows how you can provide more complex legal services if you delegate many of your existing responsibilities to a new paralegal employee. One of the advantages of working for a small firm is the lack of any set, formal structure for promotions. If the firm is expanding, the paralegal may have significant input into how and to whom responsibilities will be assigned as new personnel are hired.

Other Options.   There are many other alternatives. You may apply for a job with another firm that offers you a better position or more advancement opportunities. You may learn a new specialty or return to school for further education. You might volunteer to speak to paralegal classes and seminars and, in so doing, establish new contacts and contribute to paralegal profes-sional development. Researching and writing law-related articles for your paralegal association's newsletter or trade magazine improves your profes-sional stature in the legal community as well. Any of these activities will increase your visibility both inside and outside the firm. In a broad sense, these activities are part of networking. The people you meet when engaging in these activities may offer you employment opportunities that you did not even know existed but that are perfect for you.

KEY TERMS AND CONCEPTS

bankruptcy law 38	estate planning 41	probate 41
bonus 48	family law 44	probate court 41
civil law 37	intellectual property 42	real estate 44
corporate law 38	litigation 36	tort 37
criminal law 37	litigation paralegal 36	trust 41
damages 37	negligence 37	will 41
defendant 36	overtime wages 48	workers' compensation
environmental law 43	plaintiff 36	statutes 40

CHAPTER SUMMARY

1. The job opportunities available in today's para-legal employment market are extraordinarily varied. Traditionally, paralegals worked for law firms, and most paralegals continue to work in the law-firm environment. Increasingly, however, paralegals are finding employment in corporate legal departments, as well as other business institutions, such as banks and insurance companies. A small but growing number of paralegals work for government agencies at the federal or state level.

2. Paralegals often specialize in particular areas of law, including the following: litigation assistance, personal-injury law, criminal law, corporate law, bankruptcy law, employment and labor law, estate planning and probate administration, intellectual-property law, environmental law, real-estate law, and family law.

3. Salaries and wage rates for paralegal employees vary substantially. Factors affecting compensation include geographical location, firm size, and type of employer (law firm, corporation, or government agency). Most paralegals are salaried—that is, they are paid a specified amount per year, regardless of the number of hours worked. Overtime work is compensated through year-

end bonuses or in some other way, such as equivalent time off work. Some paralegals are paid hourly wages for all hours worked and overtime wages for all hours worked exceeding forty hours per week.

4. Career planning involves three steps: defining your long-term career goals, adjusting your goals to fit job realities (and creating short-term goals), and reevaluating your career and career goals after you have had some on-the-job experience.

5. Career goals change over time, as do job opportunities. Advancing in your career may mean educating your employer in your abilities so that you can take on more responsibility, or it may mean looking for a job in a different department of the same firm or with another firm. Active participation in paralegal professional organizations or in paralegal education is a way to achieve higher visibility in the profession and to learn of new professional opportunities.

QUESTIONS FOR REVIEW

1. Name and describe the basic types of organizations that hire paralegals. What percentage of paralegals work for each type of organization?

2. From your perspective, what would be the advantages and disadvantages of working for each of the following organizations?

    a. A small law firm.

    b. A large law firm.

    c. A corporation.

    d. A government agency.

3. List and briefly describe each of the paralegal specialties discussed in this chapter. Which specialty area or areas interest you the most? Why?

4. How are paralegals compensated? What is the average paralegal salary in your state?

5. On average, in what specialty area do paralegals receive the highest salaries?

6. What are the advantages of being paid a salary? What are the advantages of being paid an hourly wage? What are the disadvantages of each type of compensation?

7. What are overtime wages? Are employers required to pay their paralegal employees overtime wages? Would you prefer to be compensated for overtime work by overtime wages or a year-end bonus? Why?

8. What are some of the factors, other than salary or wages, that you should consider when evaluating what a job is worth?

9. What are the three basic steps that are involved in career planning? What are long-term goals? How do short-term goals relate to long-term goals?

10. What are some ways in which you can advance in your paralegal career?

ETHICAL QUESTIONS

1. Tom Brown is a legal assistant in a busy litigation firm. As Tom is walking in the door at 8:30 A.M., he passes Mike Walker, his supervising attorney, who is

on his way to court to begin a trial. As they pass, Mike says to Tom, "I need a motion and a brief for the *Jones* case. I've left the file on your desk." Mike walks out the door and down the street to court. Can Tom competently prepare the motion and brief? Why or why not? What should Tom do?

2. Laura Bronson has just started her first job with the firm of Thompson & Smith, a general law practice. Laura is asked to prepare articles of incorporation for one of the firm's corporate clients. Laura did not take corporate law while studying to be a paralegal and has never prepared articles of incorporation before. Should Laura accept the assignment? If she does accept it, what obligations does she have?

3. Dennis Walker works at a very busy law firm. On each side of his desk, there are one-foot-high stacks of work, leaving only enough room for a small work space in the center of the desk and a spot for the telephone. His floor is likewise stacked high with legal documents. Dennis constantly misses deadlines and is often in trouble for turning work in late or doing work incorrectly. Dennis has tried to get organized but feels that it is impossible to do so because he has such a heavy workload. What are Dennis's ethical obligations in this situation?

PRACTICE QUESTIONS AND ASSIGNMENTS

1. Which of the following are tasks that might be assigned to a litigation paralegal:

    a. Interviewing a client.

    b. Drafting a will.

    c. Drafting a complaint.

    d. Preparing articles of incorporation.

    e. Collecting technical data to submit to the Environmental Protection Agency.

    f. Attending a deposition.

    g. Preparing a witness for trial.

    h. Reviewing an information checklist for a divorce case.

    i. Assisting at trial.

    j. Preparing a trial notebook.

2. Start planning your career now by doing the following:

    a. Make a list of your long-term career goals.

    b. Make a list of short-term goals that could serve as "stepping stones" on the path to your long-term goals.

    c. Make a list of activities that you could undertake now, as a paralegal student, that would further your career goals.

3

REGULATION AND ETHICAL RESPONSIBILITIES

Chapter Objectives

After completing this chapter, you will know:

- Why and how legal professionals are regulated.
- Some important ethical rules governing the conduct of attorneys and how these rules affect paralegal practice.
- The extent to which the paralegal profession is regulated.
- The kinds of activities that paralegals are and are not legally permitted to perform.
- Some of the pros and cons of regulation, including the debate over paralegal licensing.
- How personal ethics and legal ethics can sometimes come into conflict.

Chapter Outline

INTRODUCTION

As discussed in the previous chapter, paralegals preparing for a career in today's legal arena have a variety of career options. Regardless of which career path you choose to follow, you should have a firm grasp of your state's ethical rules governing the legal profession. When you work under the supervision of an attorney, as most paralegals do, you and the attorney become team members. You will work together on behalf of clients and share in the ethical and legal responsibilities arising as a result of the attorney-client relationship.

In preparing for a career as a paralegal, you must know what these responsibilities are, why they exist, and how they affect you. The reason why the first part of this chapter is devoted to the regulation of attorneys is because the ethical duties imposed on attorneys by state laws also affect paralegals. If a paralegal violates one of the rules governing attorneys, that violation may result in serious consequences for the client, for the attorney, and for the paralegal.

Although attorneys are subject to direct regulation by the state, paralegals are not. Paralegals are regulated *indirectly*, however, by attorney ethical codes, by ethical codes developed and adopted by paralegal associations, and by state laws that prohibit nonlawyers from practicing law. Professional paralegal organizations, the American Bar Association, and state bar associations also have issued guidelines, and continue to do so, that serve to regulate paralegals indirectly. After examining the ways in which these codes, laws, and guidelines indirectly regulate paralegal conduct, we look at the question being explored by legal professionals (and others) today: Should paralegals be directly regulated—through licensing requirements, for example—by the state? We conclude the chapter with a discussion of a topic of interest to every paralegal—what the paralegal should do when his or her personal values conflict with professional ethical responsibilities.

THE IMPLICATIONS OF PROFESSIONAL STATUS

PROFESSION
An occupation requiring knowledge of the arts or sciences and advanced study in a specialized field, such as the law.

A **profession** is usually defined as an occupation or trade that requires a basic knowledge of the arts and sciences as well as advanced study in a specialized field. Historically, professions have been distinguished from other types of occupations by the fact that, in addition to acquiring expert knowledge in their fields of study as demonstrated by the passing of examinations, professionals are subject to standards of expertise and behavior established by their peers—other members of their profession.

SELF-REGULATION
The regulation of the conduct of a professional group by members of the group themselves. Self-regulation usually involves the establishment of ethical or professional standards of behavior with which members of the group must comply.

Professional groups usually engage in a degree of **self-regulation** by establishing ethical or professional codes to regulate their conduct while serving the public. Note that if professionals simply acquired knowledge but never offered their expert advice to the public, there would be no need to regulate professions. The need for regulation arises only when the members of the public (individuals without such specialized knowledge) rely on professionals for expert advice. The fact that individuals rely on (and pay for) professional services imposes a duty on professionals to serve those individuals' best interests.

At the heart, then, of the concept of a professional is *service to others.* In their professional capacity, lawyers strive to make sure that their clients' interests are protected under the law; physicians seek to heal and comfort patients; accountants work hard to ensure that their clients have the best accounting advice possible; and so on. In regard to the legal profession, an attorney's advice and work product can greatly affect the client's welfare. The quality of an attorney's work can determine, for example, whether a client will be imprisoned, be compensated for pain and suffering, receive a fair share of marital assets and liabilities in a divorce proceeding, or acquire rights to the exclusive proceeds of his or her invention. Because so much is at stake, attorneys are regulated both internally by members of the profession and externally by the state.

The quality of a paralegal's work can also have serious consequences for clients, so paralegals who work for attorneys are also subject to (indirect) regulation by attorney rules of conduct. Whether paralegals should also be regulated directly by state laws—through licensing requirements, for example—is a question that has elicited a great deal of controversy, as you will see later in this chapter.

THE REGULATION OF ATTORNEYS

The term *regulate* derives from the Latin term *regula,* meaning "rule." According to Webster's dictionary, to *regulate* means "to control or direct in agreement with a rule." To a significant extent, attorneys are self-regulated because they themselves establish the majority of the rules governing the profession—rules that are enforced by state authorities.

The rules governing attorneys protect the public interest in two ways. First, by establishing educational and licensing requirements, they ensure that anyone practicing law is competent to do so. Second, by defining specific ethical requirements for attorneys, the rules protect the public against unethical attorney behavior that may affect clients' welfare. We discuss these requirements and rules below. First, however, you should know how these rules are created and enforced.

Who Are the Regulators?

Key participants in determining what rules should govern attorneys and the practice of law, as well as how these rules should be enforced, are bar associations, state supreme courts, state legislatures, and, in some cases, the United States Supreme Court. Procedures for regulating attorneys vary, of course, from state to state. What follows is a general discussion of who the regulators may be.

Bar Associations.   Lawyers themselves determine the requirements for entering the legal profession and the rules of conduct they will follow. Traditionally, lawyers have joined together in professional groups, or bar associations, at the local, state, and national levels to discuss issues affecting the legal profession and to decide on standards of professional conduct.

Although membership in local and national bar associations is always voluntary, membership in the *state* bar association is mandatory in over two-thirds of the states. In these states, before an attorney can practice law, he or she must be admitted to the state's bar association. Approximately half of the lawyers in the United States are members of the American Bar Association (ABA), the voluntary national bar association discussed in Chapter 1. As you will read shortly, the ABA plays a key regulatory role by proposing model (uniform) codes, or rules of conduct, for adoption by the various states.

State Supreme Courts.   Each state's highest court, often called the state supreme court, is normally the ultimate regulatory authority in that state. The judges who sit on the bench of the highest state court decide what conditions (such as licensing requirements, discussed below) must be met before an attorney can practice law within the state and under what conditions that privilege will be suspended or revoked. In many states, the state supreme court works closely with the state bar association. The state bar association may recommend rules and requirements to the court. If the court so orders, these rules and requirements become law within the state. Under the authority of the courts, state bar associations often perform routine regulatory functions, including the initiation of disciplinary proceedings against attorneys who fail to comply with professional requirements.

State Legislatures.   State legislatures regulate the legal profession by enacting legislation affecting attorneys—statutes prohibiting the unauthorized practice of law, for example. In a few states, the states' highest courts delegate significant regulatory responsibilities to the state legislatures, which may include the power to bring disciplinary proceedings against attorneys.

The United States Supreme Court.   On rare occasions, the United States Supreme Court has decided issues relating to attorney conduct. For example, until a few decades ago, state ethical codes, or rules governing attorney conduct, prohibited lawyers from advertising their services to the public. These restrictions on advertising were challenged as an unconstitutional limitation on attorneys' rights to free speech, and ultimately, the United States Supreme Court decided the issue. In a case decided in 1977, *Bates v. State Bar of Arizona*,[1] the Supreme Court ruled that truthful advertising of the availability and price of routine legal services was protected speech under the First Amendment to the U.S. Constitution and that provisions of state ethical codes forbidding such advertising were therefore unconstitutional.

Licensing Requirements

LICENSING
A government's official act of granting permission to an individual, such as an attorney, to do something that would be illegal in the absence of such permission.

The **licensing** of attorneys, which gives them the right to practice law, is accomplished at the state level. Each state has different requirements that

---

1. 433 U.S. 350, 97 S.Ct. 2691, 53 L.Ed.2d 810 (1977). (See Chapter 9 for a discussion of how to read case citations.)

individuals must meet before they are allowed by law to practice law and give legal advice. Generally, however, there are three basic requirements:

1. A prospective attorney must have obtained a bachelor's degree from a university or college and must have graduated from an accredited law school (in most states, the school must be accredited by the ABA), which requires an additional three years of study. There are rare exceptions to this requirement.

2. A prospective attorney must pass a state bar examination—a very rigorous and thorough examination that tests the candidate's knowledge of the law and (in some states) the state's ethical rules governing attorneys. The examination covers both state law (law applicable to the particular state in which the attorney is taking the exam and wishes to practice) and multistate law (law applicable in most states, including federal law).

3. The candidate must pass an extensive personal-background investigation to verify that he or she is a responsible individual and otherwise qualifies to engage in an ethical profession. An illegal act committed by the candidate in the past, for example, might disqualify the individual from being admitted to the profession.

Only when these requirements have been met can an individual be admitted to the state bar and legally practice law within the state.

Licensing requirements for attorneys are the result of a long history of attempts to restrict entry into the legal profession. The earliest of these restrictions date to the colonial era. During the 1700s, local bar associations began to form agreements to restrict entry into their associations to those who fulfilled certain educational and apprenticeship requirements. At the same time, to curb unnecessary litigation and the detrimental effects of incompetent legal practitioners, courts began to require that individuals representing clients in court proceedings had to be licensed by the court to do so.

Beginning in the mid-1850s, restrictions on who could (or could not) practice law were given statewide effect by state statutes prohibiting the **unauthorized practice of law (UPL)**. Court decisions relating to unauthorized legal practice also date to this period. By the 1930s, virtually all states had enacted legislation prohibiting anyone but licensed attorneys from practicing law. As you will see in subsequent sections, many of the ethical issues facing the legal profession—and particularly paralegals—are directly related to these UPL statutes.

UNAUTHORIZED PRACTICE OF LAW (UPL)
Engaging in actions defined by a legal authority, such as a state legislature, as constituting the "practice of law" without legal authorization to do so.

Ethical Codes and Rules

The legal profession is regulated by the licensing requirements just discussed. Additionally, the profession is regulated through ethical codes and rules adopted by each state—in most states, by order of the state supreme court. These codes of professional conduct—the names of the codes vary from state to state—evolved over a long period of time. The first state bar to publish a code of ethics was Alabama, in 1887. A major step toward ethical regulation was taken in 1908, when the ABA approved the Canons of Ethics, which consisted of thirty-two ethical principles based on the Alabama model. In the following decades, various states adopted these canons as law.

Today's state ethical codes are based, for the most part, on two subsequent revisions of the ABA canons: the Model Code of Professional Responsibility (published in 1969) and the Model Rules of Professional Conduct (published in 1983 to replace the Model Code). Although most of the states have now adopted the Model Rules, the Model Code is still in effect in some states, so you should be familiar with the basic format and content of both the Model Code and the Model Rules.

The Model Code of Professional Responsibility. The ABA Model Code of Professional Responsibility, often referred to as simply the Model Code, consists of the nine canons listed in Exhibit 3.1. In the Model Code, each canon is followed by sections entitled "Ethical Considerations" (ECs) and "Disciplinary Rules" (DRs). The ethical considerations are "aspirational" in character—that is, they suggest ideal conduct, not behavior that is necessarily required by law. For example, Canon 6 ("A lawyer should represent a client competently") is followed by EC 6–1, which states (in part) that a lawyer "should strive to become and remain proficient in his practice." In contrast, disciplinary rules are mandatory in character—an attorney may be subject to disciplinary action for breaking one of the rules. For example, DR 6–101 (which follows Canon 6) states that a lawyer "shall not . . . [n]eglect a legal matter entrusted to him."

The Model Rules of Professional Conduct. The 1983 revision of the Model Code—referred to as the Model Rules of Professional Conduct or, more simply, as the Model Rules—represented a thorough revamping of the code. The Model Rules replaced the canons, ethical considerations, and disciplinary rules of the Model Code with a set of rules organized under eight general headings, as outlined in Exhibit 3.2. Each rule is followed by comments shedding additional light on the rule's application and how it compares with the Model Code's treatment of the same issue.

EXHIBIT 3.1
The ABA Model Code of Professional Responsibility (Canons Only)

CANON 1
A lawyer should assist in maintaining the integrity and competence of the legal profession.

CANON 2
A lawyer should assist the legal profession in fulfilling its duty to make legal counsel available.

CANON 3
A lawyer should assist in preventing the unauthorized practice of law.

CANON 4
A lawyer should preserve the confidences and secrets of a client.

CANON 5
A lawyer should exercise independent professional judgment on behalf of a client.

CANON 6
A lawyer should represent a client competently.

CANON 7
A lawyer should represent a client zealously within the bounds of the law.

CANON 8
A lawyer should assist in improving the legal system.

CANON 9
A lawyer should avoid even the appearance of professional impropriety.

EXHIBIT 3.2

The ABA Model Rules of Professional Conduct (Headings Only)

• • • • •

CLIENT-LAWYER RELATIONSHIP

1.1	Competence		1.9	Conflict of Interest: Former Client
1.2	Scope of Representation		1.10	Imputed Disqualification: General Rule
1.3	Diligence		1.11	Successive Government and Private Employment
1.4	Communication		1.12	Former Judge or Arbitrator
1.5	Fees		1.13	Organization as Client
1.6	Confidentiality of Information		1.14	Client under a Disability
1.7	Conflict of Interest: General Rule		1.15	Safekeeping Property
1.8	Conflict of Interest: Prohibited Transactions		1.16	Declining or Terminating Representation

COUNSELOR

2.1	Advisor		2.3	Evaluation for Use by Third Persons
2.2	Intermediary			

ADVOCATE

3.1	Meritorious Claims and Contentions		3.6	Trial Publicity
3.2	Expediting Litigation		3.7	Lawyer as Witness
3.3	Candor toward the Tribunal		3.8	Special Responsibilities of a Prosecutor
3.4	Fairness to Opposing Party and Counsel		3.9	Advocate in Nonadjudicative Proceedings
3.5	Impartiality and Decorum of the Tribunal			

TRANSACTIONS WITH PERSONS OTHER THAN CLIENTS

4.1	Truthfulness in Statement to Others		4.3	Dealing with Unrepresented Person
4.2	Communication with Person Represented by Counsel		4.4	Respect for Rights of Third Persons

LAW FIRMS AND ASSOCIATIONS

5.1	Responsibilities of a Partner or Supervisory Lawyer		5.4	Professional Independence of a Lawyer
5.2	Responsibilities of a Subordinate Lawyer		5.5	Unauthorized Practice of Law
5.3	Responsibilities Regarding Nonlawyer Assistants		5.6	Restrictions on Right to Practice

PUBLIC SERVICE

6.1	*Pro Bono Publico* Service		6.3	Membership in Legal Services Organization
6.2	Accepting Appointments		6.4	Law Reform Activities Affecting Client Interests

INFORMATION ABOUT LEGAL SERVICES

7.1	Communications Concerning a Lawyer's Services		7.4	Communication of Fields of Practice
7.2	Advertising		7.5	Firm Names and Letterheads
7.3	Direct Contact with Prospective Clients			

MAINTAINING THE INTEGRITY OF THE PROFESSION

8.1	Bar Admission and Disciplinary Matters		8.4	Misconduct
8.2	Judicial and Legal Officials		8.5	Jurisdiction
8.3	Reporting Professional Misconduct			

BREACH
To violate a legal duty by an act or a failure to act.

The Model Rules—A Sampling

State ethical codes of conduct provide the basic framework for all legal work, including that undertaken by paralegals. The state ethical codes are fairly uniform because they are patterned after either the Model Code or the Model Rules (except in California, whose code follows neither the Model Code nor the Model Rules). Because most state codes are guided by the Model Rules of Professional Conduct, the rules discussed below are drawn from the Model Rules. Keep in mind, though, that it is the code of conduct *adopted by your state* that is the governing authority on attorney conduct in your state. You will thus want to obtain and keep in your office (or on your desk) a copy of your state's ethical code.

To understand how the profession is regulated and your responsibilities as a paralegal, you need to have some knowledge of the ethical duties imposed on legal professionals by these codes. We look here at some of the duties that have particularly important implications for paralegal practice.

The Duty of Competence.   The first of the Model Rules states one of the most fundamental duties of attorneys—the duty of competence. Rule 1.1 of the Model Rules reads as follows:

> A lawyer shall provide competent representation to a client. Competent representation requires the legal knowledge, skill, thoroughness and preparation reasonably necessary for representation.

Competent legal representation is a basic requirement of the profession, and **breaching** (failing to perform) this duty may subject attorneys to one or more of the sanctions discussed later. As a paralegal, you should realize that when you undertake work on an attorney's behalf, you share in this duty. Deadlines—such as the dates by which certain documents must be filed with a court or other action taken—must be met. Documents must be free of errors that might jeopardize a client's legal rights. If your supervising attorney asks you to research a particular legal issue for a client, you must make sure that your research is careful and thorough—because the attorney's reputation (and the client's welfare) may depend on your performance. You should also realize that careless performance of your duties as a paralegal, if it results in substantial injury to the client's interests, may subject you personally to liability for negligence (discussed below), not to mention the loss of a job or career opportunities.

The duty of competence, because it is so fundamental and so broadly conceived, overlaps with numerous other duties, including the duty of diligence.

Diligence.   Model Rule 1.3 states that "[a] lawyer shall act with reasonable diligence and promptness in representing a client." The paralegal plays a vital role in making sure that a client's case or legal matter is handled efficiently and in a timely manner. Attorneys and paralegals often work on several cases at the same time, some of which may take years to resolve. A major challenge for paralegals and attorneys is making sure that no unnecessary delays occur.

A particularly serious problem occurs when an attorney fails to initiate action on behalf of a client within the time period established by a statute of limitations. State **statutes of limitations** establish fixed time limits within which different types of lawsuits must be filed. After the time allowed under a statute of limitations has expired, the client's right to sue is extinguished, and no action can be brought, no matter how strong the case was originally.

Communication.   Model Rule 1.4 establishes the attorney's duty to keep the client reasonably informed: "A lawyer shall keep a client reasonably informed about the status of a matter and promptly comply with reasonable requests for information." As a paralegal, you need to be aware that keeping clients reasonably informed about the progress being made on their cases goes beyond courtesy and the cultivation of a client's goodwill—it is a *legal* duty of attorneys. The meaning of "reasonably informed" varies, of course, depending on the client and on the nature of the work being done by the attorney. In some cases, a phone call every week or two will suffice to keep the client informed. In other cases, the attorney may ask the paralegal to draft a letter to a client explaining the status of the client's legal matter. Generally, as a paralegal, you should discuss with your supervising attorney how each client should be kept informed of the status of his or her case.

Fees.   Model Rule 1.5 begins with the statement, "A lawyer's fees shall be reasonable." The rule goes on to indicate what factors should be considered in determining the reasonableness of a fee. The factors include the time and labor required to perform the legal work, the fee customarily charged in the locality for similar legal services, and the experience and ability of the lawyer performing the services. A major ethical concern of the legal profession has to do with the reasonableness of attorneys' fees and the ways in which clients are billed for legal services. You will read about some of the ethical problems relating to fees and client billing procedures in Chapter 4.

In regard to fees, paralegals should also become familiar with Rule 5.4 of the Model Rules. That rule states, "A lawyer or law firm shall not share legal fees with a nonlawyer." For this reason, paralegals cannot become partners in a law partnership (because the partners share the firm's income), nor can they have a fee-sharing arrangement with an attorney in any way. One of the reasons for this rule is that it protects the attorney's independent judgment concerning legal matters. The rule against fee splitting also protects against the possibility that nonlawyers would, indirectly through attorneys, be able to engage in the practice of law, which no one but an attorney can do.

Confidentiality of Information.   Rule 1.6 of the Model Rules states that a lawyer may not reveal "information relating to representation of a client" without the client's consent to the disclosure. An attorney may make "disclosures that are impliedly authorized in order to carry out the representation," however. Clearly, such disclosure is necessary because legal representation of clients involves the attorney's assistants, and they must have access to confidential information to do their jobs.

The rule of confidentiality is one of the oldest and most important rules of the legal profession, primarily because it would be difficult for a lawyer to represent a client without such a rule. A client must be able to confide in his or her attorney so that the attorney can best represent the client's interest. Exceptions to this rule will only be made in two situations: (1) when an

STATUTE OF LIMITATIONS
A statute setting the maximum time period within which certain actions can be brought or rights enforced. After the period set out in the applicable statute of limitations has run, normally no legal action can be brought.

DEVELOPING PARALEGAL SKILLS

Prohibition on Fee Splitting

Robert Minson has worked as a paralegal for Peter H. Stonequist III for ten years. Robert has on several occasions referred cases to Peter that have been big winners. Robert has another one of those cases, and he is going into Peter's office to tell him about it.

"Peter, I have another case that you might be interested in handling—do you have a minute?" asks Robert. Peter responds, "Certainly, Robert, please come in. What kind of case is it?" Robert says, "Well, it's a personal-injury case. One of my father's friends was involved in a car accident a few months ago and was badly injured. He wants to sue the person who caused the accident, and I told my father that I'd see if you were interested in taking on the case." Robert and the attorney discuss the case, and Peter agrees with Robert that his father's friend might have a strong case against the driver of the other car.

"You know, Robert, you have referred many cases to me over the years, and I'd like to compensate you in some way for contributing to the firm's business," says Peter. Robert suggests that maybe they can work out a commission arrangement. "That presents a problem, Robert," replies Peter. "Lawyers are not allowed to split fees with nonlawyers, and they aren't allowed to pay referral fees, either. I value the business that you bring in, as well as the quality of your work, but I'm not allowed to give you a commission on your referrals because that would, in effect, be splitting fees with a nonlawyer, which I can't legally do. I've thought about it many times. Believe me, if I could, I'd make you a partner, but again, the ethical rules prohibit lawyers from entering into a partnership with nonlawyers."

"I see," Robert says. Peter, noting Robert's disappointment, then tells Robert that although attorneys cannot legally split fees with nonlawyers, there is no prohibition against increasing paralegals' salaries and bonuses when the firm is profitable. "When it's time for your performance review, your overall contribution to the firm's profitability will be considered," Peter explains to Robert. Robert smiles and replies that he certainly wouldn't object to that!

---

attorney is sued by a client and it is necessary to reveal confidential information to defend against the suit and (2) when a client reveals that he or she intends to commit a criminal act that may cause bodily harm or death to another. In the latter situation, the policy underlying the rule of confidentiality (protection of the client's legal rights) is outweighed by the policy of protecting another from imminent bodily harm or death.

What the confidentiality rule means for paralegals is that they also must assume responsibility for keeping confidential all knowledge relating to clients' cases. Because confidentiality is one of the easiest rules to violate, paralegals must take special care to refrain from saying or doing anything that might result in confidential information falling into the wrong hands. We look below at just a few ways in which paralegals can violate, inadvertently, the rule of confidentiality.

Conversations with Others.   As a paralegal, perhaps one of the greatest temptations you will face is the desire to discuss a particularly interesting case, or some aspect of a case, with a someone you know, such as a spouse, a co-worker, or a good friend. You can deal with this temptation in two ways: you can decide, as a matter of policy, never to discuss *anything* concerning your work; or you can limit your discussion to issues and comments that will not reveal the identity of your client. The latter approach is, for many paralegals, a more realistic solution, but it requires great care. Something you say may reveal a client's identity, even though you are not aware of it.

Violations of the confidentiality rule may happen simply by oversight. For example, suppose that you and the legal secretary in your office are both working on the same case and continue, as you walk down the hallway toward the elevator, a conversation about the case that you started in the office. You pause before the elevator, not realizing that your conversation is being overheard by someone around the corner from you. You have no way of knowing the person is there, and you have no way of knowing whether the confidential information that you inadvertently revealed will have any adverse effect on your client's interests. One way to avoid the possibility of unwittingly revealing confidential information to **third parties** (persons who are not directly involved in a case) is to follow this rule of thumb:

- **Never discuss confidential information when you are in a common area, such as a hallway, an elevator, or a cafeteria, where a conversation might be overheard.**

Telephone Calls and Confidentiality.   Similarly, you need to take preventive measures whenever you talk to or about a client on the telephone by making sure that your conversation will not be overheard by a third party. You may be sitting in your private office, but if your door is open, someone may overhear the conversation. Telephone calls can be particularly problematic if your work area is in or near a reception room. For example, assume that you work for a sole practitioner. Your job combines the functions of receptionist, legal secretary, and paralegal. Your desk is in the reception area of the office, and a client enters the room. While the client is waiting to see the attorney, another client calls you on the phone. You cannot even greet the caller by name without revealing confidential information to the client in your office. Similarly, if you are engaged in a phone conversation and someone enters the office, you must immediately be very guarded in what you say while the visitor is present.

Paralegals should take special care when using cellular phones. Cellular phones are not always secure because conversations on such phones can be tapped. As a precaution, you should thus never disclose confidential information when talking on cellular phones.

Other Ways of Violating the Confidentiality Rule.   There are hundreds of other ways in which you can reveal confidential information without intending to do so. A file or document sitting on your desk, if observed by a third party, may reveal the identity of a client or enough information to suggest the client's identity. A computer screen, if visible to those passing by your desk, could convey information to someone who is not authorized to

---

ETHICAL CONCERN
Misdialed Fax Numbers and Confidentiality

Sending a fax is a simple operation, but it presents a potential pitfall for the paralegal. What if you accidentally key in a wrong number? If that wrong number happens to be someone else's fax number, confidential information will end up in the hands of a third party. Sometimes, faxes are sent to the wrong person because the client has several fax numbers and the wrong one is selected. For example, you may have more than one fax number for a large corporation. If you inadvertently sent a fax to the corporate president, when you intended to send it to the firm's accountant (who had consulted with your supervising attorney about his employment relationship with the firm), the breach of confidentiality could significantly harm the accountant's interests. One way to guard against misdialing fax numbers is by double-checking the recipient's number registered on the fax machine after you have dialed the number.

THIRD PARTY
In the context of legal proceedings, a party who is not directly involved in the proceeding—that is, a party other than the plaintiff and defendant and their attorneys.

know that information. As a paralegal, you will need to be particularly careful to prevent such inadvertent disclosures of confidential information. For example, you should develop a habit of always making sure that your computer screen is blank before you leave your desk. Some law offices are now attaching a special kind of computer screen cover. This device makes it impossible for anyone to view the screen from an angle. Only the person directly facing the computer can see the document on the screen.

Confidentiality and the Attorney-client Privilege. All information relating to a client's representation is considered confidential information. Some confidential information also qualifies as *privileged* information, or information subject to the **attorney-client privilege**. The attorney-client privilege comes into play during the litigation process. As you will read in Chapter 6, prior to a trial, each attorney is permitted to obtain information relating to the case from the opposing attorney, as well as other persons, such as witnesses. This means that attorneys must exchange a certain amount of information relating to their clients. An attorney need not divulge privileged information, however—unless the client consents to the disclosure or a court orders the disclosure. Similarly, if an attorney is called to the witness stand during a trial, the attorney may not disclose privileged information unless the court orders him or her to do so.

State statutes and court cases define what constitutes privileged information. Generally, any communications concerning a client's *legal* rights or problem fall under the attorney-client privilege. For example, suppose that an attorney's client is a criminal defendant. The client tells the attorney that she actually was in the vicinity of the crime site at the time of the crime, but to her knowledge, no one noticed her presence there. This is privileged information that the attorney may only disclose with the client's consent or on a court's order to do so.

Information and documents concerning an attorney's legal strategy for conducting a case may be classified as **work product** and, as such, subject to the attorney-client privilege. Legal strategy includes the legal theories that the attorney plans to use in support of the client's claim, how the attorney interprets the evidence relating to the claim, and so on. Certain evidence gathered by the attorney to support the client's claim, however, such as financial statements relating to the client's business firm, would probably not be classified as work product. Because it is often difficult to tell what types of information (including work product) qualify as privileged, paralegals should consult closely with their supervising attorneys whenever issues arise that may require that such a distinction be made.

Conflict of Interest. A **conflict of interest** exists whenever a person's duties (or interests) come into conflict. In the legal context, a classic example of a conflict of interest exists when an attorney simultaneously represents two adverse parties in a legal proceeding. Clearly, in such a situation, the attorney's loyalties must be divided. It would be as if a football player agreed to play on both teams during a game—half of the time with one team and half of the time with the other. To ensure that clients' interests are not harmed by an attorney's divided loyalties, professional codes or rules of ethics prohibit lawyers from representing clients when doing so would result in a con-

ATTORNEY-CLIENT PRIVILEGE
A rule of evidence requiring that confidential communications between a client and his or her attorney (relating to their professional relationship) be kept confidential, unless the client consents to disclosure.

WORK PRODUCT
An attorney's mental impressions, conclusions, and legal theories regarding a case being prepared on behalf of a client. Work product normally is regarded as privileged information.

CONFLICT OF INTEREST
A situation in which two or more duties or interests come into conflict, as when an attorney attempts to represent opposing parties in a legal dispute.

flict of interest. Rule 1.7 of the Model Rules states the general rule: "A lawyer shall not represent a client if the representation of the client will be directly adverse to another client."

Simultaneous Representation.   If an attorney decides that representing two parties in a legal proceeding will not adversely affect either party's interest, then the attorney is permitted to do so—but only if both parties agree. Normally, attorneys avoid this kind of situation because what might start out as a simple, uncontested proceeding may evolve into a legal battle. Divorce proceedings, for example, may begin amicably but end up in heated disputes over child-custody arrangements or property division. The attorney then faces a conflict of interest: assisting one party will necessarily be adverse to the interests of the other.

Former Clients.   A conflict of interest may also involve former clients. Model Rule 1.9 states that "[a] lawyer who has formerly represented a client in a matter shall not thereafter represent another person in the same or substantially related matter in which that person's interests are materially adverse to the interests of the former client unless the former client consents after consultation." The rule regarding former clients is closely related to the rule on preserving the confidentiality of client information. The rationale behind the rule is that an attorney, in representing a client, is entrusted with certain information that may be unknown to others, and that information should not be used against the client—even after the represention has ended.

The rule concerning former clients does not necessarily prohibit an attorney from working at a law firm that may represent interests contrary to those of a former client. If that were the situation, many of those who have worked for very large firms would be unable ever to change jobs. Depending on the circumstances, the new firm may continue to work on a case involving the attorney's former client as long as the attorney avoids working on that particular case and refrains from disclosing any information about the former client. In theory, an impenetrable screen, or ethical wall, should be erected around the attorney so that he or she remains in ignorance about the case. Although the rules governing attorneys do not cover conflicts of interest resulting from paralegal job changes, many courts have held that walling-off procedures may suffice to shield the firm from a violation of the conflict-of-interest rules.

Walling-off Procedures.   Law offices usually have special procedures for "walling off" an attorney or other legal professional from a case when a conflict of interest exists. The firm may announce in a written memo to all employees that a certain attorney or paralegal should not have access to certain files, for example, and may set out procedures to be followed to ensure that access to those files is restricted. Computer documents relating to the case may be protected by warning messages or in some other way. Commonly, any hard-copy files relating to the case are flagged with a sticker to indicate that access to the files is restricted. Firms normally take great care to establish such procedures and observe them carefully, because if confidential information is used in a way harmful to a former client, the firm may be sued by the client and have to pay steep damages. In defending against

DEVELOPING PARALEGAL SKILLS

Erecting an Ethical Wall

 Lana Smith, a paralegal, is meeting with her supervising attorney, Fred Martin, in his office. "I asked you to meet with me because the firm is hiring a new attorney, Sandra Piper," Fred tells Lana. "Sandra is coming from Nunn & Bush. There is a conflict of interest because she represented the plaintiff in *Tymes v. Seski Manufacturing Co.*, and we're representing the defendant in that case. Because of the conflict of interest, we will need to set up some screening procedures to wall Sandra off from this case. Are you familiar with ethical walls?" Lana answers, "Yes, I know about them from my paralegal training program." "Good. Have you ever set one up before?" asks Fred. "No, I haven't," answers Lana. "Then we'll work together on it," replies Fred.

PHYSICAL LOCATION

"The first thing that you need to do is draft a memo to the office manager explaining the existence of the conflict of interest. I want you to suggest that Sandra's office should be located on a different floor from ours, maybe on the twenty-first floor. Be sure to explain the importance of the physical separation from a court's perspective. That is, explain that a court would look for proof that Sandra did not have access to the case files and that we did not have easy access to Sandra because we were physically separated," explains Fred.

COMPUTER PASSWORDS

"Next, I want you to request that the office manager's staff assign a special computer password to all computer files relating to the *Tymes* case and that only our team be given the password. This will restrict access to the documents on the computer and should also satisfy a court that Sandra was not involved in the case," says Fred.

INFORMING THE FIRM'S PERSONNEL

"We also need to prepare a memo to the firm. In the memo, we need to explain the conflict of interest and state the case name and who is involved. The memo must instruct the other members of the firm that they are to maintain a blanket of silence regarding this case whenever they talk to Sandra," instructs Fred.

CONFLICTS STICKERS

"In terms of our procedures, we need to collect all of the files on the case and place conflicts stickers on them. You should be able to find these stickers in the supply room. They are in fluorescent colors and have "ACCESS RESTRICTED" in bold letters on them. You need to place these stickers on all of the files. Then I want you to develop a procedure for keeping track of all the files, so that we do not give any of them to Sandra or anyone who works with her," says Fred. Lana asks Fred some questions and then leaves to begin her assignment.

such a suit, the firm will need to demonstrate that it took reasonable precautions to protect that client's interests.

Conflicts Checks.   Whenever a potential client consults with an attorney, the attorney will want to make sure that no potential conflict of interest exists before deciding whether to represent the client. This is a standard procedure in the law office and one that is frequently undertaken by paralegals. Before you can run a **conflicts check**, you need to know the name of the prospective client, the other party or parties that may be involved in the client's legal matter, and the legal issue involved. Normally, every law firm has some established procedure for conflicts checks, and in larger firms, there is usually a computerized database containing the names of former clients and the other information you will need in checking for conflicts of interest.

CONFLICTS CHECK
A procedure for determining whether an agreement to represent a potential client will result in a conflict of interest.

Safekeeping of Property.   Rule 1.15 imposes strict requirements on attorneys in relation to the safekeeping of property (documents, money, or other items) that they hold in trust for clients. As a paralegal, you may be responsible for safeguarding evidence in the form of documents or other property belonging to the firm's clients or others, such as witnesses. It is extremely important that these documents or other property not be mislaid or lost, or fall into the wrong hands. You may also be involved in handling client funds, particularly if you work for a small law firm. You will read more about how client funds are handled in Chapter 4.

Candor toward the Tribunal.   Rule 3.3 imposes a duty of candor on attorneys, which means, among other things, that attorneys must not make false statements, offer false evidence, or fail to disclose information that should be disclosed to a tribunal (court or other official hearing body). To ensure that the attorney for whom you work does not violate this duty of candor, you need to take special care when conducting research, preparing exhibits, drafting documents to be submitted in courts, and undertaking similar tasks. Submitting false or inaccurate evidence, for example, could lead to serious consequences, including the court's dismissal of the client's case.

Fairness to Opposing Party and Counsel.   Rule 3.4 describes a number of actions that are prohibited as unfair to the opposing party or that party's attorney. The rule states that a lawyer shall not "unlawfully obstruct another party's access to evidence or unlawfully alter, destroy or conceal a document or other material having potential evidentiary value [value as evidence]" and shall not counsel other persons to do such acts. The rule also states that attorneys may not "falsify evidence, counsel or assist a witness to testify falsely, or offer an inducement to a witness that is prohibited by law." If, as a paralegal, you are ever requested, for whatever reason, to conceal or to falsify evidence or to prevent the opposing party from obtaining evidence in the attorney's possession, do not do so. The rule speaks for itself: any such action is clearly prohibited and could result in serious consequences for both yourself and your supervising attorney.

Pro Bono* Obligations.** A goal of the legal profession that is clearly expressed in state ethical codes is to ensure that Americans, particularly the needy, are not deprived of access to legal services. Model Rule 6.1 states that "[a] lawyer should render public interest legal service" through providing legal services ***pro bono publico (for the benefit of the public) "at no fee or a reduced fee to persons of limited means." The Model Code similarly imposes an ethical obligation on attorneys to perform legal services *pro bono*.

Lawyers and law firms normally take very seriously their ethical obligation to perform *pro bono* work and, by so doing, broaden the public's access to legal services. As a paralegal, you may be involved in your firm's *pro bono* work. Alternatively, you may volunteer your assistance as a paralegal to attorneys working on behalf of needy clients at no fee or at a reduced fee.

Responsibilities Regarding Nonlawyer Assistants. Rule 5.3 of the Model Rules defines the responsibilities of attorneys in regard to nonlawyer assistants. This rule states, in part, that "a lawyer having direct supervisory authority over the nonlawyer shall make reasonable efforts to ensure that the person's conduct is compatible with the professional obligations of the lawyer." Rule 5.3 further states that "a lawyer shall be responsible for the conduct of [a nonlawyer] that would be a violation of the rules of professional conduct if engaged in by a lawyer." In sum, Rule 5.3 requires that attorneys not only supervise their assistants' work but also bear responsibility for their assistants' actions that violate professional ethical standards.

Sanctions for Rule Violations

Attorneys who violate the rules governing professional conduct are subject to disciplinary proceedings brought by the state bar association, state supreme court, or state legislature—depending on the state's regulatory scheme. In most states, unethical attorney actions are reported (by clients, legal professionals, or others) to the ethics committee of the state bar association, which is obligated to investigate each complaint thoroughly. For serious violations, the state bar association or the court initiates disciplinary proceedings against the attorney. Sanctions range from a **reprimand** (a formal "scolding" of the attorney—the mildest sanction[2]) to **suspension** (a serious sanction by which the attorney is prohibited from practicing law in the state for a given period of time, such as one month or one year, or for an indefinite period of time) to **disbarment** (revocation of the attorney's license to practice law in the state—the most serious sanction).

In addition to these sanctions, attorneys (and their paralegals) may be subject to civil liability for negligence, which is a tort (civil wrong) that occurs when a person fails to exercise a reasonable standard of care in his or her actions. As mentioned in Chapter 2, tort law allows those who are injured by others' wrongful or careless acts to bring civil lawsuits against the wrongdoers for compensation (money damages). What constitutes a reasonable standard of care differs according to the circumstances. For lawyers, the standard of care is defined by the state ethical rules discussed above. Failure

---

2. Even this mildest sanction can seriously damage an attorney's reputation within the legal community. In some states, state bar associations publish in their monthly journals the names of violators and details of the violations for all members of the bar to read.

DEVELOPING PARALEGAL SKILLS

Inadequate Supervision

 Michael Patton is a paralegal in a firm consisting of two attorneys, himself, and two secretaries. The two attorneys have been in practice together since they graduated from law school ten years ago. The firm, a general law practice, is located in a rural community.

Michael has a great deal of experience in divorce law and has just finished drafting a complaint for Muriel Chapman, one of the two attorneys. Later that day, Michael reviews the complaint. He thinks that it is complete, but he has a question about the temporary alimony that the plaintiff is requesting. He walks to Muriel's office and knocks on the door. Muriel, who is on the phone, waves him in. Muriel hangs up the phone and looks up. Michael says, "I have a question about the amount of temporary alimony the plaintiff is requesting in this case. Was it $5,000 per year or was that the total amount?"

Muriel responds, "That is the total amount." "Okay. I'll insert the $5,000 and bring the complaint back for you to review," answers Michael. But Muriel thinks otherwise and says, "Don't bother to bring it back. I know that you know as much about this as I do. Just call her and have her come in to sign it." Michael hesitates and responds, "I'd feel more comfortable if you reviewed it."

"I'll be in court or at depositions or meetings for most of the next couple of days," Muriel replies. "The client wants her divorce filed as soon as possible, so I will have to rely on you," instructs Muriel. Michael, still not comfortable with Muriel's request, says, "Actually, it will take me just a couple of minutes to insert the $5,000 figure. Could you take a moment to review it before you leave?" "Okay," responds Muriel. "You know, Michael, you are rather persistant in making me do 'the right thing.' Bring the complaint back, and I'll review it before I leave."

to abide by these rules may lead to liability under tort law for negligence (called **malpractice** when committed by a professional, such as an attorney). Of course, a client is permitted to bring a lawsuit against an attorney only if the client has suffered harm because of the attorney's failure to perform a legal duty (if there is no harm, there is no tort). Attorneys and paralegals are also subject to potential criminal liability under criminal statutes prohibiting fraud, theft, and other crimes.

MALPRACTICE
Professional misconduct or negligence—the failure to exercise due care—on the part of a professional, such as an attorney or a physician.

THE REGULATION OF PARALEGALS

The ethical codes governing attorney conduct apply directly only to attorneys, and only attorneys are subject to disciplinary proceedings for violating the ethical duties required by state codes. If a paralegal's action or inaction causes an attorney to breach a professional duty, the paralegal will not be subject to sanctions by the legal profession. Whereas attorneys can be disbarred and lose their licenses, paralegals have no licenses to be revoked.

Nonetheless, the ethical standards of the legal profession *indirectly* regulate paralegal activities because part of a paralegal's job is to ensure that he

PARALEGAL PROFILE

Litigation Paralegal and Paralegal Coordinator

JILL BURTON has a bachelor of arts degree in paralegal studies program from Eastern Kentucky University. In 1980, when Burton received her degree, there were only six students in her class. Since that time, however, the program has expanded significantly. Burton started her career with the law firm of Middleton and Reutlinger, located in Louisville, Kentucky, where she worked in the area of litigation. After three years, Burton took a position with the largest law firm in Kentucky, Brown, Todd, and Heyburn, where she currently works. In 1985, Burton assumed the role of paralegal coordinator for the firm. Her job involves hiring and training paralegals and acting as liaison between the attorneys and the paralegals. In 1993, she became the firm's legal-support manager, which involves administrative work and handling office automation.

What do you like best about your work?

"The thing I enjoy the most is that each new case I work on has a new set of facts and witnesses. I work on complex business litigation, which produces a lot of paper, and I enjoy managing all the documents. I particularly enjoy the challenge of creating and tracking the paper trail as the puzzle pieces fall together. Also, the attorneys for whom I work are super advocates for paralegals. They consistently encourage me to express my views and solicit my ideas, making me feel like an integral part of the team."

What is the greatest challenge that you face in your work?

"Really, the greatest challenge I face is convincing our attorneys to use paralegals effectively. Some of our more senior paralegals tend to become frustrated with the level of assignments they receive. New associates can also present a challenge in that they are not comfortable in relying on a paralegal for assistance. I have tried to overcome this problem by arranging for a lunch meeting with our paralegals and new associates each fall. This gives the paralegals an opportunity to share their educational backgrounds, levels of experience, and areas of expertise with the new associates. Generally, the associates are pleasantly surprised to find out that the firm has on its staff paralegals who are so talented and experienced and who are anxious to help the associates."

> **"A SUCCESSFUL LITIGATION PARALEGAL . . . HAS A 'CAN-DO' ATTITUDE."**

What advice do you have for would-be paralegals in your area of work?

"I recommend that new paralegals take on any tasks that they are assigned, and I would encourage them to avoid telling the attorney that they don't know how to do the task. I feel that new paralegals should always accept assignments and then rely on experienced paralegals, or other resources, to help get the job done. Good writing skills are extremely important, and I would encourage any would-be paralegals to take as many English and writing classes in school as possible."

What are some tips for success as a paralegal in your area of work?

"First, develop a good working relationship with other members of the litigation team. This will go a long way in getting the attorneys to let you take an active role in the litigation. Learn the facts of each case on which you are working so that you are in a position to anticipate what needs to be done without constant supervision and instruction. Be creative and look for areas in which you can apply your analytical skills. Many paralegals make the mistake of working like hourly employees who leave when the clock says it is time to go home. Be prepared to work the hours needed to get the job done even if it means leaving the office at 10 P.M. A successful litigation paralegal is one who is dedicated and resourceful and who has a 'can-do' attitude."

or she does not violate the professional rules governing attorneys. Further-more, as mentioned earlier, attorneys assume legal responsibility not only for their own ethical violations but also for those of their legal assistants. An attorney will not want to hire or maintain as an employee a paralegal whose incompetence or unfamiliarity with professional ethics could result in disci-plinary sanctions or a lawsuit against the attorney. The fact that paralegals are subject to tort liability for negligence is a further incentive for paralegals to adhere to the ethical standards regulating attorney conduct.

In this section, you will learn that paralegals are also regulated indirect-ly by ethical codes adopted by paralegal associations, by state statutes pro-hibiting the unauthorized practice of law, and by ethical guidelines concern-ing the utilization of legal assistants in today's legal arena. The controversial issue of whether paralegals should be directly regulated by the state—through licensing requirements, for example—will be addressed in the next section.

Paralegal Ethical Codes

In addition to indirect regulation through attorney ethical codes, paralegals are becoming increasingly self-regulated. Recall from Chapter 1 that the two major national paralegal associations in the United States—the National Federation of Paralegal Associations (NFPA) and the National Association of Legal Assistants (NALA)—were formed to define and represent paralegal pro-fessional interests on a national level. Soon after they were formed, both associations adopted ethical codes defining the ethical responsibilities of legal assistants.

These ethical codes, which are discussed below, establish ethical rules to guide paralegals. Note that compliance with these codes is not mandatory for paralegals. In other words, if a paralegal does not abide by a paralegal asso-ciation's code of ethics, the association cannot initiate disciplinary proceed-ings against the paralegal. The association can, however, expel the paralegal from the association, which may have significant implications for the para-legal's future career opportunities.

The NFPA Code of Ethics.   In 1977, NFPA adopted its first code of ethics, called the Affirmation of Responsibility. The Affirmation set forth six ethi-cal standards for paralegals, the sixth of which called for commitment on the part of NFPA members to professional development. The Affirmation of Responsibility was revised in 1981 and again in 1991. In 1993, NFPA replaced the Affirmation with its Model Code of Ethics and Professional Responsibility. The 1993 code reflects the influence of the Model Code of Professional Responsibility discussed earlier in this chapter by presenting ethical precepts as "canons" and by following each canon with a series of "Ethical Considerations" (ECs). NFPA's 1993 code of ethics is presented in Exhibit 3.3 on the following page.

The NALA Code of Ethics.   In 1975, NALA issued its Code of Ethics and Professional Responsibility, which has since undergone two revisions, the latest in 1988. The NALA code is also phrased as a series of canons. Exhibit 3.4 on page 80 presents the code in its entirety.

EXHIBIT 3.3

The NFPA Model Code of Ethics and Professional Responsibility

PREAMBLE

The National Federation of Paralegal Associations, Inc. ("NFPA") is a professional organization comprised of paralegal associations and individual paralegals throughout the United States. Members of NFPA have varying types of backgrounds, experience, education, and job responsibilities which reflect the diversity of the paralegal profession. NFPA promotes the growth, development and recognition of the paralegal profession as an integral partner in the delivery of legal services.

NFPA recognizes that the creation of guidelines and standards for professional conduct are important for the development and expansion of the paralegal profession. In May 1993, NFPA adopted this Model Code of Ethics and Professional Responsibility ("Model Code") to delineate the principles for ethics and conduct to which every paralegal should aspire. The Model Code expresses NFPA's commitment to increasing the quality and efficiency of legal services and recognizes the profession's responsibilities to the public, the legal community, and colleagues.

Paralegals perform many different functions, and these functions differ greatly among practice areas. In addition, each jurisdiction has its own unique legal authority and practices governing ethical conduct and professional responsibilities.

It is essential that each paralegal strive for personal and professional excellence and encourage the professional development of other paralegals as well as those entering the profession. Participation in professional associations intended to advance the quality and standards of the legal profession is of particular importance. Paralegals should possess integrity, professional skill and dedication to the improvement of the legal system and should strive to expand the paralegal role in the delivery of legal services.

CANON 1.

A PARALEGAL[1] SHALL ACHIEVE AND MAINTAIN A HIGH LEVEL OF COMPETENCE.

EC-1.1 A paralegal shall achieve competency through education, training, and work experience.

EC-1.2 A paralegal shall participate in continuing education to keep informed of current legal, technical and general developments.

EC-1.3 A paralegal shall perform all assignments promptly and efficiently.

CANON 2.

A PARALEGAL SHALL MAINTAIN A HIGH LEVEL OF PERSONAL AND PROFESSIONAL INTEGRITY.

EC-2.1 A paralegal shall not engage in any ex parte[2] communications involving the courts or any other adjudicatory body in an attempt to exert undue influence or to obtain advantage for the benefit of only one party.

CANON 2.

EC-2.2 A paralegal shall not communicate, or cause another to communicate, with a party the paralegal knows to be represented by a lawyer in a pending matter without the prior consent of the lawyer representing such other party.

EC-2.3 A paralegal shall ensure that all timekeeping and billing records prepared by the paralegal are thorough, accurate, and honest.

EC-2.4 A paralegal shall be scrupulous, thorough and honest in the identification and maintenance of all funds, securities, and other assets of a client and shall provide accurate accountings as appropriate.

EC-2.5 A paralegal shall advise the proper authority of any dishonest or fraudulent acts by any person pertaining to the handling of the funds, securities or other assets of a client.

CANON 3.

A PARALEGAL SHALL MAINTAIN A HIGH STANDARD OF PROFESSIONAL CONDUCT.

EC-3.1 A paralegal shall refrain from engaging in any conduct that offends the dignity and decorum of proceedings before a court or other adjudicatory body and shall be respectful of all rules and procedures.

EC-3.2 A paralegal shall advise the proper authority of any action of another legal professional which clearly demonstrates fraud, deceit, dishonesty, or misrepresentation.

EC-3.3 A paralegal shall avoid impropriety and the appearance of impropriety.

CANON 4.

A PARALEGAL SHALL SERVE THE PUBLIC INTEREST BY CONTRIBUTING TO THE DELIVERY OF QUALITY LEGAL SERVICES AND THE IMPROVEMENT OF THE LEGAL SYSTEM.

EC-4.1 A paralegal shall be sensitive to the legal needs of the public and shall promote the development and implementation of programs that address those needs.

EC-4.2 A paralegal shall support bona fide efforts to meet the need for legal services by those unable to pay reasonable or customary fees; for example, participation in pro bono projects and volunteer work.

EC-4.3 A paralegal shall support efforts to improve the legal system and shall assist in making changes.

EXHIBIT 3.3
Continued

CANON 5.

A PARALEGAL SHALL PRESERVE ALL CONFIDENTIAL INFORMATION[3] PROVIDED BY THE CLIENT OR ACQUIRED FROM OTHER SOURCES BEFORE, DURING, AND AFTER THE COURSE OF THE PROFESSIONAL RELATIONSHIP.

EC-5.1 A paralegal shall be aware of and abide by all legal authority governing confidential information.

EC-5.2 A paralegal shall not use confidential information to the disadvantage of the client.

EC-5.3 A paralegal shall not use confidential information to the advantage of the paralegal or of a third person.

EC-5.4 A paralegal may reveal confidential information only after full disclosure and with the client's written consent; or, when required by law or court order; or, when necessary to prevent the client from committing an act which could result in death or serious bodily harm.

EC-5.5 A paralegal shall keep those individuals responsible for the legal representation of a client fully informed of any confidential information the paralegal may have pertaining to that client.

EC-5.6 A paralegal shall not engage in any indiscreet communications concerning clients.

CANON 6.

A PARALEGAL'S TITLE SHALL BE FULLY DISCLOSED.[4]

EC-6.1 A paralegal's title shall clearly indicate the individual's status and shall be disclosed in all business and professional communications to avoid misunderstandings and misconceptions about the paralegal's role and responsibilities.

EC-6.2 A paralegal's title shall be included if the paralegal's name appears on business cards, letterhead, brochures, directories, and advertisements.

CANON 7.

A PARALEGAL SHALL NOT ENGAGE IN THE UNAUTHORIZED PRACTICE OF LAW.

EC-7.1 A paralegal shall comply with the applicable legal authority governing the unauthorized practice of law.

CANON 8.

A PARALEGAL SHALL AVOID CONFLICTS OF INTEREST AND SHALL DISCLOSE ANY POSSIBLE CONFLICT TO THE EMPLOYER OR CLIENT, AS WELL AS TO THE PROSPECTIVE EMPLOYERS OR CLIENTS.

EC-8.1 A paralegal shall act within the bounds of the law, solely for the benefit of the client, and shall be free of compromising influences and loyalties. Neither the paralegal's personal or business interest, nor those of other clients or third persons, should compromise the paralegal's professional judgment and loyalty to the client.

EC-8.2 A paralegal shall avoid conflicts of interest which may arise from previous assignments whether for a present or past employer or client.

EC-8.3 A paralegal shall avoid conflicts of interest which may arise from family relationships and from personal and business interests.

EC-8.4 A paralegal shall create and maintain an effective recordkeeping system that identifies clients, matters, and parties with which the paralegal has worked, to be able to determine whether an actual or potential conflict of interest exists.

EC-8.5 A paralegal shall reveal sufficient nonconfidential information about a client or former client to reasonably ascertain if an actual or potential conflict of interest exists.

EC-8.6 A paralegal shall not participate in or conduct work on any matter where a conflict of interest has been identified.

EC-8.7 In matters where a conflict of interest has been identified and the client consents to continued representation, a paralegal shall comply fully with the implementation and maintenance of an Ethical Wall.[5]

---

1 "Paralegal" is synonymous with "Legal Assistant" and is defined as a person qualified through education, training, or work experience to perform substantive legal work that requires knowledge of legal concepts and is customarily, but not exclusively performed by a lawyer. This person may be retained or employed by a lawyer, law office, governmental agency or other entity or may be authorized by administrative, statutory or court authority to perform this work.

2 "Ex Parte" denotes actions or communications conducted at the instance and for the benefit of one party only, and without notice to, or contestation by, any person adversely interested.

3 "Confidential Information" denotes information relating to a client, whatever its source, which is not public knowledge nor available to the public. ("Non-Confidential Information" would generally include the name of the client and the identity of the matter for which the paralegal provided services.)

4 "Disclose" denotes communication of information reasonably sufficient to permit identification of the significance of the matter in question.

5 "Ethical Wall" refers to the screening method implemented in order to protect a client from a conflict of interest. An Ethical Wall generally includes, but is not limited to, the following elements: (1) prohibit the paralegal from having any connection with the matter; (2) ban disussions with or the transfer of documents to or from the paralegal; (3) restrict access to files; and (4) educate all members of the firm, corporation or entity as to the separation of the paralegal (both organizationally and physically) from the pending matter. For more information regarding the Ethical Wall, see the NFPA publication entitled "The Ethical Wall–Its Application to Paralegals."

EXHIBIT 3.4
The NALA Code of Ethics and Professional Responsibility

PREAMBLE

It is the responsibility of every legal assistant to adhere strictly to the accepted standards of legal ethics and to live by general principles of proper conduct. The performance of the duties of the legal assistant shall be governed by specific canons as defined herein in order that justice will be served and the goals of the profession attained.

The canons of ethics set forth hereafter are adopted by the National Association of Legal Assistants, Inc. as a general guide, and the enumeration of these rules does not mean there are not others of equal importance although not specifically mentioned.

CANON 1: A legal assistant shall not perform any of the duties that lawyers only may perform nor do things that lawyers themselves may not do.

CANON 2: A legal assistant may perform any task delegated and supervised by a lawyer so long as the lawyer is responsible to the client, maintains a direct relationship with the client, and assumes full professional responsibility for the work product.

CANON 3: A legal assistant shall not engage in the practice of law by accepting cases, setting fees, giving legal advice or appearing in court (unless otherwise authorized by court or agency rules).

CANON 4: A legal assistant shall not act in matters involving professional legal judgment as the services of a lawyer are essential in the public interest whenever the exercise of such judgment is required.

CANON 5: A legal assistant must act prudently in determining the extent to which a client may be assisted without the presence of a lawyer.

CANON 6: A legal assistant shall not engage in the unauthorized practice of law and shall assist in preventing the unauthorized practice of law.

CANON 7: A legal assistant must protect the confidences of a client, and it shall be unethical for a legal assistant to violate any statute now in effect or hereafter to be enacted controlling privileged communications.

CANON 8: It is the obligation of the legal assistant to avoid conduct which would cause the lawyer to be unethical or even appear to be unethical, and loyalty to the employer is incumbent upon the legal assistant.

CANON 9: A legal assistant shall work continually to maintain integrity and a high degree of competency throughout the legal profession.

CANON 10: A legal assistant shall strive for perfection through education in order to better assist the legal profession in fulfilling its duty of making legal services available to clients and the public.

CANON 11: A legal assistant shall do all other things incidental, necessary, or expedient for the attainment of the ethics and responsibilities imposed by statute or rule of court.

CANON 12: A legal assistant is governed by the American Bar Association Model Code of Professional Responsibility and the American Bar Association Model Rules of Professional Conduct.

UPL Statutes

In addition to being regulated indirectly by attorney and paralegal ethical codes, paralegals are also regulated indirectly by statutes that prohibit the unauthorized practice of law. The corollary to licensing requirements for attorneys is, of course, that only attorneys are legally permitted to practice law. Statutes prohibiting all persons but licensed attorneys from practicing law have always presented problems for those legal practitioners who either could not or did not wish to satisfy state requirements for licensing. In the last few decades, however, these statutes have also presented problems for paralegals. No matter how expert a paralegal may be in terms of legal knowledge and skills, he or she cannot give legal advice to clients or otherwise engage in the unauthorized practice of law (UPL) as defined by state laws.

Independent Paralegals and the UPL.   One of the developments that focused attention on UPL statutes was the rise of the **independent paralegal**, or *legal technician.* A small number of paralegals practice independently—that is, they are not under an attorney's supervision. The independent-paralegal movement began in California over twenty years ago when a group of individuals with various degrees of legal training established a chain of do-it-yourself divorce centers. In these centers, paralegals, for a fee ranging between $50 and $75, supplied members of the public with the necessary forms and procedural knowledge to obtain a divorce without having to use the services of an attorney. The repercussions of this project were felt around the country as paralegals in some other states began to set up businesses (which were usually called typing services, form-preparation services, or something similar) for the purpose of assisting members of the public in relatively simple legal tasks, such as writing a will or obtaining a simple divorce.

Lawsuits brought by bar associations, clients, or other parties against independent paralegals for the unauthorized practice of law raised an issue of concern to all paralegals, including those working under attorney supervision: What kinds of tasks or activities can paralegals undertake without violating UPL statutes? This is a serious question for practicing paralegals because in at least thirty states, the unauthorized practice of law is classified as a crime. In those states, paralegals judged to have engaged in the unauthorized practice of law are subject to fines and possibly imprisonment. UPL actions are complicated by the fact that state statutes stipulating that only licensed attorneys can engage in the practice of law rarely indicate with any specificity what constitutes the "practice of law."

Definitional Problems: What Is the Practice of Law?   Some state statutes do not define the phrase *practice of law* at all. Other statutes essentially define the practice of law as being "what attorneys do." Still others attempt a definition of the practice of law and then add to that definition a phrase, such as "and any other action connected with law," that essentially nullifies the narrower definition.

The ABA's Model Code and Model Rules are also vague in this respect. For example, the Ethical Consideration to Canon 3 (EC 3–5) of the Model Code states that it is "neither necessary nor desirable to attempt the formulation of a single, specific definition of what constitutes the practice of law" and that generally "the practice of law relates to the rendition of services for others that call for the professional judgment of a lawyer."

Model Rule 5.5 essentially states that the practice of law varies from state to state, that restricting the practice of law to attorneys benefits the public interest, and that attorneys can delegate functions to paralegals as long as attorneys supervise the work and retain responsibility for it. Both the Model Code and the Model Rules also specifically prohibit lawyers from assisting in the "unauthorized practice of law."

INDEPENDENT PARALEGAL
A paralegal who offers services directly to the public, normally for a fee, without attorney supervision. Independent paralegals assist consumers by supplying them with forms and procedural knowledge relating to simple or routine legal procedures.

Because state statutes and ethical codes do not spell out what exactly constitutes the unauthorized practice of law, the courts have often been left to decide the question. In their decisions, courts have used different criteria. In some cases, courts have decided that the practice of law equates to "what attorneys usually do"—or something equally vague. In other cases, the courts have established some general standards, or tests, to use in determining whether a particular action constitutes the unauthorized practice of law. In *The Florida Bar v. Sperry*,[3] a case decided in 1962, the Florida Supreme Court held that giving advice or performing services constituted the practice of law if that advice or those services affected "important rights of a person under the law." Other courts have been guided by whether a legal task requires a lawyer's special training and expert skills. If so, the professional judgment of a lawyer is required and only a lawyer can legally perform such a task. Generally, the determination of what kinds of actions constitute the unauthorized practice of law has been decided by the courts on a case-by-case basis.

Guidelines for the Utilization of Paralegals

By the 1980s, it was clear that there was a growing need to define the role and function of paralegals within the legal arena and, more specifically, to define what tasks paralegals could and could not legally perform. In response to this need, NALA, the ABA, and numerous state bar associations have developed guidelines for the utilization of legal assistance in the performance of legal services. NALA published its Model Standards and Guidelines for the Utilization of Legal Assistants in 1984. NALA based its guidelines on specific provisions of the Model Code and the Model Rules, state ethical codes, and state court decisions relating to the unauthorized practice of law. In 1991, the American Bar Association adopted its Model Guidelines for the Utilization of Legal Assistant Services, which were based in part on the NALA guidelines. Today, over one-third of the states have adopted similar guidelines on the role and function of paralegals in legal representation. (See Appendix D and Appendix F at the end of this book for the text of the NALA guidelines and the ABA guidelines, respectively.)

The NALA Model Standards and Guidelines and the ABA Model Guidelines hold paralegals to the ethical standards governing attorneys— that is, paralegals cannot do what attorneys cannot do. These guidelines also indicate the kinds of activities that *only* attorneys are permitted to do, as determined by court interpretations of UPL statutes. Guideline VI of the NALA Model Standards and Guidelines is fairly representative of what legal actions the ABA, state bar associations, state UPL statutes, and court decisions consider to constitute the practice of law and can therefore be undertaken only by attorneys. Guideline VI states, in part, that legal assistants may *not* perform any of the following actions:

- Establish attorney-client relationships.
- Set legal fees.
- Give legal opinions or advice.
- Represent a client before a court (with some exceptions).

---

3. 140 So.2d 587 (Fla. 1962).

These activities, because they lie at the heart of the attorney-client relationship, have traditionally been regarded by the courts as activities that can only be undertaken by an attorney.

The first two prohibitions listed above are relatively straightforward. The second two prohibitions are less so, however, for the reasons discussed below.

Legal Opinions and Advice.   In regard to giving legal opinions and advice, Guideline 3 of the ABA Model Guidelines echoes NALA Guideline VI by stating that a lawyer "may not delegate to a legal assistant" the responsibility "for a legal opinion rendered to a client." Clearly, giving legal advice goes to the essence of legal practice. After all, a person would not seek out a legal expert if he or she did not want legal advice on some matter. Although a paralegal may *communicate* an attorney's legal advice to a client, the paralegal may not *give* legal advice.

Although other nonlawyers often give advice affecting others' legal rights or obligations, paralegals may not do so. For example, when an individual receives a speeding ticket, a friend or relative who is a nonlawyer might suggest that the person should argue the case before a judge and explain his or her side of the story. When a paralegal gives such advice, however, he or she may be accused of engaging in the unauthorized practice of law. Legal assistants are prohibited from giving even simple, common-sense advice because of the understandably greater weight given to the advice of someone who has legal training. Although as a legal assistant you may have developed great expertise in a certain area of law, you must refrain from advising clients in respect to their legal obligations or rights.

What constitutes the giving of legal advice is not always easy to pin down. As you will read below, paralegals are permitted to advise clients on a number of matters, and drawing the line between permissible and impermissible advice may at times be difficult. To be on the safe side (and avoid potential liability for the unauthorized practice of law), a good rule of thumb is the following:

● **Never advise a client or other person on any matter if the advice may alter the legal position or legal rights of the one to whom the advice is given.**

Whenever you are pressured to render legal advice—as you surely will be at one time or another, by your firm's clients or others—simply say that you cannot give legal advice because it is against the law to do so. Paralegals find that this frank and honest statement usually solves the problem.

The Representation of Clients.   The rule that only attorneys—with limited exceptions—can represent others in court has a long history. Recall from the discussion of attorney regulation earlier in this chapter that attorney licensing was initially required only for court representation. In the last few decades, the ethical reasoning underlying this rule has been called into question by two developments.

First, in 1975, the United States Supreme Court held that people have a constitutional right to represent themselves in court.[4] Some people have

---

4. *Faretta v. California*, 422 U.S. 806, 95 S.Ct. 2525, 45 L.Ed.2d 562 (1975).

ETHICAL CONCERN

Saying "If I were you . . ." and the UPL

Any time a paralegal says, "If I were you, I would . . . ," the paralegal is, in effect, engaging in the unauthorized practice of law—giving legal advice that could result in a client's decision to take (or not to take) a certain action. For example, suppose that a client calls your law office, and you take the call. The client, Mrs. Rabe, is an older woman who is very upset about the fact that an insurance company has not paid on a $1,000 life insurance policy that she purchased covering the life of her grandson, who has just died. Mrs. Rabe tells you all of the details, and you feel that even though she might win a lawsuit against the insurance company, she would probably spend a lot more than $1,000 in the process. Mrs. Rabe wants to know if your supervising attorney will see her about the case, and when you tell her the attorney is out of town, she presses you for advice. Finally, you say, "Well, if I were you, I'd take the case to small claims court. You would not have to hire an attorney, it would be less costly, and you might recover some of the money." What you do not realize (and thus do not tell Mrs. Rabe) is that if she sues the insurance company, she might win not just the $1,000 payment but also substantial punitive damages for the insurance company's wrongful behavior—and might also benefit by other penalties imposed under the state's insurance statute.

questioned why a person can represent himself or herself in court but cannot hire a person more educated in the law to do so unless that person is a licensed attorney. Second, the fact that paralegals are allowed to represent clients before some federal and state government agencies, such as the federal Social Security Administration and state welfare departments, has called into question the ethical underpinnings of this rule. Nonetheless, as a paralegal, you should know that you are not allowed to appear in court on behalf of your supervising attorney—although local courts in some states are carving out exceptions to this rule for *limited* purposes.

What Paralegals Can (and Should) Do

Other than the above-mentioned activities, paralegals can perform virtually any legal task as long as the work is supervised by an attorney. Guideline 2 of the ABA Model Guidelines indicates the breadth of paralegal responsibilities:

> Provided the lawyer maintains responsibility for the work product, a lawyer may delegate to a legal assistant any task normally performed by the lawyer except those tasks proscribed to one not licensed as a lawyer by statute, court rule, administrative rule or regulation, controlling authority, the ABA Model Rules of Professional Conduct, or these Guidelines.

Paralegals working for attorneys may interview clients and witnesses, investigate legal claims, draft legal documents for attorneys' signatures, attend will executions (in some states), appear at real-estate closings (in some states), and undertake numerous other types of legal work, as long as

---

THE LEGAL TEAM AT WORK
Teamwork and the Risk of UPL

One of the valuable functions of the paralegal as a member of the legal team is communicating with the the firm's clients. In some areas of legal practice, clients need more than just legal advice. They may need to be encouraged, consoled, and so on. For example, if you become a paralegal in a family-law practice, many of the firm's clients will be undergoing difficult times emotionally. They may also face economic problems. A spouse who has never been involved in the family's finances, for example, may have no idea of the extent of the value of the marital property to be distributed (the value of the home, investments, and other assets). He or she may never have balanced a checkbook before or paid routine bills. As a paralegal, you will have frequent contact with the client, and you will probably have numerous opportunities to communicate with and assist the client on one matter or another.

Your challenge is to know which kinds of statements you may legally make and which kind of statements may subject you to liability for the unauthorized practice of law. Because each client's circumstances are unique, so will be many of the questions you are asked. Unless you are absolutely certain that answering a particular question will not constitute the unauthorized practice of law, discuss the issue with your supervising attorney. Ask the attorney how you should answer the client's questions before giving the client any answer.

the work is supervised by attorneys. When state or federal law allows them to do so, paralegals can also represent clients before government agencies. Paralegals are allowed to perform freelance services for attorneys (freelance paralegals will be discussed shortly) and, depending on state law and the type of service, perform limited independent services for the public.

Legal assistants are also permitted to give information to clients on many types of matters relating to a case or other legal matter. When arranging for client interviews, they let clients know what kind of information is needed and what documents to bring to the office. They inform clients about legal procedures and what the client should expect to experience during the progress of a legal proceeding. For example, in preparing for trial, legal assistants instruct clients on trial procedures, what they should wear to the trial, and so on. Clearly, as a legal assistant, you will be permitted to give clients all kinds of information. Nonetheless, you must make sure that you know where to draw the line between giving permissible types of advice and giving "legal advice"—advice that only attorneys are licensed to give under state laws.

The specific types of tasks that paralegals are legally permitted to undertake are described throughout this book—and it would be impossible to list them all here. Generally, Guideline 2 of the ABA makes it clear that paralegals can engage in a wide spectrum of legal activities:

- **Apart from tasks that only attorneys can legally perform, paralegals may perform almost any type of legal work as long as the attorney authorizes the work and assumes responsibility for the paralegal's work product.**

Freelance Paralegals

Some paralegals, called **freelance paralegals**, own their own businesses and provide paralegal services, on a contractual basis, for attorneys. A question with important implications for such paralegals is whether work performed outside the law office or other hiring organization can be adequately supervised by attorneys. In 1992, the New Jersey Supreme Court's Committee on the Unauthorized Practice of Law rendered its opinion (Opinion 24) on exactly this question. The opinion stated that freelance paralegals lacked adequate attorney supervision and therefore were engaging in the unauthorized practice of law. When a group of freelance paralegals appealed the issue to the New Jersey Supreme Court, however, that court stated that it could find no reason why freelance paralegals could not be just as adequately supervised by the attorneys for whom they worked as those paralegals working in attorneys' offices.[5] Generally, attorneys are held responsible for the work product of freelance paralegals regardless of whether the work is performed in the attorney's office or outside the attorney's workplace.

FREELANCE PARALEGAL
A paralegal who operates his or her own business and provides services to attorneys on a contractual basis. A freelance paralegal works under the supervision of an attorney, who assumes responsibility for the paralegal's work product.

---

5. *In re Opinion No. 24 of the Committee on the Unauthorized Practice of Law*, 128 N.J 114, 607 A.2d 962 (1992). (See Chapter 9 for an explanation of how to read case citations.)

FEATURED GUEST: MICHAEL A. PENER

Ten Tips on Ethics and the Paralegal

Biographical Note

Michael A. Pener developed the paralegal program at Johnson County Community College, in Kansas, in 1977. It was approved by the American Bar Association (ABA) in 1980. He was the program's first director and continued as director until 1987, when be became one of its full-time instructors. Pener is one of the founders of the American Association for Paralegal Education (AAfPE). He served on its initial board of directors and, in 1985 and 1986, as its president. He is a member of the Ethics Advisory Services Committee and Legal Assistant Committee of the Kansas Bar Association (KBA). Since 1992, he has been serving as one of the AAfPE's representatives on the Approval Commission of the ABA Standing Committee on Legal Assistants.

As a legal-assistant educator and practicing attorney, I have developed several ethics-related "truths" for my students that I think are essential for their professional survival as working legal assistants. Each of these truths is important, and the legal assistant must adhere to all of them if he or she wants to avoid, or lessen the impact of, situations involving ethical problems. While I believe the following tips will keep you out of trouble, no list of this type is ever complete without your own input—so use it to develop ethical "rules" appropriate for your work and legal practice area.

1 Obtain Copies of State and Local Ethical Rules. Keep up with current state ethical rules for attorneys and paralegals and continually review their application in cases,

disciplinary proceedings, and ethical opinions of local, state, and national lawyer associations. Specifically, there are now many guidelines on major areas of concern to the legal profession, including the use of legal assistants by lawyers, confidentiality, the unauthorized practice of law, conflicts of interest, and legal competence.

2 Attend Continuing Legal Education (CLE) Programs on Legal Ethics. In many states, lawyers are required to have CLE hours on legal ethics. Attending CLE programs not only reminds you of what the rules require but also helps you remain current in ethical developments within the profession.

3 Network with Other Legal Assistants. Network with other legal assistants through local para-

legal organizations and education programs and through the National Federation of Paralegal Associations and the National Association of Legal Assistants. Both of the national organizations have professional ethical codes and are involved in court cases affecting paralegals.

4 Make No Assumptions about Others. In an ideal world, all legal professionals would act ethically at all times. In such a world, there would be no need for rules to govern attorney behavior and no need for disciplinary actions. As a paralegal, you may encounter situations in which you suspect unethical behavior on the part of someone with whom you work. Ignoring unethical behavior will not necessarily make it go away. Always keep your professional ethical

Disclosure of Paralegal Status

Because of the close working relationship between an attorney and a paralegal, a client may have difficulty perceiving that the paralegal is not also an attorney. To avoid misleading clients and others, the NALA guidelines strongly emphasize the importance of disclosing to clients and others the fact that a paralegal is not an attorney. When you are first introduced to a client, you should make sure that the client knows that you are not an attor-

---

FEATURED GUEST, Continued

requirements in mind. At times, this may mean you need to discuss the matter with someone in authority.

5 Double-check Your Work. Expect the unexpected, especially when dealing with unfamiliar matters or with strangers. Don't assume that the documents you produce will be checked for accuracy by others. As a legal assistant, you will need to pay the utmost attention to detail and double-check everything you do to make sure it is accurate. Also, make sure that all written communications are sent to the proper person.

6 Review All Documents That You Receive. When documents are being exchanged in the drafting stage with opposing counsel or during negotiations, always review the documents that you receive in their entirety.

7 Anticipate and Prepare for Ethical Problems. Anticipate and prepare for situations in your work and professional relationships that may give rise to ethical problems. In this chapter, you will encounter a number of "real-life" situations that test your understanding and application of legal ethics. Study them carefully, because they most likely will happen to you. Also, note that clients want to know how their

legal matters are progressing but lawyers are sometimes too busy to attend to their clients' needs in this respect. Legal assistants may end up communicating more frequently with the clients than attorneys do. If the lawyer for whom you work puts you in this role, you should feel complimented by the lawyer's confidence in you. Watch out, however, for a client who becomes too dependent on you and your judgment. Very soon, he or she may be asking you for your "legal opinion." If you respond to such a question, you will get into trouble very quickly.

8 Use Caution When Notarizing Documents or Signing Documents as a Witness. If you are a notary public, only notarize documents signed in your presence. As a notary public you have a statutory requirement to perform the duties of your appointed office. Failure to act as required may subject you to personal liability. This means that you must refuse a lawyer's request to notarize a document that was not signed in your presence. Similarly, never sign any document as a witness without first reviewing it to make sure that your signature is properly requested.

9 Maintain a Balance Between Personal and Legal Ethics. Maintain a proper balance between your

> **"DON'T ASSUME THAT THE DOCUMENTS YOU PRODUCE WILL BE CHECKED FOR ACCURACY BY OTHERS."**
> • • • •

personal ethics and legal ethics. This may be the most difficult thing for you to do. You may be a party to confidential communications that concern unethical, and even immoral, behavior on the part of clients. Your law firm may have a policy or engage in an activity that is acceptable by legal ethical standards but that you personally consider to be unethical. Professionally, you must accept this. If you personally cannot, then you may have no other choice but to seek employment elsewhere.

10 Rely on Your Common Sense and Intuition. Use your common sense and intuition. Develop a sense of what is right and wrong behavior in any given situation and then seek the answer to any legal ethical problem that you encounter.

---

ney. Similarly, in correspondence with clients or others, you should always indicate your nonattorney status by typing "Paralegal" or "Legal Assistant" after your name.

The ABA Model Guidelines also emphasize the importance of disclosing the nonattorney status of paralegals. Guideline 4 places this responsibility on attorneys: "It is the lawyer's responsibility to take reasonable measures

Disclosure of Paralegal Status

UPL problems often result from telephone conversations between a client or potential client and a paralegal. For example, a client's call to an attorney may be transferred to the attorney's paralegal if the attorney is not in the office. The paralegal may assume that the client knows that he or she is not an attorney and may speak freely with the client about a legal matter, advising the client that the attorney will be in touch with the client shortly about the matter. The client, however, may assume that the paralegal is an attorney and may make inferences based on the paralegal's comments that result in actions with harmful consequences—in which event, the paralegal might be charged with the unauthorized practice of law. To avoid such problems, you should always make sure that a client or a potential client knows that you are a paralegal and not an attorney.

GENERAL LICENSING

A type of licensing in which all individuals within a specific profession or group (such as paralegals) must meet licensing requirements imposed by the state before they may legally practice their profession.

LIMITED LICENSING

A type of licensing in which a limited number of individuals within a specific profession or group (such as independent paralegals within the paralegal profession) must meet licensing requirements imposed by the state before those individuals may legally practice their profession.

to ensure that clients, courts, and other lawyers are aware that a legal assistant, whose services are utilized by the lawyer in performing legal services, is not licensed to practice law."

THE DEBATE OVER LICENSING

One of the major issues facing legal professionals and other interested groups today is whether paralegals should be subject to direct regulation by the state through licensing requirements. Unlike certification, which was discussed in Chapter 1, *licensing* involves direct and *mandatory* regulation, by the state, of an occupational or professional group. When licensing requirements are established for a professional group, such as for attorneys, a license is required before a member of the group can practice his or her profession.

A few states have considered implementing a **general licensing** program, which would require all paralegals to meet certain educational requirements and other specified criteria before being allowed to practice their profession. The problem with general licensing has been that to license a professional group, the licensing body must first define the group to be licensed. This is difficult to do in respect to paralegals because of the diversity of paralegal tasks and the broad range of services they perform.

As an alternative to general licensing, over half the states are considering **limited licensing**, which would limit licensing requirements to those paralegals (independent paralegals, or legal technicians) who wish to provide specified legal services directly to the public. With limited licensing, qualified paralegals would be authorized to handle routine legal services traditionally rendered only by attorneys, such as advising clients on simple divorces, will executions, bankruptcy petitions, incorporation, real-estate transactions, selected tax matters, and other specified services as designated by the state licensing body. Currently, only the state of Washington has adopted a form of limited licensing. That state now permits qualifying paralegals to become licensed in one specialty area—real estate.

The two leading paralegal organizations, NFPA and NALA, are divided on whether paralegals should be directly regulated by the state. Although there are numerous other participants in the debate—including other paralegal associations, state bar associations, the American Bar Association, the courts, and various interest groups—the arguments for and against regulation set forth by NFPA and NALA indicate the basic contours of the debate.

NFPA's Position

NFPA endorses the implementation of regulation of the paralegal profession on a state-by-state basis insofar as its implementation expands the utilization of paralegals to deliver cost-efficient legal services. If it can be demonstrated that there is a public need for lower-cost legal services, NFPA is in favor of the regulation of paralegals, providing the paralegals meet certain minimum criteria and pass a licensing examination.

NFPA contends that the licensing of paralegals would accomplish several goals. First, attorneys and the public would benefit because only demonstrably qualified paralegals would be licensed to practice as paralegals. Second, attorneys' search costs in finding competent assistance would be reduced. Third, the licensing of paralegals would be a step forward in the development of the paralegal profession. Fourth, licensing would permit paralegals to perform specified tasks legally, and therefore they would not be at risk for the unauthorized practice of law to the extent they are today. And finally, the licensing of paralegals would give consumers greater access to low-cost legal assistance for routine legal matters. NFPA argues that the latter issue (access to legal services) provides a compelling reason to expand the role of paralegals.

NFPA proposes a two-tiered system of licensing: general licensing and specialty licensing. General licensing by a state board or agency would require all paralegals within the state to satisfy stipulated requirements in regard to education, experience, and continuing education; it would also subject practicing paralegals to disciplinary procedures bv the licensing body. Specialty licensing would require paralegals who wish to practice in a specialized area to demonstrate, by an examination, their proficiency in that area.

NALA's Position

While NALA supports voluntary certification, it believes that imposing licensing requirements on paralegals would be premature. Currently, paralegals perform a wide range of tasks and work in a variety of settings. In NALA's opinion, to impose mandatory, uniform requirements on a group of professionals whose function is not yet sufficiently defined would limit paralegal opportunities—it would close the door to those paralegals who could not meet the requirements for licensing and might prohibit activities that paralegals are currently authorized to undertake. NALA looks at certification and the development of paralegal education programs as being, at least at this point in time, a reasonable alternative to licensing. Furthermore, NALA emphasizes that most paralegals work under the supervision of attorneys and are thus already subject to regulation via attorney codes.

NALA's objections to specific limited-licensing proposals for independent paralegals (legal technicians) do not reflect opposition to the idea of limited licensing for independent paralegals so much as disagreement with specific aspects of the proposed regulatory schemes.

PERSONAL ETHICS AND PARALEGAL PRACTICE

So far in this chapter, we have been discussing ethical responsibilities in the context of **legal ethics**—rules and standards governing the legal profession. If you are like most paralegals, you may find that some of the ethical questions you face cannot be answered by professional rules. Rather, the solutions will rest on your own personal moral or ethical convictions. Generally, people who have a clear idea of their ethical values and priorities are best able to cope with ethical challenges. As you enter the paralegal profession, it is thus a good idea to examine carefully the meaning of ethics and your own personal ethical standards and priorities.

Ethics can be defined as that branch of philosophy that focuses on morality and the way in which moral principles are applied to daily life. Ethics has

LEGAL ETHICS
The principles, values, and rules of conduct that govern legal professionals.

ETHICS
Moral principles and values applied to social behavior.

to do with fundamental questions such as the following: What is fair? What is just? What is the right thing to do in this situation? Essentially, ethics has to do with any question relating to the fairness, justness, rightness, or wrongness of an action.

Ethics is not an abstract or a static concept. On the contrary, ethics affects and gives meaning to our everyday lives and the decisions we make. We constantly apply our values and moral convictions to our actions and decisions, frequently without even being aware of the fact that we are doing so. The clothes we buy, the music we prefer, the way we treat our friends, the books we choose to read—these and a thousand other everyday activities and decisions, if you analyze them carefully, ultimately relate, at least in part, to ethical values and goals. Your interest in paralegal work may even be rooted in some moral belief or ethical conviction that you hold.

Personal Ethics and Professional Responsibility

As a paralegal, you will be expected to abide by the ethical rules governing the legal profession, which you *must* do. But in a broader sense, ethical behavior means more than merely abiding by a particular profession's rules of conduct. A paralegal could follow each of the rules governing the legal profession meticulously and still act unethically in a broader sense.

For example, suppose that Joan, a paralegal, is looking for a job. Her father knows an attorney who is looking for a paralegal, and Joan interviews for the job. The attorney mistakenly assumes, from comments made to him by Joan's father, that Joan has more experience as a paralegal than she actually has. Joan realizes this but does nothing to correct the mistaken assumption. The employer hires Joan and never learns of Joan's implicit misrepresentation. In fact, Joan does excellent work, and no one suffers any harmful consequences from her deceptive action (or inaction). Joan has not violated any ethical rule governing the legal profession, but has she acted ethically? Many people would conclude that she has not.

Violating a professional ethical rule, such as the duty of competence or the duty of confidentiality, may expose attorneys and paralegals to legal liability. Violating a personal ethical standard usually does not, unless a professional rule is violated at the same time. There is no law, for example, that requires you to "go that extra mile" for your supervising attorney and his or her client, even when it involves working overtime. Nor is there any law that requires you to be kind to a grieving client or sensitive to the views of your co-workers.

Honesty, personal integrity, consideration for others, a commitment to excellence, dedication to hard work—these and other attributes that will be expected of you as a paralegal are not mandated by law but rooted in personal ethical convictions. Generally, paralegals are expected to have made a personal ethical commitment to their profession and to the rules that govern it.

Conflicts between Personal and Legal Ethics

As a paralegal, you may encounter situations in which your personal ethical views conflict with one or more of the ethical rules that govern the legal profession, or legal ethics. Personally, for example, you may believe that there is nothing wrong with discussing confidential information about a client with your spouse—you trust your spouse implicitly and know that the information will go no further. As a legal professional, however, you have a duty to refrain from disclosing confidential information to anyone who is not working on the case, including your spouse, unless the client consents to the disclosure.

Paralegals sometimes face similar ethical conflicts when asked by friends for legal advice. For example, suppose that a good friend asks you for legal advice concerning an issue about which you are particularly well informed. Your friend is having financial difficulties and asks you for advice on whether she should file for bankruptcy and what the consequences would be if she did. You doubt that she would ever hold you responsible for any unexpected detriment she might suffer if she followed your advice. Given the circumstances, and the fact that you want to help a friend, you feel that the "right" thing to do is answer her questions. But clearly, if you advised your friend on her legal rights, you would be engaging in the unauthorized practice of law, which is prohibited in all states and a crime under many state statutes.

Perhaps one of the most serious personal ethical conflicts occurs when you are asked to work on behalf of a client whose actions you cannot condone. For example, what if you are asked to assist an attorney who is defending a person who has been accused of drug dealing? You are morally uncomfortable about being a member of a defense team working on behalf of such a client. What is your ethical responsibility in this situation? On the one hand, you have a professional responsibility to assist the attorney in defending the client's rights. On the other hand, you feel that, by assisting in the client's defense, you may be implicitly condoning unethical (and criminal) behavior. When facing these kinds of ethical conflicts, you must place legal ethics in the larger context of the American system of justice and examine how legal ethics function within that context.

Legal Ethics and the Adversarial System of Justice

American and English courts follow the **adversarial system of justice**, in which the parties act as adversaries, or opponents. Parties to a lawsuit come before the court as contestants. In a sense, a courtroom is like a battlefield in which the parties to a lawsuit conduct a "legal battle." One side "wins" and the other "loses."

The parties do not come together in the courtroom with the idea of working out a compromise solution to their problems or of looking at the dispute from each other's point of view (although to avoid the time and expense of a lawsuit or of continuing a lawsuit, parties often do settle for a compromise solution out of court). Nor are they unbiased in their presentation of the facts to the court. Rather, they take sides and present the facts of the case in a light most favorable to their respective positions. The adversarial system of justice is founded on the assumption that the court (the judge—and the jury, if it is a jury trial), based on the evidence presented by the parties, will arrive at a true and just solution to the matter.

ADVERSARIAL SYSTEM OF JUSTICE
A legal system in which the parties to a lawsuit are opponents, or adversaries, and present their cases in a light most favorable to themselves. The court arrives at a just solution based on the evidence presented by the parties, or contestants, and determines who wins and who loses.

TODAY'S PROFESSIONAL PARALEGAL

What to Do When Your Values Clash with Those of Your Client

Sandy Brownell works as a legal assistant for a sole practitioner of law, Joe Harding. Joe has been asked to defend Dr. Wyeth Ebon, who has gained notoriety in the past few years by assisting terminally ill patients in committing suicide. Aiding a person in committing suicide is illegal under the state's criminal statutes. Dr. Ebon has been charged with the crime of assisting in the suicide of Daniel Currie, who had an advanced case of Alzheimer's disease.

AN ETHICAL DILEMMA

Joe calls Sandy into his office and tells her that he will conduct an initial client interview with Dr. Ebon tomorrow at 9 A.M. Joe wants Sandy to sit in on the interview because if he accepts the case, she will be working closely with him on it. Sandy is uncomfortable with the idea of working with Dr. Ebon, but she realizes that she has no other option. After all, she works for a sole practitioner, and she is the only legal assistant in the office. She tells Joe that she will see him at nine o'clock the next morning.

On returning to her office, Sandy cannot get Dr. Ebon off her mind. She knows that she has to work on the case; Joe expects her to. Yet she does not believe in assisted suicide for anyone, not even for the terminally ill. In her opinion, assisting another in committing suicide is ethically unjustifiable under any circumstances. By helping Joe prepare Dr. Ebon's defense, will she be compromising her own ethical beliefs and standards? As a professional, how should she deal with this situation?

RESOLVING THE DILEMMA

Once Sandy reminds herself of her professional status, the answer becomes clear. It is not up to her to judge Dr. Ebon's actions. Even though she does not agree with Dr. Ebon, she knows that as a criminal defendant, he has a right to counsel, an important constitutional right of all Americans. As a legal professional, she has an obligation to ensure that the constitutional rights of criminal defendants, including the right to counsel, are not violated. Sandy concludes that it is her professional duty to help the attorney prepare to defend Dr. Ebon against the criminal charges.

Having analyzed the situation and decided where her professional duties lay, Sandy arrives at the initial client interview with an open mind, ready to assist Joe.

ADVOCATE
As a verb, to assist, defend, or plead (argue) a cause for another. As a noun, a person (such as an attorney) who assists, defends, or pleads (argues) for another (such as a client) before a court.

The Concept of Advocacy and Legal Ethics. Attorneys are **advocates** for their clients—that is, they present and argue their clients' cases before the courts. Their job is not to judge the rightness or wrongness of their clients' actions but to help their clients obtain a favorable judgment. Although attorneys argue on behalf of their clients, they are also officers of the court. As such, they must act with integrity and comply with ethical rules when presenting a client's case or evidence relating to the case. An attorney who does not fulfill this responsibility may be held in contempt of court.

Attorneys are essential to the legal process because they know the law. They have the necessary expertise to help a client put forth the best argument possible in support of the client's position. Although parties to a dispute have the right to represent themselves in court (instead of having attorneys represent them), few persons do so—and with good reason: unless they are knowledgeable in the law and know how the law can be used in support of their claims, they will be at a serious disadvantage. As the oft-quoted adage states, "Only a fool has himself or herself for a client."

Many of the ethical rules governing attorneys, who are key participants in the litigation process, are rooted in this adversarial framework. To advocate effectively a client's cause, for example, an attorney must be able to communicate openly with his or her client. The rule of confidentiality facilitates such communication by protecting clients against unauthorized disclosures of confidential information. The rules governing conflicts of interest, which are designed both to protect clients and to ensure fairness in legal representation, also stem from the concept of advocacy. Other rules that you will read about in this text, including the rules governing court procedures and evidence, also relate to the adversarial nature of our justice system.

Professional Responsibility and Adversarial Justice.   Now, consider again the situation mentioned above, in which you are asked to assist an attorney who is defending someone whose purported behavior you cannot ethically condone. Your professional responsibility is to fulfill your supervising attorney's request. Furthermore, if you look at the question in the larger context, the question takes on a different meaning. Ultimately, the issue is, do you believe that it is right for people to be allowed to have their "day in court" and to have legal advice and guidance in presenting their cases? Do you believe that every person has a right to the "due process of law"?[6] Do you believe that it should be up to the court, and not to the attorneys (or their paralegals), to decide on truth and pronounce judgments?

If you answer "yes" to these questions, then you will probably be able to assist your supervising attorney in good conscience. Your participation on the defense team does not suggest that you condone the alleged wrongdoing allegedly committed by the client but that you believe in the American system of justice. By assisting your supervising attorney in finding evidence and legal theories in support of your client's claim, you are helping the court do its job—that of dispensing justice in a fair and equitable manner.

---

6. This right is guaranteed by the Fifth and Fourteenth Amendments to the U.S. Constitution, which provide that no person can be deprived of life, liberty, or property without due process of law. *Due process of law* means that the government must follow a set of reasonable, fair, and standard procedures in any action against a citizen.

KEY TERMS AND CONCEPTS

adversarial system of
  justice   91

advocate   92

attorney-client privilege   70

breach   66

conflict of interest   70

conflicts check   73

disbarment   74

ethics   89

freelance paralegal   85

general licensing   88

independent paralegal   81

legal ethics   89

licensing   62

limited licensing   88

malpractice   75

pro bono publico   74

profession   60

reprimand   74

self-regulation   60

statute of limitations   67

suspension   74

third party   69

unauthorized practice of law
  (UPL)   63

work product   70

CHAPTER SUMMARY

1. A professional is one who has acquired a basic knowledge of the arts and sciences in addition to specialized knowledge in a particular area. Historically, professional groups have engaged in self-regulation by establishing minimum levels of competency for membership in the profession and ethical or professional codes to regulate the conduct of those belonging to the profession. Because clients seek out and pay lawyers for their legal expertise and because the professional judgment of a lawyer can significantly affect a client's welfare, lawyers are legally obligated to act in the client's best interests.

2. Key participants in the regulation of attorneys are state bar associations, state supreme courts, state legislatures, the United States Supreme Court (very occasionally), and the American Bar Association, which establishes model rules and guidelines relating to attorney conduct to be adopted by the various states. Attorneys are regulated both through licensing requirements and through ethical codes of conduct. To obtain a license to practice law in a state, an attorney normally must receive a bachelor's degree from a college or university, graduate from an accredited law school, take and pass a state bar examination, and pass an extensive background inspection.

3. All states but California have adopted a version of either the 1969 Model Code of Professional Responsibility or the 1983 revision of the Model Code, called the Model Rules of Professional Conduct, both of which were published by the American Bar Association. The majority of the states have adopted the Model Rules. The Model Code and Model Rules spell out the ethical and professional duties governing attorneys and the practice of law.

4. Ethical rules governing attorney behavior relate to competence, diligence, communication with clients, fees, confidentiality of client information, conflicts of interest, safekeeping of property, and other areas or activities. Attorneys who violate these duties may be subject to sanctions in the form of a reprimand, a suspension, or a disbarment. Additionally, attorneys (and paralegals) may be subject to potential liability for malpractice or violation of criminal statutes.

5. Paralegals are not subject to direct regulation by the state, in the form of licensing requirements, but paralegal conduct is regulated indirectly by the codes of conduct regulating attorney behavior, by ethical codes developed and adopted by paralegal associations, by statutes prohibiting the unauthorized practice of law, and by model standards and guidelines for the utilization of legal assistants.

6. Court decisions, state attorney ethical rules, paralegal ethical codes and guidelines, and the guidelines on the use of legal assistants that have been adopted by the National Association of Legal Assistants, the American Bar Association, and several states all express a general consensus that paralegals, under attorneys' supervision, may perform virtually any legal task that an attorney can perform, with four exceptions. A paralegal may not (1) establish an attorney-client relationship, (2) set the fees to be charged for an attorney's services, (3) give legal advice or opinions, and (4) represent a client in court (with few exceptions).

7. To avoid misleading clients and others, paralegal ethical codes and guidelines emphasize the importance of disclosing to clients and others the fact that a paralegal is not an attorney. Paralegal codes and guidelines also emphasize that a paralegal should abide by the rules governing attorney conduct, including the confidentiality rule, and avoid any action that might cause his or her supervising attorney to violate an ethical rule or that might give the appearance of professional impropriety.

8. A major concern today for both legal professionals and the public is whether paralegals should be directly regulated by the state through licensing requirements. General licensing would establish minimum standards that every paralegal would have to meet in order to practice as a paralegal in the state. Limited licensing would require paralegals wishing to offer routine legal services directly to the public in certain areas, such as family law or bankruptcy law, to demonstrate their proficiency in that area. The pros and cons of direct regulation through licensing are being debated vigorously by the leading paralegal associations, state bar associations, state courts, state legislatures, and public-interest groups.

9. *Ethics* can be defined as the study of morality and how moral principles and convictions apply to various real-world situations. Questions involving the

rightness, fairness, or justness of an action are, in essence, ethical questions. Our choices and decisions are ultimately affected, consciously or unconsciously, by our ethical values and goals. Ethical conduct in the legal arena requires, at a minimum, adherence to the ethical rules of the legal profession (legal ethics). Legal professionals are also expected to have high personal ethical standards as well.

10. When facing conflicts between legal ethics and personal ethics, paralegals may find it helpful to view legal ethics in the larger context of the American system of justice. Many of the ethical rules governing attorneys are rooted in the adversarial justice system and the concept of advocacy. Often, the question turns on whether the paralegal believes in the American system of justice and the way in which the rights and duties of individuals are protected and enforced by that system.

QUESTIONS FOR REVIEW

1. How is the legal profession regulated? Who are the regulators?

2. Why is regulation needed? How is it accomplished?

3. What are the two primary sets of ethical rules that regulate attorney behavior in the United States?

4. What are some of the duties imposed on attorneys (and paralegals) by state ethical codes regulating attorney conduct?

5. Why are attorneys and paralegals required, under state ethical codes, to keep client information confidential? What are some ways in which the confidentiality rule can be violated inadvertently?

6. How is the paralegal profession regulated indirectly by attorney ethical codes? What are the names of the two paralegal ethical codes discussed in this chapter? When were they adopted?

7. What is the unauthorized practice of law (UPL)? What are the four kinds of legal work that paralegals may not undertake without violating ethical guidelines and/or UPL statutes?

8. What types of tasks may legally be performed by paralegals?

9. Should paralegals be licensed? Why or why not? Should only independent paralegals be licensed? Why or why not? How can paralegals influence the debate over licensing?

10. What is the difference, if any, between legal ethics and personal ethics? In what kinds of situations might the standards of conduct prescribed by legal ethics come into conflict with personal ethical standards? How might paralegals overcome such conflicts?

ETHICAL QUESTIONS

1. Norma Sollers works as a paralegal for a small law firm. She is a trusted, experienced employee who has worked for the firm for twelve years. One morning, Linda Lowenstein, one of the attorneys, calls in from her home and asks Norma to sign Linda's name to a document that must be filed with the court that day. Norma has just prepared the final draft of the document and placed it on Linda's desk for her review and signature. Linda explains to Norma that because her child is sick, she does not want to the leave the child to come into the office. Norma knows that she should not sign Linda's name—only the client's attorney can sign the document. She mentions this to Linda, but Linda says, "Don't worry. No one will ever know that you signed it instead of me." How should Norma handle this situation?

2. Roberta Miller works as a paralegal, secretary, and receptionist for an attorney who is a sole practitioner. She is drafting an opinion letter to a client, Gina Thomas, advising her to file for bankruptcy. The telephone rings, and she turns away from her computer to answer it, leaving the opinion letter on the screen. As she hangs up the phone, James Archer, another client, enters the reception area and asks to see her supervising attorney. She leaves her desk and the computer screen with the letter on it. While she is gone, Archer looks in the direction of the computer, and the letter to Gina Thomas catches his eye. Gina Thomas is a neighbor of his, so he reads the letter. Has an ethical violation occurred? If so, by whom and of what rule? How could the violation have been avoided?

3. Mike Robbins works for Sarah Jones, a sole practitioner. Sarah's first appointment on Monday morning is with Jeffrey Sutherland. When Sutherland leaves the office, Sarah calls Mike in and asks him to draft a complaint to initiate Sutherland's divorce action. She expresses her disbelief over the divorce of two clients whom she has known for so long. Later that week, Sutherland's wife, Melanie, calls to make an appointment with Sarah to discuss the possibility of a divorce. May Sarah represent both Jeffrey and Melanie Sutherland? Why or why not? What ethical rule is involved?

PRACTICE QUESTIONS AND ASSIGNMENTS

1. Kathryn Borstein works for the legal department of a large manufacturing corporation as a legal assistant. In the process of interviewing a middle-management accountant with the company relating to an employment-discrimination lawsuit, Kathryn discovers that a number of the top executives cheat on their income-tax returns by not declaring a substantial portion of their bonuses. Kathryn becomes disenchanted with her job with the corporation and finds a new one with a law firm. Her supervising attorney in the law firm is involved in a case against her former employer. The attorney tells Kathryn that the only way to deal with these big corporations is to get whatever dirt you can on them and then threaten to go to the press. He wants to know if she can give him any such information. Can she tell him any of the "dirt" about the executives who cheat on their income taxes? Why or why not? What ethical rules are involved in her decision?

2. According to this chapter's text, which of the following actions are paralegals legally permitted to undertake?

a. Advise a client of the date of an upcoming legal procedure and when the client should appear at the courthouse.

b. Answer a potential client's questions about what the attorney charges for legal services.

c. Interview a witness to a car accident.

d. Represent a client before an administrative agency.

e. Represent a client in court.

f. Investigate the facts of a car-accident case.

g. Work as a freelance paralegal for attorneys.

h. Inform a friend of the legal consequences of violating a child-custody order issued by the court.

4

WORKING IN A
LAW OFFICE

CHAPTER OBJECTIVES

After completing this chapter, you will know:

- How law firms organize and structure their businesses.
- The various lines of authority and accountability in a typical law partnership.
- How paralegals are evaluated.
- The importance of an efficient filing system in legal practice and some typical filing procedures.
- How clients are billed for legal services and some of the ethical implications of client billing practices.
- The importance of communication skills in the legal profession.

CHAPTER OUTLINE

THE ORGANIZATIONAL
   STRUCTURE OF LAW FIRMS

Sole Proprietorships

Partnerships

Professional Corporations

LAW-OFFICE PERSONNEL

PERFORMANCE EVALUATIONS

FILING PROCEDURES

Client Files

Work-product Files and
   Reference Materials

Forms Files

Personnel Files

FINANCIAL PROCEDURES

Fee Arrangements

Retainer Agreements

Client Trust Accounts

Billing and Timekeeping Procedures

Ethics and Client Billing Practices

COMMUNICATION SKILLS
   AND THE LEGAL PROFESSION

The Communication Process

Nonverbal Communication

Communication Skills
   and Conflict Resolution

LAW-OFFICE CULTURE AND POLITICS

Introduction

The wide variety of law-office environments makes it impossible to describe in any detail how the particular firm with which you find employment will be run. Typically, though, that firm will have specific policies and procedures relating to how many hours per day or per week you will be required to work, how you are to document the time you spend on various projects, how office supplies are maintained, how vacation time accrues, the employee benefits to which you are entitled, and so on. In some firms, particularly large law firms, these policies and procedures may be spelled out in a written document, such as an **employment policy manual**. In smaller firms, policies and procedures are often less formal and may be based largely on habit or tradition. Because most paralegals are employed by private law firms, this chapter focuses on the organization, management, and procedures characteristic of private law firms.

Part of working in a law office also involves knowing how to communicate and relate well with others. The latter part of this chapter discusses the importance of communication skills in the context of legal work.

The Organizational Structure of Law Firms

As mentioned in Chapter 2, law firms range in size from the small, one-attorney firm to the huge megafirm that consists of hundreds of attorneys. Regardless of their differences in size, though, in terms of business organization, law firms typically organize their businesses as sole proprietorships, partnerships, or professional corporations. Because the way in which a business is organized affects the law-office environment, we look briefly at each of the three major organizational forms here.

Sole Proprietorships

Many law firms, particularly smaller firms, are **sole proprietorships**. Sole proprietorships are the simplest business form and are often used by attorneys when they first set up legal practices. In a sole proprietorship, one individual—the sole proprietor—owns the business. The sole proprietor is entitled to any profits made by the firm but is also personally liable for all of the firm's debts or obligations. **Personal liability** means that the personal assets of the business owner (such as a home, automobile, savings or investment accounts, and other property) may have to be sacrificed to pay business obligations if the business fails.

An attorney who practices law as a sole proprietor is often called a *sole (solo) practitioner*. Although a sole practitioner may at times hire an associate attorney to help with the legal work, the associate will be paid a specific sum for his or her time and will not share in the profits or losses of the firm itself.

Working for a sole practitioner is a good way for a paralegal to learn about law-office procedures because the paralegal will typically perform a wide

Employment Policy Manual
A firm's handbook or written statement that specifies the policies and procedures that govern the firm's employees and employer-employee relationships.

Sole Proprietorship
The simplest form of business, in which the owner is the business. Anyone who does business without creating a formal business entity has a sole proprietorship.

Personal Liability
An individual's personal responsibility for debts or obligations. The owners of sole proprietorships and partnerships are personally liable for the debts and obligations incurred by their business firms. If their firms go bankrupt or cannot meet debts as they become due, the owners will be personally responsible for paying the debts.

variety of tasks. Many sole practitioners hire one person to perform the functions of secretary, paralegal, administrator, and manager. Paralegals holding this kind of position would probably handle the following kinds of tasks: receiving and date-stamping the mail, organizing and maintaining the filing system, interviewing clients and witnesses, bookkeeping (receiving payments from clients, preparing and sending bills to clients, and so on), conducting investigations and legal research, drafting legal documents, assisting the attorney in trial preparation and perhaps in the courtroom, and numerous other tasks, including office administration.

As mentioned, working for a sole practitioner who runs a small general practice is a good way to learn about procedures relating to different areas of legal work. You will have an opportunity to find out which area of law you most enjoy—and you may want to pursue a career as a specialist in that area with another firm. If you work for a sole practitioner who specializes in one area of law, you will have an opportunity to develop expertise in that area of law. In sum, working in a small law firm gives you a broad overview of law-office procedures and legal practice. This knowledge will help you throughout your career.

Partnerships

The majority of law firms are either partnerships or professional corporations. In a **partnership**, two or more individuals undertake to do business jointly as **partners**. A partnership may consist of just a few attorneys or over a hundred attorneys. In a partnership, each partner owns a share of the business and shares jointly in the firm's profits or losses. Like sole proprietors, partners are personally liable for the debts and obligations of the business if the business fails.

In smaller partnerships, the partners may participate equally in managing the partnership. They will likely meet periodically to make decisions relating to clients, policies, procedures, and other matters of importance to the firm. In larger partnerships, managerial decisions are usually made by a committee consisting of some of the partners, one of whom may be designated as the **managing partner**.

The partnership may hire associate attorneys, but, as in a sole proprietorship, the associates will not have ownership rights in the firm. Normally, an associate hopes to become a partner, and if the associate's performance is satisfactory, the partners may invite the associate to become a partner in the firm.

Professional Corporations

A **professional corporation (P.C.)** is owned by **shareholders**, so called because they purchase the corporation's stock, or shares, and thus own a share of the business. The shareholders share in the profits and losses of the firm in proportion to how many shares they own. Their personal liability may or may not be limited to the amount of their investment depending on the circumstances and on state law.

PARTNERSHIP

An association of two or more persons to carry on, as co-owners, a business for profit.

PARTNER

A person who has undertaken to operate a business jointly with one or more other persons. Each partner is a co-owner of the business firm.

MANAGING PARTNER

The partner in a law firm who makes decisions relating to the firm's policies and procedures and who generally oversees the business operations of the firm.

PROFESSIONAL CORPORATION (P.C.)

A business form in which shareholders (those who purchase the corporation's stock, or shares) own the firm and share in the profits and losses of the firm in proportion to how many shares they own. Their personal liability, unlike that of partners, is limited to the amount of their investment.

SHAREHOLDER

One who purchases corporate stock, or shares, and who thus becomes an owner of the corporation.

In many respects, the professional corporation is run like a partnership, and the distinction between these two forms of business organization is often more a legal formality than an operational reality. Because of this, attorneys who organize their business as a professional corporation are nonetheless sometimes referred to as partners. For the sake of simplicity, in this chapter we will refer to anyone who has ownership rights in the firm as a partner.

DEVELOPING PARALEGAL SKILLS

Types of Practice

 Jane Upton, a student in a legal-assistant program, is looking for a job for her internship course. She has some questions about some of the job postings, which she is discussing with Lorraine Burwitz, a friend who graduated from the program two years ago. "With which type of firm should I do my internship?" asks Jane. "There are so many different types and sizes of firms to consider. How do I sort it all out?"

Lorraine responds, "You need to think about the different types of practices. First, there are private law firms—you know, sole practitioners, partnerships, and professional corporations. Then there are corporations and government legal departments and offices."

Jane pulls out a job posting for a sole practitioner. It reads: "General law practice seeks legal-assistant student with strong word-processing skills. Areas of law include family law, probate, real estate, some litigation. Must be dependable and willing to take initiative. Contact the law offices of Mary T. Jones, (616) 555-9000." Jane asks Lorraine whether Mary Jones, because she is the only person listed, is a sole practitioner. "Right," responds Lorraine. "If it were a partnership, the name would read something like the name of the firm I work for, which is Culpepper, Hines, Tobin & Thomas." "What about a professional corporation? Would the name be something like Culpepper, Hines, Tobin & Thomas, P.C.?" asks Jane. "It might in some states," answers Lorraine. "In other states, though," Lorraine continues, "the names of professional corporations are followed by other initials, such as P.A., for professional association."

"What about working for these various types of firms? How does that differ?" asks Jane. "Sole practitioners usually want someone who can act as both a paralegal and a secretary and who isn't afraid to ask questions and assume a lot of responsibility. Working for a sole practitioner can be a good way to get a lot of experience," explains Lorraine. "In larger partnerships and P.C.s, paralegals tend to specialize, and you don't get to work in as many different areas. It really depends on what you feel comfortable with, but for my internship, I chose a sole practitioner's office for the varied experience. I didn't know yet which area of law I wanted to work in," says Lorraine. Jane liked that idea and decided to apply to the offices of Mary T. Jones.

LAW-OFFICE PERSONNEL

When you take a job as a legal assistant, one of the first things you will want to learn is the relative status of the office personnel. Particularly, you will want to know who has authority over you and to whom you are accountable. You also want to know who will be accountable to you—whether you have an assistant or a secretary (or share an assistant or a secretary with another paralegal), for example. In a small firm, you will have no problem learning this information. If you work for a larger law firm, however, the lines of authority may be more difficult to perceive. Your supervisor will probably instruct you, either orally or in writing, on the relative status of the firm's personnel. If you are not sure about who has authority over whom and what kinds of tasks are performed by various employees, you should ask your supervisor.

The lines of authority and accountability vary from firm to firm, depending on the firm's size and its organizational and management preferences. A sample organizational chart for a smaller law partnership is shown in Exhibit 4.1. The ultimate decision makers in the hypothetical firm represented by that chart are the partners. Next in authority are the associate attorneys and summer associates (law clerks—see Chapter 1). The paralegals in this firm are supervised by both the attorneys (in regard to legal work) and the office manager (in regard to office procedural and paralegal staffing matters). In larger

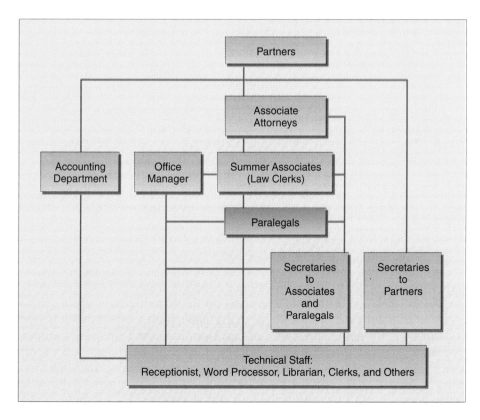

EXHIBIT 4.1
A Sample Organizational Chart for a Law Partnership

LEGAL-ASSISTANT MANAGER
An employee who is responsible for overseeing the paralegal staff and paralegal professional development.

LEGAL ADMINISTRATOR
An administrative employee of a law firm who manages the day-to-day operations of the firm. In smaller law firms, legal administrators are usually called office managers.

OFFICE MANAGER
An administrative employee who manages the day-to-day operations of a business firm. In larger law firms, office managers are usually called legal administrators.

SUPPORT PERSONNEL
Those employees who provide clerical, secretarial, or other support to the legal, paralegal, and administrative staff of a law firm.

firms, there may be a **legal-assistant manager**, who coordinates and oversees paralegal staffing and various programs relating to paralegal educational and professional development.

Law-firm personnel include, in addition to attorneys and paralegals, administrative personnel. In larger firms, the partners may hire a **legal administrator** to run the business end of the firm. The legal administrator might delegate some of his or her authority to an **office manager** and other supervisory employees. In smaller firms, such as that represented by the chart in Exhibit 4.1, an office manager handles the administrative aspects of the firm. Generally, the legal administrator or office manager makes sure that the office runs smoothly, that sufficient supplies are on hand, that office procedures are established and followed, and so on. In a small firm, the office manager might also handle client billing procedures. The hypothetical firm represented by the chart in Exhibit 4.1 has an accounting department to perform this function.

The **support personnel** in a large law office may include secretaries, receptionists, bookkeepers, file clerks, messengers, and others. Depending on their functions and specific jobs, support personnel may fall under the supervision of any number of the other personnel in the firm. In a very small firm, just one person—the legal secretary, for example—may perform all of the above-mentioned functions.

PERFORMANCE EVALUATIONS

Many law firms have a policy of conducting periodic performance evaluations. Usually, performance is evaluated annually, but some firms conduct evaluations every six months.

Because paralegal responsibilities vary from firm to firm, no one evaluation checklist applies to every paralegal. Some of the factors that may be considered during a performance evaluation are indicated in Exhibit 4.2. Typically, under each factor is a series of options—ranging from "very good" to "unsatisfactory" or something similar—for the supervisor or attorney to check. When you begin work as a paralegal, you should learn at the outset what exactly your duties will be and what performance is expected of you. This way, you will be able to prepare for your first evaluation from the moment you begin working. You will not have to wait six months or a year before you learn that you were supposed to be doing something that you failed to do.

In the busy legal workplace, you will probably not have much time available to discuss issues with your supervisor that do not relate to immediate needs. And even if you do find a moment, you may feel awkward in broaching a discussion about your performance or about problems that you face in the workplace. Performance evaluations are designed specifically to allow both the employer and the employee to exchange their views on such issues.

During performance reviews, you can learn how the firm rates your performance. You can gain valuable feedback from your supervisor, learn more about your strengths and weaknesses, and identify the areas in which you need to improve your skills or work habits. You can also give feedback to your supervisor on how you feel about the workplace. For example, if you

_____ **1. RESPONSIBILITY**
Making sure that all tasks are performed on time and following up on all pending matters.
_____ **2. EFFICIENCY**
Obtaining good results in the least amount of time.
_____ **3. PRODUCTIVITY**
Producing a sufficient quantity of work in a given time period.
_____ **4. COMPETENCE**
Knowledge level and skills.
_____ **5. INITIATIVE**
Applying intelligence and creativity to tasks and making appropriate recommendations.
_____ **6. COOPERATION**
Getting along well with others on the legal team.
_____ **7. PERSONAL FACTORS**
Appearance, grooming habits, friendliness, poise, and so forth.
_____ **8. DEPENDABILITY**
Arriving at work consistently on time and being available when needed.

EXHIBIT 4.2
A Sample Evaluation Checklist

think that your expertise is not being fully utilized, this would be a good time to discuss that issue and perhaps suggest some ways in which your knowledge and experience could be put to better use.

FILING PROCEDURES

The paperwork generated by law offices is enormous. And, for the most part, the paperwork consists of important and confidential documents that must be safeguarded yet be readily retrievable when they are needed. Efficient filing procedures are thus essential. Otherwise, important files and documents may be lost or unavailable when needed. Documents must also be filed in such a way as to protect client confidentiality.

Larger firms normally have specific procedures concerning the creation, maintenance, use, and storage of office files. If you take a job with a large firm, a supervisor will probably spend some time training you in routine office procedures, including filing procedures. The trend today, particularly in larger firms, is toward computerized filing systems. You will read about the application of computer technology to document management and filing later in this text, in Chapter 8. If you work for a small firm, filing procedures may be less formal, and you may even assume the responsibility for organizing and developing an efficient filing system. In either situation, you must take the initiative, if necessary, to learn about existing filing procedures.

Generally, law offices maintain several types of files. Typically, a law firm's filing system will include client files, work-product files and reference materials, forms files, and personnel files.

Client Files

The heart of any legal practice is its client files. Law firms could not operate without having some kind of system for organizing and maintaining client files. If a document is misfiled or a file is missing, valuable time may have to be spent tracking down the document or file. If a file is lost, the client may

PARALEGAL PROFILE

Paralegal Supervisor

JOEL WIRCHIN received his bachelor of arts degree from the State University of New York at Albany. He then enrolled in the lawyer's-assistant program at Adelphi University. He is now working on a master's degree in public administration. Wirchin is currently the director of paralegal services for Sullivan and Cromwell, a law firm specializing in corporate transactions and litigation. Wirchin started at Sullivan and Cromwell as a senior legal assistant and moved into administrative work about four and a half years ago. Prior to working at Sullivan and Cromwell, he worked in the legal department of a pharmaceutical company.

What do you like best about your work?

"I like working in an administrative position, especially because of the variety of duties involved. It is a very people-oriented job, and I consider that to be one of my greatest talents—working with others. I think I'm making a positive difference in the lives of the people whom I manage."

What is the greatest challenge that you face in your area of work?

"The biggest challenge for me is the varied scope of my work. I find it very challenging to manage and deal with such a large staff. The New York office, in which I work, employs about forty-five paralegals. I am in charge of seventy paralegals worldwide, and my duties include hiring, training, evaluating, and budgeting responsibilities, to name just a few. I also travel occasionally, mainly to Sullivan and Cromwell's office in Washington, D.C. One of my greatest challenges is working with lawyers and clients when urgent or particularly demanding circumstances arise. I feel as though I have to create miracle after miracle."

What advice do you have for would-be paralegals in your area of work?

"My advice to paralegals who are interested in administrative work is to pay close attention to the work environment—not just to the lawyers but to the law firm itself. I feel you should keep one eye on the client work and one eye on how decisions are made. This will help the paralegal get a feel for the business transactions and, really, the business of the law firm. If I were a student now, I'd focus on shooting higher and being more selective when planning my career and selecting potential employers."

> **"I THINK I'M MAKING A POSITIVE DIFFERENCE IN THE LIVES OF THE PEOPLE WHOM I MANAGE."**

What are some tips for success as a paralegal in your area of work?

"Paralegals should convey a positive, upbeat attitude. It is, of course, important to be smart, organized, and analytical, but it's also important to inspire confidence in others. Also, a paralegal's attitude comes through in his or her performance evaluation."

suffer irreparable harm. Each law firm, regardless of its size, must take special care in maintaining its case files so that the files are protected, kept confidential, and yet immediately at hand when needed.

To illustrate client filing procedures, we present below the phases in the "life cycle" of a hypothetical client's file. The name of the client is Katherine Baranski, who has just retained one of your firm's attorneys to represent her in a lawsuit that she is bringing against Tony Peretto. Because Baranski is initiating the lawsuit, she is referred to as the plaintiff. Peretto, because he has to defend against Baranski's claims, is the defendant. The name of the case is *Baranski v. Peretto.* Assume that you will be working on the case and that your supervising attorney has just asked you to open a new case file. Assume also that you have already verified, through a "conflicts check" (discussed in Chapter 3), that no conflict of interest exists.

Opening a New Client File.   The first step that you (or a secretary, at your request) will take in opening a new file is to assign the case a file number. For reasons of both efficiency and confidentiality, many firms identify their client files by numbers or some kind of numerical and/or alphabetical sequence instead of the clients' names.

The range of possibilities is virtually limitless. One frequently used technique is to identify the file by the date on which it is created. For example, a file opened on January 12, 1996, could be identified as follows: 96-0112. The advantage of identifying files by date is that the age of the file is readily apparent. Additionally, the initials of the **responsible billing partner** (the partner responsible for overseeing the case) might be added to the file number. If attorney Allen Gilmore was the responsible partner for the Baranski case, the file label might read 96-0112-AG. To ensure confidentiality, some law firms identify the responsible billing partner by a number instead of the attorney's initials. Assuming that Allen Gilmore's identifying number was six, then the file number for the Baranski file would be 96-0112-06.

Another technique is to combine letters of the names of the plaintiff and defendant in such as way as to obscure their identities. The *Baranski v. Peretto* case file might be identified by the letters BARAPE—the first four letters of the plaintiff's name followed by the first two letters of the defendant's name.

Typically, law firms maintain a master client list on which clients' names are entered alphabetically and cross-referenced to the clients' case numbers. If file numbers consist of numerical sequences, there is also a master list on which the file numbers are listed in numerical order and cross-referenced to the clients' names.

Adding Subfiles.   As the work on the Baranski case progresses and more documents are generated or received, the file will expand. To ensure that documents will be easy to locate, you will create subfiles. A special subfile might be created for client documents (such as a contract, will, stock certificate, or photograph) that the firm needs for reference or for evidence at trial. As correspondence relating to the Baranski case is generated, you will probably add a correspondence subfile. You will also want a subfile for your or the attorney's notes on the case, including research results.

As you will read in Chapter 6, litigation involves several stages. The first stage involves *pleadings.* The pleadings include the plaintiff's *complaint,* a document filed with the court to initiate a lawsuit, and the defendant's *answer,* or response to the complaint. Prior to trial, attorneys for both sides will engage in a process called *discovery.* The purpose of discovery is to gather ("discover") as much evidence as possible—from opposing parties, witnesses, and other sources—to support the claims of the parties.

As the Baranski litigation progresses through the pleadings and discovery stages, subfiles for documents relating to each stage will be added to the Baranski file. By the discovery stage of litigation, for example, the Baranski

RESPONSIBLE BILLING PARTNER
The partner in a law firm who is responsible for overseeing a particular client's case and the billing of that client.

file might contain the subfiles shown in Exhibit 4.3 on the next page. Numerous other subfiles may be created during the course of the litigation.

Documents are typically filed within each subfile in reverse chronological order, with the most recently dated document on the top. Usually, to safeguard the documents, they are punched at the top with a two-hole puncher so that they can be secured within the file with a clip. Note, though, that original client documents should not be punched or altered in any way. They should always be left loose within the file. For example, if you were holding in the file a property deed belonging to a client, you would not want to alter that document in any way.

Color Coding, Tabs, and Indexes.   Many law firms find it useful to color-code subfiles so that they can be readily identified. For example, pink file folders (or pink stickers on the file labels) might be used routinely for pleadings subfiles, orange folders for discovery subfiles, yellow folders for correspondence, and so on. Color coding may also be used in other ways—to indicate the responsible attorney for certain files, for example. Some firms use different colors of paper for different documents so that they can be quickly identified. For example, all *copies* of original documents might be made on pink paper.

A subfile is sometimes further subdivided by adding tabs to various documents within the subfile. An index attached to the inside cover of the subfile indicates what documents can be found at what tab number. Exhibit 4.3 also shows a sample index for the pleadings file in the Baranski case. Note that the sample index shown in the exhibit also includes relevant dates, such as when the complaint was filed with the court (indicated by an "F" following the date) and when the answer was received (indicated by an "R" following the date).

File Use and Storage.   Typically, files are stored in a central file room or area. Most firms require that office staff use "out cards" when removing files from the storage area. An **out card** is a piece of cardboard, about the size of a manila folder, with lines on it to indicate the date, the name of the file, and the initials of the user. When a file is removed, the card is inserted in the file's place. Even if a file is removed for only a few minutes, an out card should be used. The consistent use of out cards helps to avoid the time cost and frustration involved in trying to locate missing files. An alternative to an out card is an *out folder*, in which documents can be filed temporarily until the file is returned to storage.

The problem with out cards and out folders is that people either do not use them at all or fail to initial them. A perpetual challenge for most law firms is trying to devise a "foolproof" system for quickly locating files that have been removed from the file storage area. Valuable staff time is often spent in tracking down files that are not where they should be. As you will read in Chapter 8, computerized file-management systems can provide firms with a solution to this problem.

Note that individual documents should never be removed from a client file or subfile. Rather, the entire file or subfile should be removed for use. This ensures that important documents will not be separated from the file and possibly mislaid or lost. Many paralegals and other users make copies of

OUT CARD
A large card inserted in a filing cabinet in the place of a temporarily removed file. The out card notifies others who may need the file of the name of the person who has the file and the time and date that the file was removed.

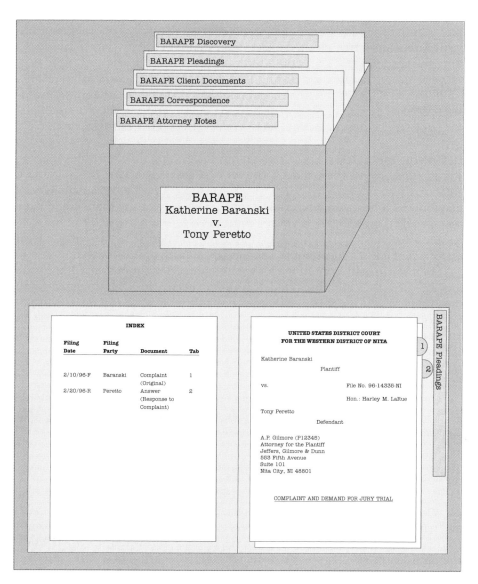

EXHIBIT 4.3
A Sample Client File

documents in the file for their use. For example, if you are working on the Baranski case and need to review the complaint, which is located in the pleadings file, you might remove the pleadings file temporarily from the storage area (inserting an out card or folder), copy the complaint, and immediately return the file to storage.

Closing a File.   Assume that the Baranski case has been settled out of court and that no further legal work on Baranski's behalf needs to be done. For a time, her file will be retained in the inactive files, but when it is fairly certain that no one will need to refer to it very often—if ever—it will be closed. Closed files are often stored in a separate area of the building or even off-site. There are warehouses that specifically cater to attorneys and other professionals who need storage space for confidential files. Such warehouses make sure that the files are secure and protected from dampness or other environmental problems that could damage their contents. Many larger law firms store the content of old files on microfilm.

Specific procedures for closing files vary from firm to firm. Typically, when a case is closed, original documents provided by the client (for example, a deed to property) are returned to the client, and extraneous materials, such as extra copies of documents or cover letters, are destroyed.

Destroying Old Files. Law firms do not have to retain client files forever, and at some point, the Baranski file will be destroyed. Law firms exercise great care when destroying client files because a court or government agency may impose a heavy fine on a law firm that destroys a file that should have been retained for a longer period of time. How long a particular file must be retained depends on many factors, including the nature of the client's legal matters and governing statutes, such as the statute of limitations.

State statutes of limitations for legal-malpractice actions vary from state to state—from six months to ten years after the attorney's last contact with the client. When the statute of limitations in your state expires is thus an important factor in determining how long to retain a client file because an attorney or law firm will need the information contained in the client's file to defend against a malpractice action. If the file has been destroyed, the firm will not be able to produce any documents or other evidence to refute the plaintiff's claim.

Only when the retention time for a client file has expired should the file be destroyed. Old files are normally destroyed by shredding them so that confidentiality is preserved.

Work-product Files and Reference Materials

Many law firms keep copies of research projects, legal memoranda, and pleadings and other case-related materials prepared by the firm's attorneys and paralegals so that these documents can be referred to in future projects. In this way, legal personnel do not have to start all over again when working on a claim similar to one dealt with in the past. These work-product files, or legal information files, are typically filed in the firm's library in alphabetical order by legal topic, with subtopics. For example, the topic of "Automobile Negligence" would include in subfiles copies of complaints, answers, legal research, and other documents relating to cases involving automobile negligence.

When a firm has its own library, someone is normally assigned the job of overseeing the library and making sure that it is kept current. This person probably also maintains a card catalog or computerized record, creating new cards or records for new additions to the library and keeping a log of who has which book or other reference materials.

FORMS FILE
A reference file containing copies of the firm's commonly used legal documents and informational forms. The documents in the forms file serve as a model for drafting new documents.

Forms Files

Every law firm keeps on hand various forms that it commonly uses. These forms may be kept in various files or, as is often the case, stored in a **forms file**. A forms file might include retainer-agreement forms, forms used for filing lawsuits in specific courts, bankruptcy forms indicating the type of information that must be obtained from clients petitioning for bankrupcy, forms used in real-estate matters, and numerous others. Often, to save time, copies of pleadings (or other documents) relating to specific types of cases are kept for future reference. Then, when the attorney or paralegal works on a similar case, the pleadings (or other documents) from the previous case can be used as a model, or guide. These forms may be kept either in a forms file or in a work-product file.

As will be discussed in Chapter 8, there is an abundance of legal software that contains forms for use in litigation and other legal specialties. Computerized forms have simplified legal practice by allowing legal personnel to generate customized documents within minutes.

Personnel Files

The firm's personnel files usually contain a complete employment record for each employee of the firm, including the employee's original employment application and résumé, performance reviews, general progress notes, and attendance records. These records are usually kept in a locked file at all times, and old personnel files are rarely stored off-site—because they must be close at hand if someone requests a job reference for a previous employee.

FINANCIAL PROCEDURES

Like any other business firm, a law firm needs to at least cover its expenses or it will fail. In the business of law, the product is legal services, which are sold to clients for a price. A foremost concern of any law firm is therefore to establish a clear policy on fee arrangements and efficient procedures to ensure that each client is billed appropriately for the time and costs associated with serving that client. Efficient billing procedures require, in turn, that attorneys and paralegals keep accurate records of the time that they spend working on a given client's case or other legal matter.

Fee Arrangements

Normally, fee arrangements are discussed and agreed on at the outset of any attorney-client relationship. Recall from Chapter 3 that the practice of law is usually defined to include the establishment of legal fees, and thus only attorneys make fee arrangements with clients. Basically, there are three forms of fee arrangements: fixed fees, hourly fees, and contingency fees.

Fixed Fees. The client may agree to pay a **fixed fee** for a specified legal service. Certain procedures, such as incorporation and simple divorce filings, are often handled on a fixed-fee basis because the attorney can estimate fairly closely how much time will be involved in completing the work. For example, an attorney may charge $500 for a simple will or $1,000 for an uncontested divorce involving no children or property.

FIXED FEE
A fee paid to the attorney by his or her client for having rendered a specified legal service, such as the creation of a simple will.

DEVELOPING PARALEGAL SKILLS

Client File Confidentiality

At the law firm of Jenkins & Fitzgerald, P.C., the client files are organized so that there is a separate folder, or subfile, for each of the following: attorney notes (research), client documents, pleadings, and discovery. All of the subfiles are kept in a large, red, accordion-shaped folder, which expands to accommodate a great number of documents. On each subfile, as well as on the large red folder, is written the name of the case, such as *Hanks v. Hardy*, the court's docket (or file) number, the firm's file number, and the client's name.

Robert James, a paralegal with the firm, was assigned a research project on *Sims v. Purdy Contracting, Inc.*, a case involving a personal-injury suit for millions of dollars against the firm's client, Mr. Purdy. Robert took the pleadings and research folders with him to the county bar association's law library to do some research. He set the files down on a table and went to the shelves to find a case reporter. While Robert was looking for the reporter, in an area several aisles away from the table on which he had left the files, Lori Langer walked by and noticed the file. Lori was an attorney and was currently doing work on behalf of Clark Construction Company, a large contractor who was considering giving Mr. Purdy's company a big job. Lori looked at the folders and saw Purdy's name, the docket number, and a law firm's file number.

Curious about the lawsuit, Laurie wrote down the docket number, left the library, and went to the court clerk's office. There she requested a copy of the court's file on the case, which was public information. Laurie read through the complaint. She could see that the plaintiff, Sims, sought a substantial amount in money damages. Laurie decided to call Mr. Clark to see if he was aware of the lawsuit. She knew that he would be hesitant to award a subcontract to Purdy if he knew that Purdy was being sued for so much money. This kind of case could bankrupt Purdy, and he might not be able to finish the job.

Later that week, Robert's supervising attorney, Lane Perkins, called Robert into his office. "It seems that Mr. Purdy lost out on a major contract with Clark Construction Company because Mr. Clark found out about Purdy's lawsuit," said Lane. "Clark told Purdy that Clark's attorney had seen a file with Purdy's name on it at the law library. Purdy is furious over the breach of client confidentiality. I have discussed this matter with my partners, and we do not hold you responsible. But we have learned a lesson: our filing system needs to be modified. We will be changing the system so that the case names and client names no longer appear on the outside of any of the files."

Hourly Fees. With the exception of litigation work done on a contingency-fee basis (discussed below), most law firms charge clients hourly rates for legal services. Hourly rates vary widely from firm to firm. Some litigation firms, for example, can charge extremely high hourly rates ($500 an hour or more) for their services because of their reputation for obtaining favorable settlements or court judgments for their clients. In contrast, an attorney just starting up a practice as a sole practitioner will have to charge a lower, more competitive rate (which may be as low as $75 per hour) to attract clients.

Today's law firms are increasingly billing clients for hourly rates for paralegal services. Because the hourly rate for paralegals is lower than that for attorneys, clients benefit from attorneys' use of paralegal services. Clients normally appreciate the flexibility of being able to contact paralegals, knowing that they will be charged less than the hourly rate for attorneys. At the initial client interview, the attorney usually explains to the client the kinds of work that will be undertaken by paralegals and the lower rates that will be charged for their services. The estimated 1995 average billable rate for paralegals is $77.[1]

Note that although your services might be billed to the client at a certain rate, say $75, that does not mean that the firm will actually pay you $75 an hour as wages. The billable rate for paralegal services, as for attorney services, has to take into account the firm's expenses for overhead (rent, utilities, employee benefits, supplies, and so on). The estimated 1995 average annual salary for paralegals who work for private law firms is $30,851. If you divide this salary by fifty-two weeks, you will see that paralegals, on average, earn $588.10 per week. If you divide this figure by forty (hours per week), the average hourly wage rate for paralegals is $14.70—substantially lower than the average *billable* hourly rate.

Contingency Fees.   A common practice among litigation attorneys, especially those representing plaintiffs in certain types of cases (such as personal-injury or negligence cases), is to charge the client on a contingency-fee basis. A **contingency fee** is contingent (dependent) on the outcome of the case. If the plaintiff wins the lawsuit and recovers damages or settles out of court, the attorney will be entitled to a certain percentage of the amount recovered. If the plaintiff loses the lawsuit, the attorney gets nothing—although the client normally will reimburse the attorney for the costs and expenses involved in preparing for trial (costs and expenses are discussed below, in regard to billing procedures).

Often, the attorney's contingency fee is one-fourth or one-third of the amount recovered. The agreement may provide for modification of the amount depending on how and when the dispute is settled. For example, an agreement that provides for a contingency fee of 25 percent of the amount recovered for a plaintiff may state that the amount will be reduced to a lower percentage if the case is settled out of court. In this situation, the agreement might provide, that if the case is settled before trial, the attorney's fee will be one-tenth of the amount recovered in the settlement.

While some people maintain that the use of contingency fees is ethically questionable (because it may motivate attorneys to resort to aggressive tactics just to win a case), the legal profession deems it ethical because it allows broader access to legal services. Contingency-fee arrangements allow

---

> **ETHICAL CONCERN**
>
> ## Handling Clients' Questions about Fees
>
> Suppose that you work as a paralegal for a sole practitioner, Marina Tesner, who is just setting up practice. You know that the attorney is soliciting new clients and that she relies on you, when she is out of the office, to make sure that potential clients are not turned away for any reason. One day, while Tesner is out of town, a man named Henry Roth calls the office. He is purchasing a home and wants to consult with an attorney before signing the final papers four days from now. You explain that Ms. Tesner is out of the office but will return in two days and could see him then. Roth says that he would wait for a couple of days if he knew what Tesner would charge for her services. Should you tell him that Ms. Tesner usually bills clients $125 an hour for her services, which is a low billable rate for your community? No, you should not. As discussed in Chapter 3, professional ethical codes prohibit anyone but an attorney from setting legal fees. If you told Roth what he wanted to know, you may be engaging in the unauthorized practice of law.

CONTINGENCY FEE
A legal fee that consists of a specified percentage (such as 30 percent) of the amount the plaintiff recovers in a civil lawsuit or if a settlement is reached in the plaintiff's favor. The fee must be paid only if the plaintiff prevails in the lawsuit (recovers damages) or an out-of-court settlement.

---

1. Authors' estimate based on the 1993 paralegal compensation survey conducted by *Legal Assistant Today* (see Carol Milano, "Salary Survey Results," *Legal Assistant Today,* May/June 1993, p. 48); the Legal Assistant Management Association's *1994 Compensation Survey;* and Bureau of Labor Statistics, *Monthly Labor Review,* various issues.

FEATURED GUEST: KATHLEEN MERCER REED

Ten Tips for Creating and Maintaining an Efficient File System

Biographical Note

Kathleen Mercer Reed holds a bachelor of science degree in legal administration from the University of Toledo and has a law degree. She currently works as an assistant professor and as the Coordinator of Legal Assistant Technology at the University of Toledo's Community and Technical College, the same program from which she received her associate's degree in 1985. A member of many legal-assistant advisory committees, Reed is a former president of the Toledo Association of Legal Assistants. She is active in national paralegal education issues and a frequent speaker on the paralegal profession.

File maintenance is one of the most important aspects of legal work. Without an organized case file, the attorney is unable to make sure that the case is on track and deadlines are being met. This can mean unhappy clients and a resulting loss of business. Generally, attorneys rely on their paralegals to assume responsibility for the essential task of maintaining (or supervising the maintenance of) the files. Filing systems vary. In some firms, they are highly structured and efficient; in other firms, they may be virtually nonexistent. If you are ever faced with the challenge of setting up (or reorganizing) a file system, here are some tips to consider.

1 Set Aside Time for Planning.
The major problem relating to filing systems is the time factor. Law offices are extremely busy places. Time is money in the law firm.

Everyone wants to get on with the important job of performing work for the client. But filing systems *must* be planned. You need to recognize this fact and allow time for the planning process.

2 Create a System That Is Simple, Yet Effective. Remember that you and the attorney will not be the only ones working with the file. Secretaries, receptionists, and file clerks may also need to use client files. Don't create a system that generates confusion about where certain documents are to be filed or where they can be found. Try to establish a simple, logical system that can be readily understood by everybody.

3 Make Sure That the Files Are Clearly Labeled. Each file should be clearly labeled so that it can be easily located. Files are more easily

recognized when the labels are consistently placed on files and consistently typed, printed, or handwritten.

4 Don't Be Afraid to Create as Many Files as You Need. Don't hesitate to create additional files, especially subfiles, if you think that they are necessary. Generally, the more subfiles you create, the better organized your file will be—and the easier it will be to retrieve specific documents.

5 Make Sure That the Filing System Ensures Client Confidentiality. When setting up your filing system, make sure that the system protects client confidentiality to the greatest possible extent. Some law firms are eliminating alphabetical systems (files in which the client's name is clearly identified on the file folder) and are using numeric filing sys-

clients who otherwise could not afford legal services to have their claims settled, in or out of court, by competent attorneys.

Note that contingency-fee agreements only apply if an attorney represents the client in a *civil* lawsuit. In a civil case, the plaintiff frequently seeks money damages from the defendant to compensate the plaintiff for harms suffered. If the plaintiff "wins" the case, the attorney's fee will be a

tems instead. Numerical file systems eliminate the risk of one client seeing another client's name when the file is opened. Remember, a firm can breach a client's right to confidentiality simply by divulging (inadvertently or otherwise) the fact that the client consulted the firm, even as a potential client.

6   Set Up Efficient Case-opening Procedures. A client file should be set up within twenty-four hours of the initial client interview and sent back to the attorney assigned to the file. This means that conflict-of-interest checks and initial file organization must be done quickly. A thorough conflict-of-interest check must be done to prevent the necessity of spending hours on a plaintiff's case only to find out that another attorney in the law firm is representing the defendant in that same case. At the same time, the file must be given to the attorney promptly so that he or she can begin working for the client and avoid missing any deadlines.

7   Establish an Efficient Checkout System. No matter how well organized your file is, you can't work on the file if you can't find it! In a very small law office, this may not be a great concern. But the larger the firm, the more difficult it becomes to locate files—because more people have access to them. A file that you or an attorney needs

urgently may be sitting on a partner's desk, but you do not know this. You need to establish and enforce some kind of sign-out system, such as placing "out cards" or "sign-out cards" in the file whenever a file folder is removed.

8   Establish Proper Procedures for Closing and Storing Files. Closed files must be properly stored and maintained for several reasons. First, a client may contact the firm—sometimes months after his or her case has been closed—to obtain documents or information from the client's file. Second, work that you did on past cases can be a great resource when working on current cases, and if old files are easily accessible, you will not have to "reinvent the wheel" whenever you work on a case that is similar to a case already in the firm's files. Third and most important, there are state and national standards governing file retention. Find out how long your law firm is *legally required* to store and maintain closed files. For all of these reasons, closed files must be maintained with as much integrity as active files.

9   Establish Proper Procedures for Destroying Files. Client confidentiality must be maintained even when destroying very old closed files. One lawyer was shocked to find out that the paper from his closed files had been made into

> **"TRY TO ESTABLISH A SIMPLE, LOGICAL SYSTEM THAT CAN BE READILY UNDERSTOOD BY EVERYBODY."**

note pads and donated to a local school! There are a number of companies nationwide that deal exclusively with the destruction of confidential files. Use one of them or encourage your firm to invest in a paper shredder.

10   Keep in Mind the Ultimate Goal of Your Filing System. When setting up and maintaining a filing system, you should always keep in mind your primary goal—to help the firm deliver legal services more efficiently and economically. With an organized case file, the attorney can make sure that the case is on track and that deadlines are being met. Clients are happier, and malpractice actions are avoided. Additionally, by getting involved in file organization, your job as a paralegal is made easier. You not only stay well informed on file contents but also don't have to waste time searching for needed files or documents.

percentage of the amount awarded. Criminal cases, in contrast, are brought by the state (through the district attorney, county attorney, or other attorney working for the government). If the court finds the defendant guilty, the state imposes a penalty (a fine and/or imprisonment) on him or her. If the defendant is deemed innocent in the eyes of the court, no money is awarded to the defendant. In criminal cases, contingency fees are thus not an option.

RETAINER AGREEMENT

A signed document stating that the attorney or the law firm has been hired by the client to provide certain legal services and that the client agrees to pay for those services in accordance with the terms set forth in the retainer agreement.

RETAINER

An advance payment made by a client to a law firm to cover part of the legal fee and/or costs that will need to be incurred on that client's behalf.

TRUST ACCOUNT

A bank or escrow account in which one party (the trustee, such as an attorney) holds funds belonging to another person (such as a client); a bank account into which funds advanced to a law firm by a client are deposited.

ETHICAL CONCERN

Trust Accounts

Suppose that a legal professional who has access to funds held in trust for clients borrows money from those funds for temporary personal use. Would such borrowing be unethical? Would it be illegal? The answer to both questions is a resounding "Yes!" By law, anyone who takes for personal use any property (including money) that is legally entrusted to his or her care commits a form of theft called embezzlement. It does not matter whether the person who used the funds *intended* to replace them the next day, week, or month. The fact is, a crime has been committed.

Retainer Agreements

Whenever a client seeks legal advice from an attorney, fee arrangements are normally discussed at the initial client interview. Most law firms require each client to agree, in a signed writing called a **retainer agreement**, to whatever fee arrangements have been made. (Some states also require, by law, that fee arrangements be stated in writing.) The agreement specifies that the client is *retaining* (hiring) the attorney and/or firm to represent the client in a legal matter and states that the client agrees to the fee arrangements set forth in the agreement. Exhibit 4.4 shows a sample retainer agreement.

Client Trust Accounts

Law firms often require new clients to pay a **retainer**—an initial advance payment to the firm to cover part of the fee and various costs that will be incurred on the client's behalf (such as mileage or other travel expenses, phone and fax charges, and so on). Former clients of the firms, if they have paid their bills promptly, may not be required to pay retainer fees.

As mentioned in Chapter 3, every law firm maintains a bank account into which funds advanced to the firm by its clients are deposited. This account is usually referred to as a **trust account** (or *escrow account*).

- **It is extremely important that the funds held in a trust account be used only for expenses relating to the costs of serving that client's needs. Misuse of such accounts constitutes a breach of the firm's duty to its client.**

An attorney's personal use of the funds, for example, can lead to disciplinary action and possible disbarment, as well as criminal penalties. Commingling (mixing together) a client's funds with the firm's funds also constitutes abuse. If you handle a client's trust account, you should be especially careful to document fully your use of the funds to protect yourself and your firm against the serious problems that may arise if there are any discrepancies in the account.

Billing and Timekeeping Procedures

As a general rule, a law firm bills its clients monthly. Each client's bill reflects the amount of time spent on the client's matter by the attorney or other legal personnel. In the context of legal work, client billing serves both a financial function (collecting payment for services rendered) and a communicative function (keeping the client informed of work being done on the client's behalf—which is an ethical obligation of the profession).

Generally, client bills are prepared by a legal secretary or a bookkeeper or, in larger firms, by someone in the accounting department. The bills are based on the fee arrangements and the time slips collected from the firm's attorneys and paralegals. The time slips (discussed below) indicate how many hours are to be charged to each client at what hourly rate.

The *legal fees* billed to clients will be based on the number of billable hours generated for work requiring legal expertise. The *costs* billed to clients

EXHIBIT 4.4

A Sample Retainer Agreement

RETAINER AGREEMENT

I, Katherine Baranski, agree to employ Allen P. Gilmore and his law firm, Jeffers, Gilmore & Dunn, as my attorneys to prosecute all claims for damages against Tony Peretto and all other persons or entities that may be liable on account of an automobile accident that caused me to sustain serious injuries. The accident occurred on August 4, 1995, at 7:45 A.M., when Tony Peretto ran a stop sign on Thirty-eighth Street at Mattis Avenue and, as a result, his car collided with mine.

I agree to pay my lawyers a fee that will be one-fourth (25 percent) of any sum recovered in this case, regardless of whether the sum is received through settlement, lawsuit, arbitration, or any other way. The fee will be calculated on the sum recovered, after costs and expenses have been deducted. The fee will be paid when any money is actually received in this case. I agree that Allen P. Gilmore and his law firm have an express attorney's lien on any recovery to ensure that their fee is paid.

I agree to pay all necessary costs and expenses, such as court filing fees, court reporter fees, expert witness fees and expenses, travel expenses, long distance telephone and facsimile costs, and photocopying charges. I understand that these costs and expenses will be billed to me by my attorney on a monthly basis and that I am responsible for paying these costs and expenses, even if no recovery is received.

I agree that this agreement does not cover matters other than those described above. It does not cover an appeal from any judgment entered, any efforts necessary to collect money due because of a judgment entered by a court, or any efforts necessary to obtain other benefits, such as insurance.

I agree to pay a carrying charge amounting to the greater of two dollars ($2.00) or two percent (2%) per month on the average daily balance of bills on my account that are thirty days overdue. If my account is outstanding by more than sixty (60) days, all work by the attorney shall cease until the account is paid in full or a monthly payment plan is agreed on.

This contract is governed by the law of the state of Nita.*

I AGREE TO THE TERMS AND CONDITIONS STATED ABOVE:

Date: 2 / 4 / 96   *Katherine Baranski*
                                 Katherine Baranski

I agree to represent Katherine Baranski in the matter described above. I will receive no fee unless a recovery is obtained. If a recovery is obtained, I will receive a fee as described above.

I agree to notify Katherine Baranski of all developments in this matter promptly, and I will make no settlement of this matter without her consent.

I AGREE TO THE TERMS AND CONDITIONS STATED ABOVE:

Date: 2 / 4 / 96   *Allen P. Gilmore*
                                 Allen P. Gilmore
                                 Jeffers, Gilmore & Dunn
                                 553 Fifth Avenue
                                 Suite 101
                                 Nita City, Nita 48801

---

*A hypothetical state.

DEVELOPING PARALEGAL SKILLS

Creating a Trust Account

 Louise Larson is a paralegal who has just begun working for Don Jones. Don is just starting his own law practice as a sole practitioner after many years of working with a medium-sized law firm in which he had nothing to do with the firm's financial management. Don has hired Louise to help him with legal matters, as well as with the practical aspects of running a law office. One of Louise's first assignments is to establish a client trust account.

Don explains that the rules of professional responsibility require that client funds not be commingled with the lawyer's funds. "They must be kept in separate accounts. It's too easy to 'borrow' a client's money when all the money is in the same account."

"What kinds of funds go into the client trust account?" asks Louise. "Attorneys receive money from clients for a variety of reasons," explains Don. "Sometimes, we request an advance from clients to cover costs relating to the client's case. Sometimes we receive checks in settlement of a lawsuit. Generally, any money that we receive from clients in payment for legal services rendered goes into the firm's account. Everything else will go into the client's trust account."

Don instructs Louise to get the necessary forms from the bank to open a client trust account. Louise obtains the forms, and the account is set up. "Now that we have the account, I want you to devise a bookkeeping method for keeping track of the money we receive and the deposits that are made into the client trust account. We also need to keep a record of the payments that are made to the clients," Don says. Louise purchases an appropriate ledger from an office-supply store. The ledger allows her to record each amount received from a client and each payment or disbursement made to a client. Louise also creates a file for the deposit slips, which prove that she deposited the money into the trust account, and a file for the canceled checks, which prove that the client was paid. In addition, she sets up a file for the monthly bank statements on the trust account, which she will have to reconcile monthly. The bookkeeping system appears to have all the features needed to meet the professional requirement that client funds be kept in a separate account to protect Jones from any potential claims that he misused or commingled client funds.

will include expenses incurred by the firm (such as court fees, travel expenses, phone and fax charges, express-delivery charges, and copying costs) on the client's behalf. If an attorney is retained on a contingency-fee basis, the client is not billed monthly for legal fees. The client is normally billed monthly for any costs incurred on the client's behalf, however.

Typically, a preliminary draft of the client's bill will be given to the responsible billing partner for that client. The responsible billing partner then reviews and possibly modifies the client's bill. The final draft of the bill is then generated and sent to the client. Exhibit 4.5 illustrates a sample client bill in its final form.

Most law firms today have computerized their billing procedures, using time-and-billing software designed specifically for law-office use. Billing proce-

EXHIBIT 4.5
A Sample Client Bill

Jeffers, Gilmore & Dunn
553 Fifth Avenue
Suite 101
Nita City, NI 48801

BILLING DATE: February 28, 1996

Thomas Jones, M.D.
508 Oak Avenue
Nita City, Nita 48802

RE: Medical-Malpractice Action Brought against Dr. Jones,
          File No. 15789

DATE	SERVICES RENDERED	PROVIDED BY	HOURS SPENT	TOTAL
1/30/96	Initial client consultation	APG (attorney)	1.00	$150.00
1/30/96	Client interview	EML (paralegal)	1.00	74.00
1/30/96	Document preparation	EML (paralegal)	1.00	74.00
2/5/96	Interview: Susanne Mathews (nurse)	EML (paralegal)	1.50	111.00
	TOTAL FOR LEGAL SERVICES			**$409.00**

DATE	EXPENSES			
2/5/96	Hospital charges for a copy of the medical documents			$75.00
	TOTAL FOR EXPENSES			**$75.00**
	TOTAL BILL TO CLIENT			**$484.00**

dures using time-and-billing software will be discussed in detail in Chapter 8, in the context of computer programs used in law offices. Here we look at traditional timekeeping and billing procedures to illustrate the basic principles involved in client billing.

Documenting Time and Expenses.   Accurate timekeeping by attorneys and paralegals is crucial because clients cannot be billed for time spent on their behalf unless that time is documented. Attorneys and paralegals normally keep track of the time they spend on each client's work by filling out **time slips**. Each time slip documents in hours and fractions of hours (commonly in tenths or quarters of an hour) the amount of time spent on a particular day

TIME SLIP
A record documenting, for billing purposes, the hours (or fractions of hours) that an attorney or a paralegal worked for each client, the date on which the work was done, and the type of work that was undertaken.

TIME SLIP

Name of timekeeper_____   Client name/number_____

File number_____   Time allocated_____

Hourly rate_____   Billable/nonbillable_____

Date service rendered_____

Brief description of legal service:_____

_____

_____

EXPENSE SLIP
A slip of paper on which any expense, or cost, that is incurred on behalf of a client (such as the payment of court fees or long-distance telephone charges) is recorded.

PERSONAL TIME DIARY
A journal or notebook used by paralegals and attorneys to record and track the hours (or fractions of hours) worked and the tasks completed on behalf of each client.

on a particular task for a particular client. Exhibit 4.6 shows a sample time slip.

When working on a client's matter, an attorney or paralegal usually records on the time slip—in addition to the time spent—his or her initials, the date, the client number, and a description of the type of legal services performed. (This description will appear on the client's bill.) Any costs incurred on behalf of clients are entered on **expense slips**. Exhibit 4.7 on page 122 shows a sample expense slip.

Keep a Personal Time Diary. One of the challenges you will face as a paralegal is keeping track of the number of hours or fractions of hours that you spend on work for various clients. Suppose, for example, that you fill out time slips at the end of each day. You may assume that you will remember accurately how you spent your time. In fact, it is very easy to forget details, such as interruptions due to telephone calls.

To ensure that you never have difficulties in accounting accurately for your time, you should keep a **personal time diary**—a journal or notebook in which you note how you spend your time. Have the time diary at hand at all times and make entries in the diary whenever you start and end a particular task for a particular client. You should include in each entry the client's name (or identifying number), a precise description of the task, and the time you spent on the task. If you are interrupted by a phone call, make a note of the minutes you spent on the phone so that those minutes are not charged to the client. Also note in your time diary when you change from one task to another and from one client's work to another client's work.

If you consistently account for your time in a personal time diary, you will find that filling out time slips at the end of the day (or week) presents few problems. Another advantage of keeping a time diary is that if a client ever challenges a bill, you will be able to produce an exact record of the work you performed for the client, when it was performed, and how long it took to complete it.

As an alternative to keeping a time diary, you might keep with you a pad of time slips throughout the day and record your time as you complete each task. The advantage of having a personal time diary is that you can enter more detail than the time-slip format may allow.

Billable versus Nonbillable Hours.   The time recorded on time slips is charged either to a client (**billable hours**) or to the firm (nonbillable hours). Billable time generally includes the hours or fractions of hours that attorneys and paralegals spend in client-related work that requires legal expertise. For example, the time you spend researching or investigating a client's claim is billable time. So is the time spent in conferences with or about a client, drafting documents on behalf of a client, interviewing clients or witnesses, and traveling (to and from the courthouse to file documents, for example).

Time spent on other tasks, such as administrative work, staff meetings, or performance reviews, is nonbillable time. For example, suppose that you spend thirty minutes photocopying forms for the forms file, time sheets, or a procedures manual for the office. That thirty minutes would not be considered billable time.

Generally, law firms have a legitimate reason for wanting to maximize their billable hours:

- **The financial well-being of a law firm depends to a great extent on how many billable hours are generated by its employees.**

Nonbillable time ultimately cuts into the firm's profits. Of course, as mentioned earlier, nonbillable time is factored into the hourly rate charged for legal services. But to remain competitive, a law firm cannot charge too high an hourly rate. Therefore, the more billable hours generated by the firm's legal professionals, the more profitable the business will be.

Law firms normally tell their paralegals and associate attorneys how many billable hours they are expected to produce and the consequences of not being able to meet that number. Some firms expect associate attorneys to produce a minimum of 2,200 billable hours per year; other firms require fewer hours or more hours. Depending on the firm, a paralegal may be expected to generate between 1,250 and 2,000 billable hours per year.[2]

Attorneys and paralegals face substantial pressure to produce billable hours for the firm. As a paralegal, you may be subject to this pressure and must learn how to handle it. For example, suppose that your employer expects you to produce 1,800 billable hours per year. Discounting vacation time and holidays (assuming a two-week vacation and ten paid holidays), this equates to 37.5 hours weekly. Assuming that you work forty hours a week, you will have 2.5 hours a week for such nonbillable events as interoffice meetings, performance reviews, coffee breaks, tidying up your desk, reorganizing your work area, or chatting with others in the office. As you can imagine, unless you are willing to work more than eight hours a day, you may have difficulty meeting the billable-hours requirement.

BILLABLE HOURS
Hours or increments of hours that are billed directly to a client for legal services performed on behalf of that client.

---

2. According to the 1993 paralegal compensation survey conducted by *Legal Assistant Today*, paralegals were expected to generate, on average, 1,519 billable hours per year. See Carol Milano, "Salary Survey Results," *Legal Assistant Today*, May/June 1993, p. 48. According to the Legal Assistant Management Association's *1994 National Compensation Survey*, the average paralegal's billable hours were approximately 1,500.

EXHIBIT 4.7
A Sample Expense Slip

```
┌─────────────────────────────────────────────────────────────────────┐
│                          EXPENSE SLIP                                 │
│                                                                       │
│   Name_____      │
│   Client name and file number_____       │
│   Billable/nonbillable_____                        │
│   Date of expense_____                         │
│   Brief description of expense incurred:_____       │
│                                                                       │
│   _____   │
│                                                                       │
│   Quantity and rate (if applicable)_____       │
└─────────────────────────────────────────────────────────────────────┘
```

Ethics and Client Billing Practices

To understand why hourly billing can present ethical problems, consider the following situation. Suppose that you are asked to travel to another city to interview a witness in a case for Client A. You spend three hours traveling in an airplane, travel time that is necessary in working on behalf of Client A. You spend two hours in the airplane summarizing a document relating to a case for Client B. Who should pay for those two hours, Client A, Client B, or both? In this situation, you could argue—as many attorneys do in similar circumstances—that you generated five billable hours, three on Client A's work and two on Client B's case. This is an example of how **double billing**—billing more than one client for the same time—can occur. Clearly, the double billing of clients is one way to meet billable-hours quotas. Lawyers, however, as mentioned in the preceding chapter, have a duty to charge their clients "reasonable fees."

Double billing also occurs when a firm bills a new client for work that was done for a previous client. For example, suppose that an attorney is working on a case for Client B that is very similar to a case handled by the firm a year ago for Client A. The firm charged Client A $2,000 for the legal services. Because much of the research, writing, and other work done on Client A's case can transfer over to Client B's case, the firm is able to complete the work for Client B in half the time. In this situation, would it be fair to bill Client B $2,000 also? After all, $1,000 of that amount represents hours spent on Client A's case (and for which Client A has already been billed). At the same time, would it be fair to Client A to bill Client B less for essentially the same services? Would it be fair to the firm if it was not allowed to profit from cost efficiencies generated by overlapping work?

Some firms today are tackling this ethical problem by what is known as "value-added" billing or "value billing"—in effect, splitting the benefits derived from cost efficiencies between the client and the firm. For example, the attorney in the above example might split the savings created by the overlapping research ($1,000) with Client B by billing Client B $1,500 instead of $2,000. Other firms still bill their clients for the time spent on previous work that transfers over to new clients' cases.

DOUBLE BILLING
Billing more than one client for the same billable time.

The American Bar Association addressed this ethical "gray area" in the legal profession—double billing—in an ethical opinion issued in 1993. In its first formal opinion on the issue, the ABA stated that attorneys are prohibited from charging more than one client for the same hours of work. Additionally, the ABA rejected the notion that the firm, and not the client, should benefit from cost efficiencies created by the firm's work for previous clients. "The lawyer who has agreed to bill solely on the basis of time spent is obliged to pass the benefit of these economies on to the client."[3] Although ABA opinions do not become legally binding on attorneys until they are adopted by the states as law, they do carry much weight in the legal profession.

COMMUNICATION SKILLS AND THE LEGAL PROFESSION

The legal profession is essentially a communications profession. Legal representation involves communicating with clients, opposing counsel, third parties (witnesses and others from whom information must be obtained), court personnel, and many others. Legal representation also involves generating, receiving, and safeguarding legal documents relating to clients' cases or legal matters. As a legal professional, you will be directly involved in this communications enterprise. You will frequently be communicating with others in person, on the telephone, or in writing.

Furthermore, each worker in a law firm—whether it be a partner, a legal assistant, or a legal secretary—is a member of the legal team whose overall goal is to serve clients' needs efficiently and effectively. Maximum efficiency and effectiveness can only be attained through cooperative work efforts, which in turn depend on the ability of team members to communicate openly and productively with one another.

In the broadest sense, **communication skills** involve all of the skills used in conveying concepts or information to another person. Writing skills are communication skills, as are speaking, reading, and listening skills. This section explains what communication means and how communication skills can be applied to the kinds of situations that you will encounter as a paralegal.

The Communication Process

The communication process involves the sending and receiving of messages. The term *message* is commonly used to mean a transmission of information only, as in "He left a message for you." As used here, however, the term refers not to the words or other symbols used in communication but rather to the *meaning* of those words and symbols. If the person receiving a message does not understand its meaning, the communication process is incomplete, and no communication has occurred.

Miscommunication and communication failure occur frequently in all walks of life, and the law office is no exception. As a paralegal, you might have difficulty communicating with a certain attorney or other staff member. Your supervising attorney, for example, might not give very clear instructions, and

---

ETHICAL CONCERN

Billable Hours

Timekeeping requirements present numerous ethical pitfalls for attorneys and paralegals. A problem occurs when you work on behalf of several clients during the same time period. Suppose that you need to go to the county courthouse to file a document for a client's case. While at the courthouse, you have to wait for ten minutes to see the court clerk, so you read through a document for another client. On your way back to the office, you stop by the library to obtain a copy of a case pertaining to yet another client's claim. In all, you have spent two hours, but how do you allocate these 120 minutes accurately to the three clients served? As you can see, part of the ethical problem in regard to billable hours is not intentionally "padding" the client's bill or double billing but devising techniques for allocating time fairly when you work on several cases during the same time period. Whenever you face questions of how to allocate your time, discuss the issue with your office manager or supervising attorney. Law firms often have established policies on how to calculate billable hours, and you need to make sure that you learn about and abide by these policies.

COMMUNICATION SKILLS
All skills that assist in the communication process. Speaking, reading, writing, and listening skills are all communication skills.

---

3. American Bar Association Formal Opinion 93–379, December 6, 1993.

thus you would not be sure what was expected of you. Similarly, you might have difficulty communicating instructions to your secretary or other employees of the firm. How can you make sure, in these situations, that communication is actually occurring? One way is to give—or ask for—feedback.

Feedback from the listener (or the person to whom a message is directed) is an essential part of the communication process. Feedback indicates whether a message has been received and understood as intended. When your supervising attorney gives you instructions, for example, you might give feedback in the form of statements summarizing the instructions or questions asking for clarification. You might want to give feedback to the attorney in the form of a memo summarizing the instructions. If you have worked with an attorney for years, you probably face few communication difficulties, and your feedback might consist of merely a nod of the head and an "Okay."

The ultimate feedback to instructions is, of course, the resulting work product. If you are instructed to draft a document containing certain information, the document that you produce will be the final "test" of whether the instructions were communicated effectively.

Nonverbal Communication

Sending and receiving messages also may involve a nonverbal dimension. Generally, the use of language to convey messages is referred to as **verbal communication.** Written documents fall into the category of verbal communication; so do the words we say, in person or on the phone, to others. **Nonverbal communication**, in contrast, results from the use of body language (such as gestures), voice tones, and other expressions that do not involve language. Nonverbal messages are often subtle, and sometimes we may even be unaware that we are sending or receiving them. The paralegal who is sensitive to nonverbal as well as verbal messages is in a better position to control the communication process to his or her advantage.

Using body language to reinforce or complement verbal messages can significantly enhance communication. For example, suppose that you are being introduced to a new legal assistant in the law firm for which you work. You say, "Nice to meet you," and you are genuinely pleased. But your expression is deadpan, you do not offer to shake hands, and you look more or less at the floor as you are saying these words. Now, imagine the same situation, but this time add a smile, a firm handshake, and eye contact to your verbal message. These nonverbal messages reinforce your verbal message and enhance the chances that your verbal communication was interpreted accurately. The meanings commonly attached to some specific gestures and other body movements are summarized in Exhibit 4.8.

Tonal qualities can also enhance verbal communication. Voice volume (shouting versus whispering, for example) alters the quality of messages, as do different levels of pitch (highness or lowness of sound). Irony and sarcasm are also conveyed by voice tones, usually in conjunction with a smile, sneer, or other facial expression or body movement. The clothes we wear, the way we wear our hair, and other things relating to personal appearance also send nonverbal messages to others about our personalities and values.

FEEDBACK
A response from the person to whom a message has been sent indicating whether the receiver received and understood the message.

VERBAL COMMUNICATION
The sending and receiving of messages using spoken or written words.

NONVERBAL COMMUNICATION
The sending and receiving of messages without using language. Nonverbal communication includes body language (such as facial gestures) and utterances or sounds that do not consist of words.

Gesture/Action	Message Commonly Attached to Gesture/Action
Maintaining eye contact	Interested, sincere, honest, or (if glaring) hostile and intimidating
Avoiding eye contact, looking away from speaker	Uninterested, suspicious, insincere, dishonest
Leaning away from speaker	Uninterested, showing dislike
Tapping fingers on desk	Uninterested, impatient
Continuing to read or work on task	Uninterested
Sighing, grimacing	Bored, disgusted
Failing to acknowledge greeting or other remark	Inconsiderate, unfriendly
Making agitated hand or arm movements	Worried, distressed
Smiling	Friendly, interested, supportive
Sneering	Sarcastic, disgusted, arrogant
Frowning	Concerned, displeased, concentrating
Raising eyebrows	Surprised, showing disbelief
Shrugging shoulders	Uninterested, uncaring
Glaring	Angry

EXHIBIT 4.8
Nonverbal Cues and Their Effects

Barriers to Communication

Anything that interferes with the communication process can result in miscommunication or communication failure. As a paralegal, you have a vital interest in communicating effectively with others. Becoming aware of communication barriers is the first step in overcoming these obstacles to effective communication.

Some listening barriers consist of sound or other activities that are distracting. If you are trying to hear what your supervising attorney is saying while someone nearby noisily opens and closes file drawers, these sounds will distract your attention. Loud radios, ringing phones or faxes, or people walking back and forth in the immediate area may also distract you. Whenever you find that you cannot listen because of these kinds of distractions, find a quiet place to hold your conversation—if you really want to listen effectively. When you interview clients, for example, you should conduct the interview in a quiet environment, such as a conference room, to prevent interruptions.

An important factor in the communication process is the timing of the message. Often, a person sending a message has no way of knowing whether the message will be received at a "good" or "bad" time. If you call someone on the phone, for example, the person may have a moment of leisure and may enjoy talking to you at that moment. Alternatively, the person may be in the midst of a personal or a work-related crisis and in no mood to talk.

- **As a courtesy, you should normally ask the person you are calling if this is a good time to speak.**

Communication Skills and Conflict Resolution

Conflict is inevitable. We all have our own set of personal needs, goals, and agendas, and it is only natural that at some point, these needs, goals, and agendas will come into conflict with those of others. The law office is not exempt from the human experience, and as you begin your career as a paralegal, you should expect to encounter conflict as a normal element in the legal workplace.

- **One way to reduce or minimize conflict is to focus on issues rather than on personalities. For example, how often do you say "I dis-**

agree with you" rather than "I disagree with that idea [opinion, statement, conclusion]"? This may seem like a subtle distinction, but it is a significant one in communication behavior.

We all have our own opinions. If someone disagrees with our views on an issue, we sometimes take it personally and become defensive of our opinions. Before we know it, an emotional element has entered the picture. Hostile words or attitudes may result, and they can lead to communication failure. Separating issues from personalities helps you to view opinions, including your own, more openly and objectively.

Another way of dealing with conflict is to address the problem openly. Communicating openly with others requires, first of all, the ability to listen effectively so that you can identify others' needs, goals, and perhaps motivations. It also requires the ability to assert your needs and opinions and, at times, your rights as an individual or as a member of the legal team. If you feel uncomfortable with a particular arrangement or sense a conflict between your goals and needs and those of others, the wisest course of action may be to assert your concern immediately to prevent the situation from worsening. Suppressing your feelings may result in growing hostility toward those responsible for the arrangement.

Note that being assertive is different from being aggressive. **Assertive communication** occurs when one person takes the initiative and lets others know his or her thoughts and feelings on issues. As a paralegal, you will have to be an assertive communicator. Other members of the legal team will rely on your input, and you will need to be forthcoming with your ideas and conclusions. You cannot play a passive role. At the same time, you do not want to let your communication cross the line between assertiveness and aggressiveness. **Aggressive communication** involves placing your own thoughts and feelings above those of others and being inattentive to others' opinions. Respecting the views of others is essential in any kind of cooperative work arrangement, including working together as a legal team.

ASSERTIVE COMMUNICATION
Stating one's opinions confidently but tactfully and with concern for the thoughts, feelings, and rights of the listener.

AGGRESSIVE COMMUNICATION
Stating one's opinions without concern for the thoughts, feelings, or rights of the listener.

THE LEGAL TEAM AT WORK
Holding the Client's Many Hands

Although attorneys and paralegals may deal daily with legal procedures, clients often do not know what to expect when initiating a lawsuit or other legal proceeding. Also, many legal matters involve an emotional element for the client. Bankruptcy petitions, divorce actions, and probate procedures (dealing with the transfer of property upon death) may be particularly upsetting emotionally. To ease a client's frustrations and anxieties, legal practitioners have traditionally engaged in what is known as "hand-holding," or gently guiding the client through the various steps involved in litigation or other legal procedures. Unfortunately, as one attorney put it, "the client has eight hands, and I only have two." Teamwork provides a solution to this problem. The attorney's hands are joined by those of paralegals (and others on the project), and each team member can observe and respond to the client's needs for information, guidance, and support.

TODAY'S PROFESSIONAL PARALEGAL

Managing Conflict

On Cheryl Hardy's first day at her new job as a legal assistant at Comp-Lease, Inc., a computer leasing corporation, Cheryl is introduced to the department staff by her boss, Dennis Hoyt. Dennis then takes her to meet the legal team. When she meets Jackie, the team secretary, Jackie gives her a frosty "Hello," without a handshake or smile, and then looks down at the desk. Cheryl does not understand why Jackie seems hostile. She has just met Jackie and has not done or said anything to offend her.

After her lunch break, Cheryl is given her first lease package to prepare. The work consists of drafting a lease (rental) agreement and giving it to the secretary to input into the computer and print out the agreement form. Cheryl prepares the draft and gives it to Jackie. Cheryl is very polite and tells Jackie not to rush because the agreement does not have to be sent out for two days. When Cheryl asks Jackie for the lease two days later, it is not done. Jackie tells Cheryl to check with her after lunch to see how it is coming. "Great," thinks Cheryl to herself, as she walks back to her desk. "My first week on the job and I'll be in trouble because of Jackie."

ANALYZING THE PROBLEM

Cheryl knows that she must do something about the situation with Jackie. She decides to talk to a co-worker, Sandy, about the problem. At lunch, Cheryl explains to Sandy that Jackie has resented her from the minute that she walked in the door. "She probably does resent you," agreed Sandy. "You see, Jackie has always wanted to be a paralegal. The company has a policy that you have to have a degree or a certificate, even if you have experience, and so she cannot move into a paralegal position without some education. She has not been able to attend a paralegal training program because of family obligations and the expense involved. I'm sure that she knows that you were a legal secretary and that you worked your way through school. When Dennis told us that he had hired a new paralegal, he made your experience and education quite clear."

"So that is why she reacted the way she did to me," says Cheryl. "Thanks, that clears up the situation a lot." Sandy says, "If you need help in getting your lease out today, just let me know. Our team secretary can probably help out." Cheryl ends up using Sandy's secretary that day and on several other occasions because Jackie always leaves Cheryl's work until last, no matter how early Cheryl gives it to her. "This has got to stop," thinks Cheryl one day. "I wonder how I can win her over."

SOLVING THE PROBLEM

Cheryl has an idea. She invites Jackie to lunch. Jackie talks about her interest in becoming a paralegal, her frustration with the company's policy, and her inability to get a certificate or degree because of her family obligations and the cost of going back to school. Cheryl tells Jackie that she was in a similar situation and that she got a scholarship from her school to pay for most of her education. She tells Jackie that she might be able to get one, too. She encourages Jackie by telling her, truthfully, that she is obviously bright enough to be a paralegal. Cheryl gives Jackie the name and phone number of Lois Allison, the director of the program that Cheryl attended. "Why don't you call her and tell her that I referred you? Explain that you are in the same situation that I was in when I started. She can tell you what might be available," suggested Cheryl.

When Cheryl returns to her office from lunch, she calls Lois Allison. She explains Jackie's situation and tells Lois that Jackie might be calling to get information on the program and scholarships. Lois replies that she will be happy to talk to Jackie and to help her if she can.

Later that afternoon, when Cheryl gives Jackie a lease package to prepare, Jackie prepares it right away. She even brings it into Cheryl's office, which she does not have to do. "I just want to thank you for going out of your way for me," says Jackie. "I called Lois Allison, and she wants me to come in and fill out some application forms. She thinks that I might qualify for a scholarship. So I might get to go to school after all."

Cheryl smiles. "I am glad that Lois could help you," she says. She feels happy knowing that she and Jackie are off to a better start in their relationship because she has resolved the conflict between them.

LAW-OFFICE CULTURE AND POLITICS

As a paralegal, you will find that each law firm you work for is unique. Even though two firms may be the same size and have similar organizational structures, they will have different cultures, or "personalities." The culture of a given legal workplace is ultimately determined by the attitudes of the firm's owners (the partners, for example) in regard to the fundamental goals of the firm.

Additionally, you will find that each firm has a political infrastructure that may have little to do with the lines of authority and accountability that are spelled out in the firm's employment manual or other formal policy statement. An up-and-coming younger partner in the firm, for example, may in fact exercise more authority than one of the firm's older partners who is about to retire. There may be rivalry between associate attorneys for promotion to partnership status, and you may be caught in the middle of it. If you are aware (and you may not be) of the rivalry and your position relative to it, you may find yourself tempted to take sides—which could jeopardize your own future with the firm.

Unfortunately, paralegals have little way of knowing about the culture and politics of a given firm until they have worked for the firm a while. Of course, if you know someone who works or has worked for a firm and value that employee's opinion, then you might gain some advance knowledge about the firm's environment from that source. Otherwise, when you start to work for a firm, you will need to learn for yourself about interoffice politics. One way to do this is to listen carefully whenever a co-worker discusses the firm's staff and ask discreet questions to elicit information from co-workers about office politics and unwritten policies. This way, you can both prepare yourself to deal with these issues and protect your own interests. Ultimately, after you've worked for the firm for a time, you will be in a position to judge whether the firm you have chosen is really the "right firm" for you.

KEY TERMS AND CONCEPTS

aggressive communication   127

assertive communication   127

billable hours   121

communication skills   123

contingency fee   113

double billing   122

employment policy manual   100

expense slip   120

feedback   124

fixed fee   111

forms file   110

legal administrator   104

legal-assistant manager   104

managing partner   101

nonverbal communication   124

office manager   104

out card   108

partner   101

partnership   101

personal liability   100

personal time diary   120

professional corporation (P.C.)   101

responsible billing partner   107

retainer   116

retainer agreement   116

shareholder   101

sole proprietorship   100

support personnel   104

time slip   119

trust account   116

verbal communication   124

Chapter Summary

1. Law firms typically have specific policies and procedures relating to compensation and employee benefits, performance evaluations, employment termination, and other rules of the workplace, such as office hours. Usually (particularly in larger firms), these policies are spelled out in an employment manual or other writing.

2. In terms of business organization, a law firm may take the form of a sole proprietorship (in which one individual owns the business), a partnership (in which two or more individuals—called partners— jointly own the business), or a professional corporation (in which two or more individuals—called shareholders—own the business). The sole proprietor is entitled to all the firm's profits, bears the burden of any losses, and is personally liable for the firm's debts or other obligations. Partners share jointly the profits or losses of the firm and are subject to personal liability for all of the firm's debts or other obligations. The owner-shareholders of a professional corporation, like partners, share the firm's profits or losses but, unlike partners, are not liable for the firm's debts or other obligations beyond the amount they invested in the corporation.

3. Law-firm personnel include the owners of the firm (partners, for example); associate attorneys, who are hired as employees and do not have ownership rights in the business; summer associates, or temporary law clerks; paralegals; administrative personnel, who are supervised by the legal administrator or office manager; and support personnel, including receptionists, secretaries, clerks, and others. Paralegals should learn, upon first taking a job in a law firm, the relative status of law-firm personnel. Particularly, they should learn to whom they are accountable and who, in turn, is accountable to them.

4. Every law firm follows certain procedures in regard to its filing system. In larger firms, these procedures may be written up in a procedural book. In smaller firms, procedures may be more casual and based on habit or tradition. A typical law firm has client files, work-product files and reference materials, forms files, and personnel files. Proper file maintenance is crucial to a smoothly functioning law firm. An efficient filing system helps to ensure that important documents will not be lost or misplaced and will be available when needed. Filing procedures must also maximize client confidentiality and the safekeeping of documents and other evidence.

5. A foremost concern of any law firm is to establish a clear policy on fee arrangements and efficient billing procedures, so that each client is billed appropriately. Types of fee arrangements include fixed fees, hourly fees, and contingency fees. As a rule, clients pay hourly fees and are billed monthly for the time spent by attorneys or other legal personnel on the clients' cases or projects. Clients who are represented on a contingency-fee basis, however, do not pay legal fees until the case or legal matter has been decided or completed. All costs incurred on behalf of clients, including those retained on a contingency-fee basis, normally are billed to the client monthly.

6. Firms require attorneys and paralegals to document how they use their time by filling out and submitting time slips. Because the firm's income depends on the number of billable hours produced by the firm's legal personnel, firms usually require attorneys and paralegals to generate a certain number of billable hours per year. This requirement subjects legal personnel to significant pressure.

7. An important ethical concern in the legal profession today concerns the double billing of clients. Double billing occurs when a law firm bills two or more clients for the same billable time. Double billing includes billing two clients for overlapping work, such as when a firm uses the research or other legal work done on a previous client's case for a present client and bills both clients for the time spent in performing that research or other legal work. In 1993, the American Bar Association, in its first ethical opinion on double billing, stated that it is unethical to ever bill two clients for the same billable hours or legal work. The ABA also stated that any cost efficiencies created by using previous work for a present client should be passed on to the client.

8. The legal profession is a communications profession, and good communications skills are essential to legal practice. The communications process involves two events: the sending of a message and the receiving of that message. Much communication takes place nonverbally, and the paralegal should also be familiar with what messages are conveyed by different types of gestures, expressions, and other actions or utterances. Anything that interferes with the communication process is a barrier to communication. Communication barriers include noises and other distractions.

9. Communication skills are helpful in managing or reducing conflict. A willingness to focus on issues instead of personalities is one way of reducing or preventing conflict. Open and assertive communication also helps to alleviate conflict.

10. Each law office has its own culture, or personality, which is largely shaped by the attitudes of the firm's owners and the qualities they look for when hiring personnel. Each firm also has a political infrastructure that is not apparent to outsiders. Law-office culture and politics make a great difference in terms of job satisfaction and comfort. Wise paralegals will learn as soon as possible after taking a job, from co-workers or others, about these aspects of the legal workplace.

QUESTIONS FOR REVIEW

1. What are the three basic organizational structures of law firms?

2. What is the difference between an associate and a partner? Who handles the administrative tasks of a law firm? Who supervises the work of paralegals in a law firm?

3. How do firms evaluate paralegal performance?

4. What kinds of files do law firms maintain? What procedures are typically followed in regard to client files?

5. How do considerations of confidentiality affect filing procedures?

6. How does a law firm arrange its fees with its clients? How do lawyers and legal assistants keep track of their time? What is the difference between billable and nonbillable hours?

7. What is double billing? What is value-added billing? What is the American Bar Association's opinion in regard to these billing practices?

8. Describe the communication process. What are nonverbal messages, and how do we send them?

9. What are some of the reasons for miscommunication or communication failure?

10. How can communication skills be used to reduce or prevent conflict? What is the difference between assertive and aggressive communication?

ETHICAL QUESTIONS

1. Marc Sims, a paralegal, is instructed by his supervising attorney, Sam Felder, to file a complaint in federal court. Because the federal courthouse is an hour's drive from their office, Sam also tells Marc to take Sam's cellular phone with him and to make a number of follow-up calls relating to other clients' cases while Marc is driving to and from the courthouse. Sam instructs Marc to record the exact amount of time that he spends driving, so that Sam can bill the client for this travel time. Sam also asks Marc to keep track of the time he spends making the telephone calls concerning the other clients' cases, so that Sam can also bill those clients for the time Marc spends making calls on their behalf. Is it ethical of Sam to bill Marc's time in this way? If Marc follows Sam's instructions, will he be acting unethically in any way?

2. Sam Martin, an attorney, receives a settlement check for a client's case. It is made out jointly to Sam and his client. Sam signs it and deposits it in his law firm's bank account because he wants to take out his fee before he gives the client his portion of the money. May Sam do this? Why or why not?

3. Tom Baker, a paralegal, has been doing research for a client using WESTLAW (a computerized research service discussed in Chapter 8). Tom's supervising attorney tells him to bill the WESTLAW charges that he just incurred on behalf of one client to another client's account. The client to be billed is a large and prosperous corporation. After he prepares a memo summarizing his WESTLAW research, he is instructed to bill his time in preparing the memo to yet another client number. What should Tom do?

PRACTICE QUESTIONS AND ASSIGNMENTS

1. Obtain a page from the "want ads" in your local newspaper or from another source that advertises for legal professionals. Try to determine from the ads whether the firms advertising openings are organized as sole proprietorships, partnerships, or professional corporations.

2. Identify the type of billing that is being used in each of the following examples:

   a. The client is billed $150 per hour for a partner's time, $100 per hour for an associate attorney's time, and $70 per hour for a legal assistant's time.

   b. The attorney's fee is one-third of the amount that the attorney recovers for the client, either through a pretrial settlement or through a trial.

   c. The client is charged $175 to change the name of the client's business firm.

3. Try an experiment the next time your supervisor or professor gives you an assignment. Try repeating the instructions to the person giving them. See if your interpretation of the instructions matched exactly the intended instructions.

5

THE AMERICAN
LEGAL SYSTEM

CHAPTER OBJECTIVES

After completing this chapter, you will know:

• What the common law tradition is and how English law influenced the development of the American legal system.
• The meaning and relative importance in the American legal system of constitutional law, statutory law, and administrative law.
• The requirements that must be met before a lawsuit can be brought in a particular court by a particular party.
• The types of courts that make up a typical state court system and the different functions of trial courts and appellate courts.
• The organization of the federal court system and the relationship between state and federal jurisdiction.
• The various ways in which disputes can be resolved outside the court system.

CHAPTER OUTLINE

INTRODUCTION

Like the legal systems of many other countries, the American legal system is based on tradition. For the most part, the colonists who first came to America were governed by English law. As a result, the law of England continued to be the paramount model for American jurists and legislators after the colonists declared their independence from England in 1776. English common law from medieval times onward thus became part of the American legal tradition as well, modified as necessary to suit conditions unique to America.

This chapter opens with a discussion of the nature of law and then examines the common law tradition. We then examine other important sources of American law, including constitutional law, statutory law, and administrative law. The remainder of the chapter focuses on another essential component of the American legal system—the court system and methods of settling disputes out of court.

WHAT IS LAW?

Paralegals spend their entire careers dealing with legal matters. But even the most seasoned paralegal might be hard pressed to give you a useful definition of *law*. What is law? There is no one answer to this question because how law is defined depends on the speaker's personal philosophy about such things as morality, ethics, and truth. As a result, there have been and will continue to be different definitions of law. Although the various definitions differ in their particulars, they all are based on the following general observation concerning the nature of **law**:

LAW
A body of rules of conduct with legal force and effect, prescribed by the controlling authority (the government) of a society.

● **Law consists of a body of rules of conduct with legal force and effect, prescribed by the controlling authority (the government) of a society.**

In the United States, these "rules of conduct" are embodied in numerous sources, including the common law, constitutions, statutes, and administrative law.

THE COMMON LAW TRADITION

Because of our colonial heritage, much of American law is based on the English legal system. After the United States declared its independence from England, American jurists continued to be greatly influenced by English law and English legal writers. Indeed, much of American law in such areas as contracts, torts (types of civil wrongs), property law, and criminal law derives in large part from the English legal system.

The Origins and Nature of the Common Law

In 1066, the Normans conquered England, and William the Conqueror and his successors began the process of unifying the country under their rule.

One of the means they used to this end was the establishment of the king's courts, or *curia regis*. Before the Norman Conquest, disputes had been settled according to the local legal customs and traditions in various regions of the country. The king's courts sought to establish a uniform set of customs for the country as a whole. What evolved in these courts was the beginning of the **common law**—a body of general rules that prescribed social conduct and applied throughout the entire English realm.

Courts developed the common law rules from the principles behind judges' decisions in actual legal controversies. Judges attempted to be consistent. When possible, they based their decisions on the principles suggested by earlier cases. They sought to decide similar cases in a similar way and considered new cases with care because they knew that their decisions would make new law. Each interpretation became part of the law on the subject and served as a legal **precedent**. Later cases that involved similar legal principles or facts could be decided with reference to that precedent. The courts were guided by traditions and legal doctrines that evolved over time.

The practice of deciding new cases with reference to former decisions, or precedents, eventually became a cornerstone of the English and American judicial systems. It forms a doctrine called ***stare decisis***[1] ("to stand on decided cases"). Under this doctrine, judges are obligated to follow the precedents established by higher courts within their jurisdictions. Sometimes a court will depart from the rule of precedent if it decides that the precedent is simply incorrect or that technological or social changes have rendered the precedent inapplicable.

The Common Law Today

The common law developed in England and still used in the United States consists of the rules of law announced in court decisions. These rules of law include interpretations of constitutional provisions, of statutes enacted by legislatures, and of regulations created by administrative agencies, such as the Environmental Protection Agency. Today, this body of law is referred to variously as the common law, judge-made law, or **case law.** The common law governs all areas not covered by *statutory law*, which (as will be discussed shortly) generally consists of those laws enacted by state legislatures and by the federal Congress.

The Common Law and the Paralegal

As a paralegal, you will find that a basic understanding of the common law tradition will serve you well whenever you need to research and analyze case law. The doctrine of *stare decisis*, the different types of judicial reasoning, and the distinction between different types of remedies—these concepts are all critical when applied to real-life situations faced by clients.

For example, suppose that a client wants to sue another party for breaching a contract to perform computer consulting services. In this situation, the common law of contracts would apply to the case. If you were

COMMON LAW

A body of law developed from custom or judicial decisions in English and U.S. courts and not attributable to a legislature.

PRECEDENT

A court decision that furnishes an example or authority for deciding subsequent cases in which identical or similar facts are presented.

STARE DECISIS

A flexible doctrine of the courts, recognizing the value of following prior decisions (precedents) in cases similar to the one before the court; the courts' practice of being consistent with prior decisions in cases involving similar facts.

CASE LAW

Rules of law announced in court decisions. Case law includes the aggregate of reported cases that interpret judicial precedents, statutes, regulations, and constitutional provisions.

---

1. Pronounced *ster*-ay dih-*si*-ses.

Legal Research and *Stare Decisis*

One of the challenges faced by legal professionals is keeping up with the ever-changing law. For example, suppose that you are asked to do research on a case involving issues similar to those in a case you researched just three months ago. If you apply your previous research results to the current client's case, you need to verify that your earlier research still applies—that is, that previous case decisions are still "good law." In three months' time, an appeals court might have created a new precedent, and failure to update your research (how to do this is explained in Chapter 9) can lead to serious consequences for the client—and for you and the attorney, if the client decides to sue the attorney for negligence (specifically, for breaching the duty of competence).

BILL OF RIGHTS
The first ten amendments to the Constitution.

asked to research the case, you would search for previous cases dealing with similar issues to see how those cases were decided. You would want to know of any precedents set by a higher court in your jurisdiction—and, of course, by the United States Supreme Court—on that issue. Even in an area governed by statutory law, you will want to find out how the courts have interpreted and applied the relevant state statute or statutory provision.

In addition to lawsuits involving contract law, the common law also applies to *tort law* (the law governing civil wrongs, such as negligence or assault and battery, as opposed to criminal wrongs). As a paralegal, you may be working on behalf of clients bringing or defending against the following types of actions, all of which involve tort law:

• *Personal-injury lawsuits*—actions brought by plaintiffs to obtain compensation for injuries allegedly caused by the wrongful acts of others, either intentionally or through negligence.
• *Malpractice lawsuits*—actions brought by plaintiffs against professionals, such as physicians and attorneys, to obtain compensation for injuries allegedly caused by professional negligence (breach of professional duties).
• *Product-liability lawsuits*—actions brought by plaintiffs to obtain compensation for injuries allegedly caused by defective products.

Numerous other areas, such as property law and employment law, are also still governed to some extent by the common law. Depending on the nature of your job as a paralegal, you may be dealing with many cases that are governed by the common law.

Constitutional Law

In addition to the common law, courts have numerous other sources of law to consider when making their decisions, including constitutional law. The federal government and the states have separate constitutions that set forth the general organization, powers, and limits of their respective governments.

The Federal Constitution

The U.S. Constitution, as amended, is the supreme law of the land. A law in violation of the Constitution (including its amendments), no matter what its source, will be declared unconstitutional if it is challenged. For example, if a state legislature enacts a law that conflicts with the federal Constitution, a person or business firm that is subject to that law may challenge its validity in a court action. If the court agrees with the complaining party that the law is unconstitutional, it will declare the law invalid and refuse to enforce it.

The U.S. Constitution sets forth the powers of the three branches of the federal government and the relationship between the three branches. The need for a written declaration of the rights of individuals eventually caused the first Congress of the United States to submit twelve amendments to the Constitution to the states for approval. Ten of these amendments, commonly known as the **Bill of Rights**, were adopted in 1791 and embody a series of protections for the individual—and in some cases, business entities—against various types of interference by the federal government.

Constitutional Rights.   Summarized below are the protections guaranteed by the Bill of Rights. The full text of the Constitution, including its amendments, is presented in Appendix H at the end of this book.

1. The First Amendment guarantees the freedoms of religion, speech, and the press and the rights to assemble peaceably and to petition the government.

2. The Second Amendment guarantees the right to keep and bear arms.

3. The Third Amendment prohibits, in peacetime, the lodging of soldiers in any house without the owner's consent.

4. The Fourth Amendment prohibits unreasonable searches and seizures of persons or property.

5. The Fifth Amendment guarantees the rights to indictment by grand jury and to due process of law, and prohibits compulsory self-incrimination and double jeopardy. The Fifth Amendment also prohibits the taking of private property for public use without just compensation.

6. The Sixth Amendment guarantees the accused in a criminal case the right to a speedy and public trial by an impartial jury and the right to counsel. The accused has the right to cross-examine witnesses against him or her and to solicit testimony from witnesses in his or her favor.

7. The Seventh Amendment guarantees the right to a trial by jury in a civil case involving at least twenty dollars.

8. The Eighth Amendment prohibits excessive bail and fines, as well as cruel and unusual punishment.

9. The Ninth Amendment establishes that the people have rights in addition to those specified in the Constitution.

10. The Tenth Amendment establishes that those powers neither delegated to the federal government nor denied to the states are reserved for the states.

The Courts and Constitutional Law.   You should realize that the rights secured by the Bill of Rights are not absolute. The broad principles enunciated in the Constitution are given form and substance by the courts. For example, even though the First Amendment guarantees the freedom of speech, we are not, in fact, free to say anything we want. In interpreting the meaning of the First Amendment's guarantee of free speech, the United States Supreme Court has made it clear that certain types of speech will not be protected. For example, speech that harms the good reputation of another is deemed a tort, or civil wrong. If the speaker is sued, he or she may be ordered by a court to pay damages to the harmed person.

Courts often have to balance the rights and freedoms enunciated in the Bill of Rights against the other rights, such as the right to be free from the harmful actions of others. Ultimately, it is the United States Supreme Court, as the final interpreter of the Constitution, that both gives meaning to our constitutional rights and determines their boundaries.

State Constitutions

Each state also has a constitution that sets forth the general organization, powers, and limits of the state government. The Tenth Amendment to the U.S. Constitution, which defines the powers and limitations of the federal government, reserves all powers not granted to the federal government to the states. Unless they conflict with the U.S. Constitution, state constitutions are supreme within the states' respective borders.

Constitutional Law and the Paralegal

Many paralegals assist attorneys in handling cases that involve constitutional provisions or rights. For example, a corporate client might claim that a regulation issued by a state administrative agency, such as the state department of natural resources, is invalid because it conflicts with a federal law or regulation. (Administrative agencies are discussed later in this chapter.) You may be assigned the task of finding out which regulation takes priority. Many cases arise in which the plaintiff claims that his or her First Amendment rights have been violated. Suppose that a plaintiff's religious beliefs forbid working on a certain day of the week. If he or she is required to work on that day, the plaintiff may claim that the employer's requirement violates the First Amendment, which guarantees the free exercise of religion.

No matter what kind of work you do as a paralegal, you will find that a knowledge of constitutional law will be beneficial. This is because the authority and underlying rationale for the substantive and procedural laws governing many areas of law are ultimately based on the Constitution. For example, a knowledge of constitutional law is helpful to paralegals working in the area of criminal law, because criminal procedures are essentially designed to protect the constitutional rights of accused persons.

STATUTORY LAW

STATUTE
A written law enacted by a legislature under its constitutional lawmaking authority.

STATUTORY LAW
Laws enacted by a legislative body.

ORDINANCE
An order, rule, or law enacted by a municipal or county government to govern a local matter unaddressed by state or federal legislation.

Laws passed by the federal Congress and the various state legislatures are called **statutes**. These statutes make up another source of law, which, as mentioned earlier, is generally referred to as **statutory law**. When a legislature passes a statute, that statute is ultimately included in the federal code of laws or the relevant state code of laws. The California Code, for example, contains the statutory law of the state of California.

Statutory law also includes local ordinances. An **ordinance** is a statute (law, rule, or order) passed by a municipal or county government unit to govern matters not covered by federal or state law. Ordinances commonly have to do with city or county land use (zoning ordinances), building and safety codes, and other matters affecting the local unit. Persons who violate ordinances may be fined or jailed, or both. No state statute or local ordinance may violate the U.S. Constitution or the state constitution.

Today, legislative bodies and administrative agencies assume an ever-increasing share of lawmaking. Much of the work of modern courts consists of interpreting what the rulemakers intended to accomplish when a particular law was drafted and enacted and deciding how the law applies to a specific set of facts.

Statutory Law and the Common Law

As mentioned earlier, the common law governs all areas not covered by statutory law. In the early years of this nation, the body of statutory law was

DEVELOPING PARALEGAL SKILLS

State versus Federal Regulation

 Stephanie Wilson works as a paralegal in the legal department of National Pipeline, Inc. National Pipeline's business is transporting natural gas to local utility companies, factories, and other sites throughout the United States. Last month, there was an explosion on one of its pipelines. The pipeline ran under a residential street in a suburb of Minneapolis, Minnesota. The explosion occurred in the middle of the night, set several homes on fire, and resulted in one death.

FEDERAL PREEMPTION

In 1968, the federal government passed the Natural Gas Pipeline Safety Act (NGPSA), which regulates the safety and maintenance of pipelines. The federal act has been effective in reducing the number of injuries and deaths associated with pipeline leaks and explosions. The Minnesota legislature decided, however, that it should further regulate the pipeline industry within its state to increase pipeline safety.

   The vice presidents of engineering and operations at National Pipeline have always believed that the NGPSA preempted state law. *Preemption* occurs when the federal government indicates its intention to regulate an area of national concern, such as aviation. A state may not pass a law that regulates a field of law that is preempted by federal law. The vice presidents remember that several years ago, in 1979, another state tried to pass a pipeline safety act, which failed because of federal preemption.

   The two vice presidents of engineering and operations meet with Stephanie's supervising attorney, Randall Holman, and ask Randall to research the issue to determine if it would be possible to challenge the proposed state legislation on the ground of federal preemption. Randall is very busy with other matters, so he assigns the research task to Stephanie.

FINDING THE FEDERAL STATUTE AND RELEVANT CASE LAW

Stephanie begins her research in the company's law library. She locates the NGPSA in the federal statutory code. The first section of the statute contains definitions of the terms used in the statute. The next section covers federal safety standards. A subsection states the minimum standards required, factors to be considered, state standards, and reporting requirements. As Stephanie reads it, she notices the following clause:

> No state agency may adopt or continue in force any such standards applicable to interstate transmission facilities. . . .

   Great, thinks Stephanie. This applies to us because we *transmit* natural gas *interstate*, or among states. Our pipeline crosses the United States. Now I will see if there are any cases in which the courts have interpreted this statute. She finds a case from a federal appeals court in which the court held that the NGPSA preempted New York state requirements regarding a pipeline project.

   Stephanie copies the relevant portions of the statute and the case. She takes them back to her office and prepares a memo summarizing the results of her research and discussing National Pipeline's chances of successfully challenging the proposed Minnesota legislation.

CODIFY
To collect and organize systematically and logically a body of concepts, principles, decisions, or doctrines.

relatively small compared to the body of common law principles and doctrines. The body of statutory law has expanded greatly since then, however, and continues to grow. To some extent, this expansion has resulted from the enactment of statutes that essentially **codify** (systematize, or arrange in a logical order) common law doctrines. For example, criminal law was at one time governed extensively by common law. Over time, common law doctrines were codified, expanded on, and enacted in statutory form. Today, criminal law is primarily statutory law.

The expansion of statutory law has also resulted from the need to regulate business and other activities for various purposes. For example, many federal and state statutes have been enacted in an attempt to protect consumers, employees, investors, and other groups from business practices that are potentially harmful to the rights or interests of these groups. Numerous statutes and regulations exist to protect the environment, and a whole body of law, antitrust law, is based on statutes passed to protect the public's interest in a freely competitive society. Another reason why the body of statutory law has expanded is to address the need for uniform laws among the states, such as the laws governing commercial transactions.

Even when legislation has been substituted for common law principles, a court's interpretation and application of a statute may become a precedent that lower courts in the jurisdiction must follow. Furthermore, courts often look to the common law when determining how to interpret a statute, on the theory that the people who drafted the statute intended to codify an existing common law rule. In a sense then, common law and statutory law are never totally separate bodies of law, because the courts must interpret and apply statutory law.

Statutory Law and the Paralegal

As a paralegal, you may often be assisting in cases that involve violations of statutory law. If you work for a small law firm, you may become familiar with the statutory law governing a wide spectrum of activities. If you specialize in one area, such as bankruptcy law, you will become very familiar with the federal statutory law governing bankruptcy and bankruptcy procedures. Here are just a few examples of the areas in which you might work that are governed extensively by statutory law:

- *Corporate law*—governed by state statutes.
- *Patent, copyright, and trademark law*—governed by federal statutes.
- *Employment law*—governed to an increasing extent by federal statutes concerning discrimination in employment, workplace safety, labor unions, pension plans, Social Security, and other aspects of employment. Each state also has statutes governing certain areas of employment, such as safety standards in the workplace and employment discrimination.
- *Antitrust law*—governed by federal statutes prohibiting specific types of anticompetitive business practices.
- *Consumer law*—governed by state and federal statutes protecting consumers against deceptive trade practices (such as misleading advertising), unsafe products, and generally any activities that threaten consumer health and welfare.

- *Wills and probate administration* (relating to the transfer of property on the property owner's death)—governed by state statutes.

A paralegal working in an area (or on a case) governed by statutory law needs to know how to both locate and interpret the relevant state or federal statutes. You will learn how to find and analyze statutory law in Chapter 9.

ADMINISTRATIVE LAW

There is virtually no way that the federal Congress or a state legislature can oversee the actual implementation of all the laws that it enacts. To assist them in their governing responsibilities, legislatures at all levels of government often delegate such tasks to **administrative agencies**, particularly when the issues relate to highly technical areas. By creating and delegating some of its authority to an administrative agency, a legislature may indirectly monitor a particular area in which it has passed legislation without becoming bogged down in the details relating to enforcement—details that are best left to specialists.

ADMINISTRATIVE AGENCY
A federal or state government agency established to perform a specific function. Administrative agencies are authorized by legislative acts to make and enforce rules relating to the purpose for which they were established.

Agency Creation and Function

To create an administrative agency at the federal level, Congress passes **enabling legislation**, which specifies the name, purpose, composition, and powers of the agency being created. The Occupational Safety and Health Act of 1970, for example, provided for the creation of the Occupational Safety and Health Administration to administer and implement the provisions of the act, to issue rules as necessary to protect employees from dangerous conditions in the workplace, and to enforce the act's provisions and the agency's rules.

ENABLING LEGISLATION
Statutes enacted by Congress that authorize the creation of an administrative agency and specify the name, purpose, composition, and powers of the agency being created.

There are dozens of federal administrative agencies, each of which has been established to perform specific governing tasks. For example, the federal Environmental Protection Agency coordinates and enforces federal environmental laws. The Food and Drug Administration enforces federal laws relating to the safety of foods and drugs. The Federal Trade Commission issues and enforces rules relating to unfair advertising or sales practices. Each state also has a number of administrative agencies, many of which parallel agencies at the federal level. For example, state environmental laws are implemented by state environmental agencies, such as a state's department of natural resources. The rules, orders, and decisions of administrative agencies at all levels of government constitute what is known as **administrative law**.

Administrative Law and the Paralegal

Paralegals frequently deal with administrative agencies. If you work for a law firm that has many corporate clients, you may be involved extensively in researching and analyzing agency regulations and their applicability to certain business activities. If you work for a corporate legal department, you will probably assist the attorneys in the department in a vital task—determining which agency regulations apply to the corporation and whether the corporation is complying with those regulations. If you work for an administrative

ADMINISTRATIVE LAW
A body of law created by administrative agencies—such as the Securities and Exchange Commission and the Federal Trade Commission—in the form of rules, regulations, orders, and decisions in order to carry out their duties and responsibilities.

agency, you may be involved in drafting new rules, in analyzing survey results to see if a new rule is necessary, in mediating disputes between a private party and an agency, in investigations to gather facts about compliance with agency rules, and numerous other tasks. In any law practice, you may be asked to assist clients who are involved in disputes with administrative agencies.

Paralegals who do *pro bono* work (work for free or at a reduced charge) or who work for legal aid societies or legal services corporations often become very familiar with administrative process when helping clients obtain needed benefits, such as Social Security benefits, from state or federal administrative agencies. You may work with local agencies in assisting the homeless obtain medical assistance, for example. Some administrative agencies, including the Social Security Administration, allow paralegals to represent clients at administrative-agency hearings and other procedures.

We list below a few federal government agencies and describe how paralegals may be involved with administrative law and procedures relating to those agencies.

• *Equal Employment Opportunity Commission (EEOC).* If a client wants to pursue a claim against his or her employer for employment discrimination, the client must first contact the EEOC. The EEOC will investigate and try to settle the claim, and only if the problem cannot be resolved by the EEOC will the client be entitled to sue the employer directly. You may be involved in contacting the EEOC and assisting the client in complying with procedures required by the EEOC for handling complaints of employment discrimination.

• *Internal Revenue Service (IRS).* If you work for a corporate law department, you might be asked to assist corporate counsel in handling corporate taxes and related IRS requirements. If you work in a law firm, a corporate client may request legal assistance in settling a dispute with the IRS or in complying with tax laws.

• *Securities and Exchange Commission (SEC).* If you work for a corporation that sells shares of stock in its company to the public, you may be asked to assist in drafting the documents necessary to fulfill registration requirements under federal securities law. If you work for a law firm, you may perform similar tasks for corporate clients. You may also assist in the defense of a client who has been charged with "insider trading" in violation of securities law (which prohibits the purchase or sale of securities, for personal gain, based on knowledge available only to corporate officers or employees and not to the general public).

• *Food and Drug Administration (FDA).* Any firm that places foods or drugs on the market must make sure that those products are safe and properly labeled. If you work for a corporation or on behalf of a corporate client that markets food or drug products, you may be involved in procedures required by the FDA for product testing and labeling or for seeking FDA approval to market a firm's product.

The American System of Justice

Before a lawsuit can be brought before a court, certain requirements must be met. We first examine these important requirements and some of the basic

PARALEGAL PROFILE LSO Paralegal

MARVALINE PRINCE is a paralegal with the Evansville Office of Legal Services Organization of Indiana, Inc. (LSOI). Prince has worked with LSOI since May 1978. She received her training directly through LSOI at its Midwest Resource Training Center. In addition to her training, Prince attended courses on advocacy, Social Security, and Medicaid. She states, however, that most of her training was acquired "on the job." The Evansville office serves ten counties. Its priority is helping underprivileged persons determine their eligibility for government benefits. Prince's area of work involves representing clients before the Social Security Administration.

What do you like best about your work?

"I find my job very challenging and rewarding. Although there are ups and downs to the job, I can't imagine not doing the work I do. I believe my job is fairly unique. Paralegals can do research and case preparation with a private firm, but they will not work as directly with the clients and the courts in most jobs as I do in mine. I also am able to go with clients to hearings and to present evidence. If a case is unusual or difficult, I consult with my supervising attorney at LSOI."

What is the greatest challenge that you face in your area of work?

"My greatest challenge is helping people with their claims for benefits. Ninety percent of my cases are SSI (Supplemental Security Income) cases, and the other 10 percent are Medicaid and food-stamp cases. I have a reputation for aggressive advocacy before the Social Security Administration, and some clients call LSOI asking that I take their case, even though they are aware that I am a paralegal and not an attorney."

What advice do you have for would-be paralegals in your area of work?

"My advice to any would-be paralegal is to obtain the best education possible. A large part of my job is assessing whether or not a client qualifies for SSI benefits, which I am able to do by determining their educational background, areas of skill, and medical history. It is important for paralegals in my area of work to have an extensive knowledge of many areas when trying to determine eligibility for a client."

> **"I CAN'T IMAGINE NOT DOING THE WORK I DO."**

What are some tips for success as a paralegal in your area of work?

"Regardless of whether a paralegal works for a private law firm or with a legal services organization, it is essential that paralegals become familiar with computers. My own desk-top computer allows me to draft memoranda in half the time that it would take me to draft it manually. Any paralegal who resists using computer technology is truly at a disadvantage. Paralegals should insist that their employers invest in computers for all staff members to use, and not just support staff."

---

features of the American system of justice. We then look at the state and federal court systems.

Types of Jurisdiction

In Latin, *juris* means "law," and *diction* means "to speak." Thus, "the power to speak the law" is the literal meaning of the term **jurisdiction**. Before any court can hear a case, it must have jurisdiction over the person against whom the suit is brought or over the property involved in the suit. The court must also have jurisdiction over the subject matter.

JURISDICTION
The authority of a court to hear and decide a specific action.

Jurisdiction over Persons.   Generally, a court can exercise personal jurisdiction (*in personam* jurisdiction) over residents of a certain geographical area. A state trial court, for example, normally has jurisdictional authority over residents of a particular area of the state, such as a county or district. A state's highest court (often called the state supreme court)[2] has jurisdictional authority over all residents within the state.

In some cases, under the authority of a long-arm statute, a court can exercise personal jurisdiction over nonresidents as well. A **long-arm statute** is a state law permitting courts to exercise jurisdiction over nonresident defendants. Before a court can exercise jurisdiction over a nonresident under a long-arm statute, though, it must be demonstrated that the nonresident had sufficient contacts (*minimum contacts*) with the state to justify the jurisdiction. For example, if an individual has committed a wrong within the state, such as causing an automobile injury or selling defective goods, a court can usually exercise jurisdiction even if the person causing the harm is located in another state. Similarly, a state may exercise personal jurisdiction over a nonresident defendant who is sued for breaching a contract that was formed within the state.

In regard to corporations, the minimum-contacts requirement is usually met if the corporation does business within the state. A Maine corporation that has a branch office or manufacturing plant in Georgia, for example, has sufficient minimum contacts with the state of Georgia to allow a Georgia court to exercise jurisdiction over the Maine corporation. If the Maine corporation advertises and sells its products in Georgia, those activities may also suffice to meet the minimum-contacts requirement.

Jurisdiction over Property.   A court can also exercise jurisdiction over property that is located within its boundaries. This kind of jurisdiction is known as *in rem* jurisdiction, or "jurisdiction over the thing." For example, suppose that a a dispute arises over the ownership of a boat in dry dock in Fort Lauderdale, Florida. The boat is owned by an Ohio resident, over whom a Florida court cannot normally exercise personal jurisdiction. The other party to the dispute is a resident of Nebraska. In this situation, a lawsuit concerning the boat could be brought in a Florida state court on the basis of the court's *in rem* jurisdiction.

Jurisdiction over Subject Matter.   Jurisdiction over subject matter is a limitation on the types of cases a court can hear. In both the state and federal court systems, there are courts of *general jurisdiction* and courts of *limited jurisdiction*. The basis for the distinction lies in the subject matter of cases heard. For example, probate courts—state courts that handle only matters relating to the transfer of a person's assets and obligations on that person's death, including matters relating to the custody and guardianship of children—have limited subject-matter jurisdiction. A common example of a federal court of limited subject-matter jurisdiction is a bankruptcy court.

LONG-ARM STATUTE
A state statute that permits a state to obtain jurisdiction over nonresident individuals and corporations. Individuals or corporations, however, must have certain "minimum contacts" with that state for the statute to apply.

---

2. As will be discussed shortly, a state's highest court is often referred to as the state supreme court, but there are exceptions. For example, in New York, the supreme court is a trial court.

Bankruptcy courts handle only bankruptcy proceedings, which are governed by federal bankruptcy law (bankruptcy law allows debtors to obtain relief from their debts when they cannot make ends meet). In contrast, a court of general jurisdiction can decide virtually any type of case.

The subject-matter jurisdiction of a court is usually defined in the statute or constitution creating the court. In both the state and federal court systems, a court's subject-matter jurisdiction can be limited not only by the subject of the lawsuit, but also by the amount of money in controversy, by whether a case is a felony (a more serious type of crime) or a misdemeanor (a less serious type of crime), or by whether the proceeding is a trial or an appeal.

Original and Appellate Jurisdiction.   The distinction between courts of original jurisdiction and courts of appellate jurisdiction normally lies in whether the case is being heard for the first time. Courts having **original jurisdiction** are courts of the first instance, or **trial courts**—that is, courts in which lawsuits begin, trials take place, and evidence is presented. In the federal court system, the *district courts* are trial courts. In the various state court systems, the trial courts are known by different names. The key point here is that normally, any court having original jurisdiction is known as a trial court. Courts having **appellate jurisdiction** act as reviewing courts, or **appellate courts**. In general, cases can be brought before them only on appeal from an order or a judgment of a trial court or other lower court. State and federal trial and appellate courts will be discussed more fully later in this chapter.

Jurisdiction of the Federal Courts

Because the federal government is a government of limited powers, the jurisdiction of the federal courts is limited. Article III of the U.S. Constitution established the boundaries of federal judicial power. Section 2 of Article III states that "[t]he judicial Power shall extend to all Cases, in Law and Equity, arising under this Constitution, the Laws of the United States, and Treaties made, or which shall be made, under their Authority."

Federal Questions.   Whenever a plaintiff's cause of action is based, at least in part, on the U.S. Constitution, a treaty, or a federal law, then a **federal question** arises, and the case comes under the judicial power of federal courts. Any lawsuit involving a federal question can originate in a federal court. People who claim that their constitutional rights have been violated can begin their suits in a federal court.

Diversity Jurisdiction.   Federal district courts can also exercise original jurisdiction over cases involving **diversity of citizenship**. Such cases may arise between (1) citizens of different states, (2) a foreign country and citizens of a state or of different states, or (3) citizens of a state and citizens or subjects of a foreign country. The amount in controversy must be more than $50,000 before a federal court can take jurisdiction in such cases. For purposes of diversity-of-citizenship jurisdiction, a corporation is a citizen of the

BANKRUPTCY COURT
A federal court of limited jurisdiction that hears only bankruptcy proceedings.

ORIGINAL JURISDICTION
The power of a court to take a case, try it, and decide it.

TRIAL COURT
A court in which most cases usually begin and in which questions of fact are examined.

APPELLATE JURISDICTION
The power of a court to hear and decide an appeal; that is, the power and authority of a court to review cases that already have been tried in a lower court and the power to make decisions about them without actually holding a trial. This process is called appellate review.

APPELLATE COURT
A court that reviews decisions made by lower courts, such as trial courts; a court of appeals.

FEDERAL QUESTION
A question that pertains to the U.S. Constitution, acts of Congress, or treaties. A federal question provides jurisdiction for federal courts. This jurisdiction arises from Article III, Section 2, of the Constitution.

DIVERSITY OF CITIZENSHIP
Under Article III, Section 2, of the Constitution, a basis for federal court jurisdiction over a lawsuit between certain parties, such as citizens of different states.

state in which it is incorporated and of the state in which its principal place of business is located. A case involving diversity of citizenship can be filed in the appropriate federal district court, or, if the case starts in a state court, it can sometimes be transferred to a federal court.

As an example of diversity jurisdiction, assume that the following events have taken place. Maria Ramirez, a citizen of Florida, was walking near a busy street in Tallahassee, Florida, one day when a large crate flew off a passing truck and hit and seriously injured her. She incurred numerous medical expenses and could not work for six months. She now wants to sue the trucking firm for $300,000 in damages. The trucking firm's headquarters are in Georgia, although the company does business in Florida.

In this situation, Maria could bring suit in a Florida court because she is a resident of Florida, the trucking firm does business in Florida, and that is where the accident occurred. She could also bring suit in a Georgia court, because a Georgia court could exercise jurisdiction over the trucking firm, which is headquartered in that state. As a third alternative, Maria could bring suit in a federal court because the requirements of diversity jurisdiction have been met—the lawsuit involves parties from different states, Florida and Georgia, and the amount in controversy (the damages Maria is seeking) exceeds $50,000. Note that in a case based on a federal question, a federal court will apply federal law. In a case based on diversity of citizenship, however, a federal court will normally apply the law of the state in which the court sits.

CONCURRENT JURISDICTION
Jurisdiction that exists when two different courts have the power to hear a case. For example, some cases can be heard in a federal or state court.

EXCLUSIVE JURISDICTION
Jurisdiction that exists when a case can be heard only in a particular court or type of court.

Exclusive versus Concurrent Jurisdiction. When both federal and state courts have the power to hear a case, as is true in suits involving diversity of citizenship (such as Maria's case described above), **concurrent jurisdiction** exists. When cases can be tried only in federal courts or only in state courts, **exclusive jurisdiction** exists. Federal courts have exclusive jurisdiction in cases involving federal crimes, bankruptcy, patents, and copyrights; in suits against the United States; and in some areas of admiralty law (law governing transportation on the seas and ocean waters). States also have exclusive jurisdiction in certain subject matters—for example, in divorce and adoptions.

When concurrent jurisdiction exists, a plaintiff bringing a lawsuit has a choice: he or she may bring the case in either a state court or a federal court. Normally, an attorney will look at several factors before advising a client on which court would be most advantageous. These factors include convenience (the physical location of the court), how long it would take in either type of court to get the case to trial (state courts often have heavier case loads, and thus the wait may be longer), and the temperaments and judicial philosophies of the judges of the courts.

Venue

VENUE
The geographical district in which an action is tried and from which the jury is selected.

Jurisdiction has to do with whether a court has authority to hear a case involving specific persons, property, or subject matter. **Venue**[3] is concerned with the most appropriate location for a trial. For example, two state courts may have

---

3. Pronounced *ven*-yoo.

DEVELOPING PARALEGAL SKILLS

Choice of Courts: State or Federal?

 Joan Dunbar is a legal assistant in a law firm. Her supervisor, Susan Radtke, is a well-known lawyer who specializes in employment law. They are meeting with a new client who wants to sue her former employer for sex discrimination. The client complained to her employer when she was passed over for a promotion, and she was fired as a result of her complaint. The client appears to have a strong case because several of her former co-workers have agreed to testify that they heard the employer say on several occasions that he would never promote a woman to a managerial position in his firm.

Susan explains to the client that both state law and federal law prohibit sex discrimination, and therefore the client's case could be brought in either a state court or a federal court. The client asks Susan about the advantages and disadvantages of each of these options.

THE PROS AND CONS OF FILING THE SUIT IN A STATE COURT

Susan asks Joan to get the newspaper and magazine clippings file on the county court. When Joan returns with it, Susan removes a newspaper article from the file entitled "Plaintiff's County, USA." Their county has earned this reputation nationwide because of the large number of million-dollar and multimillion-dollar jury verdicts that the county court awards to plaintiffs each year. The client asks if this means that she is assured of winning her case if she files in this court. "No," Susan responds. "But it will help. The disadvantage to filing here is that the county's docket is so backlogged that you are looking at three to five years before you go to trial." The client, who is unemployed, explains to Susan that she does not want to wait that long to obtain a decision, and the claimed damages, in her case.

THE PROS AND CONS OF FILING THE SUIT IN A FEDERAL COURT

Susan explains that if the client filed in federal court, the case could go to trial within six months to a year. "The disadvantage here," continues Susan, "is that you might not have a county jury that favors plaintiffs and apparently dislikes defendants, especially corporate ones." The client likes the idea of having her case decided as quickly as possible, but she also wants to win at trial and obtain damages. The client decides to let Susan choose the court. "Just remember that while I want to maximize the amount of damages awarded, it's more important that I receive damages as soon as possible. My unemployment compensation won't last forever."

MAKING THE DECISION

The client leaves, and Susan and Joan discuss the case. They both agree that because the client has a strong case, she could probably win in either court. Because of the client's concern about time, Susan decides to file the case in a federal court, even though the damages awarded might not be as high as they would be in the county court. Susan then discusses with Joan the legal theories that the complaint should contain.

Meeting Procedural Deadlines

One of the paralegal's most important responsibilities is making sure that court deadlines are met. For example, suppose that your supervising attorney asks you to file with the court a motion to dismiss (a document requesting the court to dismiss a lawsuit for a specific reason). You know that the deadline for filing the motion is three days away. You plan to deliver the motion to the court the next day, so you don't place a reminder note on your calendar. In the meantime, you place the motion in the client's file. The next morning, you arrive at work and immediately are called to help your supervising attorney with last-minute trial preparations on another case. You are busy all afternoon interviewing witnesses in still another case. You have totally forgotten about the motion to dismiss and do not think of it again until a week later—when the deadline for filing the motion has passed. Because you forgot to file the motion, your supervising attorney has breached the duty of competence. How can you make sure that you remember important deadlines? The answer is simple: *always* enter deadlines on the office calendaring system and *always* check your calendar several times a day.

the authority to exercise jurisdiction over a case, but it may be more appropriate or convenient to hear the case in one court than in the other.

Basically, the concept of venue reflects the policy that a court trying a suit should be in the geographic neighborhood (usually the county) in which the incident leading to the lawsuit occurred or in which the parties involved in the lawsuit reside. Pretrial publicity or other factors, though, may require a change of venue to another community, especially in criminal cases in which the defendant's right to a fair and impartial jury has been impaired. For example, in 1992, when four Los Angeles police officers accused of beating Rodney King were brought to trial, the attorneys defending the police officers requested a change of venue from Los Angeles to Simi Valley, California. The attorneys argued that to try the case in a Los Angeles court would prejudice the police officers' right to a fair trial. The court agreed and granted the request.

Judicial Procedures

Litigation in court, from the moment a lawsuit is initiated until the final resolution of the case, must follow specifically designated procedural rules. The procedural rules for federal court cases are set forth in the Federal Rules of Civil Procedure. State rules, which are often similar to the federal rules, vary from state to state—and even from court to court within a given state. Rules of procedure also differ in criminal and civil cases. Paralegals who work for trial lawyers need to be familiar with the procedural rules of the relevant courts. Because judicial procedures will be examined in detail in Chapter 6, we do not discuss them here.

The American System of Justice and the Paralegal

Paralegals should be familiar with such concepts as jurisdiction and venue because these concepts affect pretrial litigation procedures. For example, a defendant in a lawsuit may claim that the court in which the plaintiff filed the lawsuit cannot exercise jurisdiction over the matter—or over the defendant or the defendant's property. If you are working on behalf of the defendant, you may be asked to draft a motion to dismiss the case on this ground. You may also be asked to draft a legal memorandum in support of the motion, outlining the legal reasons why the court cannot exercise jurisdiction over the case. (Motions to dismiss and supporting documents are discussed in Chapter 6.) Additionally, a party to a lawsuit may request that a case filed in a state court should be "removed" to a federal court (if there is a basis for federal jurisdiction) or vice versa. You may also be asked to draft a document requesting a change of venue (or objecting to an opponent's request for change of venue).

If you work for a plaintiff's attorney, you might be asked to draft a complaint to initiate a lawsuit. Once the attorney reviews the facts with you, he or she may expect you to know whether concurrent jurisdiction exists. If concurrent jurisdiction exists, the attorney may expect you to ask whether the suit should be filed in a state or a federal court. If concurrent jurisdiction does not exist, the attorney may assume that you know in which court the case will be filed and that you know how to prepare the compaint for the appropriate court.

Recall from Chapter 1 that paralegal education and training emphasizes procedural law. A paralegal can be a valuable member of a legal team if he or she has substantial knowledge of the procedural requirements relating to litigation and to different types of legal proceedings. You will read in detail about litigation procedures in Chapter 6.

STATE COURT SYSTEMS

Each state has its own system of courts, and no two state systems are the same. As Exhibit 5.1 on the following page indicates, there may be several levels, or tiers, of courts within a state court system: (1) state trial courts of limited jurisdiction, (2) state trial courts of general jurisdiction, (3) appellate courts, and (4) the state's highest court (often called the state supreme court). Judges in the state court system are usually elected by the voters for a specified term.

Generally, any person who is a party to a lawsuit has the opportunity to plead the case before a trial court and then, if he or she loses, before at least one level of appellate court. Finally, if a federal statute or federal constitutional issue is involved in the decision of a state supreme court, that decision may be further appealed to the United States Supreme Court.

Trial Courts

Trial courts are exactly what their name implies—courts in which trials are held and testimony taken. You will read in detail about trial procedures in Chapter 6. In that chapter, we follow a hypothetical case through the various stages of a trial. Briefly, a trial court is presided over by a judge, who issues a decision on the matter before the court. If the trial is a jury trial (many trials are held without juries), the jury will decide the outcome of factual disputes, and the judge will issue a judgment based on the jury's conclusion. During the trial, the attorney for each side introduces evidence (such as relevant documents, exhibits, and testimony of witnesses) in support of his or her client's position. Each attorney is given an opportunity to cross-examine the opposing party's witnesses and challenge evidence introduced by the opposing party.

State trial courts have either general or limited jurisdiction. Trial courts that have general jurisdiction as to subject matter may be called county, district, superior, or circuit courts.[5] The jurisdiction of these courts is often determined by the size of the county in which the court sits. State trial courts of general jurisdiction have jurisdiction over a wide variety of subjects, including both civil disputes (such as landlord-tenant matters or contract claims) and criminal prosecutions.

Courts with limited jurisdiction as to subject matter are often called special inferior trial courts or minor judiciary courts. Courts of limited jurisdiction include domestic-relations courts, which handle only divorce actions and

---

5. The name in Ohio is Court of Common Pleas; the name in New York is Supreme Court.

EXHIBIT 5.1

State Court Systems

State court systems vary widely from state to state, and it is therefore impossible to show a "typical" state court system. This exhibit is typical of the court systems in several states, however, including Texas, California, Arizona, and Nevada.

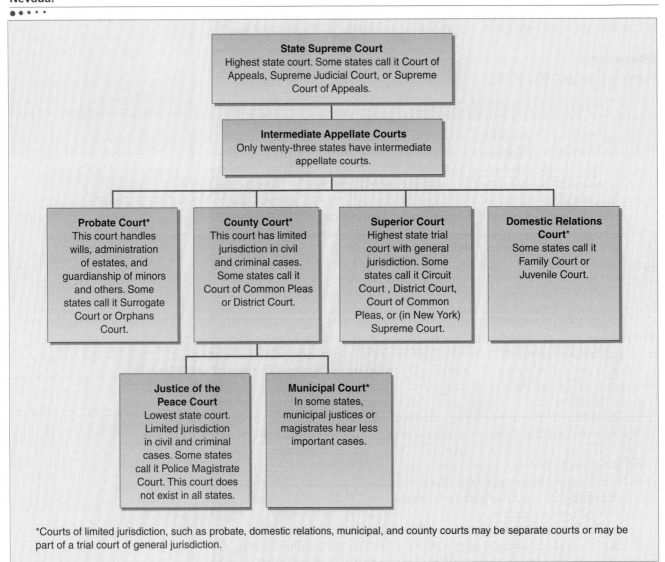

State Supreme Court
Highest state court. Some states call it Court of Appeals, Supreme Judicial Court, or Supreme Court of Appeals.

Intermediate Appellate Courts
Only twenty-three states have intermediate appellate courts.

Probate Court*
This court handles wills, administration of estates, and guardianship of minors and others. Some states call it Surrogate Court or Orphans Court.

County Court*
This court has limited jurisdiction in civil and criminal cases. Some states call it Court of Common Pleas or District Court.

Superior Court
Highest state trial court with general jurisdiction. Some states call it Circuit Court, District Court, Court of Common Pleas, or (in New York) Supreme Court.

Domestic Relations Court*
Some states call it Family Court or Juvenile Court.

Justice of the Peace Court
Lowest state court. Limited jurisdiction in civil and criminal cases. Some states call it Police Magistrate Court. This court does not exist in all states.

Municipal Court*
In some states, municipal justices or magistrates hear less important cases.

*Courts of limited jurisdiction, such as probate, domestic relations, municipal, and county courts may be separate courts or may be part of a trial court of general jurisdiction.

child-custody cases; local municipal courts, which mainly handle traffic cases; and probate courts, which, as previously mentioned, handle the administration of wills, estate-settlement problems, and related matters.

Courts of Appeals

Generally, courts of appeals (appellate courts, or reviewing courts) are not trial courts. In some states, however, trial courts of general jurisdiction may have

DEVELOPING PARALEGAL SKILLS

State Court Litigation

 David Garner is a legal assistant in a busy law firm. David's supervising attorney, Helen Schmidt, has called him into a meeting. She
wants him to draft complaints for a couple of new cases. The first
case is a medical-malpractice case against an orthopedist whose
allegedly careless treatment of the client's knee injury resulted in
unnecessary complications and expensive surgery. The client is all right
now, but she lost two months of work while she was recovering. She feels
that she is entitled to damages to cover her medical expenses and her lost
wages. Her total damages are about $7,000.

Because the state has, for the most part, a two-tiered trial court system,
David suggests to Helen that they file the case in the local district court, the
lowest-level trial court with jurisdiction. These courts have jurisdiction over
civil cases in which the amount in controversy (the damages sought by the
plaintiff) is under $10,000. Helen agrees that the district court has jurisdic-
tion to hear the case.

The second case is a product-liability case against a local automobile manufacturer. The plaintiffs are the parents of a young man whose death was
allegedly caused by a defective steering mechanism in a car produced by the
auto manufacturer. The plaintiffs are seeking damages in the millions. Helen
tells David to prepare this case to be filed with the county circuit court,
because this court has jurisdiction over civil cases that exceed $10,000 in
damages.

limited jurisdiction to hear appeals from the minor judiciary—for example,
from small claims courts or traffic courts. Every state has at least one court of
appeals, which may be an intermediate appellate court or a state supreme court.

Intermediate Appellate Courts.   Twenty-three states have intermediate
appellate courts. The subject-matter jurisdiction of these courts of appeals is
substantially limited to hearing appeals. Appellate courts do not retry cases
(conduct new trials, in which evidence is submitted to the court and witnesses are examined). Rather, an appellate court panel of three or more
judges reviews the record of the case on appeal, which includes a transcript
of the trial proceedings, and determines whether the trial court committed
an error. Appellate courts look at questions of law and procedure but usually not at questions of fact.

Normally, an appellate court will defer to a trial court's finding of fact
because the trial court judge and jury were in a better position to evaluate testimony; they could directly observe witnesses' gestures, demeanor, and nonverbal behavior generally during the trial. At the appellate level, the judges
review the written transcript of the trial, which does not include these nonverbal elements. An appellate court will challenge a trial court's finding of
fact only when the finding is clearly erroneous (that is, when it is contrary to
the evidence presented at trial) or when there is no evidence to support the
finding. For example, if a jury concluded that a manufacturer's product

harmed the plaintiff but no evidence was submitted to the court to support that conclusion, the appellate court would hold that the trial court's decision was erroneous.

State Supreme Courts. The highest appellate court in a state is usually called the supreme court but may be called by some other name. For example, in both New York and Maryland, the highest state court is called the Court of Appeals. The decisions of each state's highest court on all questions of state law are final. Only when issues of federal law are involved can a decision made by a state's highest court be overruled by the United States Supreme Court. A case involving a constitutional right, for example, might be appealed to the nation's highest court.

State Court Systems and the Paralegal

Because each state has its own unique system of courts, you will need to become familiar with the court system of your particular state. What is the official name of your state's highest court, or supreme court? How many intermediate state appellate courts are in your state, and to which of these courts should appeals from your local trial court or courts be appealed? What courts in your area have jurisdiction over what kinds of disputes?

In addition to knowing the names of your state's courts and their jurisdictional authority, you will also need to become familiar with the procedural requirements of specific courts. Paralegals frequently assist their attorneys in drafting legal documents to be filed in state courts, and the required procedures for filing these documents may vary from court to court. You will read more about court procedures in Chapters 10 and 11.

As indicated earlier and illustrated in Exhibit 7.1, state courts exercise exclusive jurisdiction over all matters that are not subject to federal jurisdiction. Family law and probate law (discussed in Chapter 2), for example, are two areas in which state courts exercise exclusive jurisdiction. If you work in these or other areas of the law over which state courts exercise jurisdiction, you will need to be familiar with procedural requirements established by state (or local) courts relating to those areas.

THE FEDERAL COURT SYSTEM

The federal court system is basically a three-tiered model consisting of (1) U.S. district courts (trial courts of general jurisdiction) and various courts of limited jurisdiction, (2) U.S. courts of appeals (intermediate courts of appeals), and (3) the United States Supreme Court. Exhibit 5.2 shows the organization of the federal court system.

According to the language of Article III of the U.S. Constitution, there is only one national Supreme Court. All other courts in the federal system are considered "inferior." Congress is empowered to create other inferior courts as it deems necessary. The inferior courts that Congress has created include those on the first and second tiers in our model—the district courts and various courts of limited jurisdiction, as well as the U.S. courts of appeals.

EXHIBIT 5.2
The Organization of the Federal Court System

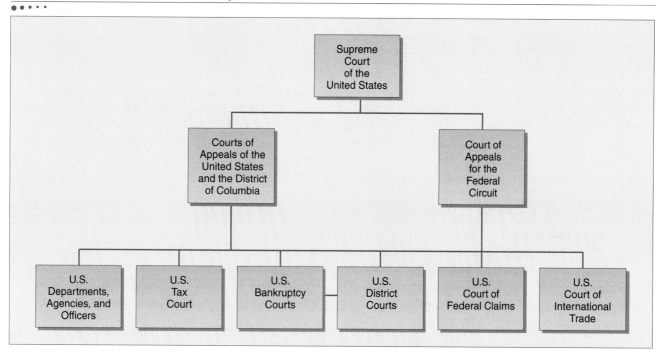

Unlike state court judges, who are usually elected, federal court judges are appointed by the president of the United States, subject to the approval of the U.S. Senate. Federal judges receive lifetime appointments (because under Article III they "hold their Offices during good Behavior").

U.S. District Courts

At the federal level, the equivalent of a state trial court of general jurisdiction is the district court. There is at least one federal district court in every state. The number of judicial districts can vary over time, primarily owing to population changes and corresponding case loads. Currently, there are ninety-six judicial districts.

U.S. district courts have original jurisdiction in federal matters. Federal cases typically originate in district courts. There are other trial courts with original, but special (or limited) jurisdiction, such as the federal bankruptcy courts and others shown in Exhibit 5.2.

U.S. Courts of Appeals

In the federal court system, there are thirteen U.S. courts of appeals—also referred to as U.S. circuit courts of appeals. The federal courts of appeals for twelve of the circuits hear appeals from the federal district courts located within their respective judicial circuits. The court of appeals for the thirteenth circuit, called the federal circuit, has national appellate jurisdiction over certain types of cases, such as cases involving patent law and cases in which the U.S. government is a defendant.

A party who is dissatisfied with a federal district court's decision on an issue may appeal that decision to a federal circuit court of appeals. As in state courts of appeals, the decisions of the circuit courts are made by a panel of three or more justices. The justices review decisions made by trial courts to see if any errors of law were made, and the justices generally defer to a district court's findings of fact. The decisions of the circuit courts of appeals are final in most cases, but appeal to the United States Supreme Court is possible. Exhibit 5.3 shows the geographical boundaries of U.S. circuit courts of appeals and the boundaries of the U.S. district courts within each circuit.

EXHIBIT 5.3
U.S. Courts of Appeals and U.S. District Courts

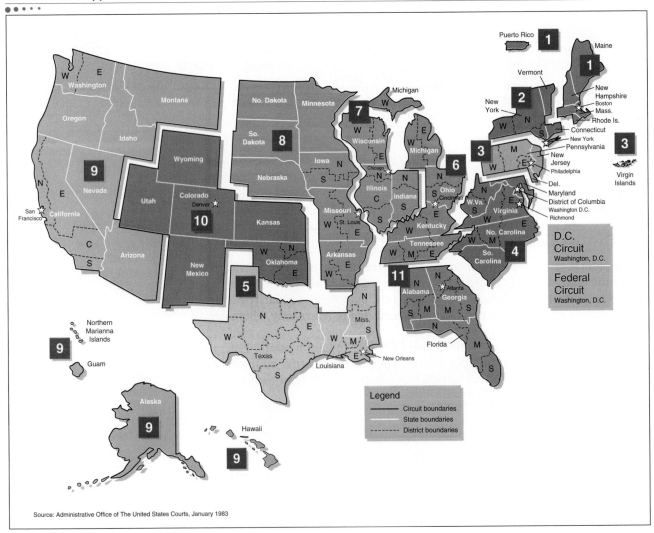

Source: Administrative Office of The United States Courts, January 1983

The United States Supreme Court

The United States Supreme Court consists of nine justices. These justices, like all federal judges, are nominated by the president of the United States and confirmed by the Senate.

The Supreme Court is given original, or trial court, jurisdiction in a small number of situations. Under Article III, Section 2, of the U.S. Constitution, the Supreme Court can exercise original jurisdiction in all cases "affecting Ambassadors, other public Ministers and Consuls, and those in which a State shall be a Party." In all other cases, the Supreme Court may exercise only appellate jurisdiction "with such Exceptions, and under such Regulations as the Congress shall make." Most of the Supreme Court's work is as an appellate court. The Supreme Court can review any case decided by any of the federal courts of appeals, and it also has appellate authority over some cases decided in the state courts.

Many people are surprised to learn that there is no absolute right of appeal to the United States Supreme Court. Thousands of cases are filed with the Supreme Court each year, yet it hears, on average, fewer than 150 of these cases. To bring a case before the Supreme Court, a party requests the Court to issue a writ of *certiorari*. A **writ of *certiorari***[4] is an order issued by the Supreme Court to a lower court requiring the latter to send it the record of the case for review. Parties can petition the Supreme Court to issue a writ of *certiorari*, but the Court is not required to issue a writ of *certiorari*, and most petitions for writs are denied. A denial is not a decision on the merits of a case, nor does it indicate agreement with the lower court's opinion. It simply means that the Supreme Court declines to grant the request (petition) for appeal. Furthermore, denial of the writ has no value as a precedent.

Typically, the petitions granted by the Court involve cases that raise important constitutional questions or that conflict with other state or federal court decisions. Similarly, if federal appellate courts are rendering inconsistent opinions on an important issue, the Supreme Court may review a case involving that issue and generate a decision to define the law on the matter.

The Federal Court System and the Paralegal

In your work as a paralegal, you will probably be dealing occasionally with the federal court system. As discussed above, certain cases involving diversity of citizenship may be brought in either a state or a federal court. Many litigants who could sue in a state court will opt for a federal court if diversity of citizenship exists for the reasons mentioned earlier.

You may also be working on behalf of plaintiffs whose claims involve a federal question. An increasing number of cases in federal courts are brought by plaintiffs who allege employment discrimination in violation of federal laws, such as Title VII of the Civil Rights Act of 1964, which prohibits employment discrimination based on race, color, national origin, gender, or religion. Other federal laws prohibit discrimination based on age or disability. Sexual harassment and pregnancy discrimination are considered by the

---

ETHICAL CONCERN

Meeting Federal Court Deadlines

As yet another example of the consequences of missing a court procedural deadline, suppose that a client of your firm has been sued in tort for the conversion of intellectual property. *Conversion* is the wrongful taking of another's property—the civil counterpart of theft. The plaintiff, an author, has filed suit against the client in a state court, alleging that the defendant has used portions of a textbook written by the plaintiff without permission. You are asked to prepare a "notice of removal" so that the case can be removed (transferred) from the state court to a federal court—because the claim is essentially a copyright claim, over which federal courts exercise jurisdiction. If the notice is not filed with the federal court within thirty days of the defendant's receipt of the complaint and summons (and nothing is filed with the state court), the defendant may lose the right to defend against the suit and may end up having to pay whatever damages the plaintiff is seeking. If this happened, the client, in turn, could then sue the attorney, and possibly the paralegal, to recover the damages that the defendant had to pay the plaintiff due to the attorney's breach of the duty of competence.

WRIT OF *CERTIORARI*
A writ from a higher court asking the lower court for the record of a case.

---

4. Pronounced sur-shee-uh-*rah*-ree.

courts to fall under the protective umbrella of Title VII's prohibition against gender discrimination, and such cases frequently come before federal courts.

As indicated earlier, federal courts exercise exclusive jurisdiction over cases relating to bankruptcy, patents, copyrights, trademarks, federal crimes, and certain other claims. If you work on such cases, you will be dealing with the federal court system and the court procedures set forth in the Federal Rules of Civil Procedure. As with state courts, you should make sure that you know the specific requirements of the particular federal court in which a client's lawsuit is to be filed, because each federal court has some discretionary authority over its procedural rules. You will read in detail about the procedural rules governing litigation proceedings in federal courts in Chapter 6.

ALTERNATIVE DISPUTE RESOLUTION

Litigation in court is generally a last resort because of the high costs associated with litigating even the simplest complaint. In addition, because of the growing backlog of cases pending in the courts, it may sometimes be several years before a case is actually tried. Finally, the legal process is beset with uncertainties. One cannot know in advance how effectively the opposing side will argue its case or how the personal views and perceptions of judges and jurors may affect the outcome of the trial.

For these reasons, more and more individuals and business firms are turning to **alternative dispute resolution (ADR)** instead of resolving their disputes in court. Approximately 95 percent of all civil lawsuits are settled without a trial. Sometimes, a claim is settled before a lawsuit has been initiated. Most frequently, a settlement is achieved after the lawsuit is filed but before a trial takes place. In such situations, pretrial investigations give the parties and their attorneys an opportunity to assess the plaintiff's damages realistically and determine the relative strengths and weaknesses of the disputants' cases. Because so many cases are settled before they reach trial, attorneys and paralegals usually devote as much attention to these possibilities as to trial preparations. We now look at the various methods employed for settling disputes outside the court system.

Negotiation and Mediation

Negotiation is one alternative means of resolving disputes. Attorneys frequently advise their clients to negotiate a **settlement** of their disputes voluntarily before they proceed to trial. During pretrial negotiation, the parties and/or their attorneys may meet informally one or more times to see if a mutually satisfactory agreement can be reached.

Another alternative method of resolving disputes is to enlist the aid of a mediator. A mediator is expected to propose solutions, but he or she does not *impose* any solution or decision on the parties. In the **mediation** process, the parties themselves must reach agreement; the role of the mediator is to help the parties view their dispute more objectively and find common grounds for agreement.

ALTERNATIVE DISPUTE RESOLUTION (ADR)
The resolution of disputes in ways other than those involved in the traditional judicial process. Negotiation, mediation, and arbitration are forms of ADR.

NEGOTIATION
A method of alternative dispute resolution in which disputing parties, with or without the assistance of their attorneys, meet informally to resolve the dispute out of court.

SETTLEMENT
An out-of-court resolution to a legal dispute, which is agreed to by the parties in writing. A settlement agreement may be reached at any time prior to or during a trial.

MEDIATION
A method of settling disputes outside of court by using the services of a neutral third party, who acts as a communicating agent between the parties; a method of dispute settlement that is less formal than arbitration.

THE LEGAL TEAM AT WORK
ADR versus Adversarial Justice

As a member of a litigation team, you will be involved in the seemingly impossible task of working simultaneously toward two mutually exclusive goals. On the one hand, you will be assisting your supervising attorney in working toward an out-of-court settlement of the dispute. On the other hand, you will be assisting in trial preparations so that, if no settlement agreement is reached, your client's case will be ready by the trial date.

Working toward these two goals simultaneously means that you will need to switch back and forth between two different approaches to the case. Preparing to litigate a case in court requires your team to view the opponent as an adversary. Implicitly, this view emphasizes the points of *disagreement* between the parties and reflects the win-lose philosophy that has traditionally characterized the adversarial system of justice. Settlement negotiations, in contrast, involve a totally different approach, one that is geared toward finding grounds for *agreement* between the parties.

The success of settlement negotiations or other method of ADR often depends on the negotiation and communication skills of the members of the legal team. There is every indication that the trend toward ADR will continue to grow and that the legal team will devote even more time in the future toward helping clients solve their problems through voluntary out-of-court settlements rather than adversarial proceedings. In preparing to work as a paralegal and legal teammate, you will thus want to improve and fine-tune your communication skills so that you will be a valuable ally in working toward settlements.

The parties may select a mediator on the basis of his or her expertise in a particular field or reputation for fairness and impartiality. The mediator may not need to be a lawyer. The mediator may be one person, such as a paralegal, an attorney, or a volunteer from the community, or a panel of mediators may be used. Usually, a mediator charges a fee, which can be split between the parties. Many state and federal courts require that parties mediate their disputes before being allowed to resolve the disputes through trials. When mediation is required by a court before the parties can have the court hear their dispute, the mediators may be appointed by the court.

Mediation usually results in the quick settlement of disputes. Initial meetings between the parties and the mediator often occur within several weeks after a voluntary request to mediate has been made by one or both parties. (See this chapter's featured-guest article entitled "Mediation and the Paralegal" for further details on the functions performed by mediators and the role played by paralegals in the mediation process.)

Arbitration

A more formal method of alternative dispute resolution is **arbitration**. The key difference between arbitration and the forms of ADR just discussed, negotiation and mediation, is that in those forms of ADR, the parties themselves settle their dispute—although a third party may assist them in doing

ARBITRATION
The settling of a dispute by submitting it to a disinterested third party (other than a court), who renders a legally binding decision.

FEATURED GUEST: ANDREA NAGER CHASEN

Mediation and the Paralegal

Biographical Note

Andrea Nager Chasen received her master's degree in public administration, specializing in the theory and practice of decision-making processes, from New York University. Four years later, she earned her law degree at the American University School of Law. Following graduation from law school, through her work as a litigator, she became interested in alternative methods of dispute resolution. Her interest led her to an in-depth exploration of mediation as one method of resolving disputes out of court. As a consequence, she has developed and taught courses in mediation and has served as a mediator. Currently, she mediates and arbitrates disputes on a full-time basis in her private practice.

With all of the attention on alternative dispute resolution (ADR) methods as tools for conflict resolution, how is the traditional law firm to respond? Will the availability of ADR result in the end of the trial as we know it and the exhaustive amount of work that goes into preparing for trial? Rest assured, there is still work (and lots of it) to be done. But the type of work will differ from what the average attorney and paralegal are used to doing. This feature focuses on just one method of ADR—mediation—and the paralegal's role in this process.[a]

WHAT DOES A MEDIATOR DO?

Before considering the paralegal's role in the mediation process, it is important to know how mediators help parties in settling their conflicts. Generally, the mediator undertakes to do the following:

1. Learn what the parties' real interests are (as opposed to the positions that the parties have put forward).
2. Assess realistically the alternative ways in which the dispute might be resolved.
3. Deal with the differences between the parties' perceptions of the issues involved in the dispute.
4. Learn (in private sessions with each party) what information the parties are unwilling to disclose to each other.
5. Devise options and solutions that meet the interests of all parties involved in the dispute.

Throughout the proceedings, the mediator maintains a neutral position and focuses on the parties' feelings and statements that can be used productively. The mediator never imposes a judgment but acts as a facilitator to help the parties reach their own agreement.

THE PARALEGAL'S ROLE IN THE MEDIATION PROCESS

What tasks does the paralegal perform in relation to the mediation process? Perhaps the best way to answer this question is to divide the mediation process into various stages and examine the role of the paralegal during each stage. Generally, as with cases that go to trial, a good deal of the paralegal's efforts will be involved in overall case management.

Stage One: Premediation. The first stage of the mediation process consists of finding out the facts about a client's claim against another party and determining whether mediation might be appropriate at this point. In divorce or custody matters, if the couple has retained attorneys but negotiations appear to be failing, then an attempt to mediate the dispute may be useful. Sometimes, the client's case will already be in the initial stages of litigation, and pretrial investigations will be underway. Mediation may also be forced

---

a. EDITOR'S NOTE: The author of this article describes some of the general features of the mediation process and the paralegal's role in mediation. Realize, however, that the mediation process may be voluntary or mandated by a court, and different states (and different courts within a state) may have different mediation procedures.

FEATURED GUEST, Continued

upon the parties by a court or other authority at almost the "eleventh hour" prior to trial—after both parties are fully prepared to present their respective cases to the court.

Paralegals play an important role during the premediation stage by investigating the factual background of the dispute, organizing the results of all preliminary investigations and other data relevant to the dispute, contacting the parties, and generally managing the case.

Stage Two: Selecting Mediation. Certain factors should be considered in reviewing the available tools (including litigation) for conflict resolution. If the disputing parties have a continuing relationship—as business partners, for example—court-imposed decisions may alienate the parties and intensify the conflict. Also, having the conflict resolved by a court can be costly and time consuming.

Generally, mediation can be arranged to meet the scheduling demands of the parties and is far less costly than litigation. Furthermore, because the mediator does not impose the decision, the parties control how the agreement is shaped. Unlike litigation, mediation is not adversarial in nature; rather, it seeks to find common grounds on which an agreement can be based. Therefore, the process tends to reduce the antagonism between the disputants and to allow them to resume their former relationship more easily.

The paralegal's role during this preliminary stage is to develop a clear understanding of the client's

needs and interests so that the attorney can better assess whether mediation would be a desirable alternative for resolving the dispute. The paralegal can also provide the attorney with a list of pre-screened, qualified mediators. (Such lists can be obtained from numerous organizations, including the American Arbitration Association, the federal Mediation and Conciliation Service, local courts, and chambers of commerce.) The parties can then select the appropriate mediator for their dispute from this list. Depending on what person or organization will be mediating the dispute, the paralegal may wish to obtain information on what kinds of procedures will be involved and secure any necessary forms.

Stage Three: Mediation Sessions. During the mediation sessions, the mediator allows both sides to present their views and spends time with the parties, either jointly or in private meetings with each party, to uncover the real interests and needs of the disputants. Sometimes, the parties may reach agreement after just one mediation session, but commonly several sessions are held so that the parties have the time and opportunity to obtain information on issues that need to be addressed. It may be necessary, for example, to obtain financial data relating to one or both of the parties. And, of course, several sessions may be required simply to reach a satisfactory agreement.

The paralegal can play a crucial role during this stage of the mediation process by helping to provide

> **"THE MEDIATOR NEVER IMPOSES A JUDGMENT BUT ACTS AS A FACILITATOR TO HELP THE PARTIES REACH THEIR OWN AGREEMENT."**

additional information for the sessions as they progress. The paralegal can also help in the drafting of any preliminary responses that are required during the course of the mediation. The paralegal may also draft the final agreement—unless that duty is assumed by the mediator.

CONCLUSION

Mediation can be useful at many stages of a dispute between parties. Mediation may help to resolve the entire dispute or just one aspect of it. Case management within the legal office is as important for the cases that are to be mediated as it is for the cases that will be tried in court. The paralegal can play a significant role in overall case management by doing the following:

1. Maintaining good methods of tracking and organizing data during the premediation stage.
2. Assisting the parties in selecting an appropriate mediator.
3. Providing necessary data and information during mediation sessions.

ARBITRATION CLAUSE
A clause in a contract that provides that, in case of a dispute, the parties will determine their rights by arbitration rather than through the judicial system.

AMERICAN ARBITRATION ASSOCIATION (AAA)
The major organization offering arbitration services in the United States.

SUMMARY JURY TRIAL (SJT)
A relatively recent method of settling disputes in which a trial is held but the jury's verdict is not binding. The verdict only acts as a guide to both sides in reaching an agreement during the mandatory negotiations that immediately follow the trial. If a settlement is not reached, both sides have the right to a full trial later.

MINI-TRIAL
A private proceeding that assists disputing parties in determining whether to take their case to court. During the proceeding, each party's attorney briefly argues the party's case before the other party and (usually) a neutral third party, who acts as an adviser. If the parties fail to reach an agreement, the adviser renders an opinion as to how a court would likely decide the issue.

so. In arbitration, the third party hearing the dispute normally makes the decision for the parties. In a sense, the arbitrator becomes a private judge, even though the arbitrator does not have to be a lawyer. Frequently, a panel of experts arbitrates the dispute. Frequently, disputes are arbitrated because of an **arbitration clause** in a contract.

Depending on the parties' circumstances and preferences, the arbitrator's decision may be legally binding or nonbinding on the parties. In nonbinding arbitration, the parties submit their dispute to a third party but remain free to reject the third party's decision. Nonbinding arbitration is more similar to mediation than to binding arbitration. As will be discussed shortly, arbitration that is mandated by the courts is often not binding on the parties. If, after mandatory arbitration, the parties are not satisfied with the results of arbitration, they may then ignore the arbitrator's decision and have the dispute litigated in court. Even if the arbitrator's decision is legally binding, a party can appeal the decision to a court for judicial review.

Arbitration services are provided by both government agencies and private organizations. The primary provider of arbitration services is the **American Arbitration Association (AAA)**. Most of the largest law firms in the nation are members of this association. Founded in 1926, the AAA now settles more than fifty thousand disputes a year in its numerous offices around the country. Settlements usually are effected quickly and, at times, in informal settings, such as a conference room or even a hotel room, depending on the preferences of the parties.

Cases brought before the AAA are heard by an expert or a panel of experts in the area relating to the dispute. Generally, about half of the panel members are lawyers. To cover its costs, the nonprofit organization charges a fee, paid by the party filing the claim. In addition, each party to the dispute pays a specified amount for each hearing day, as well as a special additional fee in cases involving personal injuries or property loss.

Other Forms of ADR

A relatively new form of ADR that has been successfully employed in the federal court system is the **summary jury trial (SJT)**. In an SJT, the parties present their arguments and supporting evidence (other than witness testimony—witnesses are not called in an SJT), and the jury then renders a verdict. Unlike in an actual trial, the jury's verdict is not binding. The verdict does, however, act as a guide to both sides in reaching an agreement during the mandatory negotiations that immediately follow the SJT. Because no witnesses are called, the SJT is much speedier than a regular trial, and frequently the parties are able to settle their dispute without resorting to an actual trial. If no settlement is reached, both sides have the right to a full trial later. Because they have proved to be a cost-effective and efficient way to settle disputes, SJTs are now held in numerous federal courts.

Another fairly recent development in the area of ADR is the use of mini-trials. Unlike court-sponsored SJTs, **mini-trials** are private proceedings. Typically, mini-trials are undertaken by business firms involved in contractual or other types of disputes to resolve disputes outside the court system. In a mini-trial, each party's attorney briefly argues the party's case before representatives of each firm who have the authority to settle the dispute. Often, a neutral third party, such as a retired judge, presides over the proceedings and acts as an adviser. If the parties fail to reach an agreement, the adviser renders an opinion as to how a court would likely decide the issue. The advantage of the mini-trial is similar to that of the SJT: it allows the parties to assess the relative strengths and weaknesses of their cases before an actual trial is held.

Other alternatives to traditional court proceedings include private "rent-a-judge" courts. This option first became available in 1976 in California, when that state's legislature enacted a statute that allowed disputing parties to bypass the formal court system by hiring former judges of the California courts to hear their disputes. The California statute provided that jurors could be selected from the public jury roll, and verdicts could be appealed to a state appellate court. The system of "private justice" spread quickly, and now hundreds of firms throughout the country offer dispute-resolution services by hired judges. Two of the leading firms in this legal industry, Endispute of Washington, D.C., and Judicial Arbitration and Mediation Services of California, have recently merged and now offer dispute-resolution services throughout the country.

Mandatory ADR

Up to this point, we have been discussing ADR that is undertaken by the parties *voluntarily*. Increasingly, the courts are *requiring* that parties attempt to settle their differences through some form of ADR before proceeding to trial. Usually, the claims involved must fall under a certain threshold amount. Since 1984, federal courts in several districts have been experimenting with court-sponsored, nonbinding arbitration for cases involving up to $100,000. Because of the success of this program (less than 10 percent of the cases referred for arbitration go to trial), federal courts continue to use this method. State courts are also increasingly turning to ADR programs as a means of relieving their burgeoning case loads. Many states now require that certain types of disputes, such as child-custody disputes, be mediated.

In the federal courts and in many state courts, when cases are referred for arbitration, the arbitrator's decision is not binding. If either party rejects the award, the case proceeds to trial, and the court reconsiders all of the evidence and legal questions pertaining to the dispute. To encourage parties to accept decisions reached through ADR as final, courts frequently make those who resort to litigation following ADR pay for the costs of the court proceedings.

ADR and the Paralegal

The time and money costs associated with litigating disputes in court continue to rise, and, as a result, disputing parties are increasingly turning to ADR as a means of settling their disputes. As a way to reduce their case loads, state and federal courts are also increasingly requiring litigants to undergo arbitration prior to bringing their suits before the courts. Although paralegals have always assisted attorneys in work relating to the negotiation of out-of-court settlements for clients, they may play an even greater role in the future. Some paralegals are qualified mediators and directly assist parties

---

ETHICAL CONCERN
Potential Arbitration Problems

Many individuals and business firms prefer to arbitrate disputes rather than take them to court. For that reason, they often include arbitration clauses in their contracts. These clauses normally specify who or what organization will arbitrate the dispute and where the arbitration will take place. To safeguard a client's interests, when drafting and reviewing arbitration clauses in contracts, the careful paralegal will be alert to the possibility that those who arbitrate the dispute might not be totally neutral or that the designated place of arbitration is so geographically distant from the client's location that it may pose a great inconvenience and expense for the client should a dispute arise that needs to be arbitrated. The paralegal should call any such problems to his or her supervising attorney's attention. The attorney can then discuss the problem with the client and help the client negotiate an arbitration clause that is more favorable to the client's position.

TODAY'S PROFESSIONAL PARALEGAL

Arbitrating Commercial Contracts

Julia Lorenz has worked as a legal assistant for International Airlines (IA) for ten years. She works in the legal department on the staff of the general counsel. Her job has been to work with Jim Manning, senior attorney. This attorney is responsible for all of the corporation's contracts, including the following: major contracts with jet manufacturers for the purchase of aircraft, contracts with catering companies to supply food during flights, fuel contracts, employment and labor contracts, and many small contracts for the purchase and lease of equipment and supplies for the many airline offices and ticket counters.

REVIEWING PROPOSED CONTRACTS

Julia's job is to review the provisions of proposed major contracts, such as the contracts to purchase jet aircraft, and to provide Jim with an article-by-article summary of the contracts' provisions. Jim then negotiates these contracts to obtain the most favorable terms possible for the airline. Once he has negotiated a contract, Julia makes the final changes and forwards it to the appropriate IA corporate official to review and sign.

ATTENDING ARBITRATION PROCEEDINGS

All of the airline's major contracts contain arbitration clauses that require all contract disputes to be resolved through binding arbitration services provided by the American Arbitration Association (AAA). On numerous occasions, Julia has attended arbitration proceedings with Jim. In preparing for arbitration, Julia obtains affidavits, prepares subpoenas, and arranges for witnesses to be present to testify. During the arbitration proceedings, she assists in presenting material into evidence. She and Jim have developed a good rapport with several arbitrators at the local AAA office, and they usually request these arbitrators when they have a case that must be arbitrated.

BECOMING AN ARBITRATOR

Julia's knowledge of arbitration procedures and her outstanding work in preparing for arbitration, as well as during the proceedings, won her significant recognition from this group of arbitrators. One of the arbitrators eventually approached Julia and suggested that she apply for approval as an arbitrator. She said that she would consider it.

Julia later mentioned the arbitrator's suggestion to Jim. He thought that Julia had been paid quite a compliment. He encouraged her to contact the AAA to inquire about the possibility of being approved as an arbitrator. When Julia called the AAA, she learned that arbitrators in the area of commercial arbitration are not required to be attorneys. She would need eight years of experience in her field and would have to meet certain educational requirements. When Julia realized that she had the necessary qualifications, she submitted an application. About two months later, she was approved as an arbitrator.

in reaching a mutually satisfactory agreement. Some paralegals serve as arbitrators. As more and more parties utilize ADR, paralegals will have increasing opportunities in this area of legal work.

KEY TERMS AND CONCEPTS

Chapter Summary

1. Law has been defined variously over the ages, yet all definitions of law rest on the following assumption about the nature of law: law consists of a body of rules of conduct with legal force and effect, prescribed by the controlling authority (the government) of a society.

2. A major source of American law is the common law, which originated in medieval England and was established in America during the colonial era. A cornerstone of the common law tradition is the doctrine of *stare decisis*, which means "to stand on decided cases." Under this doctrine, judges are bound by precedents, or previous court decisions, in their jurisdictions. Today, the common law governs all areas that are not covered by statutory law.

3. Other important sources of American law are constitutional law (the law established by the U.S. Constitution and the constitutions of the various states), statutory law (statutes enacted by the U.S. Congress and state legislatures and ordinances passed by local governing bodies), and administrative law (the rules and regulations issued and enforced by administrative agencies at both the state and federal levels).

4. Before a court can hear a case, the court must have jurisdiction over the person against whom the suit is brought or over the property involved in the suit. It must also have jurisdiction over the subject matter of the dispute. Courts of general jurisdiction can hear most types of disputes. Courts of limited jurisdiction are restricted in the types of actions they can decide. Courts having original jurisdiction are courts in which the trial of a case begins. Courts having appellate jurisdiction are reviewing courts. They do not try cases anew but review the decisions of trial courts.

5. Federal courts can exercise jurisdiction over claims involving (1) a federal question, which arises when the plaintiff's claim is based at least in part on the U.S. Constitution, a treaty, or a federal law; or (2) diversity of citizenship, which arises when the case involves citizens of different states, a foreign country and citizens of a state or different states, or citizens of a state and citizens or subjects of a foreign country. The amount in controversy must exceed $50,000 for jurisdiction based on diversity of citizenship to arise.

6. Venue has to do with the appropriate geographical area in which a case should be brought. The concept of venue reflects the policy that a court trying a suit should be in the geographic neighborhood (usually the county) in which the incident leading to the suit occurred or in which the parties involved in the suit reside.

7. The structure of state court systems varies from state to state. A typical state court system may consist of several tiers. On the bottom tier are courts of limited jurisdiction. On the next tier are usually the trial courts of general jurisdiction. Trial courts are courts of original jurisdiction—in other words, courts in which lawsuits are initiated, trials are held, and evidence is presented. The upper tier consists of appellate courts, to which trial court decisions can be appealed. Appellate courts are reviewing courts; their function is to review the trial court's decision in cases that are appealed. The highest state appellate court is typically called the state supreme court, although there are exceptions. Cases can be appealed from state supreme courts to the United States Supreme Court only if a federal question is involved.

8. The federal court system consists of U.S. district courts (trial courts), U.S. courts of appeals (intermediate appellate courts), and the United States Supreme Court. Decisions from a district court can be appealed to the court of appeals of the circuit (geographical area) in which the district court is located. There are thirteen circuit courts of appeals. Decisions rendered by these circuit courts may be appealed to the United States Supreme Court.

9. The United States Supreme Court is the highest court in the land. There is no absolute right of appeal to the Supreme Court, and the Court hears only a fraction of the cases that are filed with it each year. If the Court decides to review a case, it will issue a writ of *certiorari*, which is an order by the Supreme Court to a lower court requiring the latter to send it the record of the case for review. Generally, only those petitions that raise the possibility of important constitutional questions are granted.

10. The costs and time-consuming character of litigation, as well as the public nature of court proceedings, have caused many to turn to various forms of alternative dispute resolution (ADR) for settling their disputes. Out-of-court settlements are reached in the majority of lawsuits, usually before the trial begins.

11. Negotiation, the simplest method of ADR, may or may not involve a third party; the parties to the dispute simply try to work out their problems to avoid going to court. Mediation is a form of ADR in which the parties attempt to reach agreement with the help of a neutral third party, called a mediator (or a panel of mediators), who helps the disputants explore alternative possibilities for settling their differences as amicably as possible. The mediator proposes various solutions for the parties to consider.

12. Arbitration is the most formal method of ADR. In arbitration, a neutral third party (a lawyer, expert, panel of specialists, or other party) renders a decision after the parties present their cases and evidence in a hearing. Normally, in voluntary arbitration (as opposed to court-mandated ADR), the parties agree at the outset to be legally bound by the arbitrator's decision.

13. Other forms of ADR include summary jury trials and mini-trials. In a summary jury trial, the parties present their arguments and evidence to a jury, and the jury renders a verdict. The verdict is not legally binding but serves to guide the parties in reaching an agreement on the disputed matter. Mini-trials are private proceedings in which each party's attorney briefly argues the party's case before the other party. Often, a neutral third party, who acts as an adviser, is also present. If the parties fail to reach an agreement, the adviser renders an opinion as to how a court would likely decide the issue. "Rent-a-judge" courts have also become an attractive ADR option for many people. In these private courts, former judges are hired to hear disputes and render decisions.

14. To ease their heavy case loads, numerous state and federal courts today require that certain disputes (under a certain dollar threshold, for example) be mediated or arbitrated before they can be heard in court. If a party is not satisfied with the results of mediation or arbitration, however, that party can take the issue to court.

QUESTIONS FOR REVIEW

1. What is law? Why are there so many definitions of law?

2. Where, when, and how did the common law tradition begin? What does *stare decisis* mean? Why is it said that the doctrine of *stare decisis* became the cornerstone of English and American law?

3. What is constitutional law? If a state constitution conflicts with the U.S. Constitution, which constitution takes priority?

4. What is a statute? How is statutory law created? How does the enactment of statutes affect the common law?

5. What is an administrative agency? How are such agencies created?

6. Define *jurisdiction* and explain why jurisdiction is important. What is the difference between venue and jurisdiction?

7. Over what types of cases may federal courts exercise jurisdiction? What is the relationship between state and federal jurisdiction?

8. Describe the functions of a trial court. How do they differ from the functions of an appellate court?

9. What are the typical courts in a state court system? What are the three basic tiers, or levels, of courts in the federal court system? How do cases reach the United States Supreme Court?

10. List and explain the various methods of alternative dispute resolution.

ETHICAL QUESTIONS

1. Larry Simpson is working on a lawsuit that was recently filed in a federal district court on the basis of diversity-of-citizenship jurisdiction. Larry, a legal assistant, just received the plaintiff's answers to interrogatories (attorneys' written questions to the parties in a lawsuit), which he is summarizing. Larry discovers that the plaintiff's damages are nowhere near the $50,000 required for diversity jurisdiction. What should Larry do?

2. Suzanne Andersen's supervising attorney, Amy Lynch, works occasionally as a mediator for family-law cases in the local courts. Amy has mediated a case today involving custody and visitation rights for a wealthy businessperson, who happens also to be a defendant in another lawsuit in which Amy represents the plaintiff. As a result of her mediation today, Amy has learned some confidential financial information about this man. She now has come to Suzanne, her paralegal, and asked her to use this information to his disadvantage in the lawsuit. How should Suzanne handle this situation?

PRACTICE QUESTIONS AND ASSIGNMENTS

1. Look at the Constitution in Appendix H of this text. Locate the language in the Bill of Rights that gives U.S. citizens the following rights and protections:

    a. The right to freely exercise one's religion.
    b. Protection against unreasonable searches and seizures.
    c. Protection against self-incrimination.
    d. The right to counsel in criminal prosecutions.
    e. The right to free speech.

2. Look at Exhibit 5.3. In which federal circuit is your state located? How many federal judicial districts are located in your state?

3. Based on the information provided in this chapter, including the exhibits, determine which federal court (or courts) could hear the following cases and on what jurisdictional grounds:

    a. A case in which the Internal Revenue Service sues a taxpayer for back taxes.
    b. A case involving an automobile accident between a citizen of Chicago, Illinois, and a citizen of St. Louis, Missouri, in which the plaintiff seeks damages of $100,000.
    c. A bankruptcy case.
    d. A lawsuit claiming sexual harassment in violation of Title VII of the federal Civil Rights Act of 1964.
    e. A lawsuit claiming that the defendant violated the federal statute prohibiting racketeering crimes.

6

THE CIVIL
LITIGATION PROCESS

CHAPTER OBJECTIVES

After completing this chapter, you will know:

• The basic steps involved in the civil litigation process and the types of tasks that may be required of paralegals during each step of the process.
• How a lawsuit is initiated and what documents are filed during the pleadings stage of the civil litigation process.
• What discovery is and the kind of information that attorneys and their paralegals obtain from parties to the lawsuit and witnesses when preparing for trial.
• How attorneys prepare for trial and the ways in which paralegals assist in this task.
• The various phases of a trial and the kinds of trial-related tasks that paralegals often perform.
• The options available to the losing party after the verdict is in.

CHAPTER OUTLINE

INTRODUCTION

The paralegal plays a particularly important role in helping the trial attorney prepare for and conduct a civil trial. Popular television shows and movies tend to glamorize courtroom trials as semantic battles between quick-witted litigators, but the success of any trial depends primarily on how well the attorney and the paralegal have prepared for it.

Preparation for trial involves a variety of tasks. The law relating to the client's case must be carefully researched. Evidence must be gathered and documented. The litigation file must be created and carefully organized. Procedural requirements and deadlines for filing certain documents with the court must be met. **Witnesses**—persons who are asked to testify at trial—must be prepared in advance and must be available to testify at the appropriate time during the trial. Any exhibits, such as charts, photographs, or videotapes, to be used at the trial must be properly prepared, mounted, or filmed. Arrangements must be made to have any necessary equipment, such as a slide projector, a VCR, videodisc, or a CD-ROM player, available for use at the trial. The paralegal's efforts are of critical importance in preparing for trial, and attorneys usually rely on paralegals to ensure that nothing has been overlooked during trial preparation.

WITNESS
A person who is asked to testify under oath at a trial.

Attorneys may request that their paralegals assist them during the trial also. In the courtroom, the paralegal can perform numerous tasks. For example, the paralegal can locate documents or exhibits as they are needed. The paralegal can also observe jurors' reactions to statements made by attorneys or witnesses, check to see if a witness's testimony is consistent with sworn statements made by the witness before the trial, and perhaps give witnesses some last-minute instructions outside the courtroom before they are called to testify.

The complexity of even the simplest civil trial requires that the paralegal have some familiarity with the litigation process and the applicable courtroom procedures. Much litigation expertise, of course, can only be acquired through hands-on experience. Yet every paralegal should be acquainted with the basic phases of civil litigation and the forms and terminology commonly used in the process. In this chapter, you will learn about the stages of a civil lawsuit and the ways in which paralegals assist attorneys in the litigation process.

CIVIL LITIGATION—AN OVERVIEW

Although civil trials may vary greatly in terms of complexity, cost, and detail, they all share similar structural characteristics. They begin with an event that gives rise to the legal action, and (provided the case is not settled by the parties at some point during the litigation process—as most cases are) they end with the issuance of a **judgment**, the court's decision on the matter. In the interim, the litigation itself may involve all sorts of twists and turns. Even though each case has its own "story line," most civil lawsuits follow some version of the course charted in Exhibit 6.1.

JUDGMENT
The court's final decision regarding the rights and claims of the parties to a lawsuit.

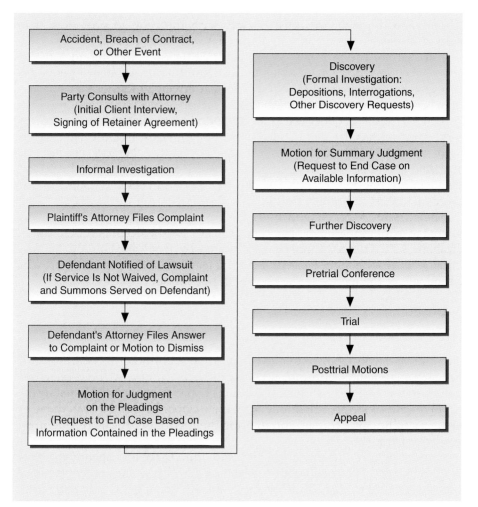

EXHIBIT 6.1
A Typical Case Flow Chart

Understanding and meeting procedural requirements is essential in the litigation process. These requirements are spelled out in the procedural rules of the court in which a lawsuit is brought. All civil trials held in federal district courts are governed by the **Federal Rules of Civil Procedure (FRCP)**.[1] These rules specify what must be done during the various stages of the federal civil litigation process. For example, FRCP 4 (Rule 4 of the FRCP) describes the procedures that must be followed in notifying the defendant of the lawsuit. Each state also has its own rules of civil procedure (which in many states are similar to the FRCP).[2] In addition, many courts have their own local rules of procedures that supplement the federal or state rules. The

FEDERAL RULES OF CIVIL PROCEDURE (FRCP)
The rules controlling all procedural matters in civil trials brought before the federal district courts.

---

1. Some practitioners use the abbreviation FRCivP to distinguish the Federal Rules of Civil Procedure from the Federal Rules of Criminal Procedure.
2. The 1993 revision of the FRCP substantially changed the rules governing some of the topics discussed in this chapter, and it is uncertain at this time whether state courts will adopt similar changes in their procedural rules. In the meantime, the revised FRCP may vary significantly from state rules, as will be discussed later in this chapter.

attorney and the paralegal must comply with the rules of procedure that apply to the specific court in which the trial will take place.

To illustrate the procedures involved in litigation, we present a hypothetical civil lawsuit. The case involves an automobile accident in which a car driven by Tony Peretto collided with a car driven by Katherine Baranski. Baranski suffered numerous injuries and incurred substantial medical and hospital costs. She also lost wages for the five months that she was unable to work. Baranski has decided to sue Peretto for damages. Because Baranski is the person initiating the lawsuit, she is the plaintiff. Peretto, because he must defend against Baranski's claims, is the defendant. The plaintiff and the defendant are referred to as the *parties* to the lawsuit. (Some cases involve several plaintiffs and/or defendants.)

The attorney for the plaintiff (Baranski) is Allen P. Gilmore. Gilmore is assisted by paralegal Elena Lopez. The attorney for the defendant (Peretto) is Elizabeth A. Cameron. Cameron is assisted by paralegal Gordon McVay. Throughout this chapter, *Case at a Glance* features in the page margins will remind you of the names of the players in this lawsuit.

CASE AT A GLANCE

The Plaintiff—
   Plaintiff: Katherine Baranski
   Attorney: Allen P. Gilmore
   Paralegal: Elena Lopez

The Defendant—
   Defendant: Tony Peretto
   Attorney: Elizabeth A.
      Cameron
   Paralegal: Gordon McVay

THE PRELIMINARIES

Katherine Baranski arranges to meet with Allen P. Gilmore, an attorney with the law firm of Jeffers, Gilmore & Dunn, to see if Gilmore will represent her in the lawsuit. Gilmore asks paralegal Elena Lopez to prepare the usual forms and information sheets, including a retainer agreement and a statement of the firm's billing procedures, and to bring them with her to the initial interview with Baranski.

During the initial client interview, Katherine Baranski explains to attorney Gilmore and paralegal Lopez the facts of her case as she perceives them. Baranski tells them that Tony Peretto, who was driving a Dodge van, ran a stop sign and crashed into the driver's side of her Ford Tempo as she was driving through the intersection of Mattis Avenue and Thirty-eighth Street in Nita City, Nita. The accident occurred at 7:45 A.M. on August 4, 1995. Baranski has misplaced Peretto's address, but she knows that he lives in another state, the state of Zero.[3] Baranski claims that as a result of the accident, she has been unable to work for five months and has lost approximately $15,000 in wages. Her medical and hospital expenses total $85,000, and the property damage to her car is estimated to be $10,000.

Gilmore agrees to represent Baranski in the lawsuit against Peretto. He explains the fee structure to Baranski, and she signs the retainer agreement.[4] He also has Baranski sign forms authorizing Gilmore to obtain relevant medical, employment, and other records relating to the claim. (These forms, which are called *release forms,* will be discussed in Chapter 7.) At the end of the interview, Gilmore also asks Lopez to schedule a follow-up interview with Baranski to obtain more details about the accident and its consequences.

---

3. Nita and Zero are fictitious states invented for the purpose of this hypothetical.
4. See Chapter 4 for a discussion of legal fees and retainer agreements.

After Baranski leaves the office, attorney Gilmore asks Lopez to undertake a preliminary investigation to glean as much information as possible concerning the factual circumstances of Baranski's accident. You will read in Chapter 7 about the steps that a paralegal, such as Lopez, can take when investigating the facts of a client's case, and therefore we will not discuss investigation here. Additionally, attorney Gilmore asks Lopez to create a litigation file for the case (see Chapter 4).

THE PLEADINGS

The next step will be for attorney Gilmore to file a complaint in the appropriate court. The **complaint**[5] is a document that states the claims the plaintiff is making against the defendant. The complaint also contains a statement regarding the court's jurisdiction over the dispute and a demand for a remedy (such as money damages).

The filing of the complaint is the initial step that begins the legal action against the defendant, Peretto. The plaintiff's complaint and the defendant's answer—both of which are discussed below—are **pleadings**. The pleadings inform each party of the claims of the other and specify the issues (disputed questions) involved in the case. We examine here the complaint and answer, two basic pleadings. Exhibit 6.2 on page 175 includes other types of pleadings that, under the FRCP, may also be filed with the court during this stage of the litigation.

Drafting the Complaint

The complaint itself may be no more than a few paragraphs long, or it may be many pages in length, depending on the complexity of the case. In the Baranski case, the complaint will probably be only a few pages long unless special circumstances justify additional details. The complaint will include the following sections, each of which we discuss below:

- Caption.
- Jurisdictional allegations.
- General allegations (the body of the complaint).
- Prayer for relief.
- Signature.
- Demand for a jury trial.

Exhibit 6.3 on pages 176 and 177 shows a sample complaint. The sections of the complaint are indicated in the marginal annotations.

Baranski's case is being filed in a federal court, so the Federal Rules of Civil Procedure (FRCP) apply. If Baranski's case were filed in a state court, paralegal Lopez might need to review the appropriate state rules of civil procedure. The rules for drafting pleadings in state courts differ from the FRCP. The rules also differ from state to state and even from court to court within the same state. Lopez could obtain pleading forms, either from "form books" available in the law firm's files or library (or on computer) or from pleadings

COMPLAINT
The pleading made by a plaintiff or a charge made by the state alleging wrongdoing on the part of the defendant.

PLEADINGS
Statements by the plaintiff and the defendant that detail the facts, charges, and defenses involved in the litigation.

> ### CASE AT A GLANCE
>
> **The Plaintiff—**
> Plaintiff: Katherine Baranski
> Attorney: Allen P. Gilmore
> Paralegal: Elena Lopez
>
> **The Defendant—**
> Defendant: Tony Peretto
> Attorney: Elizabeth A. Cameron
> Paralegal: Gordon McVay

---

5. In state courts, this document may be called a *petition*.

DEVELOPING PARALEGAL SKILLS

File Work-up

 Once a litigation file has been created, the paralegal typically "works up" the file. In the Baranski case, after paralegal Lopez has completed her initial investigation into Baranski's claim, she will review and summarize the information that she has gathered so far, including the information obtained during the initial client interview, during any subsequent client interviews, and through any research and investigation that she has conducted.

Lopez will also identify areas that might require the testimony of an expert witness. For example, if Baranski broke her hip in the accident and her doctor told her that she would always walk with a limp, Gilmore will probably want to have a medical specialist in this area give expert testimony to support Baranski's claim. Lopez will therefore prepare a list of potential expert witnesses to submit to Gilmore for his review. (How to locate expert witnesses will be discussed in Chapter 7.)

Once Lopez has worked up the file, she will write a memo to her supervising attorney, Gilmore, that contains the following:

• A summary of what information has been obtained about Baranski's case up to this point.
• A plan for further investigation into the matter (you will read about investigation plans in Chapter 7).
• Suggestions as to what further information might be obtained during discovery (discussed later in the chapter).
• A list of expert witnesses whom they might contact to give expert testimony on Baranski's claim. (Lopez might also make recommendations as to which of the expert witnesses would be preferable and why.)

This memo will provide Gilmore with a basis for his decision regarding what legal remedy or strategy should be pursued, what legal issues need to be researched, and generally how to proceed with the case.

---

drafted previously in similar cases litigated by the firm in the court in which the Baranski case will be filed.

The Caption.   All documents submitted to the court or other parties during the litigation process begin with a caption. The caption of the complaint identifies the court in which the action is being filed, the names of the parties, and the designation of the document as a "Complaint." The caption leaves a space for the court to insert the name of the judge who will be hearing the case. The caption also leaves a space for the court to insert the file number, or case number, that it assigns to the case. (The court's file number may also be referred to as the *docket number*. A **docket** is the list of cases entered on a court's calendar and thus scheduled to be heard.) Exhibit 6.3 shows how the caption will read in the case of *Baranski v. Peretto*.

Jurisdictional Allegations.   Because attorney Gilmore is filing the lawsuit in a federal district court, he will have to include in the complaint an allegation

DOCKET
The list of cases entered on a court's calendar and thus scheduled to be heard by the court.

EXHIBIT 6.2
Types of Pleadings

Initial Pleadings

Complaint—Filed by the plaintiff to initiate the lawsuit.
Answer—Filed by the defendant in response to the plaintiff's complaint.

Counterclaim and Reply

Counterclaim—Filed by the defendant against the plaintiff, asserting a claim for an injury arising from the same incident that forms the basis for the plaintiff's claim. There are two types of counterclaims:

1. A *compulsory* counterclaim must be asserted if it arises out of the same transaction or event that gave rise to the plaintiff's complaint or the right to assert the claim will be waived (forgone). Example: Defendant Peretto claims that plaintiff Baranski's negligence caused him to suffer injuries for which he should be compensated.

2. A *permissive* counterclaim arises from a separate transaction than the one forming the basis for the original lawsuit. Example: Defendant Peretto claims that plaintiff Baranski, prior to the accident, had purchased a used Rolls-Royce from him, and Baranski's check bounced. If Peretto chooses not to raise this counterclaim, he would not be precluded from filing a separate suit against Baranski in the future to recover that debt because it arose from a completely separate incident.

Reply—Filed by the plaintiff in response to the defendant's counterclaim.

Cross-claim and Answer

Cross-claim—Filed by a defendant against another defendant or a plaintiff against another plaintiff. When cross-claims are made, the defendants are suing one another (or the plaintiffs are suing one another). Example: Assume that plaintiff Baranski had been struck by two vehicles, one belonging to defendant Peretto and one belonging to Leon Balfour. If Peretto and Balfour had been named as co-defendants in Baranski's complaint, then Peretto's attorney could also file a cross-claim on behalf of Peretto against Balfour.

Answer—Filed by the party against whom a cross-claim is brought.

Third Party Complaint and Answer

Third Party Complaint—Filed by the defendant (in response to the plaintiff's complaint) or by the plaintiff (in response to the defendant's counterclaim) to bring into the litigation a third party who could be liable. Example: Defendant Peretto files a third party complaint against the manufacturer of the van that he was driving. Peretto asserts that the manufacturer should be liable for Baranski's injuries because the van's brakes were defective and therefore Peretto was unable to stop at the stop sign.

Answer—Filed by the third party in response to the third party complaint.

that the federal court has jurisdiction to hear the dispute. (An **allegation** is an assertion, claim, or statement made by one party in a pleading that sets out what the party expects to prove to the court.) Recall from Chapter 5 that federal courts can exercise jurisdiction over certain types of disputes, including those based on *diversity of citizenship.* Diversity of citizenship exists when the parties involved in the lawsuit are citizens of different states and the amount in controversy exceeds $50,000. Because Baranski and Peretto are citizens of

ALLEGATION
A party's statement, claim, or assertion made in a pleading to the court. The allegation sets forth the issue that the party expects to prove.

EXHIBIT 6.3
The Complaint

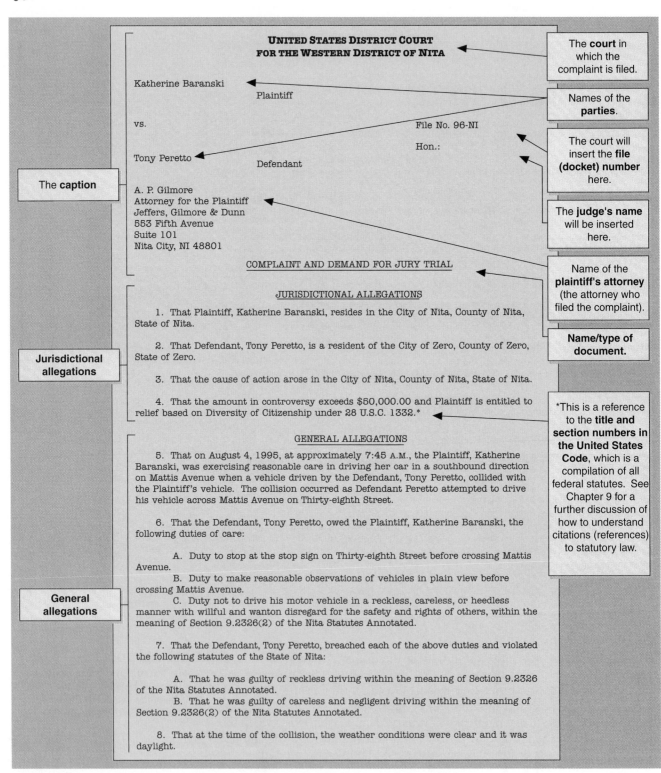

UNITED STATES DISTRICT COURT
FOR THE WESTERN DISTRICT OF NITA

The **court** in which the complaint is filed.

Katherine Baranski

Plaintiff

Names of the **parties**.

vs.

File No. 96-NI

Hon.:

The court will insert the **file (docket) number** here.

Tony Peretto

Defendant

The **caption**

A. P. Gilmore
Attorney for the Plaintiff
Jeffers, Gilmore & Dunn
553 Fifth Avenue
Suite 101
Nita City, NI 48801

The **judge's name** will be inserted here.

COMPLAINT AND DEMAND FOR JURY TRIAL

Name of the **plaintiff's attorney** (the attorney who filed the complaint).

JURISDICTIONAL ALLEGATIONS

1. That Plaintiff, Katherine Baranski, resides in the City of Nita, County of Nita, State of Nita.

Name/type of document.

2. That Defendant, Tony Peretto, is a resident of the City of Zero, County of Zero, State of Zero.

Jurisdictional allegations

3. That the cause of action arose in the City of Nita, County of Nita, State of Nita.

4. That the amount in controversy exceeds $50,000.00 and Plaintiff is entitled to relief based on Diversity of Citizenship under 28 U.S.C. 1332.*

*This is a reference to the **title and section numbers in the United States Code**, which is a compilation of all federal statutes. See Chapter 9 for a further discussion of how to understand citations (references) to statutory law.

GENERAL ALLEGATIONS

5. That on August 4, 1995, at approximately 7:45 A.M., the Plaintiff, Katherine Baranski, was exercising reasonable care in driving her car in a southbound direction on Mattis Avenue when a vehicle driven by the Defendant, Tony Peretto, collided with the Plaintiff's vehicle. The collision occurred as Defendant Peretto attempted to drive his vehicle across Mattis Avenue on Thirty-eighth Street.

6. That the Defendant, Tony Peretto, owed the Plaintiff, Katherine Baranski, the following duties of care:

    A. Duty to stop at the stop sign on Thirty-eighth Street before crossing Mattis Avenue.
    B. Duty to make reasonable observations of vehicles in plain view before crossing Mattis Avenue.
    C. Duty not to drive his motor vehicle in a reckless, careless, or heedless manner with willful and wanton disregard for the safety and rights of others, within the meaning of Section 9.2326(2) of the Nita Statutes Annotated.

General allegations

7. That the Defendant, Tony Peretto, breached each of the above duties and violated the following statutes of the State of Nita:

    A. That he was guilty of reckless driving within the meaning of Section 9.2326 of the Nita Statutes Annotated.
    B. That he was guilty of careless and negligent driving within the meaning of Section 9.2326(2) of the Nita Statutes Annotated.

8. That at the time of the collision, the weather conditions were clear and it was daylight.

9. That at the time of the collision, the Plaintiff, Katherine Baranski, was a generally healthy female, twenty-five years of age.

10. That as a result of the collision, the Plaintiff, Katherine Baranski, suffered severe physical injuries, which prevented her from working for five months, and property damage to her vehicle. The costs that the Plaintiff, Katherine Baranski, incurred as a result of the collision included $85,000 in medical bills, $15,000 in lost wages, and $10,000 in automobile-repair costs.

11. That the injuries sustained by the Plaintiff as a result of the collision were solely caused by the negligence of the Defendant, Tony Peretto.

WHEREFORE, the Plaintiff prays for the following relief:

The prayer for relief.

A. That the Plaintiff be awarded appropriate compensatory damages;
B. That the Plaintiff be awarded an amount deemed fair and just by a Jury to compensate the Plaintiff for damages sustained as presented by the evidence in this case;
C. That the Plaintiff be awarded such other further relief as the Court deems proper. Plaintiff Katherine Baranski claims judgment against the Defendant in an amount in excess of $50,000 in actual, compensatory, and exemplary damages together with attorneys' fees, court costs, and other costs as provided by law.

Date: 2/10/96

The signature of the plaintiff's attorney.

Jeffers, Gilmore & Dunn

Allen P. Gilmore

Allen P. Gilmore
Attorney for Plaintiff
553 Fifth Avenue
Suite 101
Nita City, NI 48801

Katherine Baranski, being first duly sworn, states that she has read the foregoing Complaint by her subscribed and that she knows the contents thereof, and the same is true, except those matters therein stated to be upon information and belief, and as to those matters, she believes to be true.

Katherine Baranski

Plaintiff

Affidavit (and plaintiff's signature).

Sworn and subscribed before me this 10th day of February, 1996,

Leela M Shay

Notary Public, Nita County, State of Nita

My Commission Expires:

March 10, 1999

DEMAND FOR A JURY TRIAL

The Plaintiff demands a trial by jury.

Demand for a jury trial.

Date: 2/10/96

Jeffers, Gilmore & Dunn

Allen P. Gilmore

Allen P. Gilmore
Attorney for the Plaintiff
553 Fifth Avenue
Suite 101
Nita City, Nita 48801

different states (Nita and Zero, respectively) and because the amount in controversy exceeds $50,000, the case meets the requirements for diversity-of-citizenship jurisdiction. Gilmore thus asserts that the federal court has jurisdiction on this basis, as illustrated in Exhibit 6.3.

General Allegations (the Body of the Complaint).   The body of the complaint contains a series of allegations, stated in numbered paragraphs. In plaintiff Baranski's complaint, the allegations outline the factual events that gave rise to Baranski's claims.[6] As Exhibit 6.3 shows, the numbers of the paragraphs in the body of the complaint continue the sequence begun in the section on jurisdictional allegations.

When drafting the complaint, paralegal Lopez will present the facts forcefully and in a way that supports the client's claim. Lopez must be careful, however, not to exaggerate the facts or make false statements. The most effective complaints are those that are clear and concise. Moreover, brevity and simplicity are required under FRCP 8(a). As in all legal writing, Lopez should strive for clarity.

What if her research into the case had given Lopez reason to believe that a fact was probably true even though she could not be certain as to its validity? She could still include the statement in the complaint by prefacing it with the phrase, "On information and belief. . . ." This language would indicate to the court that the plaintiff, Baranski, had good reason to believe the truth of the statement but that the evidence for it either had not yet been obtained or might not hold up under close scrutiny.

After telling plaintiff Baranski's story, paralegal Lopez will add one or more paragraphs outlining the harms suffered by the plaintiff and the remedy (in money damages) that the plaintiff seeks.

Prayer for Relief and Signature.   Paralegal Lopez will include at the end of the complaint a paragraph, similar to that shown in Exhibit 6.3, asking that judgment be entered for the plaintiff and appropriate relief be granted. This "prayer for relief" will indicate that plaintiff Baranski is seeking money damages to compensate her for the harms that she suffered. In federal practice, the signature following the prayer for relief certifies that the plaintiff's attorney (or the plaintiff, if he or she is not represented by an attorney) has read the complaint and that the facts alleged are true to the best of his or her knowledge. In addition to the attorney's signature, some courts require an affidavit signed by the plaintiff verifying that the complaint is true to the best of the plaintiff's knowledge. **Affidavits** are sworn statements attesting to the existence of certain facts. They are acknowledged by a notary public or another official authorized to administer such oaths or affirmations. Exhibit 6.3 illustrates an affidavit for the Baranski complaint.

AFFIDAVIT
A written statement of facts, confirmed by the oath or affirmation of the party making it and made before a person having the authority to administer the oath or affirmation.

---

6. The body of the complaint described in this section is a *fact pleading,* in which sufficient factual circumstances must be alleged to convince the court that the plaintiff has a cause of action. State courts often require fact pleadings, whereas federal courts only require *notice pleading.* FRCP 8(a) requires only that the complaint have "a short and plain statement of the claim showing that the pleader is entitled to relief." Fact pleading and notice pleading are not totally different—that is, the same allegation of facts could be in the body of a complaint submitted to either a federal or a state court. Federal courts simply have fewer requirements in this respect, and therefore they are often more attractive to litigants.

Demand for a Jury Trial.   The Seventh Amendment to the U.S. Constitution guarantees the right to a jury trial in federal courts in all "suits at common law" when the amount in controversy exceeds $20. Most states have similar guarantees in their own constitutions, although many states put a higher minimum dollar restriction on the guarantee (for example, in Iowa the minimum amount is $1,000). If this threshold requirement is met, either party may request a jury trial. The right to a trial by jury does not have to be exercised, and many cases are tried without one. If plaintiff Baranski wants a jury trial, Gilmore will ask his paralegal, Lopez, to include a demand for jury trial (similar to the one illustrated in Exhibit 6.3) with the complaint.

Filing the Complaint

Once the complaint has been prepared, carefully checked for accuracy, and signed by attorney Gilmore, paralegal Lopez will file the complaint with the court in which the action is being brought. To file the complaint, Lopez will deliver it to the clerk of the court, together with a check payable to the court in the amount of the required filing fee. (If Lopez is not aware of the court's specific procedures for filing the complaint, she should call the court clerk to verify the amount of the filing fee and how many copies of the complaint need to be filed.) The court clerk files the complaint by stamping the date on the document; assigning the case a file number, or docket number; and assigning the case to a particular judge. (In state courts, the file number may not be assigned until later.)

Although the complaint is normally delivered personally to the court clerk, the 1993 revision of Rule 5(a) of the FRCP provides that federal courts may permit filing by fax (facsimile) or "other electronic means." In the future, filing court documents electronically will likely become a more common method of filing.

After the complaint has been filed, the court will consult with the attorneys for both sides, often through a **scheduling conference**. Following this meeting, the judge will enter a *scheduling order* that sets out the time limits within which pretrial events (such as the pleadings, discovery, and the final pretrial conference) must be completed and the date of the trial. Under FRCP 16(b), the scheduling order should be entered "as soon as practicable and in no event more than 120 days after the complaint is filed."

SCHEDULING CONFERENCE
A meeting (conducted shortly after a plaintiff's complaint is filed) attended by the judge and the attorneys for both parties to the lawsuit. Following the conference, the judge issues a scheduling order for the pretrial events and the trial date.

Service of Process

Before the court can exercise jurisdiction over the defendant—in effect, before the lawsuit can begin—the court must have proof that the defendant was notified of the lawsuit. If defendant Peretto did not agree to *waive* service of process (waiver of service will be discussed below) or if the case against Peretto had been filed in a state court, Peretto would be served with a summons. Serving the summons and complaint—that is, the delivery of these documents to the defendant in a lawsuit—is referred to as **service of process**.

The Summons.   The **summons** identifies the parties to the lawsuit, as well as the court in which the case will be heard, and directs the defendant to

SERVICE OF PROCESS
The delivery of the summons and the complaint to a defendant.

SUMMONS
A document served on a defendant in a lawsuit informing a defendant that a legal action has been commenced against the defendant and that the defendant must appear in court on a certain date to answer the plaintiff's complaint.

DEVELOPING PARALEGAL SKILLS

Federal Court Rules—
Creating a Complaint Checklist

 Ann Marsdon, a paralegal, has been assigned the task of preparing a checklist for drafting complaints to be filed in federal court. The checklist will be used by the other paralegals and lawyers in her medium-sized law firm. She will base her checklist on Rules 8, 10, and 11 of the Federal Rules of Civil Procedure (FRCP), which specify the kind of information that should be included in complaints filed in federal courts.

COMPLAINT CHECKLIST

Ann begins her task by making a list of all the things that she does before she sits down to draft a complaint:

• Get the file and review my notes and memos from the client interview or use whatever notes are in the file.
• Check the date on which the injury or other action that harmed the plaintiff occurred and find out when the statute of limitations expires.
• Review any reports—such as police reports, insurance investigators' reports, or other similar documents—in the file. This information is necessary to describe how and when the injury occurred.
• Find out the plaintiff's and the defendant's correct legal names. Contact the secretary of state to obtain the legal name of a defendant corporation.
• Look for notes that may indicate in which court the complaint will be filed. If that information is not included, discuss the issue with the attorney.
• Obtain the appropriate complaint form for the type of case involved from either the forms file or a forms book.
• Review the court rules of the court in which the complaint will be filed to ensure that we comply with that court's requirements for the complaint.

REVIEWING THE RULES

Ann pulls a copy of the FRCP off her bookshelf to review the complaint requirements. She reads through Rule 8, which tells her that a complaint has to contain a statement showing that the court has jurisdiction over the case, another statement showing that the plaintiff is entitled to the damages or other relief for which he or she is asking, and a demand for a judgment for that relief. Ann then looks at Rule 10, which outlines the format for a complaint.

Rule 11 says that the complaint must be signed by an attorney, if the plaintiff is represented by one. This is interesting, thinks Ann. It says here that the attorney's signature means that the attorney has read the complaint and that to the best of the attorney's "knowledge, information and belief, formed after an inquiry reasonable under the circumstances," the allegations (claims, or contentions) of fact can be supported by evidence, are warranted by existing law, and are not being used for an improper purpose, such as to harass or delay. If a complaint is signed in violation of these rules, sanctions may be imposed. After reading through Rule 11, Ann continues drafting her checklist and includes in it the requirements for a complaint under the FRCP.

respond to the complaint within a specified period of time. In the Baranski case, paralegal Lopez, will prepare a summons by filling out a form similar to that shown in Exhibit 6.4 on the following page.

If the case were being brought in a state court, paralegal Lopez would deliver the summons to the court clerk at the same time she delivered the complaint. (In federal court cases, as will be discussed below, the complaint may already have been filed under the new FRCP provisions relating to waiver of notice.) After the clerk files the complaint and signs, seals, and issues the summons, attorney Gilmore will be responsible for making sure that the documents are served on defendant Peretto. The service of the complaint and summons must be effected within a specified time—120 days under FRCP 4(m)—after the complaint has been filed.

Serving the Complaint and Summons.   How service of process occurs depends on the rules of the court or jurisdiction in which the lawsuit is brought. Under FRCP 4(c)(2), service of process in federal court cases may be effected "by any person who is not a party and who is at least 18 years of age." Paralegal Lopez, for example, could serve the summons by personally delivering it to defendant Peretto or leaving it at his home or with someone living in his home. Alternatively, she could make arrangements for someone else to do so, subject to the approval of attorney Gilmore. In some types of cases, Gilmore might request that the court have a U.S. marshal or other federal official serve the summons.

Under FRCP 4(e)(1), service of process in federal court cases may also be effected "pursuant to the law of the state in which the district court is located." Many state courts require that the complaint and summons be served by a public officer, such as a sheriff.

Regardless of how the summons is served, attorney Gilmore will need some kind of proof that defendant Peretto actually received the summons. In federal court cases, unless service is made by a U.S. marshal or other official, proof of service can be established by having the process server fill out and sign a form similar to the **return-of-service form** shown in Exhibit 6.5 on page 183. This form can then be submitted to the court as evidence that service has been effected.

RETURN-OF-SERVICE FORM
A document signed by a process server and submitted to the court to prove that a defendant received a summons.

Paralegal Lopez must be very careful to comply with the service requirements of the court in which plaintiff Baranski's suit has been filed. If service is not properly made, defendant Peretto will have a legal ground (basis) for asking the court to dismiss the case against him, thus delaying the litigation. As mentioned earlier, the court will not be able to exercise jurisdiction over Peretto until he has been properly notified of the lawsuit being brought against him.

Serving Corporate Defendants.   In cases involving corporate defendants, the summons and complaint may be served on an officer or *registered agent* (representative) of the corporation. The name of a corporation's registered agent is usually obtainable from the secretary of state's office in the state in which the company incorporated its business (and, usually, the secretary of state's office in any state in which the corporation does business).

EXHIBIT 6.4
A Summons in a Civil Action

United States District Court

_____WESTERN_____ DISTRICT OF _____NITA_____

Katherine Baranski

SUMMONS IN A CIVIL ACTION

V.

CASE NUMBER:

Tony Peretto

TO:

Tony Peretto
1708 Johnston Drive
Zero City, ZE 59806

YOU ARE HEREBY SUMMONED and required to file with the Clerk of this Court and serve upon

PLAINTIFF'S ATTORNEY
    Allen P. Gilmore
    Jeffers, Gilmore & Dunn
    553 Fifth Avenue
    Suite 101
    Nita City, NI 48801

an answer to the complaint which is herewith served upon you, within _____20_____ days after service of this summons upon you, exclusive of the day of service. If you fail to do so, judgment by default will be taken against you for the relief demanded in the complaint.

C. H. Hynek
_____
CLERK

February 10, 1996
_____
DATE

John Dolan
_____
BY DEPUTY CLERK

Notice and Waiver of Service—FRCP 4(d)

The 1993 revision of the FRCP added Rule 4(d), allows for a simpler and less costly alternative to service of process. Under this rule, a plaintiff's attorney is permitted to notify the defendant directly, through the mails or "other reliable means," of the lawsuit. After the complaint has been filed, attorney Gilmore will thus probably ask paralegal Lopez to follow the procedures outlined in FRCP 4(d).

To comply with FRCP 4(d), Lopez will need to fill out two forms. Form 1A, which is shown in Exhibit 6.6 on page 184, is entitled "Notice of Lawsuit and Request for Waiver of Service of Summons." This form, which must be signed by attorney Gilmore, requests defendant Peretto to waive the

EXHIBIT 6.5
A Return-of-Service Form

AO 440 (Rev. 5/85) Summons in a Civil Action

RETURN OF SERVICE

Service of the Summons and Complaint was made by me[1]	DATE 2/11/96
NAME OF SERVER Elena Lopez	TITLE Paralegal

Check one box below to indicate appropriate method of service

[X] Served personally upon the defendant. Place where served: ___Defendant Peretto's Home: 1708 Johnston Drive, Zero City, Zero 59806___

[ ] Left copies thereof at the defendant's dwelling house or usual place of abode with a person of suitable age and discretion then residing therein. Name of person with whom the summons and complaint were left: _____

[ ] Returned unexecuted: _____

[ ] Other (specifiy): _____

STATEMENT OF SERVICE FEES

TRAVEL 40 miles @ 25¢/mile	SERVICES 1 hour @ $25/hour	TOTAL $35.00

DECLARATION OF SERVER

I declare under penalty of perjury under the laws of the United States of America that the foregoing information contained in the Return of Service and Statement of Service Fees is true and correct.

Executed on ___2/11/96___
               Date

Elena Lopez
Signature of Server

308 University Avenue, Nita City, Nita 48804

Address of Server

---

1) As to who may serve a summons see Rule 4 of the Federal Rules of Civil Procedure.

● ● ● ● ●

EXHIBIT 6.6
Form 1A—Notice of Lawsuit and Request for Waiver of Service of Summons

● ● ● ● ●

TO:_____(A)_____

[as_____(B)_____ of _____(C)_____]

    A lawsuit has been commenced against you (or the entity on whose behalf you are addressed). A copy of the complaint is attached to this notice. It has been filed in the United States District Court for the_____(D)_____ and has been assigned docket number_____(E)_____.

    This is not a formal summons or notification from the court, but rather my request that you sign and return the enclosed waiver of service in order to save the cost of serving you with a judicial summons and an additional copy of the complaint. The cost of service will be avoided if I receive a signed copy of the waiver within_____(F)_____ days after the date designated below as the date on which this Notice and Request is sent. I enclose a stamped and addressed envelope (or other means of cost-free return) for your use. An extra copy of the waiver is also attached for your records.

    If you comply with this request and return the signed waiver, it will be filed with the court and no summons will be served on you. The action will then proceed as if you had been served on the date the waiver is filed, except that you will not be obligated to answer the complaint before 60 days from the date designated below as the date on which this notice is sent (or before 90 days from that date if your address is not in any judicial district of the United States).

    If you do not return the signed waiver within the time indicated, I will take appropriate steps to effect formal service in a manner authorized by the Federal Rules of Civil Procedure and will then, to the extent authorized by those Rules, ask the court to require you (or the party on whose behalf you are addressed) to pay the full costs of such service. In that connection please read the statement concerning the duty of parties to waive the service of the summons, which is set forth on the reverse side (or at the foot) of the waiver form.

    I affirm that this request is being sent to you on behalf of the plaintiff, this_____ day of_____ ,____ .

_____
Signature of Plaintiff's Attorney or
Unrepresented Plaintiff

Notes:
    A-Name of individual (or name of officer or agent of corporate defendant)
    B-Title, or other relationship of individual to corporate defendant
    C-Name of corporate defendant, if any
    D-District
    E-Docket number of action
    F-Addressee must be given at least 30 days (60 days if located in foreign country) in which to return waiver

requirement that he be notified of the lawsuit by having a summons served on him. Next, Lopez will fill out Form 1B, entitled "Waiver of Service of Summons." Exhibit 6.7 indicates the information that must be included in this form. Once these forms are filled out and attorney Gilmore has reviewed and signed them, paralegal Lopez will send to defendant Peretto a packet containing the following contents:

- Two copies each of Form 1A and Form 1B.
- A copy of the complaint.
- An addressed, stamped envelope for defendant Peretto to use when returning Form 1B.

    If defendant Peretto agrees to waive service of process, he will need to sign and return the waiver to attorney Gilmore within thirty days after the

EXHIBIT 6.7
Form 1B—Waiver of Service of Summons

TO: _____(name of plaintiff's attorney or unrepresented plaintiff)_____

I acknowledge receipt of your request that I waive service of a summons in the action of _(caption of action)_, which is case number ___(docket number)___ in the United States District Court for the _____(district)_____. I have also received a copy of the complaint in the action, two copies of this instrument, and a means by which I can return the signed waiver to you without cost to me.

I agree to save the cost of service of a summons and an additional copy of the complaint in this lawsuit by not requiring that I (or the entity on whose behalf I am acting) be served with judicial process in the manner provided by Rule 4.

I (or the entity on whose behalf I am acting) will retain all defenses or objections to the lawsuit or to the jurisdiction or venue of the court except for objections based on a defect in the summons or in the service of the summons.

I understand that a judgment may be entered against me (or the party on whose behalf I am acting) if an answer or motion under Rule 12 is not served upon you within 60 days after ____(date request was sent)____, or within 90 days after that date if the request was sent outside the United States.

_____
Date

Signature _____
Printed/typed name: _____
[as_____]
[of_____]

To be printed on foot of or on reverse side of form:

DUTY TO AVOID UNNECESSARY COSTS OF SERVICE OF SUMMONS

Rule 4 of the Federal Rules of Civil Procedure requires parties to cooperate in saving unnecessary costs of service of the summons and complaint. A defendant located in the United States, who, after being notified of an action and asked by a plaintiff located in the United States to waive service of a summons, fails to do so will be required to bear the cost of such service unless good cause be shown for its failure to sign and return the waiver.

It is not good cause for a failure to waive service that a party believes that the complaint is unfounded, or that the action has been brought in an improper place or in a court that lacks jurisdiction over the subject matter of the action or over its person or property. A party who waives service of the summons retains all defenses and objections (except any relating to the summons or to the service of the summons), and may later object to the jurisdiction of the court or to the place where the action has been brought.

A defendant who waives service must within the time specified on the waiver form serve on the plaintiff's attorney (or unrepresented plaintiff) a response to the complaint and must also file a signed copy of the response with the court. If the answer or motion is not served within this time, a default judgment may be taken against that defendant. By waiving service, a defendant is allowed more time to answer than if the summons had been actually served when the request for waiver of service was received.

waiver form was sent by Gilmore. (For defendants located in a foreign country, the time period is extended to sixty days.)

The aim of FRCP 4(d) is to eliminate the costs associated with service of process and to foster cooperation among adversaries. To encourage defendants to agree to the waiver of service, FRCP 4(d)(3) provides that defendants who return the required waiver are not required to respond to the complaint for sixty days (ninety days for defendants outside the United States) after the date on which the request for waiver of service was sent. In contrast, if a defendant does not agree to waive service and a complaint and summons must be served, then (under FRCP 12) the defendant must respond to the complaint within twenty days after process is served.

The Defendant's Response

Once a defendant receives the plaintiff's complaint, either via mail or through service of process, the defendant must respond to the complaint within a specified time period (in federal cases, within the time periods specified above). If the defendant fails to respond within that time period, the court, on the plaintiff's motion, will enter a **default judgment** against the defendant. The defendant will then be liable for the entire amount of damages that the plaintiff is claiming and will lose the opportunity to either defend against the claim in court or settle the issue with the plaintiff out of court.

In the Baranski case, assume that defendant Peretto consults with an attorney, Elizabeth A. Cameron, to decide on a course of action. Before Cameron advises Peretto on the matter, she will want to investigate plaintiff Baranski's claim and obtain evidence of what happened at the time of the accident. She may ask her paralegal, Gordon McVay, to call anyone who may have witnessed the accident and any police officers who were at the scene. Attorney Cameron will also ask McVay to gather relevant documents, including the traffic ticket that Peretto received at the time of the accident and any reports that might have been filed by the police. If all goes well, attorney Cameron and paralegal McVay will complete their investigation in a few days and then meet to assess the results. In deciding how best to respond to the complaint, Peretto's attorney, Cameron, must consider whether to file an answer or a motion to dismiss the case.

The Answer.   A defendant's **answer** must respond to each allegation in the plaintiff's complaint. FRCP 8(b) permits the defendant to admit or deny the truth of each allegation. Defendant Peretto's attorney may advise Peretto to admit to some of the allegations in plaintiff Baranski's complaint, because doing so narrows the number of issues in dispute. For example, paragraph 5 of Peretto's answer might read "Defendant admits the allegations contained in paragraph 5 of the Plaintiff's complaint." If Peretto wishes to deny an allegation, such as the plaintiff's allegation in paragraph 11, he may state in his answer, "Defendant denies the allegation of negligence contained in paragraph 11 of the Plaintiff's complaint." Another option for the defendant is to state in the answer that he or she does not have sufficient information on which to base an admission or a denial. For example, paragraph 9 of the answer might state that the defendant "lacks sufficient information to form a belief as to the truth of the allegation contained in paragraph 9 of the Plaintiff's complaint."

Like the complaint, the answer begins with a caption and ends with the attorney's signature. It may also include, following the attorney's signature, an affidavit signed by the defendant, as well as a demand for a jury trial.

A defendant may assert, in the answer, a reason why he or she should not be held liable for the plaintiff's injuries even if the facts, as alleged by the plaintiff, are true. This is called raising an **affirmative defense**. For example,

---

DEFAULT JUDGMENT
A judgment entered by a clerk or court against a party who has failed to appear in court to answer or defend against a claim that has been brought against him or her by another party.

CASE AT A GLANCE

The Plaintiff—
Plaintiff: Katherine Baranski
Attorney: Allen P. Gilmore
Paralegal: Elena Lopez

The Defendant—
Defendant: Tony Peretto
Attorney: Elizabeth A. Cameron
Paralegal: Gordon McVay

ANSWER
A defendant's response to a plaintiff's complaint.

AFFIRMATIVE DEFENSE
A response to a plaintiff's claim that does not deny the plaintiff's facts but attacks the plaintiff's legal right to bring an action.

Peretto might claim that someone else was driving his Dodge van when it crashed into Baranski's car. Although affirmative defenses are directed toward the plaintiff, the plaintiff is not required to file additional pleadings in response to these defenses.

Motion to Dismiss.   A **motion** is a procedural request submitted to the court by an attorney on behalf of his or her client. When one party files a motion with the court, they must also send to, or serve on, the opposing party a *notice of motion.* The notice of motion informs the opposing party that the motion has been filed and indicates when the court will hear the motion. The notice of motion gives the opposing party an opportunity to prepare for the hearing and argue before the court why the motion should not be granted.

The **motion to dismiss**, as the phrase implies, requests the court to dismiss the case for reasons provided in the motion. Defendant Peretto's attorney, for example, could file a motion to dismiss if she believed that Peretto had not been properly served, that the complaint had been filed in the wrong court, that the statute of limitations for that type of lawsuit had expired, or that the complaint did not state a claim for which relief (a remedy) could be granted. See Exhibit 6.8 on the next page for an example of a motion to dismiss.

If defendant Peretto's attorney decides to file a motion to dismiss plaintiff Baranski's claim, she may want to attach one or more supporting affidavits—sworn statements as to certain facts that may contradict the allegations made in the complaint. Peretto's attorney may also have her paralegal draft a **memorandum of law** (which is called a *brief* in some states) to be submitted along with the motion to dismiss and the accompanying affidavits. The memorandum of law will present the legal basis for the motion, citing any statutes and cases that support it. A supporting affidavit gives factual support to the motion to dismiss, while the memorandum of law provides the court with the legal grounds for the dismissal of the claim.[7]

PRETRIAL MOTIONS

Many motions may be made during the pretrial litigation process, including those listed and described in Exhibit 6.9 on page 190. Some pretrial motions, if granted by the court, will end a case before trial. These motions include the motion to dismiss (which has already been discussed), the motion for judgment on the pleadings, and the motion for summary judgment. Here we examine the latter two motions.

Once the two attorneys in the Baranski case, Gilmore and Cameron, have finished filing their respective pleadings, either one of them may file a **motion for judgment on the pleadings**. Motions for judgment on the pleadings are often filed when it appears from the pleadings that the plaintiff has failed to state a cause of action for which relief may be granted. They may also be filed

---

7. The memorandum of law described here should not be confused with the legal memorandum discussed in Chapter 9. The latter is an internal memorandum (that is, a memo submitted—usually by the paralegal—to his or her supervising attorney).

MOTION
A procedural request or application presented by an attorney to the court on behalf of a client.

MOTION TO DISMISS
A pleading in which a defendant admits the facts as alleged by the plaintiff but asserts that the plaintiff's claim fails to state a cause of action (that is, has no basis in law) or that there are other grounds on which a suit should be dismissed.

MEMORANDUM OF LAW
A document (known as a *brief* in some states) that delineates the legal theories, statutes, and cases on which a motion is based.

MOTION FOR JUDGMENT ON THE PLEADINGS
A motion, which can be brought by either party to a lawsuit after the pleadings are closed, for the court to decide the issue without proceeding to trial. The motion will be granted only if no facts are in dispute and the only issue concerns how the law applies to a set of undisputed facts.

CASE AT A GLANCE

The Plaintiff—
Plaintiff: Katherine Baranski
Attorney: Allen P. Gilmore
Paralegal: Elena Lopez

The Defendant—
Defendant: Tony Peretto
Attorney: Elizabeth A. Cameron
Paralegal: Gordon McVay

EXHIBIT 6.8
A Motion to Dismiss

**UNITED STATES DISTRICT COURT
FOR THE WESTERN DISTRICT OF NITA**

Katherine Baranski

               Plaintiff   File No. 96-14335-NI

vs.

                                       Hon. Harley M. LaRue

Tony Peretto

               Defendant

Elizabeth A. Cameron
Attorney for the Defendant
Cameron & Strauss, P.C.
310 Lake Drive
Zero City, ZE 59802

MOTION TO DISMISS

    The Defendant, Tony Peretto, by his attorney, moves the court to dismiss the above-named action because the statute of limitations governing the Plaintiff's claim has expired, as demonstrated in the memorandum of law that is being submitted with this motion. The Plaintiff therefore has no cause of action against the Defendant.

                                 Cameron & Strauss, P.C.

Date: 2/20/96

                                  Elizabeth A. Cameron
                                  Attorney for the Defendant
                                  310 Lake Drive
                                  Zero City, ZE 59802

MOTION FOR SUMMARY JUDGMENT
A motion requesting the court to enter a judgment without proceeding to trial. The motion can be based on evidence outside the pleadings and will be granted only if no facts are in dispute and the only issue concerns how the law applies to a set of undisputed facts.

when the pleadings indicate that no facts are in dispute and the only question is how the law applies to a set of undisputed facts. For example, assume for a moment that in the Baranski case, defendant Peretto admitted to all of plaintiff Baranski's allegations in his answer and raised no affirmative defenses. In this situation, Baranski's attorney, Gilmore, would file a motion for judgment on the pleadings in Baranski's favor.

A **motion for summary judgment** is similar to a motion for judgment on the pleadings in that the party filing the motion is asking the court to grant a judgment in its favor without a trial. As with a motion for judgment on the pleadings, a court will only grant a motion for summary judgment if it determines that no facts are in dispute and the only question is how the law applies to a set of facts agreed on by both parties.

When the court considers a motion for summary judgment, it can take into account *evidence outside the pleadings.* This distinguishes the motion for summary judgment from the motion to dismiss and the motion for judgment on the pleadings. To support a motion for summary judgment, one party can submit evidence obtained at any point prior to trial (including during the discovery stage of litigation—to be discussed shortly) that refutes the other party's factual claim. In the Baranski case, for example, suppose that Peretto was in another state at the time of the accident. Defendant Peretto's attorney could make a motion for summary judgment in Peretto's favor and

PARALEGAL PROFILE   Litigation Paralegal

AL SANCHEZ received an associate's degree in design and drafting in 1971 from Don Bosco Technical Institute. He then worked for sixteen years as an engineering drafter for the aerospace industry. Sanchez decided to become a paralegal in 1987. In 1992, he received his paralegal degree from Rio Hondo College. He now works for an attorney who practices personal-injury law.

What do you like best about your work?

"The best aspect of my job is having people appreciate the work that I've done for them. I feel like I go the extra mile, and it's nice to be appreciated."

What is the greatest challenge that you face in your area of work?

"The greatest challenge is dealing with and balancing the volume of work involved in my case load and still giving clients personal attention. I do everything from the initial client interview to settlement or litigation support. I have a lot of contact with clients, insurance companies, and doctors. I also do some office management. It is also a challenge to keep up with changes in both substantive law and procedural law."

What advice do you have for would-be paralegals in your area of work?

"My advice is to gain computer skills and take psychology classes to help you better understand clients and their problems. Organizational skills and the ability to prioritize are also very important. I feel that my job is a 'good fit' because I am a 'people person,' and my job allows me to deal more with the public. It is also important to learn more about the law and attend continuing-education seminars to keep current with the law."

What are some tips for success as a paralegal in your area of work?

"I feel it is important to spend some time in the courthouse observing various proceedings. Also, try to remember that your clients are people, not just case numbers. Finally, keep in mind that quality work takes time and attention to detail. Therefore, paralegals need to put in a lot of hours."

> **"...TRY TO REMEMBER THAT YOUR CLIENTS ARE PEOPLE, NOT JUST CASE NUMBERS."**

attach to the motion a witness's sworn statement that Peretto was in the other state at the time of the accident. Unless plaintiff Baranski's attorney could bring in sworn statements by other witnesses that Peretto was at the scene of the accident, Peretto would normally be granted his motion for summary judgment.

DISCOVERY

Before a trial begins, the parties can use a number of procedural devices to obtain information and gather evidence about the case. Plaintiff Baranski's attorney, for example, will want to know how fast defendant Peretto was driving, whether he had been drinking, whether he saw the stop sign, and so on. The process of obtaining information from the opposing party or from other witnesses is known as **discovery**.

DISCOVERY
Formal investigation prior to trial. During discovery, opposing parties use various methods, such as interrogatories and depositions, to obtain information from each other and other persons, such as witnesses, to prepare for trial.

EXHIBIT 6.9
Pretrial Motions

MOTION TO DISMISS

A motion filed by the defendant in which the defendant asks the court to dismiss the case for a specified reason, such as improper service, lack of personal jurisdiction, or the plaintiff's failure to state a claim for which relief can be granted.

MOTION TO STRIKE

A motion filed by the defendant in which the defendant asks the court to strike (delete from) the complaint certain of the paragraphs contained in the complaint. Motions to strike help to clarify the underlying issues that form the basis for the complaint by removing paragraphs that are redundant or irrelevant to the action.

MOTION TO MAKE MORE DEFINITE AND CERTAIN

A motion filed by the defendant to compel the plaintiff to clarify the basis of the plaintiff's cause of action. The motion is filed when the defendant believes that the complaint is too vague or ambiguous for the defendant to respond to it in a meaningful way.

MOTION FOR JUDGMENT ON THE PLEADINGS

A motion that may be filed by either party in which the party asks the court to enter a judgment in its favor based on information contained in the pleadings. A judgment on the pleadings will only be made if there are no facts in dispute and the only question is how the law applies to a set of undisputed facts.

MOTION TO COMPEL DISCOVERY

A motion that may be filed by either party in which the party asks the court to compel the other party to comply with a discovery request. If a party refuses to allow the opponent to inspect and copy certain documents, for example, the party requesting the documents may make a motion to compel production of documents.

MOTION FOR SUMMARY JUDGMENT

A motion that may be filed by either party in which the party asks the court to enter judgment in its favor without a trial. Unlike a motion for judgment on the pleadings, a motion for summary judgment can be supported by evidence outside the pleadings, such as witnesses' affidavits, answers to interrogatories, or other evidence obtained prior to or during discovery.

PRIVILEGED INFORMATION
Confidential communications between certain individuals, such as an attorney and his or her client, that are protected from disclosure except under court order.

The FRCP and similar rules in the states set forth the guidelines for discovery activity. Discovery includes gaining access to witnesses, documents, records, and other types of evidence. The rules governing discovery are designed to make sure that a witness or a party is not unduly harassed, that **privileged information** (communications that may not be disclosed in court) is safeguarded, and that only matters relevant to the case at hand are discoverable. Currently, the trend is toward allowing more discovery and thus fewer surprises. The 1993 revision of the FRCP significantly changed the rules governing discovery in federal court cases. To the extent that state courts decide to follow the new federal rules, discovery in such cases will also be affected. You will learn how the revised rules affect the traditional discovery process later in this section.

Traditional discovery devices include interrogatories, depositions, requests for documents, requests for admissions, and requests for examinations. Each of these discovery tools is examined below.

Interrogatories

Interrogatories are written questions that must be answered, in writing, by the parties to the lawsuit and then signed by the parties under oath. Typically, the paralegal drafts the interrogatories for the attorney's review and approval. In the Baranski case, for example, attorney Gilmore will probably ask paralegal Lopez to draft interrogatories to be sent to defendant Peretto.

All discovery documents, including interrogatories, normally begin with a caption similar to the complaint caption illustrated earlier in this chapter. Following the caption, Lopez will add the name of the party who must answer the interrogatories, instructions to be followed by the party, and definitions of certain terms that are used in the interrogatories. The body of the document consists of the interrogatories themselves—that is, the questions that the opposing party must answer. The interrogatories should end with a signature line for the attorney below which appears the attorney's name and address.

Before drafting the questions, Lopez will want to review carefully the contents of the case file (including the pleadings and the evidence and other information that she obtained during her preliminary investigation into plaintiff Baranski's claim) and consult with attorney Gilmore on what litigation strategy should be pursued. For further guidance, she might consult form books containing sample interrogatories as well as interrogatories used in similar cases previously handled by the firm. For a discussion of how to draft effective interrogatories, see this chapter's featured-guest article entitled "Ten Tips for Drafting Interrogatories."

Depending on the complexity of the case, interrogatories may be few in number, or they may run into the hundreds. Exhibit 6.10 on the next page shows the first page of a sample set of interrogatories. Realize that some state courts now limit the number of interrogatories that can be used, and the 1993 revision of FRCP 33 limits the number of interrogatories in federal court cases to twenty-five (unless a greater number is allowed by stipulation of the parties or by court order). Therefore:

- **Before drafting interrogatories, the paralegal should always check the rules of the court in which an action is being filed to find out if that court limits the number of interrogatories that can be used.**

Upon receiving the interrogatories, defendant Peretto would have to answer them within a specified time period (thirty days under FRCP 33) in writing and under oath, as mentioned above. Very likely, he will have substantial guidance from his attorney and his attorney's paralegal in forming his answers. Peretto must answer each question truthfully, of course, because he is under oath. His attorney would counsel him, though, on how to phrase his answers so that they are both truthful and strategically sound. For example, the attorney would advise Peretto on how to limit his answers to prevent disclosing more information than is necessary.

INTERROGATORIES
A series of written questions for which written answers are prepared and then signed under oath by a party to a lawsuit (the plaintiff or the defendant).

ETHICAL CONCERN
Keeping Client Information Confidential

As it happens, attorney Gilmore's legal assistant, Lopez, is a good friend of plaintiff Baranski's daughter. Lopez learns from the results of Baranski's medical examination that Baranski has a terminal illness. Lopez is sure that the daughter, who quarreled with her mother two months ago and hasn't spoken to her since, is unaware of the illness and would probably be very hurt if she learned that Lopez knew of it and didn't tell her. Should Lopez tell her friend about the illness? No. This is confidential information at this point, which Lopez only became aware of by virtue of her job. Should the information be revealed publicly during the course of the trial, then Lopez would be free to disclose it to her friend if the friend still remained unaware of it. In the meantime, Lopez is ethically (and legally) obligated not to disclose the information to anyone who is not working on the case, including her friend.

EXHIBIT 6.10
Sample Interrogatories (Excerpt)

UNITED STATES DISTRICT COURT
FOR THE WESTERN DISTRICT OF NITA

Katherine Baranski

          Plaintiff

vs.

          File No. 96-14335-NI

          Hon. Harley M. LaRue

Tony Peretto   Defendant

A. P. Gilmore
Attorney for the Plaintiff
Jeffers, Gilmore & Dunn
553 Fifth Avenue
Suite 101
Nita City, NI 48801

PLAINTIFF'S FIRST INTERROGATORIES TO DEFENDANT

    PLEASE TAKE NOTICE that the following Interrogatories are directed to you under the provisions of Rule 26(a)(5) and Rule 33 of the Federal Rules of Civil Procedure. You are requested to answer these Interrogatories and to furnish such information in answer to the Interrogatories as is available to you.

    You are required to serve integrated Interrogatories and Answers to these Interrogatories under oath, within thirty (30) days after service of them upon you. The original answers are to be retained in your attorney's possession and a copy of the answers are to be served upon Plaintiff's counsel.

    The answers should be signed and sworn to by the person making answer to the Interrogatories.

    When used in these Interrogatories the term "Defendant," or any synonym thereof, is intended to and shall embrace and include, in addition to said Defendant, all agents, servants and employees, representatives, attorneys, private investigators, or others who are in possession or who may have obtained information for or on behalf of the Defendant.

    These Interrogatories shall be deemed continuing and supplemental answers shall be required immediately upon receipt thereof if Defendant, directly or indirectly, obtains further or different information from the time answers are served until the time of trial.

1.   Were you the driver of an automobile involved in an accident with plaintiff on the _____ day of _____, 19 ___, at about _____ o'clock _____ A.M. at the intersection of _____ and _____, in the city of _____ in the county of _____, state of_____? If so, please state the following:

    (a) Whether your name is correctly spelled in the complaint in this cause of action;
    (b) Any other names by which you have been known, including the dates during which you have used those names;
    (c) Your Social Security number and place and date of birth;
    (d) Your height, weight, and eye and hair color;
    (e) Your address at the time of the accident;
    (f) The names, addresses, and phone numbers of your present and former spouses (if any) and all of your children, whether natural or adopted, who were residing with you at the time of the accident (if any).

2.   Please list your places of residence for the last five years prior to your current residence, including complete addresses and dates of residence as well as the names of owners or managers.

Depositions

Like interrogatories, **depositions** are given under oath. Unlike interrogatories, however, depositions are usually conducted orally (except in certain circumstances, such as when the party being deposed is at a great distance and cannot be deposed via telephone). Furthermore, they may be taken from witnesses. As indicated earlier, interrogatories can only be taken from the parties to the lawsuit. The attorney wishing to depose a party must give that party's attorney reasonable notice in writing.

When an attorney takes the deposition of a party or witness, the attorney is able to question the person being deposed (the **deponent**) in person and then follow up with any other questions that come to mind. Even though the deposition is usually taken at the offices of one of the party's attorneys, the fact that the deponent has sworn to tell the truth necessitates that both the attorney and the deponent treat the deposition proceedings as seriously as they would if the deponent were on the witness stand in court. Depositions are conducted by attorneys. Although paralegals may attend depositions, they do not ask questions during the deposition. Deposition questions are often drafted by paralegals, however.

FRCP 30, as revised in 1993, prohibits the taking of any depositions in federal court cases before the parties have made the disclosures required under revised Rule 26 and discussed in the next section. Revised Rule 30 also states that the court's approval is required if, without written agreement by the parties, either attorney wants to take more than one deposition from the same party or witness, or more than a total of ten depositions.

The Role of the Deponent's Attorney.   The deponent's attorney will attend the deposition, but the attorney's role will be limited. The attorney may make occasional objections to the opposing attorney's questions if the questions appear to be irrelevant to the case or ask for privileged information. If plaintiff Baranski were to be deposed by defendant Peretto's attorney, Cameron, then Baranski's attorney, Gilmore, would object to any of Cameron's questions that were misleading or ambiguous or that wandered too far from the issues relating to the claim.

Gilmore would also caution Baranski to limit her responses to the questions and not to engage in speculative answers that might prejudice her claim. If plaintiff Baranski was asked whether she had ever been involved in an automobile accident before, for example, Gilmore would probably caution her to use a simple (but truthful) "yes" or "no" answer. Attorney Gilmore normally would permit Baranski to volunteer additional information only in response to precisely phrased questions.

As will be discussed below, deposition proceedings are recorded. If both attorneys agree to do so, however, they can go "off the record" to clarify a point or discuss a disputed issue. Depositions are stressful events, and tempers often flare. In the event that the deposition can no longer be pursued in an orderly fashion, the attorney conducting the deposition may have to terminate it.

The above description of the role of the deponent's attorney at a deposition is typical for cases filed in state courts and, until the 1993 revision of the FRCP, in federal courts as well. The revised FRCP, however, imposes

DEPOSITION

A pretrial question-and-answer proceeding, usually conducted orally, in which an a party or witness answers an attorney's questions. The answers are given under oath, and the session is recorded.

DEPONENT

A party or witness who testifies under oath during a deposition.

CASE AT A GLANCE

The Plaintiff—
   Plaintiff: Katherine Baranski
   Attorney: Allen P. Gilmore
   Paralegal: Elena Lopez

The Defendant—
   Defendant: Tony Peretto
   Attorney: Elizabeth A. Cameron
   Paralegal: Gordon McVay

strict limitations on an attorney's right to object to questions asked of his or her client during a deposition. Rule 30(d)(1) now requires that an attorney may instruct a deponent not to answer only "when necessary to preserve a privilege, to enforce a limitation on evidence directed by the court, or to present a motion [to terminate the deposition]." The revised rule also states that all objections during a deposition must be stated concisely and in a nonargumentative, nonsuggestive manner. This rule is consistent with the revised FRCP 26, which imposes an ongoing duty on each party to disclose relevant information to the other party in the lawsuit.

The Deposition Transcript.   Every utterance made during a deposition is recorded. A court reporter will usually record the deposition proceedings and create an official **deposition transcript.** Methods of recording a deposition include stenographic recording (a traditional method that involves the use of a shorthand machine), tape recording, videotape recording, or some combination of these methods. Revised Rule 30(b)(2) of the FRCP states that unless the court orders otherwise, a deposition "may be recorded by sound, sound-and-visual, or stenographic means."

The deposition transcript may be used by either party during the trial to prove a particular point or to **impeach** (call into question) the credibility of a witness who says something during the trial that is different from what he or she stated during the deposition. For example, a witness in the Baranski case might state during the deposition that defendant Peretto *did not* stop at the stop sign before proceeding to cross Mattis Avenue. If at trial, the witness states that Peretto *did* stop at the stop sign before crossing Mattis Avenue, plaintiff Baranski's attorney (Gilmore) could challenge the witness's credibility on the basis of the deposition transcript. Exhibit 6.11 shows a page from a transcript of a deposition conducted by attorney Gilmore in the Baranski case. The deponent was Julia Williams, an eyewitness to the accident. On the transcript, the letter "Q" precedes each question asked by Gilmore, and the letter "A" precedes each of Williams's answers.

Summarizing and Indexing the Deposition Transcript.   Typically, the paralegal will summarize the deposition transcript. The summary, which along with the transcript will become part of the litigation file, allows the members of the litigation team to review quickly the information obtained from the deponent during the deposition.

In the Baranski case, assume that paralegal Lopez is asked to summarize the deposition transcript of Julia Williams. A commonly used format for deposition summaries is to summarize the information sequentially—that is, in the order that it was given during the deposition—as shown in Exhibit 6.12 on page 196. Notice that the summary includes the page and line numbers in the deposition transcript where the full text of the information can be found.

Often, in addition to summarizing the transcript, the paralegal provides an index to the document. The index consists of a list of topics (such as education, employment status, injuries, medical costs, and so on) followed by the relevant page and line numbers of the deposition transcript. Together, the summary and the index allow anyone involved in the case to locate information quickly.

DEPOSITION TRANSCRIPT
The official transcription of the recording taken during a deposition.

IMPEACH
To call into question the credibility of a witness by challenging the truth or accuracy of his or her trial statement.

67	Q: Where were you at the time of the accident?
68	A: I was on the southwest corner of the intersection.
69	Q: Are you referring to the intersection where Thirty-eighth Street crosses Mattis Avenue?
70	A: Yes.
71	Q: Why were you there at the time of the accident?
72	A: Well, I was on my way to work. I usually walk down Mattis Avenue to the hospital.
73	Q: So you were walking to work down Mattis Avenue and you saw the accident?
74	A: Yes.
75	Q: What did you see?
76	A: Well, as I was about to cross the street, a dark green van passed within three feet of me and ran the
77	stop sign and crashed into another car.
78	Q: Can you remember if the driver of the van was a male or a female?
79	A: Yes. It was a man.
80	Q: I am showing you a picture. Can you identify the man in the picture?
81	A: Yes. That is the man who was driving the van.
82	Q: Do you wear glasses?
83	A: I need glasses only for reading. I have excellent distance vision.
84	Q: How long has it been since your last eye exam with a doctor?
85	A: Oh, just a month ago, with Dr. Sullivan.

page 4

EXHIBIT 6.11
A Deposition Transcript (Excerpt)

Other Discovery Requests

During the discovery phase of litigation, attorneys often request documents so that they may familiarize themselves with specific facts or events that were earlier disclosed by the parties or learned on investigation. In federal court cases, the revised FRCP 34 authorizes each party to request documents and other forms of evidence held by other parties and witnesses, but such requests cannot be made until after the initial prediscovery meeting of the parties (discussed below) has taken place. In most state courts, and depending on the nature of the case, the inspection of documents may be the first step in the discovery process if document inspection will facilitate the widest possible scope of discovery.

During discovery, a party can also request that the opposing party admit the truth of matters relating to the case. For example, plaintiff Baranski's attorney can request that defendant Peretto admit that he did not stop at the

EXHIBIT 6.12

A Deposition Summary (Excerpt)

Case:	Baranski v. Peretto	Attorney: Allen P. Gilmore
	Plaintiff 15773	Legal Assistant: Elena Lopez

Deponent:	Julia Williams	Date: March 16, 1996
	3801 Mattis Avenue	
	Nita City, Nita 48800	

Page	Line(s)	

* * * *

4	72-77	Williams stated that she was on the way to work at the time of the accident. She was about to cross the street when Peretto's car ("a dark green van") passed within three feet of her, ran the stop sign, and crashed into Baranski's car.
4	80-81	When shown a picture of Peretto, she identified him as the driver of the green van.
4	82-83	Williams has excellent distance vision and does not require corrective lenses. She does need reading glasses for close work.

* * * *

CASE AT A GLANCE

The Plaintiff—
Plaintiff: Katherine Baranski
Attorney: Allen P. Gilmore
Paralegal: Elena Lopez

The Defendant—
Defendant: Tony Peretto
Attorney: Elizabeth A.
Cameron
Paralegal: Gordon McVay

stop sign before crossing Mattis Avenue at Thirty-eighth Street. Such admissions save time at trial because the parties will not have to spend time proving facts on which they already agree. Any matter admitted under such a request is conclusively established as true for the trial. FRCP 36 permits requests for admission, but the 1993 revision of this rule stipulates that a request for admission cannot be made, without the court's permission, prior to the prediscovery meeting of the attorneys. In view of the limitations on the number of interrogatories under the revised FRCP (and under some state procedural rules that impose similar limitations), requests for admissions are a particularly useful discovery tool.

During discovery, the defendant's attorney may also want to verify the nature and extent of any injuries alleged by the plaintiff. If a defendant has genuine doubts as to the nature of the injuries suffered by the plaintiff, then the defendant may petition the court to order that the plaintiff submit to a medical examination. Although a medical examination may appear to be overly intrusive, FRCP 35(a) permits such an examination when the existence of the plaintiff's claimed injuries is in dispute. The examination, however, must be preceded by a court order. Because plaintiff Baranski is suing defendant Peretto for injuries arising from the accident, the existence, nature, and extent of her injuries is vitally important in calculating the damages that she might be able to recover from Peretto. Consequently, Baranski will probably be ordered by the court to undergo a physical examination if Peretto's attorney submits a request for a medical examination.

Revised Discovery Procedures under FRCP 26

The 1993 amendments to the FRCP significantly changed discovery procedures in the federal courts. Under the revised rules, each party to a lawsuit has a duty to disclose to the other party specified types of information prior to the discovery stage of litigation. Under revised Rule 26(f), once a lawsuit is brought, the parties (the plaintiff and defendant and/or their attorneys, if the parties are represented by counsel) must schedule a prediscovery meeting to discuss the nature of the lawsuit, any defenses that may be raised against the claims being brought, and possibilities for promptly settling or otherwise resolving the dispute. The meeting should take place as soon as practicable but at least fourteen days before a scheduling conference is held or a scheduling order issued. Either at this prediscovery meeting or within ten days after it, the parties must also make certain initial disclosures and submit to the court a plan for discovery.

Initial disclosures that must be made by the attorneys include the names and addresses of persons who are likely to have "discoverable information" and the nature of that information, all documents or data in the possession of the parties that are relevant to the dispute, the materials on which a computation of the damages being claimed by the disclosing party, and copies of any relevant insurance policies. As the trial date approaches, the attorneys must make subsequent disclosures relating to witnesses, documents, and other information that is relevant to the case.

The new discovery rules do not replace the traditional methods of discovery discussed in the preceding section. Rather, the revised rules impose a duty on attorneys to disclose automatically specified information to opposing counsel early in the litigation process so that the time and costs of traditional discovery methods can be reduced. Under the revised rules, attorneys may still use the traditional discovery tools (depositions, interrogatories, and so on) to obtain information, but they cannot use these methods until the prediscovery meeting has been held and initial disclosures have been made. Also, to save the court's time, the revised rules give attorneys a freer hand in crafting a discovery plan that is appropriate to the nature of the claim, the parties' needs, and so on.[8]

PREPARING FOR TRIAL

As the trial date approaches, the attorneys for the plaintiff and the defendant and their respective paralegals complete their preparations for the trial. The paralegals collect and organize all of the documents and other evidence relating to the dispute. Plaintiff Baranski's attorney, Gilmore, will focus on legal strategy and how he can best use the information learned during the pleadings and discovery stages when presenting Baranski's case to the court. He will meet with his client and with his key witnesses to make last-minute preparations for trial. He might also meet with defendant Peretto's attorney to try once more to settle the dispute. Gilmore's legal assistant, Elena Lopez,

CASE AT A GLANCE

The Plaintiff—
Plaintiff: Katherine Baranski
Attorney: Allen P. Gilmore
Paralegal: Elena Lopez

The Defendant—
Defendant: Tony Peretto
Attorney: Elizabeth A. Cameron
Paralegal: Gordon McVay

---

8. The 1993 revision of the FRCP, including the revision of Rule 26 governing discovery requirements, has created substantial controversy. Revised Rule 26(a)(1) allows federal district courts to modify, or opt not to follow, these rules requiring early disclosures. As of mid-1994, of the ninety-six federal districts in the United States, thirty-two districts had adopted the early-disclosure rule, thirty-one districts had adopted a modified version of the rule, and twenty-three districts had opted out of the rule. See Mark Hansen, "Early Disclosure Hits Snag," *ABA Journal,* May 1994, p. 35.

will be notifying witnesses of the trial date and helping Gilmore prepare for trial. For example, she will make sure that all exhibits to be used during the trial are ready and verify that the trial notebook (discussed below) is in order.

Contacting and Preparing Witnesses

Typically, the paralegal is responsible for ensuring that witnesses are available and in court on the day of the trial. In the Baranski case, attorney Gilmore and paralegal Lopez will have lined up witnesses to testify on behalf of their client, plaintiff Baranski. In preparing for the trial, Lopez will inform each of the witnesses that the trial date has been set and that they will be expected to appear at the trial to testify. A **subpoena**—an order issued by the court clerk directing a person to appear in court—will be served on each of the witnesses to ensure their presence in court. A subpoena to appear in a federal court is shown in Exhibit 6.13. (Although not shown in the exhibit, a return-of-service form similar to the one illustrated in Exhibit 6.5 will be attached to the subpoena to verify that the witness received it.)

Unless she is already familiar with the court's requirements, paralegal Lopez will want to check with the court clerk to find out about what fees and documents she needs to take to the court to obtain the subpoena. The subpoena will then be served on the witness. Most subpoenas to appear in federal court can be served by anyone who is eighteen years of age or older, including paralegals, who often serve subpoenas. Subpoenas to appear in state court are often served by the sheriff or other process server.

No prudent attorney ever puts a party or a witness on the stand unless the attorney has discussed the testimony beforehand with the party or witness. Prior to the trial, attorney Gilmore and paralegal Lopez will meet with each witness and prepare the witness for trial. Gilmore will prepare the witness for the types of questions to expect from himself and from opposing counsel during the trial. He might do some role playing with the witness to help the witness understand how the questioning will proceed during the trial and to prepare the witness for the opposing attorney's questions. Gilmore will also review with the witness any sworn statements the witness made during discovery—during a deposition, for example. Additionally, Gilmore will review the substantive legal issues involved in the case and how the witness's testimony will affect the outcome of those issues.

Lopez will handle other aspects of witness preparation. She will advise the witness on trial procedures, when and where the witness will testify, and so on. Lopez might take the witness to the courtroom in which the trial will take place (if the courtroom is not in use) and familiarize the witness with the courtroom environment. She will show the witness where he or she will sit while giving testimony, where the judge and jurors will be, and where the attorneys will be seated.

Exhibits and Displays

Paralegals are frequently asked to prepare exhibits or displays that will be presented at trial. Attorney Gilmore may wish to present to the court a photograph of plaintiff Baranski's car taken after the accident occurred, a diagram of the intersection, an enlarged document (such as a police report), or other

SUBPOENA
A document commanding a person to appear at a certain time and place to give testimony concerning a certain matter.

ETHICAL CONCERN

Why Subpoena Friendly Witnesses?

The beginning paralegal might logically ask why it is necessary to subpoena friendly witnesses. The answer to this question is twofold. First, subpoena's make it easier for witnesses to be excused from their jobs and any other obligations on the date that they are to appear in court. Second, attorneys must take reasonable steps (and serving witnesses with subpoenas is a reasonable measure) to ensure that the clients' interests are best served. If a witness had not been subpoenaed and for some reason failed to appear at trial, the lack of his or her crucial testimony could jeopardize the client's chances of winning the case. By serving the witness with a subpoena, the attorney has proof that he or she has not breached the duty of competence to the client.

United States District Court	DISTRICT	Nita
Katherine Baranski	DOCKET NO.	96-14335-NI
v.	TYPE OF CASE	☒ CIVIL ☐ CRIMINAL
Tony Peretto	SUBPOENA FOR	☒ PERSON ☐ DOCUMENT(S) or OBJECT(S)

TO: Julia Williams
      3765 Mattis Avenue
      Nita City, NI 48803

YOU ARE HEREBY COMMANDED to appear in the United States District Court at the place, date, and time specified below to testify in the above-entitled case.

PLACE	COURTROOM
4th and Main Nita City, NI	B
	DATE AND TIME
	8/4/96 10:00 A.M.

YOU ARE ALSO COMMANDED to bring with you the following document(s) or Object(s):

☐ *See additional information on reverse*

This subpoena shall remain in effect until you are granted leave to depart by the court or by an officer acting on behalf of the court.

U.S. MAGISTRATE OR CLERK OF COURT	DATE
C. H. Hynek	July 13, 1996
(BY) DEPUTY CLERK *John Dolan*	

This subpoena is issued upon application of the:

☒ Plaintiff   ☐ Defendant   ☐ U.S. Attorney

ATTORNEY'S NAME AND ADDRESS
Allen P. Gilmore
Jeffers, Gilmore & Dunn
553 Fifth Avenue, Suite 101
Nita City, NI 48801

EXHIBIT 6.13
A Subpoena

evidence. Paralegal Lopez will be responsible for making sure that all exhibits are properly prepared and ready to introduce at trial. If any exhibits require special equipment, such as an easel or a VCR, Lopez must also make sure that these will be available in the courtroom and properly set up when they are needed.

The Trial Notebook

To present plaintiff Baranski's case effectively, attorney Gilmore will need to have in the courtroom all of the relevant documents; he will also need to be able to locate them quickly. To accomplish both of these ends, Lopez will prepare a **trial notebook**. The notebook will contain copies of the pleadings,

TRIAL NOTEBOOK
A binder that contains copies of all of the documents and information that an attorney will need to have at hand during the trial.

FEATURED GUEST: JAMES W. H. McCORD

Ten Tips for Drafting Interrogatories

Biographical Note

Since 1978, James McCord has been active in paralegal education as the director of paralegal programs at Eastern Kentucky University. He has served as president of the American Association for Paralegal Education, is a member of the American Bar Association Legal Assistant Program Approval Commission, and chairs the Kentucky Bar Association Committee on Paralegals. He received his law degree from the University of Wisconsin and practiced law before taking the position at Eastern Kentucky University. McCord is the author of *The Litigation Paralegal: A Systems Approach,* which is now in its second edition; *ABA Approval: An Educator's Guide;* and (as co-author) *Criminal Law and Procedure for the Paralegal.* He lives in Richmond, Kentucky, with his wife and son.

Interrogatories that are well thought out and carefully phrased can help to clarify the factual circumstances of the case, the types of evidence that can be obtained, and the issues in dispute. Because they help to define and shape a lawsuit, your ability to draft good interrogatories will make you a valued member of the litigation team. Here are some tips that you might find useful when you are asked to draft interrogatories.

1　Know the Limits of Interrogatories. Interrogatories have limits. The questions must seek information that is relevant to the issues or that will lead to relevant facts. The number of questions may be limited by the relevant rules or by the judge. Ethical standards explicitly forbid using interrogatories to harass a party or for the primary purpose of swamping the opponent with paperwork. Objections to interrogatories cause unwanted delay and possible loss of valuable information. Opponents usually object to questions that are irrelevant, vague or ambiguous, unduly burdensome, too numerous, or too broad in scope (covering too great a time span, for example). An attorney will also object to questions

that seek protected information (such as the privileged communication between spouses or between an attorney and his or her client) or the ideas and strategies that make up the attorney's work product.

2　Develop Objectives for the Interrogatories. Review the case file to familiarize yourself with its contents. Meet with your supervising attorney to discuss the attorney's approach to the case. Identification of the key issues in the case, as well as the strategies and directions the attorney intends to pursue at trial, will help you streamline your work. With your attention focused on only the pertinent matters, reread the complaint, answer, and any other pleadings. Identify the elements to be proved and the defenses to be asserted, then list possible evidence that would support or disprove those elements or defenses. Divide the list into three parts: the information you already possess, information you have that needs to be clarified, and information that you need but do not yet possess. For items in the last two groups, indicate likely persons, files, documents, or other sources that will provide the information or give you leads to the information.

3　Refer to Forms Books or Previous Interrogatories. Collections of commonly used interrogatories can be found in the firm's library, a law library, or practice manuals. These are frequently categorized by the type of case—personal injury, contract, antitrust, and so on. Check interrogatories from similar cases in the firm's files to locate pertinent questions. Local examples keyed to local practice are especially helpful. Use the gathered examples as a guide only, then shape your questions to the unique needs of your case. Input useful examples into your computer and edit them to your satisfaction. Add your own questions to fully address the elements of the case at hand.

4　Use Preliminary Sections to Define and Instruct. Following the desired case caption, draft an introductory paragraph stating the name of the person to whom the questions are directed, that answers to the questions are requested, the date answers are due, and the applicable rule or rules of procedure. A subsequent section should define any terms or identify any acronyms that will be repeated in the questions. This promotes clarity and avoids repetitive language. It reduces evasiveness by giving you the power to define the terms as broadly or as narrowly as needed. Interrogatories from previous cases define commonly repeated terms, such as *document, identify, you,* and *corporate officer,* and thus are good sources for the definitions section. Review your proposed definitions in light of your case to make sure that they do not exclude a particularly valuable area of information. The definition and instruction sections should not be so long that they are difficult to read.

5 Cover the "Who, What, Why, When, Where, and How." When planning your interrogatories, try to cover the "who, what, why, when, where, and how." Focus on the pleadings. Include in the interrogatories questions that will elicit the basis for each allegation and each denial made in the pleadings. Also include questions that will help you locate evidence that go beyond the allegations and denials in the pleadings. You might draft questions that ask, for example, for the address and custodian of certain documents, physical evidence, exhibits and witnesses to be relied on, and other items. (Under the revised FRCP, much of the information will already have been disclosed by the parties.)

6 Phrase Your Questions Simply, Concisely, and Accurately. The questions should be written simply and concisely. Try to eliminate all unnecessary adjectives and adverbs. Break complex questions into shorter and simpler components. Avoid giving the defendant options that allow the defendant to select the easiest and least informative answer. Be reasonable in the scope of your requests. For example, you

should limit the time span for which records or other kinds of information are sought.

Also, make sure that no words are misspelled. Misspellings create an impression of incompetence and may allow respondents to answer legitimately that they have no knowledge of the whereabouts of "Mr. Fones" when you need information about "Mr. Jones."

7 Avoid Questions Calling for a "Yes" or "No" Answer. Questions that permit a "yes" or "no" response are of little value unless you include follow-up questions. Questions should determine if the person's statement is based on personal observation or secondhand knowledge. "Why" questions are easily circumvented with such responses as "That is what he wanted to do," or "He believed he should."

8 Make Effective Use of Opinion and Contention Questions. Opinion and contention questions are permitted by federal and most state rules. They identify where the opponent stands on key factual questions. For example, "Do you contend that the intersection light was red before the defendant entered the intersection? If so, on what do you base your contention? What persons have knowledge of these facts?" and so forth. The answers to these types of questions identify the facts in contention and the evidence on which the contention is based. This is extremely useful because other discovery devices do not get at the reasons or evidence that forms the basis for a contention or opinion. It is best to reserve this kind of question for a time later in the discovery process when previous discovery has

"YOUR ABILITY TO DRAFT GOOD INTERROGATORIES WILL MAKE YOU A VALUED MEMBER OF THE LITIGATION TEAM."

revealed the contentions and most of the investigation in the case is completed. Otherwise, "I do not know yet" is a likely response.

9 Add Concluding or Summary Interrogatories. Include one or more questions to provide some protection for anything you forgot to address. This may prevent the opponent from using evidence at trial that you should have learned about earlier. A concluding request might be, "Identify any additional information pertinent to this lawsuit but not set out in your previous answers."

10 Employ the Evasiveness Test and Submit the Document to Your Supervising Attorney. Proofread the drafted interrogatories. Test your questions by placing yourself in the position of the other party and seeing if you can weasel your way around and out of providing such information. Redraft questions if necessary. Once this is done, give the document to your supervising attorney for any final review and signature. Have the interrogatories served on defendant.

interrogatories, deposition transcripts and summaries, pretrial motions, a list of exhibits and when they will be used, a witness list and the order in which the witnesses will testify, relevant cases or statutes that Gilmore plans to cite, and generally any document or information that will be important to have close at hand during the trial.

● **Unless the paralegal knows from prior experience what his or her supervising attorney wants to include in the trial notebook and how it should be organized, the paralegal should discuss these matters with the attorney.**

Typically, the trial notebook is a three-ring binder (or several binders, depending on the complexity of the case). The contents of the notebook are separated by divider sheets with tabs on them. Paralegal Lopez will create a general index to the notebook's contents and place this index at the front of the notebook. She may also create an index for each section of the binder and place those indexes at the beginnings of the sections. Some paralegals use a computer notebook and a software retrieval system to help them quickly locate documents, especially in complicated cases involving thousands of documents.

When preparing the trial notebook, always remember the following:

● **The documents in the trial notebook should not be the original documents but rather copies of them.**

The original documents (unless they are needed as evidence at trial) should always remain in the firm's files, both for reasons of security (should the trial notebook be misplaced) and to ensure that Lopez or others in the office will have access to the documents while the notebook is in court with the attorney.

Pretrial Conference

Before the trial begins, the attorneys usually meet with the trial judge in a **pretrial conference** to explore the possibility of resolving the case and, if a settlement is not possible, at least agree on the manner in which the trial will be conducted. In particular, the parties may attempt to clarify the issues in dispute and establish ground rules to restrict such things as the admissibility of certain types of evidence. Once the pretrial conference has concluded, both parties will turn their attention to the trial itself. Assuming that the trial will be heard by a jury, however, one more step is necessary before the trial begins: selecting the jurors who will hear the trial and render a verdict on the dispute.

Jury Selection

Before the trial gets under way, a panel of jurors must be assembled. The clerk of the court usually notifies local residents by mail that they have been selected for jury duty. The process of selecting the names of these prospective jurors varies, depending on the court, but often they are randomly selected by the court clerk from lists of registered voters or those within a state to

PRETRIAL CONFERENCE
A conference prior to trial in which the judge and the attorneys litigating the suit discuss settlement possibilities, clarify the issues in dispute, and agree on how the trial will be conducted.

DEVELOPING PARALEGAL SKILLS

Trial Support

 Scott Greer, a paralegal with the firm of Dewey & Stone, is assisting an attorney, Sue Jefferson, in a personal-injury lawsuit. The lawsuit was brought by a client who was injured in an automobile accident. Scott has received a memo from attorney Jefferson requesting him to prepare a diagram of the accident and to arrange to have a "day-in-the-life" videotape created for presentation in court. The videotape will show what a typical day in the life of the plaintiff is like as a result of injuries sustained in the accident.

Scott begins his tasks by contacting Trial Support Services, Inc., a firm that specializes in litigation support services. Included in these services are investigations, photographic services, and the preparation of videotapes and other demonstrative evidence, such as graphs, charts, and scale drawings. Scott explains that he needs a day-in-the-life tape made that details the day-to-day living experiences of the plaintiff, who is now a paraplegic as a result of the accident. This video will be shown to the jury to make them aware of the kind of life the plaintiff now leads as a result of the defendant's negligence. Scott arranges to meet with an employee of Trial Support Services at the plaintiff's home on the following day so that the videotape can be made.

Because Scott has so many other responsibilities in preparing for this trial, he does not have time to prepare the graphs and charts on his computer at the office, as he often does. Scott arranges to have Trial Support Services enlarge the diagram of the accident site so that it can be viewed clearly by the jury. The diagram will help the jury understand how the accident occurred. Scott delivers the diagram, which measures 8½ by 11 inches, to Trial Support Services that afternoon and asks them to enlarge it to 2½ by 4½ feet. Scott further requests that the enlarged diagram be done in color and placed on an easel, which Trial Support Services can also provide.

Trial Support Services agrees to deliver a VCR, a television set, the enlarged diagram, copies of the diagram for the jurors, and the easel to the courtroom prior to the trial. Scott makes a deposit on the equipment, and Trial Support Services agrees to bill the firm for the balance. Scott will have to contact the judge's clerk to arrange for a convenient time for the delivery of these items. He will also have to meet with an employee of Trial Support Services in the courtroom prior to the trial so that the employee can show Scott how to work the video equipment and set up the easel.

Now that Scott has performed the work assigned to him, he prepares a memo detailing the arrangements that he has made and puts it in the file. He sends a copy of the memo to his supervising attorney so that she knows that he has completed the assignment.

whom driver's licenses have been issued. The persons selected then report to the courthouse on the date specified in the notice. At the courthouse, they are gathered into a single pool of jurors, and the process of selecting those jurors who will actually hear the case begins. Although some types of trials require twelve-person juries, most civil matters can be heard by a jury of six persons.

VOIR DIRE

A French phrase meaning "to speak the truth." The phrase is used to describe the preliminary questions that attorneys for the plaintiff and the defendant ask prospective jurors to determine whether potential jury members are biased or have any connection with a party to the action or with a prospective witness.

CHALLENGE

An attorney's objection, during *voir dire,* to the inclusion of a particular person on the jury.

CHALLENGE FOR CAUSE

A *voir dire* challenge for which an attorney states the reason why a prospective juror should not be included in the jury.

PEREMPTORY CHALLENGE

A *voir dire* challenge to exclude a potential juror from serving on the jury without any supporting reason or cause. Peremptory challenges based on racial or gender criteria are illegal.

CASE AT A GLANCE

The Plaintiff—
   Plaintiff: Katherine Baranski
   Attorney: Allen P. Gilmore
   Paralegal: Elena Lopez

The Defendant—
   Defendant: Tony Peretto
   Attorney: Elizabeth A.
      Cameron
   Paralegal: Gordon McVay

Each attorney will question prospective jurors in a proceeding known as *voir dire.*[9] Legal assistants often work with their attorneys to write up the questions that will be asked of jurors during *voir dire.* Because all of the jurors will have previously filled out forms giving basic information about themselves, the attorneys and their paralegals can tailor their questions accordingly. They fashion the questions in such a way as to uncover any biases on the part of prospective jurors and to find persons who might identify with the plights of their respective clients. When large numbers of jurors are involved, during the *voir dire* process, the attorneys may direct their questions to groups of jurors, as opposed to individual jurors, to minimize the amount of time needed to choose the jurors who will sit on the jury. Note that in some courts, judges may question the jurors, using questions prepared by the attorneys.

During *voir dire,* the attorney for each side may exercise a certain number of **challenges** to prevent particular persons from being allowed to serve on the jury. Both attorneys can exercise two types of challenges: challenges "for cause" and peremptory challenges. If attorney Gilmore concludes that a particular prospective juror is biased against Baranski for some reason, Gilmore may exercise a **challenge for cause** and request that the prospective juror not be included in the jury. Each attorney may also exercise a limited number of **peremptory challenges**. Attorneys may exercise peremptory challenges without giving any reason for their desire to exclude a particular juror. Peremptory challenges based on racial criteria or gender, however, are illegal.[10]

After both sides have completed their challenges, those jurors who have been excused are permitted to leave. The remaining jurors, those found to be acceptable by both attorneys, will be seated in the jury box.

THE TRIAL

During the trial, the attorneys, Allen Gilmore and Elizabeth Cameron, will present their cases to the jury. Because the attorneys will be concentrating on the trial, it will fall to their paralegals to coordinate the logistical aspects of the trial and observe as closely as possible the trial proceedings. Because paralegal Lopez is thoroughly familiar with the case and Gilmore's legal strategy, she will be a valuable ally during the trial. She will be able to anticipate Gilmore's needs and provide appropriate reminders or documents as Gilmore needs them. She will also monitor each witness's testimony to ensure that it is consistent with previous statements made by the witness.

Generally, Lopez will also act as a second pair of eyes and ears during the trial. She will observe how the jury is responding to various witnesses and their testimony or to the attorneys' demeanor and questions. She will take

---

9. A French phrase meaning "to speak the truth." Pronounced vwahr *deehr.*
10. Discriminating against prospective jurors on the basis of race was prohibited by the United States Supreme Court in *Batson v. Kentucky,* 476 U.S. 79, 106 S.Ct. 1712, 90 L.Ed.2d 69 (1986). Discriminating against prospective jurors on the basis of gender was prohibited by the Supreme Court in *J.E.B. v. Alabama ex rel. T.B.,* ____U.S.____, 114 S. Ct. 1419, 128 L.Ed.2d 89 (1994). See Chapter 9 for an explanation of how to read court citations.

THE LEGAL TEAM AT WORK
In the Courtroom

Many paralegals, like Elena Lopez, attend trials with their attorneys. And many attorneys say that they do not know how they could manage the many things that need to be done during the trial without such assistance. Suppose, for example, that an attorney wants to check on the contents of a document that was not included in the trial notebook. There is no way that the attorney can leave the courtroom while the court is in session. His paralegal, however, can. If the paralegal brought a cellular phone with him or her, as many paralegals who attend trials do, the paralegal can simply step out into the hallway, dial a number, and get the information from the office over the phone or arrange to have documents brought to the courthouse immediately. (The legal assistant must take care when using a cellular phone to preserve confidentiality. For example, he or she must not reveal the client's name or any other information that could identify the client because conversations over cellular phones may be tapped. As with any phone call, paralegals must also be careful to make sure that the conversation is not overheard by any third party, such as someone in the hallway of the courthouse.)

The paralegal can also assist at trial by comparing statements made in court by a witness for the opponent to statements made earlier by that witness during his or her deposition. If the witness gives testimony that is inconsistent with earlier statements, the attorney will want to prove this inconsistency to the court by pointing to the relevant page of the deposition transcript. The paralegal, if he or she was checking the testimony against the deposition transcript, will have the relevant page numbers of the transcript at hand and can quickly direct the attorney's attention to those pages.

The old adage "Two heads are better than one" is certainly true in the context of trial work. Although their duties and functions differ, the lawyer and the paralegal both play essential roles in representing the client's best interests in the courtroom.

notes during the trial on these observations as well as on the points being stressed and the types of evidence introduced by the opposing counsel, Cameron. At the end of the day, Lopez and Gilmore may review the day's events, and Lopez's "trial journal" will provide a ready reference to the major events that transpired in the courtroom.

Opening Statements

The trial both opens and closes with attorneys' statements to the jury. In their **opening statements**, the attorneys will give a brief version of the facts and the supporting evidence that they will use during the trial. Because some trials can drag on for weeks or even months, it is extremely helpful for jurors to hear a summary of the story that will unfold during the trial. Otherwise, they may be left wondering how a particular piece of evidence fits into the dispute. In short, the opening statement is a kind of "road map" that describes the destination that each attorney hopes to reach and outlines how he or she plans to reach it.

OPENING STATEMENT
An attorney's statement to the jury at the beginning of the trial. The attorney briefly outlines the evidence that will be offered during the trial and the legal theory that will be pursued.

CASE AT A GLANCE

The Plaintiff—
Plaintiff: Katherine Baranski
Attorney: Allen P. Gilmore
Paralegal: Elena Lopez

The Defendant—
Defendant: Tony Peretto
Attorney: Elizabeth A.
   Cameron
Paralegal: Gordon McVay

DIRECT EXAMINATION
The examination of a witness by the attorney who calls the witness to the stand to testify on behalf of the attorney's client.

CROSS-EXAMINATION
The questioning of an opposing witness during the trial.

REDIRECT EXAMINATION
The questioning of a witness following the adverse party's cross-examination.

RECROSS-EXAMINATION
The questioning of an opposing witness following the adverse party's redirect examination.

MOTION FOR A DIRECTED VERDICT (MOTION FOR JUDGMENT AS A MATTER OF LAW)
A motion requesting that the court grant judgment in favor of the party making the motion on the ground that the other party has not produced sufficient evidence to support his or her claim.

The Plaintiff's Case

Once the opening statements have been made, Gilmore will present the plaintiff's case first. Because he is the plaintiff's attorney, he has the burden of proving that defendant Peretto was negligent. Attorney Gilmore will call several eyewitnesses to the stand and ask them to tell the court about the sequence of events that led to the accident. This form of questioning is known as **direct examination**. After attorney Gilmore has finished questioning a witness on direct examination, defendant Peretto's attorney, Cameron, will begin her **cross-examination** of that witness. During her cross-examination, Cameron will be primarily concerned with reducing the witness's credibility in the eyes of the jury and the judge. Cameron must confine her cross-examination to matters brought up during direct examination and matters that relate to a witness's credibility.

After Cameron has finished cross-examining each witness, plaintiff Baranski's attorney, Gilmore, will need to repair any damage done to the credibility of the witness's testimony—or, indeed, to the case itself. Gilmore will do this by again questioning the witness and allowing the witness to explain his or her answer. This process is known as **redirect examination**. Following Gilmore's redirect examination, defendant Peretto's attorney, Cameron, will be given an opportunity for **recross-examination**. When both attorneys have finished with the first witness, Gilmore will call the succeeding witnesses in plaintiff Baranski's case, each of whom will be subject to cross-examination (and redirect and recross, if necessary).

After attorney Gilmore has presented his case for plaintiff Baranski, then Cameron, as counsel for defendant Peretto, may decide to make a **motion for a directed verdict** (now also known as a **motion for judgment as a matter of law** in federal courts). Through this motion, attorney Cameron will be saying to the court that the plaintiff's attorney, Gilmore, has not offered enough evidence to support a claim against defendant Peretto. If the judge agrees to grant the motion, then a judgment will be entered for defendant Peretto, plaintiff Baranski's case against him will be dismissed, and the trial will be over. The motion for a directed verdict (judgment as a matter of law) is seldom granted. If the judge had believed that Baranski's case was that weak before the trial started, then the judge would probably have granted a pretrial motion to dismiss the case, thereby avoiding the expense of a trial. Occasionally, however, the occurrence of certain events—such as the death of a key witness—might mean that the plaintiff has no evidence at all to support his or her allegations. In that event, the court may grant the defendant's motion for a directed verdict, or judgment as a matter of law.

The Defendant's Case

Assuming that the motion for directed verdict (motion for judgment as a matter of law) is denied by the court, the two attorneys, Gilmore and Cameron, will now reverse their roles. Attorney Cameron will now begin to present evidence demonstrating the weaknesses of plaintiff Baranski's claims against defendant Peretto. Cameron will call witnesses to the stand

and question them. After Cameron's direct examination of each witness, that witness will be subject to possible cross-examination by Gilmore, redirect examination by Cameron, and recross-examination by Gilmore.

Once Cameron has finished presenting her case on behalf of defendant Peretto, Gilmore will be permitted to offer evidence to *rebut* (refute) evidence introduced by Cameron in Peretto's behalf. After Gilmore's rebuttal, if any, both attorneys will make their closing arguments to the jury.

Closing Arguments

In their **closing arguments**, the attorneys summarize their presentations and argue in their clients' favor. Both attorneys will want to organize their presentations so that they can explain to the jury their respective arguments and show how their arguments are supported by the evidence. Once both attorneys have completed their remarks, the case will be submitted to the jury and the attorneys' role in the trial will be finished.

CLOSING ARGUMENT
An argument made by each side's attorney after the cases for the plaintiff and defendant have been presented. Closing arguments are made prior to the jury charge.

The Verdict

Before the jurors begin their deliberations, the judge gives the jury a **charge**, in which the judge sums up the case and instructs the jurors on the rules of law that apply to the issues involved in the case. Following its receipt of the charge, the jury begins its deliberations. Once it has reached a decision, the jury issues a **verdict** in favor of one of the parties. If the verdict is in favor of the plaintiff, the jury will specify the amount of damages to be paid by the defendant. Following the announcement of the verdict, the jurors are discharged. Usually, immediately after the verdict has been announced and the jurors discharged, the party in whose favor the verdict was issued makes a motion asking the judge to issue a *judgment*—which is that court's final word on the matter—consistent with the jury's verdict. For example, if the jury in the Baranski case finds that defendant Peretto was negligent and awards plaintiff Baranski damages in the amount of $75,000, the judge will order defendant Peretto to pay the plaintiff that amount.

CHARGE
The judge's instruction to the jury following the attorneys' closing arguments setting forth the rules of law that the jury must apply in reaching its decision, or verdict.

VERDICT
A formal decision made by a jury.

POSTTRIAL MOTIONS AND PROCEDURES

Every trial must have a winner and a loser. Although civil litigation is an expensive and cumbersome process, the losing party may wish to pursue the matter further after the verdict has been rendered. Assume that plaintiff Baranski wins at trial and is awarded $75,000 in damages. Also assume that defendant Peretto's attorney, Cameron, believes that the verdict for the plaintiff is not supported by the evidence. In this situation, she may file a **motion for judgment notwithstanding the verdict** (also known as a *motion for*

MOTION FOR JUDGMENT NOTWITHSTANDING THE VERDICT
A motion (also referred to as a motion for judgment as a matter of law in federal courts) requesting that the court grant judgment in favor of the party making the motion on the ground that the jury verdict against him or her was unreasonable and erroneous.

TODAY'S PROFESSIONAL PARALEGAL

Drafting *Voir Dire* Questions Like a Pro

Andrea Leed, a legal assistant, is preparing for trial. Her boss is a famous trial attorney, Mary Marshall. Mary rarely loses a case. One of her many secrets to success is that she always draws up a jury profile and prepares carefully for *voir dire*.

Mary is defending a corporation in an environmental liability case. The case has many complex engineering and scientific issues that the jury will need to understand in order to reach its verdict. It is a common practice in these types of cases to select a "blue ribbon" jury—a jury consisting of persons who are very well educated. Mary has suggested that Andrea hire a psychologist to prepare a jury profile.

CONSULTING WITH AN EXPERT WITNESS

Andrea contacts TrialPsych, Inc., a consulting firm headed by Dr. Linda Robertson, who specializes in jury selection. Dr. Robertson would be delighted to work on the case, but her services are very expensive, and Andrea must find out whether the client is willing to pay Dr. Robertson's fee. The client agrees to pay the fee, so Andrea meets with Dr. Robertson to discuss the case. Andrea explains that the client is a corporation and that the case involves complex scientific and engineering issues. Dr. Robertson consults her files for statistical information on these types of cases. She finds that the ideal jury would be made up of white-collar professionals holding advanced degrees in engineering or another applied science. Also, the prospective jurors would ideally be against extensive government regulation of the corporate world.

DRAFTING *VOIR DIRE* QUESTIONS

Andrea returns to the office and conveys this information to Mary in a meeting. Mary asks Andrea to draft some questions for *voir dire*. Andrea then drafts a list of about twenty questions, including such questions as the following:

1. Please state your name and address.
2. Where are you employed, and how long have you been employed there?
3. What is the highest level of education that you have attained: high school diploma, some college but no degree, college degree, advanced degree (please specify)?
4. If you have attended college or received a college degree, what was your field of study?
5. Have you ever been fired by a corporate employer in a way that you believed was unfair?
4. Have you ever worked for a government regulatory agency, and if so, what were your responsibilities in that position?
5. Have you, or persons or business firms with whom you are or have been associated, ever been sued for violating environmental statutes or regulations? If so, what were the violations?
6. In your opinion, what should be the government's role in regulating a company's operations?

REVIEWING THE *VOIR DIRE* QUESTIONS

Andrea faxes the list of questions to Dr. Robertson, who reviews them and faxes back some suggested changes, which Andrea incorporates. When the final list of questions is drawn up, Andrea presents it to Mary and places a copy of the list in the trial notebook. Mary asks Andrea to call Dr. Robertson and ask her if she is available to sit in on the actual *voir dire* process to ensure that jury selection goes smoothly.

---

judgment as a matter of law in the federal courts).[11] By filing this motion, attorney Cameron asks the judge to enter a judgment in favor of defendant

---

11. Amendments to the FRCP in 1991 designated both the motion for a directed verdict and the motion for judgment notwithstanding the verdict as motions for judgment as a matter of law. One of the reasons for the change was to allow both the preverdict and postverdict motions to be referred to with a terminology that does not conceal their common identity (both motions claim, at different times during the proceedings, that there is insufficient evidence against the defendant to justify a claim—or a verdict—against the defendant). Many judges and attorneys continue to use the former names of these motions, however, so we include them in our discussion.

Peretto on the ground (basis) that the jury verdict in favor of the plaintiff was unreasonable and erroneous. Cameron may file this motion only if she previously filed a motion for a directed verdict (or judgment as a matter of law) during the trial and the motion was denied at that time. Rule 50 of the Federal Rules of Civil Procedure permits either party to file a **motion for a new trial**. Such a motion may be submitted along with a motion for a judgment notwithstanding the verdict. A motion for a new trial is a far more drastic tactic because it asserts that the trial was so pervaded by error or otherwise fundamentally flawed that a new trial should be held. Because such a motion reflects adversely on the way in which the judge conducted the trial, it should only be filed if the attorney truly believes that a miscarriage of justice will otherwise result. For a motion for a new trial to have a reasonable chance of being granted, the motion must allege such serious problems as jury misconduct, prejudicial jury instructions, excessive or inadequate damages, or the existence of newly discovered evidence (but not if the evidence could have been discovered earlier through the use of reasonable care).

If attorney Cameron's posttrial motions are unsuccessful or if she decides not to file them, she may still file an **appeal**. No new evidence will be presented to the appellate court, and there is no jury. The appellate court will review the trial court's proceedings to decide whether the trial court erred in applying the law to the facts of the case, in instructing the jury, or in administering the trial generally. Appellate courts rarely tamper with a trial court's findings of fact because the judge and jury were in a better position than the appellate court to evaluate the credibility of witnesses, the nature of the evidence, and so on.

When a case is appealed, the attorneys for both parties submit written *briefs* that present their positions regarding the issues to be reviewed by the appellate court. The briefs outline each party's view of the proper application of the law to the facts. After the appellate court has had an opportunity to review the briefs, the court sets aside a time for both attorneys to argue their positions before the panel of judges. Following the oral arguments, the judges will decide the issue and then issue a formal written opinion, which normally will be published in the relevant reporter (see Chapter 9 for a detailed discussion of how court opinions are published).

MOTION FOR A NEW TRIAL
A motion asserting that the trial was so fundamentally flawed (because of error, newly discovered evidence, prejudice, or other reason) that a new trial is needed to prevent a miscarriage of justice.

APPEAL
The process of seeking a higher court's review of a lower court's decision for the purpose of correcting or changing the lower court's judgment or decision.

KEY TERMS AND CONCEPTS

affidavit   178

affirmative defense   186

allegation   175

answer   186

appeal   209

challenge   204

challenge for cause   204

charge   208

closing argument   207

complaint   173

cross-examination   206

default judgment   186

deponent   193

deposition   193

deposition transcript   194

direct examination   206

discovery   189

docket   174

Federal Rules of Civil Procedure (FRCP)   171

impeach   194

interrogatories   191

judgment   170

memorandum of law   187

motion   187

motion for a directed verdict   206

motion for judgment as a matter of law   206

motion for judgment notwithstanding the verdict   209

motion for judgment on the pleadings   187

CHAPTER SUMMARY

1. Although civil lawsuits vary from case to case in terms of their complexity, cost, and detail, all civil litigation involves similar procedural steps, as described in Exhibit 6.1.

2. The first step in the civil litigation process occurs when the attorney initially meets with a client who wishes to bring a lawsuit against another party or parties. Once the attorney agrees to represent the client in the lawsuit and the client has signed the retainer agreement, the attorney and the paralegal undertake a preliminary investigation into the matter to ascertain the facts alleged by the client and gain other factual information relating to the case. A litigation file is also created for the case.

3. The pleadings—which consist of the plaintiff's complaint, the defendant's answer, and any counterclaim or other pleadings listed in Exhibit 6.2—inform each party of the claims of the other and delineate the details of the dispute. The complaint, which initiates the lawsuit, is filed with the clerk of the appropriate court. Typically, the defendant is notified of a lawsuit by the delivery of the complaint and a summons (service of process). In federal court cases, revised FRCP 4 permits the plaintiff's attorney to notify the defendant, by first-class mail or other reliable means, of the lawsuit and enclose with the notice a form that the defendant can sign to waive the requirement of service of process. If the defendant does not sign and return the form, then the plaintiff's attorney will arrange to have the defendant served with the complaint and summons.

4. On receiving the complaint (and summons, if process is served), the defendant has several options. The defendant may submit an answer. The answer may deny any wrongdoing, or he or she might assert an affirmative defense against the plaintiff's claim. Alternatively or simultaneously, the defendant might make a motion to dismiss the case, perhaps on the ground that the relevant statute of limitations has expired.

5. A motion for judgment on the pleadings is a pretrial motion that may be filed by either party after all pleadings have been filed. The motion may be granted if it can be shown that no factual dispute exists. A motion for summary judgment may be filed by either party during or after the discovery stage of litigation. In determining whether to grant the latter motion, the judge can consider evidence apart from the pleadings—such as evidence contained in affidavits, depositions, and interrogatories. The motion for summary judgment will not be granted if any facts are in dispute.

6. In preparing for trial, the attorney for each party undertakes a formal investigative process called discovery to obtain evidence helpful to his or her client's case. Traditional discovery tools include interrogatories and depositions, as well as various requests, including a request for documents in the possession of the other party or opposing counsel (or a third party), a request for admission (of the truth of certain statements) by the opposing party, and a request for examination (to establish the truth of claimed injuries or health status).

7. In federal court cases, revised FRCP 26 requires that the attorneys cooperate in forming a discovery plan early in the litigation process. The rule also requires attorneys to automatically disclose relevant information. Under FRCP 26, only after initial disclosures have been made can attorneys resort to the use of traditional discovery tools.

8. Before the trial begins, attorneys for both sides and their paralegals gather and organize all evidence, documents, and other materials relating to the case. Paralegals often assist in contacting and issuing subpoenas to witnesses, as well as in making sure that all exhibits and displays are ready by the trial date and that the trial notebook is prepared. The attorneys for both sides meet with the trial judge in a pretrial conference to decide whether a settlement is possible or, if not, to decide how the trial will be conducted and what types of evidence will be admissible.

9. The attorneys also engage in the jury-selection process, called *voir dire.* The attorneys can exclude certain persons in the jury pool from sitting on the jury through the exercise of challenges for cause and a limited number of peremptory challenges.

10. At the trial, the paralegal, if he or she attends the trial, coordinates witnesses' appearances, tracks the testimony of witnesses and compares it with sworn statements that the witnesses made prior to the trial, and provides the attorney with appropriate reminders or documents when necessary. The paralegal generally acts as a second set of eyes and ears for the attorney during the trial.

11. The trial begins with opening statements in which both attorneys briefly give their versions of the facts of the case and the evidence supporting their views. The plaintiff's attorney then presents evidence supporting the plaintiff's claim, including the testimony of witnesses. The attorney's questioning of the witnesses whom he or she calls is referred to as direct examination. The defendant's attorney may then cross-examine the witness, after which the plaintiff's attorney may again question the witness on redirect examination (followed by possible recross-examination by the defendant's attorney).

12. After the plaintiff's case has been presented, the defendant's attorney may make a motion for a directed verdict, also called a motion for judgment as a matter of law. This motion asserts that the plaintiff has not offered enough evidence to support the validity of the plaintiff's claim against the defendant. If the judge grants the motion, the case will be dismissed. If the motion is not granted, the attorneys then reverse their roles, and the defendant's attorney presents evidence and testimony to refute the plaintiff's claims. Any witnesses called to the stand by the defendant's attorney will be subject to direct examination by that attorney, cross-examination by the plaintiff's attorney, and possibly redirect examination and recross-examination.

13. After the defendant's attorney has finished his or her presentation, both attorneys give their closing arguments, after which the judge gives the jury a charge—instructions on the applicable law and a review of the facts as they were presented during the trial. The jury then begins its deliberations. When the jury has reached a decision, it issues a verdict in favor of one party or the other.

14. The losing party's attorney may file a motion for judgment notwithstanding the verdict (now also called a motion for judgment as a matter of law in federal courts), alleging that the judge should enter a judgment in favor of the losing party in spite of the verdict because the verdict was not supported by the evidence or was otherwise erroneous. In conjunction with the motion, or in the alternative, the attorney may also file a motion for a new trial, asserting that the trial was so flawed—by judge or juror misconduct or by other pervasive errors—that a new trial should be held. Finally, the attorney may, depending on the client's wishes, appeal the decision to an appellate court for further review and decision.

QUESTIONS FOR REVIEW

1. What are the basic steps in the litigation process prior to the trial? How does the paralegal assist the attorney in each of these steps?

2. What documents constitute the pleadings in a civil lawsuit? How are defendants notified of lawsuits that have been brought against them? What new procedures are included in revised FRCP 4 for notifying the defendant of a lawsuit?

3. Name three pretrial motions and state the purpose of each motion.

4. What is discovery? When does it take place? List three discovery devices that can be used to obtain information prior to trial.

5. How have the 1993 amendments to the FRCP affected the discovery process in federal court cases?

6. What is involved in preparing witnesses, exhibits, and displays for trial? What role does the paralegal play? How can the paralegal assist the attorney in preparing the trial notebook?

7. What is a pretrial conference? What issues are likely to be raised and decided at a pretrial conference?

8. How are jurors selected? What is the difference between a peremptory challenge and a challenge for cause?

9. Describe the basic procedures involved in a trial. What role does the paralegal play during a trial? What types of trial-related tasks may the paralegal perform?

10. Name the posttrial motions that are available. In what situation is each of them used? Describe the procedure for filing an appeal.

ETHICAL QUESTIONS

1. Scott Emerson takes a job as a paralegal with a large law firm that specializes in defending clients against product-liability claims. The firm's clients are some of the largest manufacturing companies in the country. Mark Jones, an associate attorney, assigns Scott the job of drafting and sending out interrogatories to the plaintiff in a case brought against one of the firm's clients. Specifically, Scott is told to send out a standard set of one hundred interrogatories, each with five parts. Scott eventually learns that one of the favorite discovery tactics of the firm is to inundate plaintiffs with discovery requests, interrogatories, and depositions to cause continuous delays and to outspend the plaintiffs. Scott knows that the relevant state court rules do not limit the number of interrogatories that can be used, but he suspects that the firm's tactics are ethically questionable. Are they? What should Scott do?

2. Anthony Paletti, a paralegal, is attending a trial with his supervising attorney. Anthony leaves the courtroom to go meet a witness. On his way down the hall, he runs into the defendant in the case. The defendant says to Anthony, "You work for the plaintiff's attorney, don't you? I have a question for you about that contract that your attorney offered into evidence." Should Anthony answer the defendant's question? Why or why not?

3. A client claiming to have severely injured his back at work comes into the office of a law firm. The client, in a wheelchair, seeks legal advice about filing a lawsuit, and the attorney decides to take the case. Two days later, Alvin Kerrigan, the attorney's paralegal, sees the new client on the roof of a building installing shingles. What should Alvin do?

4. During a lunch break in the course of a trial, Louise Lanham, a paralegal, was washing her hands in the restroom. One of the members of the trial jury came up to her and said, "I don't understand what negligence is. Can you explain it to me?" How should Louise answer this question?

PRACTICE QUESTIONS AND ASSIGNMENTS

1. Assume that you work for attorney Tara Jolans of Adams & Tate, 1000 Town Center, Suite 500, White Tower, MI 48892. Jolans has decided to represent Sandra Nelson in her lawsuit against David Namisch. Based on the following information, draft a complaint to be filed in the U.S. District Court for the Eastern District of Michigan.

Sandra Nelson is a plaintiff in a lawsuit resulting from an automobile accident.

Sandra was turning left at a traffic light at the intersection of Jefferson and Mack Streets, while the left-turn arrow was green, when she was hit from the side by a car driven by David Namisch, who failed to stop at the light. The accident occurred on Friday, June 3, 1995, at 11:30 P.M. David lived in New York, was visiting his family in Michigan, and just prior to the accident had been out drinking with his brothers. Several witnesses saw the accident. One of the witnesses called the police.

Sandra was not wearing her seat belt at the time of the accident, and she was thrown against the windshield, sustaining massive head injuries. When the police and ambulance arrived, they did not think that she would make it to the hospital alive, but she survived. She wants to claim damages of $500,000 for medical expenses, $65,000 for lost wages, and $35,000 for property damage to her Rolls Royce. The accident was reported in the local newspaper, complete with photographs.

2. Draft a subpoena for a friendly witness using the following facts:

Simon Kolstad of 100 Schoolcraft Road, Del Mar, CA 91428, is a witness to be subpoenaed in *Sumner v. Hayes,* a civil lawsuit filed in the U.S. District court for the Eastern District of Michigan, docket number 123492–96. He is being subpoenaed by the plaintiff's attorney, Marvin W. Green, whose office is located at 300 Penobscot Building, Detroit, MI 94202. Kolstad is to appear in room number 6 of the courthouse, which is located at 231 Lafayette Boulevard, Detroit, MI 48203, at 2:00 P.M. on January 10, 1996. Kolstad is to bring with him a letter from the defendant to Kolstad dated February 9, 1993.

7

CONDUCTING INTERVIEWS AND INVESTIGATIONS

CHAPTER OBJECTIVES

After completing this chapter, you will know:

• What kinds of skills are employed during the interviewing process.
• How to prepare for an interview with a client or witness and the types of client interviews commonly conducted by paralegals.
• How to create an investigation plan.
• Some basic principles that guide legal investigators.
• The variety of sources that you can use when trying to locate information or witnesses.
• Some useful techniques for interviewing witnesses and how to prepare witness statements.

CHAPTER OUTLINE

Introduction

Paralegals frequently interview clients. After the initial client interview (which is usually conducted by the supervising attorney), the paralegal may conduct one or more subsequent interviews to obtain detailed information from the client. How the paralegal relates to the client has an important effect on the client's attitude toward the firm and toward the attorney or legal team handling the case. Paralegals also often interview witnesses. As part of a preliminary investigation into a client's claim, for example, the paralegal may interview one or more witnesses to gain as much information as possible.

Because factual evidence is crucial to the outcome of a legal problem, investigation is necessarily an important part of legal work. Attorneys often rely on paralegals to conduct investigations, and you should be prepared to accept the responsibility for making sure that an investigation is conducted thoroughly and professionally.

Learning how to conduct interviews and investigations is thus an important part of preparing for your career as a paralegal. In this chapter, you will read about the basic skills and concepts that you can apply when interviewing clients or witnesses. You will also read about the basics of legal investigation.

Interviewing Skills

INTERVIEWEE
The person who is being interviewed.

The primary goal of any interview is to obtain factual information from the **interviewee**—the person being interviewed. Interviewing skills are essentially any skills—particularly interpersonal and communication skills—that help you to attain this goal. In this section, you will learn how the use of interpersonal and communication skills can help you establish a comfortable relationship with the interviewee. Then, you will read about specific questioning and listening techniques that can help you control the interview and elicit various types of information.

Interpersonal Skills

At the outset of any interview, remember that your primary goal is to obtain information from the client or witness being interviewed. Although some people communicate information and ideas readily and effectively, others may need considerable coaching and encouragement. If they feel comfortable in your presence and in the interviewing environment, they will generally be more willing to disclose information. Here we look at some techniques that you can employ to put the interviewee at ease and establish a good working relationship with that person.

Put the Interviewee at Ease.   As you begin an interview, you should remember that the interviewee may be very nervous or at least uncomfortable. Because the time you have to talk with a client or witness will be limited, you should put that individual at ease as quickly as possible. A minute or two spent chatting casually with the client or witness is time well spent. Also, saying or doing something that shows your concern for the interviewee's physical comfort helps to make the interviewee feel more relaxed. For example, you might offer the individual a cup of coffee or other beverage.

Use Language that Communicates.   Using language that the interviewee will understand is essential in establishing a good working relationship with that person. If you are interviewing a client with only a grade-school education, for example, do not use the phrase "facial lacerations" when talking about "cuts on the face." If you are interviewing a witness who does not speak English very well, arrange to have an interpreter present unless you are fluent in the witness's native language.

When conducting interviews, you should be particularly attentive to the following fact:

● **Most clients and witnesses are not familiar with legal terminology. You should generally avoid using legal terms that will not be clearly understood by the interviewee.**

If you must use a specific legal term to express an idea, be sure that you define the term and that it is clearly understood.

Instill a Sense of Confidence and Trust.   When you conduct an interview, you represent the firm for which you work—you are a member of a professional team. From the outset, you should try to instill in the client or witness a sense of confidence in your professional ability to deal with the matter at hand. You can do several things to accomplish this goal, including the following:

• Confidently greet the interviewee and give him or her your full attention.
• Make sure that the interviewee is aware of the relationship between specific questions and the general topic being explored during the interview. If you do not, the interviewee might assume that he or she is being placed in a subservient position and may be less willing to communicate. Also, by understanding the context, the interviewee can respond to the questions more appropriately.
• Use appropriate verbal language (avoid using slang and legalese, speak clearly, use grammatically correct sentences, and so on).
• Use appropriate nonverbal language (body language and facial gestures that show you are interested in what the interviewee is saying).
• Prevent unnecessary interruptions—hold all phone calls, for example—so that you can give your full attention to the interviewee.

In deciding what actions you might take to gain the interviewee's trust and confidence, you should also use common sense. Place yourself in the interviewee's position. What would cause you to trust or have confidence in an interviewer in a similar situation?

Questioning Skills

When questioning witnesses or clients, you should remember to remain objective at all times and gather as much relevant factual information as possible. Sometimes, you may have difficulty remaining objective when questioning witnesses because you sympathize with the client and may not want to hear about facts that are contrary to the client's position. But relevant factual information includes those details that adversely affect the client's case as well as those that support the client's position. Indeed, your supervising attorney must know *all* of the facts, especially any that might damage the client's case in court.

The experienced legal interviewer uses certain questioning techniques to prompt the interviewees to communicate the information needed. There are several types of questions, including open-ended, closed-ended, hypothetical, pressure, and leading questions. Here, we look at how you can apply these question formats when you interview clients or witnesses.

OPEN-ENDED QUESTION
A question that is phrased in such a way that it elicits a relatively detailed discussion of an experience or event.

Open-ended Questions.   The **open-ended question** is a broad, exploratory question that invites any number of possible responses. The open-ended question can be used when you want to give the interviewee an opportunity to talk at some length about a given subject. "What happened on the night of October 28—the night of the murder?" is an open-ended question. Other examples of open-ended questions are "And what happened next?" and "What did you see as you approached the intersection?" When you ask a question of this kind, be prepared for a lengthy response. If a witness has difficulty in narrating the events that he or she observed or if a lull develops during the explanation, you will need to encourage the witness to continue through the use of various prompting responses (which will be discussed shortly in the context of listening skills).

Open-ended questions are useful in interviewing clients or friendly witnesses (witnesses who favor the client's position). This is because these kinds of interviewees are usually forthcoming, and you will be able to gain information from them by indicating in broad terms what you want them to describe.

CLOSED-ENDED QUESTION
A question that is phrased in such a way that it elicits a simple "yes" or "no" answer.

Closed-ended Questions.   The **closed-ended question**, in contrast, is intended to elicit a "yes" or "no" response from the interviewee. "Did you see the murder weapon?" is an example of a closed-ended question. Although closed-ended questions tend to curb communication, they are useful in some situations. For example, if an interviewee tends to digress frequently from the topic being discussed, using closed-ended questions can help keep him or her on track. Closed-ended questions, because they invite specific answers, also may be useful in relaxing the interviewee in preparation for more difficult questions that may follow later in the interview. In addition, closed-ended questions may help to elicit information from adverse witnesses (those who are not favorable to the client's position) who may be reluctant to volunteer information.

HYPOTHETICAL QUESTION
A question based on hypothesis, conjecture, or fiction.

Hypothetical Questions.   As a paralegal, you may be asked to interview an expert witness either to gather information about a case or to evaluate whether that person would be an effective expert witness at trial (expert witnesses will be discussed later in this chapter). The **hypothetical question** is frequently used with expert witnesses. Hypothetical questions allow you to obtain an answer to an important question without giving away the facts (and confidences) of a client's case. For example, you might invent a hypothetical situation involving a certain type of knee injury (the same kind of injury as that sustained by a client) and then ask an orthopedic surgeon what kind of follow-up care would ordinarily be undertaken for that type of injury.

Pressure Questions.   Sometimes, interviewers use a type of question known as a pressure question. **Pressure questions** are intended to make the interviewee feel uncomfortable and to induce the interviewee to respond emotionally. The pressure question may be useful in eliciting a response from an interviewee who is reluctant to discuss a matter with you. If an eyewitness, for example, refuses to state whether he or she saw the murderer, an interviewer might pressure him or her into responding by asking a question such as the following: "The murder weapon—a heavy board—was found a mile from the victim's body. Did you know that the board was traced to the construction site right next door to your store?"

Note that pressure questions should be used only as a last resort and then used very carefully. As an interviewer, you want to enlist the interviewee's cooperation, not alienate him or her.

PRESSURE QUESTION
A question intended to make the interviewee feel uncomfortable and respond emotionally. Pressure questions are sometimes used by interviewers to elicit answers from interviewees who may otherwise be unresponsive.

Leading Questions.   The **leading question** is one that suggests to the listener the answer to the question. "Isn't it true that you were only ten feet away from where the murder took place?" is a leading question. This question, of course, invites a "yes" answer. Leading questions are very effective for drawing information out of eyewitnesses or clients, particularly when they are reluctant to disclose information. They are also useful when interviewing witnesses who are reluctant to communicate information that may be helpful to the client's position. When used with clients and friendly witnesses, however, leading questions have a major drawback:

LEADING QUESTION
A question that suggests, or "leads to," a desired answer. Interviewers may use leading questions to elicit responses from witnesses who otherwise would not be forthcoming.

● **Leading questions may lead to distorted answers because the client or witness may tailor the answer to fit his or her perception of what the interviewer wants to know.**

For this reason, in the interviewing context, leading questions should be used cautiously and only when the interviewer is fully aware of the possible distortions that might result.

Listening Skills

The interviewer's ability to listen is perhaps the most important communication skill used during the interviewing process. Whenever you conduct an interview, you will want to absorb fully the interviewee's verbal answers as well as his or her nonverbal messages. Prior to the interview, you should make sure that the room in which the interview is to be held will be free of noises, phone calls, visitors, and other interruptions or distractions. Recall from Chapter 4 that noises and other distractions impede the communication process because they make attentive listening difficult. During the interview itself, you can use several listening techniques to maximize communication and guide the interviewee toward the fullest disclosure of needed information.

Active Listening.   Communication is an interactive process that requires the listener to engage in active listening. **Active listening** requires the listener to pay close attention to what the speaker is saying. Paying attention

ACTIVE LISTENING
The act of listening attentively to the speaker's verbal or nonverbal messages and responding to those messages by giving appropriate feedback.

to every detail of the discussion is critical to a productive interview. Lack of attention means that important details may be missed, and ultimately, the client will suffer.

● **If you ever find your attention wandering during an interview, have the interviewee repeat what he or she just said to make sure that you have not missed anything.**

You do not have to admit that your attention was wandering, of course. Simply say that you want to make sure that your impression of what the interviewee said is accurate.

Active listening also involves feedback. As a listener, you can give feedback, in the form of both verbal and nonverbal cues, to encourage the speaker to continue discussing a topic. An example of a verbal cue is "I'm listening, please go on." A nonverbal cue can be any facial expression or body language that shows you are interested in what is being said. Nodding positively, for example, is an effective way to convey, nonverbally, your interest.

Finally, active listening involves the ability to analyze on the spot the interviewee's comments in the context of the larger picture. Often, something that the interviewee says opens a door to another area that should be explored. When this happens, you need to decide whether to explore that area now or later—perhaps at a subsequent interview.

● **In general, you need to be constantly analyzing your interviewee's responses and deciding how those responses should direct your further questioning.**

RETENTIVE LISTENING
The act of listening attentively to what the speaker is saying for the purpose of remembering, or retaining, the information communicated.

Retentive Listening. Whenever your primary goal in listening is to remember what somebody is saying, you are engaging in **retentive listening**. Retentive listening requires, first of all, that you understand exactly what was said. We often assume that we understand messages only to learn later, when we act on them or try to relay them to another person, that we are not really clear on what was said. A good way to test your understanding of a message is to rephrase it in your own words. If you are not sure of what an interviewee means by a certain statement or phrase, for example, rephrase it in your own words and ask the interviewee if that is what he or she meant by the statement. For example, if a witness says, "I saw him do it," you might clarify the meaning of that statement by saying, "Do you mean that you saw the person throw the heavy board into the pond?"

Once a message is clarified, you will want to retain it. Taking notes during the interview facilitates the retention of important information. How extensively you take notes and what information you include in your notes will depend, to some extent, on whether the interview is being tape-recorded. (The use of tape recorders for interviews will be discussed later.)

Supportive Listening. There may be times during an interview when you must show support for the interviewee. For example, suppose that you are conducting a preliminary investigation on behalf of a client who was seriously injured in a car accident. You are interviewing an eyewitness to the accident, who happens to be a good friend of the client. Although your primary interest is in the information being disclosed, you must also show that you are concerned for the witness's feelings and that you understand how difficult it is for the witness to describe the crash. This kind of listening is sometimes referred to as **supportive listening**.

In the interviewing context, supportive listening may be employed effectively to encourage a client or witness to continue speaking about his or her perceptions or feelings in regard to a certain matter. Let the speaker know that you are listening attentively by giving appropriate feedback. Maintaining eye contact and murmuring an "uh huh" here or a "hmm" there may suffice. Alternatively, you might give supportive feedback in the form of a question or two, such as "And then what happened?" Asking questions not only provides feedback but it also allows the speaker to elaborate on the message being sent.

> **SUPPORTIVE LISTENING**
> The act of providing comments, utterances, or gestures that convey to the speaker an interest in what the speaker is saying and that encourage the speaker to continue speaking.

Reading Body Language.   In the courtroom, the credibility, or believability, of a witness giving testimony is strongly affected by body language. The ability to read body language is also an important skill for the interviewer. As experienced interviewers know, some of the most informative communication is transmitted nonverbally through facial expressions, other body movements, and general demeanor (how one sits, stands, moves, and so on). By carefully observing body language, you can, in effect, "listen between the lines." The paralegal interviewing a witness may ask the question, "Why were you in the store at the time of the murder?" The witness's response, "To buy a few groceries," may seem insincere if she shifts around in her seat, crosses and uncrosses her legs, and clears her throat before answering the question.

Learning how to read nonverbal communication may help you not only to interpret an interviewee's responses more accurately but also to determine whether a client or potential witness will be able to testify effectively on the client's behalf (discussed later in this chapter).

PLANNING THE INTERVIEW

Planning an interview involves organizing many details. As a paralegal, you may be responsible for scheduling the interview, determining where the interview should take place, arranging for the use of one of the firm's conference rooms or other office space for the interview, and other related details. The following discussion will help prepare you to plan either client or witness interviews.

Scheduling the Interview

When scheduling an interview, you should make sure that sufficient time is set aside for the interview session. When the session will be attended by other members of the law firm, such as an attorney or another paralegal specialist, their schedules must also be coordinated. The time required for an interview varies depending on the purpose of the interview. An initial client interview may require forty-five minutes or more. A subsequent interview with the client may require fifteen minutes or an hour or more, depending on how much information must be gathered. With experience, the paralegal interviewer becomes adept at judging how long a given interview will take, when to schedule it, and which members of the firm or legal team should attend the interview.

Preparing the Interviewee

You should give the client or witness ample notice of the upcoming interview. You should also indicate what items or documents the interviewee should bring to the interview. At times, the request may be very general ("Bring any information you have relating to the problem"); at other times, the request will be more specific ("Bring in your bank statements for the months of June and July"). When a client petitioning for bankruptcy is to be interviewed, you may want to ask him or her to bring in numerous financial documents. If an expert witness, such as a handwriting expert, is to be interviewed, you may ask the witness to bring credentials sufficient to verify his or her expertise.

Once an interview is scheduled and the interviewee is notified (usually by phone), you might want to send the interviewee a follow-up, confirming letter as a reminder. The letter will state the time and place of the interview and list the documents or items that the interviewee should bring to the interview.

Preparing Questions

Prior to any interview, you should have clearly in mind the kind of information you want to obtain from the client or witness. You should know what questions you want to ask and have them prepared in advance. Crucial to the success of any interview is how well you are prepared for it. Advance preparation for an interview depends, of course, on the type of interview being conducted.

Preprinted or Computerized Forms. In many situations, the paralegal (or the firm) will already have created specific preprinted or computerized forms indicating what kind of information should be gathered during client interviews relating to particular types of claims. Using preprinted forms ensures that all essential information will be obtained.

If you are interviewing a client who is petitioning for bankruptcy, for example, you will need to obtain from the client the types of information that must be included in the bankruptcy forms to be submitted to the court. The bankruptcy forms will serve as a checklist for you to follow during the client interview. Similarly, if your firm frequently handles personal-injury cases, you will probably have available a preprinted or computerized personal-injury intake sheet, such as that shown in Exhibit 7.1 on pages 224 and 225, to use as a guide when obtaining client information during the initial client interview.

Preparing Your Own Checklist. At times, you will need to devise your own checklist of questions to ask during an interview. For example, suppose that a client of your firm was injured in an automobile accident and is bringing a lawsuit against the driver of the other car for negligence. You are conducting a preliminary investigation into the case and have scheduled an

---

ETHICAL CONCERN

Handling Client Documents

Clients frequently give paralegals important documents relating to their cases during interviews. As stressed in Chapter 3, state codes of ethics impose strict requirements on attorneys in regard to the safekeeping of clients' funds and other property, including documents. Suppose, for example, that a client gives you, during an interview, the only copy she has of her divorce agreement. You should never rely on memory when it comes to client documents. Instead, immediately after the conclusion of the interview, you should record the receipt of any documents or other items received from the client. The information may be recorded in an evidence log or otherwise, depending on the procedures established by your firm to govern the receipt and storage of such property. An evidence log or other method of recording documents and items received from clients provides you with evidence—should it be necessary—of what you did (or did not) receive from a client.

interview with an eyewitness to the accident. In this situation, you may not have a prepared form to guide you. The kinds of questions that you will need to ask the witness will be determined by a number of factors, including the factual background of the case already known to you and your supervising attorney, the law governing the client's claim, and your supervising attorney's legal strategy. You will read in further detail about the kinds of information that are obtained from witnesses during preliminary investigations later in this chapter.

Whether you use a prepared form or a checklist that you create yourself, you should always abide by the following rule:

● **Never let the form or checklist become a substitute for human interaction.**

In other words, do not let a printed form or checklist constrain a client's comments on a legal matter or concern—so long as the client does not stray too far from relevant topics, of course. Part of your value as a team member lies in your ability to relate to clients on a personal, human level. Also, as will be discussed later in this chapter, much valuable information may be learned through casual or unanticipated comments made by a client during an interview.

Preparing the Interview Environment

Usually, clients are interviewed at the law firm's offices. Witnesses may be interviewed in their homes or at some other place convenient to them. When you are deciding where an interview should take place within your firm's offices, a foremost concern is confidentiality (see the *Ethical Concern* in the margin of this page). Also, you should prevent potential distractions and interruptions by making sure that the environment is quiet and that you will not be interrupted by phone calls or by other employees entering or leaving the area during the interview.

A large table may be useful if the interviewee will be bringing documents to be examined. Prepare the room by setting out anything you might want to have at hand during the interview, such as pencils, note pads, or any special documents to which you might want to refer (or show to the client). If you plan to tape-record the session (to be discussed shortly), have the equipment set up, tested, and ready to operate before the interview begins.

Recording the Interview

Some interviewers tape-record their interviews. Before you tape-record an interview, you should always do the following:

● **Obtain permission to tape-record the interview from both your supervising attorney and the person being interviewed.**

When you are using a tape recorder, you should state at the beginning of the tape the following identifying information:

• The name of the person being interviewed and any other information about the interviewee that is relevant.

• The name of the person conducting the interview.

ETHICAL CONCERN

Confidentiality and Interviews

When you interview a client or a witness, a major concern on your part is to make sure that you fulfill the duty of confidentiality. If possible, arrange for the interview to be held in a conference room so that the interview will not be overheard by third parties. If a conference room is not available and you interview someone in your office, make sure that your desk and office are cleared of any confidential materials relating to other clients, and avoid taking phone calls in the presence of the interviewee. Also, escort the interviewee from the reception area to your office or to the conference room (and back to the reception area when the interview is over). Greeting a client or witness in the reception area and escorting him or her to the interviewing site is not only a courteous act but also helps to prevent the interviewee from overhearing or seeing confidential information.

DEVELOPING PARALEGAL SKILLS
Preparing for a Telephone Interview

 Adam Haskell, a legal assistant for a sole practitioner, is going to conduct a telephone interview of a witness to a car accident. The witness lives in a distant state but happened to be visiting the area when the accident occurred. For economic reasons, the initial interview will be conducted over the telephone, with a follow-up interview to be done in person if Adam's supervising attorney wants to have the witness, Sam Toole, testify at trial.

Adam had previously arranged with the witness to conduct the phone interview today at 10:30 A.M. Adam prepared a list of questions yesterday and is now making final preparations for the interview. First, he gathers all of the materials that he will need for the interview: the client file, the list of prepared questions, a note pad, and a couple of pens. Next, he takes his tape recorder from his desk. He takes a blank tape from the drawer and inserts it into the recorder. If Sam Toole consents, Adam will hook up the recorder to the telephone and tape-record the interview.

Adam then walks to the secretary's desk and asks for the portable fax machine. There is an extra phone jack for a fax machine in the conference room, which was installed for this purpose. Having the fax machine available will allow the witness to fax any relevant documents or other items, such as a drawing of the accident. Adam checks the fax machine to make sure that it has enough paper in it. Then he takes all of the materials that he has gathered to the conference room. He sets up the tape recorder and the fax machine, turns them on, and tests them to make certain that they are in operating condition before the interview begins.

Adam's final step in preparing for his phone interview is to make sure that he will not be interrupted. He returns to the secretary's desk and tells her that he will be involved in a telephone interview and that he does not want to be interrupted. He asks her to hold all of his calls and not to come in with any messages or let anyone else in the conference room. Adam walks back into the conference room and dials Sam's telephone number. The interview begins.

progresses, a remark made by the interviewee that did not seem important at the time of the interview may take on added significance in view of evidence gathered after the interview was held.

There are also some disadvantages to tape-recording interviews. A major disadvantage is that some clients and witnesses may be uncomfortable and less willing to disclose information freely if they know that everything they are saying is being recorded. Such reluctance is understandable in view of the fact that the interviewee cannot know in advance what exactly will transpire during the course of the interview or how the tape may later be used. When asking an interviewee for his or her permission to tape-record an interview, you should therefore evaluate carefully how the interviewee responds to this question. Depending on the interviewee's response, you might consider taking notes instead of tape-recording the session.

INTERVIEWING CLIENTS

The primary objective of any interview session, whether it is a client or a witness who is being interviewed, is to acquire information that will ultimately assist in the legal representation of the client. The various types of client interviews include the initial client interview, subsequent client interviews to obtain further information, and informational interviews, or meetings, to inform the client of the status of his or her case and to prepare the client for trial or other legal proceedings. We look below at each of these types of interviews.

The Initial Client Interview

When a client seeks legal advice from an attorney, the attorney normally holds an initial interview with the client. During this interview, the client explains his or her legal problem so that the attorney can advise the client on possible legal options and the legal fees that may be involved. Either then or at a later time, the client and the attorney will agree on the terms of the representation, if the attorney decides to take the case.

Paralegals often attend initial client interviews. Although the attorney normally conducts this first interview, the paralegal plays an important role. Usually, you will observe the client, take notes on what the client is saying, and provide the client with forms, statements explaining the firm's fees, and other prepared information that is normally given to new clients. Following the interview, you and the attorney may compare your impressions of the client and of what the client said during the interview.

All of the law-firm personnel present at the interview should be introduced to the client, their titles given, and the reason for their presence at the interview made known to the client. In introducing you, the paralegal, to the potential client, the attorney will probably stress that you are not a lawyer.

- **If your supervising attorney does not indicate your nonattorney status to the client, you must do so.**

If a firm decides to take a client's case, the client should be introduced to every member of the legal team who will be working on the case.

Subsequent Client Interviews

Paralegals are often asked to conduct additional interviews with clients whose cases have been accepted. For example, assume that a client wants to obtain a divorce. After the initial interview, your supervising attorney may ask you to arrange for a subsequent interview with the client to obtain all the information necessary to prepare the divorce pleadings. When scheduling the interview, you should tell the client what kinds of documents or other data the client should bring to the interview. During the interview, you will fill out the form that the firm uses to record client information in divorce cases. Paralegals often assume responsibility for gathering most of the information needed to file for a divorce or to begin child-custody proceedings.

ETHICAL CONCERN

Interviewing Clients and the Unauthorized Practice of Law

Paralegals must be especially careful not to give legal advice when interviewing clients. Suppose that you are conducting a follow-up interview of a client, Sue Collins. Collins was injured in a car accident and is suing the driver of the other car involved in the accident for negligence. During the initial client interview, Collins told you and your supervising attorney that the accident was totally the result of the other driver's negligence. During the course of your follow-up interview, however, Collins presents you with an interesting hypothetical. She says to you, "What would happen, in a lawsuit such as mine, if the plaintiff was not watching the road when the accident occurred? What if the plaintiff was looking in the back seat to see why her baby was crying? Could the plaintiff still expect to win in court?" You know that under the laws of your state, contributory negligence on the part of the plaintiff is an absolute bar to the recovery of damages. Should you explain this to Collins? No. Even though the question is phrased as a hypothetical, it is possible that your answer could affect Collins's future actions. Your best option is tell Collins that you are not permitted to give legal advice but that you will relay the "hypothetical" question to your supervising attorney.

When conducting a client interview, the paralegal should always disclose his or her nonlawyer status if this fact was not made clear at an earlier session. Remember, even if you had been introduced to the client as a "legal assistant," the client may not realize that a legal assistant is not an attorney. To protect yourself against potential claims that you have engaged in the unauthorized practice of law, you should clearly state to the client that you are "not an attorney."

The Informational Interview

The informational interview, or meeting, is an interview in which the client is brought in to discuss upcoming legal proceedings. Most clients know very little about the procedures involved in litigation, and firms often have their paralegals explain these procedures to clients and prepare clients for the trial experience. For example, the paralegal can describe to clients what will take place during the trial, how to groom themselves appropriately for trial, where to look when they testify, and so on. The informational interview helps the client understand why certain proceedings are taking place and his or her role in those proceedings.

Summarizing the Interview

The interviewing process does not end with the close of the interview. A final and crucial step in the process involves summarizing the results of the interview for the legal team working on the case. As a paralegal, you will create an intake memorandum following each initial client interview. If the firm has a prepared intake form for particular types of cases, such as the personal-injury

---

THE LEGAL TEAM AT WORK
Humanizing Legal Practice

Clients know that attorneys often face busy schedules and that an attorney's time is costly. For both of these reasons, clients are often reluctant to talk to their attorneys about matters that do not seem essential to the legal representation. The team approach opens the door to improved attorney-client communications by involving paralegals and support staff in the legal work for the client. Some firms that use the teamwork approach advise clients at the outset that whenever they want to contact the office, it is to their advantage to contact the paralegal first because the paralegal's time is less costly. If the paralegal can handle a client's question or problem, the client will not have to bear the greater expense involved in a consultation with the attorney. Clients tend to communicate more frequently—and more freely—with paralegals and support staff than they do with the attorneys because of the lower cost involved. Details that the client might have been reluctant to discuss with the attorney, but that may be critical to a successful resolution of the client's case, may thus emerge in the course of a casual conversation with the paralegal. As many attorneys have realized, the team approach not only increases communication possibilities but also adds a more personal, human touch to legal practice.

DEVELOPING PARALEGAL SKILLS

The Tape-recorded Interview

 Justin Hooper, a paralegal, is preparing for an interview that will be tape-recorded. Justin has already received permission to tape-record the interview from his supervising attorney and from the witness to be interviewed. The first step is to set up the tape recorder in the conference room in which the interview will take place. After Justin sets it up, he inserts a new, blank tape into the recorder and tests it to make sure that the tape and the recorder work.

The witness arrives and is shown into the conference room by the receptionist. From a file folder, Justin removes a prepared statement containing the introductory remarks typically used in a tape-recorded interview. He reads it into the tape recorder: "My name is Justin Hooper, a paralegal at the law firm of Smith & Howard, representing Mr. Barry Buckner, the defendant in *Jones v. Buckner*. What follows is a taped interview with Ms. Jennifer Tompkins, a witness to the accident that is the subject of the *Jones v. Buckner* litigation. This tape-recorded interview is taking place in the law offices of Smith & Howard on January 6, 1996. The time is two o'clock P.M."

Justin then turns to the witness and asks, "Ms. Tompkins, will you please state and spell your first and last name for the record?" Ms. Tompkins responds accordingly. Next, Justin asks, "Ms. Tompkins, may we record the interview that we are about to conduct?" Ms. Tompkins answers, "Yes, you have my permission to record today's interview." Justin then begins the interview.

---

intake sheet referred to earlier and illustrated in Exhibit 7.1, the completed form might constitute the interview summary. Information obtained during any subsequent interviews with a client should be analyzed and summarized in a memo for your supervising attorney or other team members to review and for later inclusion in the client's file.

Your interview summary should be created immediately after the interview, while the session is still fresh in your mind. When summarizing the results of a client interview, you should carefully review your notes and, if the session was tape-recorded, review the tape. You should never rely totally on your memory of the statements made during the interview. It is very easy to forget the client's exact words, and it may be very important later to know exactly how the client phrased a certain comment or response. Relying on memory is also risky because, as mentioned earlier, sometimes a statement that seemed irrelevant at the time of the interview may turn out to be very important to the case. You should thus make sure that the facts are accurately recorded and are as reliable as possible.

CONDUCTING AN INVESTIGATION—THE FIRST STEPS

The more factual evidence that can be gathered in support of a client's claim, the better the client's chances in court—or in any other dispute-settlement proceeding. If a client alleges that she was injured by a negligent driver, the

PARALEGAL PROFILE

Administrative Paralegal

DAVID L. HAY has an associate's degree from the legal-assistant program at El Centro Community College in Dallas, Texas. While working as an administrative assistant for a Wisconsin company, Hay had taken some classes in the legal-assistant program at an area technical college and discovered his interest in the legal field. He also worked as a legal secretary for a time. Hay currently works for the general counsel for the Dallas County Community College. Communication and interviewing skills are important in Hay's work. His responsibilities include contributing to the policy manual used by the college, researching and interpreting federal law, preparing memos, and often providing the first contact to students who call with a legal question.

What do you like best about your work?

"I like the variety. In my job, there is never a dull moment. I also like the freedom to set my own priorities. I'm often involved in investigations to locate people, and I enjoy my contact with students."

What is the greatest challenge that you face in your area of work?

"My greatest challenge is working with administrators to communicate what needs to be done. When new laws require a change, it is my responsibility to make the administrators understand what changes need to be put into effect. I also have the challenge of educating people as to what a paralegal is, because many persons assume that I am a lawyer. I clarify immediately that I am not a lawyer and remind them that I cannot give legal advice."

What advice do you have for would-be paralegals in your area of work?

"My advice is to take advantage of the informational interview process, internships, and community-service programs to learn more about different types of paralegal work and the kinds of jobs available. The informational interview allows the paralegal to interview the firm: it's a learning process. The paralegal can find out what the firm looks for in a paralegal in terms of qualifications or credentials and can learn about the type of work that is available. Internships and community-service programs also provide opportunities for paralegals to 'test the waters.' Often, such programs lead to full-time positions. It's much better to find out by trial and error which areas of law you want to work in than to go into the work force as unprepared and uninformed employees. By getting involved with informational interviews, internships, and community-service programs, you will know which direction to pursue as a paralegal."

> **"IN MY JOB THERE IS NEVER A DULL MOMENT."**

What are some tips for success as a paralegal in your area of work?

"One important tip is to follow up and not delay if someone is waiting for a response from you. I also recommend interviewing and checking several sources for a more complete picture. Don't be afraid to probe and schedule other interviews for further information—a second or third interview might reveal information the first interview did not."

attorney will want to investigate the circumstances surrounding the accident to verify that the client's allegations are supported by factual evidence.

Assume that you work for Allen Gilmore, the attorney who represented the plaintiff in the hypothetical case discussed in Chapter 6. Recall that the plaintiff in that case, Katherine Baranski, sued Tony Peretto for negligence. Peretto had run a stop sign at an intersection and as a result, his car collided with Baranski's. Further assume that the case is still in its initial stages. Attorney Gilmore has just met with Katherine Baranski for the initial client interview. You sat in on the interview, listened carefully to Baranski's description of the accident and of the damages she sustained as a result (medical expenses, lost wages, and so on), and took thorough notes.

After the interview, Gilmore asks you to do a preliminary investigation into Baranski's claim. It is now your responsibility to find the answers to a number of questions. Did the accident really occur in the way perceived by the client, Katherine Baranski? Exactly where and when did it happen? How does the police report describe the accident? Were there any witnesses? Was Tony Peretto insured and, if so, by what insurance company? What other circumstances (such as weather) are relevant? Your supervising attorney will want to know the answers to these and other questions before advising Baranski as to what legal action should be pursued.

Where Do You Start?

In undertaking any legal investigation, your logical point of departure is the information you have already acquired about the legal claim or problem. In the Baranski case, this information consists of the statements made by Baranski during the initial client interview and summarized in your notes. Baranski had described what she remembered about the accident, including the date and time it occurred. She said she thought that the police investigator had the names of some persons who had witnessed the accident. She also stated that she was employed as an assistant professor in the math department at Nita State University, earning approximately $36,000 a year. By using common sense and a little imagination, you can map out a fairly thorough investigation plan based on this information.

Create an Investigation Plan

An **investigation plan** is simply a step-by-step list of the tasks that you plan to take to verify or obtain factual information relating to a legal problem. The order in which the steps are listed should follow a logical pattern. In other words, if you need to get information from source A (such as a police report of an accident) before you can contact source B (such as an eyewitness whose name and address are in the police report), source A should precede source B on your list. For each step, you should indicate what kind of information you plan to request or obtain and how you plan to obtain it. When creating your plan, you can add columns for "date requested" and "date received" beside each item; this way, your plan will also serve as a checklist on the status of your investigation.

In the Baranski case, the steps in your investigation plan would include those summarized in Exhibit 7.2 on the following pages and discussed below.

Contact the Police Department.   The initial step in your plan should be to contact the police department. You will want to look at a copy of the police report of the accident, view any photographs that were taken at the scene, obtain the names of persons who may have witnessed the accident, and, if possible, talk to the investigating officer.

Contact and Interview Witnesses.   Next, you will want to contact and interview any known witnesses and document their descriptions of what took place at the time of the accident. Known witnesses include the driver

INVESTIGATION PLAN
A plan that lists each step involved in obtaining and verifying the facts and information that are relevant to the legal problem being investigated.

EXHIBIT 7.2
An Investigation Plan

INVESTIGATION PLAN
File No. 15773

	Date Requested	Date Received
1. Contact Police Department		
—To obtain police report	_____	_____
—To ask for photographs of accident scene	_____	_____
—To talk with investigating officer	_____	_____
—SOURCE: Nita City Police Dept.		
—METHOD: Request in person or by mail		
2. Contact Known Witnesses		
—Tony Peretto, van driver	_____	_____
—Michael Young, police officer at accident scene	_____	_____
—Julia Williams, witness at accident scene	_____	_____
—Dwight Kelly, witness at accident scene	_____	_____
—SOURCE: Police report		
—METHOD: Contact witnesses by initial phone call and personal interview when possible		
3. Obtain Employment Records		
—To learn employment status and income of Mrs. Baranski	_____	_____
—SOURCE: Nita State University		
—METHOD: Written request by mail with Mrs. Baranski's release enclosed		
4. Obtain Hospital Records		
—To learn necessary information about Mrs. Baranski's medical treatment and costs	_____	_____
—SOURCE: Nita City Hospital		
—METHOD: Written request by mail with Mrs. Baranski's release enclosed		

(Tony Peretto) of the vehicle that hit Katherine Baranski, the police officer at the scene, and the other witnesses noted in the police investigation report. Keep in mind that if Tony Peretto is aware of Baranski's intention to sue him, he will probably have retained an attorney. If he has, then you are not permitted to contact him directly—all communications with him will have to be through his attorney.

Obtain Medical and Employment Records.   To justify a claim for damages, you will need to ascertain the nature of the injuries sustained by Baranski as a result of the accident, the medical expenses that she incurred, and her annual or monthly income (to determine the amount of wages she lost as a result of the accident). To obtain this information, you will need copies of her medical and employment records.

Note that the institutions holding these records will not release them to you unless Katherine Baranski authorizes them to do so. Therefore, you will also need to arrange with Baranski to sign release forms to include with your requests for copies. A sample authorization form to release medical records

EXHIBIT 7.2
Continued

	Date Requested	Date Received

5. Contact National Weather Service
—To learn what the weather conditions were on the day of the accident

—SOURCE: National Weather Service or newspaper
—METHOD: Phone call or written request

6. Obtain Title and Registration Records
—To verify Tony Peretto's ownership of the vehicle

—SOURCE: Department of Motor Vehicles
—METHOD: Order by mail

7. Contact Tony Peretto's Insurance Co.
—To find out about insurance coverage
—To check liability limits

—SOURCE: Insurance Company
—METHOD: Written request by mail

8. Use a Professional Investigator
—To contact such witnesses as
 —ambulance attendants
 —doctors
 —residents in neighborhood of accident scene
—To inspect vehicle
—To take photos of accident site
—To investigate accident scene, etc.

—SOURCE: Regular law-firm investigator
—METHOD: In person

is shown in Exhibit 7.3 on the next page. You should make sure that Baranski signs these forms before she leaves the office after the initial interview. Otherwise, waiting for her to return the signed forms may delay your investigation.

Contact the National Weather Service. Weather conditions at the time of the accident may have an important bearing on the case. If it was snowing heavily at the time of the Baranski-Peretto accident, for example, Peretto's attorney may argue that Peretto did not see the stop sign or that ice on the road prevented him from stopping. You will therefore want to ascertain what the weather conditions were at the time of the accident by contacting the National Weather Service. Also, when you interview eyewitnesses, you should ask them about weather conditions at the place and time of the accident.

Obtain Vehicle Title and Registration Records. To verify that Tony Peretto owns the vehicle that he was driving at the time of the accident, you will

EXHIBIT 7.3
Authorization to Release Medical Records

TO: Nita City Hospital & Clinic
Nita City, NI 48803

PATIENT: Katherine Baranski
335 Natural Boulevard
Nita City, NI 48802

You are hereby authorized to furnish and release to my attorney, Allen P. Gilmore of Jeffers, Gilmore & Dunn, all information and records relating to my treatment for injuries incurred on August 4, 1995. Please do not disclose information to insurance adjusters or to other persons without written authority from me. The foregoing authority shall continue in force until revoked by me in writing, but for no longer than one year following the date given below.

Date: January 30, 1996.

Katherine Baranski

Katherine Baranski

Please attach your invoice for any fee or photostatic costs and send it with the information requested above to my office.

Thank you,

Allen P. Gilmore

Allen P. Gilmore
Jeffers, Gilmore & Dunn
Attorneys at Law
553 Fifth Avenue
Suite 101
Nita City, NI 48801

Helena Moritz

Helena Moritz
Notary Public State of Nita
Nita County
My Commission Expires November 12, 2000

need to obtain title and registration records. Usually, these can be obtained from the state department of motor vehicles, although in some states, the secretary of state's office handles such records. The requirements for obtaining such information vary from state to state and may include the submission of special forms and fees. Therefore, you should call the relevant state department or office in advance to find out what procedures should be followed.

Contact the Insurance Company. If you learned the name of Peretto's insurance company from Baranski or from the police report, you will want to contact that company to find out what kind of insurance coverage Peretto has and the limits of his liability under the insurance policy. Insurance companies usually are reluctant give this information to anyone other than the policy-holder. They sometimes cooperate with such requests, however, because they know that if they do not, the information can be obtained during discovery, should a lawsuit be initiated.

Consider Using a Professional Investigator's Services.   Some law firms routinely use the services of professional investigators. Depending on the circumstances, your supervising attorney may decide to use a professional investigator for certain tasks, including those described above. You might be responsible for working with the investigator. For example, you might arrange for the investigator to inspect and take photographs of the accident scene.

Locating certain witnesses (witnesses who have moved, for example) may be difficult and time consuming. This is another task that your super-vising attorney may prefer the professional investigator to handle, particu-larly if the attorney needs your assistance in the office. The investigator might also be asked to locate other witnesses, such as the ambulance driver or attendants, physicians who treated Baranski, or residents in the area who might have observed the accident.

Consult with Your Supervising Attorney

In planning and conducting your preliminary investigation, you will want to work closely with your supervising attorney. Primarily, this is because you will need to learn what legal theories the attorney wants to pursue and in what order of priority. The attorney may also know of additional sources that you should consult or may indicate that there is no need to investigate a certain area of a client's claim. Also, for strategic reasons, the attorney might want you to concentrate more on some areas than others. Once you have formed your investigation plan, you should submit it to your super-vising attorney for review and evaluation.

Investigation during Discovery

Investigators should be familiar with the pretrial discovery procedures dis-cussed in Chapter 6. If a lawsuit is initiated, further investigation can be con-ducted during the discovery phase of the litigation. As a paralegal, you will be able to use discovery tools—such as depositions, interrogatories, requests for admissions or documents, and subpoenas—to obtain evidence that might not be made available to you during your preliminary investigation.

In planning and pursuing your investigation, you should make notes of any documents or information that you are unable to obtain now and that you will want to obtain during discovery. In the Baranski case, for example, you may have to wait until discovery to obtain information from Peretto's insurance company about Peretto's insurance coverage and liability limits, because the company may not release this information without a subpoena. (Note that under the revised Federal Rules of Civil Procedure governing dis-covery, this information will be automatically disclosed—see Chapter 6.)

Conducting an Investigation—Basic Principles

There is no one correct way to conduct a legal investigation. This is because each person has unique attributes and personality characteristics. While a low-key, methodical style might work for one person, it might not be appropriate for a more aggressive person who likes to have several things happening at once. Over time and with practice, you will learn what approach works best for you and will acquire your own particular style of investigation. Generally, you will find that your greatest allies in investigatory work are common sense, good organizational skills, and creative thinking.

Although investigative approaches vary from person to person, all legal investigators can use the basic principles discussed below to help them achieve their goal of uncovering and verifying relevant facts.

Focus on the Who, What, and Where

Before undertaking any step on your investigation plan, you should know which people you need to contact, what information you want to uncover or verify, and where information sources can be found. For example, if you want to obtain information from a large organization, such as a government agency, make sure that you contact the appropriate person—that is, the person who has the expertise and authority to answer your questions or fulfill your request. Your firm may have directories of various federal, state, and local agencies that will give you this information. If not, you may have to contact several people within an agency before you learn which employee is authorized to handle your request.

If you need to visit a geographical area with which you are unfamiliar, do some preliminary investigation to find out what the area is like. If the neighborhood is a high-crime area, you may want to conduct your investigation with a partner and during the day, when you will be less at risk, or hire a private investigator to handle that aspect of the investigatory work.

Develop and Maintain Personal Contacts

Experienced investigators rely to a great extent on contacts they have established during previous investigations. By knowing the right people in the right places, investigators are able to obtain reports or other information quickly and efficiently. Whenever you conduct an investigation, keep an eye toward your future needs as an investigator and cultivate good relationships with people whose cooperation might be helpful to you at a later time. For example, you may need to obtain documents and reports from the county clerk on a regular basis. If you establish a good relationship with that person, he or she may be more willing to respond quickly to your requests and thus make your task easier. Similarly, if during an investigation you need to contact an employee at the police department, take time to cultivate the employee's goodwill. You never know when you might need that person's assistance again.

You should create a special notebook or file in which you keep a record of the information you learned about each person you contact. You can refer to the information when you contact that person again. A three-ring binder is useful for this purpose, because you can use dividers to create sections for different categories of contacts. For example, you might have a section for police-department personnel, one for court personnel, and so on.

During the course of your investigation, you will find that some people are more cooperative, perceptive, or pleasant than others. Regardless of these differences, you should always follow this cardinal rule of investigation:

- **Treat all of the individuals you meet with respect and courtesy.**

A sure way to make your investigation less productive and more difficult is to disregard this rule. You also may make future investigations more difficult if you alienate a person whose assistance would be valuable to you. Also remember that as a paralegal, you represent the firm for which you work. Even if someone is stubborn and difficult, you should remain professional and courteous at all times because how you conduct yourself is a reflection on your firm.

Be Flexible

In many ways, conducting an investigation is similar to interviewing a client or witness. Before an interview begins, you normally prepare for that interview by creating a checklist of the topics you wish to discuss and the kind of information you want to obtain from the client or witness. But you do not let that checklist constrain you. Similarly, when conducting a legal investigation, you form an investigation plan, but you should also allow room for some unexpected twists. One source of information may lead you to other sources of which you were unaware.

For example, assume that you are interviewing Julia Williams, an eyewitness to the Baranski-Peretto auto accident. Williams mentions that a local furniture company's delivery truck was just behind Peretto's van and probably had a good view of the accident. The witness had not remembered to tell the police about the truck when they questioned her at the time of the accident. The driver of that truck, though, would be a valuable witness, so you make a note to call the furniture company and make some inquiries to see if you can find out who the driver was.

Generally, you will want to be able to adjust your schedule to follow up on any new leads that surface during the course of your investigation. For example, even though you had not planned to interview yet another witness and want to conclude your investigation quickly, you realize that the testimony of the furniture company's truck driver may be valuable. You therefore contact the truck driver and set up an appointment to interview him.

Be Open Minded and Objective

Even though your goal is to uncover or verify information helpful to your client, you should not let that goal close your mind to facts that may adversely affect the client. Remember that as an investigator, you play a neutral role and not that of a judge or jury member. Your job is to gather factual information as objectively as possible, regardless of how it may affect your client's interests.

FEATURED GUEST: MELANIE A. P. ROWAND

Ten Tips for Pre-discovery Investigation

Biographical Note

Melanie A. Pirozzolo Rowand serves as litigation counsel for American Protective Services, Inc. (APS), which is headquartered in Oakland, California. The legal department of APS provides legal services to over seventy offices across the United States. Rowand obtained her bachelor of arts degree in education and her master of arts degree in communication. Before becoming an attorney, Rowand was a legal assistant for approximately ten years. As a legal assistant, she worked as a supervisor for several large San Francisco law firms that specialized in litigation. She has also worked in Hawaii as an aide in that state's legislature, as well as a court clerk. Rowand currently teaches introductory law courses at California State University, Hayward, at San Francisco State University, and at the University of California, Berkeley.

The basic rule to follow when conducting an investigation is that of the news reporter—learn the "who, what, when, where, and why" of your case. What was done? Who did it? When was it done? Where did it occur? Why was it done? To these "five Ws" of the journalist, the legal investigator should add "how": How did the event or action occur? Listed below are ten tips for paralegals undertaking legal investigations. Each tip indicates a source to which you can turn for factual information. By identifying significant facts during the pre-discovery stage, paralegals will gain an early insight into strategies to be pursued during discovery. Uncovering critical information before the discovery process begins may also result in an early settlement of the claim.

1 **Personally Interview Witnesses, Including Your Client.** Remember, your firm's client is your key witness. If after the initial client interview you find you need more information, arrange for another interview with the client. Instruct him or her to produce all documents that relate to the incident, and indicate which types of docu-

ments may be relevant. These documents might include tax statements, photographs of the incident, police reports, personnel files, insurance company reports, workers' compensation reports, repair estimates, and others. Personally interview witnesses to determine courtroom appeal. Try to determine beforehand if the individual to be interviewed will be a friendly or a hostile witness. Look to your supervising attorney for guidance on this and on the type of information you should gather during each interview.

2 **Obtain the Police Report.** Most police departments will provide you with a copy of a police report for a nominal fee. Some departments, however, require a written explanation as to why the report is being requested. This can take the form of a letter that simply states that the issues raised in the police report are currently being litigated. Specific identification of the case name, case number, and court will add credibility to your request. Be aware that issues involving juvenile matters will usually require a subpoena.

3 **Check for Newspaper and Magazine Accounts.** Public libraries are wonderful resources for the legal investigator. Generally, larger libraries keep back issues of newspapers and magazines on microfilm. Some libraries maintain newspaper microfilm files for issues dated as far back as fifty years. Computerized research services, such as WESTLAW and LEXIS, also offer access to printed publications from around the country. Check with your supervising attorney about these services.

4 **Photograph the Scene of the Incident.** Photograph the scene of the incident, any property that was damaged, and any injury that was sustained by the harmed individual. Arrange to photograph the scene and visit the area at the time of day the incident occurred. This will give you a more accurate picture of how the scene may have appeared at the time of the incident—how busy the intersection was, for example, or how well lighted the area was. A photograph will "preserve the scene" for the record. If the claim is litigated, it may be two or three years before it reaches trial,

FEATURED GUEST, Continued

and photographic documentation may be crucial evidence. Even if the location has changed since the date of the incident, take photographs anyway. Talk with residents in the neighborhood to learn why the changes occurred.

5 Obtain an Accurate Map of the Location of the Incident. A map of the locale in which the incident took place, as well as of the surrounding area, could make or break your case. Maps can shed light on a variety of claims, particularly those involving real property. Don't forget to obtain this commonly overlooked necessity.

6 Check Census Publications. The population of the area in which the incident occurred could be a critical factor. Census publications provide key information to those working on certain types of cases, such as cases relating to real property or business development. Contact your local census bureau for more information.

7 Request Reports from Government Agencies. In addition to census reports, other information compiled by government agencies may sometimes provide key information concerning an incident that you are investigating. If a claim involves an alleged violation of an environmental law or regulation, for example, a report prepared by the federal Environmental Protection Agency or your state's environmental agency or department may provide important information relating to the incident.

8 For Claims Involving Corporations, Contact the Secretary of State's Office in Your State. Corporations must register with the state secretary of state's office for incorporation purposes.[a] To gain information about a corporation, a paralegal can phone the secretary of state's office. Most offices allow two inquiries per call. Information available from this office includes the names of the officers and directors of a corporation, the corporation's principal place of business, and the name of the individual who has been designated to receive service of process on behalf of the corporation. Computer databases, such as Information America, provide direct access to the secretary of state's office in most states.

9 Obtain All Relevant Records. To obtain nonpublic records relating to your client, such as medical records, have your client sign a written authorization to release those records. Medical, business, and other records relating to an opposing party normally must be subpoenaed. Deeds and titles to property can be obtained from the county recorder's office.[b] Such information will enable you to prepare a property profile of a potential litigant. Records relating to previous litigation by a party can be obtained from the county court or the courts in surrounding counties. Such information will indicate

> **"UNCOVERING CRITICAL INFORMATION BEFORE THE DISCOVERY PROCESS BEGINS MAY ALSO RESULT IN AN EARLY SETTLEMENT OF THE CLAIM."**

to the investigator whether an individual is litigious (has a history of bringing lawsuits), is legally sophisticated, or has a history of litigating issues similar to the issue being investigated.

10 Obtain Publications of Local and Special-interest Organizations. These types of publications may provide additional insight into the standards of an industry and may eventually assist in the selection of expert witnesses. For example, if you are investigating a car accident, you might check with *Consumer Reports* and other consumer publications to find out if the make and model of the car involved in the incident has a history of malfunctioning.

---

a. While this is true in most states, a few states require incorporation papers to be filed with a different state department, such as the department of commerce.

b. Called the register of deeds office in many counties.

For example, in the Baranski case, it might be important to know whether Katherine Baranski was exercising reasonable care when she was driving down Mattis Avenue just before the accident occurred. You might therefore ask a witness whether the witness had observed Baranski's car immediately before the accident—to find out if she was speeding, for example, or looking away from the road at the time the accident occurred. Even though the witness's answers to these questions might be detrimental to your client's interests, your supervising attorney will want to know these and any other facts that might have a bearing on the case so that the attorney can prepare in advance for opposing counsel's arguments.

As another example, suppose that the following developments take place. You interview the furniture company's truck driver and are surprised to learn that his perception of what happened just prior to the accident is quite different from that of another eyewitness, Julia Williams. Williams had told you that she saw Peretto's green van run the stop sign and crash into Baranski's car. Now, the furniture company's truck driver states that he is quite sure that the green van ahead of him stopped at the stop sign before proceeding across Mattis Avenue.

Realize that if you were able to learn about and locate this witness (the furniture truck driver), defendant Peretto's attorney and paralegal will probably also be able to do so should Baranski bring suit against Peretto. Therefore, you need to find out as much as possible about the truck driver's perceptions of the accident. In view of his statements, your supervising attorney, Gilmore, may decide not to take Baranski's case. If Gilmore does accept the case, he will need to determine how to deal with the truck driver's testimony if opposing counsel offers it in court.

Be Imaginative

The creative investigator keeps the goal of the investigation in mind at all times. In the Baranski case, for example, one of Baranski's goals is to obtain damages from Tony Peretto, the potential defendant. To achieve that goal, your supervising attorney must have evidence that (1) Peretto was indeed negligent (driving carelessly or recklessly, in breach of a duty and in violation of the law) and (2) Peretto has sufficient assets or insurance coverage to pay the amount of damages Baranski seeks to obtain. In determining how to find the necessary evidence, give your imagination free rein.

In addition to investigating the police report of the accident and interviewing police officers and other witnesses, try to think of other possible information that might be helpful in establishing that Peretto was negligent. Did Peretto have a record of careless driving and traffic violations? If so, his driving record (if allowed in court) would help convince a jury that he might have been negligent in the Baranski case. Did Peretto have a medical condition that required the use of medication that might have affected his driving? Did he have any vision problems that required corrective lenses for driving? If so, was he wearing corrective lenses at the time of the accident?

Focusing on the desired outcome of the case—and the kind of evidence that will help to bring about that outcome—gives direction to your imaginative and creative efforts. Inevitably, there will be times during an investigation when you think you have reached a dead end or exhausted all possible sources. Whether you are trying to locate witnesses or other types of information, you will find that your imagination is always a great resource in identifying further potential sources.

LOCATING WITNESSES

Perhaps one of the most challenging tasks for the legal investigator is locating a witness whose address is unknown or who has moved from a previous, known address. Suppose, for example, that in the Baranski case, the police investigation report lists the name, address, and telephone number of Edna Ball, a witness to the accident. When you call her number, a recording informs you that the phone has been disconnected. You go to her address, and the house appears to be vacant. What is your next step?

At this point, many paralegals suggest to their supervising attorneys that a professional investigator take over the search. But if you alone must locate the witness, there are several sources to which you can turn. A good starting point is to visit other homes in the neighborhood. Perhaps someone living nearby knows Edna Ball and can give you at least some leads as to where she is or what happened to her. Other sources are discussed below.

Telephone and City Directories

The telephone directory can sometimes be a valuable source of information for the investigator. In trying to locate Edna Ball, for example, you might check to see if her name is still listed in the current directory and, if so, whether it is listed jointly with someone, such as her husband. Your local telephone information service might have a new number listed for her. If the information-service operator indicates that the number is unlisted, you can explain the nature of your concern and request that the operator phone Edna Ball at that number to see if she is willing to call you.

City directories are also good potential sources of information. Such directories may be available in the local library or the law firm's library. A city directory generally contains more information than a phone book. For example, some city directories list places of employment and spouses' names in addition to addresses and telephone numbers. Typically, city directories provide a listing of names and phone numbers by street address. In the Baranski case, if you wanted to obtain the telephone numbers of persons who live in the area of the Baranski-Peretto accident, you could consult a city directory for addresses near the intersection where the accident occurred.

Other Information Sources

Other sources of information are media reports (newspaper and magazine articles and television videos covering the event being investigated); court records (probate proceedings, lawsuits, etc.); deeds to property (usually located in the county courthouse); birth, marriage, and death certificates; voter registration lists; the post office (to see if the witness left a forwarding address); credit bureaus; the tax assessor's office; and city utilities, such as the local electric or water company.

Professional organizations may be useful sources as well. For example, if you have learned from one of Edna Ball's neighbors that she is a paralegal, you can check with state and local paralegal associations to see if they have current information on her.

You might also check with governmental agencies or bureaus to see if the information contained in public records will be helpful in locating Edna Ball. It is possible to obtain information from federal agencies, such as the Social Security Administration, and from state departments or agencies, such as the state revenue department or the secretary of state's office. If you wish to obtain information from any government files or records, you should check with the specific agency or department to see what rules apply.

The Freedom of Information Act (FOIA), which was enacted by Congress in 1966, requires the federal government to disclose certain "records" to "any person" on request. A request that complies with the FOIA procedures need only contain a reasonable description of the information sought. Exhibit 7.4 illustrates the proper format for a letter requesting information under the FOIA. Note that the FOIA exempts some types of information from the disclosure requirement, including classified information (information concerning national security), confidential material dealing with trade secrets, government personnel rules, and personal medical files.

INTERVIEWING WITNESSES

Interviewing witnesses is in many ways similar to interviewing clients. A major difference between clients and witnesses, however, is that the latter may not always be friendly to the client's position.

Types of Witnesses

Witnesses include expert witnesses, lay witnesses, eyewitnesses, friendly witnesses, and adverse (or hostile) witnesses.

EXPERT WITNESS
A witness with professional training or substantial experience qualifying him or her to testify on a particular subject.

Expert Witnesses.   An **expert witness** is an individual who has professional training, advanced knowledge, or substantial experience in a specialized area, such as medicine, computer technology, ballistics, or construction techniques. Paralegals often arrange to hire expert witnesses either to testify in court or to render an opinion on some matter relating to the client's case. Expert witnesses are often used in cases involving medical malpractice and product liability to establish the duty, or standard of care, that the defendant owed to the plaintiff. For example, if a client of your firm is suing a physician for malpractice, your supervising attorney might arrange to have another physician testify as to the standard of care owed by a physician to a patient in similar circumstances.

LAY WITNESS
A witness who can truthfully and accurately testify on a fact in question without having specialized training or knowledge; an ordinary witness.

Lay Witnesses.   Most witnesses in court are lay witnesses. In contrast to expert witnesses, **lay witnesses** do not possess any particular skill or expertise relating to the matter before the court. They are people who happened

EXHIBIT 7.4
**Freedom of Information
Act Request Form**

Agency Head or FOIA Officer
Title
Name of Agency
Address of Agency
City, State, Zip

Re: Freedom of Information Act Request.

Dear_____:

    Under the provisions of the Freedom of Information Act,
5 U.S.C. 552, I am requesting access to (identify the records as clearly
and specifically as possible).

    If there are any fees for searching for, or copying, the records I have
requested, please inform me before you fill the request. (Or:...please supply
the records without informing me if the fees do not exceed $_____.)

    [Optional] I am requesting this information (state the reason for your
request if you think it will assist you in obtaining the information).

    [Optional] As you know, the act permits you to reduce or waive fees
when the release of the information is considered as "primarily benefiting
the public." I believe that this request fits that category and I therefore
ask that you waive any fees.

    If all or any part of this request is denied, please cite the specific
exemption(s) that you think justifies your refusal to release the information,
and inform me of the appeal procedures available to me under the law.

    I would appreciate your handling this request as quickly as possible,
and I look foward to hearing from you within 10 days, as the law stipulates.

Sincerely,

Signature
Name
Address
City, State, Zip

EXHIBIT 7.4
**Freedom of Information
Act Request Form**

Source: U.S. Congress, House Committee on Government Operations, *A Citizen's Guide on How to Use the Freedom of Information Act and the Privacy Act Requesting Government Documents*, 95th Congress, 1st Session (1977).

to observe or otherwise have factual knowledge about an event. A professional or expert in one field may be a lay witness in regard to another field about which he or she does not have expert knowledge. A physician involved in a fraud claim, for example, might give testimony about the fraud as a lay witness but not as an expert witness.

Eyewitnesses. In attempting to gain more information about an event relating to a client's legal claim, paralegals may be required to interview eyewitnesses. **Eyewitnesses** are lay witnesses who have witnessed an event and may testify in a court of law as to what they observed. The term *eyewitness* is deceiving. An eyewitness may have firsthand knowledge of an event, but this knowledge need not have been derived from the sense of sight—that is, from actually *seeing* the event. An eyewitness may be someone who listened in on a telephone conversation between an accused murderer and his or her

EYEWITNESS
A witness who testifies about an event that he or she observed or has experienced.

DEVELOPING PARALEGAL SKILLS

Accessing Government Information

Ellen Simons has started a new job as a paralegal for Smith & Case, a firm that handles federal Superfund cases. The federal Superfund law requires responsible parties to pay for the clean-up of hazardous-waste sites that, due to leakage or other emissions, pose a threat to the environment. (Responsible parties include owners and operators of the sites, as well as parties who created or transported the hazardous waste.) If the responsibile parties do not undertake clean-up operations, the law authorizes the Environmental Protection Agency (EPA) to clean up the sites with funds set aside for that purpose (hence the name "Superfund"). The EPA then recovers the costs of the clean-up operations from the responsible parties.

There are often many defendants in these cases because for any one toxic-waste site, there may be many responsible parties. The EPA has numerous documents in its files relating to the types of pollution present at the site and the potentially responsible parties.

Ellen is about to request copies of EPA documents pertaining to a case on which she is working, which involves the Suburban Landfill Superfund site. Her supervisor has given her the standard FOIA (Freedom of Information Act) form to submit to the EPA. Ellen reads through it and sees that several different types of requests may be made. The first is a request for all information that the EPA has in its files pertaining to the site. The second is a request for specific documents. Ellen decides to review the file and see what kinds of information she needs to obtain from the EPA. After all, there is no reason to request all of the documents if they are not necessary.

CONTACTING THE EPA'S REGIONAL OFFICE

Ellen's review of the file indicates that all she needs from the EPA is the "waste in–waste out" report, a document that gives the total volume of hazardous

accomplice. A blind man may have been an eyewitness to a car crash, because he heard it.

In interviews, eyewitnesses are ordinarily asked to describe an event, in their own words and as they recall it, that relates to the client's case. Eyewitness accounts may be lengthy, and the paralegal may want to tape-record the interview session to ensure accuracy. The experienced paralegal may also find that different eyewitnesses to the same event have contradictory views on what actually took place. People's perceptions of reality differ, as paralegals often find when comparing eyewitness reports.

Friendly Witnesses. Some witnesses to an event may be the client's family, friends, co-workers, neighbors, or other persons who know the client and who want to be helpful in volunteering information. These witnesses are regarded as **friendly witnesses.** You may think that friendly witnesses are the best kind to interview, and they often are. They may also be biased in the client's favor, however, so the paralegal should look closely for the actual

FRIENDLY WITNESS
A witness who gives voluntary testimony at an attorney's request on behalf of the attorney's client; a witness who is prejudiced against the client's adversary.

DEVELOPING PARALEGAL SKILLS, Continued

waste at the site and lists the parties that may be potentially responsible. Ellen decides to call the regional office of the EPA in the area in which the site is located to ask if it has this information, and, if so, what would be involved in copying it.

Ellen calls and speaks to Christopher Peters, a paralegal who processes FOIA requests for the EPA. Ellen identifies herself as a paralegal from the law firm of Smith & Case, which is representing a client involved with the Suburban Land-fill Superfund site. She is greeted with an icy silence. Ellen, wondering what she might have said to offend him, asks him if the EPA has the waste in–waste out document.

CULTIVATING A GOOD RELATIONSHIP WITH AN AGENCY EMPLOYEE

Christopher responds, in a surprised voice, that they do have the documents. "Is that all that you want?" he asks. "Yes, that's all that we need now, until we determine our client's involvement at the site," responds Ellen. "Are you new?" asks Christopher. "Is it that obvious?" jokes Ellen. "No, not really," replied Christopher. "It's just that the paralegal before you always just sent in a FOIA request for everything that we had in our files, and it took weeks to respond to a request from your firm. Believe me, your firm has quite a reputation around here."

Ellen knows that she has handled things the right way. She smiles to herself and tells Christopher that she would submit the FOIA request for only the item that she has mentioned over the phone. "No one will believe that this request is from Smith & Case," laughs Christopher. Ellen knows that she is off to a good start in her new job and with an important legal assistant at the EPA.

---

facts (and not the witness's interpretation of the facts) when interviewing friendly witnesses.

Adverse Witnesses.   Witnesses who may be prejudiced against your client or friendly to your client's adversary are regarded as **adverse witnesses** (often referred to as **hostile witnesses**). Interviewing adverse witnesses can be challenging. Sometimes, hostile witnesses refuse to be interviewed. On learning that the alternative might be a subpoena, however, a hostile witness may consent to at least a limited interview. If you plan to interview hostile witnesses, keep in mind the following rule of thumb:

ADVERSE (HOSTILE) WITNESS
A witness for the opposing side in a lawsuit or other legal proceeding.

- **Contact and interview hostile witnesses in the early stages of your investigation. The longer you wait, the greater the chance that they may be influenced by the opposing party's attorney or the opinions of persons sympathetic to the opposing party.**

When interviewing hostile witnesses, you need to be especially careful to be objective, fair, and unbiased in your approach. This does not mean that you have to ignore your client's interests. On the contrary, you will best serve those interests by doing all you can to keep from further alienating a witness whose information might ultimately help your client's case.

Questioning Witnesses

How you approach witnesses, what kinds of questions you ask, how you ask those questions, and how you respond to the witnesses' answers—all of these factors affect your chances of achieving your goal of eliciting as much relevant information as possible from each witness. Many of the interviewing skills discussed earlier in this chapter apply, of course, to all interviews. This section describes some basic skills and principles that are particularly relevant to investigative interviews. As mentioned earlier, each investigator uses whatever approach works best for him or her. Similarly, when interviewing witnesses, you will ultimately discover what tactics or strategies work best for you in different situations with different types of witnesses.

When you are asking questions as a legal investigator, you should follow this rule of thumb:

- **Phrase your questions so that they lead to the most complete answer possible.**

Investigative questions should be open ended. Compare, for example, the following two questions:

1. "Did you see the driver of the green van run the stop sign?"
2. "What did you see at the time of the accident?"

The first question calls for a "yes" or "no" answer. The second question, in contrast, invites the witness to explain fully what he or she actually saw. Something else that the witness saw could be important to the case—but unless you allow room for the witness's full description, you will not learn about this information.

Notice that the first question also assumes a fact—that the driver of the green van ran the stop sign. The second question, however, makes no assumptions and conveys no information to the witness that may influence his or her answer. Generally, the less the witness knows about other witnesses' descriptions, the better, because those other descriptions could influence the witness's perception of the event. You want to find out exactly what the witness observed, in his or her own words.

Check the Witness's Qualifications

When you are interviewing a witness during the course of an investigation, you often will not know whether the testimony of that witness will be needed in court or even whether the claim you are investigating will be litigated. Nonetheless, you should operate under the assumption that each witness is a potential court witness. Thus, you should make sure that the witness is competent to testify and reliable. Is there any indication that the witness has a physical or mental disability that might interfere with the accuracy of his or her perception of the witnessed event? Has the witness ever been convicted of a crime? Does he or she abuse drugs or have a reputation in the community as a troublemaker? As discussed earlier, if it can be shown that a witness is unreliable or incompetent to testify, the witness's testimony normally will not be admitted in court.

Also investigate the witness's possible biases. Does the witness have an interest in the claim being investigated that would tend to make his or her testimony prejudicial? Is the witness a relative or close friend of one of the parties involved in the claim? Does the witness hold a grudge against one of the parties? If the answer to any of these questions is yes, the witness's testimony may be discredited in court. In any event, it will probably not be as convincing as testimony given by a neutral, unbiased witness.

Witness Statements

Whenever you interview a witness, you should take notes and prepare a memorandum of the interview. Depending on the procedures followed by your firm, you may want to have the witness—particularly if he or she is a hostile witness—sign a statement. A **witness statement** is a written statement setting forth what the witness said during the interview. Statutes and court rules vary as to the value of witness statements as evidence. Usually, statements made by witnesses during interviews cannot be introduced as evidence in court, but they can be used for other purposes. For example, if a hostile witness's testimony in court contradicts something that he or she said during your interview, the witness statement may be used to impeach the witness—that is, to call into question the witness's testimony or demonstrate that the witness is unreliable. Witness statements also can be used to refresh a witness's memory.

WITNESS STATEMENT
The written transcription of a statement made by the witness during an interview and signed by the witness.

The Content of a Witness Statement.   A witness statement should begin by identifying the witness, the interviewer, the time and place of the interview, and the event that was witnessed. In some circumstances—if you suspect that a witness might change his or her mind about what was said during the interview, for example—you may want to create a handwritten statement for the witness to sign immediately. In other situations, you may want to return to the office and type up a statement for the witness to sign later.

When writing or typing a witness statement, you should—to the extent possible or feasible—include the witness's own words. The statement should conclude with an attestation clause, which is a sentence indicating that the witness has read the statement and attests to its accuracy or truth. Some investigators have the witness initial each page of the statement; others simply add to the final attestation clause the number of pages—for example, "I affirm that the information given in the three pages of this statement are accurate and true to the best of my knowledge." Exhibit 7.5 on the following page presents a portion of a sample witness statement.

Recording Interviews.   Some investigators tape-record their interviews as an alternative to writing up statements—providing, of course, that the witness agrees to have the interview tape-recorded. As pointed out earlier, if you are using a tape recorder, you need to state at the beginning of the tape the name of the witness; other relevant witness information; the name of the

EXHIBIT 7.5

A Sample Witness Statement (Excerpt)

STATEMENT OF JULIA WILLIAMS

I, Julia Williams, am a thirty-five-year-old female. I reside at 3801 Mattis Avenue, Nita City, Nita 48800, and my home telephone number is (408) 555-8989. I work as a nurse at the Nita City Hospital & Clinic, 412 Hospital Way, Nita City, Nita 48802. My work telephone number is (408) 555-9898. I am making this statement in my home on the afternoon of February 8, 1996. The statement is being made to Elena Lopez, a paralegal with the law firm of Jeffers, Gilmore & Dunn.

In regard to the accident on the corner of Mattis Avenue and Thirty-eighth Street on August 4, 1995, at approximately 7:45 A.M. on that date, I was standing at the southwest corner of that intersection, waiting to cross the street, when I observed . . .

* * * *

I affirm that the information given in this statement is accurate and true to the best of my knowledge.

Julia Williams
Julia Williams

person who conducted the interview; the date, time, and place of the interview; and other information that would normally appear in a written statement. If more than one tape is used, you should indicate at the end of each tape that the interview will be continued on the next tape in the series, and each subsequent tape should contain identifying information.

Some of the advantages and disadvantages of tape-recording interviews have already been discussed. In regard to tape-recorded witness statements, you should check with your supervising attorney to learn the firm's preferences with respect to tape-recorded versus written witness statements.

THE INVESTIGATION SUMMARY

The final step in any investigation is summarizing the results. How you organize your summary depends to a large extent on your own organizational preferences and the scope of the investigation. Generally, though, your investigation report should provide the following:

• An overall summary of your findings.
• A summary of the facts and information gathered from each source that you investigated.
• Your general conclusions and recommendations based on the information obtained during the investigation.

The overall summary of the investigation should thoroughly describe for the reader all of the facts that you have gathered about the case. This section should be written in such a way that someone not familiar with the case could read it and become adequately informed of the factual background.

TODAY'S PROFESSIONAL PARALEGAL

Locating a Witness

Darin Styles, a legal assistant in a litigation firm, is trying to locate a missing witness in a product-liability case. The witness, Bob Morey, saw the plaintiff's hand being crushed by a press in the factory where both he and the plaintiff worked. Morey helped the plaintiff remove his hand from the press and obtain medical treatment.

LOCATING THE WITNESS

Darin has tried to contact Morey by telephoning him and by going to his listed address, but Morey has apparently moved. He also no longer works at the factory where the accident occurred. When Darin was unable to find Morey at his home, he asked some of the neighbors if they knew where Morey now lived, but he had no success in finding a forwarding address.

Darin has now decided to go to the post office. He approaches the counter and asks if there is a forwarding address for Bob Morey of 1234 Grove Street, Appleton, Michigan. The clerk gives Darin a form to fill out. The clerk then checks the records and finds a forwarding address for Bob Morey. Darin copies it down, thanks her, and leaves. He drives to the address. It appears that someone is living in the house. Darin gets out of the car, goes to the door, and knocks.

INTERVIEWING THE WITNESS

A man answers the door. Darin introduces himself and explains the reason for his visit. The man is Bob Morey. Morey tells Darin that he is concerned about giving a statement because he lost his job as a result of com-plaining about the working conditions after the accident happened. He is afraid that if he gets involved in a lawsuit, he will have an even harder time finding another job.

Darin tries to persuade Morey to cooperate. He tells Morey to think about the serious injury that his friend suffered and about how his friend may never work again because of his crushed hand. Darin also tells Morey that his testimony might help others and prevent this type of accident from happening again in the future. "If we win this case and others like it, the manufacturers of presses are going to have to change the design of their presses so they won't have to pay huge sums of money to people who are injured by their apparently negligent design," explains Darin.

Morey thinks about this. "Well, maybe if it will help others," he murmurs. "I don't know. I'll have to think about it. I'll let you know." Darin has not wanted to threaten Morey with a subpoena and turn him into a hostile witness, but he senses that if he does not mention the possibility of one now, he may have to use a subpoena to make Morey testify.

Darin says, "You know, Mr. Morey, you're a very important witness in this case. We need your testimony, and we'd like to get it voluntarily. But you're so important that we can get a court order—a subpoena—to require you to testify, if we have to." "You mean you can make me testify, even if I don't want to?" asks Morey. "Yes," answers Darin. "Well, in that case, I might as well tell you everything and help you as much as I can," responds Morey. Darin takes out his note pad and begins to interview Morey.

A second step is to create a list of your information sources, including witnesses, and summarize the facts gleaned from each of these sources. Each "source section" should contain all of the information gathered from that source, including direct quotes from witnesses. Each source section should also contain a subsection giving your personal comments on that particular source. You might comment on a witness's demeanor, for example, or on whether the witness's version of the facts was consistent or inconsistent with that of other witnesses. Your impressions of the witness's competence or reliability could be noted. If the witness provided you with further leads to be explored, this information could also be included.

In the final section, you will present your overall conclusions about the investigation, as well as any suggestions that you have on the development of the case. Attorneys rely heavily on their investigators' impressions of witnesses and evaluations of investigative results because the investigators have firsthand knowledge of the sources. Your impression of a potentially important witness, for example, may help the attorney decide whether to arrange for a follow-up interview with the witness. Usually, the attorney will want to interview only the most promising witnesses, and your impressions and comments will serve as a screening device. Based on your findings during the investigation, you might also suggest to the attorney what further information can be obtained during discovery, if necessary, and what additional research needs to be done.

KEY TERMS AND CONCEPTS

active listening   219

adverse (hostile) witness   245

closed-ended question   218

expert witness   242

eyewitness   243

friendly witness   244

hypothetical question   218

interviewee   216

investigation plan   231

lay witness   242

leading question   219

open-ended question   218

pressure question   219

retentive listening   220

supportive listening   221

witness statement   247

CHAPTER SUMMARY

1. Paralegals often interview clients and witnesses. The paralegal may interview an individual alone on behalf of the firm or as part of a legal team that includes an attorney. Becoming a successful interviewer takes practice, dedication, and good interviewing skills.

2. Interviewing skills include interpersonal skills, questioning skills, and communication skills, particularly listening skills. Interpersonal skills are helpful in establishing a comfortable and productive relationship with the interviewee. Establishing a rapport with the client or witness and putting him or her at ease is the cornerstone of an effective interview. To communicate effectively with the interviewee, the interviewer should use language that is familiar to that person. Particularly, the paralegal should avoid using legal terminology unless the terms are defined clearly for the interviewee (or the interviewee is familiar with legal terms).

3. Paralegals can use several types of questions during the interviewing process, including open-ended, closed-ended, hypothetical, pressure, and leading questions. Understanding how these questions function and what types of responses they elicit helps the para-

legal control the interview and maximize the amount of information obtained from the interviewee.

4. Good listening skills are essential for the interviewer. Interruptions and distractions should be kept to a minimum so that both the interviewer and the interviewee can concentrate on the subject being discussed. The paralegal should be an active participant in the communication process even while listening. Active listening involves paying careful attention to what is being said, giving appropriate feedback to the speaker, and analyzing what is being said in light of the larger picture. Retentive listening—listening to retain information—is particularly important in the interviewing context. At times, the paralegal needs to engage in supportive listening, in which the listener responds to the emotional needs of the speaker.

5. Successful interviews require careful preparation. Prior to the interview, the paralegal schedules the session, notifies the interviewee of what (if any) documents or items should be brought to the interview, and prepares a list of questions for the client or witness to answer. The paralegal also prepares the interview environment to ensure that interruptions and delays will be minimized, that the client will be

comfortable, and that any necessary supplies and equipment are at hand. If an interview is to be tape-recorded, the paralegal must obtain permission from both his or her supervising attorney and the interviewee to tape the session.

6. There are basically three types of client interviews: the initial interview, the subsequent interview, and the informational interview (or meeting). The initial interview is usually conducted by the attorney but often is attended by the paralegal (and possibly other members of the legal team). The paralegal is ordinarily responsible for documenting and summarizing the results of the initial session. Preprinted or computerized forms are often used to obtain initial information about a client and the client's legal problem. If the firm accepts the case, a subsequent interview may be scheduled to gather additional information. This session is often conducted by the paralegal alone. The informational interview, or meeting, is also handled by the paralegal. In this interview, the client is updated on case progress, procedures, trial dates, and other information that the paralegal is authorized to convey to clients. As soon as possible after an interview is concluded, the paralegal should summarize in a written memorandum the information gathered in the interview.

7. Before starting an investigation, the paralegal should create an investigation plan. The plan should be a step-by-step list of what sources will be investigated to obtain specific types of information. The paralegal should discuss the plan with his or her supervising attorney before embarking on the investigation.

8. Each person develops his or her own unique style of investigation—what works for one person may not work for another. As a general rule, however, all investigators benefit from abiding by certain basic principles. These principles include (a) focusing on the who, what, and where at all times; (b) maximizing the use of personal contacts; (c) maintaining flexibility; (d) being open minded and objective; and (e) being imaginative and creative in searching out relevant information and potential information sources.

9. There are several information sources available to paralegals who wish to locate factual information regarding witnesses or other persons involved in a lawsuit. These sources include telephone and city directories, media reports, court records, utility companies, professional organizations, and information recorded, compiled, or prepared by federal, state, and local government entities. The Freedom of Information Act of 1966 requires that federal agencies disclose certain of their records to any person on request, providing that the form of the request complies with the procedure mandated by the act.

10. Witnesses interviewed by paralegals include expert witnesses, lay witnesses, eyewitnesses, friendly witnesses, and adverse (hostile) witnesses. Expert witnesses have specialized training in a given area, making their educated opinions helpful when certain facts and issues related to a given case are difficult to understand. Lay witnesses are ordinary witnesses who have factual information about the matter before the court but who are not experts in that area. Eyewitnesses are those who have observed or have first-hand knowledge about an incident. Friendly witnesses are often relatives or friends of the client and are generally supportive of the client's position. Adverse, or hostile, witnesses are prejudiced against the client and often have an interest in the outcome of the case that is adverse to the client's interests.

11. For whichever type of witness is interviewed, the paralegal creates a witness statement. This statement identifies the witness, discloses what was discovered during the interview, and is signed by the witness, who attests that the written statement is a fair representation of his or her own words.

12. When the investigation is complete, the paralegal should summarize the results. The summary should include an overall summary, a source-by-source summary, and a final section giving the paralegal's conclusions and recommendations.

QUESTIONS FOR REVIEW

1. What kinds of skills do interviewers employ during interviews?

2. What are the different types of questions that can be used in an interview? When would you use each type?

3. What are the steps involved in preparing for an interview? Why is each step important?

4. What types of client interviews are commonly conducted by paralegals? What is the purpose of each type?

5. How do you create an investigation plan? Why might investigation plans differ for different cases?

6 What are the basic principles for conducting an investigation?

7. List five sources that you would consult in attempting to locate a witness. Which would be the most useful? The least useful? Why?

8. What is the difference between an expert witness and a lay witness? What is the difference between a friendly witness and an adverse (or hostile) witness?

9. What is a witness statement? How is it used?

10. What is included in an investigation summary? Why should one be prepared?

ETHICAL QUESTIONS

1. Thomas Lent is a new legal assistant with a law firm that specializes in personal-injury cases. He is reviewing a "Request to Produce Documents" that was recently received in a case that his supervising attorney is handling for the plaintiff. The document requests the plaintiff's medical records, but it does not state specifically which records or for what injuries. Thomas's supervising attorney instructs Thomas to obtain copies of all of the plaintiff's medical records. The plaintiff's medical-records file is several inches thick because of the plaintiff's age and various medical problems. Thomas is instructed to bury the relevant medical records in the stack and not to make them obvious to the defendant's attorney. If she wants these records, she will have to sort through the file, says the attorney. What should Thomas do? Can the attorney be disciplined for this kind of behavior?

2. In response to a discovery request, Lynnette Banks, a paralegal in a corporate law firm, receives a package of documents in the mail. She opens the package and begins to read through the documents. As she reads, she discovers documents with the words "Privileged and Confidential" stamped on them. She scans a document and realizes that it is a letter from the opposing counsel to his client. The letter reveals the opposing attorney's legal strategy in the case on which Lynnette is now working. What should Lynnette do?

PRACTICE QUESTIONS AND ASSIGNMENTS

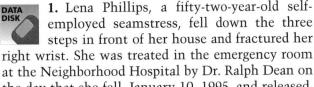

1. Lena Phillips, a fifty-two-year-old self-employed seamstress, fell down the three steps in front of her house and fractured her right wrist. She was treated in the emergency room at the Neighborhood Hospital by Dr. Ralph Dean on the day that she fell, January 10, 1995, and released. On January 17, January 25, and February 11, 1995, she visited Dr. Dean's office for follow-up care to make sure that the wrist was healing properly. It appeared that the wrist was healing properly during the month in which she was treated by Dr. Dean. She noticed, however, that even though she had a full range of motion in her wrist, the wrist angled inward somewhat. When she queried Dr. Dean about this, he told her that some angling of the wrist was inevitable.

Over the course of the following year, her wrist became increasingly crooked and bent inward. She went to an orthopedist, Dr. Alicia Byerly, on March 30, 1996. Dr. Byerly tried a splint, but without success. She eventually performed surgery on the wrist at the Neighborhood Hospital on May 3, 1996, but was unable to correct the problem. Dr. Byerly told Ms. Phillips that she should have had surgery on the wrist during the first three weeks after it was broken to correct the angling problem.

Lena Phillips has come to the firm for which you work, the law firm of Samson & Goren, 5000 West Avenue, Northville, New Hampshire 12345, because she wants to sue Dr. Dean for medical malpractice. On May 15, 1996, you are asked to investigate her case. Draft an investigation plan.

2. Using the information in this chapter on questioning skills, identify the following types of questions:

   a. "From January 10, 1995, until January 17, 1995, you were on a cruise in the Bahamas, Mr. Johnson. Your credit-card records, which were subpoenaed, indicate that you purchased two tickets. If your wife did not accompany you on that cruise, who did?"

   b. "Did you go on a cruise in the Bahamas with another woman, Mr. Johnson?"

   c. "Isn't it true, Mr. Johnson, that someone other than your wife accompanied you on a cruise in the Bahamas?"

   d. "Mr. Johnson, will you please describe your whereabouts between January 10, 1995, and January 17, 1995?"

8

COMPUTERS AND THE
LEGAL PROFESSION

CHAPTER OBJECTIVES

After completing this chapter, you will know:

• The effect of computers on law-office operations and on the nature of the work performed by paralegals.
• The types of computers in use, the types of components used in computer systems, and the types of external devices on which computer data and files can be stored.
• The difference between operating-system software and application software.
• How networking and electronic-mail systems can be used to share data and software or transmit communications via computer.
• The three basic types of application software and some of the specific types of application programs used in law offices.

CHAPTER OUTLINE

SOFTWARE
Computer programs that instruct and control the computer's hardware and operations.

HARDWARE
The physical components (mechanical, magnetic, electronic, and so on) of the computer, including the computer itself, the keyboard, the monitor, and other peripheral devices attached to the computer.

ETHICAL CONCERN

Accuracy in Data Entry

Paralegals are ethically obligated to abide by the ethical duties imposed on attorneys, including the duty of competence. When working on computers, paralegals must, among other things, take special care in checking and double-checking the accuracy of data entered into computers. This is because, once entered, the data may appear on numerous future drafts, as well as in other related documents. Assume, for example, that you work as a paralegal specializing in real estate. Your work is made simpler by a computer program specifically designed for real-estate transactions. One day, you mistakenly key in the buyer's deposit as $9,800 instead of $8,900. The erroneous amount is replicated on a number of other forms produced by the program that relate to the same transaction, and the mistake is not detected until an audit at the end of the month reveals a $900 discrepancy in the buyer's account. You have just learned the hard way how important it is to ensure that initial entries of data are accurate.

INTRODUCTION

Computers have simplified the tasks of paralegals enormously. They have changed the pace of document preparation and have made law-office operations more efficient. They have also made it possible for paralegals to spend more time performing substantive legal work and less time engaging in mechanical tasks, such as retyping documents to incorporate revisions. In the area of legal research, computerized legal-research services such as WESTLAW and LEXIS (discussed later in this chapter) have made it possible for attorneys and paralegals to access court cases, statutes, regulations, articles in law journals, and numerous other information sources and data without leaving the law office.

Because of the widespread use of computers in today's law offices, computer literacy is a must for paralegals. No one textbook chapter can cover all of the various ways in which computers are used by the firms and other organizations that hire paralegals or all of the computer programs used in law offices. Even if it could, you would not benefit by learning about *all* computer systems and programs for two reasons. First, much of what you need to know will be determined to a great extent by where you work. Each law firm, corporation, government agency, or other organization that hires paralegals has its own computer system and software applications with which you will need to become familiar. (**Software** consists of computer programs that instruct the computer to perform certain functions or tasks.) Second, specific features of computer systems and specific software applications become outdated very quickly—because newer and better computer programs are produced regularly. Although we mention some specific computer programs in this chapter, bear in mind that by the time you read this book, other improved programs will probably be available for law-office use.

We present in this chapter an overview of computer technology and how computers are used in legal practice. The information contained in the following pages will furnish you with a basic knowledge of computer systems, computer networks, the basic types of application software commonly used in law offices, and some of the benefits and costs involved in computerized legal research. You can consider this chapter a stepping stone on the way to computer literacy. Once you begin working as a paralegal, you can take the further step of learning how to operate the specific computer system and software used in your workplace—or, if little computer technology is used, how it might be applied to the tasks performed in your office.

COMPUTER HARDWARE

The term **hardware** is used to describe the physical components of a computer system. Computer hardware varies with the type of system in use. Here we look at the types of computers and computer components frequently used in legal offices.

Types of Computers

Computers range in size and capacity from large mainframe computers to small personal, or desktop, computers.

The Mainframe Computer.   At one time, all computers were mainframe computers. A **mainframe computer** is a centralized, large computer processing unit that can handle and store vast amounts of data. Because of the expense of purchasing and maintaining mainframe computers, typically they are used only by very large organizations and government agencies. For example, databases provided by computerized legal-research services, such as WESTLAW and LEXIS, are stored and processed by mainframe computers. Airline companies track their reservation and scheduling systems through mainframes. The Internal Revenue Service and state government tax bureaus use mainframes to handle tax returns. The college or university that you are attending probably uses a mainframe computer. Only a few of the largest law firms, or megafirms, own mainframes.

Multiple *terminals* can be connected to a mainframe so that its computing ability and data can be accessed by a number of users. Access to databases in mainframe computers is typically restricted to authorized users. Paralegals who access mainframe computers therefore normally will be assigned a **security code**, or **password**. (See Exhibit 8.1 for a photograph of a mainframe computer.)

Minicomputers and Servers.   Today, computer technology has made it possible for law offices to obtain, at a significantly lower cost, smaller computer systems with sufficient memory and computing ability to serve their needs. The **minicomputer** is a computer with more power and capabilities than most individual users need, but its capabilities are not as great as those of a mainframe computer. The minicomputer is frequently found in large departments or in middle-sized businesses or law firms. Typically, as with a mainframe, the minicomputer is connected to a number of terminals so that

MAINFRAME COMPUTER
A large, centralized computer processing unit that can service multiple terminals simultaneously and that is capable of storing, handling, and retrieving vast amounts of data (used by large organizations, such as megafirms, government agencies, and universities).

SECURITY CODE (PASSWORD)
A predetermined series of numbers and/or letter characters that an authorized user keys in to gain access to a computer system or data contained in computer files.

MINICOMPUTER
A computer with more power and capacity than a microcomputer but less than a mainframe computer. Like the mainframe, the minicomputer (server) can be connected to a number of terminals (clients) simultaneously.

EXHIBIT 8.1
An IBM ES/9000 Mainframe

EXHIBIT 8.2
**A DEC Microvax
Minicomputer System**

PERSONAL COMPUTER (PC)

A desktop computer, or microcomputer, with its own central processing unit, which is ordinarily used for applications that are tailored to the user's employment, domestic, or educational needs.

HARD DRIVE

A unit that enables a personal computer to store software programs and data files in permanent memory. The hard drive contains a hard disk.

CENTRAL PROCESSING UNIT (CPU)

The part of a computer that controls the function of the other computer components, stores the information contained in software programs, and executes the operator's keyboard commands.

MONITOR

A black-and-white or multicolor display screen that displays the current activities of the computer.

KEYBOARD

A computer input device with alphanumeric characters (arranged similarly to the traditional typewriter) and function keys.

it can be used simultaneously by a number of users. Often, the term *server* is used for a minicomputer, and the terminals that are connected to it are called *clients*. A law firm might use a server/client system to permit numerous users to have access to the data in the minicomputer. Exhibit 8.2 shows a minicomputer system.

The Personal Computer.   Often, a paralegal is assigned an individual processing unit and monitor, commonly referred to as a **personal computer (PC)**, a desktop computer, or a microcomputer. This unit will be used for applications tailored to the individual's assignments. Personal computers normally contain **hard drives** (or hard disk drives). The hard drive allows the computer to store, in its permanent memory, software and data files that are tailored to the paralegal's needs and work assignments. Without the hard drive, the software and data would have to be "loaded" from diskettes each time the user turned on the computer. Legal professionals can use personal computers and modems (discussed below) to access the data contained in the mainframes of service bureaus such as WESTLAW and LEXIS.

Components

Every computer, whether it is a large mainframe unit or a personal computer, is composed of several parts (see Exhibit 8.3), which we discuss below. We also describe other components of a computer system, including optical scanners, printers, and modems.

The Central Processing Unit.   The **central processing unit (CPU)** is the component of a computer system that controls the interpretation and execution of instructions. In a sense, it is the "brain" of the computer. The CPU controls the functions of the other computer components. It temporarily stores the information contained in the computer programs, or software, and executes the operator's commands as they are input through the keyboard. Each personal computer has its own CPU. In a mainframe system, in contrast, only the mainframe computer itself has a CPU. Each terminal normally contains only a monitor and a keyboard with which the user can access the central CPU, or mainframe.

The Monitor.   The **monitor** is a screen, like a television screen, that displays the current activities of the computer. The technology of monitors varies, and different software programs require different levels of technology. Monitors also come in different sizes. Additionally, some monitors display data or information only in shades of black and white, while others offer full-color displays.

The Keyboard.   The **keyboard** is used to send information to the computer's processing unit; in turn, this information is displayed on the monitor. The keyboard looks much like a typewriter keyboard but differs from a typewriter keyboard in several ways. In addition to containing the letters of the alphabet and numbers, the computer keyboard usually has specialized *function keys* designed for communicating with the computer's processing unit. The keyboard usually also contains a separate numeric keypad to speed the input of arithmetic data.

Computers, because they allows paralegals to "cut and paste" part or all of the contents of one document to another, reduce to some extent the need for "perfect" typing skills. Nonetheless, the ability to type quickly and accurately is an essential paralegal skill. Experienced paralegals find that the better they are at keyboarding, the more efficiently and accurately they can produce necessary documents.

The Mouse.   Many computers use a **mouse**, which is a pointing device that lets the user give commands without using the keyboard. The mouse, which is usually no larger than a person's hand, contains a rotating ball inside it. Moving the mouse across the desk rotates the ball and creates corresponding movements in the *cursor*, a symbol indicating where the next character—if keyed in—will appear on the monitor. An alternative to a mouse is a *trackball*, in which the rotating ball is mounted in a fixed base.

Optical Scanners.   Law firms are increasingly utilizing optical-imaging technology for data-input purposes. An *optical scanner* (see Exhibit 8.4) is a device that, when moved over a document, "scans" and copies the contents of the document in a form readable by the computer. Optical scanning is thus an alternative input device to a keyboard. You will read more about the benefits of optical imaging for the law office in the *Today's Professional Paralegal* feature at the end of this chapter.

Printers.   A printer transfers data that you see on your computer screen and from computer files to a permanent, readable form. In some offices, each CPU is linked to an individual printer; in other offices, computers are linked to a shared printer. The computer document transferred to paper is referred to as a *hard copy*. There are a variety of types of printers. Law firms typically use *laser printers* because of their speed and the high quality of the printed results. (See Exhibit 8.5 on the next page for a photograph of a LaserJet printer.)

Modems.   A **modem** is a device that, when connected to a computer and a telephone line, allows computer users to transmit and receive information and documents directly from other computers. The modem converts outgoing data from the digital signals used by the computer to analog sound waves that can be transmitted over a telephone line. The receiving computer's modem then translates the incoming data from analog form to digital form so that the information can be displayed by the receiving computer's screen. Specialized *communications software* is needed to convert data to a form that can be communicated via modem over telephone lines.

Storage Devices

Storage devices are used to store programs, data, and work performed on the computer. Personal computers generally contain internal hard drives (or hard disk drives), as mentioned earlier. The internal hard drive is built into the computer unit. The computer user can store software and work files on the computer's hard drive, where they are accessible whenever the computer is switched on.

EXHIBIT 8.5
HP LaserJet 4MV Printer

Many users store work on their computer hard drives. The amount of data that can be stored on hard drives varies, depending on the computer. Internal hard drives are sold with various storage capacities ranging from as little as forty megabytes up to several thousand megabytes. Note that computer memory is measured in units called *bytes*. A byte may represent a character, such as a letter or numeral, or a character space. A *kilobyte* is a thousand bytes; a *megabyte* is a million bytes.

Most computer users also "back up" their work on external storage devices. For one thing, users commonly need extra storage space. For another, users usually wish to create back-up copies of their work so that the documents or files are not lost if the computer system fails. We will look shortly at the importance of "saving" computer-generated work to an internal hard drive and of backing up work on an external storage device. Here we look at some of the external storage devices currently in use.

External Hard Drives. An external hard drive (which is similar to the internal hard drive discussed above) can be connected to a computer to provide ongoing storage opportunities. In other words, while using the computer, you can periodically transfer documents and data to the external hard drive for storage without having to insert a diskette or other storage device into the computer.

Diskettes. Removable diskettes (see Exhibit 8.6) are commonly used to back up and store computer files and data. A diskette can be inserted into the disk drive of the computer, and data from the computer can be transferred, or

EXHIBIT 8.6
Diskettes

THE LEGAL TEAM AT WORK
Communications Systems and Teamwork

We have stressed earlier in this text how important communication is to effective teamwork. To ensure that nothing crucial is overlooked in preparing for a trial or other legal proceeding, each team member must be kept informed of what the other team members are doing and the current status of each member's work. Communicating with team members would not be difficult if all of the attorneys and paralegals working on a case were at all times in close physical proximity to each other. But that is not always the situation. Attorneys frequently have to attend meetings, conferences, or other proceedings outside their offices—sometimes in distant cities or even other countries. Similarly, paralegals sometimes need to leave their offices for significant time periods, as when traveling to other cities to interview witnesses, obtain evidence, or perhaps do legal research.

Being physically distant from one another no longer poses the communication problems for team members that it once did. Today, using modems and communications software, an attorney or paralegal can transfer documents and other information from a home computer to the office computer or, while traveling within the United States or even in other countries, from a hotel room or other site (using a notebook computer with a built-in modem) to the home office. Increasingly, judges are permitting attorneys to use computer equipment in the courtroom. In some trials, paralegals and attorneys no longer have to leave the courtroom to call their offices on the phone. Instead, they can send and receive E-mail messages while in the courtroom. If necessary, they can transmit documents via modem back and forth between their offices and the courtroom, as well as access legal-research databases, such as WESTLAW and LEXIS, from the courtroom to conduct research.

---

backed up on, the diskette for storage and safekeeping. Most computers accept 3½-inch diskettes, but others use 5¼-inch diskettes (the latter are almost never used anymore, however). Although diskettes provide a convenient way to store data, their storage capacity is usually limited to two megabytes or less.

Optical Disks.   Law firms can now purchase recordable optical disk drives and optical disks, such as those shown in Exhibit 8.7 on the next page, to record and store data. Each 3½-inch optical disk can store 230 megabytes of data—the equivalent of a typical hard drive. To store data on an optical disk, you insert the disk into the optical disk drive, which (usually) is an external device connected to the computer.

CD-ROMs.   A more recent technological breakthrough allows vast amounts of data to be accessed through a *compact disk, read-only memory (CD-ROM)*. CD-ROM technology allows the legal researcher to access a variety of legal data on a small, compact laser disk, much like the compact disks that have revolutionized the world of music. CD-ROM libraries combine the power of personal computers with traditional legal-research techniques. A CD-ROM holds the equivalent of over 600 megabytes of data. This means that one CD-ROM can store approximately 300,000 pages, or over one hundred volumes of legal reference material. CD-ROMs thus can contain material that, in printed form, would fill many shelves in a library. For

EXHIBIT 8.7
An Optical Disk

example, the entire 215-volume *United States Code Annotated* (discussed in Chapter 9) is contained on only two CD-ROMs. Federal government publications and other research sources will be increasingly available in CD-ROM format.

CD-ROMs are accessed through a CD-ROM reader, which is similar to a disk drive. The CD-ROM reader is designed to read and display the contents of the CD-ROM inserted into the reader. Depending on the computer system, the CD-ROM reader, or drive, can either be an internal drive or be attached through cables and appear as a separate, external part of the computer system. The software program, which allows the computer operating system to communicate with the CD-ROM, will be installed when the CD-ROM reader is installed.

As technology improves, more and more law firms will also be purchasing CD-ROM recording machines to record their own CD-ROMs. A recordable CD-ROM is basically the same as a diskette and can be used instead of a diskette to store data.

Magnetic Tape. Another type of storage device for high volumes of information is a *magnetic-tape system* (see Exhibit 8.8). Unlike most CD-ROM devices, magnetic tape systems can both read *and write* data. In other words, in addition to accessing information contained on a magnetic tape, a computer user can transfer data from a hard drive to a magnetic tape for back-up storage.

The magnetic tape can be used in two formats, either small cartridges of magnetic tape or larger reels of tape. Magnetic-tape systems are typically used to make back-up copies of large quantities of data. There is now a *digital audiotape* (DAT) that has even greater storage capability. A DAT is typically smaller than a regular cassette and can hold as much data as a CD-ROM.

EXHIBIT 8.8
A Magnetic Tape in a Magnetic Tape Drive

Saving and Backing Up Your Work

An important aspect of proficiency in computer use involves two process-es—saving your work and backing it up on an external storage device.

Saving Your Work.   Whenever you perform work on a computer, you should save your work at frequent intervals. *Saving* refers to the process in which the work you are currently performing on the computer is transferred to, or saved on, the internal hard drive of your computer. For example, suppose that you are revising a document on a personal computer that has an internal hard drive. While you are performing this work, your changes or additions to the document are stored in the computer's temporary memory. Should a power failure cause your computer to shut down, all work stored in temporary memory will be lost.

To store work in permanent memory, you need to use the "Save" command on your computer. Computer users today install special software that automatically saves your work to the computer's hard drive at frequent intervals, such as every two minutes. Many such "auto-save" programs are available. Because it is difficult to remember to save your work periodically, to protect yourself against the possibility of losing valuable work time, you should take special note of the following advice:

● **Whatever program you are using, make sure that you have an automatic-save system in place that transfers your current work to the computer's hard drive every two minutes.**

Backing Up Your Work.   Another important aspect of computer proficiency is remembering to *back up* your work on a diskette or another external storage device at the end of each project (or at the end of each day). If work is not backed up on an external storage device, it can easily be lost. For example, if your computer system "crashes," you may not be able to retrieve the data that have been saved on your hard drive. In this situation, you will lose valuable documents or data that may have taken hours (or days) to create and that may not be replaceable.

OPERATING-SYSTEM SOFTWARE

Computers work according to certain *operating systems*. **Operating-system software** controls the communication between the computer system and application software. **Application software** is the term used to describe computer programs that instruct the CPU how to perform specific tasks, such as word processing or arithmetic computations. Application software designed for one operating system will not usually function on a computer that uses a different operating system. We look below at disk operating systems and the problem of compatibility in regard to application software.

OPERATING-SYSTEM SOFTWARE
A program allowing the computer to control the sequencing and processing of application software programs so that the computer responds correctly to the operator's commands.

APPLICATION SOFTWARE
Computer programs designed to instruct the central processing unit on the operation and performance of certain tasks.

User Interface
The computer connection, or link, between the software and the hardware that controls the image that an operator views on the monitor and the method of accomplishing a given task.

Disk Operating System (DOS) and Alternatives

One of the most common operating systems is the *disk operating system (DOS)* developed by Microsoft Corporation. Because Microsoft (MS) developed this system, it is often referred to as *MS-DOS*. IBM and IBM-compatible computers typically operate using the DOS system. An alternative for these computers is *System 2*, offered by IBM.

The primary alternative to IBM and IBM-compatible computers in law offices is Apple's *Macintosh* computer. Macintosh computers have used some version of an operating system called *System 7* for a few years. New versions are available regularly, the latest of which is *Mac OS*. Newspapers and magazines often contain advertisements for various new operating systems and for updates to existing operating systems.

Compatibility

As mentioned, application software is typically manufactured for use with a particular operating system. New technology, however, is allowing both operating-system and application-software manufacturers to claim that their operating-system or application software is *compatible* (workable) with other systems or software. An expert computer user should be consulted about all questions related to the compatibility of one system with another.

Traditionally, personal computer systems used in law offices have been either IBM (or IBM-compatible) systems or Macintosh systems. Each has had its own typical operating system and applications programs. Thus, work done on an IBM system using DOS could be transferred only to another IBM or IBM-compatible computer. Today, however, special software programs allow users to translate data created on DOS systems to Macintosh computers and vice versa.

User Interfaces

One of the major differences between operating systems has traditionally been something called the **user interface**. The user interface controls what the user sees on the computer screen. For DOS, the user must learn—or consult the user's manual for—commands and codes to communicate with the computer. Macintosh users do not have to learn as many codes and keyboard commands, because the Macintosh system provides icons, or pictures (such as a picture of a file), to illustrate various functions. To open a computer file using a Macintosh computer, for example, you use the mouse to direct the cursor on the screen to a particular file, double-click on the mouse, and the file opens.

The user interface called *Windows* was developed for use with DOS. The most recent version of this user interface is *Windows 95*, which became available in the spring of 1995. The Windows program provides an interface involving icons. For Windows to work, however, the computer system must meet certain requirements related to processing speed and specific kinds of internal memory.

Another aspect of the user interface is the appearance of the screen when the computer is turned on, before any software program has been loaded. The operating system also controls this aspect of the interface. With a computer using DOS, for example, the computer screen usually shows C:—which is known as the *C-prompt.* The C-prompt indicates that the computer is ready to accept user commands. The most typical command is for the computer to *load* a software system of the user's choice. Some law offices use an interface or menu program with DOS. Such a program may provide an introductory screen featuring icons (as with Windows) or a *menu*—a list of the software programs available to the user. Computers can also be set up so that a preferred software program is automatically loaded into the system when the power is turned on.

OFFICE NETWORK SYSTEMS

While individual computer users can share files or information through the use of modems, law firms may want to have individual computers share information on a more consistent and routine basis. Networks serve this purpose.

Local and Wide Area Networks

A **local area network (LAN)** connects personal computers or minicomputers in a local area, such as a room or a building, so that they can communicate with each other and share software or data. The network also allows the linked computer units to use the same printer, hard drive, or other *peripheral* (support) devices. Using a LAN also allows one user on the network to view on his or her computer screen a document created by another user. For example, suppose that you have finished drafting a complaint that needs to be filed very soon with the court. Your supervising attorney's office is at the other end of the building. Using a LAN, your supervising attorney could review the complaint on his or her computer screen. If revisions need to be made, you could make them and print out the final draft of the document.

A **wide area network (WAN)** allows multiple computer users located across a large geographical area to enjoy the benefits of direct communication. National and international law firms can take advantage of WANs to share a common pool of data and office or operations information.

Network Design

Firms use two basic models of network design. The first, the *client/server* model, was discussed earlier in the section on minicomputers. This model requires a powerful server computer to act as an information manager for client personal computers in the network. The server contains master software, files, and data. The client computers can access the wealth of tools and information available on the server and can also use the server as an electronic "post office" to send and receive electronic-mail (**E-mail**) messages. Users of client computers cannot communicate directly with each other unless they communicate through the server. Creating a client/server network usually requires professional assistance, both to *configure,* or set up, the hardware system and to select and install software to support the network.

LOCAL AREA NETWORK (LAN)
A system of physically dispersed computers that are interconnected, via telecommunications, within a local area, such as an office building. Users at each connected computer can share information and software with other computers connected to the network.

WIDE AREA NETWORK (WAN)
A system of computers, physically dispersed over a large geographical area, in which the users are able to communicate directly with each other via computer.

E-MAIL
An abbreviation for electronic mail; an electronic message sent over a computer network from one computer terminal to another or others.

PARALEGAL PROFILE   Corporate Paralegal

ARIE MARIE BAGGETT started her career as a legal secretary in a Chicago law firm with thirteen attorneys, who worked in various areas of the law. In 1983, she received her paralegal certificate from Roosevelt University, in Chicago. After receiving her certificate, she continued to work for the same firm, mainly performing research in the areas of bankruptcy, litigation, and securities law. In 1986, when the firm moved to Texas, she was hired by Information Resources, Inc., a marketing research corporation. The company creates and sells software that assists retailers and manufacturers in researching and analyzing their sales of consumer products. Baggett's responsibilities at Information Resources include trademark searches, some patent applications, records automation, and general records management.

What do you like best about your work?

"The thing that I like best about my job is the variety. I am always working on a little bit of everything and am continually learning new things. I also like the fact that the variety of work I do allows me to utilize all of my skills and educational training. I had experience in records automation at my previous job, so I took the initiative and started automating the files. So far, I've automated about half of them. Other departments in the corporation, including the accounting and engineering departments, now can call for data and get results much faster due to the automation. I also enjoy the contacts I have with a variety of people, including department heads and people in foreign countries, as well as the fact that I am able to work to a great extent on my own and at my own pace."

> **"COMPUTER TECHNOLOGY CAN HELP ATTORNEYS AND PARALEGALS BE MORE PRODUCTIVE"**

What is the greatest challenge that you face in your area of work?

"The most challenging aspect of my job is taking on new responsibilities. When I first take on an area of responsibility, it is challenging until I master it. For example, at first I thought that dealing with document discovery was very challenging, especially if it involved a major litigation case. But now I feel much more comfortable with this area of work. Another challenging area at first was how to treat plaintiffs' attorneys when they want to look at documents. It is a sensitive position. Often, the plaintiff's attorney is waiting downstairs while I am going through the files to see what documents might be privileged. I never make decisions on what is privileged myself and always present the documents to the attorneys so that they can make that decision."

What advice do you have for would-be paralegals in your area of work?

"If I were a student now, I would be more attentive to everything, especially to topics (such as securities, bankruptcy, and intellectual property) that I thought were boring when I was in school. Now I work in corporate law and deal with matters relating to these topics on a daily basis. You never know what you're going to be using when you get out into the field, and it is important to realize that everything you study may be of critical importance on the job."

What are some tips for success as a paralegal in your area of work?

"The most important attributes for a paralegal to have in the area of corporate law are dependability, initiative, and self-motivation. I also feel that it is very important to continue to take classes and educate yourself. Additionally, I recommend circulating new or updated information to the attorneys. Many attorneys may be hesitant to take advantage of computer technology that goes beyond simple word processing or other basic functions. I have been able to show how computer technology can help attorneys and paralegals be more productive."

The second model for designing a network is a file-sharing system, in which every personal computer acts as both a client and a server. The individual computer user determines which files and programs to make available to the network. The file-sharing (or "peer-to-peer") network is easier to set up and operate than the client/server network. The file-sharing model cannot be used effectively, however, for more than twenty or thirty computers.

Both network systems require certain expertise that is not normally associated with the use of the stand-alone personal computer. Network users must learn to transmit and receive information. They must also be aware of security procedures, so that unauthorized users cannot gain access to files.

Electronic Mail

Law offices frequently take advantage of the ability of computers to communicate with each other by establishing an electronic-mail bulletin board, or E-mail system. E-mail allows people in offices to send messages directly to one another's computer screens. Interoffice communications and even client-attorney communications can be speeded up through the use of E-mail. To ensure the privacy and confidentiality of E-mail communications, many people today invest in software programs, called *encryption programs*, that encode, or encrypt, data transmitted or received via E-mail.

Millions of individuals today send E-mail messages over the Internet, an international network connecting over thirty-five thousand educational, corporate, and research computer networks around the world. Internet can be accessed through colleges and universities, most of which are directly connected to the Internet, and through commercial on-line services such as Delphi, CompuServe, Prodigy, and others. Clearly, because of the vast number of individuals using the Internet, confidential E-mail messages should be encoded for transmission via the Internet. You will read more about using the Internet in Appendix B at the end of this text.

APPLICATION SOFTWARE

Application software, as indicated earlier, creates a dialogue between the computer user and the central processing unit and determines the kinds of tasks that the computer will perform. The same CPU can run different software programs at different times. This section describes the law-office activities that benefit from computer assistance and the types of application software that are frequently used to perform these activities.

Generally, application software falls into three categories: word-processing software, database management systems, and spreadsheet software. We look at each of these types of software in the following sections.

Word-processing Software

Virtually all law firms now use word-processing programs on their computer systems to prepare documents. **Word-processing software** is a term used to describe computer programs that allow the user to create the text of documents and save, edit, or otherwise change the content and the appearance of those documents.

WORD-PROCESSING SOFTWARE
Specialized application software that allows a computer user to create, edit, revise, save, and generally manipulate textual material and document formatting.

DEVELOPING PARALEGAL SKILLS

Out-of-town Hearing

 Barbara Holmes, a corporate legal assistant, is attending a regulatory hearing in Washington, D.C., along with three attorneys from her corporation. The corporation, TexMex Transmission, Inc., is a natural gas pipeline company. The Federal Energy Regulatory Commission (FERC) is holding the hearing to determine whether to grant permission to the pipeline industry to vastly expand current lines to provide much-needed additional service to the northeastern states. The hearing is expected to last almost a year, so Barbara and the attorneys from her department—along with representatives of the marketing, rates, engineering, and public relations departments—have rented the top five floors of a Washington hotel for their use during the hearing. The top floor contains their offices. They have brought along their secretaries and computer equipment to supply word-processing, electronic-mail, and fax capabilities.

WITNESS SCHEDULES AND TESTIMONY

Barbara's duties include coordinating witnesses' schedules, assisting in their travel arrangements when necessary, and summarizing each day the transcripts of the witnesses' testimony. These summaries are then circulated for use by the witnesses and attorneys. They are also forwarded to the general corporate counsel at the home office in Dallas, Texas, so that the boss can monitor the hearing without having to be present for the entire procedure.

HEARING SCHEDULES

The commission is hearing testimony from the last of the local gas utility companies in Boston, Massachusetts, and has issued the schedule of New York companies, whose testimony will be heard next. The testimony of the New York companies will help the commission determine if there is enough demand to justify expanding the pipelines. Barbara, using the wide area network (WAN) established prior to the hearing, has finished keying in the schedule for the New York companies on her computer and has just transmitted the schedule to the general counsel in Dallas.

COMMUNICATING WITH THE HOME OFFICE

While waiting for a response from Dallas, Barbara accesses her E-mail and reads through the messages that she has received today. There are some interesting memos from the personnel department concerning some changes in health insurance, but otherwise things are quiet on the Dallas front. She then begins to read through the transcripts of yesterday's hearing so that she can summarize them, distribute them to the attorneys present, and then forward them to the general counsel for his review. The general counsel will have the transcripts edited and distributed to others in the corporation.

Form Documents. Recall from Chapter 4 that law offices and legal practitioners in other environments frequently maintain a forms file for routinely created documents, such as wills and contracts. For example, in each state, a will must meet specific requirements established by state law. If your forms file contains a sample copy of a will that addresses all of these requirements, you can use that form as a model and modify it as necessary when you are drafting a will for a client.

In the past, preprinted forms were routinely used. Now, software programs, such as *West's Desktop Practice Systems,* supply those same preprinted forms on disk. The user can choose forms from a table of contents or search the entire contents of the disk automatically. Once a form is chosen, the user can fill in the blanks using the software and move the form into a word processor for editing and printing. A customized document—instead of a form with the blanks filled in—is the result. It is no longer easy to tell from the face of the document which language or provisions are **boilerplate** (terms and clauses used in all such documents) and which have been specially prepared for the individual client. Also, document revision is much simpler when using computerized forms.

Document Revision.   Documents must frequently be revised—that is, phrases, paragraphs, or sections must be added, deleted, or otherwise modified. Word-processing software allows such changes to be made simply and speedily. Page length, margins, and other formatting features can be changed by simple commands, and some word-processing software even allows for automatic paragraph renumbering.

For example, suppose that you have been asked to create a last will and testament for a client, Anne Lampher. You locate the diskette containing sample forms for wills and find a form for a will that is similar to the one you want to create for Lampher. You insert the diskette into the computer's disk drive, copy the selected form to your hard drive, and ask the computer to save the document as "LAMPHER1." Then you open the form document and modify it as necessary to meet Lampher's specific wishes, periodically commanding the computer to save the revised document to your hard drive (unless you have special software on your computer that automatically saves your work at specified intervals).

Once you have prepared a first draft of the will, you can print out the document for your supervising attorney to review. Assuming that some modifications are necessary, you will again open the document and make the necessary changes. Once the changes are made, you may want either to replace the first document with the revised document or to retitle the revised document "LAMPHER2."

Naming Documents.   The name you assign to a document or file must be unique—that is, one that is not already entered for another document that is stored on your hard drive. If there is already a document on your hard drive named "LAMPHER1" (as there would be in the above hypothetical scenario), you may be asked whether you would like to replace the existing document under the same name. If you say yes, the preexisting file will be erased, or destroyed—just as if you had taken the only paper copy of a document and run it through a shredder. Generally, you should abide by the following rule when naming computer files:

● **Before you replace any existing document on a computer, you need to know what the existing document is and whether you or another employee of your firm will want to keep it.**

ETHICAL CONCERN

Software Piracy

Computer software can be very costly to create and to purchase. If you own a personal computer, you could avoid having to pay for computer software already purchased by your employer for the office computer system. It would be simple—just make a back-up copy (or use the original copy) of the software, take it home, load it onto your hard disk, and return it to the office the next morning. It is relatively easy to convince yourself that because no one is being deprived of anything in a situation such as this, no theft has occurred. But remember that the company that produced that software has ownership rights in the intellectual property (see Chapter 8). By using the software company's property without authorization, you are engaging in an unethical (and probably illegal) action.

BOILERPLATE
Certain terms or clauses that are normally included in specific types of legal documents.

If you are at all uncertain, the safest step is to assign your new work product a new file name and leave the existing document as it is.

Law offices have different policies as to the retention of various versions of a document or file. Because attorneys and paralegals often bill their clients based on the hours spent performing the client's work, firms may wish to keep a record of the various steps they have taken in order to reach the end results desired by the clients. You should determine, therefore, whether your office would like you to give each revision of a document a separate name and retain it on your computer. If so, you will call the revision of Lampher's will "LAMPHER2," and the original draft ("LAMPHER1") will be retained in the computer's memory. Your office may instead prefer that you keep a paper copy, or hard copy, of the first version on file to avoid cluttering the computer's hard drive. In any event, you will need to be familiar with the document-retention policy of your firm before you can be certain that you are performing this function correctly.

Commonly Used Word-processing Features and Terms.   Although many different types of word-processing systems are used in law offices, certain features and terms are typically used in all systems. Exhibit 8.9 shows some of the more commonly used terms and features used in word-processing software.

Database Management Systems

Attorneys and paralegals typically deal with large collections of information. A law firm may want to send a mailing to each of its clients to announce the opening of a new office, track discovery documents in a complex trial, or maintain a list of expert witnesses in different specialty areas. A **database management system** allows users to organize data in specific ways, create reports, and print out information in a variety of formats. Exhibit 8.10 on page 272, for example, shows part of a specialized expert-witness database. Like word-processing software, database software uses a specialized vocabulary to describe its features. Exhibit 8.11 on page 272 lists and defines some basic terms commonly used in database software.

Law offices and legal practitioners in other environments use database management systems to perform certain functions with the data, or information, that the systems contain. For these functions to be performed effectively, information about the intended use of the database should be carefully gathered. The database should then be planned according to its intended use. A first step in creating a database is, of course, deciding what information it must contain. The information is then organized logically into fields, records, and files (see Exhibit 8.11 for definitions of these terms). Exhibit 8.12 on page 273 presents some basic rules for planning a database.

An important consideration in planning and creating a database is the ability to *search* the database. When the database is organized so that each key item is placed in its own field, the user can locate the item easily by commanding the database to perform a search of the fields. For example, to find a dentist in the expert-witness database shown in Exhibit 8.10, the user could have the program search for the term *dentistry*. This greatly speeds the process of finding needed information.

DATABASE MANAGEMENT SYSTEM
Software that makes it possible to store information in fields, records, and files for easy retrieval and manipulation by the operator.

EXHIBIT 8.9
Terms Commonly Used in Word Processing

• • • • •

CURSOR: The symbol on the computer screen indicating the position at which the user's changes or additions will appear. The cursor can appear as a blinking hyphen, as a shaded line, or in some other fashion. The cursor must be positioned at the place at which changes, additions, or deletions should be made. The user moves around a document by changing the position of the cursor.

EDITING: The word processor's ability to allow changes, additions, deletions, and formatting changes without the necessity of retyping or recreating the entire document.

FONT: The kind of typeface selected for a document. Most word processors offer a variety of sizes and types of font. For example, *ten-point italic will look like this, and eight-point italic will look like this.* Many word processors allow the user to go back and change the font selected for the document after the document has already been prepared. Word processors also allow multiple fonts to be used in the same document.

FOOTNOTES: Legal documents frequently require citations (see Chapter 9) for cases, articles, and other sources used as authority for the author's statement. These citations are indicated by placing a footnote number immediately following the statement, with the corresponding number placed at the bottom of the page together with the associated information as to the name of the source being cited and in what publication the source can be found. Word processors allow footnotes to be inserted, edited, and deleted as an editing feature. Word processors also place the footnote at the bottom of the correct text page or at the end of the document—depending on the user's preference.

FORMATTING: The same text can vary in appearance, depending on whether it is single or double spaced, the font used, the location of page numbers, the size of the margins, and whether the margins are ragged or justified (see below, under margins). The word processor gives the user many formatting options. A document can be reformatted (after it has been created) as well.

INSERT: A method of editing in which new text or information is added at the place in the document where the cursor is positioned.

MARGINS: The amount of space between the top, bottom, right edge, or left edge of a page and the text printed on the page. Word-processing software allows you to change the margins of a document after the document has been created. Word processors also give you the option of creating a justified, or smooth, right margin.

MOVE AND BLOCK (or cut and paste): A word-processing editing capability that allows you to move text from one section of a document to another.

SEARCH AND REPLACE: A word-processing editing capability that allows you to find each occurrence of a certain word or symbol in a document and replace the word or symbol with a new choice. If, for example, a client of your firm proposed to lease Suite 1420, which is mentioned twenty-three times in the lease agreement, but later decided to lease Suite 1755, you could substitute 1755 for 1420 automatically with the search-and-replace function. The search-and-replace function is often used in revising a document originally prepared for a previous client by changing the previous client's name with that of the present client for whom the document is being prepared.

SPELL CHECKER: A feature that allows you to check the spelling of each word in a document by comparing it against a dictionary that is part of the word processor. The spell checker highlights words that are either misspelled or not contained in the dictionary. (For example, a spell checker might highlight a client's name if it does not find the name in its dictionary.) Note that the spell checker cannot find user errors that involve incorrect word use rather than incorrect spelling. If, for example, you use *there* instead of *their*, the spell checker will not highlight the word *there*, because it is spelled correctly.

GRAMMAR CHECKER: A feature that allows you to check your document to see if it contains any grammatical errors, such as errors in subject-verb agreement (as in "The clients wants a will prepared"), and make suggestions for correcting any errors that are found. The grammar checker may also point out the sentences in which the passive voice has been used (see Chapter 18), how many words the documents contains, and the line length of the document.

WORD WRAP: On typewriters, a person must press the "return" key at the end of every line. With word-processing systems, the typist can continue from line to line without interruption because of word wrap. The lines automatically wrap, or move from one line to the beginning of the next line.

EXHIBIT 8.10
An Expert-witness Database (Excerpt)

Last Name	First Name	Address	City	State	Zip Code	Telephone Number	Specialty	Fee
Allen	Fred	34 Cedar Street	Miami	FL	33156	(503) 555-1908	Construction	$400
Dobbs	Susan	55 Spruce Drive	Portland	ME	04112	(207) 555-9320	Pediatrics	$350
Menkin	Gerald	320 Park Avenue	New York	NY	10166	(212) 555-9690	Psychiatry	$550
Olin	Barbara	Four Square Drive	Chicago	IL	60690	(312) 555-6641	Internal Medicine	$800
Payne	Daniel	214 Illinois Street	Austin	TX	78711	(512) 555-3823	Dentistry	$650

As mentioned, database systems allow users to create reports and print information in a variety of formats. The user can ask the database to sort, or organize, information in various ways. The sort function allows you to create a variety of end products using the same data.

Database Software for Tracking Litigation Documents.   The discovery and trial phases of litigation involve preparing, distributing, and receiving numerous documents. Database systems are useful in managing and tracking the flow of documents and evidence, as well as in locating particular information when needed. Specialized database software, such as *FoxPro* and *Paradox*, allows attorneys and paralegals to consolidate and manage documents involved in complex litigation, such as litigation involving multiple plaintiffs and defendants. For example, a case involving liability for cleaning up a site contaminated by toxic waste may involve hundreds of potentially responsible parties as litigants and thousands of exhibits and documents. Storing and retrieving such data through automated systems can allow the

EXHIBIT 8.11
Terms Commonly Used in Database Software

FIELD: An individual item of data is a field. If a database is to contain client records, for example, a field might be established for each client's last name. Another field would contain the client's telephone number. Information is added to a database field by field. Determining what fields will be included in the database is an important function when planning and creating a database.

RECORD: Fields exist in logical relation to one another. A group of fields treated as a unit is referred to as a record. For example, a particular name, address, city, state, zip code, telephone number, and case number would together be referred to as a record.

FILE: A collection of records intended to be used as a unit is referred to as a file. For example, the entire list of client names, addresses, and telephone numbers would be stored in the database as the client file. If the firm also had a collection of records for prospective clients, these would be kept in a separate file. Some database management systems refer to files by other names, such as *tables* or *databases*.

EXHIBIT 8.12
Rules for Planning a Database
● ● ● ● ●

RULES FOR PLANNING A DATABASE

Keep the following rules in mind when planning a database.

1. **Get Started:** Many times, a computerized database's design is based on a manual system. Start the process by enumerating what you like and dislike about the manual system. For example, suppose that you are designing a client database. If your law firm previously used a manual card system for keeping track of clients, this would be a good starting point for designing the computerized version.

2. **Plan Ahead:** Plan ahead for the future. If you think you might need an extra field later, add it now for safety. For example, in the client database, if you think you might eventually want a field for a work phone number, go ahead and include it now even though you may not use it right away. Try to anticipate your future needs.

3. **Keep Fields in Logical Order:** When you create the database or design an entry screen (the screen that you see to enter additional records), make sure the fields are put in a logical order that flows well. For example, in the client database, you would not want the Last Name field followed by the Zip Code field. Design the entry screen so that it is easy for additional records to be entered.

4. **Allow Plenty of Space for Each Field:** If you have to enter a maximum field length, leave plenty of space. If you have plenty of space available on your hard disk or other storage device, a good rule is to estimate how many characters you think you will need and then double it for safety. For instance, if you only allowed for five digits for a Zip Code field, you would have a problem, since some Zip Codes today are nine digits.

5. **Separate Data into Small Fields:** It is almost always better to separate data into small fields, rather than having multiple kinds of information in large fields. Instead of using one name field (Name), for example, use two smaller name fields (Last Name and First Name). Also, always separate city, state, and zip code instead of combining them. Sometime in the future you may want to sort or search using these specified fields.

6. **Make Field Names as Small as Possible:** When you are naming the fields for your database, make the names as small as possible. When you print the data, large field names get in the way, especially when the data they contain have only a few characters.

7. **Anticipate How the Database Will Be Used:** Before you make the design, think about how the information will be searched, how it will be sorted, and what format your reports and printouts will take. Most databases that fail do so because this rule was not followed.

8. **Always Test the Design:** No matter how good you think a design is, always test it before you put in hundreds of records, only to find out it is faulty.

SOURCE: Adapted from Brent D. Roper, *Computers in the Law: Concepts and Applications* (St. Paul: West Publishing Co., 1992), pp. 145-146.

legal team to access critical information in seconds—versus the minutes or hours that might otherwise be required to find the information.

Docket-control Software.   As mentioned in previous chapters, a docket is a schedule, or calendaring system, used by courts to list the cases that it will hear on certain dates. Law firms also use a docketing, or calendaring, system

Efficiently Organizing Deposition Transcripts

Eric Hawk is an experienced litigation paralegal. Part of his job is to summarize deposition transcripts. Thanks to the computer software that has been developed over the past decade, such as *Discovery ZX* and *Summation II*, his job is much easier than it used to be. Before these programs existed, he used to have to read and reread deposition transcripts several times to find and mark critical testimony. Then he had to photocopy each page containing this testimony, highlight what he needed on each page, and dictate a summary of the transcript.

With these programs, Eric's job is much easier because he can receive the deposition transcript on a diskette, which can be inserted into his computer. Using *Discovery ZX* or *Summation II*, Eric only needs to read the deposition transcript once. He can locate the critical testimony through word searches and use the software to organize the summary in any order he chooses—by page or by line, chronologically, or by category—and then print out his finished summary. Let's see how he does it.

REVIEWING AND ANNOTATING THE TRANSCRIPT

Eric begins reading a 265-page transcript of a physician's deposition. The physician will serve as an expert witness in a medical-malpractice case. He receives the transcript on both hard copy and diskette. Because Eric attended this deposition with the attorney, he is very familiar with the testimony, so he chooses to review it on the disk. When he is unfamiliar with the testimony, he uses the hard copy because it is easier to read. Eric needs to include the physician's credentials, which are included at the beginning of the transcript. He highlights this information on the computer. If Eric had not known the location of this information, he would have done a word search for the term "credentials," and it would have been located for him by the computer. He makes a note next to the credentials section.

He also needs to include the physician's exact testimony regarding the standard of care in the case. He decides to perform a search for the words "reasonable" (because standard of care is closely linked to reasonable care under the circumstances), "standard," and "care." He locates several pages of testimony on this topic. He makes more margin notes and highlights this portion of the testimony as well. Then he continues to look through the transcript. He comes across a reference to some medical records with which he is not familiar. He highlights the reference and makes another margin note to himself to request a copy of these records.

PREPARING THE DEPOSITION SUMMARY

When Eric finishes reviewing the transcript, he is ready to prepare his summary. He wants to summarize the important testimony by the pages and lines on which it appears. He chooses the page/line summary format. All of the lines that he highlighted begin to appear on the screen. Next, he uses the *sort* function to organize the information in the order in which he wants it to appear. When he prints it, it will appear with his notes first, followed by any excerpted testimony that he has highlighted.

to make sure that they comply with the multiple deadlines and requirements involved in the cases on which they are working. To assist them in this effort, they use specialized software, called *docket-control software.* Docket-control software helps track important dates and deadlines, such as court appearances and the dates by which certain documents must be filed with the court. A built-in reminder—or "tickler"—system gives advance notice of an approaching deadline so that the needed work can be completed at the appropriate time. Typical calendar display screens for docket-control software are shown in Exhibit 8.13.

Legal professionals also use docket-control software to help them monitor deadlines in other areas. For example, if you are assisting an attorney who is involved in a complex acquisition or financing transaction, docket-control software makes it easier for you to monitor the various deadlines set forth in the contract or loan documents. Docket-control software is also useful in scheduling routine firm meetings. Suppose that you have been asked to schedule a meeting of the partners and paralegals who are working on a particular case. The software will typically advise you of the dates and times when members of the team will be free to meet and enter your suggested meeting time and date on each team member's calendar.

A docket-control program typically includes a perpetual calendar. Unlike paper calendars, it will not become obsolete at the end of a year. In addition,

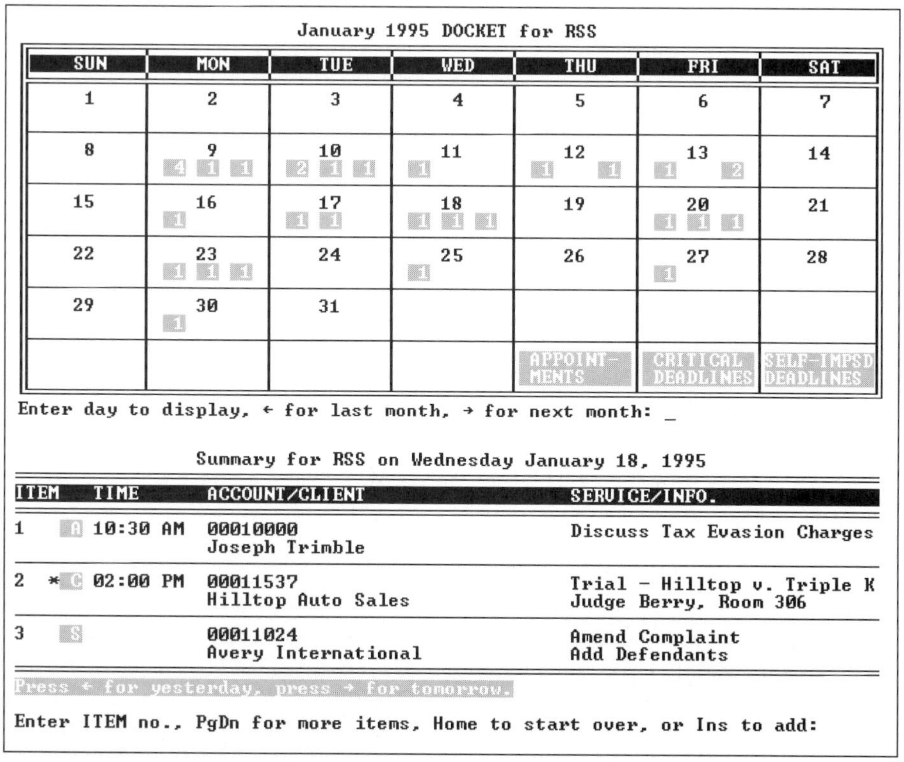

EXHIBIT 8.13
Typical Calendar Display Screens

FEATURED GUEST: JAN RICHMOND

Keeping Current on Computer Technology

Biographical Note

Jan Richmond is currently pursuing her master of arts degree in legal studies at Webster University in St. Louis, Missouri. As an undergraduate, she specialized in systems and data processing. She received her undergraduate degree from Washington University. Richmond has been an adjunct faculty member in the legal-assisting program at St. Louis Community College since 1989. Her teaching schedule includes courses in Computers and the Law, Advanced Computer Utilization, and Legal Administration, in addition to classes in WordPerfect 5.1 and 6.0, and Windows, Excel, Lotus, and numerous other software applications. Richmond has been a consultant in law-office training for nine years. For the past four summers, she has offered computer classes for the Missouri Bar Association.

Computer technology is developing at such a rapid pace that you can almost rest assured that what's here today will be changed or gone tomorrow. That means that paralegals must learn to tackle the tremendous problem of keeping their computer systems up to date.

There are several ways that you can learn about current developments in the area of computer technology and software. One way is to read computer magazines, such as those listed and described below. Other ways include attending computer workshops and seminars, participating in user groups, and attending software demonstrations or obtaining demonstration software diskettes, or "demos."

COMPUTER MAGAZINES

There are a number of monthly or bimonthly publications to which you or your firm can subscribe. By routinely scanning through some or all of these publications, you can keep abreast of what's happening in the computer world in regard to technology or software relating to law offices and legal research.

The Lawyer's PC (published by Shepard's/McGraw-Hill, P. O. Box 35300, Colorado Springs, CO 80935-3530) is a monthly publica-

tion for lawyers who use personal computers. Each month, a different topic is addressed. One issue, for example, featured an article entitled "Changing the Way We Work: Where Are Computers Taking Us?" The topic was right on target for attorneys and paralegals who wish to assess the impact of computer technology on their work habits. Each November, the entire issue is devoted to a list of software applications for the law office. The list is particularly helpful because it groups the software according to specific legal fields (such as bankruptcy) or specific functions in the law office (such as calendar and docket control). Information on vendors (sellers), prices, and software capabilities is also included. *The Perfect Lawyer*, a similar type of monthly publication also published by Shepard's/McGraw-Hill, deals with WordPerfect word-processing software and legal applications specific to that software.

Law Office Technology is a bimonthly publication that covers a wide variety of topics and deals with all aspects of law and computing. Topics covered range from the most commonly used WordPerfect macros to automating the job of estate management. To obtain

information on this magazine, write to *Law Office Technology*, 3520 Cadillac Avenue, Suite E, Costa Mesa, CA 92626.

Computer Counsel is similar to *The Lawyer's PC* in that it discusses different types of software applications specifically designed for the law office. For information, contact *Computer Counsel*, 641 West Lake Street, Suite 403, Chicago, IL 60661.

Legal Assistant Today (3520 Cadillac Avenue, Suite E, Costa Mesa, CA 92626) and *Legal Professional* (6060 North Central Expressway, Suite 670, Dallas, TX 75206-9947) are less oriented toward computer technology but do contain computing articles of interest and offer differing points of view on particular topics.

Last but not least are *PC Week* (P. O. Box 1769, Riverton, NJ 08077-7369) and other similar computing magazines. These publications differ from those just discussed because they deal with computer hardware and software that are not directly related to the legal area. They are very informative, though, in regard to new developments in computer technology, current prices, and new versions of software that can be used to

FEATURED GUEST, Continued

upgrade your current system. The material in these magazines is usually easy to read and understand.

WORKSHOPS AND SEMINARS

Every professional organization offers workshops and seminars dealing with computers. If you are a member of an association for paralegals, you will have an opportunity to meet and exchange ideas with others doing similar work. Check with your state, city, or county organization—or with the American Bar Association—to find out when seminars or workshops will be offered and on what specific topics. Computer workshops and seminars are not just for the technologically astute; even the novice can benefit from this type of meeting.

Seminars may be attended by attorneys, legal assistants, systems administrators, technical support personnel, and general support staff. If you attend a seminar dealing with computers, you can find out how computers are currently being used in other offices as well as gain ideas on how your office can maximize the computing capabilities available. You can learn how a particular software package can automate a task, and you benefit from candid information on the problems that attend almost every product. You can also exchange ideas and establish connections with others in your profession during these meetings.

USER GROUPS

User groups come in two varieties: specific and generic. Specific groups deal with one particular product, such as WordPerfect. I have attended meetings of WordPerfect users in several cities and have found that those attending these meetings have the same common goal: to get the most out of the product. You can gain invaluable information from both knowledgeable members attending these meetings and Word-Perfect personnel. You will pick up tips from both groups that can help make your tasks easier.

Generic groups include groups formed by IBM-computer users, Macintosh users, and others. Such groups often meet on a monthly basis and discuss different software application packages that operate on personal computers. Usually, vendors attend these meetings and give away software to the groups for their use. Although the group's interests may not be the same as yours, you will not know until you attend a meeting or two.

Bar associations are beginning to sponsor special-interest groups that exchange information. In addition, a number of state bar association meetings now address special topics at the end of each meeting. These topics may include vendor displays of new computer products and programs relating to law-office management, litigation, and so on.

SOFTWARE DEMONSTRATIONS

When a new software product piques your interest, you will not want to purchase it without having first had an opportunity to explore its capabilities and how it can be applied to your firm's needs. One way of evaluating new software is by contacting the vendor and requesting a demonstration by a local dealer. You might also request from the vendor the names of some other firms in your area using the product. Then make some telephone calls to those firms to see if they might be willing to discuss with you the advantages and disadvantages of the product. Usually, people are anxious to tell you about the problems they have experi-

> **"PARALEGALS MUST LEARN TO TACKLE THE TREMENDOUS PROBLEM OF KEEPING THEIR COMPUTER SYSTEMS UP TO DATE."**

enced—which would be most helpful for you.

You can also ask the vendor for a demonstration diskette with supporting literature. Demonstration diskettes are usually very simple to use and very informative. Others in your firm can also view them and help in the evaluating process. Literature is always helpful because it will give you the hardware requirements of the program, such as how much space will be needed on the hard drive and how much internal memory is required for the program to run smoothly. The down side of demonstration diskettes is that you may receive an abbreviated version of the software and thus may not be able to see its full capabilities.

CONCLUSION

Computer technology is an everchanging field. New kinds of hardware and software seem to appear every day. Keeping current in regard to computer technology can be frustrating, but it is also exciting. Generally, the best way to keep current is by reading computer literature and by communicating with others who share your needs and concerns.

a "recurring entry"—an event that will take place periodically at set intervals—need only be entered once. Also, a docket-control program can adjust related dates to correspond to a change in one of the dates. For example, court procedures may require that certain actions be taken at certain predetermined intervals. If a scheduled date for one of the actions is changed, the docket-control program can automatically adjust subsequent dates to correspond to the required time interval.

Docket programs can also be used to generate reports and personal schedules. A paralegal may want to know what events and deadlines have been scheduled over the next thirty days. A managing partner may want to know all activities or appearances scheduled in a client's behalf. Docket-control software allows the rapid and painless acquisition and analysis of such scheduling information.

Spreadsheet Programs and Accounting Software

SPREADSHEET PROGRAM
A computer program that completes calculations, does numerical tracking, and allows the operator to manipulate numeric data for statistical and reporting purposes (such as budget reporting).

Law offices use **spreadsheet programs** to expedite and automate functions requiring numerical tracking, calculation, and manipulation. If, for example, a firm is preparing a budget report on its income and expenses, all expenses and income can be entered on a spreadsheet, and calculations will be performed automatically. If one attorney's salary was omitted or incorrectly entered the first time, the correct data can be entered, and the spreadsheet will automatically adjust related computations. Spreadsheet entries for a law firm's budget are shown in Exhibit 8.14.

Spreadsheets have many uses. For example, assume that you are a litigation paralegal. Your firm has been retained by a large insurance company, which is a defendant in a malpractice suit against a brain surgeon. The plaintiff is one of the surgeon's patients, who is now disabled, allegedly because of the surgeon's negligence. The plaintiff's attorney is trying to prove that the plaintiff will suffer a loss of earnings over his lifetime of $4 million. You are preparing a series of projections—based on different hypothetical recovery periods and different future wage rates—to show that even if the physician was negligent, the loss of earnings would be no more than $500,000. Instead of having to recalculate, retype, and then proofread each projection as you change one of the variables (recovery period or wage rate), you will use a spreadsheet program. When one number changes, appropriate calculations are made automatically by the program, based on formulas that you have entered.

A spreadsheet is organized in a grid of vertical *columns* and horizontal *rows*, which create individual cells. (You can see these elements in Exhibit 8.14.) Spreadsheet software, like word-processing software, has a cursor that points to your present location within the spreadsheet. The cursor needs to be at the cell in which you wish to make an entry (or a change). You can enter either data (words or numbers) or formulas in the cells.

In addition to general-purpose software such as *Lotus 1-2-3, Excel,* and *Quattro Pro,* law firms use specialized spreadsheet programs. For example, one specialized program makes calculations for loan amortizations. The user can enter the loan amount, the interest rate, and the number of payments to be made, and the spreadsheet will calculate the monthly payment. Additional specialized programs are discussed below.

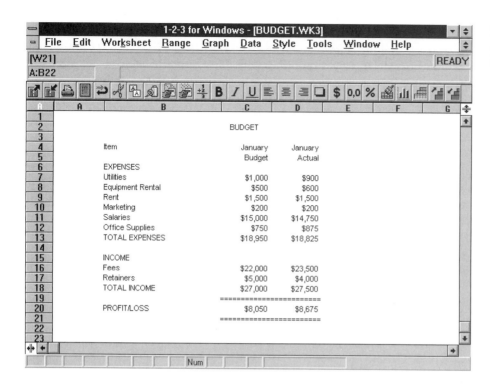

EXHIBIT 8.14

A Law Firm's Budget

Client Trust Accounts. Spreadsheet programs also exist to handle client trust accounts. As discussed in Chapter 4, law firms typically have a trust account in which they place funds being held for clients—advance funds for costs that the firm may incur, funds received through the settlement of a legal claim, and so on. Some firms have more than one trust account, but often, the trust account contains funds held for numerous clients. The firm is ethically and legally obligated to keep a strict record of the amount of funds deposited into and disbursed from the trust account on behalf of each client, as well as the current balance of funds being held for each client. Using a spreadsheet program, the paralegal or attorney can enter an amount deposited or disbursed on behalf of a particular client, and the program will make the appropriate calculations and create a new balance.

Tax-return Software. Federal, state, and local taxation requires accurate record keeping and complicated analyses of income, expenses, and other data to determine tax liabilities. Specialized *tax-return software* allows tax attorneys to view more easily client financial information, analyze tax liabilities, and prepare corresponding tax returns. Many programs generate not only the information to be inserted in the form but also the form itself. Computerized preparation of tax returns offers a major advantage when changes or corrections are required after the form has already been prepared. Tax software often automatically recalculates tax liabilities and then produces a revised and corrected form.

Time-and-billing Software. One way that law offices have adapted the concept of spreadsheet software to their particular needs is through *time-and-billing software,* which integrates features of database programs with the accounting capabilities of spreadsheet software. Some programs in widespread use include *Verdict, TABS II, Juris, Timeslips, Profit$ource,* and *AccountMate.* The programs differ not only in their operating features but also in the amount and complexity of information that they support. Thus, some of the programs are better suited for small or medium-sized firms, while others are most effectively used in large national or international firms.

Tracking Time and Expenses. As discussed in Chapter 4, the cost of the law firm's services is often measured by the amount of time spent by attorneys, paralegals, and legal secretaries on the client's legal matter. The procedure used to track and bill the number of hours that firm professionals devote to each client's business is thus critical. In addition to timekeeping, the firm needs to track its expenses on behalf of the client so that it can be reimbursed by the client for these expenses. Furthermore, it is not sufficient for the firm to know merely that one attorney or one paralegal spent one hour on a client's business; the firm will typically tell the client the particular nature of the work that was done.

For example, a statement produced for client Thomas Jones, M.D., will not simply indicate that paralegal Elena Lopez spent 1.5 hours on "work relating to the Jones case" but will specifically indicate what work was performed during the 1.5 hours. The statement may read "Interview: Susan Mathews (nurse): 1.5 hours." Even if the more specific information is not presented on the billing statement, the firm will want easy access to more detailed information so that it can respond to any questions that the client may have about the bill.

The time-and-billing program does not relieve the firm's employees from the important responsibility of keeping track of their time. Often, this first tracking stage is performed manually, when the timekeeper fills out a paper time slip (discussed and illustrated in Chapter 4). The time slip is then entered into the computer by someone on the firm's staff who understands the importance of accuracy at this key step. The firm also enters into the computer information about the billing arrangement with the client. The computer program can then merge the billable hours with the billing rate and calculate the sum to be billed to the client.

Reviewing and Finalizing the Client's Bill. Once the bill has been calculated, the attorney in charge of the client's work will review a "prebilling report"—a draft version of the bill. The attorney reviews the bill for accuracy and may also determine that the amount calculated from the time slips should be modified.

Once the billing statement is adjusted to reflect any changes made by the responsible attorney, the program generates a final bill to be mailed to the client. The program should also generate management reports, which indicate the total amount of time billed by each attorney or paralegal for the month and possibly for the year to date. The report also indicates the amount billed, client by client, for the firm as a whole. Many programs allow the firm to track payments as they are made by the clients; management reports can then also indicate the status of the firm's collections for the amounts billed.

Integrated, Special-use Programs

Most software programs can be described as word-processing software, database programs, or spreadsheet programs. Many law-office tasks require a combination of these processing tools, however. Law offices frequently take advantage of specially integrated programs—software that has been developed to assist in the practice of a particular area of the law.

For example, an area of practice in which the integration of word-processing, database, and financial spreadsheet capabilities is useful is bankruptcy law. A paralegal assisting a bankruptcy attorney may be asked to handle pleadings and court documents, advise creditors of the status of the proceedings, and produce financial reports. An integrated program keyed to the requirements of federal bankruptcy practice can simplify, expedite, and even improve the quality of legal work in this area.

COMPUTER-ASSISTED LEGAL RESEARCH (CALR)

One of the great benefits of computer technology for legal practitioners is *computer-assisted legal research (CALR)*. As you will read in Chapter 9, thorough and up-to-date legal research requires access to voluminous source materials, including cases decided by state and federal courts and state and federal statutory law. Additionally, the legal researcher often needs to refer to publications, such as legal encyclopedias, law books, and articles in legal periodicals, that provide background information on a particular legal issue.

CALR has made it possible to access databases containing many of the most important legal resources. By accessing databases provided through computerized legal-research services, such as WESTLAW and LEXIS, legal professionals can obtain within seconds or minutes, without leaving their offices, case law or statutory law governing a particular issue. Although not all printed legal sources are contained on these databases, many of them are. See, for example, Exhibit 8.15 on page 284, which shows the directory of research sources available through WESTLAW.

Advantages of CALR

An obvious advantage of CALR is that you can locate and print out court cases, statutory provisions, and other legal documents within a matter of minutes without leaving your work station. Of course, if the firm for which you work has an extensive law library and the case or statute you need to find is contained in that library, it would make sense to refer to the printed source. But many small law offices have neither the money nor space available to acquire a very extensive law library. For attorneys and paralegals working in such environments, it may be cost-effective to access needed information using CALR instead of traveling to the nearest law library to obtain it—especially if the nearest law library is over a hundred miles away.

As you will read in Chapter 9, a key advantage of CALR is that new case decisions and changes in statutory law are entered almost immediately into the database. In other words, legal sources on databases accessed through WESTLAW or LEXIS are more current than printed sources.

DEVELOPING PARALEGAL SKILLS

Computerized Legal Research

 Kathleen Connors has been assigned the task of researching an issue on WESTLAW. John Ralstrom, one of the firm's clients, has been sued by a friend who attended Ralstrom's annual Christmas party. The friend, David Wheeler, was drunk when he left the party and got into a car accident in which he severely injured his left leg. As a result of the accident, Wheeler lost 70 percent of his use of the leg. Because he is a high school gym teacher, Wheeler's leg injury has greatly impaired his ability to work. Wheeler wants to obtain compensatory damages, including lost wages, from Ralstrom in the lawsuit.

THE PRELIMINARIES

Kathleen will be researching state statutes and case law to determine whether Ralstrom can be held liable for Wheeler's injury. She begins by familiarizing herself with the issue. She consults a legal encyclopedia to find background information on the topic, which will help her define the issue. After some preliminary research, Kathleen decides what the central issue is and writes it down: What is the liability of a social host with respect to serving intoxicating beverages?

Now Kathleen needs to choose the specific WESTLAW database that she will be using. She knows that she wants Illinois cases, because the lawsuit is being brought in an Illinois state court, so she chooses the Illinois Courts database, *IL-CS.* She will also be researching in the Illinois Statutes Annotated database, *IL-ST.* She enters the names of these databases on the form.

DRAFTING THE QUERY

The next step is to draft a query, which creates an index of terms for the computer to search. Kathleen selects the important terms relating to her issue: *social, host, liability,* and *alcohol.* Because the computer will only retrieve cases containing the terms that the user gives it, she chooses some

---

If your supervising attorney is preparing for trial, for example, the attorney will want to base his or her legal argument on current legal authorities. A precedential case that may have been "good law" three months ago may be "bad law" today. The case may have been overturned by a higher court since then, and the only way you would know this would be through CALR (because the case would not yet be included in printed sources).

● **Making sure that your research results reflect current law is a crucial step in legal research.**

Charges for Legal-research Services

To use a computerized legal-research service, such as WESTLAW or LEXIS, a law firm or other user signs a contract with the provider of the service. Charges for the service are typically based on either on-line time (WESTLAW) or the number of database searches performed (LEXIS). Although the com-

alternative terms as well. She chooses *guest* as an alternative to *host* because these types of cases often discuss liability to social guests. She chooses *responsibility, culpability*, and *negligence* as alternatives to *liability*. For *alcohol*, she uses *intoxicating, inebriating, liquor*, and *drunk*.

Then she has to decide if she needs to use the root expander (!) or the universal character (*) in her query. If she places the root expander at the end of the root, the program will give her all forms of a term. For example, *liab!* will give her *liable, liability*, and so on. The universal character is a variable character that may be placed in the middle or at the end of a term to retrieve various forms of the term. For example, *dr*nk* retrieves *drank* and *drunk*. Kathleen uses both the root expander and the universal character for the term *drunk: dr*nk!* She uses the root expander for all of the terms describing liability and alcohol.

The last step is to decide how to connect the terms. She connects *social* and *host!* with *A/S*, which means that they should appear within the same sentence. All of the the terms are connected with *A/P* to indicate that they should appear within the same paragraph.

ACCESSING WESTLAW

Now that her query is drafted, Kathleen accesses WESTLAW on her computer and signs on, using her password. When she sees the *Welcome to WESTLAW* screen, she enters the client file number. At the *WESTLAW Directory* screen, she types *IL-CS* for the Illinois Courts database. The next screen that she sees is the *Enter Query* screen. The screen says that she may enter a query in Natural Language—a search method on WESTLAW that lets you type your search request in plain English. For this research session, however, Kathleen decides to use the traditional terms-and-connectors search method, as she had planned, because she is familiar with this traditional method of searching. For someone less familiar with the terms-and-connectors method, using natural language would be an attractive alternative.

---

puter terminal gains access to the service through a modem over a telephone line, the cost of the long-distance connection is built into the price of using the service. In other words, the entity paying for the service generally does not pay long-distance charges as well.

Using Legal-research Services

There are several ways to access cases, statutes, and other sources provided by legal-research services, such as WESTLAW and LEXIS. When you know the citation[1] to a case or statute, it may be entered using one of several commands. The service will then display the case or statute requested. When the researcher wants to retrieve a group of cases or statutes relating to a certain

---

1. As will be explained in Chapter 9, a citation indicates the abbreviated name and volume number of the publication in which a case, statute, or regulation can be found, as well as the page number within that volume on which the case, statute, or regulation begins.

ETHICAL CONCERN

Cutting the Cost of Legal Research

As a paralegal, you have an ethical duty to the client to minimize costs, including the cost of computerized research—which, after all, is paid for by the client. One way you can reduce research costs is to plan your inquiries carefully before accessing a service such as LEXIS or WESTLAW. This way, you do not have to spend on-line time making such decisions.

EXHIBIT 8.15
**Directory of Research Sources
Available through WESTLAW**

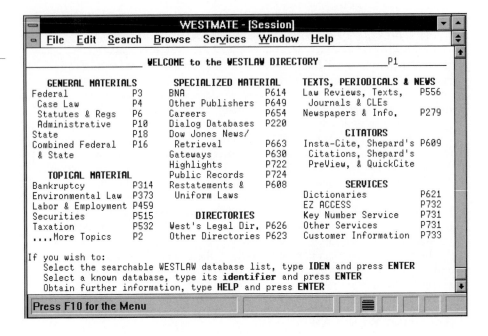

issue, a word search can be performed. This requires the researcher to input a group of the most important terms from the legal issue, called a *query*.

Drafting Queries. To best utilize computerized legal-research services, you should make sure that you draft your queries effectively. For example, suppose that one of your firm's clients is suing a restaurant for serving her "tainted oysters." Apparently, the oysters were tainted by bacteria that caused the client to become critically ill after eating them and to sustain permanent nerve damage. You have been asked to research case law to find similar cases. You want to make sure that your query is not too broad (as it would be if you entered just the term *restaurant*). Your search will be futile because so many thousands of documents contain that term.

Similarly, if your query is to narrow (as it would be if you entered the terms *restaurant* and *tainted oysters*), you might not retrieve any documents. Over time, you will learn how to phrase queries in such a way that the documents you retrieve from the computerized database are relevant to your research goal. For further information on how to draft a query using the traditional "terms-and-connectors" approach, see this chapter's *Developing Paralegal Skills* features entitled "Computerized Legal Research." Exhibit 8.16 shows how the query on the legal issue discussed in that feature would appear on the WESTLAW query screen.

Both WESTLAW and LEXIS have made it easier for legal professionals to search their databases by allowing for "natural-language" (WESTLAW) or "associative-language" (LEXIS) searching. WESTLAW's system is called WIN (Westlaw is Natural), while LEXIS's system is called FREESTYLE. Using the WIN or FREESTYLE method of searching, you can draft a query using ordinary language. For example, in researching the tainted-oyster case, you might draft a natural-language query on WESTLAW as follows: "What is the liability of a restaurant owner to a customer who suffers injury from food

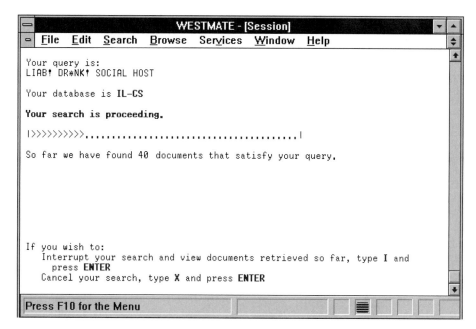

EXHIBIT 8.16
A WESTLAW Query Screen

prepared and served by the restaurant?" WESTLAW will then retrieve a maximum of twenty cases that most closely match your description.

West Publishing Company has developed a voice-recognition system, called *LawTalk*, that can be integrated into the WIN system. If you have LawTalk available for CALR, you can simply give voice commands to the computer, rather than keying in your queries. Note that LawTalk is an add-on product—that is, it does not come with WESTLAW and WIN. Special software, as well as a significant amount of computer power, is required.

Passwords and File Names.   Because users are billed for using the database, the user needs a password to access the service. In some firms, each paralegal using legal-research services will be assigned a separate access code; in other firms, each department, practice group, or attorney is assigned a code.

Charges for CALR constitute an expense that ultimately will be paid for by the client. Therefore, a separate research file should be opened for each client. WESTLAW assists this function by asking the user to enter the file name each time the system is accessed. The paralegal should remember to enter a separate file name for each client if several research projects are undertaken for different clients during the same WESTLAW session. This can be done by typing CLIENT when you wish to open a new file.

A WORD OF CAUTION

We have seen how the computer in the law-office setting has revolutionized the way that legal work is done. By eliminating duplicative, routine tasks, computers have allowed law offices to increase their productivity and often the quality of their work. But computers have also placed a premium on the careful planning of projects and on the painstaking review of entries that will

TODAY'S PROFESSIONAL PARALEGAL

Dedicated Imaging Systems

Ashley Wagner is a legal assistant in an environmental-law practice. Her firm's client is responding to an Environmental Protection Agency (EPA) information request. The client, a manufacturing company, is being investigated by the EPA for potential violations of its requirements relating to air permits. These permits are required for the company to emit into the air the wastes that result from its production process. Ashley is responsible for organizing the ten thousand documents needed to respond to the information request.

Ashley is used to managing documents because environmental cases usually involve a tremendous number of them. She uses a computer to summarize each document and to index and code all of the documents so that they can be located. In this case, she needs to be able to access and retrieve, quickly and easily, any document when requested.

FINDING A SOLUTION TO STORAGE AND RETRIEVAL PROBLEMS

Ashley needs to find a reliable way to access and retrieve all of the documents. She begins by calling a computer consulting firm, CompuLaw, Inc., whose services she and others in her law firm often use. She speaks with Sandra Bossin, a consultant. Ashley describes the situation to Sandra and asks Sandra if she has anything that could help the storage and retrieval problems presented by this case. Sandra tells Ashley that imaging technology might provide a solution for Ashley's problem and offers to demonstrate the technology for Ashley. They agree to meet at Ashley's office the following day.

DEDICATED IMAGING SYSTEMS

The next day, Sandra arrives with some equipment that resembles a personal computer. She calls it a dedicated imaging system and explains that it contains an optical scanner that allows it to scan a document and copy it, much as a photocopy machine does. Images of all of the documents that are copied are then stored on either disks or tapes. The documents on the disks or tapes can be indexed so that the user can view them on a PC. The firm would still have to assign an employee to scan all of the documents.

Ashley is impressed. The imaging systems could save much time and office space. She excuses herself and walks across the hall to the office of her supervising attorney, Nate Wenger. She had arranged previously for Nate to attend the demonstration if she thought that Sandra had a solution to their problem. He had agreed and said that he would be in his office at the time of Ashley's meeting with Sandra.

Ashley returns to her office with Nate. She asks Sandra to demonstrate how the optical scanner works. Ashley gives Sandra a form from a forms file, and Sandra runs the scanner over it. Sandra then shows Nate the image that was created and stored on the disk. She explains all of the system's benefits to Nate.

AN ALTERNATIVE—CONTRACTING FOR IMAGING SERVICES

Sandra also tells Nate and Ashley that there are companies that provide imaging services. "You submit your documents, and they return either the disks or tapes to you. They create the indexes and do all of the scanning so that you don't have to," explains Sandra. Nate says that he thinks optical scanning is a great idea and asks Sandra if she has some literature on the system that she had just demonstrated, as well as the names of the companies that provide imaging services and the approximate costs.

After Sandra leaves the office, Ashley meets with Nate. They discuss how useful this system would be and how much time it would save. Nate tells Ashley that he thinks it might be better to start with an outside service, because the firm does not have a full-time employee available to scan the documents. He makes it clear that her job cannot include that task because it is too time consuming. Ashley agrees with the idea of starting with a scanning service. Nate then asks Ashley to "shop around" and find out what rates the different companies charge for the service. "Once I have the cost data," explains Nate, "I can discuss the issue with the other partners at the next partnership meeting."

be automatically replicated at many stages of a project. Detailed planning and review require a significant amount of time. While outside consultants may be retained to minimize the time spent on planning, consultants are expensive. Also, a carefully devised system for backing up computer data on external storage devices is essential. If a system fails and data are not backed up, crucial information may be lost. If back-up copies are made but are difficult to locate, much valuable time may be required to find the back-up copies. In sum, computers have simplified law-office work, but they have not replaced the human management skills that are required to use the technology as productively as possible.

KEY TERMS AND CONCEPTS

application software 263	keyboard 258	password 257
boilerplate 269	local area network (LAN) 265	personal computer (PC) 258
central processing unit (CPU) 258	mainframe computer 257	security code 257
	minicomputer 257	software 256
database management system 270	modem 259	spreadsheet program 278
	monitor 258	user interface 264
E-mail 265	mouse 259	wide area network (WAN) 265
hard drive 258	operating-system software 263	word-processing software 267
hardware 256		

CHAPTER SUMMARY

1. Computers have made it possible for paralegals to spend less time on mechanical tasks (such as retyping entire documents to incorporate revisions) and more time exercising their professional skills and abilities.

2. Hardware consists of the physical components of a computer system. Computers range in size and capacity from large mainframe computers to minicomputers to personal, or desktop, computers. Because of the expense involved in purchasing and maintaining mainframes, they are normally used only by very large organizations and firms. Minicomputers are less powerful than mainframes and are typically used by middle-sized firms—law firms with fifty or so lawyers, for example. Most law firms today use personal computers, often linked to other computers in the same office.

3. Components of a computer system include the central processing unit (CPU), which controls the functions of the computer components; the monitor, which displays the current activities of the computer; the keyboard, which sends input to the computer's CPU, which in turn displays the information on the monitor; and the mouse, which directs the cursor on

the monitor. In addition to the keyboard, there are other input devices, including optical scanners, which "scan" and copy the contents of documents in a form readable by computers. Output devices, such as printers, transfer data from the computer to permanent, readable forms (on hard copy, for example). Modems, when used with specialized communications software, allow the user to transfer data from one computer to another.

4. Storage devices include internal hard disk drives, external hard disk drives, removable diskettes, optical disks, CD-ROMs, and magnetic-tape systems (which can be used in two formats, cartridges and reels).

5. Operating-system software controls the communication between the computer system and the application software used by the computer. IBM and IBM-compatible computers have typically used the disk operating system (DOS). Traditionally, computer operating systems have been manufactured to operate with either IBM and IBM-compatible computers or the Apple Macintosh family of computers. Translation programs allow data created on one operating system to be translated into a format compatible with a different operating system. Each operating system has a special user interface, which controls what the computer user sees on the screen and how the user gives commands to the computer.

6. Office network systems link personal computers together so that data and software can be shared. These systems include local area networks (LANs), which link computers in an office or building, and wide area networks (WANs), which link multiple computers over a wide geographical area. Networking can also be done via electronic-mail (E-mail) systems, by which users can send messages from one computer to another.

7. Application software consists of computer programs that instruct the computer on how to perform specific tasks. Three basic types of application software are word-processing software, database management systems, and spreadsheet software.

8. Word-processing software allows users to create documents and save, edit, and otherwise change the content and appearance of those documents. Form documents can be customized using word-processing software.

9. Database management systems offer an alternative to manual indexing or filing systems. Database systems allow users to organize data in specific ways, create reports, and print out information in a variety of formats. Database software also allows legal professionals to track litigation documents, and docket-control software can help track important deadlines, such as court appearances and the dates by which cer-

tain documents must be filed with the court.

10. Spreadsheet programs automate functions requiring numerical tracking, calculation, and manipulation. Spreadsheets are computerized grids of vertical columns and horizontal rows. The user can enter data or formulas to instruct the computer to perform certain calculations, such as totaling a column of figures. Software utilizing spreadsheets includes time-and-billing software and tax-return software.

11. Integrated, special-use programs combine various features of word-processing, database, and spreadsheet programs. Integrated, special-use programs are generally developed for a particular legal area, such as bankruptcy.

12. Computer-assisted legal research (CALR) has revolutionized the way in which many paralegals and attorneys conduct legal research. Widely used in the legal arena are computerized legal-research services, such as WESTLAW and LEXIS. These services provide access to databases that contain comprehensive law libraries. For a fee, which is normally based on either on-line time or the number of searches performed, legal professionals can access relevant case law, statutory law, or other legal authorities on particular legal issues within minutes without leaving their offices. A key advantage of CALR is that legal professionals can obtain the most current law, because new court decisions, statutory law, and other legal documents are available through computerized legal-research services shortly after the decisions or changes in the law have been made.

QUESTIONS FOR REVIEW

1. What kinds of work do legal assistants perform on computers?

2. List the various types of computers that are in use. What are their components?

3. What are some of the external storage devices currently in use? Why are saving and backing up computer work essential to computer proficiency?

4. What is the difference between operating-system software and application software? What is DOS? On what types of computers has it traditionally been used?

5. What are the two primary types of networks? What is electronic mail? How are networks used to share data and software or transmit communications via the computer?

6. How is word-processing software used? List and define five terms that are commonly used in word processing.

7. What is a database? What is the difference between a field and a record? How can the use of database software enhance the efficiency of legal work?

8. What are spreadsheet programs? How are they used by legal professionals?

9. What are integrated, special-use programs? Give an example of one.

10. What are some of the benefits for legal professionals of computer-assisted legal research? Who pays for the cost of using computerized legal-research services?

ETHICAL QUESTIONS

1. Tom Malcomb works as a paralegal in a large law firm. The firm recently hired two attorneys and a paralegal from another firm. Before they were hired, the attorneys and the paralegal had worked as a team on the opposite side of a major case Tom's firm is handling, *Black v. Walker Manufacturing Co.* As a result, Tom's firm faced a potential conflict of interest. Under the code of ethics adopted in Tom's state, the firm could continue to represent its client in the case but only if it erected an "ethical wall" to prevent the new team from participating in the case in any way. As part of the ethical wall, Tom's firm created a special password. This password was required to access any computerized files relating to this case.

Tom has just printed out a research memo concerning an important issue in the case. Because the copier on his floor is not working, he takes the elevator up to the next floor to the copier there. Tom accidentally drops the card that contains the *Black v. Walker Manufacturing Co.* password. Tom makes his copy and returns to his office. Susan Hines, the paralegal on the newly hired team, finds the card on the floor next to the copier that Tom used. What ethical obligation does Susan have?

2. Amelia and Richard are paralegals in the same law firm, and they have both been working on the same brief, the written argument that will be submitted to the appellate court in support of a client's position. Each of them has researched and written sections on specific issues. Amelia, however, has a great deal of expertise on one of Richard's issues. Amelia does not agree with the way he has prepared the brief on that issue, and she is unable to persuade him to follow her suggestions on how it should be written. While Richard is at lunch, Amelia accesses his portion of the brief on the firm's computer network and changes it. Richard does not notice the changes until after the brief is reviewed by the supervising attorney and filed with the court. He can look at the directory and tell that Amelia accessed the brief and changed it. What should Richard do?

3. Judy Harris works as a paralegal for a small law firm. She has worked for the last three hours on a legal memorandum summarizing her research results on a case being litigated by her supervising attorney. Normally, whenever Judy creates or modifies documents on the personal computer she uses, she periodically enters the *Save* command so that her work will be saved on the computer's hard disk. Today, however, she has been so engrossed in her task that she has forgotten to take this precaution. Suddenly, her computer screen "freezes," and she realizes that there is no way that she can save her memo. She will have to shut down and restart her system, and she will have to recreate everything she had written in the last three hours. She spends another three hours redoing the previous work and spends an additional two hours to complete the memo—all the time saving her work at frequent intervals. When the memo is finished, she enters on a time slip the name of the client and the nature of the work performed on the client's behalf. She looks at the space where she needs to enter the number of hours spent on the task and is faced with a dilemma. Should she bill the client for five hours (the time it would have taken to complete the job had the computer failure not occurred) or eight hours (the actual time she had to spend creating the memorandum)? What would you do if you were in Judy's position?

PRACTICE QUESTIONS AND ASSIGNMENTS

1. What types of software would do the following?

a. Prevent you from missing deadlines.

b. Manage documents in complex litigation.

c. Perform legal research.

    d. Find quickly and summarize in a report all scheduled appearances for a particular client.

    e. Store and organize information on expert witnesses.

2. What type of computer would you select for the following offices?

    a. A small law firm in which the legal assistant also serves as the legal secretary.

    b. A medium-sized law firm in which there is a large number of legal assistants who frequently draft documents.

    c. A large law firm with 350 attorneys, 90 legal assistants, and 190 secretaries, all of whom need or want computers on their desks for drafting documents, creating tables and graphs, performing financial projections and analyses, and the like.

    d. A megafirm of 900 attorneys.

3. Your supervising attorney is the chairperson of the state bar association's probate and estate section, which has 275 members. The attorney wants you to create a database for the section members. The database should include the members' names and bar (license) numbers (for those members who are attorneys), as well as their law firms' names, addresses, and telephone numbers. The database should also include the names of the committees—such as the estate-planning committee, trust committee, or tax committee—on which the the members serve. What fields and records would you create in generating your database?

Introduction

For many paralegals, legal research is a fascinating part of their jobs. They find it intrinsically interesting to read the actual words of a court's opinion on a legal question or the text of a statute. They also acquire a firsthand knowledge of the law and how the law applies to actual people and events. Research is also a crucial part of the paralegal's job, and the ability to conduct research thoroughly yet efficiently enhances a paralegal's value to the legal team. As a paralegal, you may be asked to perform a variety of research tasks. Some research tasks will be simple. You may be asked to locate and copy a court case, for example. Other research tasks may take days or even weeks to complete.

As discussed in the preceding chapter, computers have greatly simplified the task of legal research. Many paralegals now conduct research without even entering a law library. Computerized legal services such as WESTLAW and LEXIS allow legal professionals to find the text of cases, statutes, and other legal documents without leaving their desks. An increasing number of law firms today are also purchasing reference materials on CD-ROMs. To a great extent, how you do your research—that is, whether you conduct research via a computer or in a law library—will depend on your employer and the computer facilities available to you. In some workplaces, paralegals are expected to conduct much of their research using computerized legal services. In other workplaces, paralegals may be asked to do the bulk of their legal research using printed legal sources in law libraries.

Regardless of whether legal research is conducted via computer or in a law library, it is essential to know what sources to consult for different types of information. In this chapter, you will learn what these sources are, how to analyze these sources, and how to make sure that the law you find is up to date and still "good law." Legal research also involves legal writing. When you complete a research assignment, for example, you will need to summarize your results in writing. As a paralegal, you will also be expected to draft legal correspondence and documents. Because legal writing is also an important part of paralegal work, we conclude the chapter with a discussion of that subject.

Primary and Secondary Sources

Primary Source
In legal research, a document that establishes the law on a particular issue, such as a case decision, legislative act, administrative rule, or presidential order.

Secondary Source
In legal research, any publication that indexes, summarizes, or interprets the law, such as a legal encyclopedia, a treatise, or an article in a law review.

Generally, research sources fall into two broad categories—primary sources and secondary sources. Printed decisions of the various courts in the United States, statutes enacted by legislative bodies, rules and regulations created by administrative agencies, presidential orders, and generally any documents that *establish* the law are **primary sources** of law. **Secondary sources** of law consist of books and articles that summarize, systematize, compile, or otherwise interpret the law. Legal encyclopedias, which summarize the law, are secondary sources of law.

Normally, researchers in any field or profession begin their research with secondary sources. Secondary sources are often referred to as *finding tools*, because they help the researcher to find primary sources on the topics they are researching and to learn how those sources have been interpreted by others. When you are asked to undertake a research assignment, you should do likewise. You should first refer to secondary sources to learn about the issue and find relevant primary sources concerning it. Then, you can go to the primary sources themselves (such as statutes or court cases) to research the established law on the issue.

In the following sections, you will read about the primary and secondary sources that are most frequently used in researching case law, statutory law and legislative history, administrative law, and constitutional law.

THE RESEARCH PROCESS

Any research project normally involves the following five steps:

- Defining the issue(s) to be researched.
- Determining the goal(s) of the research project.
- Consulting relevant secondary sources.
- Researching relevant primary sources.
- Summarizing research results.

To illustrate how you would follow these steps when researching case law, we present a hypothetical case. The case involves one of your firm's clients, Trent Hoffman, who is suing Better Homes Store for negligence. During the initial client interview, Hoffman explained to you and your supervising attorney that he had gone to the store to purchase a large mirror. As he was leaving the store through the store's side entrance, carrying the bulky mirror, he ran into a large pole just outside the door. He did not see the pole because the mirror blocked his view. Upon hitting the pole, the mirror broke, and a piece of glass entered Hoffman's left eye, causing permanent loss of eyesight in that eye. Hoffman claims that the store was negligent in placing a pole so close to the exit and is suing the store for $3 million in damages.

After undertaking a preliminary investigation of the matter and obtaining evidence supporting Hoffman's account of the facts, your supervising attorney asks you to do some research. Your job now is to research case law to find other cases with similar fact patterns and see how the courts decided the issue in those cases. Before you can begin your actual research into the matter, you need to know what issue you are researching and what your research goals are. In clarifying the legal issue to be researched, you may need to consult some secondary sources of law. In this section, you will read about these first three steps in the research project.

Defining the Issue

You can probably tell—simply by reviewing the facts of Hoffman's case and Hoffman's allegation that Better Homes Store was negligent—that the issue in Hoffman's case has to do with the tort theory of *negligence.* Recall from Chapter 3 that negligence occurs when someone fails to fulfill a legal duty or to observe a reasonable standard of care under the circumstances. You will thus want to find out the nature of the duty owed by retail business owners to their customers. Although at this point your issue is very broadly defined,

DEVELOPING PARALEGAL SKILLS

Defining the Issues to Be Researched

 Bernie Berriman was observed by federal government agents in his parked car talking on his car phone. Later, other cars were seen driving up to Bernie's car and stopping. The drivers received brown bags in exchange for money. Bernie was questioned, and his car was searched. Cocaine was found in the car. He was arrested for transporting and distributing a controlled substance, and his car and phone were taken by the police. Natalie Martin, a legal assistant with the U.S. attorney's office, has been assigned the task of researching federal statutes and cases to determine if the government had the authority to require Bernie to forfeit his car and car phone.

Before Natalie can begin her research project, she must thoroughly review the facts of the case to determine what specific issues need to be researched. Using a method described in *Sample Pages*, a West Publishing Company publication that she used in school, she breaks the facts down into five categories: parties, places and things, basis of action or issue, defenses, and relief sought. On a sheet of paper, she writes down these categories to use as headings and inserts the appropriate information for this case under each heading.

Natalie begins by identifying the *parties*. What people are involved in the action? Under this heading, she writes "U.S. attorney and drug-enforcement officers" and "Bernie Berriman and drug dealer." She then turns to the next category, *places and things*. Under this heading, she lists "car," "car phone," and "cocaine." Under the third heading, *basis of action or issue*, Natalie writes that the reason for the action is the transportation and distribution of a controlled substance.

The fourth category is *defenses*. Natalie thinks for a time and then decides that Berriman, the defendant, will probably argue that his constitutional rights were violated because the agents did not have sufficient evidence to justify searching the vehicle. She writes this down as a defense. The defendant might also argue that the government did not have the authority to require him to forfeit his car and car phone, so Natalie also includes this argument as a defense. The last category is *relief sought*, which is the legal remedy sought in a civil case by the plaintiff. Because this is a criminal case, Natalie crosses out the word *relief* and inserts *penalty* instead, so that the heading reads *penalty sought*. Under this heading, Natalie writes that the government is seeking the forfeiture of the vehicle and the car phone. Now Natalie is ready to go to the library to begin her research.

you can narrow it down by consulting secondary sources to learn more about the specific legal questions presented by the facts in Hoffman's case.

Understanding Your Research Goals

Your next step is to determine what it is you want to find—that is, your research goal or goals. Generally, whenever researching case law, you will want to find cases that are both on point and mandatory authorities. Depending on what you find, you may wish to locate persuasive authorities as well.

Cases on Point.   One of your goals will be to find **cases on point** (other cases with similar fact patterns and issues) and see how the courts decided the issue in those cases. The ideal case on point, of course, would be a case in which all four elements of a case (the parties, the circumstances, the legal issues involved, and the remedies sought) are very similar. Such a case is called a **case on "all fours."**[1]

Mandatory Authorities.   You also want to find cases that are mandatory authorities. A **mandatory authority** is any authority that the court *must* rely on in its determination of the issue. A mandatory authority may be a statute, regulation, or constitution that governs the issue, or it may be a previously decided court case that is controlling in your jurisdiction. For a case to serve as mandatory authority, it must be on point and decided by a superior court. A lower court is bound to follow the decisions set forth by a superior court in its jurisdiction. An appellate court's decision in a case involving facts and issues similar to a case brought in a trial court in the same jurisdiction would thus be a mandatory authority—the trial court would be bound to follow the appellate court's decision on the issue. A higher court is never required to follow an opinion written by a lower court in the same jurisdiction, however.

State courts have the final say on state law, and federal courts have the final say on federal law. Thus, except in deciding an issue that involves federal law, state courts do not have to follow the decisions of federal courts. In deciding issues that involve federal law, however, state courts must abide by the decisions of the United States Supreme Court.

● **When you are performing research, look for cases on point decided by the highest court in your jurisdiction, because those cases carry the most weight.**

Persuasive Authorities.   In contrast to a mandatory authority, a **persuasive authority** is not binding on a court. In other words, the court is not required to follow that authority in making its decision. Examples of persuasive authorities include prior opinions made by courts in other jurisdictions, which, although they are not binding, may be suggestive as to how a particular case should be decided. Scholarly articles and texts that describe how the law has been applied in the past may also serve as persuasive authorities.

Often, a court refers to persuasive authorities when deciding a *case of first impression*, which is a case involving an issue that has never been addressed by the courts in your jurisdiction before. For example, if in your research of Hoffman's claim you find that no similar cases have ever reached a higher court in your jurisdiction, you would look for similar cases decided by courts in other jurisdictions. If courts in other jurisdictions have faced a similar issue, the court may be guided by those other courts' decisions when deciding Hoffman's case. Your supervising attorney will want to know about these persuasive authorities so that he can present them to the court for the court's consideration.

CASE ON POINT
A case involving factual circumstances and issues that are similar to the case at bar (before the court).

CASE ON "ALL FOURS"
A case in which all four elements of a case (the parties, the circumstances, the legal issues involved, and the remedies sought) are very similar.

MANDATORY AUTHORITY
Any source of law that a court must follow when deciding a case. Mandatory authorities include constitutions, statutes, and regulations that govern the issue at bar and court decisions made by a superior court in the jurisdiction.

PERSUASIVE AUTHORITY
Any legal authority, or source of law, that a court may look to for guidance but on which it need not rely in making its decision. Persuasive authorities include cases from other jurisdictions and secondary sources of law, such as scholarly treatises.

---

1. Some scholars maintain that this phrase originated from the Latin adage that "nothing similar is identical unless it runs on all four feet."

Consulting Secondary Sources

In researching the Hoffman issue, your next step will be to consult secondary sources of law to learn more about negligence theory and how negligence theory applies to the factual circumstances in Hoffman's case. You will also want to define more precisely the legal issue that needs to be researched and find references to relevant cases or other primary sources relating to that issue. The secondary sources described below will help you accomplish these aims.

Legal Encyclopedias.   Legal encyclopedias cover topics of law in a general manner. They explain subjects, define terms, and provide detailed summaries of legal concepts and rules. They are also helpful in finding primary sources of authority. The two major legal encyclopedias are *Corpus Juris Secundum (C.J.S.)*, published by West Publishing Company, and *American Jurisprudence 2d* (Am.Jur.2d)—"2d" means second edition—published by the Lawyers Cooperative Publishing Company. Each of these encyclopedias divides the law into more than four hundred topics. The legal discussions in these encyclopedias are valuable for the researcher because they provide both broad statements of accepted law and extensive footnotes to other legal sources, both primary and secondary.

Another helpful secondary source is *Words and Phrases,* a forty-six-volume encyclopedia of definitions and interpretations of legal terms and phrases published by West Publishing Company. The words and phrases covered are arranged in alphabetical order, and each word or phrase is followed by brief summary statements from federal or state court decisions in which that word or phrase has been interpreted or defined.

In researching Hoffman's claim, you could review the topic of *negligence* in a legal encyclopedia to learn more about the issue you are researching. The encyclopedia would also discuss the leading cases relating to that issue. A good starting point might be to look in *Words and Phrases* to find out how various courts have defined *negligence*. Part of the entry for this term is shown in Exhibit 9.1.

Some states also have encyclopedias, such as *Texas Jurisprudence 3d*. A less technical reference is *The Guide to American Law: Everyone's Legal Encyclopedia*, which is published by West Publishing Company.

Digests.   In addition to legal encyclopedias, digests are helpful finding tools for the legal researcher. **Digests** are indexes to American case law. There are digests for both the federal and state court systems. Digests consist primarily of case summaries, which are arranged topically, from each jurisdiction. The advantage of a digest is that researchers can review cases from, for example, all appellate courts for a ten-year period. The *American Digest System*, published by West Publishing Company, provides a master index of all cases published in West's National Reporter System (to be discussed later). The *American Digest System* includes the *Decennial Digest Series*, which is published every ten years,[2] and the *General Digest Series*, which is issued

Digest
A compilation in which brief statements regarding court cases are arranged by subject and subdivided by jurisdiction and courts.

---

2. Because of the increased number of reported cases, West now publishes the "Decennial" digest every five years.

EXHIBIT 9.1
Excerpt from *Words and Phrases*

NEGLIGENCE

Estoppel by Negligence
Fault
General Negligence
Gross Negligence
Hazardous Negligence
Heedlessness
High Degree of Negligence
Homicide by Negligence
Imputed Contributory Negligence
Imputed Negligence
Incurred Without Fault or Negligence
Independent Act of Negligence
Independent Negligence
Injury Resulting from Negligence
Insulated Negligence
Intentional Negligence
Joint Negligence
Legal Negligence
Liability Created by Law
Marine Cause
Mistake, Error or Negligence
Mutual Contributory Negligence
Negligent
Notice of Negligence
Nuisance
Nuisance Dependent Upon Negligence
Ordinary Care
Ordinary Negligence
Otherwise
Persistent Negligence
Preponderance
Presumption of Negligence
Prima Facie Case of Negligence
Prima Facie Negligence
Prior Negligence
Proof of Negligence
Proximate Contributory Negligence
Reckless; Recklessly; Recklessness
Separate Negligence
Simple Negligence
Situation Created by Actor's Negligence
Slight Negligence
Specific Negligence
Subsequent Negligence
Supervening Negligence
Trespass
Wanton Negligence
Wantonness
Willful and Intentional Negligence
Willful Negligence
Willfulness
Without Negligence

In general

"Negligence", in absence of statute, is defined as the doing of that thing which a reasonably prudent person would not have

In general—Cont'd

done, or the failure to do that thing which a reasonably prudent person would have done, in like or similar circumstances. Biddle v. Mazzocco, Or., 284 P.2d 364, 368.

"Negligence" is a departure from the normal or what should be the normal, and is a failure to conform to standard of what a reasonably prudent man would ordinarily have done under the circumstances, or is doing what such man would not have done under the circumstances. Moran v. Pittsburgh-Des Moines Steel Co., D.C.Pa., 86 F. Supp. 255, 266.

"Negligence" being failure to do that which ordinarily prudent man would do or doing of that which such a man would not do under same circumstances, an ordinary custom, while relevant and admissible in evidence of negligence, is not conclusive thereof, especially where it is clearly a careless or dangerous custom. Tite v. Omaha Coliseum Corp., 12 N.W.2d 90, 94, 144 Neb. 22, 149 A.L.R. 1164.

Whether or not an act or omission is "negligence" seems to be determined by what under like circumstances would men of ordinary prudence have done. Cleveland, C., C. & St. L. R. Co. v. Ivins, Ohio, 12 O.C.D. 570.

"Negligence" means simply the want of ordinary care under the circumstances surrounding that particular case and the transaction in question, and "negligently" simply means doing an act in such a manner that it lacks the care which men of ordinary prudence and foresight use in their everyday affairs of life under the same or similar circumstances. Smillie v. Cleveland Ry., Ohio, 31 O.C.D. 323, 325, 20 Cir.Ct.R.,N.S., 302.

"Negligence" is the failure to do what a reasonable and prudent man would ordinarily have done under circumstances of situation or doing what such a person, under existing circumstances, would not have done. Judt v. Reinhardt Transfer Co., 17 Ohio Supp. 105, 107, 32 O.O. 161.

By "negligence" is meant negligence of such character that in the discretion of the court, the defendant should have inflicted upon him the punative penalties of having his license suspended and that the public required such protection. Com. v. Galley, 17 Som. 54.

"Negligence" is a failure to use ordinary care, that is, such care as persons of ordinary prudence are accustomed to exercise

EXHIBIT 9.2
American Law Reports

ANNOTATION

A brief statement, comment, or explanation of a legal point, which is found in a case digest or other legal source.

periodically between publications of the *Decennial Digest Series*. There are also a number of subject-matter digests and jurisdictional digests, which are simply extractions of digested cases from the master index.

Although West is the only publisher of comprehensive digests, other publishers offer digests for specific jurisdictions and specialized interest areas. For example, the *Lawyers' Edition of the Digest of the Supreme Court Reports*, published by the Lawyers Cooperative Publishing Company, provides an index to cases decided by the United States Supreme Court. This digest, which is similar in organizational style to the West digests, also includes cross-references to the *American Law Reports* (discussed below) and other legal publications of the Lawyers Cooperative Publishing Company. Some publishers also publish state-specific digests, such as Callahan's *Michigan Digest*.

Annotations: *American Law Reports.*   The *American Law Reports (A.L.R.)* and *American Law Reports Federal (A.L.R.Fed.)*, published by the Lawyers Cooperative Publishing Company, are also useful resources for the legal researcher. A photograph of an *A.L.R.* volume is shown in Exhibit 9.2. These reports are multivolume sets that present the full text of selected cases in numerous areas of the law. They are helpful in finding cases from jurisdictions throughout the country with similar factual and legal issues. There are five different series of *American Law Reports,* covering case law since 1919. The fifth series *(A.L.R.5th)* is the current edition. *A.L.R. Federal*, the current edition for coverage of federal decisions, began in 1969.

The cases presented in the *A.L.R.* are followed by **annotations** (commentaries). In the *A.L.R.*, annotations consist of articles that focus on specific issues; these reports can therefore be an excellent source to turn to in researching case law. The annotations also present an overview of the specific area of law addressed by the case, indicate current trends in that area, and refer to other case law relating to the specific issue or issues.

Restatements of the Law.   Another source of general background information is found in the Restatements of the Law, produced by the American Law Institute, an organization established in 1923 by a group of prominent judges, law professors, and practicing attorneys. The Restatements present an overview of the basic principles of the common law in ten specific fields: agency law, conflict of laws, contracts, foreign-relations law, judgments, property, restitution, security, torts, and trusts. Most of the Restatements have been updated by the issuance of second or third editions. The *Restatement of the Law of Torts,* for example, a photograph of which is shown in Exhibit 9.3, is now in its second edition.[3] The Restatements are often abbreviated when referred to by legal professionals. The *Restatement of the Law of Torts*, Second Edition, is often referred to as the *Restatement (Second) of the Law of Torts*, or, more simply, as the *Restatement (Second) of Torts*.

Restatements are helpful resources when researching issues involving common law doctrines, such as negligence. Each section included in the Restatements contains a general statement of the principles of law that are generally accepted by the courts and/or embodied in statutes on the topic,

---

3. Plans are in progress to publish a third edition of the *Restatement of the Law of Torts*.

followed by a discussion of these principles. The Restatements are useful research tools because they present particular cases as examples and also discuss variations on the general propositions of the law. Although the Restatements are *not* primary sources of law and therefore are not binding on the courts, they are highly respected secondary sources of law and are often referred to by the courts as the basis for their decisions.

Treatises.   Law **treatises** are written by legal scholars and specialists on certain subjects. Longer treatises are frequently published in multiple volumes. There are treatises for virtually all of the major topics of law. When updated, treatises are usually accurate explanations of the law in a particular area and a good source to turn to when beginning one's legal research. In reviewing the tort of negligence, for example, you might consult the classic treatise on tort law, *Prosser and Keeton on Torts.* This scholarly summary of tort law is frequently referred to by legal professionals, including court judges, as a (persuasive) authority on tort principles and doctrines.

Legal Periodicals.   Legal periodicals, such as law reviews, are also important secondary sources of law. The contents of most law reviews include (1) commentaries about the law, usually written by law professors, judges, or practicing attorneys; (2) reviews of books recently written about the law; (3) comments by student writers explaining the meaning of selected recent cases; and (4) student notes on specific topics of law. Almost every accredited law school publishes a law review. The *Harvard Law Review* is one of the most prestigious law reviews. There are many more of equal quality. In addition to the general law reviews, many law schools also publish law journals on specific topics, such as environmental law or product liability.

To locate law-review articles relevant to your research topic, you can begin by looking in the subject index of a guide to legal periodicals. Every law library provides periodical guides, and if you are unfamiliar with them, ask the reference librarian for assistance.

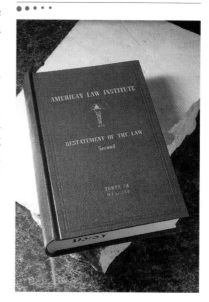

EXHIBIT 9.3
Restatement (Second) of the Law of Torts

TREATISE
In legal research, a text, such as a hornbook, that provides a systematic, detailed, and scholarly review of a particular legal subject.

FINDING AND ANALYZING CASE LAW

The primary sources of case law are, of course, the cases themselves. Once you have learned what cases are relevant to the issue that you are researching, you need to find the cases and examine the exact words of the court opinions.

Assume, for example, that in researching the issue in Hoffman's case, you learn that your state's supreme court, a few years ago, issued a decision on a case with a very similar fact pattern. In that case, the state supreme court upheld a lower court's judgment that a retail business owner had to pay extensive damages to a customer who was injured on the store's premises. You know that the state supreme court's decision is a mandatory authority, and to your knowledge, the decision has not been overruled or modified. Therefore, the case will likely provide weighty support to your attorney's arguments in support of Hoffman's claim. At this point, however, you have only read *about* the case in secondary sources. To locate the case itself and make sure that it is applicable, you need to understand the case reporting system and the legal "shorthand" employed in referencing court cases.

FEATURED GUEST: E. J. YERA

Ten Tips for Effective Legal Research

Biographical Note

E. J. Yera graduated from the University of Miami School of Law in 1987 and served as a research instructor at the school until 1989. He then clerked in the U.S. District Court for the Southern District of Florida until 1993. He has lectured and taught in paralegal programs, including the programs at Miami Dade Community College in Miami, Florida, and Barry University in Miami Shores, Florida. He has twice been named to *Who's Who in American Law* and has authored and published works on intellectual property. Yera is licensed to practice law in Florida and Washington, D.C. He is currently the assistant corporate counsel at Holmes Regional Medical Center in Melbourne, Florida.

If you perform legal research frequently, you will develop a routine. The purpose of this article is not to give you ironclad rules but to set out ten guidelines that will help you find the routine that is most comfortable for you. You may come back to this article and reread it over time. Now, however, as you read it for the first time, think about how you can use the tips in your future research tasks.

1 Before You Start, Make Sure That You Know Exactly What Legal Issue Is to Be Researched. You would be surprised at how many students, paralegals, and lawyers research a question for hours only to find that the reason they are getting nowhere is because they do not know what the question is. Before you start your research, you should determine what the legal question, or issue, is that needs to be researched. You might learn this from reviewing information you already have available, such as a summary of a client interview. If you have an opportunity to ask questions of the attorney giving you a research assignment, do so. What counts, in the end, is coming back with the correct answers, not

impressing the attorney by appearing to understand the research task completely when you first hear about it. It will take you twice as long to finish the assignment if you research the wrong issue or if you are unsure what the issue is.

2 Understand the Language of the Issue. Often, the researcher finds that he or she cannot find the answer because the legal terms used in defining the problem are unfamiliar to him or her. Legal terms, or "terms of art," as they are often called, are as unfamiliar to many people as a foreign language. If you are uncertain about the meaning of any term or phrase, look it up in a law dictionary or encyclopedia to get a basic idea of its meaning. Depending on how broad the term is, you may want to read a hornbook on the topic to give you a basic understanding. For example, assume that you are researching an issue relating to securities law. If you do not have a clear understanding of what securities are, there is no way in the world that you can conduct effective research on this issue. You will need to acquire some background knowledge before you focus on the particular research topic.

3 Be Aware of the Circular Nature of Legal Research and Use It to Your Advantage. Students often ask whether primary or secondary sources should be researched first. The answer is that it does not matter, as long as you always research both types of sources. By researching both primary and secondary sources on a topic, you can be assured that you are almost always double-checking your own work. For example, in a case (a primary source of law) on a particular issue, the judge writing the opinion will discuss any pertinent statutes on the issue. Similarly, most annotated versions of a statute (the annotations are secondary sources of law) give a listing, following the text of the statute, of cases applying the statute and the context in which the statute was applied. The reason that you check both sources is to make sure that you have found all of the relevant materials.

4 Until You Hand in the Assignment, Always Assume That There are Additional Relevant Materials to Find. You need to keep on your toes until you complete your research task. Always assuming that further relevant materials

FEATURED GUEST, Continued

must be located will help you do this. Of course, there comes a point when you have to assume that you *have* covered the research territory, and knowing when to stop doing research is perhaps one of the hardest things to learn. Certain legal issues can be researched for months and even years. The intention of this tip, though, is to encourage you not to cut corners when conducting research.

5 Keep a List of What Sources You Have Found and to What Sources They Have Led You. You do not want to spend valuable time wondering if you have already checked certain sources. Therefore, it is important to construct a "road map" of where you have been and where you are going.

6 Take the Time to Become Familiar with the Sources That You Are Using. It probably seems obvious that you need to become familiar with your sources, yet this requirement is sometimes overlooked. For example, a case digest (a volume summarizing cases) may indicate on its spine that the digest covers the years "1961 to Date." "To Date," however, does not mean that it is the most current digest; it only means that the digest covers cases up to the date of publication of the new digest replacing it. You should take the time to read the first few pages of the digest to verify its contents. This is true generally for any source you are using— look it over carefully before assuming that it contains the sources you need to find.

7 Always Be Aware of the Jurisdiction and the Time Frame That

You Are Researching. If you are researching an issue that will be resolved by a Florida state court, then your emphasis should be on Florida cases. Of course, there are times when no case law is available, and you must then find cases on point from other states to use as persuasive authorities. You must also be aware of the time frame covered by the source you are using (as mentioned in Tip 6). Be aware when researching any area of the law that very often there is either a loose-leaf service or a pamphlet or pocket part (the latter is a small booklet that slips into a pocket of the bound volume) containing newer information. Always ask yourself the following question: Where can the most up-to-date material be found? If you don't know, ask a law librarian who does.

8 Always Use *Shepard's* to Make Sure That the Cases You Are Using Are Up to Date. *Shepard's Citations* is a set of volumes that helps the researcher of case law in two ways. First, it tells you what other cases have cited the cases that you have found. This information is helpful because if another case has cited a case you have found, that other case may also be relevant to your issue, and thus you may be able to use it. Also, cases that cite your case are more recent, and using one or more of those cases may thus be advantageous. Second, *Shepard's* tells you, among other things, whether the cases that you have found are still "good law"—that is, whether the cases have been overruled, reversed, or the like. Knowing this information is crucial—because presenting a case to your attorney that no longer represents good law could

"WHAT COUNTS, IN THE END, IS COMING BACK WITH THE CORRECT ANSWERS."

• • • •

well be a short cut to the unemployment line.

9 Use Computerized Legal Research Services to Update Your Research Results. Computerized legal databases such as WESTLAW and LEXIS allow you to update your research results by "Shepardizing" cases by computer. Also, these services allow you to search the available case law for words or phrases. By doing so, you can actually create your own indexing system.

10 Twice a Year, Take Three or Four Hours and Browse through Your Local Law Library. You cannot use sources effectively if you do not know that they exist. You should periodically—say, twice a year— spend an afternoon in the law library browsing through the shelves. Read the first few pages of each new source, and then make a note of what the source contains. Ask the librarian for new sources in your area. The time you save later will more than compensate for an afternoon's time spent in the library. You will be surprised at how quickly the new sources you discovered or were told about at the law library come quickly to mind when you receive a new research assignment, and they may figure significantly in your research.

Finding Case Law

New York and a few other states publish selected opinions of their trial courts, but most state trial court decisions are not published. Decisions from the state trial courts are usually just filed in the office of the clerk of the court, where they are available for public inspection. Written decisions of the appellate courts, however, are usually published and distributed. The reported appellate decisions are published—in chronological order by date of decision—in **reporters,** the term generally given to any publication that "reports" (publishes) cases decided by the courts.

State Court Decisions.   State appellate court decisions are found in the reports of that particular state. State court decisions are usually published in both official and unofficial reporters. The official reports are designated as such by the state legislature, are issued by the individual courts, and serve as the authoritative texts of case decisions. A few of the states, including New York and California, have more than one official state reporter.

West's National Reporter System.   Additionally, state court opinions appear in regional units of the *National Reporter System,* published by West Publishing Company. Most libraries have the West reporters because they report cases more quickly and are distributed more widely than the state-published reports. In fact, many states have eliminated their own reporters in favor of West's National Reporter System.

The National Reporter System divides the states into the following geographical areas: *Atlantic* (A. or A.2d), *South Eastern* (S.E. or S.E.2d), *South Western* (S.W. or S.W.2d), *North Western* (N.W. or N.W.2d), *North Eastern* (N.E. or N.E.2d), *Southern* (So. or So.2d), and *Pacific* (P. or P.2d). Note that the *2d* in the preceding abbreviations refers to *Second Series.* The states included in each of these regional divisions are indicated in Exhibit 9.4, which illustrates West's National Reporter System.

Citation Format.   After an appellate decision has been published, it is normally referred to (*cited*) by the name of the case (often called the *style* of the case) and the volume number, abbreviated name, and page number of each reporter in which the case has been published. This information is included in what is called the **citation.** When more than one reporter contains the text of the same case, a reference to the other reporter or reporters in which the case can be found—called a **parallel citation**—is also included. The first citation will be to the state's official reporter (if different from West's National Reporter System). Note that in every citation to a reporter, the number preceding the abbreviated name of the reporter will be the volume number, and the first number following it will be the page number of the first page of the case.

To illustrate how to find case law from citations, suppose that you want to find the following case: *Ward v. K-Mart Corp,* 136 Ill.2d 132, 554 N.E.2d 223 (1990). You can see that the opinion in this case may be found in volume 136 of the official *Illinois Reports, Second Series,* on page 132. The parallel citation is to volume 554 of West's *North Eastern Reporter, Second Series,* page 223. Exhibit 9.5 on page 306 further illustrates how to read citations to state court decisions.

REPORTER
A publication in which court cases are published, or reported.

CITATION
In case law, a reference to the volume number, name, and page number of the reporter in which a case can be found. In statutory and administrative law, a reference to the title number, name, and section of the code in which a statute or regulation can be found.

PARALLEL CITATION
A second (or third) citation to another case reporter in which a case has been published. When a case is published in more than one reporter, each citation is a parallel citation to the other(s).

EXHIBIT 9.4

National Reporter System—Regional and Federal

Regional Reporters	Coverage Beginning	Coverage
Atlantic Reporter (A. or A.2d)	1885	Connecticut, Delaware, Maine, Maryland, New Hampshire, New Jersey, Pennsylvania, Rhode Island, Vermont, and District of Columbia.
North Eastern Reporter (N.E. or N.E.2d)	1885	Illinois, Indiana, Massachusetts, New York, and Ohio.
North Western Reporter (N.W. or N.W.2d)	1879	Iowa, Michigan, Minnesota, Nebraska, North Dakota, South Dakota, and Wisconsin.
Pacific Reporter (P. or P.2d)	1883	Alaska, Arizona, California, Colorado, Hawaii, Idaho, Kansas, Montana, Nevada, New Mexico, Oklahoma, Oregon, Utah, Washington, and Wyoming.
South Eastern Reporter (S.E. or S.E.2d)	1887	Georgia, North Carolina, South Carolina, Virginia, and West Virginia.
South Western Reporter (S.W. or S.W.2d)	1886	Arkansas, Kentucky, Missouri, Tennessee, and Texas.
Southern Reporter (So. or So.2d)	1887	Alabama, Florida, Louisiana, and Mississippi.
Federal Reporters		
Federal Reporter (F., F.2d, or F. 3d)	1880	U.S. Circuit Court from 1880 to 1912; U.S. Commerce Court from 1911 to 1913; U.S. District Courts from 1880 to 1932; U.S. Court of Claims (now called U.S. Court of Federal Claims) from 1929 to 1932 and since 1960; U.S. Court of Appeals since 1891; U.S. Court of Customs and Patent Appeals since 1929; and U.S. Emergency Court of Appeals since 1943.
Federal Supplement (F.Supp.)	1932	U.S. Court of Claims from 1932 to 1960; U.S. District Courts since 1932; and U.S. Customs Court since 1956.
Federal Rules Decisions (F.R.D.)	1939	U.S. District Courts involving the Federal Rules of Civil Procedure since 1939 and Federal Rules of Criminal Procedure since 1946.
Supreme Court Reporter (S.Ct.)	1882	U.S. Supreme Court since the October term of 1882.
Bankruptcy Reporter (Bankr.)	1980	Bankruptcy decisions of U.S. Bankruptcy Courts, U.S. District Courts, U.S. Courts of Appeals, and U.S. Supreme Court.
Military Justice Reporter (M.J.)	1978	U.S. Court of Military Appeals and Courts of Military Review for the Army, Navy, Air Force, and Coast Guard.

NATIONAL REPORTER SYSTEM MAP

EXHIBIT 9.5
How to Read Case Citations

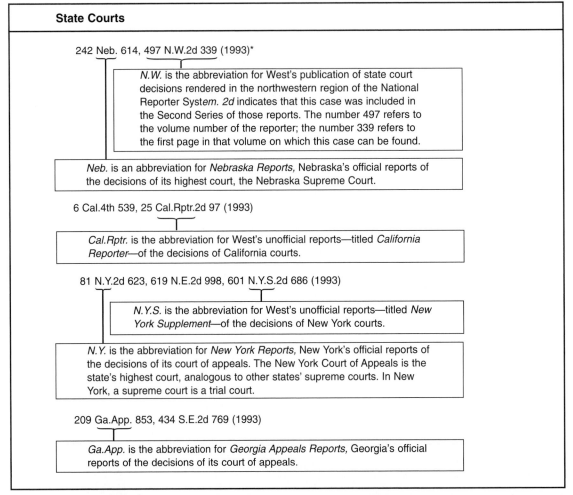

*   The case names have been deleted from these citations to emphasize the publications. It should be kept in mind, however, that the name of a case is as important as the specific page numbers in the volumes in which it is found. If a citation is incorrect, the correct citation may be found in a publication's index of case names. The date of a case is also important because, in addition to providing a check on error in citations, the value of a recent case as an authority is likely to be greater than that of earlier cases.

When conducting legal research, you need to include in your research notes the citations to the cases or other legal sources that you have consulted, quoted, or want to refer to in a written summary of your research results. Several guides have been published on how to cite legal sources. The most widely used guide is a book entitled *A Uniform System of Citation,* which is published by the Harvard Law Review Association. The Bluebook, as this book is often called (because of its blue cover), explains the proper format for citing cases, statutes, constitutions, regulations, and other legal sources. It is a good idea to memorize the basic format for citations to cases and statuto-

EXHIBIT 9.5
Continued

Federal Courts

___ U.S. ___, 114 S.Ct. 1164, 127 L.Ed.2d 500 (1994)

> *L.Ed.* is an abbreviation for *Lawyers' Edition of the Supreme Court Reports*, an unofficial edition of decisions of the United States Supreme Court.

> *S.Ct.* is the abbreviation for West's unofficial reports—titled *Supreme Court Reporter*—of United States Supreme Court decisions.

> *U.S.* is the abbreviation for *United States Reports*, the official edition of the decisions of the United States Supreme Court. Volume and page numbers are not included in this citation because they have not yet been assigned.

Statutory and Other Citations

15 U.S.C. Section 1262(e)

> *U.S.C.* denotes *United States Code,* the codification of *United States Statutes at Large.* The number 15 refers to the statute's U.S.C. title number and 1262 to its section number within that title. The letter e refers to a subsection within the section.

UCC 2-206(1)(a)

> *UCC* is an abbreviation for *Uniform Commercial Code.* The first number 2 is a reference to an article of the UCC and 206 to a section within that article. The number 1 refers to a subsection within the section and the letter a to a subdivision within the subsection.

Restatement (Second) of Torts, Section 568

> *Restatement (Second) of Torts* refers to the second edition of the American Law Institute's *Restatement of the Law of Torts.* The number 568 refers to a specific section.

16 C.F.R. Section 453.2

> *C.F.R.* is an abbreviation for *Code of Federal Regulations*, a compilation of federal administrative regulations. The number 16 is a reference to the regulation's title number and 453.2 to a specific section within that title.

---

ry law because these legal sources are frequently cited in legal writing.[4] Another popular guide is a small booklet entitled *The Unversity of Chicago*

---

4. Because the rules presented in the Bluebook may be difficult to understand, you might want to refer to Alan L. Dworsky, *User's Guide to the Bluebook* (Littleton, Colo.: F. B. Rothman, 1988).

DEVELOPING PARALEGAL SKILLS
Understanding Case Citations

Wendy Morgan is a legal secretary studying to become a paralegal. She has just read a chapter in her text on legal research and is studying the section on case citations. She shows a citation to Janet Honner, a legal assistant at the office, and asks Janet to go over the case citation with her. The name of the case is *O'Driscoll v. Hercules, Inc.*, and its citation is 12 F.3d 176 (10th Cir. 1994). Janet tells Wendy that the names in the case title are the names of the parties to the lawsuit. Next is the volume number, which is 12. This number is imprinted on the outside binding of the book, or reporter, in which the case is contained. The name of the reporter is indicated by F.3d, which is the abbreviation for West's *Federal Reporter, Third Series*. The next number, 176, indicates that the case begins on page 176 of volume 12. The information in parentheses shows that the case was decided by the federal Court of Appeals for the Tenth Circuit in 1994.

Next, Wendy wants to check her understanding by explaining a citation to Janet. She finds a citation to *Gypsy Moth v. Rose*, 652 F.Supp. 1109 (S.D.N.Y. 1975) and says, "This case appears in volume 652 of the *Federal Supplement* on page 1109. The information in parentheses is the name of the court. I know that this case is from a federal district court because the reporter is the *Federal Supplement*, which is the unofficial reporter for the federal district courts. So the S.D.N.Y. must mean a district in New York. Is it the southern district?" "Yes," responds Janet. Finally, Wendy determines that the case was decided in 1975.

Manual of Legal Citation, which is often referred to as the Maroon Book (because of its maroon cover).

Federal Court Decisions. Court decisions from the U.S. district courts (federal trial courts) are published in West's *Federal Supplement* (F.Supp.), and opinions from the circuit courts of appeals are reported in West's *Federal Reporter* (F., F.2d, or F.3d). These are both unofficial reporters (there are no official reporters for these courts). Both the *Federal Reporter* and the *Federal Supplement* incorporate decisions from specialized federal courts. West also publishes separate reporters, such as its *Bankruptcy Reporter*, that contain decisions in certain specialized fields under federal law. Sample citations for federal court decisions are also listed and explained in Exhibit 9.5.

United States Supreme Court Decisions. Opinions from the United States Supreme Court are published in several reporters. The *United States Reports* (U.S.), published by the federal government, is the official edition of all decisions of the United States Supreme Court for which there are written opinions.

Supreme Court cases are also published in West Publishing Company's *Supreme Court Reporter* (S.Ct.). West's *Supreme Court Reporter*, which is an unofficial edition of Supreme Court opinions, includes a brief **syllabus**

SYLLABUS

A brief summary of the holding and legal principles involved in a reported case, which is followed by the court's official opinion.

(which summarizes the case) and **headnotes** (which summarize points of law or legal principles addressed by the case and the court's ruling on those issues) prepared by West editors.

Another unofficial edition of Supreme Court decisions is the *Lawyers' Edition of the Supreme Court Reports* (L.Ed.), published by the Lawyers Cooperative Publishing Company of Rochester, New York. Each case published in the *Lawyers' Edition, Second Series,* is preceded by a full summary of the case and a detailed discussion of selected cases of special interest to the legal profession. Also, the *Lawyers' Edition* is the only reporter of Supreme Court opinions that provides summaries of the briefs presented by counsel.

Virtually all Supreme Court decisions, as well as the text of many treaties and statutes, are now available in electronic format on the Internet. Supreme Court opinions are available on the Internet within minutes after their release. Thus, if you have access to the Internet and want to read the text of a Supreme Court decision made yesterday or even just hours ago, you may be able to view it on your computer screen. (The Internet is discussed in detail in Appendix B.)

Analyzing Case Law

One of the difficulties that all legal professionals face in analyzing case law is the sheer length and complexity of some court opinions. While certain court opinions may be only two or three pages in length, others can occupy hundreds of pages. Understanding the components of a case—that is, the basic format in which cases are presented—can simplify your task of reading and analyzing case law. You will find that over time, as you acquire experience, reading and analyzing cases becomes easier.

The Components of a Case.   Reported cases contain much more than just the court's decision. Cases have many different parts, and you should understand why each part is there and what information it communicates. To illustrate the components of a case, fold-out Exhibit 9.6 presents excerpts from an actual case that was decided by the United States Supreme Court in 1994. The lawsuit was initiated by Acuff-Rose Music, Inc., which held the copyright to a popular song entitled "Oh, Pretty Woman." The rap group 2 Live Crew authored and profited from a parody (satiric rendition) of the song. Federal copyright law allows writers, artists, and other authors of creative works to have the exclusive right to reproduce those works. Copyright *infringement* occurs when someone reproduces a copyrighted work without the author's permission to do so.

Important sections, terms, and phrases in the case are defined or discussed in the margins. You will note also that triple asterisks (* * *) and quadruple asterisks (* * * *) frequently appear in the exhibit. The triple asterisks indicate that we have deleted a few words or sentences from the opinion for the sake of readability or brevity. Quadruple asterisks mean that an entire paragraph (or more) has been omitted. Also, when the opinion cites another case or legal source, the citation to the referenced cases or sources has been omitted to save space and to improve readability.

HEADNOTE
A note near the beginning of a reported case summarizing the court's ruling on an issue.

ETHICAL CONCERN
Citing Sources

A good habit to develop as you are doing research is to make sure—before returning a legal source to the library shelf (or signing off a computerized legal-research service)—that you have included in your research notes the proper reference or citation for that authority. If you are reviewing a court opinion, for example, remember to include in your notes the proper case citation, including parallel citations, and to double-check the case title to make sure that you have spelled it correctly. If you forget to cite your source, you will have to spend additional time relocating the source to obtain the citation. As has been stressed elsewhere, your time is a valuable resource for your attorney and a costly one for your client. If you have to spend another hour's time going to and from a library to obtain a citation that you should have included in your notes in the first place, who will pay for that hour's time? If your time is charged directly to the client, the client may not agree that paying for that hour's time is reasonable—and attorneys have a duty to charge their clients reasonable fees.

Case Format.   The case presented in fold-out Exhibit 9.6 follows the typical format used in most case reporters. First, the case title, citation, and docket number are given. These are followed by the dates that the case was argued and decided, and the syllabus (in this case, prepared by the West editors). In the WESTLAW printout of this case, following the syllabus were a series of headnotes and the names of the lawyers representing the parties. We have not included these components in Exhibit 9.6 for reasons of space. The name of the judge or justice who authored the opinion in the case appears just above the opinion.

OPINION
A statement by the court expressing the reasons for its decision in a case.

The Opinion.   As you may have noted in previous chapters, the term *opinion* is often used loosely to refer to a court case or decision. In fact, the term has a precise meaning. The formal **opinion** of the court contains the analysis and decision of the judge or judges that heard and decided the case. When researching case law, the opinion itself should receive your greatest attention. The other components of a case, including the syllabus and headnotes, are helpful guides to understanding the case, but they are not authoritative sources of law and should not be quoted or cited in your research summary.

When all of the judges unanimously agree in their legal reasoning and their decision, the opinion is deemed a *unanimous* opinion. When the opinion is not unanimous, a *majority* opinion is written, outlining the views of the majority of the judges deciding the case. There may also be a *concurring* opinion or a *dissenting* opinion. A concurring opinion is written by a judge who agrees with the majority's conclusion but who wants to either offer a different legal basis for the conclusion or shed additional light on the issue. A dissenting opinion is written by a judge who disagrees with the majority's decision. Although only the majority opinion is controlling (that is, mandatory authority for lower courts in that jurisdiction), concurrent and dissenting opinions may have future value as persuasive authorities.

The Court's Conclusion.   In the opinion, the judges will indicate their conclusion, or decision, on the issue or issues before the court. If several issues are involved, as often happens, there may be a conclusion at the end of the discussion of each issue. Often, at the end of the opinion, the conclusions presented within the opinion will be briefly reiterated and summarized, or, if no conclusions were yet presented, they will be presented in the concluding section of the opinion.

An appellate court also specifies what the *disposition* of a case should be. As discussed in Chapter 6, if the appellate court agrees with a lower court's decision, it will *affirm* that decision, which means that the decision of the lower court remains unchanged. If the appellate court concludes that the lower court erred in its interpretation of the law, the court may *reverse* the lower court's ruling. Sometimes, if an appellate court concludes that further factual findings are necessary or that a case should be retried and a decision made that is consistent with the appellate court's conclusions of law, the appellate court will *remand* the case to the lower court for further proceedings consistent with its opinion. In the sample case presented in fold-out Exhibit 9.6, the United States Supreme Court reversed the lower court's decision and remanded the case.

Guidelines for Reading Cases.   When reading case law, you will inevitably find that some opinions are easier to understand than others. Some judges write more clearly and logically than others. You may need to reread a case (or a portion of a case) several times to understand what is being said, why it is being said at that point in the case, and what the judge's underlying legal reasoning is. Some cases contain several pages describing facts and issues of previous cases and how those cases relate to the one being decided by the court. You will need to distinguish between comments made in the previous case and comments that are being made about the case at bar (before the court).

Often, the judge writing the opinion provides some guideposts, perhaps by indicating sections and subsections within the opinion by numbers, letters, or subtitles. Note that in fold-out Exhibit 9.6, Roman numerals are used to divide the opinion into basic sections. Scanning through the opinion for these types of indicators can help orient you to the opinion's format.

In cases that involve dissenting or concurring opinions, you need to make sure that you identify these opinions so that you do not mistake one of them for the majority opinion. Generally, you should scan through the case a time or two to identify its various components and sections and then read the case (or sections of the case) until you understand the facts and procedural history of the case, the issues involved, the applicable law, the legal reasoning of the court, and how the reasoning leads to the court's conclusion on the issue or issues.

Summarizing and Briefing Cases.   A method that is commonly used by legal researchers, including paralegals, to summarize a case is the **IRAC method**. IRAC stands for **I**ssue, **R**ule, **A**pplication, and **C**onclusion. The IRAC approach helps to focus your attention on the essential aspects of the case in both the prewriting and writing stages of a research project. The format for the IRAC method is shown in Exhibit 9.7 on page 312. Note that in cases involving more than one issue, you will use IRAC to analyze each separate issue.

Another method of summarizing a case is called **briefing a case**. There is a fairly standard format that you can use when you brief any court case. Although the format may vary, typically it will present the essentials of the case under headings such as those illustrated and described in Exhibit 9.8 on page 312. As you can see in the exhibit, the headings used in a case brief are similar to those used in the IRAC method. The difference is that in a case brief, the background and facts leading up to the lawsuit are included. Also, when more than one issue is involved in a case, the issues are combined in the *Issue* section, the decisions regarding each issue may be combined under the *Decision* section, and so on. Depending on the issue you were researching, you would add a conclusion to the brief indicating how the Supreme Court's ruling affected that issue.

IRAC METHOD
IRAC is a mnemonic for issue, rule, application, and conclusion. The IRAC method helps legal researchers and writers focus on the four critical elements of a case.

BRIEFING A CASE
Summarizing a case. A typical case brief will indicate the case title and citation and then briefly state the factual background and procedural history of the case, the issue or issues raised in the case, the court's decision, the applicable rule of law and the legal reasoning upon which the decision is based, and conclusions or notes concerning the case made by the one who is briefing it.

RESEARCHING STATUTORY LAW

Because of the tremendous growth in statutory and regulatory law in the last century, the legal issues dealt with by attorneys are frequently governed by statutes and administrative regulations. Indeed, in researching any legal issue, you will often find that you need to look not only at case law but also at statutory law, or vice versa. Although the issue in Hoffman's case will probably be decided on the basis of common law principles governing torts,

EXHIBIT 9.7
The IRAC Method

ISSUE: What issue is being addressed by the court?

RULE: What rule of law applies to the issue? The rule of law may be a rule stated by the courts in previous decisions, a state or federal statute, or a state or federal administrative-agency regulation.

APPLICATION: How does the court apply the rule of law to the facts involved in this particular case?

CONCLUSION: What is the court's conclusion?

as enunciated by the courts, other issues that you may be asked to research may be governed by statutory law.

To find the relevant statutory law governing a particular legal issue or area, you will need to know, first of all, the names of the various publications in which statutory law can be found. In this section, we look first at how federal statutes are published and how you can find, within these publications, statutes governing the issue you are researching. We then look at a more difficult task: how to read and analyze a statutory law.

Finding Statutory Law

When the U.S. Congress passes laws, they are collected in a publication entitled *United States Statutes at Large.* When state legislatures pass laws, they are collected in similar state publications. These publications arrange laws by date of enactment. Most frequently, however, laws are referred to in their codified form—that is, the form in which they appear in the federal and state codes. (A **code** is a systematic and logical presentation of laws, rules, or regulations.) Codes arrange statutory provisions by topic. When you are researching statutory law, a good beginning point is to review the topical index to a state, federal, or local code of laws to see if you can find statutes relevant to your issue.

CODE
A systematic and logical presentation of laws, rules, or regulations.

EXHIBIT 9.8
Format for Briefing a Case

1. **NAME (TITLE, OR STYLE) OF CASE.** Give the full name of the case.

2. **CASE CITATION.** Give the full citation for the case, including all parallel citations, the date the case was decided, and the name of the court deciding the case.

3. **FACTS.** Briefly indicate (a) the reasons for the lawsuit; (b) the identity and arguments of the plaintiff(s) and defendant(s); and (c) if the case was decided by an appellate court, the lower court's opinion on the issues.

4. **ISSUE.** Concisely phrase the essential legal issue(s) before the court.

5. **DECISION (RULING, HOLDING).** Indicate here the court's decision on the issue(s).

6. **REASON.** Summarize as briefly as possible the legal reasoning on which the court based its decision.

The *United States Code.* Federal statutes enacted by Congress are published in their final form in the *United States Code (U.S.C.)*, which is published by the U.S. government. The *U.S.C.* is divided into fifty topic classifications. As shown in Exhibit 9.9, each of these topics, called *titles* of the code, carries a descriptive title and a number. For example, laws relating to commerce and trade are collected in Title 15, and laws concerning the courts or judicial procedures are collected in Title 28. Titles are subdivided into *chapters* (sections) and *subchapters* (subsections). A citation to the *U.S.C.* includes title and section numbers. Thus, a reference to "28 U.S.C. Section 1346" means that the statute can be found in Section 1346 of Title 28. "Section" may also be designated by the symbol §, and "Sections" by §§.

One approach to finding statutory law in the *U.S.C.* is simply to refer to the title descriptions listed in the front of each volume. This approach is

---

TITLES OF UNITED STATES CODE

*1. General Provisions.	27. Intoxicating Liquors.
2. The Congress.	*28. Judiciary and Judicial Procedure; and Appendix.
*3. The President.	
*4. Flag and Seal, Seat of Government, and the States.	29. Labor.
	30. Mineral Lands and Mining.
*5. Government Organization and Employees; and Appendix.	*31. Money and Finance.
	*32. National Guard.
†6. [Surety Bonds.]	33. Navigation and Navigable Waters.
7. Agriculture.	
8. Aliens and Nationality.	‡34. [Navy.]
*9. Arbitration.	*35. Patents.
*10. Armed Forces; and Appendix.	36. Patriotic Societies and Observances.
*11. Bankruptcy; and Appendix.	*37. Pay and Allowances of the Uniformed Services.
12. Banks and Banking.	
*13. Census.	*38. Veterans' Benefits.
*14. Coast Guard.	*39. Postal Service.
15. Commerce and Trade.	40. Public Buildings, Property, and Works.
16. Conservation.	41. Public Contracts.
*17. Copyrights.	42. The Public Health and Welfare.
*18. Crimes and Criminal Procedure; and Appendix.	43. Public Lands.
	*44. Public Printing and Documents.
19. Customs Duties.	
20. Education.	45. Railroads.
21. Food and Drugs.	*46. Shipping; and Appendix.
22. Foreign Relations and Intercourse.	47. Telegraphs, Telephones, and Radiotelegraphs.
*23. Highways.	
24. Hospitals and Asylums.	48. Territories and Insular Possessions.
25. Indians.	*49. Transportation; and Appendix.
26. Internal Revenue Code.	50. War and National Defense; and Appendix.

*This title has been enacted as law. However, any Appendix to this title has not been enacted as law.
†This title was enacted as law and has been repealed by the enactment of Title 31.
‡This title has been eliminated by the enactment of Title 10.

Page III

EXHIBIT 9.9
Titles in the *United States Code*

most beneficial for researchers who can quickly find the applicable title for the statute they are researching. Alternatively, the researcher can consult the index to the *U.S.C.* The index provides an alphabetical listing of all federal statutes by subject matter and by the name of the act. The index provides the exact location of the statute, by title and section number.

Sometimes a researcher may know the popular name of a legislative act but not its official name. In this situation, the researcher can consult the *U.S.C.* volume entitled *Popular Name Table,* which lists statutes by their popular names. Many legislative bills enacted into law are commonly known by a popular name. Some have descriptive titles reflecting their purpose; others are named after their sponsors. The Labor-Management Reporting and Disclosure Act of 1959, for example, is also known as the Landrum-Griffin Act. Searching by popular name will allow the researcher to find the title and section of the statute and therefore locate the statute in the *U.S.C.*

Unofficial Versions of the Federal Code. There are two unofficial versions of the federal code. These versions are similar to the *U.S.C.,* but they contain some important differences. They provide annotations describing cases and other sources that have applied or interpreted a given statute. Additionally, they contain more cross-references to related sections of the code than does the *U.S.C.*

One of these unofficial versions is the *United States Code Annotated (U.S.C.A.),* published by West Publishing Company. The *U.S.C.A.* contains the full text of the *U.S.C.,* the U.S. Constitution, the Federal Rules of Evidence, and various other rules, including the Rules of Civil Procedure and the Rules of Criminal Procedure. This set of approximately two hundred volumes offers historical notes relating to the text of each statute and any amendments to the act. Locating statutory law in the *U.S.C.A.* is similar to locating statutes in the *U.S.C.* Researchers can use the topical or index approach and, if necessary, look through the *Popular Name Table.*

The second unofficial statutory code is the *United States Code Service (U.S.C.S.),* published by the Lawyers Cooperative Publishing Company. The *U.S.C.S.* offers some of the same features offered by the *U.S.C.A.,* such as annotations. The *U.S.C.S.* and the *U.S.C.A.* are distinguishable by the research tools they provide. The research section of the *U.S.C.S.* provides references and citations to some sources that are not contained in the *U.S.C.A.,* including non-West publications such as *American Law Reports,* legal periodicals, and *American Jurisprudence.* Paralegals can begin statutory research in the *U.S.C.S.* by reviewing the subject index or tables listing the popular names of statutes. Both annotated codes also have conversion charts listing all public acts by public law number (P.L. number), *Statutes at Large* references, and *U.S.C.* title and section numbers.

State Codes. State codes follow the *U.S.C.* pattern of arranging statutes by subject. They may be called codes, revisions, compilations, consolidations, general statutes, or statutes, depending on the preference of the states. In some codes, subjects are designated by number. In others, they are designated by name. For example, "13 Pennsylvania Consolidated Statutes Section 1101" means that the statute can be found in Section 1101 of Title 13 of the Pennsylvania code. "California Commercial Code Section 1101" means that the statute can be found in Section 1101 under the heading "Commercial" in the California code. Abbreviations may be used. For example, a reference to "13 Pennsylvania Consolidated Statutes Section 1101" may be abbreviated to "13 Pa.C.S. § 1101," and a reference to "California Commercial Code Section 1101" may be abbreviated to "Cal. Com. Code § 1101."

In many states, official codes are supplemented by annotated codes published by private publishers. Annotated codes follow the numbering scheme set forth in the official state code but provide outlines and indexes to assist in locating information. These codes also provide references to case law, legislative history sources, and other documents in which the statute has been considered or discussed.

Analyzing Statutory Law

As with court cases, some statutes are more difficult to read than others. Some are extremely wordy or lengthy or difficult to understand for some other reason. The kinds of information you want to look for when reading a statute will vary, depending on the nature of the issue you are researching. Generally, though, you should find answers to the following types of questions:

- Why was the statute enacted?
- When does the statute take effect? (The effective date of a statute may be a year or more after the statute was enacted by Congress.)
- To what class or group of people does the statute apply?
- What kind of conduct is being regulated by the statute, and in what circumstances is that conduct prohibited, required, or permitted?
- Are there any exceptions to the statute's applicability?

By carefully reading and rereading a statute, you can usually find answers to these questions.

Generally, when trying to understand the meaning of statutes, you should do as the courts do. When a court is unsure of how a particular statute applies to a given set of circumstances, the court will often research case law to see how other courts have applied the statute. You can find citations to court cases relating to specific statutes by referring to the annotated versions of state or federal statutory codes discussed above.

Another technique used by courts in interpreting a statute's meaning and applicability is to research the legislative history of the statute to discern what the legislators intended when they enacted the law. In researching the legislative history of a statute, you will want to locate and read through the reports of congressional committees, transcripts of congressional debates and proceedings, and other relevant documents. The easiest way to locate these sources is to refer to unofficial annotated versions of statutory codes. Unofficial versions of the federal code, such as the *U.S.C.A.*, often include references to sources that will provide you with more detailed information on a statute's legislative history.

RESEARCHING ADMINISTRATIVE LAW

Administrative rules and regulations also constitute a source of American law. As discussed in Chapter 5, Congress frequently delegates authority to

DEVELOPING PARALEGAL SKILLS

Researching the *U.S.C.A.*

 Natalie Martin has completed her factual analysis of the case involving Bernie Berriman (see the *Developing Paralegal Skills* feature entitled "Defining the Issues to Be Researched) and begins her research. The issue she is researching is whether the government, which arrested Bernie for the transportation and distribution of cocaine, had the authority to confiscate Bernie's car and car phone. Natalie's supervising attorney has told her to start her research by looking at the relevant federal statutes.

USING *U.S.C.A.* INDEXES

Natalie goes to the firm's library and selects the general index to the *United States Code Annotated (U.S.C.A.).* The general index is the best place to start, unless the specific *U.S.C.A.* title is known. (If the specific *U.S.C.A.* title—that is, topic—is known, then the research should begin in the title index, which is a detailed index in the volume where the title appears.) Natalie decides that she could look under several topics in the general index, including *drugs, controlled substances, distribution of controlled substances,* and *forfeiture.* She selects the topic "Drugs" and removes from the shelf the general index volume labeled "Di–F." She turns to "Drugs" and finds several entries under that general heading. She scans the column until she comes to the entry "Fines, penalties, and forfeitures." Below that subtopic is another subtopic, "Property subject to forfeiture to U.S." Still another subtopic under that entry is "Enumeration, 21 sec. 881." Natalie concludes that the term *enumerated* must mean *listed.* Therefore, the entry must mean that the property subject to forfeiture is listed in Section 881 of Title 21. Natalie copies down the citation.

She continues to peruse the pages under the topic "Drugs" until she comes to the subtopic "Process." Under that subtopic is another subtopic, "Forfeiture, property subject to, issuance, 21 sec. 881." "This is the same citation I just found," Natalie says to herself. Continuing to scan the columns, Natalie comes to the subtopic "Vehicle" and notices under this entry the subtopic "Used for illegal conveyance of controlled substances, 21 sec. 881." The same section again. Natalie decides to take a look at it.

Natalie returns the index to the shelf and takes down the volume containing "Title 21—Food and Drugs." She opens it up to Section 881 and reads through the section. It says that vehicles are subject to forfeiture if they are used or intended to be used to transport controlled substances. "That gives the prosecutor the right to confiscate the car," thinks Natalie. "I had better

administrative agencies through enabling legislation. All regulations issued by federal administrative agencies are published in their final form in the federal *Code of Federal Regulations (C.F.R.),* a U.S. government publication. The regulations are compiled from the *Federal Register,* a daily government publication in which regulations and presidential orders are initially published. The *C.F.R.* uses the same titles as the *U.S.C.* (shown previously in Exhibit 9.9). Each title of the *C.F.R.* is similarly divided into sections and subsections.

> ## DEVELOPING PARALEGAL SKILLS, Continued
>
> check the pocket part to see if this statute has been amended, though." She finds that the relevant part of the statute that she was reading has not been changed. She makes a note to check on the statute using the firm's computerized legal-research service. The computer database will include recent modifications to the law that might not yet be available in printed research materials.
>
> ### FINDING RELEVANT CASE LAW
>
> So the government has the authority to confiscate the car, but what about the car phone? She turns several pages until she comes to the case annotations following Section 881. She does not find any annotations in the main volume, so she turns to the pocket part. There she finds a case entitled *U.S. v. One 1978 Mercedes Benz*, 711 F.2d 1297 (5th Cir. 1983). The annotation states as follows:
>
> > Although automobile was properly forfeited to government on basis of its use in violation of drug control laws, automobile telephone attached to automobile, which was easily removable, had identity and use separate from automobile, and was separately insured, was not subject to forfeiture with automobile itself, especially where there was no evidence that the telephone was used in furtherance of the underlying crime.
>
> "Well," thinks Natalie, "this case verifies that a car may be properly forfeited to the government, but it limits the forfeiture of the car phone to very specific circumstances. The government is not permitted to confiscate the car phone if the car phone is easily removable, is separately insured, and has not been shown to have been used in furtherance of the crime. I'll have to go back to the file and find out if there are any more facts regarding Bernie's car phone. If the file doesn't contain the information, I'll have to go to the impoundment lot and take a look at it."
>
> Natalie takes the case reporter—the *Federal Reporter, Second Series*—from the shelf and locates the case. She makes a copy of it to read closely later, to see if there are any additional factors that were not contained in the annotation but that could affect the interpretation of the rule regarding car phones. She also makes a note to verify the recent history of this case by using the firm's computerized legal-research service, just to make sure that the case hasn't been recently reversed or modified by a subsequent court decision. She then returns to the office to continue her factual research.

If you are searching for administrative regulations in the *C.F.R.*, you should begin with the index section of the *Index and Finding Aids* volume. This index will allow you to locate the relevant title and the section of the *C.F.R.* that pertains to your issue. The *Congressional Information Service (C.I.S.)* also provides an index to the *C.F.R.* The *C.I.S.* index is helpful in locating *C.F.R.* regulations by subject matter and also in determining the geographical areas affected by the regulation. The *American Digest System* can be of additional help because it provides coverage of court cases dealing with administrative questions. The digests, however, do not contain any agency rulings. Whenever you need to research administrative law, you may discover that the most efficient way to find what you are looking for is simply to call the agency and ask agency personnel how to access information relevant to your research topic.

Regulations issued by administrative agencies are as challenging to read as the laws, or statutes, enacted by legislatures. Generally, in reading and interpreting administrative law, you should apply the same techniques as you would when analyzing statutory law.

Finding Constitutional Law

The federal government and each of the fifty states have their own constitutions describing the powers, responsibilities, and limitations of the various branches of government. Constitutions can be replaced or amended, and it is important that researchers have access to both current and older versions.

The text of the U.S. Constitution can be found in a number of publications. A useful source of federal constitutional law is *The Constitution of the United States of America*, published under the authority of the U.S. Senate and available through the Library of Congress. It includes the full text of the U.S. Constitution, corresponding United States Supreme Court annotations, and a discussion of each provision, including background information on its history and interpretation. Additional constitutional sources are found in the *U.S.C.A.* and the *U.S.C.S.*, both of which contain the text of the U.S. Constitution and its amendments, as well as citations to cases discussing particular constitutional provisions. Annotated state codes provide a similar service for their state constitutions. State constitutions are usually included in the publications containing state statutes.

Updating the Law

Almost every day, new court decisions are made, new regulations are issued, and new statutes are enacted or existing statutes amended. Because the law is ever changing, a critical factor to consider when researching a topic or point of law is whether a given court opinion, statute, or regulation is still valid. A case decided six months ago may prove to be "bad law" today (if it has been reversed or significantly modified on appeal, for example). Similarly, statutes are frequently amended and new statutes enacted. This means that statutory law, too, is constantly changing. When conducting research, you must never assume that the law on a specific issue is the same today as it was last year or even last month.

● **Updating the law—making sure that your research results are still valid—is a crucial step in the research process.**

One way to update your research results is to make sure that you check any supplemental publications to legal sources. For example, legal encyclopedias, case digests, and other sources are updated periodically by the publication of pamphlets or **pocket parts** (small pamphlets that slip into the back cover of a bound volume).

Pocket Part
A separate pamphlet containing recent cases or changes in the law that is used to update hornbooks, legal encyclopedias, and other legal authorities. It is called a "pocket part" because it slips into a sleeve, or pocket, in the back binder of the volume.

DIANE SOROKO has a bachelor of arts degree from Georgia State University and received her paralegal certificate, with honors, from the National Center of Paralegal Training in Atlanta. Soroko has worked for about four years in the area of administrative law, which deals mainly with industries regulated by the federal and state governments.

PARALEGAL PROFILE   Administrative-law Paralegal

What do you like best about your work?

"What I like most about my job is the client contact. I work primarily with immigration and naturalization, telecommunications, and health care. A typical day for me involves monitoring meetings and assisting clients. I enjoy working with people and building relationships to achieve goals. The failure or success of our efforts in such areas as immigration can dramatically affect clients' lives."

What is the greatest challenge that you face in your area of work?

"The greatest challenge for me is the cross-cultural dimension of my job. I deal with many international clients, and cultural differences can be challenging. I have to be sensitive to other perspectives, viewpoints, and customs."

What advice do you have for would-be paralegals in your area of work?

"I recommend a focus on both communication and writing skills. Organizational skills are also critical for all paralegal work and especially in the area of administrative law."

What are some tips for success as a paralegal in your area of work?

"Tips for success as an administrative-law paralegal include having excellent writing, communication, and computer skills. People skills are also an important asset. Don't be afraid to carve out a niche for yourself and aggressively seek what you want to do."

> **"THE GREATEST CHALLENGE FOR ME IS THE CROSS-CULTURAL DIMENSION OF MY JOB."**

You should also consult a citator to make sure that a law, such as a statute or case, has not been modified or overruled since the statute was enacted or the case decided. A **citator** provides a list of legal references that have cited or interpreted the case or law. A *case citator* provides, in addition, a history of the particular case.

Shepard's Citations

Shepard's Citations, which is published by Shepard's/McGraw-Hill, Inc., is a research tool with which all paralegals should become familiar. *Shepard's Citations* contains the most comprehensive system of case citators in the United States. *Shepard's* lists every case published in an official or unofficial reporter by its citation. *Shepard's* citators are available for many different jurisdictions. *Shepard's United States Citations* covers the decisions of the United States Supreme Court. *Shepard's* citators also exist for the reports of every state, the District of Columbia, and Puerto Rico. Every region of the National Reporter System is covered by *Shepard's.* Additionally, *Shepard's*

CITATOR
A book or on-line service that provides the subsequent history and interpretation of a court decision, statute, or regulation and a list of the cases, statutes, and regulations that have interpreted, applied, or modified a statute or regulation.

EXHIBIT 9.10
Shepard's Citations

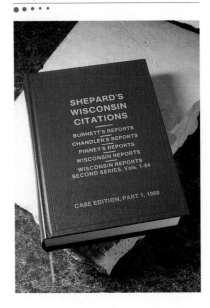

citators cover statutory law, administrative regulations, constitutional law, and legal periodicals. Exhibit 9.10 shows a *Shepard's* citator.

You can use *Shepard's* citators to accomplish several research objectives. For example, *Shepard's* provides parallel citations for the cited case, thus allowing you to locate the case in other official or unofficial reporters. *Shepard's* also lists other cases ("citing cases") that have cited the main case (the "cited case"), which may provide you with useful information. For example, suppose that in researching Hoffman's claim you have found a case on point. You can check *Shepard's Citations* to see what other courts have cited the case (indicating that those courts must have discussed one or more of the issues involved in the cited case). Some of these citing cases may be on point and valuable to your research.

One of the most valuable functions of *Shepard's* is that it provides you with a means to verify the history of a case. For example, if you want to know whether a certain court decision has been reversed by a higher court, *Shepard's* provides that information. Note, though, that it takes some time before the printed versions of *Shepard's* citators are updated. To make absolutely sure that your research is truly up to date, you will want to use one of the on-line citators provided by computerized legal-research services.

On-line Citators

Several computerized legal research services provide on-line citators. On-line citators are extremely useful to legal researchers because they are more up to date than *Shepard's* printed citators. Computerized legal-research services, such as WESTLAW and LEXIS, provide access to several types of citators, including the following:

• *Shepard's Citator Services*—Provides information not yet included in *Shepard's* printed citations (available through both WESTLAW and LEXIS).
• *Shepard's PreView*—Updates *Shepard's* citators with the most recent cases reported in West reporters (available through WESTLAW).
• *QuickCite*—Provides a list of all cases citing a case, including the most recent cases (available through WESTLAW).
• *LexCite*—Provides a listing of the most recent cases citing a case (available through LEXIS).
• *Insta-Cite*—Summarizes the prior and subsequent history of the cited case, and includes references to the cited case made in the *Corpus Juris Secundum* (available through WESTLAW).
• *Auto-Cite*—Summarizes the prior and subsequent history of the cited case, and includes references to the cited case made in *American Law Reports* annotations (available through LEXIS).

These and other on-line citators allow you to update the law within seconds. If you want to learn the direct history of a case, you can go to *Insta-Cite* (on WESTLAW) or *Auto-Cite* (on LEXIS) and immediately find the information you need. For example, suppose that you want to learn if there has been any subsequent history in relation to the case *Ward v. K-Mart Corp,* 136 Ill.2d 132, 554 N.E.2d 223 (1990). If you were using WESTLAW, you would first call up the case by entering *FI* (for "find") and then one of the parallel citations. Within a second or two, the beginning page of the case would appear on the screen. Then you would enter the command to call up *Insta-Cite.* A second or two later, you would view the screen presented in Exhibit 9.11.

If you want more information on the case, such as a list of other cases that have cited it, you could access *Shepard's* citators—or "Shepardize" the case—using either LEXIS or WESTLAW. Again, you would call up the case in question and enter the appropriate command to call up *Shepard's.* Exhibit 9.12 on the next page shows a sample page from the citator for the *North Eastern Reporter* as it appears on the WESTLAW screen.

LEGAL WRITING

As mentioned in this chapter's introduction, legal research and writing often go hand in hand. When you brief cases during the research process, for example, you are engaging in a form of legal writing. When you complete your research, you will need to create a memorandum in which you summarize the results of your research for your supervising attorney to review. As a paralegal, you will find that in addition to drafting research summaries, you will be expected to draft numerous other types of materials. In fact, much of your work as a paralegal will involve writing assignments. In the remainder of this chapter, we look at some of the basic requirements of legal writing and at the kinds of legal materials that paralegals create.

Important Considerations in Legal Writing

As mentioned in Chapter 4, the legal profession is primarily a communications profession. Effective written communications are particularly crucial

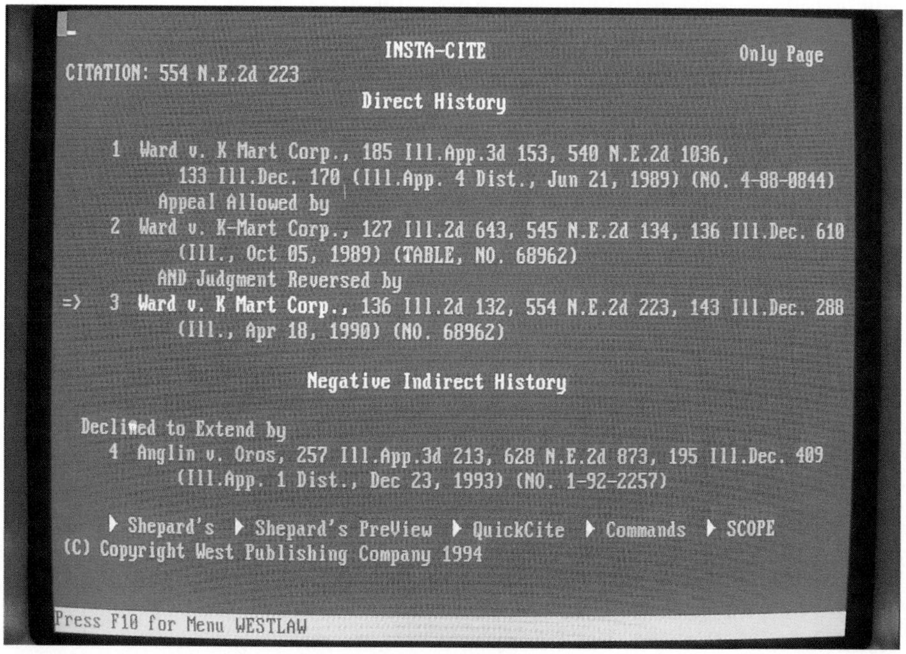

INSTA-CITE Only Page
CITATION: 554 N.E.2d 223
Direct History

1 Ward v. K Mart Corp., 185 Ill.App.3d 153, 540 N.E.2d 1036, 133 Ill.Dec. 170 (Ill.App. 4 Dist., Jun 21, 1989) (NO. 4-88-0844)
Appeal Allowed by
2 Ward v. K-Mart Corp., 127 Ill.2d 643, 545 N.E.2d 134, 136 Ill.Dec. 610 (Ill., Oct 05, 1989) (TABLE, NO. 68962)
AND Judgment Reversed by
=> 3 Ward v. K Mart Corp., 136 Ill.2d 132, 554 N.E.2d 223, 143 Ill.Dec. 288 (Ill., Apr 18, 1990) (NO. 68962)

Negative Indirect History

Declined to Extend by
4 Anglin v. Oros, 257 Ill.App.3d 213, 628 N.E.2d 873, 195 Ill.Dec. 409 (Ill.App. 1 Dist., Dec 23, 1993) (NO. 1-92-2257)

▶ Shepard's ▶ Shepard's PreView ▶ QuickCite ▶ Commands ▶ SCOPE
(C) Copyright West Publishing Company 1994

Press F10 for Menu WESTLAW

EXHIBIT 9.11
A Sample *Insta-Cite* Screen Format

EXHIBIT 9.12
A *Shepard's* Screen Format on WESTLAW

```
                    SHEPARD'S  (Rank 1 of 2)      Page 2 of 13
CITATIONS TO: 554 N.E.2d 223
CITATOR: NORTHEASTERN REPORTER CITATIONS
DIVISION: North Eastern Reporter 2nd
Retrieval                                        Headnote
  No.    —Analysis——  ———Citation———             No.
  1    F  Followed     563 N.E.2d 1228, 1229     5
  2                    565 N.E.2d 687, 689        3
  3    F  Followed     566 N.E.2d 239, 241
  4                    566 N.E.2d 239, 243        4
  5                    567 N.E.2d 423, 426
  6    F  Followed     567 N.E.2d 423, 427        9
  7                    569 N.E.2d 214, 215
  8    D  Distinguished 569 N.E.2d at 216         7
  9    D  Distinguished 569 N.E.2d at 216         9
 10                    569 N.E.2d 579, 583        2
 11                    569 N.E.2d 579, 583        3
 12                    570 N.E.2d 1218, 1222      3
 13    E  Explained    571 N.E.2d 479, 481        4
 14                    571 N.E.2d 815, 817
  ▶ Insta-Cite    ▶ Shepard's PreView   ▶ QuickCite   ▶ Commands  ▶ SCOPE
  Copyright (C) 1994 McGraw-Hill, Inc.; Copyright (C) 1994 West Publishing Co.
Press F10 for Menu WESTLAW
```

ETHICAL CONCERN

The Importance of Finding Current Law

It is easy to forget that the law is continually changing and, in certain areas, changing very quickly. Even though you might have researched a certain legal issue as recently as three months ago—and for a case very similar to the one your supervising attorney is now litigating—it is a mistake to assume that the earlier research results are still valid. Between then and now, a leading case on the issue might have been overruled or a statute amended or a regulatory guideline changed. Even though you may have checked the relevant volume of *Shepard's Citations,* you need to realize that the most recent changes in the law will not be included in printed legal reference materials. To make absolutely certain that your research results are still valid, you should use an on-line citator to see if recent cases or modifications to statutes or regulations affect your research. Failure to update your research results may seriously harm your attorney's chances at success in arguing a client's case. In sum, if your attorney trusts you to do legal research, never rely on yesterday's law.

in the legal arena. For paralegals, good writing skills therefore go hand in hand with successful job performance. The more competent a writer you are, the more likely it is that your finished products will be satisfactory to the attorney with whom you are working. You should also keep in mind that some of your written work, such as correspondence, represents the firm for which you work. A well-written document is a positive reflection on the firm and upholds the firm's reputation for good work. Other important considerations in legal writing include those discussed below.

Accuracy.   A crucial factor in legal writing is accuracy. All experienced writers in any business or other environment normally strive to produce accurate documents. In legal writing, however, accuracy is vital. A word or phrase that is ambiguous, erroneous, or unintentionally omitted from a document could jeopardize a client's legal rights. Generally, you should take special care to proofread carefully any document you write. You want to make sure not only that the document is free of grammatical or spelling errors but also that the information in the document is accurate in every respect and that no crucial clause or information has been omitted.

Legal Terminology.   Always keep in mind that the purpose of any legal document is to *communicate* information. If you are writing a document to be read by an attorney, the use of legal terms presents no problem. When writing to nonlawyers, however, you need to be especially careful when using legal terminology. Although a certain amount of legal terminology in legal writing is unavoidable, you should minimize the use of language that may confuse the reader. If you are writing a letter to a client, for example, either avoid using legal terms that the client may not understand or define such terms as you use them. For example, if you are advising a client of the date on which *voir dire* will take place, consider saying "jury selection"—or per-haps "*voir dire* (jury selection)"—instead.

Writing Approach.   Another consideration in legal writing has to do with writing approach. You should determine at the outset of any writing assign-ment what type of writing is required. Many of your writing assignments will require *objective analysis,* which either focuses on facts or discusses fairly both sides of a legal matter. When you write a memorandum to your supervising attorney summarizing your research results, for example, you will want to be as objective as possible in summarizing how the law applies to a client's case. The attorney will need to know not only of those cases or other laws that support the client's position but also of any cases or laws that favor the opponent's position. To advise the client properly and develop a strategy for litigating or settling the dispute, the attorney must be aware of both the strengths and weaknesses of the client's case.

Other types of writing assignments will require *advocacy,* which involves presenting the facts and issues in a light most favorable to your client. If the writing assignment is intended to advocate a position, the style of writing will be somewhat different from the style in an objective discus-sion of the law. In advocating a position, you are primarily concerned with convincing the reader that the argument proposed is stronger than the oppos-ing party's position. You will need to develop supportive legal arguments and present the matter in the light most favorable to the client. For example, sup-pose that you are asked to draft a *settlement letter* (a letter to an opposing party requesting that a case be settled out of court) to the defendant, Better Homes Store, in the Hoffman case. Your goal in writing is to convince the defendant of the strength of Hoffman's case against the store.

Pleadings and Discovery Documents

Many writing tasks undertaken by paralegals involve forms that must be submitted to the court or to opposing counsel before a trial begins or after the trial has commenced. These documents were discussed in Chapter 6. You can review that chapter for explanations and illustrations of the forms required for pretrial procedures (pleadings, discovery procedures, and pretri-al motions) and for motions made during or just following the trial.

It is especially important that such documents contain the required information and be presented in the appropriate format. Form books and computerized forms offer guidelines, but you should always become famil-iar with the rules of the court with which the documents are being filed to ensure that you use the proper format.

General Legal Correspondence

Paralegals are often asked to draft letters to clients, witnesses, opposing counsel, and others. In this section, you will read about some typical require-ments relating to legal correspondence. Keep in mind, though, that the par-ticular law firm, corporate legal department, or government agency for which you work will probably have its own specific procedures and require-ments that you will need to follow.

ETHICAL CONCERN

"Confidential" Correspondence

As a paralegal, you may be faced with the question of whether you should open let-ters to the attorney for whom you work when the letters are marked "Confidential." For example, suppose that you work for an attorney who is out of the country for two weeks. Because she will be hard to reach during this time, she has instructed you to open all of her mail for her and respond appropriately to certain matters. She has explicitly told you to call her only if an emergency arises. While she is gone, you receive a letter to the attorney that is marked "Confidential." You recognize the sender's name (an attorney who is defend-ing against a lawsuit brought by one of your supervising attorney's clients) and suspect that the letter pertains to the lawsuit. Should you open the letter? Should you hold it until your attorney returns? Or should you try to contact your attorney for advice? To avoid this kind of situation, ask your employer in advance how you should handle confi-dential mail. Some attorneys routinely have their para-legals open this type of mail; others do not.

INFORMATIVE LETTER
A letter that conveys certain information to a client, a witness, an adversary's counsel, or other person regarding some legal matter (such as the date, time, place, and purpose of a meeting).

CONFIRMATION LETTER
A letter that states the substance of a previously conducted verbal discussion to provide a permanent record of the oral conversation.

OPINION (ADVISORY) LETTER
A letter from an attorney to a client that contains a legal opinion on an issue raised by the client's question or legal claim. The opinion is based on a detailed analysis of the law.

DEMAND LETTER
An adversarial letter that attempts to persuade the reader that he or she should accept a position that is favorable to the writer's client—that is, demanding that the reader do or not do a certain thing.

ADDRESS BLOCK
That part of a letter that indicates to whom the letter is addressed. The address block is placed in the upper left-hand portion of the letter, above the salutation (or reference line, if one is included).

Types of Legal Letters. There are several types of legal correspondence, and each type serves a different purpose. An **informative letter** conveys information to another party. As a paralegal, you will write many such letters—to clients, for example, to inform them of current developments in their cases or of upcoming procedures. Informative letters are also sent to opposing counsel, witnesses, or other persons that may be involved in a trial. Additionally, they may be used as transmittal (cover) letters when documents or other materials are sent to a client, a court, opposing counsel, or some other person. Paralegals also frequently write **confirmation letters**—letters that put into written form the contents of an oral discussion. In addition to providing attorneys with a permanent record of earlier conversations, confirmation letters also safeguard against any misinterpretation or misunderstanding of what was communicated orally.

The function of an **opinion letter**, or *advisory letter*, is to provide information and advice. In contrast to informative letters, opinion letters actually give a legal opinion about the matter discussed. Opinion letters provide a detailed analysis of the law as it applies to a particular claim or issue and gives the firm's conclusion, or opinion, on the matter.

- **Because opinion letters issued by a firm reflect legal expertise and advice on which a client may rely, they must always be signed by attorneys.**

The signature of an attorney represents the attorney's acceptance of responsibility for what is stated in the document and can serve as the basis for liability.

Another basic type of letter is the demand letter. **Demand letters** are adversarial in nature and seek to advance the interests of a client. Whatever the content of a demand letter, its purpose is to demand something of the recipient on behalf of the client. A common form of demand letter in litigation firms is a settlement letter. Another example of a demand letter is a letter to a client's debtor, demanding payment for an amount owed.

General Format for Legal Correspondence. Although there are many types of legal letters, the format used for each of these letters is very similar. A legal letter normally includes the components discussed below and illustrated and annotated in Exhibit 9.13 on page 326.

Date, Method of Delivery, and Address Block. All legal correspondence must be *dated*. Dates serve an important function in legal matters. The date of a letter may be important in matters involving legal notice of a particular event. Additionally, legal correspondence normally is filed chronologically. Without any indication of when the letter was written, accurate filing of the letter would be difficult, if not impossible. As a general rule, you should always place a date on every written item that you create, including telephone messages, memos to file, and personal reminders to yourself.

Below the date is a line indicating how the letter was sent (if other than by U.S. mail) and the **address block**, which shows to whom the letter is addressed. This information is located on the upper part of the page at the left-hand margin. If the letter was sent by Federal Express, the line before the recipient's name and address will read VIA FEDERAL EXPRESS. If the letter

---

DEVELOPING PARALEGAL SKILLS

Writing to Clients

 Leslie Linden works as a paralegal for Sandra O'Connell, a sole practitioner who owns a small family-law practice. Sandra asks Leslie to draft a letter to a client, Karen Young, explaining that her divorce hearing is scheduled for June 3, 1995, and informing her that she needs to be present in court on that date. Leslie is also supposed to tell the client what the procedure will be and ask her to call the office to make an appointment to discuss the proceeding before June 3.

Leslie sits down at her word processor and begins to draft the letter to the client. First, she types the date, the address block, and the salutation. Because it is a formal letter, she uses "Dear Mrs. Young" in the salutation. Next, she begins the body of the letter:

> The hearing for your divorce is scheduled to take place on Monday, June 3, 1995, at 10 A.M. The hearing will be conducted in Room 2B of the Jefferson County Courthouse in Jefferson City. Please arrive at the courthouse by 9:30 A.M.
>
> Because this is a no-fault divorce state, your divorce is not contested, and we have worked out your property settlement in advance, the hearing will be brief. We expect you to be on the stand for only fifteen minutes at the most. You will be asked to make a statement concerning your marital situation, and the judge will ask you a few questions.
>
> Ms. O'Connell would like you to call the office and schedule an appointment, at your convenience, to prepare you for the hearing. She will discuss with you at that time what you will say on the stand and the kinds of questions that the judge will probably ask you. Please contact the office at your earliest convenience.

Leslie then inserts the closing, leaves four lines, and types her name and just below it her title, Legal Assistant. She prints the letter on the firm's stationery, proofreads it carefully, and sends it to Mrs. Young.

---

is hand delivered, the line will read BY HAND DELIVERY. Communication by facsimile can be described by the words BY FAX or BY FACSIMILE. The address block should contain the name of the person to whom the letter is written, the person's title, and the name and address of the person's firm or place of business.

Reference Line and Salutation. Following the method of delivery and the address block, the writer may include a **reference line** identifying the matter discussed in the letter. In a letter regarding a pending lawsuit, the reference line may contain the name of the case, its case file (or docket) number, and a brief notation of the nature of the legal dispute. Many attorneys also include the firm's file number for the case. In an informative letter, the reference line may take the form of a title. For example, a reference line in a letter concerning the closing procedures for a financing transaction may read "RE: Closing Procedures for ABC Company's $4,000,000 Financing Package."

REFERENCE LINE
The portion of the letter that indicates the matter to be discussed in the letter, such as "RE: Summary of Cases Applying the Family and Medical Leave Act of 1993." The reference line is placed just below the address block and above the salutation.

EXHIBIT 9.13
Components of a Legal Letter
• • • • •

Jeffers, Gilmore & Dunn
553 Fifth Avenue
Suite 101
Nita City, NI 48801

Telephone (616) 555-9690
Fax (616) 555-9679

Date	June 1, 1995
Method of Delivery	VIA FEDERAL EXPRESS
Address Block	John Francis Doyle, Jr., Esq. Doyle & Associates 100 Peachtree Street, N.E. Atlanta, Georgia 30303
Reference Line	RE: <u>Lindstrom v. Bente-Friedman & Co.</u>, Civ. #89-110987
Salutation	Dear Mr. Doyle:
Body of Letter	After reviewing the materials that you sent pursuant to my document request, I have concluded that you have not complied with the request. In my request, I sought "all documents pertaining to the financial condition of Bente-Friedman & Co. during 1992." You have responded by producing financial information for only two months of 1992. This response is unsatisfactory. I therefore ask again that you provide me with all documents pertaining to the financial condition of Bente-Friedman & Co. during 1992. Should you have any questions regarding this matter, please do not hesitate to call me.
Closing	Very truly yours,
Signature and Title	Allen P. Gilmore Attorney at Law
Initials of Attorney and Legal Secretary	APG/ec
Others Receiving Copies of Letter	cc: W. Danforth Adams, Jr., Esq. Charlotte Baer Lindstrom

SALUTATION
The formal greeting to the addressee of the letter. The salutation is placed just below the reference line.

The **salutation**, which appears just below the reference line, is a greeting to the addressee. Because legal correspondence is a professional means of communication, the salutation, as well as the body of the letter, should be formal in tone. There are, of course, circumstances in which a formal greeting may not be necessary. For example, if the addressee is someone you know quite well, it may be appropriate to address the person by his or her first name, rather than by "Mr." or "Ms." In these situations, you must use your discretion to determine the appropriate level of formality. Generally, when in doubt, use a formal salutation.

Body and Closing.   The main part of the letter is the body of the letter. The body of the letter should be formal and should effectively communicate information to the reader. As a representative of the firm, the paralegal must be careful to proofread all outgoing correspondence to ensure that the letter contains accurate information, is clearly written, and is free of any grammatical or spelling errors.

Following the body of the letter are standard concluding sentences. These final sentences are usually courteous statements such as "Thank you for your time and attention to this matter," or "Should you have any questions or comments, please call me at the above-listed number." These brief concluding statements are followed by the **closing**. The closing in legal correspondence is formal—for example, "Sincerely yours" or "Very truly yours."

Finally, you should always include your title in any correspondence written by you on behalf of the firm. Your title ("Paralegal" or "Legal Assistant" or other title) should immediately follow your name. This, of course, is not a concern when you prepare correspondence for an attorney who will provide a signature.

CLOSING
A final comment to a letter that is placed above the signature, such as "Very truly yours."

The Internal Memorandum

The internal legal memorandum, as the term implies, is prepared for internal use within a law firm, legal department, or other organization or agency. As a paralegal, you may be asked to draft a legal memorandum for your supervising attorney. Generally, the legal memo presents a thorough summary and analysis of a particular legal problem.

The attorney for which the document is prepared may be relying on the memo for a number of reasons. For example, the attorney may be preparing a brief on behalf of a client or an opinion letter regarding a client's claim. Thus, if you are asked to draft the memo, you will want it to be extremely thorough and clearly written. Because the legal memo is directed to attorneys who are knowledgeable in the law, there is no need to avoid sophisticated legal terminology or to define basic legal theories or procedures.

The purpose of the memo is to provide an attorney with all relevant information regarding the case, so the document is written objectively. It is an explanatory memo informing the attorney of all sides of the issues presented, including both the strengths and weaknesses of the client's claim or defense. You should keep the following in mind:

● **Your goal in drafting a legal memorandum is to inform, explain, and evaluate the client's claim or defense.**

A legal memorandum is organized in a logical manner. Although there is no one way to structure the legal memo, most are divided into sections that perform distinct functions. Of course, if the law firm or the attorney for whom you are working prefers a particular format, that format should be followed. Generally, legal memos contain the following sections:

- Heading.
- Statement of the facts.
- Questions presented.
- Brief conclusion to questions presented.
- Discussion and analysis of the facts and the applicable law.
- Conclusion.

Heading.   The *heading* of a legal memorandum is analogous to the address block in a letter. It contains four pieces of information:

- The name of the person for whom the memo was prepared.
- The name of the person submitting the memo.
- The date on which the memo is submitted.
- A brief description of the matter, usually in the form of a reference line.

Exhibit 9.14 illustrates a sample heading for a legal memorandum.

Statement of the Facts.   The *statement of the facts* describes the factual elements of the dispute. Only the relevant facts are included in this section, and the facts must be presented objectively. As indicated earlier in this section on legal writing, a legal memorandum requires *objective* analysis and writing. Therefore, you should never omit facts that are unfavorable to the client's claim or defense. The attorney for whom you work needs to know all of the facts that will influence the outcome of the case.

Presenting the factual events chronologically often helps to clarify the factual pattern in a case. Alternatively, facts relating to the same issue can be grouped together. The latter organizational technique is especially useful when the facts are complicated and numerous legal issues are presented.

Exhibit 9.15 indicates what kinds of information are typically included in a statement of the facts. It also shows what writing style is generally used.

Questions Presented.   The *questions presented* section sets forth the legal issues presented by the factual circumstances described in the statement-of-the-facts section. The questions should be specific and straightforward. They should refer to the parties by name, succinctly set out the

EXHIBIT 9.14
Legal Memorandum—Heading

MEMORANDUM

DATE: August 6, 1995

TO: Allen P. Gilmore, Partner

FROM: Elena Lopez, Paralegal

RE: Neely, Rachel: Emotional Distress—File No. 95-2146
        Neely, Rachel, and Melanie: Emotional Distress—File
            No. 95-2147

EXHIBIT 9.15
Legal Memorandum—Statement of the Facts

STATEMENT OF THE FACTS

Ms. Rachel Neely ("Neely") and Ms. Melanie Neely ("Melanie"), our clients, seek advice in connection with possible emotional distress claims against Mr. Miles Thompson ("Thompson"). The claims arose as a result of (1) Neely's distress at hearing a car crash, caused by Thompson and involving her eleven-year-old daughter, Melanie, and subsequently viewing Melanie's injuries; and (2) Melanie's distress related to statements made by Thompson.

In February 1993, Neely and Melanie moved to Union City from San Francisco. Neely immediately began working for an investment firm in downtown Union City. At that firm, she became acquainted with the defendant, Thompson. Thompson was Neely's boss. At first, the two had a friendly, professional relationship. During this time, Thompson and Neely spent much time together socially and learned much about each other. Thompson, for example, knew that Neely had left San Francisco after her marriage ended. Neely had confided in Thompson that the divorce and the events preceding it were extremely traumatic for herself and for Melanie. Melanie knew Thompson and was comfortable with him. Thompson had spent time with Melanie and knew that Melanie had suffered emotionally because of her parents' bitter divorce.

The relationship between Thompson and Neely became strained approximately six months after Neely began working with Thompson. Tension between the parties arose as a result of Thompson's expression of romantic interest in Neely. Neely, who was dating someone else, had no romantic interest in Thompson and communicated to him her lack of interest in pursuing that type of relationship with him.

On April 2, 1995, Thompson visited the Neely home. Melanie was not fully aware of the problem her mother was having with Thompson. Thompson came to the door, and Melanie, who was alone in the house, let him in. Thompson invited Melanie for a ride in his Corvette. Melanie willingly went with him. Meanwhile, Neely, who had gone to the grocery store to buy some milk, returned to the house to find Melanie missing. She panicked, called the neighbors, and then called the police.

Thompson, who claims that he took Melanie for a ride so that she could be informed about her mother's "bad behavior," drove around Union City with Melanie for approximately thirty minutes. During this ride, Thompson told Melanie that her mother was a "wicked, selfish, woman, who could care less about Melanie." Thompson also told Melanie that her mother was a "no good, sex-crazed woman who would leave Melanie once the right man came along." Upon returning to the Neely home, Thompson made a left turn from Oak Street onto Maple Road, and his car was hit by an oncoming vehicle. According to the police report of the accident, Thompson's blood-alcohol level indicated that he was intoxicated.

The Neely home is located on the corner of the intersection of Maple Road and Oak Street. Neely heard the crash and ran outside. Seeing the accident and recognizing Thompson's car, she approached the site of the accident. There she saw Melanie bleeding profusely from head injuries. As a result of the accident, Melanie spent two days at Union City Memorial Hospital, where she was kept under observation for possible internal injuries. Melanie continues to be severely depressed and emotionally unstable as a result of Thompson's comments. Additionally, she has frequent nightmares and finds it difficult to speak without stuttering. Since the time of the accident, she has been under psychiatric therapy for these problems. Neely, who fainted after viewing her daughter's injuries, spent one day in Union City Memorial Hospital for extreme anxiety and trauma.

legal problem, and specifically indicate the important and relevant events. The questions-presented section may involve just one simple issue or a number of complex issues. Regardless of the complexity of the matter, this section helps bring the main points of the conflict into focus. See Exhibit 9.16 for an example of how questions presented might be phrased.

EXHIBIT 9.16
Legal Memorandum—Questions Presented

QUESTIONS PRESENTED

1. Does Neely have a claim for the negligent infliction of emotional distress as a result of viewing the injuries sustained by her daughter in a car accident caused by Thompson's negligence?

2. Does Melanie have a claim for the intentional infliction of emotional distress arising out of Thompson's statements to her on April 2, 1995?

Brief Conclusion. The *brief conclusion* sets forth succinct responses to the questions presented in the previous section. The responses may vary in length. For example, as indicated in Exhibit 9.17, certain questions can be answered simply by a "yes," "no," "probably so," or "probably not," followed by a brief sentence summarizing the reason for that answer. For complicated legal questions, a more detailed statement might be appropriate. Even so, each conclusion should be limited to one paragraph.

Discussion and Analysis. The *discussion and analysis* section, as the phrase implies, discusses and analyzes each issue to be resolved. If the facts of the dispute concern only one legal issue, the entire discussion will revolve around that. When multiple issues are involved, as is often the situation, you should organize the discussion into separate parts so that each legal issue can be analyzed separately. For example, if the dispute involves two potential legal claims, the discussion could be divided into two sections with a descriptive heading for each section.

The discussion section should contain a thorough analysis of the law as it applies to each issue, and you should support any conclusions you have drawn on the points of law discussed by including proper citations to legal authorities. Sometimes, it is effective to quote directly from the text of a statute, court opinion, or other legal source. You should not rely too heavily on quoted material, however. Although quotations from a case or other legal authority can lend extremely helpful support, you should always keep the following fact in mind:

EXHIBIT 9.17
Legal Memorandum—Brief Conclusion

BRIEF CONCLUSION

1. Probably not. Neely cannot recover under the rule that is currently applied in this jurisdiction. This rule requires that the plaintiff be present at the scene when the accident occurs.

2. Most likely, yes. Thompson's conduct toward Melanie appears to have been (1) reckless, (2) outrageous and extreme, and (3) the direct cause of Melanie's severe emotional distress.

- **The attorney for whom the memo is prepared wants to see your analysis, not a reiteration of a court's opinion.**

Exhibit 9.18 presents a portion of a discussion section in a legal memorandum.

Conclusion.   The *conclusion* presents your opinion of how the issues discussed may be resolved. Exhibit 9.19 on page 333 shows an example of a conclusion to a legal memorandum. The concluding section may acknowledge the fact that research into a particular area bore little fruit. The conclusion also may inform the attorney that more information is needed or that a certain issue needs to be evaluated further. Finally, this section presents you with an opportunity to make strategical suggestions. Paralegals should feel comfortable—especially after a careful legal analysis—in recommending a course of action. Not only do your recommendations reflect thorough analysis, but they also indicate that you are willing to exercise initiative and make a mature judgment, which will be helpful to your supervising attorney.

EXHIBIT 9.18

Legal Memorandum—Discussion

DISCUSSION (excerpt)

I. Negligent Infliction of Emotional Distress

Recovery Restriction

An individual's right to emotional tranquility is recognized by the law protecting persons against the negligent infliction of emotional distress. The method for determining whether protection should be afforded for emotional distress caused by the knowledge of a third person's injury as a result of a defendant's negligent action is clear in this jurisdiction. The rule adopted in this jurisdiction is the "impact rule."

The impact rule requires that a plaintiff alleging emotional distress must also suffer an impact (directly and physically) from the same force that injured the victim. Saechao v. Matsakoun, 717 P.2d 165, 168 (Or.App. 1986). This test provides the courts with a "bright line" from which they can easily determine the relationship between compensability and the defendant's breach of a duty owed to the victim. Id. at 169. The impact rule, which evolved as a result of the law's early reluctance to acknowledge the authenticity of emotional distress claims, avoids the problems of floodgate litigation. Id. at 169. It strictly limits a victim's recovery.

Some strong arguments can be made against the application of the impact rule. Although the rule limits a defendant's liability and offers an easy decision-making criterion for the courts, it also lends itself to arbitrary and often unjust results. The impact rule makes an after-the-fact determination of duty, protecting those suffering from emotional distress only if they also suffered harm directly and physically as a result of the defendant's negligence. Id. at 171.

The impact rule has been applied by the Union County courts. The rule's bright line immediately eliminates Neely's possibility of recovery. She was in her house when the accident occurred and witnessed the accident scene after the crash had occurred. Thompson would not owe a duty to protect Neely from negligently inflicted emotional distress under the impact rule.

Mapping Out a Research Strategy

Bill Cather is a paralegal in a criminal-defense firm located in a major metropolitan area. Bill has been assigned a research project on a case involving one of the firm's clients, who was arrested for drug dealing. The police had seen the client making phone calls from a public telephone booth and suspected that he was engaged in drug trafficking. The police placed an electronic device into the phone booth—without a warrant—and learned that what they suspected was true. Bill is now going to map out his research strategy before he undertakes the project.

STEP ONE: IDENTIFYING THE ISSUE

Bill's first step is to analyze the facts and identify the issue involved. He knows that the police may search certain areas without a warrant. The courts determine which areas are entitled to the protection of a warrant by considering whether a person has a reasonable expectation of privacy in the area. Bill wonders whether a person has a reasonable expectation of privacy in a public phone booth. Do people customarily expect others to hear what they are saying on the phone when they are in a phone booth with the door closed? Bill will have to research the issue. If a person using a phone booth is entitled to a reasonable expectation of privacy, then probably the police would have to obtain a search warrant before using an electronic device to listen to—and record—any telephone conversation within a public phone booth.

STEP TWO: IDENTIFYING SECONDARY SOURCES

Because he is not familiar with the topic that he is going to research, Bill will begin by doing some background research. He can choose from a variety of secondary sources, such as legal encyclopedias and treatises. He prefers legal encyclopedias because they are easy to read and understand. He particularly prefers the *Corpus Juris Secundum (C.J.S.)* because it provides numerous citations to cases. He writes "*C.J.S.*" on his list as the first source to consult.

STEP THREE: IDENTIFYING PRIMARY SOURCES

Next he will want to consult the various primary sources of law. He will want to look at the Fourth Amendment to the U.S. Constitution to find the exact wording of the amendment's guarantee of freedom from unreasonable searches and seizures and the warrant requirement. He can find the Constitution in the *U.S.C.A.* He writes "Constitution" on his list as a primary source to consult. He will also want to consult state and federal statutory codes to find out whether the police's action violated a wiretapping statute, if one exists, so he writes "federal and state statutory codes" on his list. To find cases on point—in addition to those cited in the *C.J.S.*—relating to the topic, Bill can consult case digests.

STEP FOUR: UPDATING AND VERIFYING RESEARCH RESULTS

After Bill finds and reads through relevant cases, he will have to Shepardize them to verify that they are still good law. *Shepard*'s will also provide an additional source of case law because it includes every subsequent case that cited the case being Shepardized. He writes "*Shepard's*" on his list.

Bill will also want to either run a computer search or return to the secondary sources, such as an encyclopedia, to make certain that he has not overlooked any case law. As a final measure, he will want to use an online citator to verify that his research results are as up to date as possible. Bill writes "*C.J.S.* and citators—WESTLAW or LEXIS" as the final item on his list. Once Bill is comfortable with the results of his research, he will return to his office and prepare a memorandum of law to inform his supervisor of his findings.

CONCLUSION

It is unlikely that Neely has a cause of action against Thompson for the emotional distress that she allegedly suffered due to Thompson's negligence.

It is likely that Melanie has a cause of action for the intentional infliction of emotional distress based on Thompson's outrageous comments to her about her mother.

Note that Neely might pursue, on her own behalf, a claim for the intentional infliction of emotional distress against Thompson for Thompson's reckless behavior in taking Melanie from her home and telling Melanie outrageous things. I recommend that we speak with Neely about the effect on her of Thompson's statements to Melanie. This, in my opinion, is a strong claim. I believe that we could argue successfully that Thompson intended to injure Neely through this egregious act.

EXHIBIT 9.19
Legal Memorandum—Conclusion

KEY TERMS AND CONCEPTS

address block 324	demand letter 324	pocket part 318
annotation 300	digest 298	primary source 294
briefing a case 311	headnote 309	reference line 325
case on "all fours" 297	informative letter 324	reporter 304
case on point 297	IRAC method 311	salutation 326
citation 304	mandatory authority 297	secondary source 294
citator 319	opinion 310	syllabus 308
closing 327	opinion letter 324	treatise 301
code 312	parallel citation 304	
confirmation letter 324	persuasive authority 297	

CHAPTER SUMMARY

1. Primary sources of law consist of all documents that establish the law, including court decisions, statutes, regulations, constitutions, and presidential orders. Secondary sources of law are sources written about the law, such as legal encyclopedias, case digests, annotations, Restatements of the Law, treatises, and periodicals.

2. The research process involves five steps: defining the issue, determining the goals of the research project, consulting secondary sources, researching primary sources, and summarizing research results. In researching case law, the researcher's goal is to find cases that are both on point (ideally, cases on "all fours") and mandatory authorities. Mandatory author-

ities are all legal authorities (statutes, regulations, constitutions, or cases) that courts must follow in making their decisions. In contrast, courts are not bound to follow persuasive authorities (such as cases decided in other jurisdictions).

3. Most state and federal trial court decisions are not published in printed volumes. State appellate court opinions, including those of state supreme courts, are normally published in state reporters, although many states have eliminated their own reporters in favor of West's National Reporter System. Federal trial court opinions are published unofficially in West's *Federal Supplement,* and opinions from the federal circuit courts of appeals are published unofficially in West's

Federal Reporter. United States Supreme Court opinions are published officially in the *United States Reports,* published by the federal government, and unofficially in West's *Supreme Court Reporter* and the *Lawyers' Edition of the Supreme Court Reports.* The latter is published by the Lawyers Cooperative Publishing Company.

4. In reading and analyzing case law, it is essential to understand the significance of the various components of a case. The IRAC (Issue, Rule, Application, and Conclusion) method is a helpful tool in summarizing the essential aspects of a case. Legal professionals often use an analytical technique called case briefing to reduce the content of the case to its essentials. The case brief is similar to an IRAC analysis, but it also includes background and facts.

5. Federal statutes are published officially in the *United States Code (U.S.C.).* The *U.S.C.* organizes statutes into fifty subjects, or titles, and further subdivides each title into chapters (sections) and subchapters. The researcher can find a statute in the *U.S.C.* by searching through the topical outlines, by looking in the index, or by looking under the act's popular name in the volume entitled *Popular Name Table.* The *United States Code Annotated* and the *United States Code Service* are unofficial publications of federal statutes. Both of these sources are useful to researchers because they provide annotations and citations to other resources.

6. Reading and analyzing statutory language is often difficult. In reading statutory law, you should note the statute's provisions concerning its coverage and effective date, the class or groups of people to whom it applies, the type of conduct being regulated by the statute, and any exception to the statute's coverage. In interpreting statutory law, the paralegal can turn to previous judicial interpretations of the statute, if any exist, and the legislative history of the statute.

7. Regulations issued by federal administrative agencies are primary sources of law. Agency regulations are published in the *Code of Federal Regulations (C.F.R.),* which follows a format similar to that of the *U.S.C.* The U.S. Constitution can be found in a number of publications, including the extensively annotated official publication, which is available through the Library of Congress. Annotated versions of state constitutions are also available.

8. A critical requirement in legal research is making sure that the research results obtained are still valid. Printed legal sources are commonly updated through the periodic publication of supplemental pamphlets or pocket parts. The various volumes of *Shepard's Citations* allow the researcher to verify whether a case, statute, or regulation represents current law by indicating whether the case has been overruled or reversed, the statute repealed or amended, the regulation voided or superseded, and the like. On-line citators, including *Auto-Cite* (LEXIS) and *Insta-Cite* (WESTLAW) enable the researcher to access recent cases, statutes, or regulations (or amendments or modifications to existing statutes or regulations) and thus ensure that research results are as up to date as possible.

9. Legal writing requires excellent writing skills, and special care must be taken to ensure that legal documents are free of grammatical and spelling errors. Other important considerations in legal writing include making sure that legal documents are accurate in every respect, using legal terminology appropriately, and knowing whether a writing project calls for an objective or adversarial writing approach.

10. Much legal writing consists of documents relating to litigation procedures, such as pleadings and discovery documents. These important forms of legal writing were discussed in Chapter 6.

11. Paralegals commonly draft the following types of letters: informative letters (to notify clients or others of some action or procedure or to transmit documents), confirmation letters (to create a written record of an oral transaction or agreement), opinion letters (to convey to a client or other party a formal legal opinion or advice on an issue), and demand letters (to advance the client's cause by demanding something from an adversarial party on the client's behalf).

12. The internal legal memorandum is a thoroughly researched and objectively written summation of the facts, issues, and applicable law relating to a particular legal claim. The purpose of the memo is to inform the attorney for whom the document is written of the strengths and weaknesses of the client's position. Generally, the legal memo is presented in a format that includes the following sections: heading, statement of the facts, questions presented, brief conclusion, discussion and analysis of the facts and the applicable law, and conclusion.

QUESTIONS FOR REVIEW

1. What is the difference between primary and secondary sources of law? How are these sources used in legal research?

2. What is a case on point? What is a case on "all fours"? Why is finding such a case important when researching case law? What is the difference between a mandatory authority and a persuasive authority?

3. How are court decisions published? What information is contained in a case citation? What is a parallel citation? In what reporter would you find a case decided by a U.S. court of appeals?

4. What are the various components of a case? What is the IRAC method? What is meant by "briefing a case"?

5. In what official publications would you find federal statutes and administrative regulations? How could you locate constitutional law?

6. What are some techniques for interpreting and analyzing statutory law?

7. Why is it important to find the most current law? How can you verify that your research results are up to date?

8. What are some important considerations in legal writing? What is the difference between objective and adversarial writing? When would each approach be appropriate?

9. What are the components of a legal letter? Name and describe four types of legal correspondence.

10. What are the components of an internal legal memorandum? What is the purpose of the memo, and for whom is it written?

ETHICAL QUESTIONS

1. Barbara Coltiers is a legal assistant in a very busy litigation practice. She gets a call from a nervous attorney in her firm thirty minutes before the attorney is to appear in court. He wants her to do some research before he goes to court. He has just heard about a case that might help him win and gives her the citation. Because he is in a hurry, he gives her the wrong volume number. She has a hard time finding the case, but after about fifteen minutes of searching turns to the table of cases and locates the citation. She quickly copies the case and runs to his office with it so that he can hurry across the street to the court for his appearance. She is in such a hurry that she forgets to use *Insta-Cite* to check the subsequent history of the case.

It turns out that the case had been overruled by the state supreme court and was therefore no longer controlling in the jurisdiction. The attorney is chastised by the judge for citing it. In fact, the judge is so annoyed with the attorney for making an argument that was not based on existing law that he denies the attorney's motion and makes the attorney pay the other side's court costs. When the client finds out

why the motion was denied, she is irate. Does the client have any remedy against the attorney? Against Barbara?

2. John Hernandez is studying at a local college to be a legal assistant. The college has WESTLAW for its students to use. The software license specifically prohibits the faculty or students of the college from using the program for personal work. John knows that Kathy has a part-time job with a law firm, and he becomes aware that Kathy is using WESTLAW regularly to do research for her supervising attorney in that firm. What should John do?

3. David Thomas is sending out a letter to a client. It is an informative letter advising the client of the status of her case and explaining what the next step in the litigation process will be. David signs the letter without including his title. He mails the letter to the client. The client has questions, and she calls David, thinking that he is an attorney. How should David handle this situation? What should he have done to prevent it?

PRACTICE QUESTIONS AND ASSIGNMENTS

1. Mr. John D. Consumer bought a new car eight months ago. The car frequently stalls. The problem began the first week after he purchased the vehicle. It stalled late at night on an expressway while he was returning home from a business trip. It has stalled at least monthly since then, often in potentially dangerous areas. Not only has he taken the car to the dealer, who has repeatedly attempted to repair the problem without success, but he has also notified the manufacturer in writing of the problem. Most states have a lemon law that requires dealers to replace vehicles that cannot be repaired, even if the warranty has expired. Does your state have a lemon law? If so, would it help Mr. Consumer?

Research this question and try to find the answer to Mr. Consumer's problem. Begin by making a list of legal and factual terms that are relevant to the issue. Then do the following:

a. Locate the index to the annotated version of your state statutes. Using your list of terms, look in the index for citations to relevant statutes. Write down the citations.

b. Now that you have found relevant citations, go to the volume of the statutory code containing the cited sections and read those sections. (Be sure to check the pocket part of the volume.) What answer does the statute in your state give to John D. Consumer's problem?

2. Using the annotated version of your state statutes, look for relevant case law on Mr. Consumer's problem. If no annotated version of your state statute exists or if no cases appear in the annotated version—or if you want to learn to use another source—locate a state digest. Find the relevant section(s) and locate cases that interpret the statute and that are as similar to Mr. Consumer's problem as possible.

a. Write down the citations to no more than three relevant cases. Now look up those cases in the case reporters.

b. Read through the syllabus and headnotes of each case. Do the cases appear to be relevant? If not, go back to the annotated statute or digest and look for other cases that are relevant.

c. What did you find? Did the courts' application of the statute change your answer to Mr. Consumer's problem?

3. Shepardize one of the cases you found in researching Mr. Consumer's problem. Write down the results. Is the case still good law? If you find a citation to a subsequent case on the same issue, look at that case. Does the subsequent case change your answer to Practice Question 2 above? If you have access to WESTLAW, use *Insta-Cite* to check the recent history of the subsequent case cited in *Shepard's*. Does the information you found using *Insta-Cite* affect your answer to Practice Question 2?

APPENDICES

APPENDIX A

MASTERING *WEST'S PARALEGAL TODAY:* HOW TO STUDY LEGAL CONCEPTS AND PROCEDURES

The law sometimes is considered a difficult subject because it uses a specialized vocabulary and also requires substantial time and effort to learn. Those who work with and teach law believe that the subject matter is exciting and definitely worth your efforts. Everything in *West's Paralegal Today: The Essentials,* including this appendix, has been written for the precise purpose of helping you learn the most important aspects of law and legal procedures.

Learning is a lifelong process. Your learning of legal concepts and procedures will not end when you finish your paralegal studies. On the contrary, your paralegal studies mark the beginning of your learning process in regard to law and legal procedures. Just as valuable to you as the knowledge base you can acquire from mastering the legal concepts and terms in *West's Paralegal Today* is a knowledge of *how to learn* those legal concepts and terms. The focus in this appendix, therefore, is on developing learning skills that you can apply to any subject matter and any time throughout your career.

The suggestions and study tips offered in this appendix can help you "learn how to learn" law and procedures and maximize your chances of success as a paralegal student. They can also help you build lifelong learning habits that you can use in other classes and throughout your career as a paralegal.

MASTERING YOUR TEXT

A mistake commonly made by students is the assumption that the best way to understand the content of written material is to read and reread that material. True, if you read through a chapter ten times, you probably have acquired a knowledge of its contents, but think of the time you have spent in the process. What you want to strive for is using your time *effectively*. We offer here some suggestions on how to study the chapters of *West's Paralegal Today* most effectively.

Read One Section at a Time

A piano student once said to her teacher, "This piece is so complicated. How can I possibly learn it?" The teacher responded, "It's simple: measure by measure." That advice can be applied to any challenging task. As a paralegal student, you are faced with the task of learning complicated legal concepts and procedures. By dividing up your work into manageable units, you will find that before long, you have achieved your goal. Each chapter in *West's Paralegal Today* is divided into several major sections. By concentrating on sections, rather than chapters, you will find it easier to master the chapter's contents.

Once you have read through a section, do not stop there. Go back through the section again and organize the material in your mind. Outlining the section is one way to mentally organize what you have read.

Make an Outline

An outline is simply a method for organizing information. The reason an outline can be helpful is that it illustrates visually how concepts relate to each other. Outlining can be done as part of your reading of each section, but your outline will be more accurate (and helpful later on) if you have already read through a section and have a general understanding of the topics covered within that section.

The Benefits of Outlining.   Although you may not believe that you need to outline, our experience has been that the act of *physically* writing an outline for a chapter helps most students to improve greatly their ability to retain and master the material being studied. Even if you make an outline that is no more than the headings in the text, you will be studying more efficiently than you would be otherwise.

Outlining is also a paralegal skill. As a paralegal, you will need to present legal concepts and fact patterns in an outline format. For example, paralegals frequently create legal memoranda to summarize their research results. The legal memorandum is usually presented in an outline format, which indicates how the topics covered in the memo relate to one another logically or sequentially. There is no better time to master the skill of outlining than the present, while you are a student. You can learn this skill by outlining sections and chapters of *West's Paralegal Today.*

Identify the Main Concepts in Each Section.   You can use the chapter outlines at the beginning of each chapter as a starting point on your outlines for each section and chapter. The chapter-opening outlines include the headings of each major section within the chapter and the basic subheadings within each section. You use these headings as a guide when creating a more thorough and detailed outline of each section. Be careful, though. To make an effective outline you have to be selective. Outlines that contain all the information in the text are not very useful. Your objective in outlining is to identify main concepts and to arrange more detailed concepts under those main concepts. Therefore, in outlining, your first goal is to *identify the main concepts in each section.* Often the large, first-level headings within your textbook and in the chapter-opening outlines are sufficient as identifiers of the major concepts within each section. You may decide, however, that you want to phrase an identifier in a way that is more meaningful to you.

Outline Format.   Your outline should consist of several levels written in a standard outline format. The most important concepts are assigned an upper-case roman numeral; the second most important, a capital letter; the third most important, numbers; the fourth most important, lower-case letters; and the fifth most important, lower-case roman numerals. The number of levels you use in an outline varies, of course, with the complexity of the subject matter. In some outlines, or portions of outlines, you may need to use only two levels. In others, you may need as many as five or more levels.

Consider Marking Your Text

From kindergarten through high school, you typically did not own your own textbooks. They were made available by the school system. You were told not to mark in them. Now that you own your own text for a course, your learning can be greatly improved by marking your text. There is a trade-off here. The more you mark up your textbook, the less you will receive from your bookstore when you sell it back at the end of the semester. The benefit is a better understanding of the subject matter, and the cost is the reduction in the price you receive for the resale of the text. Additionally, if you want a text that you can mark with your own notations, you necessarily have to buy a new one or a used one that has no markings. Both carry a higher price tag than a used textbook with markings.

The Benefits of Marking.   Marking is helpful because it helps you to become an *active* participant in the mastery of the material. Researchers have shown that the physical act of marking, just like the physical act of outlining, helps you better retain the material. The better the material is organized in your mind, the more you will remember. There are two types of readers—passive and active. The active reader outlines and/or marks. Active readers typically do better on exams. Perhaps one of the reasons that active readers retain more is because the physical act of outlining and/or marking requires greater concentration. It is through greater concentration that more is remembered.

Different Ways of Marking.   The most commonly used form of marking is to underline important points. The second most commonly used method is to use a felt-tipped highlighter, or marker, in yellow or some other transparent color. Marking also includes circling, numbering, using arrows, brief notes, or any other method that allows you to locate things when you go back to skim the pages in your textbook prior to an exam—or when creating your outline, if you mark your text first and then outline it.

Points to Remember When Marking.   Here are two important points to remember when marking your text:

1. *Read through the entire section before you begin marking.* You cannot mark a section until you know what is important, and you cannot know what is important until you read through the whole section.
2. *Do not mark too extensively.* You should mark your text selectively. If you fill up each page with arrows, asterisks, circles, and underlines, marking will be of little use. When you go back to review the material, you will not be able to find what was important. The key is *selective* activity. Mark each page in a way that allows you to see the most important points at a glance.

Memory Devices

During the course of your study of *West's Paralegal Today*, you will encounter numerous legal terms that are, most likely, new to you. Your challenge will be to remember these terms and incorporate them into your own "working" vocabulary. You will also need to remember legal concepts and principles. We look here at some techniques for learning and retaining legal terms and concepts.

Flash Cards.   Using flash cards is a remarkably effective method of learning new terms or concepts. Through sheer repetition, or drilling, flash cards force you to recall certain ideas and repeat them. Although published flash cards are available in many bookstores, you should try to create your own by writing terms or concepts on index cards. Write the key term or concept on one side and the definition, process, or description on the other side.

There are several advantages to creating your own flash cards. First, the exercise of actually writing the information will help you insert the term into your permanent memory. Second, you do not need flash cards for terms that you already know or that you will not need to know for your particular course. Third, you can phrase the answer in a meaningful way, with unique cues that are designed just for your purposes. This personalizes the flash card, making the information easier to remember. Finally, you can modify the definition, if need be, so that it matches more closely the particular definition preferred by your instructor.

It is helpful to create your flash cards consistently and routinely at a given point in the learning process. One good moment is when you are reading or outlining your text. Make a flash card for each boldfaced term and write the margin definition on the flash card. Also include pronunciation instructions, if appropriate, on the card.

Take your flash cards with you anywhere. Review them at lunch, while you wait in line, or when your ride on the bus. When a flash card contains a term that is difficult to pronounce, say the term aloud, if possible, as often as you can. When you have a term memorized, set that card aside but save it as an exam-review device for later in the term. Prepare new cards as you cover new terms or concepts in class.

Mnemonics.   One method that students commonly employ to remember legal concepts and principles is the use of mnemonic (pronounced "nee-*mahn*-ick) devices. Mnemonic devices are merely aids to memory. A mnemonic device can be a word, a formula, or a rhyme. As an aid to remembering the basic activities that paralegals may not legally undertake, for example, you might use the mnemonic FACt, in which the letters represent the following concepts:

F represents "fees"—paralegals may not set legal fees.
A represents "advice"—paralegals may not give legal advice.
Ct represents "court"—paralegals, with some exceptions, may not represent clients in court.

Whenever you want to memorize various components of a legal doctrine or concept, consider devising a mnemonic. Mnemonics need not make sense in themselves. The point is, if they help you remember something, then use them. Any association you can make with a difficult term to help you pronounce it, spell it, or define it more easily is a useful learning tool.

Identify What You Do Not Understand

One of the most important things you can do prior to class is clarify in your mind which terms, concepts, or procedures you *do not* understand. You can do this when marking your text by placing check marks or question marks by material that you find difficult to understand. Similarly, you can include queries in your outline.

Once you have outlined and marked you text, go back to any problem areas that you have encountered and *think about them.* You will find that it is very exciting to figure out difficult material on your own. If you still do not understand a concept thoroughly, make a note to follow up on this topic later, in the classroom. Perhaps the instructor's lecture will clarify the issue. If not, make a point of asking for clarification.

As a paralegal, you may be frequently asked to undertake preliminary investigations of legal claims. Identifying what facts are *not known* is the starting point for any investigation and focuses investigatory efforts. As a student, you might think about class time as an opportunity to "investigate" further the subject matter of your course. Identifying before class what you do not know about a topic allows you to focus your "investigative" efforts, particularly your listening efforts, during class and to maximize classroom opportunities for learning.

LEARNING IN THE CLASSROOM

The classroom is the heart of your learning experience as a paralegal student. Each instructor develops an overall plan for a course that includes many elements, which are integrated, or brought together, during class sessions. A major element in your instructor's course plan will be, of course, the material presented in your textbook, *West's Paralegal Today.* As discussed in the preceding section, reading your textbook assignments thoroughly, before class, is one way to enhance your chances of truly mastering the subject matter of the course. Equally important to this goal, though, are listening carefully to your instructor and taking good notes.

Be an Active Listener

In Chapter 7 of *West's Paralegal Today*, the authors discuss different types of listening skills. Periodically reviewing that chapter's sections on active listening and retentive listening will help you learn to listen effectively in the classroom. The ability to listen actively is a learned skill and one that will benefit you throughout your career as a paralegal. When your supervising attorney gives instructions, for example, it is crucial that you understand those instructions clearly. If you do not, you will need to ask the attorney to further clarify the instructions until you know exactly what your assignment is. Similarly, when you are interviewing clients or witnesses, you will need to be constantly interacting, mentally, with the information the client or witness is giving you so that you can follow up, immediately if necessary, on that information with further questions or actions.

As a paralegal student, you can practice listening skills in the classroom that you will need to exercise later on the job. The more immediate benefit of listening actively is, of course, a better chance of obtaining an excellent course grade.

In a nutshell, active listening as a student requires you to do the following:

1. *Listen attentively.* For anything to be communicated verbally by one person to another, the listener has to pay attention or no communication will take place. If you find your attention wandering in the classroom, make a conscious effort to become attentive and focus on what is being said.

2. *Mentally interact with what is being said.* Active listening involves mentally "acting" on the information being conveyed by the speaker (your instructor). For example, if your instructor is discussing the elements required for a cause of action in negligence, you do not want simply to write down, word for word, what the instructor is saying. Rather, you first make sure that you *understand* the meaning of what is being said. This requires you to think about what is being said in the context of what else you know about the topic. Does the information make sense within that context? Does what you are hearing raise further questions in your mind? If so, make a note of them.

3. *Ask for clarification.* If you do not understand what the instructor is saying or if something is unclear, ask for clarification. How you do this will depend to some extent on the size of your class and the degree of classroom formality. In some classes, you might feel comfortable raising your hand and questioning the instructor at that point during the lecture or discussion. In other classes, you might make a note to talk to the instructor about the topic after class or later, during the instructor's office hours.

Take Good Notes

The ability to take good notes is another skill that will help you excel both in your paralegal studies and on the job as a paralegal. Ideally, you will understand clearly everything that is being said in the classroom, and note taking will simply consist of jotting down, in your own words, brief phrases and sentences to remind you of what was stated. Often, however, you may not understand fully what the instructor is talking about, or it may take half of the class period before it becomes clear to you where your instructor is going with a certain idea or topic. In the meantime, should you take notes?

The best answer to this question is, of course, "Ask for clarification." But in some situations, interrupting a lecturer may be awkward or perceived as discourteous. In such circumstances, the wiser choice might be to take notes. Write down, to the extent possible, what the instructor is saying, including brief summaries of any examples the instructor is presenting. Later, when you have more knowledge of the subject, what the instructor said during that period may fall into place. If not, find an opportunity to ask for clarification.

Two other suggestions for taking good notes and making effective use of them are the following: (1) develop and use a shorthand system and (2) review and summarize your notes as soon as possible after class.

Develop and Use a Shorthand System. There may be times during a lecture when you want to take extensive notes. For example, your instructor may be discussing a hypothetical scenario to illustrate a legal concept. Because you know that hypothetical examples are very useful in understanding (and later reviewing) legal concepts, you want to include a description of the hypothetical example in your notes. Using abbreviations and symbols can help you include more information in your notes in less time.

In taking notes of a hypothetical example, consider designating a single letter as representative of each person or entity involved in the example. This eliminates the need to write and rewrite the names of each person or entity as they are used. For example, if a hypothetical involves three business firms, you could designate each firm by a letter: *A* could stand for Abel Electronics, *B* for Brentwood Manufacturing, and *C* for Crandall Industries.

Certain symbols and abbreviations, including those listed below, are fairly widely used as a kind of "shorthand" by legal professionals and others to designate certain concepts, parties, or procedures:

Δ	defendant
π	plaintiff
≈	similar to
≠	not equal to, not the same as
∴	therefore
a/k/a	also known as
atty	attorney
b/c or **b/cz**	because
b/p	burden of proof
cert	*certiorari*
dely	delivery
dep	deposition
disc	discovery
JML	judgment as a matter of law
JOP	judgment on the pleadings
juris	jurisdiction
K	contract
mtg	mortgage
n/a	not applicable
neg	negligence
PL	paralegal
Q	as a consequence, consequently
re	regarding
§ or **sec**	section
s/b	should be
S/L	statute of limitations

You will want to expand on this short list by creating and using other symbols or abbreviations. Once you develop a workable shorthand system, routinely use it in the classroom and then carry it over to your job. Most firms or corporations you will work for will also commonly use symbols and abbreviations, which you can add to your shorthand system later. It may also be helpful to become familiar with the dictionary's proofing symbols, which are listed under "proofreading" in the dictionary.

Review and Revise Your Notes after Each Class.   An excellent habit to form is reviewing and revising your class notes as soon as possible after the class period ends. Often, at the moment you write certain notes, you are not sure of how they fit in the overall design of the lecture. After class, however, you usually have a better perspective and know how the "pieces of the puzzle" fit together. Reviewing and summarizing your notes while the topic is still fresh in your mind—at the end of each day, for example—gives you the opportunity to reorganize them in a logical manner.

If you have a computer available, consider also typing up your notes. That way, when you want to review them, you will be able to read them quickly. Using a basic outline format when typing your notes (or rewriting them, if you do not have a computer available) will be particularly helpful later. You can tell at a glance the logical relationships between the various statements made in class.

Although reviewing and summarizing your notes each day or at other frequent intervals may seem overly time-consuming, in the long run it pays off. First, as with outlining and marking a text, reviewing your notes after class allows you to learn actively—you can think about what was covered during the class period, place various concepts in perspective, and decide what you do or do not understand after you complete your review. Second, you have probably already learned that memory is fickle. Even though we think we will not forget something we learned, in fact, we often do. When preparing for an exam, for example, you will want to remember what the instructor said in class about a particular topic. But, if you are like most people, your memory of that day and that class period may be rather fuzzy several weeks later. If you have taken good notes and summarized them legibly and logically, you will be able to review the topic quickly and effectively.

Networking in the Classroom

Several times in *West's Paralegal Today*, the authors, the featured-guest authors, and the paralegals profiled have all mentioned the importance of networking. The best time to begin networking is in the classroom. Consciously make an effort to get to know your instructor. Let him or her come to know you and your interests. Later, when looking for a job, you may want to ask that instructor for a reference.

Similarly, make an effort to become acquainted with other students in your class. Compared to students who are taking other college courses, such as math courses and history courses, there is a greater likelihood those of you in paralegal studies will be working in the same geographic area and may eventually belong to the same paralegal associations. Establishing connections with your classmates now may lead to networking possibilities later, on the job, which offers many benefits for paralegals. One good way to establish long-term relationships with other students is by forming a study group.

SHOULD YOU FORM A STUDY GROUP?

Many paralegal students join together in study groups to exchange ideas, to share the task of outlining subjects, to prepare for examinations, and to lend support to each other generally. If you want to start a study group, a good way to find potential members is to observe your classmates and decide which students participate actively and frequently in class. Then approach those individuals with your idea of forming a study group. The number of participants in a study group can vary. Ordinarily, three to five members is sufficient for a good discussion. A study group with more than six members may defeat the goal of having each member actively participate, to the greatest extent possible, in group discussions.

Some paralegal students form study groups that meet on an "as needed" basis. For example, any member could call a meeting when there is an upcoming exam or difficult subject matter to be learned. Other students establish ongoing study groups that meet throughout the year (and sometimes for the entire paralegal program). The group works as a team and as such is an excellent preparatory device for working as part of a legal team in a law firm. Study groups can also continue on after course work is completed to prepare for certification exams as paralegals. These groups are also a great way to build relationships with other future paralegals with which you may want to network later, on the job.

Meeting Times and Places. It is helpful to set up a regular meeting time and hold that time sacred. The members must be committed to the meeting times and to completing their assignments, or the group will not serve its purpose. Study groups can meet anywhere. You might meet in a classroom, another school room, a member's home, a park, or a restaurant. Many paralegal schools and colleges have multipurpose rooms or study areas available to students who wish to meet in small groups. Some rooms are equipped with easels or drawing boards, which help facilitate discussions. Audiovisual equipment may also be available for the group's use, such as a television with a VCR for viewing videotaped lectures. The group should select a meeting place that has limited distractions and sufficient space to accommodate each member's opened books, notes, and other materials.

Work Allocation. Teamwork is very important in the paralegal profession. Study groups can help you learn to function as a member of a team by distributing the workload among the group. Work (such as outlining chapters) should be allocated among the group members. It is important to define clearly who will be doing what work. It may be a good idea at the close of each meeting to have each member state out loud what work he or she will be responsible for completing prior to the next meeting. Whatever work one member does, he or she should make copies to distribute to the other members at the meeting.

Evaluating Your Group. You should realize from the outset that your study group will be of little help if you are doing most of the work. You need to make sure that everyone who joins the group is as committed to learning the material as you are and that you make this concern known to the others. The teamwork approach is only effective if everybody does his or her share. As mentioned several times in *West's Paralegal Today*, teamwork involves trust and reliance. If you cannot trust one of the members to form an accurate outline of a topic, you will not be able to rely on that outline. You will end up doing the work yourself, just as a precaution. Therefore, be very selective about whom you invite to join the group. If you joined an already existing group, leave it if it turns out to be a waste of your time.

ORGANIZING YOUR WORK PRODUCT

A part of the learning experience takes place through special homework assignments, research projects, and possibly study-group meetings. For example, if you are studying pretrial litigation procedures, you will read about these procedures in Chapter 6 of *West's Paralegal Today*. Your instructor will also likely devote class time to a discussion of these procedures. Additionally, you may be asked to create a sample complaint or to check your state's rules governing the filing of complaints in state courts. You also might have notes on a study-group discussion of these procedures.

How can you best organize all the materials generated during the coverage of a given topic? Here are a few suggestions that you might find useful. If you follow these suggestions, you will find that reviewing your work prior to exams is relatively easy—most of the work will already have been done.

Consider Using a Three-ring Binder.   The authors have found that an excellent way to integrate what you have learned is by using a three-ring binder and divider sheets with tabs for the different topics you cover. As you begin studying *West's Paralegal Today*, for example, consider having a different section in your binder for each chapter. Within that section, you can place your chapter outline (formed while reading the text), notes taken in the classroom or during other reading assignments, samples of projects you have done relating to topics in that chapter, and so on.

Integrate Your Notes into One Document, If Possible.   If you have used a computer to key in your chapter outlines and class notes, consider incorporating everything you have learned about a topic into one document—a master, detailed outline of the topic. This can be done relatively easily by using the "cut and paste" feature of word-processing programs. The result will be a comprehensive outline of a particular topic that will make reviewing the topic prior to an exam (and perhaps later, on the job) a simple matter.

THE BENEFITS OF USING A COMPUTER

Many of the paralegals profiled in *West's Paralegal Today* mentioned that if they were a student again, they would spend more time developing computer skills. You should consider acquiring a personal computer, if possible. If not, see if you can arrange with someone else to use his or her personal computer on a routine basis. If your school or college has computers available in the library or other place for student use, you might also use one of those computers. Find out when there is usually a computer available—such as early in the morning—and use the computer routinely at this time.

Using a computer provides many benefits. First, you can practice your keyboarding and word-processing skills (essential paralegal skills) simultaneously as you take notes or work on research or other class projects. Second, if you have a computer available, you can type up and better organize your notes. Such time is well spent because it not only increases your knowledge of the topics but also makes it easy to review what you have learned prior to exams.

Finally, a key benefit of using a computer is the quality of any work product or homework assignment that you submit to your instructor. The editing and formatting features of word-processing programs allow you to correct misspelled words, reorganize your presentation, and generally revise your document with little effort. The spell-checker and grammar-checker features help you avoid glaring errors. The formatting features allow you to present your document in an attractive format. You can change margins, use different fonts (such as italics or boldface) to emphasize certain words or phrases. As a paralegal, you will be using a computer and a word-processing system to generate your work. You will also be expected to know how to use computers to create "quality work products." The more you can learn about computers and word processing as a student, the easier it will be for you to perform your job as a paralegal.

PREPARING FOR EXAMS

Being prepared for exams is crucial to doing well as a paralegal student. If you have followed the study tips and suggestions given in the preceding pages of this appendix, you will have little problem preparing for an exam. You will have at your fingertips detailed outlines of the topics covered, a marked textbook that allows you to review major concepts quickly and easily, and class notes. If you have integrated your outlines and class notes in one comprehensive, detailed outline, you will have an even easier task when it comes time to prepare for an examination.

In addition to mastering the material in *West's Paralegal Today* and in the classroom, if you want to do well on an exam, you should develop an exam-taking strategy. For example, prior to any exam, you should find answers to the following questions:

- What type of exam are you going to take—essay, objective, or both?
- What reading materials and lectures will be covered on the exam?
- What materials should you bring to the exam? Will you need paper to write on, or will paper be provided?
- Will you be allowed to refer to your text or notes during the exam (as in an open-book exam)?
- Will the exam be computerized? If so, you will probably need to bring several no. 2 pencils to the exam.
- How much time will be allowed for the exam?

The more you can find out in advance about an exam, the better you can prepare for it. For example, if you learn that there will an essay question on the exam, one way to prepare for the question is to practice writing timed essays. In other words, find out in advance how much time you will have for each essay question, say fifteen minutes, and then practice writing an answer to a sample essay question during a fifteen-minute time period. This is the only way you will develop the skills needed to pace yourself for an essay exam. Because most essay exams are "closed book," do your timed essay practice without using the book.

Usually, you can anticipate certain essay exam questions. You do this by going over the major concept headings, either in your lecture notes or in your text. Search for the themes that tie the materials together, and then think about questions that your instructor might ask you. You might even list possible essay questions as a review device. Then write a short outline for each of the questions that will most likely be asked. Some instructors give their students a list of questions from which the essay questions on the exam will be drawn. This gives you an opportunity to prepare answers for each of the questions in advance. Even though you cannot take your sample essays to class and copy them there, you will have organized the material in your mind.

TAKING EXAMS

There are several strategies you can employ while taking exams to better your grade, including those discussed below.

Following Instructions

Students are often in such a hurry to start an exam that they take little time to read the instructions. The instructions can be critical, however. In a multiple-choice exam, for example, if there is no indication that there is a penalty for guessing, then you should never leave a question unanswered. Even if there are only a few minutes remaining at the end of the exam, you should guess at the answers for those questions about which you are uncertain.

You also need to make sure that you are following the specific procedures required for the exam. Some exams require that you use a no. 2 lead pencil to fill in the dots on a machine-graded answer sheet. Other exams require underlining or circling. In short, you have to look at the instructions carefully.

Finally, check to make sure that you have all the pages of the examination. If you are uncertain, ask the instructor or the exam proctor. It is hard to justify not having done your exam correctly because you failed to answer all of the questions. Simply stating that you did not have them will pose a problem for both you and your instructor.   Do not take a chance.   Double-check to make sure.

Use Exam Time Effectively

Examinations are often timed. This can make an otherwise straightforward question more difficult because of the *time pressure* that the student faces. Timed examinations require that a question or cluster of questions be answered within a specified period of time. If you must complete thirty multiple-choice questions in one hour, then you have two minutes to work on each individual question. If you finish fifteen of those questions in one minute instead of two, then you will have banked fifteen minutes that can be spent elsewhere on the examination or used to double-check your answers.

Consider the following example. Assume that you have ninety minutes for the entire exam: thirty minutes to answer the multiple-choice questions, fifteen minutes to answer the true-false questions, and forty-five minutes to answer a long essay question. If you could shave ten minutes off the time it takes to answer the multiple-choice section and five minutes off the time it takes to answer the true-false questions, you will have fifteen additional minutes to complete the long essay question.

Taking Objective Examinations

The most important point to discover initially with any objective test is if there is a penalty for guessing. If there is none, you have nothing to lose by guessing. In contrast, if a point or portion of a point will be subtracted for each incorrect answer, then you probably should not answer any question for which you are purely guessing.

Students usually commit one of two errors when they read objective-exam questions: (1) they read things into the questions that do not exist, or (2) they skip over certain words or phrases.

Most test questions include key words such as:

all
always
never
only

If you miss these key words you will be missing the "trick" part of the question. Also, you must look for questions that are only *partly* correct, particularly if you are answering true/false questions.

Never answer a question without reading all of the alternatives. More than one of them may be correct. If more than one of them seems correct, make sure you select the answer that seems the *most* correct.

Whenever the answer to an objective question is not obvious, start with the process of elimination. Throw out the answers that are clearly incorrect. Even with objective exams in which there is a penalty for guessing, if you can throw out several obviously incorrect answers, then you may wish to guess among the remaining ones because your probability of choosing the correct answer is relatively high. Typically, the easiest way to eliminate incorrect answers is to look for those that are meaningless, illogical, or inconsistent. Often, test authors put in choices that make perfect sense and are indeed true, but they are not the answer to the question you are to answer.

Writing Essay Exams

As with objective exams, you need to read the directions to the essay questions carefully. It is best to write out a brief outline *before* you start writing. The outline should present your conclusion in one or two sentences, then your supporting argument. You should take care not to include in your essay information that is irrelevant, even if you think it is interesting. It is important to stay on the subject. We can tell you from first-hand experience that no instructor likes to read answers to unasked questions.

Finally, write as legibly as possible. Again speaking from experience, the authors can tell you that it is easier to be favorably inclined to a student's essay if we do not have to reread it several times to decipher the handwriting.

THE NALA CODE OF ETHICS AND PROFESSIONAL RESPONSIBILITY

PREAMBLE

It is the responsibility of every legal assistant to adhere strictly to the accepted standards of legal ethics and to live by general principles of proper conduct. The performance of the duties of the legal assistant shall be governed by specific canons as defined herein in order that justice will be served and the goals of the profession attained.

The canons of ethics set forth hereafter are adopted by the National Association of Legal Assistants, Inc. [NALA], as a general guide, and the enumeration of these rules does not mean there are not others of equal importance although not specifically mentioned.

Canon 1

A legal assistant shall not perform any of the duties that lawyers only may perform nor do things that lawyers themselves may not do.

Canon 2

A legal assistant may perform any task delegated and supervised by a lawyer so long as the lawyer is responsible to the client, maintains a direct relationship with the client, and assumes full professional responsibility for the work product.

Canon 3

A legal assistant shall not engage in the practice of law by accepting cases, setting fees, giving legal advice or appearing in court (unless otherwise authorized by court or agency rules).

Canon 4

A legal assistant shall not act in matters involving professional legal judgment as the services of a lawyer are essential in the public interest whenever the exercise of such judgment is required.

Canon 5

A legal assistant must act prudently in determining the extent to which a client may be assisted without the presence of a lawyer.

Canon 6

A legal assistant shall not engage in the unauthorized practice of law and shall assist in preventing the unauthorized practice of law.

Canon 7

A legal assistant must protect the confidences of a client, and it shall be unethical for a legal assistant to violate any statute now in effect or hereafter to be enacted controlling privileged communications.

Canon 8

It is the obligation of the legal assistant to avoid conduct which would cause the lawyer to be unethical or even appear to be unethical, and loyalty to the employer is incumbent upon the legal assistant.

Canon 9

A legal assistant shall work continually to maintain integrity and a high degree of competency throughout the legal profession.

Canon 10

A legal assistant shall strive for perfection through education in order to better assist the legal profession in fulfilling its duty of making legal services available to clients and the public.

Canon 11

A legal assistant shall do all other things incidental, necessary, or expedient for the attainment of the ethics and responsibilities imposed by statute or rule of court.

Canon 12

A legal assistant is governed by the American Bar Association Model Code of Professional Responsibility and the American Bar Association Model Rules of Professional Conduct.

Adopted May, 1975
Revised November, 1979
Revised September, 1988

THE NALA MODEL STANDARDS AND GUIDELINES FOR UTILIZATION OF LEGAL ASSISTANTS ANNOTATED

INTRODUCTION

The purpose of this annotated version of the National Association of Legal Assistants, Inc. (NALA) Model Standards and Guidelines for the Utilization of Legal Assistants is to provide references to the existing case law and other authorities where the underlying issues have been considered. The authorities cited will serve as a basis upon which conduct of a legal assistant may be analyzed as proper or improper.

The Guidelines represent a statement of how the legal assistant may function in the law office. The Guidelines are not intended to be a comprehensive or exhaustive list of the proper duties of a legal assistant. Rather, they are designed as guides to what may or may not be proper conduct for the legal assistant. In formulating the Guidelines, the reasoning and rules of law in many reported decisions of disciplinary cases and unauthorized practice of law cases have been analyzed and considered. In addition, the provisions of the American Bar Association's Model Code of Professional Responsibility and the Model Rules of Professional Conduct, as well as the ethical promulgations of various state courts and bar associations have been considered in development of the Guidelines.

While the Guidelines may not have universal application, they do form a sound basis for the legal assistant and the supervising attorney to follow in the operation of a law office. The Model will serve as a definitive and well-reasoned guide to those considering voluntary standards and guidelines for legal assistants. If regulation is to be imposed in a given jurisdiction the Model may serve as a comprehensive resource document.

I.   PREAMBLE

Proper utilization of the services of legal assistants affects the efficient delivery of legal services. Legal assistants and the legal profession should be assured that some measures exist for identifying legal assistants and their role in assisting attorneys in the delivery of legal services. Therefore, the National Association of Legal Assistants, Inc., hereby adopts these Model Standards and Guidelines as an educational document for the benefit of legal assistants and the legal profession.

Comment

The three most frequently raised questions concerning legal assistants are (1) How do you define a legal assistant; (2) Who is qualified to be identified as a legal assistant; and (3) What duties may a legal assistant perform? The definition adopted answers the first question insofar as legal assistants serving attorneys are concerned. The Model sets forth minimum education, training, and experience through standards which will assure that one denominated as a legal assistant has the qualifications to be held out to the public in that capacity. The Guidelines identify those acts which the reported cases hold to be proscribed and give examples of services which the legal assistant may perform under the supervision of an attorney.

The three fundamental issues in the preceding paragraph have been raised in various cases for the past fifty years. In *Ferris v. Snively,* 19 P.2d 942 (Wash. 1933), the Court stated [that] work performed by a law clerk[,] to be proper and not the unauthorized practice of law[,] required supervision by the employing attorney. The Court stated:

> *We realize that law clerks have their place in a law office, and we recognize the fact that the nature of their work approaches in a degree that of their employers. The line of demarcation as to where their work begins and where it ends cannot always be drawn with absolute distinction or accuracy. Probably as nearly as it can be fixed, and it is sufficient to say that it is work of a preparatory nature, such as research, investigation of details, the assemblage of data and other necessary information, and such other work as will assist the employing attorney in carrying the matter to a completed product, either by his personal examination and approval thereof or by additional effort on his part. The work must be such, however, as loses its separate identity and becomes either the product, or else merged in the product, of the attorney himself. (19 P.2d at pp. 945–46.) (See Florida EC3–6, infra, at Section IV.)*

The NALA Guidelines constitute a statement relating to services performed by non-lawyer employees as approved by court decisions and other sources of authority. The purpose of the Guidelines is not to place limitations or restrictions on the legal profession. Rather, the Guidelines are intended to outline for the legal profession an acceptable course of conduct. By voluntary recognition and utilization of the Model Standards and Guidelines the legal profession will avoid many problems.

II.   DEFINITION

Legal assistants* are a distinguishable group of persons who assist attorneys in the delivery of legal services. Through formal education, training, and experience, legal assistants have knowledge and expertise regarding the legal system and substantive and procedural laws which qualify them to do work of a legal nature under the supervision of an attorney.

---

*Within this occupational category some individuals are known as paralegals.

Comment

This definition has been used to foster a distinction between a legal assistant as one working under the direct supervision of an attorney and a broader class of paralegals who perform tasks of similar nature, but not necessarily under the supervision of an attorney. In applying the standards and guidelines it is important to remember that they in turn were developed to apply to the legal assistant as defined therein.

III.   STANDARDS

A legal assistant should meet certain minimum qualifications. The following standards may be used to determine an individual's qualifications as a legal assistant:

1. Successful completion of the Certified Legal Assistant ("CLA") certifying examination of the National Association of Legal Assistants, Inc.;

2. Graduation from an ABA approved program of study for legal assistants;

3. Graduation from a course of study for legal assistants which is institutionally accredited but not ABA approved, and which requires not less than the equivalent of 60 semester hours of classroom study;

4. Graduation from a course of study for legal assistants, other than those set forth in (2) and (3) above, plus not less than six months of in-house training as a legal assistant;

5. A baccalaureate degree in any field, plus not less than six months in-house training as a legal assistant;

6. A minimum of three years of law-related experience under the supervision of an attorney, including at least six months of in-house training as a legal assistant; or

7. Two years of in-house training as a legal assistant.

For purposes of these Standards, "in-house training as a legal assistant" means attorney education of the employee concerning legal assistant duties and these Guidelines. In addition to review and analysis of assignments the legal assistant should receive a reasonable amount of instruction directly related to the duties and obligations of the legal assistant.

Comment

The Standards set forth suggested minimum qualifications for a legal assistant. These minimum qualifications as adopted recognize legal related work backgrounds and formal education backgrounds, both of which should provide the legal assistant with a broad base in exposure to and knowledge of the legal profession. This background is necessary to assure the public and the legal profession that the one being identified as a legal assistant is qualified.

The Certified Legal Assistant ("CLA") examination offered by NALA is the only voluntary nationwide certification program for legal assistants. The "CLA" designation is a statement to the legal profession and the public that the legal assistant has met the high levels of knowledge and professionalism required by NALA's certification program. Continuing education requirements, which all certified legal assistants must meet, assure that high standards are maintained. Certification through NALA is available to any legal assistant meeting the educational and experience requirements.

IV.   GUIDELINES

These Guidelines relating to standards of performance and professional responsibility are intended to aid legal assistants and attorneys. The responsibility rests with an attorney who employs legal assistants to educate them with respect to the duties they are assigned and to supervise the manner in which such duties are accomplished.

Comment

In general, a legal assistant is allowed to perform any task which is properly delegated and supervised by an attorney, so long as **the attorney is ultimately responsible to the client and assumes complete professional responsibility for the work product.**

The Code of Professional Responsibility of the American Bar Association, EC3–6 states:

ABA Model Rules of Professional Conduct, Rule 5.3 provides:

With respect to a non-lawyer employed or retained by or associated with a lawyer:

(a) a partner in a law firm shall make reasonable efforts to ensure that the firm has in effect measures giving reasonable assurance that the person's conduct is compatible with the professional obligations of the lawyer;

(b) a lawyer having direct supervisory authority over the non-lawyer shall make reasonable efforts to ensure that the person's conduct is compatible with the professional obligations of the lawyer; and

(c) a lawyer shall be responsible for conduct of such a person that would be a violation of the rules of professional conduct if engaged in by a lawyer if:

(1) the lawyer orders or, with the knowledge of the specific conduct ratifies the conduct involved; or

(2) the lawyer is a partner in the law firm in which the person is employed, or has direct supervisory authority over the person, and knows of the conduct at a time when its consequences can be avoided or mitigated but fails to take reasonable remedial action.

The Florida version of EC3–6 provides:

A lawyer or law firm may employ non-lawyers such as secretaries, law clerks, investigators, researchers, legal assistants, accountants, draftsmen, office administrators, and other lay personnel to assist the lawyer in the delivery of legal services. A lawyer often delegates tasks to such persons. Such delegation is proper if a lawyer retains a direct relationship with his client, supervises the delegated work, and has complete professional responsibility for the work product.

The work which is delegated is such that it will assist the employing attorney in carrying the matter to a completed product either by the lawyer's personal examination and approval thereof or by additional effort on the lawyer's part. The delegated work must be such, however, as loses its separate identity and becomes either the product or else merged in the product of the attorney himself.

The Kentucky Paralegal Code defines a legal assistant as:

. . . a person under the supervision and direction of a licensed lawyer, who may apply knowledge of law and legal procedures in rendering direct assistance to lawyers engaged in legal research; design, develop or plan modifications or new procedures, techniques, services, processes or applications; prepare or interpret legal documents and write detailed procedure for practicing in certain fields of law; select, compile and use technical information from such references as digests, encyclopedias or practice manuals; and analyze and follow procedural problems that involve independent decisions.

Kentucky became the first state to adopt a Paralegal Code, which sets forth certain exclusions to the unauthorized practice of law:

For purposes of this rule, the unauthorized practice of law shall not include any service rendered involving legal knowledge or advice, whether representation, counsel or advocacy, in or out of court, rendered in respect to the acts, duties, obligations, liabilities or business relations of the one requiring services where:

A. The client understands that the paralegal is not a lawyer;
B. The lawyer supervises the paralegal in the performance of his duties; and
C. The lawyer remains fully responsible for such representation, including all actions taken or not taken in connection therewith by the paralegal to the same extent as if such representation had been furnished entirely by the lawyer and all such actions had been taken or not taken directly by the attorney. Paralegal Code, Ky. S.Ct. R 3.700, Sub-Rule 2.

While the Kentucky rule is an exception, it does provide a basis for expanding services which may be performed by legal assistants.

There are many interesting and complex issues involving the use of legal assistants. One issue which is not addressed in the Guidelines is whether a legal assistant, as defined herein, may make appearances before administrative agencies. This issue is discussed in Remmer, *Representation of Clients Before Administrative Agencies: Authorized or Unauthorized Practice of Law?*, 15 Valparaiso Univ.L.Rev. 567 (1981). The State Bar of California Standing Committee on Professional Responsibility and Conduct, in opinion 1988–103 (2/8/89)[,] has stated a law firm can delegate authority to a legal assistant employee to file petitions, motions and make other appearances before the Workers' Compensation Appeals Board provided adequate supervision is maintained by the attorney and the client is informed and has consented to the use of legal assistant in such fashion.

In any discussion of the proper role of a legal assistant attention must be directed to what constitutes the practice of law. The proper delegation of work and duties to legal assistants is further complicated and confused by the lack of adequate definition of the practice of law and the unauthorized practice of law.

In *Davis v. Unauthorized Practice Committee,* 431 S.W.2d 590 (Tex., 1968), the Court found that the defendant was properly enjoined from the unauthorized practice of law. The Court, in defining the "practice of law," stated:

> *According to the generally understood definition of the practice of law, it embraces the preparation of pleadings and other papers incident to actions of special proceedings, and the management of such actions in proceedings on behalf of clients before judges in courts. However, the practice of law is not confined to cases conducted in court. In fact, the major portion of the practice of any capable lawyer consists of work done outside of the courts. The practice of law involves not only appearance in court in connection with litigation, but also services rendered out of court, and includes the giving of advice or the rendering of any service requiring the use of legal skill or knowledge, such as preparing a will, contract or other instrument, the legal effect of which under the facts and conclusions involved must be carefully determined.*

The important distinguishing fact between the defendant in *Davis* and a legal assistant is that the acts of the legal assistant are performed under the supervision of an attorney.

EC3–5 of the Code of Professional Responsibility states:

> *It is neither necessary nor desirable to attempt the formulation of a single, specific definition of what constitutes the practice of law. Functionally, the practice of law relates to the rendition of services for others that call for the professional judgment of a lawyer. The essence of the professional judgment of the lawyer is his educated ability to relate the general body and philosophy of law to a specific legal problem of a client; and thus, the public interest will be better served if only lawyers are permitted to act in matters involving professional judgment. Where this professional judgment is not involved, non-lawyers, such as court clerks, police officers, abstractors, and many governmental employees, may engage in occupations that require a special knowledge of law in certain areas. But the services of a lawyer are essential in the public interest whenever the exercise of professional legal judgment is required.*

There are many cases relating to the unauthorized practice of law, but the most troublesome ones in attempting to define what would or would not form the unauthorized practice of law for acts performed by a legal assistant are those such as *Crawford v. State Bar of California,* 355 P.2d 490 (Calif. 1960), which states that any act performed in a law office is the practice of law because the clients have sought the attorney to perform the work because of the training and judgment exercised by attorneys.

See also, Annot. "Layman's Assistant to Parties in Divorce Proceedings as Unauthorized Practice of Law," 12 ALR4 656; Annot. "Activities of Law Clerks as Illegal Practice of Law," 13 ALR3 1137; Annot. "Sale of Books or Forms Designed to Enable Layman to Achieve Legal Results Without Assistance of Attorney as Unauthorized Practice of Law," 71 ALR3 1000; Annot. "Nature of Legal Services or Law-Related Services Which May Be Performed for Others By Disbarred or Suspended Attorney," 87 ALR3 272. See also, Karen B. Judd, CLA, "Beyond the Bar: Legal Assistants and the Unauthorized Practice of Law," *Facts and Findings*, Vol. VIII, Issue 6, National Association of Legal Assistants, May-June, 1982.

V.

Legal assistants should:

1. Disclose their status as legal assistants at the outset of any professional relationship with a client, other attorneys, a court or administrative agency or personnel thereof, or members of the general public;

2. Preserve the confidences and secrets of all clients; and

3. Understand the attorney's Code of Professional Responsibility and these guidelines in order to avoid any action which would involve the attorney in a violation of that Code, or give the appearance of professional impropriety.

Comment

Routine early disclosure of the legal assistant's status when dealing with persons outside the attorney's office is necessary to assure that there will be no misunderstanding as to the responsibilities and role of the legal assistant. Disclosure may be made in any way that avoids confusion. If the person dealing with the legal assistant already knows of his or her status, further disclosure is necessary. If at any time in written or in oral communication the legal assistant becomes aware that the other person may believe the legal assistant is an attorney, it should be made clear that the legal assistant is not an attorney.

The attorney should exercise care that the legal assistant preserves and refrains from using any confidence or secrets of a client, and should instruct the legal assistant not to disclose or use any such confidences or secrets.

DR4–101(D), ABA Code of Professional Responsibility, provides in part that:

A lawyer shall exercise reasonable care to prevent his employees, associates, and others whose services are utilized by him from disclosing or using confidences or secrets of a client. . .

This obligation is emphasized in EC4–2:

It is a matter of common knowledge that the normal operation of a law office exposes confidential professional information to non-lawyer employees of the office, particularly secretaries and those

having access to the files; and this obligates the lawyer to exercise care in selecting and training his employees so that the sanctity of all confidences and secrets of his clients may be preserved.

The ultimate responsibility for compliance with approved standards of professional conduct rests with the supervising attorney. *In the Matter of Martinez*, 107 N.M. 171, 754 P.2d 842 (N.M. 1988). However, the legal assistant should understand what he may or may not do. The burden rests upon the attorney who employs a legal assistant to educate the latter with respect to the duties which may be assigned and then to supervise the manner in which the legal assistant carries out such duties. However, this does not relieve the legal assistant from an independent obligation to refrain from illegal conduct. Additionally, and notwithstanding that the Code is not binding upon non-lawyers, the very nature of a legal assistant's employment imposes an obligation not to engage in conduct which would involve the supervising attorney in a violation of the Code. NALA has adopted the ABA Code as a part of its Code of Ethics.

VI.

Legal assistants should not:

1. Establish attorney-client relationships; set legal fees, give legal opinions or advice; or represent a client before a court; nor
2. Engage in, encourage, or contribute to any act which could constitute the unauthorized practice of law.

Comment

Reported cases holding which acts can and cannot be performed by a legal assistant are few:

The legal assistant cannot create the attorney-client relationship. *DeVaux v. American Home Assur. Co.*, 444 N.E.2d 355 (Mass. 1983).

The legal assistant cannot make court appearances. The question of what constitute[s] a court appearance is also somewhat vague. See, for example, *People v. Alexander*, 53 Ill.App.2d 299, 202 N.E.2d 841 (1964), where preparation of a court order and transmitting information to court was not the unauthorized practice of law, and *People v. Belfor*, 611 P.2d 979 (Colo. 1980), where the trial court found that the acts of a disbarred attorney did not constitute an appearance and the Supreme Court of Colorado held that only the Supreme Court could make the determination of what acts constituted an appearance and the unauthorized practice of law.

The following cases have identified certain areas in which an attorney has a duty to act, but it is interesting to note that none of these cases state[s] that it is improper for an attorney to have the initial work performed by a legal assistant. This again points out the importance of adequate supervision by the employing attorney.

Courts have found that attorneys have the duty to check bank statements, preserve a client's property, review and sign all pleadings, ensure that all communications are opened and answered, and make inquiry when items of dictation are not received. *Attorney Grievance Commission of Maryland v. Goldberg,* 441 A.2d 338, 292 Md. 650 (1982). See also *Vaughn v. State Bar of California,* 100 Cal.Rptr. 713, 494 P.2d 1257 (1972).

The legal assistant cannot exercise professional legal judgment or give legal advice. In *Louisiana State Bar v. Edwins,* 540 So.2d 294 (La. 1989) the court held a paralegal was engaged in activities constituting the unauthorized practice of law, which included evaluation of claims and giving advice on settlements. The attorney who delegated the exercise of these acts aided in the unauthorized practice of law. See also, *People of the State of [Colorado] v. Felker,* 770 P.2d 402 (Col. 1989).

Attorneys have the responsibility to supervise the work of associates and clerical staff. *Moore v. State Bar Association,* 41 Cal.Rptr. 161, 396 P.2d 577 (1964); *Attorney Grievance Committee of Maryland v. Goldberg, supra.*

An attorney must exercise sufficient supervision to ensure that all monies received are properly deposited and disbursed. *Black v. State Bar of California,* 103 Cal.Rptr. 288, 499 P.2d 968 (1972); *Fitzpatrick v. State Bar of California,* 141 Cal.Rptr. 169, 569 P.2d 763 (1977).

The attorney must [ensure] that his staff is competent and effective to perform the work delegated. *In re Reinmiller,* 325 P.2d 773 (Ore., 1958). See also, *State of Kansas v. Barrett,* 483 P.2d 1106 (Kan., 1971); *Attorney Grievance Committee of Maryland v. Goldberg, supra.*

The attorney must make sufficient background investigation of the prior activities and character and integrity of his employees to [ensure] that legal assistants have not previously been involved in unethical, illegal, or other nefarious schemes which demonstrate such person unfit to be associated with the practice of law. See *In the Matter of Shaw,* 88 N.J. 433, A.2d 678 (1982), wherein the Court announced that while it had no disciplinary jurisdiction over legal assistants, it directed that disciplinary hearings make specific findings of fact concerning paralegals' collaboration in nefarious schemes in order that the court might properly discipline any attorney establishing an office relationship with one who had been implicated previously in unscrupulous schemes.

VII.

Legal assistants may perform services for an attorney in the representation of a client, provided:

1. The services performed by the legal assistant do not require the exercise of independent professional legal judgment;
2. The attorney maintains a direct relationship with the client and maintains control of all client matters;
3. The attorney supervises the legal assistant;
4. The attorney remains professionally responsible for all work on behalf of the client, including any actions taken or not taken by the legal assistant in connection therewith; and
5. The services performed supplement, merge with and become the attorney's work product.

Comment

EC3–6, ABA Code of Professional Responsibility, recognizes the value of utilizing the services of legal assistants, but provides certain conditions to such employment:

A lawyer often delegates tasks to clerks, secretaries, and other lay persons. Such delegation is proper if the lawyer maintains a direct relationship with his client, supervises the delegated work, and has complete professional responsibility for the work product. This delegation enables a lawyer to render legal services more economically and efficiently.

VIII.

In the supervision of a legal assistant, consideration should be given to:

1. Designating work assignments that correspond to the legal assistant's abilities, knowledge, training and experience.
2. Educating and training the legal assistant with respect to professional responsibility, local rules and practices, and firm policies;
3. Monitoring the work and professional conduct of the legal assistant to ensure that the work is substantially correct and timely performed.
4. Providing continuing education for the legal assistant in substantive matters through courses, institutes, workshops, seminars and in-house training; and
5. Encouraging and supporting membership and active participation in professional organizations.

Comment

Attorneys are responsible for the actions of their employees in both malpractice and disciplinary proceedings. The attorney cannot delegate work to a legal assistant which involves activities constituting the unauthorized practice of law. *See Louisiana State Bar v. Edwins*, 540 So.2d (La. 1989), and *People of the State of Colorado v. Felker*, 770 P.2d 402 (Colo. 1989). In the vast majority of the cases, the courts have not censured attorneys for the particular act delegated to the legal assistant, but rather, have been critical of imposed sanctions against attorneys for failure to adequately supervise the legal assistants. See e.g., *Attorney Grievance Commission of Maryland v. Goldberg, supra.*

The attorney's responsibility for supervision of legal assistants must be more than a willingness to accept responsibility and liability for the legal assistant's work. The attorney must monitor the work product and conduct of the legal assistant to [ensure] that the work performed is substantially correct and completely performed in a professional manner. This duty includes the responsibility to provide continuing legal education for the legal assistant.

Supervision of legal assistants must be offered in both the procedural and substantive legal areas in the law office.

In *Spindell v. State Bar of California*, 118 Cal.Rptr. 480, 530 P.2d 168 (1975), the attorney was suspended from practice because of the improper legal advice given by a secretary. The case illustrates that it is important that both attorneys and legal assistants confirm all telephonic advice by letter.

In all instances where the legal assistant relays information to a client in response to an inquiry from the client, the advice relayed telephonically by the legal assistant should be confirmed in writing by the attorney. This will eliminate claims if the client acts contrary to the advice given. It will establish that the legal advice given is in fact that of the attorney, not the legal assistant, and obviate any confusion resulting from transmission of the advice through the legal assistant.

The *Spindell* case is an example of an attorney's failure to supervise and educate his staff. Not only was the secretary uneducated as to the substantive provisions of the law, but more importantly, she was uneducated as to her duty and authority as an employee of the attorney.

IX.

Except as otherwise provided by statute, court rule or decision, administrative rule or regulation, or the attorney's Code of Professional Responsibility; and within the preceding parameters and proscriptions, a legal assistant may perform any function delegated by an attorney, including but not limited to the following:

1. Conduct client interviews and maintain general contact with the client after the establishment of the attorney-client relationship, so long as the client is aware of the status and function of the legal assistant, and the client contact is under the supervision of the attorney.

2. Locate and interview witnesses, so long as the witnesses are aware of the status and function of the legal assistant.

3. Conduct investigations and statistical and documentary research for review by the attorney.

4. Conduct legal research for review by the attorney.

5. Draft legal documents for review by the attorney.

6. Draft correspondence and pleadings for review by and signature of the attorney.

7. Summarize depositions, interrogatories, and testimony for review by the attorney.

8. Attend executions of wills, real estate closings, depositions, court or administrative hearings and trials with the attorney.

9. Author and sign letters provided the legal assistant's status is clearly indicated and the correspondence does not contain independent legal opinions or legal advice.

Comment

The United States Supreme Court has recognized the variety of tasks being performed by legal assistants and has noted that use of legal assistants encourage cost effective delivery of legal services. *Missouri v. Jenkins*, 491 U.S. 274, 109 S.Ct. 2463, 2471, n. 10 (1989). In *Jenkins*, the court further held that legal assistant time should be included in compensation for attorney fee awards at the prevailing practice in the relevant community to bill legal assistant time.

Except for the specific proscription contained in Section VI, the reported cases, such as *Attorney Grievance Commission of Maryland v. Goldberg, supra,* do not limit the duties which may be performed by a legal assistant under the supervision of the attorney. The Guidelines were developed from generally accepted practices. Each supervising attorney must be aware of the specific rules, decisions and statutes applicable to legal assistants within his jurisdiction.

Appendix D

The NFPA Model Code of Ethics and Professional Responsibility

Preamble

The National Federation of Paralegal Associations, Inc. ("NFPA") is a professional organization comprised of paralegal associations and individual paralegals throughout the United States. Members of NFPA have varying types of backgrounds, experience, education, and job responsibilities which reflect the diversity of the paralegal profession. NFPA promotes the growth, development and recognition of the paralegal profession as an integral partner in the delivery of legal services.

NFPA recognizes that the creation of guidelines and standards for professional conduct are important for the development and expansion of the paralegal profession. In May 1993, NFPA adopted this Model Code of Ethics and Professional Responsibility ("Model Code") to delineate the principles for ethics and conduct to which every paralegal should aspire. The Model Code expresses NFPA's commitment to increasing the quality and efficiency of legal services and recognizes the profession's responsibilities to the public, the legal community, and colleagues.

Paralegals perform many different functions, and these functions differ greatly among practice areas. In addition, each jurisdiction has its own unique legal authority and practices governing ethical conduct and professional responsibility.

It is essential that each paralegal strive for personal and professional excellence and encourage the professional development of other paralegals as well as those entering the profession. Participation in professional associations intended to advance the quality and standards of the legal profession is of particular importance. Paralegals should possess integrity, professional skill and dedication to the improvement of the legal system and should strive to expand the paralegal role in the delivery of legal services.

Canon 1

A paralegal[1] shall achieve and maintain a high level of competence.

---

1. "Paralegal" is synonymous with **"Legal Assistant"** and is defined as a person qualified through education, training, or work experience to perform substantive legal work that requires knowledge of legal concepts and is customarily, but not exclusively performed by a lawyer. This person may be retained or employed by a lawyer, law office, governmental agency or other entity or may be authorized by administrative, statutory or court authority to perform this work.

EC–1.1 A paralegal shall achieve competency through education, training, and work experience.

EC–1.2 A paralegal shall participate in continuing education to keep informed of current legal, technical and general developments.

EC–1.3 A paralegal shall perform all assignments promptly and efficiently.

Canon 2

A paralegal shall maintain a high level of personal and professional integrity.

EC–2.1 A paralegal shall not engage in any *ex parte*[2] communications involving the courts for any other adjudicatory body in an attempt to exert undue influence or to obtain advantage for the benefit of only one party.

EC–2.2 A paralegal shall not communicate, or cause another to communicate, with a party the paralegal knows to be represented by a lawyer in a pending matter without the prior consent of the lawyer representing such other party.

EC–2.3 A paralegal shall ensure that all timekeeping and billing records prepared by the paralegal are thorough, accurate, and honest.

EC–2.4 A paralegal shall be scrupulous, thorough and honest in the identification and maintenance of all funds, securities, and other assets of a client and shall provide accurate accountings as appropriate.

EC–2.5 A paralegal shall advise the proper authority of any dishonest or fraudulent acts by any person pertaining to the handling of the funds, securities or other assets of a client.

Canon 3

A paralegal shall maintain a high standard of professional conduct.

EC–3.1 A paralegal shall refrain from engaging in any conduct that offends the dignity and decorum of proceedings before a court or other adjudicatory body and shall be respectful of all rules and procedures.

EC–3.2 A paralegal shall advise the proper authority of any action of another legal professional which clearly demonstrates fraud, deceit, dishonesty, or misrepresentation.

EC–3.3 A paralegal shall avoid impropriety and the appearance of impropriety.

Canon 4

A paralegal shall serve the public interest by contributing to the delivery of quality legal services and the improvement of the legal system.

EC–4.1 A paralegal shall be sensitive to the legal needs of the public and shall promote the development and implementation of programs that address those needs.

EC–4.2 A paralegal shall support bona fide efforts to meet the need for legal services by those unable to pay reasonable or customary fees; for example, participation in *pro bono* projects and volunteer work.

---

2. ***"Ex Parte"*** denotes actions or communications conducted at the instance and for the benefit of one party only, and without notice to, or contestation by, any person adversely interested.

EC–4.3 A paralegal shall support efforts to improve the legal system and shall assist in making changes.

Canon 5

A paralegal shall preserve all confidential information[3] provided by the client or acquired from other sources before, during, and after the course of the professional relationship.

EC–5.1 A paralegal shall be aware of and abide by all legal authority governing confidential information.
EC–5.2 A paralegal shall not use confidential information to the disadvantage of the client.
EC–5.3 A paralegal shall not use confidential information to the advantage of the paralegal or of a third person.
EC–5.4 A paralegal may reveal confidential information only after full disclosure and with the client's written consent; or, when required by law or court order; or, when necessary to prevent the client from committing an act which could result in death or serious bodily harm.
EC–5.5 A paralegal shall keep those individuals responsible for the legal representation of a client fully informed of any confidential information the paralegal may have pertaining to that client.
EC–5.6 A paralegal shall not engage in any indiscreet communications concerning clients.

Canon 6

A paralegal's title shall be fully disclosed.[4]

EC–6.1 A paralegal's title shall clearly indicate the individual's status and shall be disclosed in all business and professional communications to avoid misunderstandings and misconceptions about the paralegal's role and responsibilities.
EC–6.2 A paralegal's title shall be included if the paralegal's name appears on business cards, letterhead, brochures, directories, and advertisements.

Canon 7

A paralegal shall not engage in the unauthorized practice of law.

EC–7.1 A paralegal shall comply with the applicable legal authority governing the unauthorized practice of law.

Canon 8

A paralegal shall avoid conflicts of interest and shall disclose any possible conflict to the employer or client, as well as to the prospective employers or clients.

---

3. **"Confidential Information"** denotes information relating to a client, whatever its source, which is not public knowledge nor available to the public. (**"Non-Confidential Information"** would generally include the name of the client and the identity of the matter for which the paralegal provided services.)
4. **"Disclose"** denotes communication of information reasonably sufficient to permit identification of the significance of the matter in question.

EC–8.1 A paralegal shall act within the bounds of the law, solely for the benefit of the client, and shall be free of compromising influences and loyalties. Neither the paralegal's personal or business interest, nor those of other clients or third persons, should compromise the paralegal's professional judgment and loyalty to the client.

EC–8.2 A paralegal shall avoid conflicts of interest which may arise from previous assignments whether for a present or past employer or client.

EC–8.3 A paralegal shall avoid conflicts of interest which may arise from family relationships and from personal and business interests.

EC–8.4 A paralegal shall create and maintain an effective recordkeeping system that identifies clients, matters, and parties with which the paralegal has worked, to be able to determine whether an actual or potential conflict of interest exists.

EC–8.5 A paralegal shall reveal sufficient nonconfidential information about a client or former client to reasonably ascertain if an actual or potential conflict of interest exists.

EC–8.6 A paralegal shall not participate in or conduct work on any matter where a conflict of interest has been identified.

EC–8.7 In matters where a conflict of interest has been identified and the client consents to continued representation, a paralegal shall comply fully with the implementation and maintenance of an Ethical Wall.[5]

---

5. **"Ethical Wall"** refers to the screening method implemented in order to protect a client from a conflict of interest. An Ethical Wall generally includes, but is not limited to, the following elements: (1) prohibit the paralegal from having any connection with the matter; (2) ban discussions with or the transfer of documents to or from the paralegal; (3) restrict access to files; and (4) educate all members of the firm, corporation or entity as to the separation of the paralegal (both organizationally and physically) from the pending matter. For more information regarding the Ethical Wall, see the NFPA publication entitled "The Ethical Wall—Its Application to Paralegals."

APPENDIX E

THE ABA MODEL GUIDELINES FOR THE UTILIZATION OF LEGAL ASSISTANT SERVICES

PREAMBLE

State courts, bar associations, or bar committees in at least seventeen states have prepared recommendations[1] for the utilization of legal assistant services.[2] While their content varies, their purpose appears uniform: to provide lawyers with a reliable basis for delegating responsibility for performing a portion of the lawyer's tasks to legal assistants. The purpose of preparing model guidelines is not to contradict the guidelines already adopted or to suggest that other guidelines may be more appropriate in a particular jurisdiction. It is the view of the Standing Committee on Legal Assistants of the American Bar Association [ABA], however, that a model set of guidelines for the utilization of legal assistant services may assist many states in adopting or revising such guidelines. The Standing Committee is of the view that guidelines will encourage lawyers to utilize legal assistant services effectively and promote the growth of the legal assistant profession.[3] In undertaking this project, the Standing Committee has attempted to state guidelines that conform with the American Bar Association's Model Rules of

---

1. An appendix identifies the guidelines, court rules, and recommendations that were reviewed in drafting these Model Guidelines. [This appendix is not included in *West's Paralegal Today.*]
2. On February 6, 1986, the ABA Board of Governors approved the following definition of the term "legal assistant":

   A legal assistant is a person, qualified through education, training, or work experience, who is employed or retained by a lawyer, law office, governmental agency, or other entity in a capacity or function which involves the performance, under the ultimate direction and supervision of an attorney, of specifically delegated substantive legal work, which work, for the most part, requires a sufficient knowledge of legal concepts that, absent such assistant, the attorney would perform the task.
   In some contexts, the term "paralegal" is used interchangeably with the term legal assistant. [Note: The ABA has since modified this decision. See Chapter 1.]
3. While necessarily mentioning legal assistant conduct, lawyers are the intended audience of these Guidelines. The Guidelines, therefore, are addressed to lawyer conduct and not directly to the conduct of the legal assistant. Both the National Association of Legal Assistants (NALA) and the National Federation of Paralegal Associations (NFPA) have adopted guidelines of conduct that are directed to legal assistants. See NALA, "Code of Ethics and Professional Responsibility of the National Association of Legal Assistants, Inc." (adopted May 1975, revised November 1979 and September 1988); NFPA, "Affirmation of Responsibility" (adopted 1977, revised 1981).

Professional Conduct, decided authority, and contemporary practice. Lawyers, of course, are to be first directed by Rule 5.3 of the Model Rules in the utilization of legal assistant services, and nothing contained in these guidelines is intended to be inconsistent with that rule. Specific ethical considerations in particular states, however, may require modification of these guidelines before their adoption. In the commentary after each guideline, we have attempted to identify the basis for the guideline and any issues of which we are aware that the guideline may present; those drafting such guidelines may wish to take them into account.

Guideline 1

A lawyer is responsible for all of the professional actions of a legal assistant performing legal assistant services at the lawyer's direction and should take reasonable measures to ensure that the legal assistant's conduct is consistent with the lawyer's obligations under the ABA Model Rules of Professional Conduct.

Comment to Guideline 1.   An attorney who utilizes a legal assistant's services is responsible for determining that the legal assistant is competent to perform the tasks assigned, based on the legal assistant's education, training, and experience, and for ensuring that the legal assistant is familiar with the responsibilities of attorneys and legal assistants under the applicable rules governing professional conduct.[4]

Under principles of agency law and rules governing the conduct of attorneys, lawyers are responsible for the actions and the work product of the non-lawyers they employ. Rule 5.3 of the Model Rules[5] requires that partners and supervising attorneys ensure that the conduct of non-lawyer assistants is compatible with the lawyer's professional obligations. Several state guidelines have adopted this language. E.g., Commentary to Illinois Recommendation (A), Kansas Guideline III(a), New Hampshire Rule 35, Sub-Rule 9, and North Carolina Guideline 4. Ethical Consideration 3–6 of the Model Code encouraged lawyers to delegate tasks to legal assistants provided the lawyer maintained a direct relationship with the client, supervised appropriately, and had complete responsibility for the work product. The adoption of Rule 5.3, which incorporates these principles, implicitly reaffirms this encouragement.

---

4. Attorneys, of course, are not liable for violation of the ABA Model Rules of Professional Conduct ("Model Rules") unless the Model Rules have been adopted as the code of professional conduct in a jurisdiction in which the lawyer practices. They are referenced in this model guideline for illustrative purposes; if the guideline is to be adopted, the reference should be modified to the jurisdiction's rules of professional conduct.

5. The Model Rules were first adopted by the ABA House of Delegates in August of 1983. Since that time many states have adopted the Model Rules to govern the professional conduct of lawyers licensed in those states. Since a number of states still utilize a version of the Model Code of Professional Responsibility ("Model Code"), which was adopted by the House of Delegates in August of 1969, however, these comments will refer to both the Model Rules and the predecessor Model Code (and to the Ethical Considerations and Disciplinary Rules found under the canons in the Model Code).

Several states have addressed the issue of the lawyer's ultimate responsibility for work performed by subordinates. For example, Colorado Guideline 1.c, Kentucky Supreme Court Rule 3.700, Sub-Rule 2.C, and Michigan Guideline I provide: "The lawyer remains responsible for the actions of the legal assistant to the same extent as if such representation had been furnished entirely by the lawyer and such actions were those of the lawyer." New Mexico Guideline X states "[the] lawyer maintains ultimate responsibility for and has an ongoing duty to actively supervise the legal assistant's work performance, conduct and product." Connecticut Recommendation 2 and Rhode Island Guideline III state specifically that lawyers are liable for malpractice for the mistakes and omissions of their legal assistants.

Finally, the lawyer should ensure that legal assistants supervised by the lawyer are familiar with the rules governing attorney conduct and that they follow those rules. See Comment to Model Rule 5.3; Illinois Recommendation (A)(5), New Hampshire Supreme Court Rule 35, Sub-Rule 9, and New Mexico, Statement of Purpose; see also NALA's Model Standards and Guidelines for the Utilization of Legal Assistants, guidelines IV, V, and VIII (1985, revised 1990) (hereafter "NALA Guidelines").

The Standing Committee and several of those who have commented upon these Guidelines regard Guideline 1 as a comprehensive statement of general principle governing lawyers who utilize legal assistant services in the practice of law. As such it, in effect, is a part of each of the remaining Guidelines.

Guideline 2

Provided the lawyer maintains responsibility for the work product, a lawyer may delegate to a legal assistant any task normally performed by the lawyer except those tasks proscribed to one not licensed as a lawyer by statute, court rule, administrative rule or regulation, controlling authority, the ABA Model Rules of Professional Conduct, or these Guidelines.

Comment to Guideline 2.   The essence of the definition of the term legal assistant adopted by the ABA Board of Governors in 1986 is that, so long as appropriate supervision is maintained, many tasks normally performed by lawyers may be delegated to legal assistants. Of course, Rule 5.5 of the Model Rules, DR 3–101 of the Model Code, and most states specifically prohibit lawyers from assisting or aiding a non-lawyer in the unauthorized practice of law. Thus, while appropriate delegation of tasks to legal assistants is encouraged, the lawyer may not permit the legal assistant to engage in the "practice of law." Neither the Model Rules nor the Model Code define the "practice of law." EC 3–5 under the Model Code gave some guidance by equating the practice of law to the application of the professional judgment of the lawyer in solving clients' legal problems. Further, ABA Opinion 316 (1967) states: "A lawyer can employ lay secretaries, lay investigators, lay detectives, lay researchers, accountants, lay scriveners, nonlawyer draftsmen or nonlawyer researchers. In fact, he may employ nonlawyers to do any task for him except counsel clients about law matters, engage directly in the practice of law, appear in court or appear in formal proceedings as part of the judicial process, so long as it is he who takes the work and vouches for it to the client and becomes responsible for it to the client.

Most state guidelines specify that legal assistants may not appear before courts, administrative tribunals, or other adjudicatory bodies unless their rules authorize such appearances; may not conduct depositions; and may not give legal advice to clients. E.g., Connecticut Recommendation 4; Florida EC 3–6 (327 So.2d at 16); and Michigan Guideline II. Also see NALA Guidelines IV and VI. But it is also important to note that, as some guidelines have recognized, pursuant to federal or state statute legal assistants are permitted to provide direct client representation in certain administrative proceedings. E.g., South Carolina Guideline II. While this does not obviate the attorney's responsibility for the legal assistant's work, it does change the nature of the attorney supervision of the legal assistant. The opportunity to use such legal assistant services has particular benefits to legal services programs and does not violate Guideline 2. See generally ABA Standards for Providers of Civil Legal Services to the Poor, Std. 6.3, at 6.17–6.18 (1986).

The Model Rules emphasize the importance of appropriate delegation. The key to appropriate delegation is proper supervision, which includes adequate instruction when assigning projects, monitoring of the project, and review of the completed project. The Supreme Court of Virginia upheld a malpractice verdict against a lawyer based in part on negligent actions of a legal assistant in performing tasks that evidently were properly delegable. *Musselman v. Willoughby Corp.*, 230 Va. 337, 337 S.E.2d 724 (1985). See also C. Wolfram, Modern Legal Ethics (1986), at 236, 896. All state guidelines refer to the requirement that the lawyer "supervise" legal assistants in the performance of their duties. Lawyers should also take care in hiring and choosing a legal assistant to work on a specific project to ensure that the legal assistant has the education, knowledge, and ability necessary to perform the delegated tasks competently. See Connecticut Recommendation 14, Kansas Standards I, II, and III, and New Mexico Guideline VIII. Finally, some states describe appropriate delegation and review in terms of the delegated work losing its identity and becoming "merged" into the work product of the attorney. See Florida EC 3–6 (327 So.2d at 16).

Legal assistants often play an important role in improving communication between the attorney and the client. EC 3–6 under the Model Code mentioned three specific kinds of tasks that legal assistants may perform under appropriate lawyer supervision: factual investigation and research, legal research, and the preparation of legal documents. Some states delineate more specific tasks in their guidelines, such as attending client conferences, corresponding with and obtaining information from clients, handling witness execution of documents, preparing transmittal letters, maintaining estate/guardianship trust accounts, etc. See, e.g., Colorado (lists of specialized functions in several areas follow guidelines); Michigan, Comment to Definition of Legal Assistant; New York, Specialized Skills of Legal Assistants; Rhode Island Guideline II; and NALA Guideline IX. The two-volume Working with Legal Assistants, published by the Standing Committee in 1982, attempted to provide a general description of the types of tasks that may be delegated to legal assistants in various practice areas.

There are tasks that have been specifically prohibited in some states, but that may be delegated in others. For example, legal assistants may not supervise will executions or represent clients at real estate closings in some jurisdictions, but may in others. Compare Connecticut Recommendation 7 and Illinois State Bar Association Position Paper on Use of Attorney Assistants in Real Estate Transactions (May 16, 1984), which proscribe legal assistants conducting real estate closings, with Georgia "real estate job description," Florida Professional Ethics Committee Advisory Opinion 89–5 (1989), and Missouri, Comment to Guideline I, which permit legal assistants to conduct real estate closings. Also compare Connecticut Recommendation 8 (prohibiting attorneys from authorizing legal assistants to supervise will executions) with Colorado "estate planning job description," Georgia "estate, trusts, and wills job description," Missouri, Comment to Guideline I, and Rhode Island Guideline II (suggesting that legal assistants may supervise the execution of wills, trusts, and other documents).

Guideline 3

A lawyer may not delegate to a legal assistant:

   (a) **Responsibility for establishing an attorney-client relationship.**
   (b) **Responsibility for establishing the amount of a fee to be charged for a legal service.**
   (c) **Responsibility for a legal opinion rendered to a client.**

Comments to Guideline 3.   The Model Rules and most state codes require that lawyers communicate with their clients in order for clients to make well-informed decisions about their representation and resolution of legal issues. Model Rule 1.4. Ethical Consideration 3–6 under the Model Code emphasized that "delegation [of legal tasks to nonlawyers] is proper if the lawyer *maintains a direct relationship with his client,* supervises the delegated work and has complete professional responsibility for the work product." (Emphasis added.) Accordingly, most state guidelines also stress the importance of a direct attorney-client relationship. See Colorado Guideline 1, Florida EC 3–6, Illinois Recommendation (A)(1), Iowa EC 3–6(2), and New Mexico Guideline IV. The direct personal relationship between client and lawyer is necessary to the exercise of the lawyer's trained professional judgment.

An essential aspect of the lawyer-client relationship is the agreement to undertake representation and the related fee arrangement. The Model Rules and most states require that fee arrangements be agreed upon early on and be communicated to the client by the lawyer, in some circumstances in writing. Model Rule 1.5 and Comments. Many state guidelines prohibit legal assistants from "setting fees" or "accepting cases." See, e.g., Colorado Guideline 1 and NALA Guideline VI. Connecticut recommends that legal assistants be prohibited from accepting or rejecting cases or setting fees "if these tasks entail any discretion on the part of the paralegals." Connecticut Recommendation 9.

EC 3–5 states: "[T]he essence of the professional judgment of the lawyer is his educated ability to relate the general body and philosophy of law to a specific legal problem of a client; and thus, the public interest will be better served if only lawyers are permitted to act in matters involving professional judgment." Clients are entitled to their lawyers' professional judgment and opinion. Legal assistants may, however, be authorized to communicate legal advice so long as they do not interpret or expand on that advice. Typically, state guidelines phrase this prohibition in terms of legal assistants being forbidden from "giving legal advice" or "counseling clients about legal matters." See, e.g., Colorado Guideline 2, Connecticut Recommendation 6, Florida DR 3–104, Iowa EC 3–6(3), Kansas Guideline I, Kentucky Sub-Rule 2, New Hampshire Rule 35, Sub-Rule 1, Texas Guideline I, and NALA Guideline VI. Some states have more expansive wording that prohibits legal assistants from engaging in any activity that would require the exercise of independent legal judgment. Nevertheless, it is clear that all states, as well as the Model Rules, encourage direct communication between clients and a legal assistant insofar as the legal assistant is performing a task properly delegated by a lawyer. It should be noted that a lawyer who permits a legal assistant to assist in establishing the attorney-client relationship, communicating a fee, or preparing a legal opinion is not delegating responsibility for those matters and, therefore, may be complying with this guideline.

Guideline 4

It is the lawyer's responsibility to take reasonable measures to ensure that clients, courts, and other lawyers are aware that a legal assistant, whose services are utilized by the lawyer in performing legal services, is not licensed to practice law.

Comment to Guideline 4.   Since, in most instances, a legal assistant is not licensed as a lawyer, it is important that those with whom the legal assistant deals are aware of that fact. Several state guidelines impose on the lawyer responsibility for instructing a legal assistant whose services are utilized by the lawyer to disclose the legal assistant's status in any dealings with a third party. See, e.g., Michigan Guideline III, part 5, New Hampshire Rule 35, Sub-Rule 8, and NALA Guideline V. While requiring the legal assistant to make such disclosure is one way in which the attorney's responsibility to third parties may be discharged, the Standing Committee is of the view that it is desirable to emphasize the lawyer's responsibility for the disclosure and leave to the lawyer the discretion to decide whether the lawyer will discharge that responsibility by direct communication with the client, by requiring the legal assistant to make the disclosure, by a written memorandum, or by some other means. Although in most initial engagements by a client it may be prudent for the attorney to discharge the responsibility with a writing, the guideline requires only that the lawyer recognize the responsibility and ensure that it is discharged. Clearly, when a client has been adequately informed of the lawyer's utilization of legal assistant services, it is unnecessary to make additional formalistic disclosures as the client retains the lawyer for other services.

Most state guidelines specifically endorse legal assistants signing correspondence so long as their status as a legal assistant is indicated by an appropriate title. E.g., Colorado Guideline 2; Kansas, Comment to Guideline IX; and North Carolina Guideline 9; also see ABA Informal Opinion 1367 (1976). The comment to New Mexico Guideline XI warns against the use of the title "associate" since it may be construed to mean associate-attorney.

Guideline 5

A lawyer may identify legal assistants by name and title on the lawyer's letterhead and on business cards identifying the lawyer's firm.

Comment to Guideline 5.   Under Guideline 4, above, an attorney who employs a legal assistant has an obligation to ensure that the status of the legal assistant as a non-lawyer is fully disclosed. The primary purpose of this disclosure is to avoid confusion that might lead someone to believe that the legal assistant is a lawyer. The identification suggested by this guideline is consistent with that objective, while also affording the legal assistant recognition as an important part of the legal services team.

Recent ABA Informal Opinion 1527 (1989) provides that non-lawyer support personnel, including legal assistants, may be listed on a law firm's letterhead and reiterates previous opinions that approve of legal assistants having business cards. See also ABA Informal Opinion 1185 (1971). The listing must not be false or misleading and "must make it clear that the support personnel who are listed are not lawyers."

Nearly all state guidelines approve of business cards for legal assistants, but some prescribe the contents and format of the card. E.g., Iowa Guideline 4 and Texas Guideline VIII. All agree the legal assistant's status must be clearly indicated and the card may not be used in a deceptive way. New Hampshire Supreme Court Rule 7 approves the use of business cards so long as the card is not used for unethical solicitation.

Some states do not permit attorneys to list legal assistants on their letterhead. E.g., Kansas Guideline VIII, Michigan Guideline III, New Hampshire Rule 35, Sub-Rule 7, New Mexico Guideline XI, and North Carolina Guideline 9. Several of these states rely on earlier ABA Informal Opinion 619 (1962), 845 (1965), and 1000 (1977), all of which were expressly withdrawn by ABA Informal Opinion 1527. These earlier opinions interpreted the predecessor Model Code and DR 2–102(A), which, prior to *Bates v. State Bar of Arizona*, 433 U.S. 350 (1977), had strict limitations on the information that could be listed on letterheads. States which do permit attorneys to list names of legal assistants on their stationary, if the listing is not deceptive and the legal assistant's status is clearly identified, include: Arizona Committee on Rules of Professional Conduct Formal Opinion 3/90 (1990); Connecticut Recommendation 12; Florida Professional Ethics Committee Advisory Opinion 86–4 (1986); Hawaii, Formal Opinion 78–8–19 (1978, as revised 1984); Illinois State Bar Association Advisory Opinion 87–1 (1987); Kentucky Sub-Rule 6; Mississippi State Bar Ethics Committee Opinion 93 (1984); Missouri Guideline IV; New York State Bar Association Committee on Professional Ethics Opinion 500 (1978); Oregon, Ethical Opinion No. 349 (1977); and Texas, Ethics Committee Opinion 436 (1983). In light of the United States Supreme Court opinion in *Peel v. Attorney Registration and Disciplinary Commission of Illinois*, 496 U.S. 91, 110 S.Ct. 2281 (1990), it may be that a restriction on letterhead identification of legal assistants that is not deceptive and clearly identifies the legal assistant's status violates the First Amendment rights of the lawyer.

Guideline 6

It is the responsibility of a lawyer to take reasonable measures to ensure that all client confidences are preserved by a legal assistant.

Comment to Guideline 6.   A fundamental principle underlying the free exchange of information in a lawyer-client relationship is that the lawyer maintain the confidentiality of information relating to the representation. "It is a matter of common knowledge that the normal operation of a law office exposes confidential professional information to non-lawyer employees of the office. This obligates a lawyer to exercise care in selecting and training his employees so that the sanctity of all confidences and secrets of his clients may be preserved." EC 4–2, Model Code.

Rule 5.3 of the Model Rules requires "a lawyer who has direct supervisory authority over the nonlawyer [to] make reasonable efforts to ensure that the person's conduct is compatible with the professional obligations of the lawyer." The Comment to Rule 5.3 makes it clear that lawyers should give legal assistants "appropriate instruction and supervision concerning the ethical aspects of their employment, particularly regarding the obligation not to disclose information relating to the representation of the client." DR 4–101(D) under the Model Code provides that: "A lawyer shall exercise reasonable care to prevent his employees, associates and others whose services are utilized by him from discharging or using confidences or secrets of a client. . . ."

It is particularly important that the lawyer ensure that the legal assistant understands that *all* information concerning the client, even the mere fact that a person is a client of the firm, may be strictly confidential. Rule 1.6 of the Model Rules expanded the definition of confidential information ". . . not merely to matters communicated in confidence by the client but also to all information relating to the representation, whatever its source."[6] It is therefore the lawyer's obligation to instruct clearly and to take reasonable steps to ensure the legal assistant's preservation of client confidences. Nearly all states that have guidelines for the utilization of legal assistants require the lawyer "to instruct legal assistants concerning client confidences" and "to exercise care to ensure that legal assistants comply" with the Code in this regard. Even if the client consents to divulging information, this information must not be used to the disadvantage of the client. See, e.g., Connecticut Recommendation 3: New Hampshire Rule 35, Sub-Rule 4; NALA Guideline V.

Guideline 7

A lawyer should take reasonable measures to prevent conflicts of interest resulting from a legal assistant's other employment or interests insofar as such other employment or interests would present a conflict of interest if it were that of the lawyer.

---

6. Rule 1.05 of the Texas Disciplinary Rules of Professional Conduct (1990) provides a different formulation, which is equally expansive:

"Confidential information" includes both "privileged information" and "unprivileged client information." "Privileged information" refers to the information of a client protected by the lawyer-client privilege of Rule 503 of the Texas Rules of Evidence or the Rule 503 of the Texas Rules of Criminal Evidence or by the principles of attorney-client privilege governed by Rule 501 of the Federal Rules of Evidence for United States Courts and Magistrates. "Unprivileged client information" means all information relating to a client or furnished by the client, other than privileged information, acquired by the lawyer during the course of or by reason of the representation of the client.

Comment to Guideline 7. A lawyer must make "reasonable efforts to ensure that [a] legal assistant's conduct is compatible with the professional obligations of the lawyer." Model Rule 5.3. These professional obligations include the duty to exercise independent professional judgment on behalf of a client, "free of compromising influences and loyalties." ABA Model Rules 1.7 through 1.13. Therefore, legal assistants should be instructed to inform the supervising attorney of any interest that could result in a conflict of interest or even give the appearance of a conflict. The guideline intentionally speaks to other employment rather than only past employment, since there are instances where legal assistants are employed by more than one law firm at the same time. The guideline's reference to "other interests" is intended to include personal relationships as well as instances where a legal assistant may have a financial interest (i.e., as stockholder, trust beneficiary or trustee, etc.) that would conflict with the client's in the matter in which the lawyer has been employed.

"Imputed Disqualification Arising from Change in Employment by Non-lawyer Employee," ABA Informal Opinion 1526 (1988), defines the duties of both the present and former employing lawyers and reasons that the restrictions on legal assistants' employment should be kept to "the minimum necessary to protect confidentiality" in order to prevent legal assistants from being forced to leave their careers, which "would disserve clients as well as the legal profession." The Opinion describes the attorney's obligations (1) to caution the legal assistant not to disclose any information and (2) to prevent the legal assistant from working on any matter on which the legal assistant worked for a prior employer or respecting which the employee has confidential information.

If a conflict is discovered, it may be possible to "wall" the legal assistant from the conflict area so that the entire firm need not be disqualified and the legal assistant is effectively screened from information concerning the matter. The American Bar Association has taken the position that what historically has been described as a "Chinese wall" will allow non-lawyer personnel (including legal assistants) who are in possession of confidential client information to accept employment with a law firm opposing the former client so long as the wall is observed and effectively screens the non-lawyer from confidential information. ABA Informal Opinion 1526 (1988). See also Tennessee Formal Ethics Opinion 89–F–118 (March 10, 1989). The implication of this Informal Opinion is that if a wall is not in place, the employer may be disqualified from representing either party to the controversy. One court has so held. *In re: Complex Asbestos Litigation*, No. 828684 (San Francisco Superior Court, September 19, 1989).

It is not clear that a wall will prevent disqualification in the case of a lawyer employed to work for a law firm representing a client with an adverse interest to a client of the lawyer's former employer. Under Model Rule 1.10, when a lawyer moves to a firm that represents an adverse party in a matter in which the lawyer's former firm was involved, absent a waiver by the client, the new firm's representation may continue only if the newly employed lawyer acquired no protected information and did not work directly on the matter in the former employment. The new Rules of Professional Conduct in Kentucky and Texas (both effective January 1, 1990) specifically provide for disqualification. Rule 1.10(b) in the District of Columbia, which became effective January 1, 1991, does so as well. The Sixth Circuit, however, has held that the wall will effectively insulate the new firm from disqualification if it prevents the new lawyer-employee from access to information concerning the client with the adverse interest. *Manning v. Waring, Cox, James, Sklar & Allen,* 849 F.2d 222 (6th Cir. 1988). [As a result of the Sixth Circuit opinion, Tennessee revised its formal ethics opinion, which is cited above, and now applies the same rule to lawyers, legal assistants, law clerks, and legal secretaries.] See generally NFPA, "The Chinese Wall—Its Application to Paralegals" (1990).

The states that have guidelines that address the legal assistant conflict of interest refer to the lawyer's responsibility to ensure against personal, business or social interests of the legal assistant that would conflict with the representation of the client or impinge on the services rendered to the client. E.g., Kansas Guideline X, New Mexico Guideline VI, and North Carolina Guideline 7. Florida Professional Ethics Opinion 86–5 (1986) discusses a legal assistant's move from one firm to another and the obligations of each not to disclose confidences. See also Vermont Ethics Opinion 85–8 (1985) (a legal assistant is not bound by the Code of Professional Responsibility and, absent an absolute waiver by the client, the new firm should not represent client if legal assistant possessed confidential information from old firm).

Guideline 8

A lawyer may include a charge for the work performed by a legal assistant in setting a charge for legal services.

Comment to Guideline 8.   The U.S. Supreme Court in *Missouri v. Jenkins,* 491 U.S. 274 (1989), held that in setting a reasonable attorney's fee under 28 U.S.C. §1988, a legal fee may include a charge for legal assistant services at "market rates" rather than "actual cost" to the attorneys. This decision should resolve any question concerning the propriety of setting a charge for legal services based on work performed by a legal assistant. Its rationale favors setting a charge based on the "market" rate for such services, rather than their direct cost to the lawyer. This result was recognized by Connecticut Recommendation 11, Illinois Recommendation D, and Texas Guideline V prior to the Supreme Court decision. See also Fla.Stat.Ann. §57.104 (1991 Supp.) (adopted in 1987 and permitting consideration of legal assistant services in computing attorney's fees) and Fla.Stat.Ann. §744.108 (1991 Supp.) (adopted in 1989 and permitting recovery of "customary and reasonable charges for work performed by legal assistants" as fees for legal services in guardianship matters).

It is important to note, however, that *Missouri v. Jenkins* does not abrogate the attorney's responsibilities under Model Rule 1.5 to set a reasonable fee for legal services and it follows that those considerations apply to a fee that includes a fee for legal assistant services. Accordingly, the effect of combining a market rate charge for the services of lawyers and legal assistants should, in most instances, result in a lower total cost for the legal service than if the lawyer had performed the service alone.

Guideline 9

A lawyer may not split legal fees with a legal assistant nor pay a legal assistant for the referral of legal business. A lawyer may compensate a legal assistant based on the quantity and quality of the legal assistant's work and the value of that work to a law practice, but the legal assistant's compensation may not be contingent, by advance agreement, upon the probability of the lawyer's practice.

Comment to Guideline 9.   Model Rule 5.4 and DR 3–102(A) and 3–103(A) under the Model Code clearly prohibit fee "splitting" with legal assistants, whether characterized by splitting of contingent fees, "forwarding" fees, or other sharing of legal fees. Virtually all guidelines adopted by state bar associations have continued this prohibition in one form or another.[7] It appears clear that a legal assistant may not be compensated on a contingent basis for a particular case or paid for "signing up" clients for a legal practice.

Having stated this prohibition, however, the guideline attempts to deal with the practical consideration of how a legal assistant properly may be compensated by an attorney or law firm. The linchpin of the prohibition seems to be the advance agreement of the lawyer to "split" a fee based on a pre-existing contingent agreement.[8] There is no general prohibition against a lawyer who enjoys a particularly profitable period recognizing the contribution of the legal assistant to that profitability with a discretionary bonus. Likewise, a lawyer engaged in a particularly profitable specialty of legal practice is not prohibited from compensating the legal assistant who aids materially in that practice more handsomely than the compensation generally awarded to legal assistants in that geographic area who work in law practices that are less lucrative. Indeed, any effort to fix a compensation level for legal assistants and prohibit greater compensation would appear to violate the federal antitrust laws. See, e.g., *Goldfarb v. Virginia State Bar,* 421 U.S. 773 (1975).

Guideline 10

A lawyer who employs a legal assistant should facilitate the legal assistant's participation in appropriate continuing education and *pro bono publico* activities.

Comment to Guideline 10.   While Guideline 10 does not appear to have been adopted in the guidelines of any state bar association, the Standing Committee on Legal Assistants believes that its adoption would be appro-

---

7. Connecticut Recommendation 10; Illinois Recommendation D; Kansas Guideline VI; Kentucky Supreme Court Rule 3.700, sub-rule 5; Michigan Guideline III, part 2; Missouri Guideline II; New Hampshire Rule 35, Sub-Rules 5 and 6; New Mexico Guideline IX; Rhode Island Guideline VIII and IX; South Carolina Guideline V; Texas Guideline V.
8. In its Rule 5.4, which [became] effective on January 1, 1991, the District of Columbia will permit lawyers to form legal service partnerships that include nonlawyer participants. Comments 5 and 6 to that rule, however, state that the term "nonlawyer participants" should not be confused with the term "nonlawyer assistants" and that "[n]onlawyer assistants under Rule 5.3 do not have managerial authority or financial interests in the organization."

priate.[9] For many years the Standing Committee on Legal Assistants has advocated that the improvement of formal legal assistant education will generally improve the legal services rendered by lawyers employing legal assistants and provide a more satisfying professional atmosphere in which legal assistants may work. See, e.g., ABA Board of Governors, Policy on Legal Assistant Licensure and/or Certification, Statement 4 (February 6, 1986); ABA, Standing Committee on Legal Assistants, "Position Paper on the Question of Legal Assistant Licensure or Certification" (December 10, 1985), at 6 and Conclusion 3. Recognition of the employing lawyer's obligation to facilitate the legal assistant's continuing professional education is, therefore, appropriate because of the benefits to both the law practice and the legal assistants and is consistent with the lawyer's own responsibility to maintain professional competence under Model Rule 1.1. See also EC 6–2 of the Model Code.

The Standing Committee is of the view that similar benefits will accrue to the lawyer and legal assistant if the legal assistant is included in the *pro bono publico* legal services that a lawyer has a clear obligation to provide under Model Rule 6.1 and, where appropriate, the legal assistant is encouraged to provide such services independently. The ability of a law firm to provide more *pro bono publico* services will be enhanced if legal assistants are included. Recognition of the legal assistant's role in such services is consistent with the role of the legal assistant in the contemporary delivery of legal services generally and is consistent with the lawyer's duty to the legal profession under Canon 2 of the Model Code.

THE STANDING COMMITTEE ON LEGAL ASSISTANTS
OF THE AMERICAN BAR ASSOCIATION
May 1991

ADOPTED BY ABA HOUSE OF DELEGATES
August 1991

---

9. While no state has apparently adopted a guideline similar to Model Guideline 10, parts 4 and 5 of NALA Guideline VIII suggest similar requirements. Sections III and V of NFPA's "Affirmation of Professional Responsibility" recognize a legal assistant's obligations to "maintain a high level of competence" (which "is achieved through continuing education") and to "serve the public interest." NFPA has also published a guide to assist legal assistant groups in developing public service projects. See NFPA, "Pro Bono Publico (For the Good of the People)" (1987).

APPENDIX F

PARALEGAL ASSOCIATIONS

NFPA ASSOCIATIONS

Region I

Alaska Association of Legal Assistants
P.O. Box 101956
Anchorage, AK 99510–1956

Arizona Association of Professional
Paralegals, Inc.
P.O. Box 25111
Phoenix, AZ 85002

Hawaii Association of Legal
Assistants
P.O. Box 674
Honolulu, HI 96809

Los Angeles Paralegal Association
P.O. Box 7803
Van Nuys, CA 91409 [(818) 347–1001]

Oregon Legal Assistants Association
P.O. Box 8523
Portland, OR 97207 [(503) 796–1671]

Sacramento Association of Legal
Assistants
P.O. Box 453
Sacramento, CA 95812–0453
[(916) 763–7851]

San Diego Association of Legal
Assistants
P.O. Box 87449
San Diego, CA 92138–7449
[(619) 491–1994]

San Francisco Association of Legal
Assistants
P.O. Box 26668
San Francisco, CA 94126–6668
[(415) 777–2390]

Washington State Paralegal
Association
P.O. Box 232
Ardenvoir, WA 98811 [(509) 784–9772]

Region II

Dallas Association of Legal Assistants
P.O. Box 12533
Dallas, TX 75225 [(214) 991–0853]

Gateway Paralegal Association*
P.O. Box 50233
St. Louis, MO 63105

Illinois Paralegal Association
P.O. Box 8089
Bartlett, IL 60103–8089
[(708) 837–8088]

Kansas City Association of Legal
Assistants
P.O. Box 13223
Kansas City, MO 64199
[(913) 381–4458]

Kansas Legal Assistants Society
P.O. Box 1675
Topeka, KS 66601

Legal Assistants of New Mexico
P.O. Box 1113
Albuquerque, NM 87103–1113
[(505) 260–7104]

Manitoba Association of Legal
Assistants, Inc.*
22–81 Tyndall Avenue
Winnipeg, Manitoba R2X 2W2

Minnesota Association of Legal
Assistants
2626 E. 82nd Street, Suite 201
Minneapolis, MN 55425
[(612) 853–0272]

New Orleans Paralegal Association
P.O. Box 30604
New Orleans, LA 70190

Northwest Missouri Paralegal
Association*
Box 7013
St. Joseph, MO 64507

Paralegal Association of
Wisconsin, Inc.
P.O. Box 92882
Milwaukee, WI 53202
[(414) 272–7168]

Rocky Mountain Legal Assistants
Association
P.O. Box 304
Denver, CO 80201 [(303) 369–1606]

Region III

Baltimore Association of Legal
Assistants
P.O. Box 13244
Baltimore, MD 21203
[(301) 576–BALA]

Cincinnati Paralegal Association
P.O. Box 1515
Cincinnati, OH 45201

Cleveland Association of Paralegals
P.O. Box 14247
Cleveland, OH 44114 [(216) 575–6090]

Columbia Legal Assistants
Association
P.O. Box 11634
Columbia, SC 29211–1634

Georgia Association of Legal
Assistants
P.O. Box 1802
Atlanta, GA 30301 [(404) 433–5252]

Greater Dayton Paralegal Association
P.O. Box 515, Mid-City Station
Dayton, OH 45402

---

*Affiliate member.

Greater Lexington Paralegal
    Association, Inc.
P.O. Box 574
Lexington, KY 40586

Indiana Paralegal Association
P.O. Box 44518
Indianapolis, IN 46204

Legal Assistants of Central Ohio
P.O. Box 15182
Columbus, OH 43215–0182
    [(614) 224–9700]

Louisville Association of Paralegals
P.O. Box 962
Louisville, KY 40201

Memphis Paralegal Association
P.O. Box 3646
Memphis, TN 38173–0646

Michiana Paralegal Association
P.O. Box 11458
South Bend, IN 46634

Mobile Association of Legal
    Assistants*
P.O. Box 1852
Mobile, AL 36633

National Capital Area Paralegal
    Association
P.O. Box 19124
Washington, DC 20036–9998
    [(202) 659–0243]

Northeastern Ohio Paralegal
    Association
P.O. Box 9236
Akron, OH 44305

Roanoke Valley Paralegal Association
P.O. Box 1505
Roanoke, VA 24007

Region IV

Central Connecticut Association of
    Legal Assistants
P.O. Box 230594
Hartford, CT 06123–0594

Central Massachusetts Paralegal
    Association
P.O. Box 444
Worcester, MA 01614

---

*Affiliate member.

Central Pennsylvania Paralegal
    Association
P.O. Box 11814
Harrisburg, PA 17108

Connecticut Association of Paralegals,
    Inc. (Fairfield County)
P.O. Box 134
Bridgeport, CT 06601

Connecticut Association of Paralegals
    (New Haven)
P.O. Box 862
New Haven, CT 06504–0862

Delaware Paralegal Association
P.O. Box 1362
Wilmington, DE 19899

Long Island Paralegal Association
c/o Valerie A. Murphy
58 Twin Lawns Ave.
Hicksville, NY 11801

Manhattan Paralegal Association, Inc.
521 Fifth Ave., 17th Floor
New York, NY 10175

Massachusetts Paralegal Association
P.O. Box 423
Boston, MA 02102 [(617) 469–7077]

Paralegal Association of
    Rochester, Inc.
P.O. Box 40567
Rochester, NY 14604

Philadelphia Association of Paralegals
2 Pen Center Plaza, Suite 200
Philadelphia, PA 19102
    [(215) 854–6352]

Pittsburgh Paralegal Association
P.O. Box 2845
Pittsburgh, PA 15230 [(412) 642–2745]

Rhode Island Paralegal Association
P.O. Box 1003
Providence, RI 02901

South Jersey Paralegal Association
P.O. Box 355
Haddonfield, NJ 08033

Southern Tier Association of
    Paralegals
P.O. Box 2555
Binghamton, NY 13902

West/Rock Paralegal Association
Suite 381–309 Mamaroneck Ave.
White Plains, NY 10601

Western Massachusetts Paralegal
    Association
P.O. Box 30005
Springfield, MA 01102

Western New York Paralegal
    Association, Inc.
P.O. Box 207, Niagara Square Station
Buffalo, NY 14202 [(716) 635–8250]

York County Paralegal Association
P.O. Box 2584
York, PA 17405–2584

NALA STATE AND
LOCAL AFFILIATES

(As of August 1994)
For addresses and telephone numbers
contact:
NALA Headquarters
1516 South Boston, Suite 200,
Tulsa, OK 74119
Phone: (918) 587-6828
FAX: (918) 582-6772

ALABAMA

Legal Assistant Society of Southern
    Institute/PJC
President: Douglas Ingram
Birmingham, AL

Alabama Association of Legal
    Assistants
President: Miriam Rosario, CLA
Birmingham, AL
NALA Liaison: Michael C. Ivey
Birmingham, AL

Samford Paralegal Association
President: Rebecca King
Birmingham, AL

ALASKA

Fairbanks Associations of Legal
    Assistants
President: Carolyn Bollman, CLA
North Pole, AK
NALA Liaison: Barbara A. Johnson,
    CLA
Fairbanks, AK

ARIZONA

Arizona Paralegal Association
President: Pamela J. Kieffer, CLAS
Glendale, AZ

NALA Liaison: Marian Johnson, CLA
Tempe, AZ

Legal Assistants of Metropolitan
    Phoenix
President: Ruth M. Murphy, CLA
Phoenix, AZ
NALA Liaison: Merilyn Ferrara, CLA
Phoenix, AZ

Tucson Association of Legal
    Assistants
President: Shirley L. Duran, CLA
Tucson, AZ
NALA Liaison: Mary Butera, CLA
Tucson, AZ

ARKANSAS

Arkansas Association of Legal
    Assistants
President: Patrice Carey
Little Rock, AR
NALA Liaison: Deborah J. Moon
Pine Bluff, AR

CALIFORNIA

Legal Assistants Association of Santa
    Barbara
President: Sonja B. Youngdahl
Santa Barbara, CA
NALA Liaison: Lana J. Clark, CLA
Santa Barbara, CA

Paralegal Association of Santa Clara
    County
President: Jean M. Cushman, CLA
San Jose, CA
NALA Liaison: Jo E. Floch, CLA
San Jose, CA

Ventura County Association of Legal
    Assistants
President: Cynthia J. Adams, CLA
Ventura, CA
NALA Liaison: Pamela K. Jansz, CLA
Oxnard, CA

COLORADO

Association of Legal Assistants of
    Colorado
President: Donna Coble, CLAS
Greeley, CO

FLORIDA

Florida Legal Assistants, Inc.
President: Donnajeanne B. Halder,
    CLAS
St. Petersburg, FL
NALA Liaison: Carol D. Holler, CLAS
Ft. Lauderdale, FL

Bay Area Legal Academy Student
    Association
President: George House, Jr.
Tampa, FL
NALA Liaison: Dr. Darline R. Root
Tampa, FL

Dade Association of Legal Assistants
President: Judith W. Kingman, CLA
Ft. Lauderdale, FL
NALA Liaison: Iris Krinsky, CLAS
Miami, FL

Gainesville Association of Legal
    Assistants
President: Melissa Flanagan
Gainesville, FL
NALA Liaison: Pamela S. Craig
Gainesville, FL

Jacksonville Legal Assistants
President: Tana J. Stringfellow, CLA
Jacksonville, FL
NALA Liaison: Mary Cathy Cassels,
    CLA
Jacksonville, FL

Orlando Legal Assistants
President: Jennifer H. Cooper, CLA
Orlando, FL
NALA Liaison: Lisa Vander Weide,
    CLA
Orlando, FL

Pensacola Legal Assistants
President: Carol G. Skipper
Pensacola, FL
NALA Liaison: Teresa M. Shimek,
    CLA
Pensacola, FL

Volusia Association of Legal
    Assistants
President: Mary Joan Harrington
Ormond Beach, FL
NALA Liaison: Theresa J. Thornton-
    Hill, CLA
Holly Hill, FL

GEORGIA

Georgia Legal Assistants
President: Elaine H. Hall, CLA
Alma, GA
NALA Liaison: Phyllis H. Driver,
    CLA
Waycross, GA

Professional Paralegals of Georgia
President: Judith W. McCutcheon,
    CLA
Atlanta, GA
NALA Liaison: Donita C.
    Berckemeyer, CLA
Atlanta, GA

Southeastern Association of Legal
    Assistants of Georgia
President: Linda Phipps, CLAS
Savannah, GA
NALA Liaison: Kathy J. Ulmer
Savannah, GA

South Georgia Association of Legal
    Assistants
President: Perry D. Wendel, CLA
Lake Park, GA
NALA Liaison: Michelle D. Adkins,
    CLA
Valdosta, GA

IDAHO

Gem State Association of Legal
    Assistants
President: Susan Carlson, CLA
Kethcum, ID
NALA Liaison: Ruby A. Becker, CLA
Kethcum, ID

ILLINOIS

Central Illinois Paralegal Association
President: Darlene G. Johnson, CLA
Bloomington, IL
NALA Liaison: Carolyn S. Pitts, CLA
Champaign, IL

Heart of Illinois Paralegal Association
President: Amy DeTrempe-Williams
Peoria, IL
NALA Liaison: Sharon R. Moke
Peoria, IL

INDIANA

Indiana Legal Assistants
President: Tina M. Keller
Terre Haute, IN
NALA Liaison: Dorothy M. French,
    CLA
Evansville, IN

KANSAS

Kansas Association of Legal
    Assistants
President: Marie T. Martin, CLA
Wichita, KS
NALA Liaison: Sharon K. Engle, CLA
Wichita, KS

KENTUCKY

Western Kentucky Paralegals
President: Lora L. Roberts, CLAS
Murray, KY
NALA Liaison: Lora L. Roberts, CLAS
Murray, KY

LOUISIANA

Louisiana State Paralegal Association
President: Sandra A. Smith, CLAS
Alexandria, LA
NALA Liaison: Karen L. McKnight,
    CLA
Alexandria, LA

Northwest Louisiana Paralegal
    Association
President: Karen M. Greer, CLAS
Shreveport, LA
NALA Liaison: Cindy L. Vucinovich,
    CLAS
Shreveport, LA

MAINE

Maine State Association of Legal
    Assistants
President: Ann Hartzler, CLA
Portland, ME
NALA Liaison: Judith A. Allen, CLA
Portland, ME

MICHIGAN

Legal Assistants Association of
    Michigan
President: Darcy L. Dustin
Kalamazoo, MI
NALA Liaison: Charlotte G. Curiston
Dearborn, MI

MINNESOTA

Minnesota Paralegal Association
President: Monica Sveen-Ziebell
Rochester, MN
NALA Liaison: Muriel L. Hinrichs
Rochester, MN

MISSISSIPPI

Mississippi Association of Legal
    Assistants
President: Debra D. Hammack
Jackson, MS
NALA Liaison: Gail Lucas, CLAS
Hattiesburg, MS

Mississippi College Society of Legal
    Assistants
President: LaTricia M. Nelson
Jackson, MS
NALA Liaison: Dawn Crosby, CLA
Clinton, MS

Society for Paralegal Studies
University of Southern Mississippi
Jamie B. Thomas, President
Franklinton, LA
Advisor: Gail L. Lucas, CLAS
Hattiesburg, MS

MISSOURI

St. Louis Association of Legal
    Assistants
President: Stacia Sanders
St. Louis, MO
NALA Liaison: Shirley A. Bettis
Cedar Hill, MO

MONTANA

Montana Association of Legal
    Assistants
President: Barbara Jo Wilson, CLA
Missoula, MT
NALA Liaison: Myrna L. O'Hare
Missoula, MT

NEBRASKA

Nebraska Association of Legal
    Assistants
President: Stefanie A. Neisen
Lincoln, NE
NALA Liaison: Lorrie C. Dahl
Lincoln, NE

NEVADA

Clark County Organization of Legal
    Assistants, Inc.
President: Dorothy C. Lappin, CLA
Las Vegas, NV
NALA Liaison: Betsy Branyan Kidder,
    CLAS
Las Vegas, NV

Sierra Nevada Association of
    Paralegals
President: Candace R. Jones, CLAS
Reno, NV
NALA Liaison: Carol A. Hunt
Reno, NV

NEW HAMPSHIRE

Paralegal Association of New
    Hampshire
President: Lorinda B. Gaillard
Concord, NH
NALA Liaison: Deborah A. West
Concord, NH

NEW JERSEY

The Legal Assistants Association of
    New Jersey, Inc.
President: Manny Ferrao
Rahway, NJ
NALA Liaison: Wendy Van Duyne
Elizabeth, NJ

NORTH CAROLINA

Coastal Carolina Paralegal Club
President: Nadine Nash
Jacksonville, NC
NALA Liaison: Col. Robert E. Switzer
Jacksonville, NC

North Carolina Paralegal
    Association, Inc.
President: Mary F. Haggerty, CLA
Charlotte, NC
NALA Liaison: Karen L. Grimes, CLA
Cary, NC

NORTH DAKOTA

Red River Valley Legal Assistants
President: Linda Brastrup Johnson,
    CLA
Moorhead, MN
NALA Liaison: Eileen Tronnes
    Nelson, CLA
Grand Forks, ND

Western Dakota Association of Legal
    Assistants
President: Candy L. Peterson, CLAS
Minot, ND
NALA Liaison: Connie L. Sundby,
    CLA
Williston, ND

OHIO

Toledo Association of Legal Assistants
President: Denise Wright
Maumee, OH
NALA Liaison: Cynthia L. Getzinger,
    CLA
Toledo, OH

OKLAHOMA

Oklahoma Paralegal Association
President: Lennis D. Alley, CLA
Ponca City, OK
NALA Liaison: Stephanie K. Mark,
    CLAS
Tulsa, OK

Rose State Paralegal Association
President: Judy Shaw
Midwest City, OK

Student Association of Legal
    Assistants
Rogers State College
President: Michelle K. Price
Claremore, OK

TJC Student Association of Legal
    Assistants
President: Judy Tucker
Tulsa, OK

Tulsa Association of Legal Assistants
President: Judy K. Johnson, CLA
Tulsa, OK
NALA Liaison: Toni Goss Johnson,
    CLAS
Broken Arrow, OK

OREGON

Pacific Northwest Legal Assistants
President: Perri L. Judd, CLA
Rosenburg, OR
NALA Liaison: Gayla K. Austin, CLA
Albany, OR

PENNSYLVANIA

Keystone Legal Assistant Association
President: Catrina L. Nuss, CLA
Harrisburg, PA
NALA Liaison: JoAnna M. Samosky,
    CLA
Pottsville, PA

SOUTH CAROLINA

Central Carolina Technical College
    Paralegal Association
President: Fay Steigerwalt
Sumter, SC
Faculty Advisor: Jim Curzan
Sumter, SC

Greenville Association of Legal
    Assistants
President: Linda J. Burns, CLAS
Greenville, SC
NALA Liaison: Paula Jones, CLA
Greenville, SC

Paralegal Association of Beaufort
    County South Carolina
President: Cynthia A. McClelland,
    CLAS
Hilton Head Island, SC

Tri-County Paralegal Association
President: Sylvia D. Pratt, CLA
Charleston, SC

SOUTH DAKOTA

South Dakota Legal Assistants
    Association, Inc.
President: Dory M. Maks
Rapid City, SD
NALA Liaison: Beverly McCracken,
    CLA
Rapid City, SD

TENNESSEE

Greater Memphis Legal Assistants,
    Inc.
President: Carol Scoggins, CLAS
Bartlett, TN
NALA Liaison: Wanda D. Howard,
    CLA
Memphis, TN

Tennessee Paralegal Association
President: Caleeta L. Beagles, CLA
Chattanooga, TN
NALA Liaison: Ann S. Burns, CLAS
Jackson, TN

TEXAS

Capital Area Paralegal Association
President: Gail ViDana Maskey
Pflugerville, TX
NALA Liaison: Christine Levy, CLA
Austin, TX

El Paso Association of Legal
    Assistants
President: Rosella A. Aguayo, CLAS
El Paso, TX
NALA Liaison: Martha G. Parton,
    CLA
El Paso, TX

Legal Assistant Association/Permian
    Basin
President: Len Redmon
Odessa, TX
NALA Liaison: Jo T. Behrends, CLA
Odessa, TX

Northeast Texas Association of Legal
    Assistants
President: Diane Hall, CLA
Longview, TX
NALA Liaison: Barbara J. Hensley,
    PLS
Longview, TX

Nueces County Association of Legal
    Assistants
President: Lillie E. Bordelon
Corpus Christi, TX
NALA Liaison: Evelyn Just, CLA
Corpus Christi, TX

Southeast Texas Association of Legal
    Assistants
President: Brenda E. Jenkins, CLA
Beaumont, TX
NALA Liaison: Lucinda (Cindy)
    Wagner, CLA
Beaumont, TX

Texarkana Association of Legal
    Assistants
President: Diane Plunkett, CLA
Texarkana, TX
NALA Liaison: Myra J. Conaway,
    CLA
Texarkana, TX

Texas Panhandle Association of Legal
    Assistants
President: Brenda Cole
Amarillo, TX
NALA Liaison: Julie Winkelman
Amarillo, TX

Tyler Area Association of Legal
Assistants
President: Carolyn S. Burton, CLA
Tyler, TX
NALA Liaison: Kathy C. Geoffrion,
CLAS
Tyler, TX

West Texas Association of Legal
Assistants
President: Ruth H. Bagwell, CLA
Lubbock, TX
NALA Liaison: Juanita Fortenberry,
CLA
Littlefield, TX

Wichita County Student Association
President: Kathy M. Parker, CLA
Wichita Falls, TX
NALA Liaison: Billie Ruth Goss
Wichita Falls, TX

UTAH

Legal Assistants Association of Utah
President: Marilu Peterson, CLAS
Salt Lake City, UT
NALA Liaison: Jan S. Mahoney, CLA
Salt Lake City, UT

VIRGINIA

Peninsula Legal Assistants, Inc.
President: Victoria Quadros
Poquoson, VA
NALA Liaison: Phyllis T. Anderson,
CLAS
Newport News, VA

Richmond Association of Legal
Assistants
President: Nellie J. Foley, CLA
Ashland, VA
NALA Liaison: Sheila H. Komito,
CLAS
Richmond, VA

Tidewater Association of Legal
Assistants
President: Carla L. Nagel, CLA
Poquoson, VA
NALA Liaison: Susan N.
Bawtinhimer, CLA
Norfolk, VA

VIRGIN ISLANDS

Virgin Islands Association of Legal
Assistants
President: Ann Clayton
Charlotte Amalie, VI
NALA Liaison: Jonetta Darden-
Vincent
Charlotte Amalie, VI

WASHINGTON

Association of Paralegals and Legal
Assistants of Washington State

President: Sheila M. White, CLAS
Spokane, WA

Columbia Basin College Paralegal
Association
President: Regina A. Stevens
Kennewick, WA
NALA Liaison: Kerri Wheeler Feeney,
CLAS
Richland, WA

WEST VIRGINIA

Legal Assistants of West Virginia, Inc.
President: Joyce A. Wilson
Charleston, WV
NALA Liaison: Joanne W. Rini, CLA
Charleston, WV

WISCONSIN

Madison Area Legal Assistants
Association
President: Beverly A. Potts, CLA
Madison, WI
NALA Liaison: Kristine Caldwell,
CLA
Madison, WI

WYOMING

Legal Assistants of Wyoming
President: Anita K. Schroeder, CLAS
Casper, WY
NALA Liaison: Carol D. Martin,
CLAS
Rawlins, WY

OTHER LAW-RELATED ASSOCIATIONS

American Association of Law
Libraries (AALL)
53 West Jackson Boulevard, Suite 940
Chicago, IL 60604
(312) 939–4764

American Association for Paralegal
Education (AAfPE)
P.O. Box 40244
Overland Park, KS 66204
(913) 381–4458

American Bar Association (ABA)
Standing Committee on Legal
Assistants
750 North Lake Shore Drive
Chicago, IL 60611
(312) 988–5000

Association of Legal Administrators
(ALA)
104 Wilmot Road, Suite 205
Deerfield, IL 60015–5195
(312) 940–9240

Legal Assistant Management
Association (LAMA)
P.O. Box 40129
Overland Park, KS 66204
(913) 381–4458

National Association for Independent
Paralegals
585 5th St. West
Sonoma, CA 95476

National Paralegal Association
P.O. Box 406
Solebury, PA 18963
(215) 297–8333

APPENDIX G

INFORMATION ON THE NALA's CERTIFIED LEGAL ASSISTANT (CLA) AND CERTIFIED LEGAL ASSISTANT SPECIALIST (CLAS) EXAMINATIONS*

CERTIFICATION—A PROFESSIONAL GOAL

Certification bestows a measure of professional recognition to those persons who achieve significant competence in the field.

This opportunity for the legal assistant profession is provided by the National Association of Legal Assistants, Inc. [NALA], through its national certification program. The CLA Certifying program consists of successful completion of a comprehensive two day examination. Thereafter, evidence of continuing legal education must be submitted periodically in order to maintain certification. The program is administered by the National Association of Legal Assistants through its Certifying Board which consists of a minimum of five legal assistants who have the Certified Legal Assistant and CLA Specialist designations, two attorneys and two paralegal educators. In 1994, the number of Certified Legal Assistants throughout the nation surpassed 6,500—legal assistants in 49 states, the District of Columbia and the Virgin Islands have been certified by NALA.

Although the goal of becoming a Certified Legal Assistant is a voluntary commitment, the Certified Legal Assistant designation is recognized in the legal field as denoting high standards of professionalism and excellence. The legal community recognizes Certified Legal Assistants have proven that their experience and knowledge are not restricted to a few limited areas but that they have a general knowledge and understanding of the entire profession and capabilities for exceeding minimal requirements.

The NALA CLA Certifying examination program involves successful completion of a two day examination administered in the Spring, in mid-July, and in cooperation with NALA Affiliated Associations in December. The body of knowledge required to attain the Certified Legal Assistant designation is great. Although the NALA Certifying Board recognizes the expertise required of a legal assistant cannot be reduced to a formula, certain basic

---

*This appendix presents excerpts from NALA's booklet entitled *The Certified Legal Assistant Program.* For information on upcoming CLA and CLAS examination dates and testing centers, contact NALA headquarters at (918) 587–6828.

skills common to the profession are measurable: verbal and written communication skills; judgment and analytical abilities; and an understanding of ethics, human relations, legal terminology, and legal research. The examination covers these areas as well as substantive knowledge of law and procedures. The substantive law section requires each candidate to complete a section on the American legal system and to choose and complete four of eight sections: litigation; estate planning and probate; real estate; criminal law; bankruptcy; contract; business organizations; and administrative law. As a standardized national examination, all sections are on the federal level—no state laws or procedures are tested.

As with all NALA programs, the purpose of the examination program is to help the legal assistant profession by serving as a means of distinguishing and recognizing excellence among legal assistants and by serving as a stabilizing force and directional tool in the growth on the profession. The Certified Legal Assistant program is not rigid—its foundation allows methodical and thoughtful change. It helps by attesting to the competency of certified legal assistants and by serving as a guideline for colleges and schools offering legal assistant programs. While the profession grows the individuals within must, too. Legal assistants are an integral part of the legal team and must strive to improve the profession. NALA's voluntary certification program is one answer to those needs.

OUTLINE—THE CERTIFIED LEGAL ASSISTANT EXAMINATION

Each section of the examination contains objective questions, such as multiple choice, true/false and matching. The sections on Communications and Judgment and Analytical Ability each contain short answer and/or essay questions.

Communications

This section of the Certified Legal Assistant examination covers the following areas of communications:

Word Usage	Correspondence
Punctuation	Concise Writing
Capitalization	Vocabulary
Grammar	Rules of Composition
Nonverbal Communication	

Ethics

This section deals with ethics in the legal assistant's contacts with employers, clients, co-workers and the general public. Unauthorized practice, ethical rules, practice rules and confidentiality are among the topics tested by this section.

Knowledge of the American Bar Association Rules of Professional Conduct and the National Association of Legal Assistants, Inc., Code of Ethics and Professional Responsibility is required by this examination.

Human Relations and Interviewing Techniques

The Human Relations portion encompasses professional and social contacts with the employer, clients and other office visitors, co-workers, including subordinates, and the public outside of the law office. For this reason, the legal assistant should be familiar with: authorized practice, ethical rules, practice rules, delegation of authority, consequences of delegation and confidentiality.

Interviewing Techniques confers basic principles, as agreed upon by most authors on the subject, definitions of terms of basic principles and handling of specialized interviews. Subject areas included in this section of the examination are:

- General considerations for the interviewing situation: courtesy, empathy, physical setting, body language.
- Initial Roadblocks—lapse of time, prejudiced, etc.
- Manner of questions
- Use of checklists for specific matters
- Special handling situations: the elderly, the very young
- Both initial and subsequent interviews are included as are both client and witness interviews.

Judgment and Analytical Ability

The sections of this part deal with (1) analyzing and categorizing facts and evidence; (2) the legal assistant's relationship with the lawyer, the legal secretary, the client, the courts and other law firms; (3) the legal assistant's reaction to specific situations; (4) handling telephone situations; and (5) reading comprehension and data interpretation. The section also contains an essay question which requires analysis of a research request and applicable law and the writing of a responsive memo.

Familiarity with the Rules of Professional Conduct of the American Bar Association and the Code of Ethics and Professional Responsibility of the National Association of Legal Assistants, Inc., will also be helpful. Knowledge of logical reasoning and experience as a legal assistant are valuable assets.

Legal Research

It is extremely important for the legal assistant to be able to use the most important "tool" of the legal profession—the law library. The purpose of the Legal Research section of the CLA Certifying Examination is to test your knowledge of the use of state and Federal codes, the statutes, the digests, case reports, various legal encyclopedias, court reports, Shepardizing and research procedure.

The amount of study and practice you will need to pass this section of the examination will depend on your current knowledge and experience with legal research. You can get excellent practice by researching various topics on your own.

Legal Terminology

The sections of this part deal with (1) Latin phrases; (2) legal phrases or terms in general; and (3) utilization and understanding of common legal terms.

The questions involve legal terminology and procedures used in general practice.

Substantive Law

The Substantive Law section of the CLA Certifying examination is divided into nine parts:

1. General (includes the American Legal System)
2. Administrative Law
3. Bankruptcy
4. Contract
5. Business Organization
6. Criminal
7. Litigation
8. Probate & Estate Planning
9. Real Estate

Each examinee will be required to take the general section and must select four out of the remaining eight specialty tests.

Those persons who are taking the examination, but have not had formal law courses, would benefit from a study of a current textbook in the area.

A great deal of the material covered in this section of the examination is acquired through work experience in the legal field. The Substantive Law mini-tests are designed to test the legal assistant's general knowledge of the fields of law.

STUDY METHODS

Generally, legal assistants study individually for the CLA Certifying Examination. A list of study references for each examination section and sample questions may be found in the Mock Examination and Study Guide available through NALA Headquarters. In addition to providing study references for this examination, this material will aid applicants in developing their own study programs.

Affiliated state and local legal assistant associations of the National Association of Legal Assistants have begun sponsoring study groups or review seminars for those interested in the CLA Certifying Examination. Notices of these programs are included in FACTS & FINDINGS, NALA's quarterly publication, and in the membership newsletter when available. Non-members may call NALA Headquarters for this information or contact state or local associations direct.

The NALA CLA Exam Preparation Manual is available through West Publishing Company. Authored by Attorney Virginia Koerselman, in association with NALA, this manual is a useful tool for preparing to take the NALA Certifying Examination. Copies may be obtained by calling West Publishing Company at (800) 328–9352.

Formal education courses are recommended, especially in assisting a candidate to prepare for the substantive law section. Should you choose this as a study option be sure to keep in mind that all substantive law sections are based on federal rules, codes, practice and procedure. No state laws, codes or procedures are tested.

★ ★ ★ ★

GRADING AND RETAKE POLICY

A passing score of 70% is required for each of the examination sections. The substantive law section is graded as a whole. From a total of 500 points, 350 points is passing regardless of the distribution of points among the five parts.

Results are announced by the Certifying Board in writing to all examinees. Results are not available by telephone or by FAX.

Of the seven sections of the CLA Certifying examination, four sections must be successfully completed in order to retake only those sections failed.

Applicants in retake status may attend a maximum of five retake sessions within a three year period. Applicants in retake status will be allowed to choose which sections will be retaken during any retake session. Again, an applicant can only attend a retake session five times within the three year period. The examination must be successfully completed within five retake sessions in a three year period, or credit for all passed sections will be forfeited. If less than four sections are successfully completed, the applicant must reapply for the full applications.

ELIGIBILITY REQUIREMENTS

An applicant for the Certified Legal Assistant examination must meet at least one of the three eligibility requirements listed on the Certified Legal Assistant application form [in the section of that form presented at the end of this appendix].

★ ★ ★ ★

MAINTENANCE OF CERTIFIED LEGAL ASSISTANT DESIGNATION

In recognition of the continuing change in laws and procedures that have a direct impact on the quality of work performed by legal assistants, Certified Legal Assistants are required to maintain their certified status by submitting proof of continuing education. The CLA Certifying designation is for a period of five years and if the Certified Legal Assistant submits proof of attendance in accordance with the requirements[,] . . . the certificate is renewed for another five years and the process begins again. Lifetime certification is not available.

The Certified Legal Assistant designation may be revoked for any one of the following reasons:

1. Falsification of information on application form.
2. Subsequent conviction of the unauthorized practice of law.
3. Failure to meet continuing legal education requirements as required by the Certifying Board.
4. Divulging the contents of any Examination Questions.
5. Subsequent conviction of a felony.
6. Violation of the NALA Code of Ethics and Professional Responsibility.

Individuals currently serving a prison term are ineligible to sit for the CLA examination.

★ ★ ★ ★

SPECIALTY CERTIFICATION

NALA has instituted the second phase of the CLA program—certification for those who specialize in a particular area of the law. Specialty Certification involves successful completion of a four hour in-depth examination.

Specialty Examination Descriptions

In July of 1982, the Certifying Board announced the availability of specialty certification in the two areas of Civil Litigation and Probate and Estate Planning to any CLA in good standing. In March 1984 a Corporate and Business Law specialty examination was added, Criminal Law and Procedure was added for the July 1984 testing, Real Estate Specialty examination was added in July 1987 and a Bankruptcy specialty was added in December 1992. These four hour examinations are administered during the same time as the full CLA examination. Specialty certification will be available in other practice areas in the future.

Bankruptcy   is a comprehensive examination testing knowledge of the Bankruptcy Code (Title 11 U.S.C. and Title 28 U.S.C.), bankruptcy rules and procedures, including the applicable Federal Rules of Civil Procedure and Federal Rules of Evidence, with regard to debtors and creditors.

Civil Litigation   will comprehensively test an applicants' knowledge in the areas of civil procedure, substantive law and litigation techniques. The examination covers the federal rules of civil [procedure], evidence and appellate procedure; civil substantive law (i.e., personal injury, products liability, contracts, etc.); legal terminology; and legal research. Applicants should also be familiar with document control, drafting of pleadings, abstracting information and general litigation techniques.

Probate and Estate Planning   covers general probate and trust law, federal estate tax, fiduciary income tax, drafting wills and trusts, and estate planning concepts.

Corporate and Business Law   covers the knowledge and applications of those principles of contract, tort, property, agency, employment, administrative, tax as it relates to business organizations, corporate, and partnership law which commonly constitute the subject matter known as business law. Examinees should be thoroughly familiar with the Uniform Commercial Code, Uniform Partnership Act, Uniform Limited Partnership Act, Model Business Corporate Act, as well as with the regulatory authority of those federal agencies which affect the business relationship such as the IRS, SEC, FTC, OSHA and EPA.

Criminal Law and Procedure specialty examination is a comprehensive examination testing an applicant's knowledge in the area of criminal procedure and law from arrest through trial. The examination covers components of substantive criminal law, procedural matters, and constitutional rights guaranteed to defendants. Applicants should be thoroughly familiar with the Federal Rules of Criminal Procedure, Evidence, and major United States Supreme Court Cases. The American Law Institute's Model Penal Code or any nutshell series, such as West, would be a good general reference for this examination.

Real Estate is a comprehensive examination testing the applicant's knowledge in the area of real estate purchases, sales, terminology, actions affecting title, oil, and gas, landlord/tenant relations, easements, abstracts, title insurance, liens, cluster developments, types of conveyances, methods of passing title included in conveyances, legal remedies associated with real estate and legal description of real estate.

The level of testing will require substantial experience in the specialty area. The examinations are offered at the same time as the regular examination.

Legal Assistants are becoming more and more specialized—the CLA Certifying examination tests the broad general skills required of all legal assistants. Specialty certification is a goal for those who want to be recognized for achieving significant competence in a particular field. Further, a legal assistant may want to take more than one specialty examination if a specialty changes over time.

Certified Legal Assistants are awarded two (2) units of continuing legal assistant education (CLAE) credit towards maintenance of the Certified Legal Assistant designation upon successful completion of a specialty examination.

Specialty Eligibility Requirements

The only eligibility requirement for the specialty examination is that an applicant must be a Certified Legal Assistant in good standing. Those who have allowed their certification to lapse through nonadherence to the continuing education requirements or those whose certification has been revoked, are not eligible to sit for a specialty examination.

★ ★ ★ ★

Specialty Grading and Retake Policy

Specialty examinations are four (4) hours in length and are divided into two (2) sections. There is a break after Section 1. An applicant cannot return to the first part of the examination after the break. The examination is graded as a whole and a score of 70% is the passing score for each specialty examination.

Specialty Examination Data: Certified Legal Assistant Specialists (Through April 1994)

Bankruptcy	25
Civil Litigation	286
Probate & Estate Planning	66
Corporate & Business Law	24
Criminal Law & Procedure	27
Real Estate Specialists	96
Total Specialists	524

REQUIREMENTS FOR MAINTAINING CERTIFIED LEGAL ASSISTANT STATUS

All Certified Legal Assistants must submit evidence of completion of five (5) units of Continuing Legal Assistant Education every five (5) years to maintain valid certification. A completed Recertification Audit Verification plus a fee of $50 will also be required at the time of recertification. Notice of one (1) year probation will be given to all Certified Legal Assistants failing to submit evidence of completion of the five (5) units of CLAE within the five (5) year period. If the Certified Legal Assistant fails to complete the above recertification requirements in this time certification will be revoked, with notice to the legal assistant.

All requests for CLAE credit are subject to Certifying Board approval. Relevancy is subject to approval by the NALA Certifying Board who may request employer attestation.

The categories of CLAE with unit values are:

Category A: Successful completion of a NALA Specialty Examination—2 units per Specialty Examination

Category B: Successful completion (Grade C or better) of a relevant course for a minimum of 3 quarter hours or 2 semester hours at an accredited institution of higher education. Relevancy may be requested by employer attestation and NALA Certifying Board approval—2 units per course.

Auditing of a relevant course, or completion of a relevant course not meeting above listed minimums—1 unit per course

(Clarification of hours: Institutions of higher education generally are organized into quarters—10–12 weeks in length and give "quarter hours" as unit of course measurement or into semesters 14–15 weeks in length and give "semester hours" as unit of course measurement. A 2 semester hour course is usually equal to a 3 quarter hour course. Minimums are specified only.

Clarification of "accredited": By any nationally recognized accrediting agency.)

Category C: Attendance at conferences, seminars, workshops, etc., on relevant topics for working legal assistants, with actual hours recorded. Minimum content of one hour required for consideration. Actual educational hours will be recorded and copy of brochure and/or program indicating schedule must be attached (unless a NALA-sponsored event.) Units will be recorded on the basis of ten hours of continuing education equaling one CLAE unit.

Category D: Certified Legal Assistant may petition NALA Certifying Board for credit for unusual experiences which may be considered for credit. Examples: teaching experience; extensive research beyond employment requirements on a topic related to the work of a practicing legal assistant which results in publication—limited to 2 units per petition.

Mechanics: It is the obligation of Certified Legal Assistants to secure supporting data (transcripts, employer and coordinator attestations, articles, etc.) to be submitted to NALA Headquarters as events are attended. These documents will be reviewed by the full Certifying Board for action. Request forms are available from NALA Headquarters, 1516 South Boston, Suite 200, Tulsa, Oklahoma 74119–4464.

NOTE: Effective October 1982, for recertification purposes, except in Category A, units for attending seminars in areas other than substantive law are limited to one unit maximum for any five year period.

Adopted 10/10/77; Amended 6/81; 8/82; 5/85; 5/87; 2/88; 5/88; 10/88; 3/93

CLA is a certification mark duly registered with the U.S. Patent and Trademark Office (No. 1131999). Any unauthorized use is strictly forbidden.

CLA Specialist is a certification mark duly registered with the U.S. Patent and Trademark Office (No. 1751731). Any unauthorized use is strictly forbidden.

Certified Legal Assistant Examination Application Form

NATIONAL ASSOCIATION OF LEGAL ASSISTANTS, INC.
1516 South Boston, Suite 200   Tulsa, Oklahoma 74119
(918) 587–6828   FAX (918) 582–6772

QUALIFICATIONS

Candidates for certification must meet one of the following requirements outlined in Categories 1, 2 or 3 below, at the time of filing this application form. Select the appropriate category based on your experience and training and complete the corresponding parts of this application form, beginning on the next page. Individuals currently serving a prison term are ineligible to sit for the CLA certifying examination.

Category 1

QUALIFICATIONS: Graduation from a legal assistant program that is:
  a) Approved by the American Bar Association, or
  b) An associate degree program, or
  c) A post-baccalaureate certificate program in legal assistant studies, or
  d) A bachelor's degree program in legal assistant studies, or
  e) A legal assistant program which consists of a minimum of 60 semester (or equivalent quarter)* hours of which at least 15 semester hours (or equivalent quarter hours)** are substantive legal courses.

  * *900 clock hours of a legal assistant program will be considered equivalent to 60 semester hours.*
  90 quarter hours of a legal assistant program will be considered equivalent to 60 semester hours.
  ** *225 clock hours of substantive legal courses will be considered equivalent to 15 semester hours.*
  22½ quarter hours of legal courses will be considered equivalent to 15 semester hours.

All applicants applying under this category must submit with this application form a copy of the school's official transcript showing all courses taken and date of graduation. For those applying under "c" a letter or copy of a certificate of completion must be submitted. The letter or certificate must include a statement that the certificate program is a post-baccalaureate program. **The application form will be considered incomplete without a copy of the school's official transcript, and the post-baccalaureate statement if applying under "c".**

Category 2

QUALIFICATIONS: A bachelor's degree in any field plus one (1) year's experience as a legal assistant*. Copy of official transcript showing date of graduation must be attached to the application form.
* *Successful completion of at least 15 semester hours (or 22½ quarter hours or 225 clock hours) of substantive legal assistance courses will be considered equivalent to one year experience as a legal assistant.*

All applicants applying under this category must submit with this application form a copy of the school's official transcript showing receipt of a bachelor's degree and date of completion. Those applying under the provision allowing for additional course work in lieu of the one year's work experience, must submit an official school transcript showing complete course work. **The application form will be considered incomplete without a copy of the school's official transcript, along with either verification of experience or official school transcript equivalent courses in lieu of experience.**

Category 3

QUALIFICATIONS: A high school diploma or equivalent plus seven (7) years' experience as a legal assistant under the supervision of a member of the Bar plus evidence of a minimum of twenty (20) hours of continuing legal education credit to have been completed within a two-year period prior to application for the exam.

Within this category, "legal assistant" is defined as: *legal assistants are a distinguishable group of persons who assist attorneys in the delivery of legal services. Through formal education, training and experience, legal assistants have knowledge and expertise regarding the legal system and substantive and procedural law which qualify them to do work of a legal nature under the supervision of an attorney.*

Evidence of continuing education credit is documented by the attorney/employer attestation that must be signed to complete this application form. No further documentation is required.

Appendix H

The Constitution of the United States

Preamble

We the People of the United States, in Order to form a more perfect Union, establish Justice, insure domestic Tranquility, provide for the common defence, promote the general Welfare, and secure the Blessings of Liberty to ourselves and our Posterity, do ordain and establish this Constitution for the United States of America.

Article I

Section 1. All legislative Powers herein granted shall be vested in a Congress of the United States, which shall consist of a Senate and House of Representatives.

Section 2. The House of Representatives shall be composed of Members chosen every second Year by the People of the several States, and the Electors in each State shall have the Qualifications requisite for Electors of the most numerous Branch of the State Legislature.

No Person shall be a Representative who shall not have attained to the Age of twenty five Years, and been seven Years a Citizen of the United States, and who shall not, when elected, be an Inhabitant of that State in which he shall be chosen.

Representatives and direct Taxes shall be apportioned among the several States which may be included within this Union, according to their respective Numbers, which shall be determined by adding to the whole Number of free Persons, including those bound to Service for a Term of Years, and excluding Indians not taxed, three fifths of all other Persons. The actual Enumeration shall be made within three Years after the first Meeting of the Congress of the United States, and within every subsequent Term of ten Years, in such Manner as they shall by Law direct. The Number of Representatives shall not exceed one for every thirty Thousand, but each State shall have at Least one Representative; and until such enumeration shall be made, the State of New Hampshire shall be entitled to chuse three, Massachusetts eight, Rhode Island and Providence Plantations one, Connecticut five, New York six, New Jersey four, Pennsylvania eight, Delaware one, Maryland six, Virginia ten, North Carolina five, South Carolina five, and Georgia three.

When vacancies happen in the Representation from any State, the Executive Authority thereof shall issue Writs of Election to fill such Vacancies.

The House of Representatives shall chuse their Speaker and other Officers; and shall have the sole Power of Impeachment.

Section 3.   The Senate of the United States shall be composed of two Senators from each State, chosen by the Legislature thereof, for six Years; and each Senator shall have one Vote.

Immediately after they shall be assembled in Consequence of the first Election, they shall be divided as equally as may be into three Classes. The Seats of the Senators of the first Class shall be vacated at the Expiration of the second Year, of the second Class at the Expiration of the fourth Year, and of the third Class at the Expiration of the sixth Year, so that one third may be chosen every second Year; and if Vacancies happen by Resignation, or otherwise, during the Recess of the Legislature of any State, the Executive thereof may make temporary Appointments until the next Meeting of the Legislature, which shall then fill such Vacancies.

No Person shall be a Senator who shall not have attained to the Age of thirty Years, and been nine Years a Citizen of the United States, and who shall not, when elected, be an Inhabitant of that State for which he shall be chosen.

The Vice President of the United States shall be President of the Senate, but shall have no Vote, unless they be equally divided.

The Senate shall chuse their other Officers, and also a President pro tempore, in the Absence of the Vice President, or when he shall exercise the Office of President of the United States.

The Senate shall have the sole Power to try all Impeachments. When sitting for that Purpose, they shall be on Oath or Affirmation. When the President of the United States is tried, the Chief Justice shall preside: And no Person shall be convicted without the Concurrence of two thirds of the Members present.

Judgment in Cases of Impeachment shall not extend further than to removal from Office, and disqualification to hold and enjoy any Office of honor, Trust, or Profit under the United States: but the Party convicted shall nevertheless be liable and subject to Indictment, Trial, Judgment, and Punishment, according to Law.

Section 4.   The Times, Places and Manner of holding Elections for Senators and Representatives, shall be prescribed in each State by the Legislature thereof; but the Congress may at any time by Law make or alter such Regulations, except as to the Places of chusing Senators.

The Congress shall assemble at least once in every Year, and such Meeting shall be on the first Monday in December, unless they shall by Law appoint a different Day.

Section 5.   Each House shall be the Judge of the Elections, Returns, and Qualifications of its own Members, and a Majority of each shall constitute a Quorum to do Business; but a smaller Number may adjourn from day to day, and may be authorized to compel the Attendance of absent Members, in such Manner, and under such Penalties as each House may provide.

Each House may determine the Rules of its Proceedings, punish its Members for disorderly Behavior, and, with the Concurrence of two thirds, expel a Member.

Each House shall keep a Journal of its Proceedings, and from time to time publish the same, excepting such Parts as may in their Judgment require Secrecy; and the Yeas and Nays of the Members of either House on any question shall, at the Desire of one fifth of those Present, be entered on the Journal.

Neither House, during the Session of Congress, shall, without the Consent of the other, adjourn for more than three days, nor to any other Place than that in which the two Houses shall be sitting.

Section 6.   The Senators and Representatives shall receive a Compensation for their Services, to be ascertained by Law, and paid out of the Treasury of the United States. They shall in all Cases, except Treason, Felony and Breach of the Peace, be privileged from Arrest during their Attendance at the Session of their respective Houses, and in going to and returning from the same; and for any Speech or Debate in either House, they shall not be questioned in any other Place.

No Senator or Representative shall, during the Time for which he was elected, be appointed to any civil Office under the Authority of the United States, which shall have been created, or the Emoluments whereof shall have been increased during such time; and no Person holding any Office under the United States, shall be a Member of either House during his Continuance in Office.

Section 7.   All Bills for raising Revenue shall originate in the House of Representatives; but the Senate may propose or concur with Amendments as on other Bills.

Every Bill which shall have passed the House of Representatives and the Senate, shall, before it become a Law, be presented to the President of the United States; If he approve he shall sign it, but if not he shall return it, with his Objections to the House in which it shall have originated, who shall enter the Objections at large on their Journal, and proceed to reconsider it. If after such Reconsideration two thirds of that House shall agree to pass the Bill, it shall be sent together with the Objections, to the other House, by which it shall likewise be reconsidered, and if approved by two thirds of that House, it shall become a Law. But in all such Cases the Votes of both Houses shall be determined by Yeas and Nays, and the Names of the Persons voting for and against the Bill shall be entered on the Journal of each House respectively. If any Bill shall not be returned by the President within ten Days (Sundays excepted) after it shall have been presented to him, the Same shall be a Law, in like Manner as if he had signed it, unless the Congress by their Adjournment prevent its Return in which Case it shall not be a Law.

Every Order, Resolution, or Vote, to which the Concurrence of the Senate and House of Representatives may be necessary (except on a question of Adjournment) shall be presented to the President of the United States; and before the Same shall take Effect, shall be approved by him, or being disapproved by him, shall be repassed by two thirds of the Senate and House of Representatives, according to the Rules and Limitations prescribed in the Case of a Bill.

Section 8. The Congress shall have Power To lay and collect Taxes, Duties, Imposts and Excises, to pay the Debts and provide for the common Defence and general Welfare of the United States; but all Duties, Imposts and Excises shall be uniform throughout the United States;

To borrow Money on the credit of the United States;

To regulate Commerce with foreign Nations, and among the several States, and with the Indian Tribes;

To establish an uniform Rule of Naturalization, and uniform Laws on the subject of Bankruptcies throughout the United States;

To coin Money, regulate the Value thereof, and of foreign Coin, and fix the Standard of Weights and Measures;

To provide for the Punishment of counterfeiting the Securities and current Coin of the United States;

To establish Post Offices and post Roads;

To promote the Progress of Science and useful Arts, by securing for limited Times to Authors and Inventors the exclusive Right to their respective Writings and Discoveries;

To constitute Tribunals inferior to the supreme Court;

To define and punish Piracies and Felonies committed on the high Seas, and Offenses against the Law of Nations;

To declare War, grant Letters of Marque and Reprisal, and make Rules concerning Captures on Land and Water;

To raise and support Armies, but no Appropriation of Money to that Use shall be for a longer Term than two Years;

To provide and maintain a Navy;

To make Rules for the Government and Regulation of the land and naval Forces;

To provide for calling forth the Militia to execute the Laws of the Union, suppress Insurrections and repel Invasions;

To provide for organizing, arming, and disciplining, the Militia, and for governing such Part of them as may be employed in the Service of the United States, reserving to the States respectively, the Appointment of the Officers, and the Authority of training the Militia according to the discipline prescribed by Congress;

To exercise exclusive Legislation in all Cases whatsoever, over such District (not exceeding ten Miles square) as may, by Cession of particular States, and the Acceptance of Congress, become the Seat of the Government of the United States, and to exercise like Authority over all Places purchased by the Consent of the Legislature of the State in which the Same shall be, for the Erection of Forts, Magazines, Arsenals, dock-Yards, and other needful Buildings;—And

To make all Laws which shall be necessary and proper for carrying into Execution the foregoing Powers, and all other Powers vested by this Constitution in the Government of the United States, or in any Department or Officer thereof.

Section 9. The Migration or Importation of such Persons as any of the States now existing shall think proper to admit, shall not be prohibited by the Congress prior to the Year one thousand eight hundred and eight, but a Tax or duty may be imposed on such Importation, not exceeding ten dollars for each Person.

The privilege of the Writ of Habeas Corpus shall not be suspended, unless when in Cases of Rebellion or Invasion the public Safety may require it.

No Bill of Attainder or ex post facto Law shall be passed.

No Capitation, or other direct, Tax shall be laid, unless in Proportion to the Census or Enumeration herein before directed to be taken.

No Tax or Duty shall be laid on Articles exported from any State.

No Preference shall be given by any Regulation of Commerce or Revenue to the Ports of one State over those of another: nor shall Vessels bound to, or from, one State be obliged to enter, clear, or pay Duties in another.

No Money shall be drawn from the Treasury, but in Consequence of Appropriations made by Law; and a regular Statement and Account of the Receipts and Expenditures of all public Money shall be published from time to time.

No Title of Nobility shall be granted by the United States: And no Person holding any Office of Profit or Trust under them, shall, without the Consent of the Congress, accept of any present, Emolument, Office, or Title, of any kind whatever, from any King, Prince, or foreign State.

Section 10.   No State shall enter into any Treaty, Alliance, or Confederation; grant Letters of Marque and Reprisal; coin Money; emit Bills of Credit; make any Thing but gold and silver Coin a Tender in Payment of Debts; pass any Bill of Attainder, ex post facto Law, or Law impairing the Obligation of Contracts, or grant any Title of Nobility.

No State shall, without the Consent of the Congress, lay any Imposts or Duties on Imports or Exports, except what may be absolutely necessary for executing its inspection Laws: and the net Produce of all Duties and Imposts, laid by any State on Imports or Exports, shall be for the Use of the Treasury of the United States; and all such Laws shall be subject to the Revision and Controul of the Congress.

No State shall, without the Consent of Congress, lay any Duty of Tonnage, keep Troops, or Ships of War in time of Peace, enter into any Agreement or Compact with another State, or with a foreign Power, or engage in War, unless actually invaded, or in such imminent Danger as will not admit of delay.

ARTICLE II

Section 1.   The executive Power shall be vested in a President of the United States of America. He shall hold his Office during the Term of four Years, and, together with the Vice President, chosen for the same Term, be elected, as follows:

Each State shall appoint, in such Manner as the Legislature thereof may direct, a Number of Electors, equal to the whole Number of Senators and Representatives to which the State may be entitled in the Congress; but no Senator or Representative, or Person holding an Office of Trust or Profit under the United States, shall be appointed an Elector.

The Electors shall meet in their respective States, and vote by Ballot for two Persons, of whom one at least shall not be an Inhabitant of the same State with themselves. And they shall make a List of all the Persons voted for, and of the Number of Votes for each; which List they shall sign and certify, and transmit sealed to the Seat of the Government of the United States, directed to the President of the Senate. The President of the Senate shall, in the Presence of the Senate and House of Representatives, open all the Certificates, and the Votes shall then be counted. The Person having the greatest Number of Votes shall be the President, if such Number be a Majority of the whole Number of Electors appointed; and if there be more than one who have such Majority, and have an equal Number of Votes, then the House of Representatives shall immediately chuse by Ballot one of them for President; and if no Person have a Majority, then from the five highest on the List the said House shall in like Manner chuse the President. But in chusing the President, the Votes shall be taken by States, the Representation from each State having one Vote; A quorum for this Purpose shall consist of a Member or Members from two thirds of the States, and a Majority of all the States shall be necessary to a Choice. In every Case, after the Choice of the President, the Person having the greater Number of Votes of the Electors shall be the Vice President. But if there should remain two or more who have equal Votes, the Senate shall chuse from them by Ballot the Vice President.

The Congress may determine the Time of chusing the Electors, and the Day on which they shall give their Votes; which Day shall be the same throughout the United States.

No person except a natural born Citizen, or a Citizen of the United States, at the time of the Adoption of this Constitution, shall be eligible to the Office of President; neither shall any Person be eligible to that Office who shall not have attained to the Age of thirty five Years, and been fourteen Years a Resident within the United States.

In Case of the Removal of the President from Office, or of his Death, Resignation or Inability to discharge the Powers and Duties of the said Office, the same shall devolve on the Vice President, and the Congress may by Law provide for the Case of Removal, Death, Resignation or Inability, both of the President and Vice President, declaring what Officer shall then act as President, and such Officer shall act accordingly, until the Disability be removed, or a President shall be elected.

The President shall, at stated Times, receive for his Services, a Compensation, which shall neither be increased nor diminished during the Period for which he shall have been elected, and he shall not receive within that Period any other Emolument from the United States, or any of them.

Before he enter on the Execution of his Office, he shall take the following Oath or Affirmation: ``I do solemnly swear (or affirm) that I will faithfully execute the Office of President of the United States, and will to the best of my Ability, preserve, protect and defend the Constitution of the United States.''

Section 2.   The President shall be Commander in Chief of the Army and Navy of the United States, and of the Militia of the several States, when called into the actual Service of the United States; he may require the Opinion, in writing, of the principal Officer in each of the executive Departments, upon any Subject relating to the Duties of their respective Offices, and he shall have Power to grant Reprieves and Pardons for Offenses against the United States, except in Cases of Impeachment.

He shall have Power, by and with the Advice and Consent of the Senate to make Treaties, provided two thirds of the Senators present concur; and he shall nominate, and by and with the Advice and Consent of the Senate, shall appoint Ambassadors, other public Ministers and Consuls, Judges of the supreme Court, and all other Officers of the United States, whose Appointments are not herein otherwise provided for, and which shall be established by Law; but the Congress may by Law vest the Appointment of such inferior Officers, as they think proper, in the President alone, in the Courts of Law, or in the Heads of Departments.

The President shall have Power to fill up all Vacancies that may happen during the Recess of the Senate, by granting Commissions which shall expire at the End of their next Session.

Section 3.   He shall from time to time give to the Congress Information of the State of the Union, and recommend to their Consideration such Measures as he shall judge necessary and expedient; he may, on extraordinary Occasions, convene both Houses, or either of them, and in Case of Disagreement between them, with Respect to the Time of Adjournment, he may adjourn them to such Time as he shall think proper; he shall receive Ambassadors and other public Ministers; he shall take Care that the Laws be faithfully executed, and shall Commission all the Officers of the United States.

Section 4.   The President, Vice President and all civil Officers of the United States, shall be removed from Office on Impeachment for, and Conviction of, Treason, Bribery, or other high Crimes and Misdemeanors.

ARTICLE III

Section 1.   The judicial Power of the United States, shall be vested in one supreme Court, and in such inferior Courts as the Congress may from time to time ordain and establish. The Judges, both of the supreme and inferior Courts, shall hold their Offices during good Behaviour, and shall, at stated Times, receive for their Services a Compensation, which shall not be diminished during their Continuance in Office.

Section 2.   The judicial Power shall extend to all Cases, in Law and Equity, arising under this Constitution, the Laws of the United States, and Treaties made, or which shall be made, under their Authority;—to all Cases affecting Ambassadors, other public Ministers and Consuls;—to all Cases of admiralty and maritime Jurisdiction;—to Controversies to which the United States shall be a Party;—to Controversies between two or more States;—between a State and Citizens of another State;—between Citizens of different States;—between Citizens of the same State claiming Lands under Grants of different States, and between a State, or the Citizens thereof, and foreign States, Citizens or Subjects.

In all Cases affecting Ambassadors, other public Ministers and Consuls, and those in which a State shall be a Party, the supreme Court shall have original Jurisdiction. In all the other Cases before mentioned, the supreme Court shall have appellate Jurisdiction, both as to Law and Fact, with such Exceptions, and under such Regulations as the Congress shall make.

The Trial of all Crimes, except in Cases of Impeachment, shall be by Jury; and such Trial shall be held in the State where the said Crimes shall have been committed; but when not committed within any State, the Trial shall be at such Place or Places as the Congress may by Law have directed.

Section 3. Treason against the United States, shall consist only in levying War against them, or, in adhering to their Enemies, giving them Aid and Comfort. No Person shall be convicted of Treason unless on the Testimony of two Witnesses to the same overt Act, or on Confession in open Court.

The Congress shall have Power to declare the Punishment of Treason, but no Attainder of Treason shall work Corruption of Blood, or Forfeiture except during the Life of the Person attainted.

ARTICLE IV

Section 1. Full Faith and Credit shall be given in each State to the public Acts, Records, and judicial Proceedings of every other State. And the Congress may by general Laws prescribe the Manner in which such Acts, Records and Proceedings shall be proved, and the Effect thereof.

Section 2. The Citizens of each State shall be entitled to all Privileges and Immunities of Citizens in the several States.

A Person charged in any State with Treason, Felony, or other Crime, who shall flee from Justice, and be found in another State, shall on Demand of the executive Authority of the State from which he fled, be delivered up, to be removed to the State having Jurisdiction of the Crime.

No Person held to Service or Labour in one State, under the Laws thereof, escaping into another, shall, in Consequence of any Law or Regulation therein, be discharged from such Service or Labour, but shall be delivered up on Claim of the Party to whom such Service or Labour may be due.

Section 3. New States may be admitted by the Congress into this Union; but no new State shall be formed or erected within the Jurisdiction of any other State; nor any State be formed by the Junction of two or more States, or Parts of States, without the Consent of the Legislatures of the States concerned as well as of the Congress.

The Congress shall have Power to dispose of and make all needful Rules and Regulations respecting the Territory or other Property belonging to the United States; and nothing in this Constitution shall be so construed as to Prejudice any Claims of the United States, or of any particular State.

Section 4. The United States shall guarantee to every State in this Union a Republican Form of Government, and shall protect each of them against Invasion; and on Application of the Legislature, or of the Executive (when the Legislature cannot be convened) against domestic Violence.

ARTICLE V

The Congress, whenever two thirds of both Houses shall deem it necessary, shall propose Amendments to this Constitution, or, on the Application of the Legislatures of two thirds of the several States, shall call a Convention for proposing Amendments, which, in either Case, shall be valid to all Intents and Purposes, as part of this Constitution, when ratified by the Legislatures of three fourths of the several States, or by Conventions in three fourths thereof, as the one or the other Mode of Ratification may be proposed by the Congress; Provided that no Amendment which may be made prior to the Year One thousand eight hundred and eight shall in any Manner affect the first and fourth Clauses in the Ninth Section of the first Article; and that no State, without its Consent, shall be deprived of its equal Suffrage in the Senate.

ARTICLE VI

All Debts contracted and Engagements entered into, before the Adoption of this Constitution shall be as valid against the United States under this Constitution, as under the Confederation.

This Constitution, and the Laws of the United States which shall be made in Pursuance thereof; and all Treaties made, or which shall be made, under the Authority of the United States, shall be the supreme Law of the Land; and the Judges in every State shall be bound thereby, any Thing in the Constitution or Laws of any State to the Contrary notwithstanding.

The Senators and Representatives before mentioned, and the Members of the several State Legislatures, and all executive and judicial Officers, both of the United States and of the several States, shall be bound by Oath or Affirmation, to support this Constitution; but no religious Test shall ever be required as a Qualification to any Office or public Trust under the United States.

ARTICLE VII

The Ratification of the Conventions of nine States shall be sufficient for the Establishment of this Constitution between the States so ratifying the Same.

AMENDMENT I [1791]

Congress shall make no law respecting an establishment of religion, or prohibiting the free exercise thereof; or abridging the freedom of speech, or of the press; or the right of the people peaceably to assembly, and to petition the Government for a redress of grievances.

AMENDMENT II [1791]

A well regulated Militia, being necessary to the security of a free State, the right of the people to keep and bear Arms, shall not be infringed.

AMENDMENT III [1791]

No Soldier shall, in time of peace be quartered in any house, without the consent of the Owner, nor in time of war, but in a manner to be prescribed by law.

AMENDMENT IV [1791]

The right of the people to be secure in their persons, houses, papers, and effects, against unreasonable searches and seizures, shall not be violated, and no Warrants shall issue, but upon probable cause, supported by Oath or affirmation, and particularly describing the place to be searched, and the persons or things to be seized.

AMENDMENT V [1791]

No person shall be held to answer for a capital, or otherwise infamous crime, unless on a presentment or indictment of a Grand Jury, except in cases arising in the land or naval forces, or in the Militia, when in actual service in time of War or public danger; nor shall any person be subject for the same offence to be twice put in jeopardy of life or limb; nor shall be compelled in any criminal case to be a witness against himself, nor be deprived of life, liberty, or property, without due process of law; nor shall private property be taken for public use, without just compensation.

AMENDMENT VI [1791]

In all criminal prosecutions, the accused shall enjoy the right to a speedy and public trial, by an impartial jury of the State and district wherein the crime shall have been committed, which district shall have been previously ascertained by law, and to be informed of the nature and cause of the accusation; to be confronted with the witnesses against him; to have compulsory process for obtaining witnesses in his favor, and to have the Assistance of Counsel for his defence.

AMENDMENT VII [1791]

In Suits at common law, where the value in controversy shall exceed twenty dollars, the right of trial by jury shall be preserved, and no fact tried by jury, shall be otherwise re-examined in any Court of the United States, than according to the rules of the common law.

AMENDMENT VIII [1791]

Excessive bail shall not be required, nor excessive fines imposed, nor cruel and unusual punishments inflicted.

AMENDMENT IX [1791]

The enumeration in the Constitution, of certain rights, shall not be construed to deny or disparage others retained by the people.

AMENDMENT X [1791]

The powers not delegated to the United States by the Constitution, nor prohibited by it to the States, are reserved to the States respectively, or to the people.

AMENDMENT XI [1798]

The Judicial power of the United States shall not be construed to extend to any suit in law or equity, commenced or prosecuted against one of the United States by Citizens of another State, or by Citizens or Subjects of any Foreign State.

AMENDMENT XII [1804]

The Electors shall meet in their respective states, and vote by ballot for President and Vice-President, one of whom, at least, shall not be an inhabitant of the same state with themselves; they shall name in their ballots the person voted for as President, and in distinct ballots the person voted for as Vice-President, and they shall make distinct lists of all persons voted for as President, and of all persons voted for as Vice-President, and of the number of votes for each, which lists they shall sign and certify, and transmit sealed to the seat of the government of the United States, directed to the President of the Senate;—The President of the Senate shall, in the presence of the Senate and House of Representatives, open all the certificates and the votes shall then be counted;—The person having the greatest number of votes for President, shall be the President, if such number be a majority of the whole number of Electors appointed; and if no person have such majority, then from the persons having the highest numbers not exceeding three on the list of those voted for as President, the House of Representatives shall choose immediately, by ballot, the President. But in choosing the President, the votes shall be taken by states, the representation from each state having one vote; a quorum for this purpose shall consist of a member or members from two-thirds of the states, and a majority of all states shall be necessary to a choice. And if the House of Representatives shall not choose a President whenever the right of choice shall devolve upon them, before the fourth day of March next following, then the Vice-President shall act as President, as in the case of the death or other constitutional disability of the President.—The person having the greatest number of votes as Vice-President, shall be the Vice-President, if such number be a majority of the whole number of Electors appointed, and if no person have a majority, then from the two highest numbers on the list, the Senate shall choose the Vice-President; a quorum for the purpose shall consist of two-thirds of the whole number of Senators, and a majority of the whole number shall be necessary to a choice. But no person constitutionally ineligible to the office of President shall be eligible to that of Vice-President of the United States.

AMENDMENT XIII [1865]

Section 1.   Neither slavery nor involuntary servitude, except as a punishment for crime whereof the party shall have been duly convicted, shall exist within the United States, or any place subject to their jurisdiction.

Section 2.   Congress shall have power to enforce this article by appropriate legislation.

AMENDMENT XIV [1868]

Section 1.   All persons born or naturalized in the United States, and subject to the jurisdiction thereof, are citizens of the United States and of the State wherein they reside. No State shall make or enforce any law which shall abridge the privileges or immunities of citizens of the United States; nor shall any State deprive any person of life, liberty, or property, without due process of law; nor deny to any person within its jurisdiction the equal protection of the laws.

Section 2.   Representatives shall be apportioned among the several States according to their respective numbers, counting the whole number of persons in each State, excluding Indians not taxed. But when the right to vote at any election for the choice of electors for President and Vice President of the United States, Representatives in Congress, the Executive and Judicial officers of a State, or the members of the Legislature thereof, is denied to any of the male inhabitants of such State, being twenty-one years of age, and citizens of the United States, or in any way abridged, except for participation in rebellion, or other crime, the basis of representation therein shall be reduced in the proportion which the number of such male citizens shall bear to the whole number of male citizens twenty-one years of age in such State.

Section 3.   No person shall be a Senator or Representative in Congress, or elector of President and Vice President, or hold any office, civil or military, under the United States, or under any State, who having previously taken an oath, as a member of Congress, or as an officer of the United States, or as a member of any State legislature, or as an executive or judicial officer of any State, to support the Constitution of the United States, shall have engaged in insurrection or rebellion against the same, or given aid or comfort to the enemies thereof. But Congress may by a vote of two-thirds of each House, remove such disability.

Section 4.   The validity of the public debt of the United States, authorized by law, including debts incurred for payment of pensions and bounties for services in suppressing insurrection or rebellion, shall not be questioned. But neither the United States nor any State shall assume or pay any debt or obligation incurred in aid of insurrection or rebellion against the United States, or any claim for the loss or emancipation of any slave; but all such debts, obligations and claims shall be held illegal and void.

Section 5.   The Congress shall have power to enforce, by appropriate legislation, the provisions of this article.

AMENDMENT XV [1870]

Section 1.   The right of citizens of the United States to vote shall not be denied or abridged by the United States or by any State on account of race, color, or previous condition of servitude.

Section 2.   The Congress shall have power to enforce this article by appropriate legislation.

AMENDMENT XVI [1913]

The Congress shall have power to lay and collect taxes on incomes, from whatever source derived, without apportionment among the several States, and without regard to any census or enumeration.

AMENDMENT XVII [1913]

Section 1.   The Senate of the United States shall be composed of two Senators from each State, elected by the people thereof, for six years; and each Senator shall have one vote. The electors in each State shall have the qualifications requisite for electors of the most numerous branch of the State legislatures.

Section 2.   When vacancies happen in the representation of any State in the Senate, the executive authority of such State shall issue writs of election to fill such vacancies: *Provided*, That the legislature of any State may empower the executive thereof to make temporary appointments until the people fill the vacancies by election as the legislature may direct.

Section 3.   This amendment shall not be so construed as to affect the election or term of any Senator chosen before it becomes valid as part of the Constitution.

AMENDMENT XVIII [1919]

Section 1.   After one year from the ratification of this article the manufacture, sale, or transportation of intoxicating liquors within, the importation thereof into, or the exportation thereof from the United States and all territory subject to the jurisdiction thereof for beverage purposes is hereby prohibited.

Section 2.   The Congress and the several States shall have concurrent power to enforce this article by appropriate legislation.

Section 3.   This article shall be inoperative unless it shall have been ratified as an amendment to the Constitution by the legislatures of the several States, as provided in the Constitution, within seven years from the date of the submission hereof to the States by the Congress.

AMENDMENT XIX [1920]

Section 1.   The right of citizens of the United States to vote shall not be denied or abridged by the United States or by any State on account of sex.

Section 2.   Congress shall have power to enforce this article by appropriate legislation.

AMENDMENT XX [1933]

Section 1.   The terms of the President and Vice President shall end at noon on the 20th day of January, and the terms of Senators and Representatives at noon on the 3d day of January, of the years in which such terms would have ended if this article had not been ratified; and the terms of their successors shall then begin.

Section 2.   The Congress shall assemble at least once in every year, and such meeting shall begin at noon on the 3d day of January, unless they shall by law appoint a different day.

Section 3.   If, at the time fixed for the beginning of the term of the President, the President elect shall have died, the Vice President elect shall become President. If the President shall not have been chosen before the time fixed for the beginning of his term, or if the President elect shall have failed to qualify, then the Vice President elect shall act as President until a President shall have qualified; and the Congress may by law provide for the case wherein neither a President elect nor a Vice President elect shall have qualified, declaring who shall then act as President, or the manner in which one who is to act shall be selected, and such person shall act accordingly until a President or Vice President shall have qualified.

Section 4.   The Congress may by law provide for the case of the death of any of the persons from whom the House of Representatives may choose a President whenever the right of choice shall have devolved upon them, and for the case of the death of any of the persons from whom the Senate may choose a Vice President whenever the right of choice shall have devolved upon them.

Section 5.   Sections 1 and 2 shall take effect on the 15th day of October following the ratification of this article.

Section 6.   This article shall be inoperative unless it shall have been ratified as an amendment to the Constitution by the legislatures of three-fourths of the several States within seven years from the date of its submission.

AMENDMENT XXI [1933]

Section 1.   The eighteenth article of amendment to the Constitution of the United States is hereby repealed.

Section 2.   The transportation or importation into any State, Territory, or possession of the United States for delivery or use therein of intoxicating liquors, in violation of the laws thereof, is hereby prohibited.

Section 3.   This article shall be inoperative unless it shall have been ratified as an amendment to the Constitution by conventions in the several States, as provided in the Constitution, within seven years from the date of the submission hereof to the States by the Congress.

AMENDMENT XXII [1951]

Section 1.   No person shall be elected to the office of the President more than twice, and no person who has held the office of President, or acted as President, for more than two years of a term to which some other person was elected President shall be elected to the office of President more than once. But this Article shall not apply to any person holding the office of President when this Article was proposed by the Congress, and shall not prevent any person who may be holding the office of President, or acting as President, during the term within which this Article becomes operative from holding the office of President or acting as President during the remainder of such term.

Section 2.   This article shall be inoperative unless it shall have been ratified as an amendment to the Constitution by the legislatures of three-fourths of the several States within seven years from the date of its submission to the States by the Congress.

AMENDMENT XXIII [1961]

Section 1.   The District constituting the seat of Government of the United States shall appoint in such manner as the Congress may direct:
A number of electors of President and Vice President equal to the whole number of Senators and Representatives in Congress to which the District would be entitled if it were a State, but in no event more than the least populous state; they shall be in addition to those appointed by the states, but they shall be considered, for the purposes of the election of President and Vice

President, to be electors appointed by a state; and they shall meet in the District and perform such duties as provided by the twelfth article of amendment.

Section 2.   The Congress shall have power to enforce this article by appropriate legislation.

AMENDMENT XXIV [1964]

Section 1.   The right of citizens of the United States to vote in any primary or other election for President or Vice President, for electors for President or Vice President, or for Senator or Representative in Congress, shall not be denied or abridged by the United States, or any State by reason of failure to pay any poll tax or other tax.

Section 2.   The Congress shall have power to enforce this article by appropriate legislation.

AMENDMENT XXV [1967]

Section 1.   In case of the removal of the President from office or of his death or resignation, the Vice President shall become President.

Section 2.   Whenever there is a vacancy in the office of the Vice President, the President shall nominate a Vice President who shall take office upon confirmation by a majority vote of both Houses of Congress.

Section 3.   Whenever the President transmits to the President pro tempore of the Senate and the Speaker of the House of Representatives his written declaration that he is unable to discharge the powers and duties of his office, and until he transmits to them a written declaration to the contrary, such powers and duties shall be discharged by the Vice President as Acting President.

Section 4.   Whenever the Vice President and a majority of either the principal officers of the executive departments or of such other body as Congress may by law provide, transmit to the President pro tempore of the Senate and the Speaker of the House of Representatives their written declaration that the President is unable to discharge the powers and duties of his office, the Vice President shall immediately assume the powers and duties of the office as Acting President.

Thereafter, when the President transmits to the President pro tempore of the Senate and the Speaker of the House of Representatives his written declaration that no inability exists, he shall resume the powers and duties of his office unless the Vice President and a majority of either the principal officers of the executive department or of such other body as Congress may by law provide, transmit within four days to the President pro tempore of the Senate and the Speaker of the House of Representatives their written declaration and the President is unable to discharge the powers and duties of his office. Thereupon Congress shall decide the issue, assembling within forty-eight hours for that purpose if not in session. If the Congress, within twenty-one days after receipt of the latter written declaration, or, if Congress is not in session, within twenty-one days after Congress is required to assemble, determines by two-thirds vote of both Houses that the President is unable to discharge the powers and duties of his office, the Vice President shall continue to discharge the same as Acting President; otherwise, the President shall resume the powers and duties of his office.

AMENDMENT XXVI [1971]

Section 1.   The right of citizens of the United States, who are eighteen years of age or older, to vote shall not be denied or abridged by the United States or by any State on account of age.

Section 2.   The Congress shall have power to enforce this article by appropriate legislation.

AMENDMENT XXVII [1992]

No law, varying the compensation for the services of the Senators and Representatives, shall take effect, until an election of Representatives shall have intervened.

APPENDIX I

SPANISH EQUIVALENTS FOR IMPORTANT LEGAL TERMS IN ENGLISH

Abandoned property: bienes abandonados

Acceptance: aceptación; consentimivo; acuerdo

Acceptor: aceptante

Accession: toma de posesión; aumento; accesión

Accommodation indorser: avalista de favor

Accommodation party: firmante de favor

Accord: acuerdo; convenio; arregio

Accord and satisfaction: transacción ejecutada

Act of state doctrine: doctrina de acto de gobierno

Administrative law: derecho administrativo

Administrative process: procedimiento o metódo administrativo

Administrator: administrador (-a)

Adverse possession: posesión de hecho susceptible de proscripción adquisitiva

Affirmative action: acción afirmativa

Affirmative defense: defensa afirmativa

After-acquired property: bienes adquiridos con posterioridad a un hecho dado

Agency: mandato; agencia

Agent: mandatorio; agente; representante

Agreement: convenio; acuerdo; contrato

Alien corporation: empresa extranjera

Allonge: hojas adicionales de endosos

Answer: contestación de la demande; alegato

Anticipatory repudiation: anuncio previo de las partes de su imposibilidad de cumplir con el contrato

Appeal: apelación; recurso de apelación

Appellate jurisdiction: jurisdicción de apelaciones

Appraisal right: derecho de valuación

Arbitration: arbitraje

Arson: incendio intencional

Articles of partnership: contrato social

Artisan's lien: derecho de retención que ejerce al artesano

Assault: asalto; ataque; agresión

Assignment of rights: transmisión; transferencia; cesión

Assumption of risk: no resarcimiento por exposición voluntaria al peligro

Attachment: auto judicial que autoriza el embargo; embargo

Bailee: depositario

Bailment: depósito; constitución en depósito

Bailor: depositante

Bankruptcy trustee: síndico de la quiebra

Battery: agresión; física

Bearer: portador; tenedor

Bearer instrument: documento al portador

Bequest or legacy: legado (de bienes muebles)

Bilateral contract: contrato bilateral

Bill of lading: conocimiento de embarque; carta de porte

Bill of Rights: declaración de derechos

Binder: póliza de seguro provisoria; recibo de pago a cuenta del precio

Blank indorsement: endoso en blanco

Blue sky laws: leyes reguladoras del comercio bursátil

Bond: título de crédito; garantía; caución

Bond indenture: contrato de emisión de bonos; contrato del ampréstito

Breach of contract: incumplimiento de contrato

Brief: escrito; resumen; informe

Burglary: violación de domicilio

Business judgment rule: regla de juicio comercial

Business tort: agravio comercial

Case law: ley de casos; derecho casuístico

Cashier's check: cheque de caja

Causation in fact: causalidad en realidad

Cease-and-desist order: orden para cesar y desistir

Certificate of deposit: certificado de depósito

Certified check: cheque certificado

Charitable trust: fideicomiso para fines benéficos

Chattel: bien mueble

Check: cheque

Chose in action: derecho inmaterial; derecho de acción

Civil law: derecho civil

Close corporation: sociedad de un solo accionista o de un grupo restringido de accionistas

Closed shop: taller agremiado (emplea solamente a miembros de un gremio)

Closing argument: argumento al final

Codicil: codicilo

Collateral: garantía; bien objeto de la garantía real

Comity: cortesía; cortesía entre naciones

Commercial paper: instrumentos negociables; documentos a valores commerciales

Common law: derecho consuetudinario; derecho común; ley común

Common stock: acción ordinaria

Comparative negligence: negligencia comparada

Compensatory damages: daños y perjuicios reales o compensatorios

Concurrent conditions: condiciones concurrentes

Concurrent jurisdiction: competencia concurrente de varios tribunales para entender en una misma causa

Concurring opinion: opinión concurrente

Condition: condición

Condition precedent: condición suspensiva

Condition subsequent: condición resolutoria

Confiscation: confiscación

Confusion: confusión; fusión

Conglomerate merger: fusión de firmas que operan en distintos mercados

Consent decree: acuerdo entre las partes aprobado por un tribunal

Consequential damages: daños y perjuicios indirectos

Consideration: consideración; motivo; contraprestación

Consolidation: consolidación

Constructive delivery: entrega simbólica

Constructive trust: fideicomiso creado por aplicación de la ley

Consumer-protection law: ley para proteger el consumidor

Contract: contrato

Contract under seal: contrato formal o sellado

Contributory negligence: negligencia de la parte actora

Conversion: usurpación; conversión de valores

Copyright: derecho de autor

Corporation: sociedad anómina; corporación; persona juridica

Co-sureties: cogarantes

Counterclaim: reconvención; contrademanda

Counteroffer: contraoferta

Course of dealing: curso de transacciones

Course of performance: curso de cumplimiento

Covenant: pacto; garantía; contrato

Covenant not to sue: pacto or contrato a no demandar

Covenant of quiet enjoyment: garantía del uso y goce pacífico del inmueble

Creditors' composition agreement: concordato preventivo

Crime: crimen; delito; contravención

Criminal law: derecho penal

Cross-examination: contrainterrogatorio

Cure: cura; cuidado; derecho de remediar un vicio contractual

Customs receipts: recibos de derechos aduaneros

Damages: daños; indemnización por daños y perjuicios

Debit card: tarjeta de dé bito

Debtor: deudor

Debt securities: seguridades de deuda

Deceptive advertising: publicidad engañosa

Deed: escritura; título; acta translativa de domino

Defamation: difamación

Delegation of duties: delegación de obligaciones

Demand deposit: depósito a la vista

Depositions: declaración de un testigo fuera del tribunal

Devise: legado; deposición testamentaria (bienes inmuebles)

Directed verdict: veredicto según orden del juez y sin participación activa del jurado

Direct examination: interrogatorio directo; primer interrogatorio

Disaffirmance: repudiación; renuncia; anulación

Discharge: descargo; liberación; cumplimiento

Disclosed principal: mandante revelado

Discovery: descubrimiento; producción de la prueba

Dissenting opinion: opinión disidente

Dissolution: disolución; terminación

Diversity of citizenship: competencia de los tribunales federales para entender en causas cuyas partes intervinientes son cuidadanos de distintos estados

Divestiture: extinción premature de derechos reales

Dividend: dividendo
Docket: orden del día; lista de causas pendientes
Domestic corporation: sociedad local
Draft: orden de pago; letrade cambio
Drawee: girado; beneficiario
Drawer: librador
Duress: coacción; violencia

Easement: servidumbre
Embezzlement: desfalco; malversación
Eminent domain: poder de expropiación
Employment discrimination: discriminación en el empleo
Entrepreneur: empresario
Environmental law: ley ambiental
Equal dignity rule: regla de dignidad egual
Equity security: tipo de participación en una sociedad
Estate: propiedad; patrimonio; derecho
Estop: impedir; prevenir
Ethical issue: cuestión ética
Exclusive jurisdiction: competencia exclusiva
Exculpatory clause: cláusula eximente
Executed contract: contrato ejecutado
Execution: ejecución; cumplimiento
Executor: albacea
Executory contract: contrato aún no completamente consumado
Executory interest: derecho futuro
Express contract: contrato expreso
Expropriation: expropiación

Federal question: caso federal
Fee simple: pleno dominio; dominio absoluto
Fee simple absolute: dominio absoluto

Fee simple defeasible: dominio sujeta a una condición resolutoria
Felony: crimen; delito grave
Fictitious payee: beneficiario ficticio
Fiduciary: fiduciaro
Firm offer: oferta en firme
Fixture: inmueble por destino, incorporación a anexación
Floating lien: gravamen continuado
Foreign corporation: sociedad extranjera; U.S. sociedad constituída en otro estado
Forgery: falso; falsificación
Formal contract: contrato formal
Franchise: privilegio; franquicia; concesión
Franchisee: persona que recibe una concesión
Franchisor: persona que vende una concesión
Fraud: fraude; dolo; engaño
Future interest: bien futuro

Garnishment: embargo de derechos
General partner: socio comanditario
General warranty deed: escritura translativa de domino con garantía de título
Gift: donación
Gift *causa mortis*: donación por causa de muerte
Gift *inter vivos*: donación entre vivos
Good faith: buena fe
Good-faith purchaser: comprador de buena fe

Holder: tenedor por contraprestación
Holder in due course: tenedor legítimo
Holographic will: testamento ológrafo

Homestead exemption laws: leyes que exceptúan las casas de familia de ejecución por duedas generales
Horizontal merger: fusión horizontal

Identification: identificación
Implied-in-fact contract: contrato implícito en realidad
Implied warranty: guarantía implícita
Implied warranty of merchantability: garantía implícita de vendibilidad
Impossibility of performance: imposibilidad de cumplir un contrato
Imposter: imposter
Incidental beneficiary: beneficiario incidental; beneficiario secundario
Incidental damages: daños incidentales
Indictment: auto de acusación; acusación
Indorsee: endorsatario
Indorsement: endoso
Indorser: endosante
Informal contract: contrato no formal; contrato verbal
Information: acusación hecha por el ministerio público
Injunction: mandamiento; orden de no innovar
Innkeeper's lien: derecho de retención que ejerce el posadero
Installment contract: contrato de pago en cuotas
Insurable interest: interés asegurable
Intended beneficiary: beneficiario destinado
Intentional tort: agravio; cuasi-delito inteciónal
International law: derecho internaciónal
Interrogatories: preguntas escritas sometidas por una parte a la otra o a un testigo

***Inter vivos* trust:** fideicomiso entre vivos

Intestacy laws: leyes de la condición de morir intestado

Intestate: intestado

Investment company: compañia de inversiones

Issue: emisión

Joint tenancy: derechos conjuntos en un bien inmueble en favor del beneficiario sobreviviente

Judgment *n.o.v.*: juicio no obstante veredicto

Judgment rate of interest: interés de juicio

Judicial process: acto de procedimiento; proceso jurídico

Judicial review: revisión judicial

Jurisdiction: jurisdicción

Larceny: robo; hurto

Law: derecho; ley; jurisprudencia

Lease: contrato de locación; contrato de alquiler

Leasehold estate: bienes forales

Legal rate of interest: interés legal

Legatee: legatario

Letter of credit: carta de crédito

Levy: embargo; comiso

Libel: libelo; difamación escrita

Life estate: usufructo

Limited partner: comanditario

Limited partnership: sociedad en comandita

Liquidation: liquidación; realización

Lost property: objetos perdidos

Majority opinion: opinión de la mayoría

Maker: persona que realiza u ordena; librador

Mechanic's lien: gravamen de constructor

Mediation: mediación; intervención

Merger: fusión

Mirror image rule: fallo de reflejo

Misdemeanor: infracción; contravención

Mislaid property: bienes extraviados

Mitigation of damages: reducción de daños

Mortgage: hypoteca

Motion to dismiss: excepción parentoria

Mutual fund: fondo mutual

Negotiable instrument: instrumento negociable

Negotiation: negociación

Nominal damages: daños y perjuicios nominales

Novation: novación

Nuncupative will: testamento nuncupativo

Objective theory of contracts: teoria objetiva de contratos

Offer: oferta

Offeree: persona que recibe una oferta

Offeror: oferente

Order instrument: instrumento o documento a la orden

Original jurisdiction: jurisdicción de primera instancia

Output contract: contrato de producción

Parol evidence rule: regla relativa a la prueba oral

Partially disclosed principal: mandante revelado en parte

Partnership: sociedad colectiva; asociación; asociación de participación

Past consideration: causa o contraprestación anterior

Patent: patente; privilegio

Pattern or practice: muestra o práctica

Payee: beneficiario de un pago

Penalty: pena; penalidad

Per capita: por cabeza

Perfection: perfeción

Performance: cumplimiento; ejecución

Personal defenses: excepciones personales

Personal property: bienes muebles

Per stirpes: por estirpe

Plea bargaining: regateo por un alegato

Pleadings: alegatos

Pledge: prenda

Police powers: poderes de policia y de prevención del crimen

Policy: póliza

Positive law: derecho positivo; ley positiva

Possibility of reverter: posibilidad de reversión

Precedent: precedente

Preemptive right: derecho de prelación

Preferred stock: acciones preferidas

Premium: recompensa; prima

Presentment warranty: garantía de presentación

Price discrimination: discriminación en los precios

Principal: mandante; principal

Privity: nexo jurídico

Privity of contract: relación contractual

Probable cause: causa probable

Probate: verificación; verificación del testamento

Probate court: tribunal de sucesiones y tutelas

Proceeds: resultados; ingresos

Profit: beneficio; utilidad; lucro

Promise: promesa

Promisee: beneficiario de una promesa

Promisor: promtente

Promissory estoppel: impedimento promisorio

Promissory note: pagaré; nota de pago

Promoter: promotor; fundador
Proximate cause: causa inmediata o próxima
Proxy: apoderado; poder
Punitive, or exemplary, damages: daños y perjuicios punitivos o ejemplares

Qualified indorsement: endoso con reservas
Quasi contract: contrato tácito o implícito
Quitclaim deed: acto de transferencia de una propiedad por finiquito, pero sin ninguna garantía sobre la validez del título transferido

Ratification: ratificación
Real property: bienes inmuebles
Reasonable doubt: duda razonable
Rebuttal: refutación
Recognizance: promesa; compromiso; reconocimiento
Recording statutes: leyes estatales sobre registros oficiales
Redress: reporacíon
Reformation: rectificación; reforma; corrección
Rejoinder: dúplica; contrarréplica
Release: liberación; renuncia a un derecho
Remainder: substitución; reversión
Remedy: recurso; remedio; reparación
Replevin: acción reivindicatoria; reivindicación
Reply: réplica
Requirements contract: contrato de suministro
Rescission: rescisión
Res judicata: cosa juzgada; res judicata
Respondeat superior: responsabilidad del mandante o del maestro
Restitution: restitución

Restrictive indorsement: endoso restrictivo
Resulting trust: fideicomiso implícito
Reversion: reversión; sustitución
Revocation: revocación; derogación
Right of contribution: derecho de contribución
Right of reimbursement: derecho de reembolso
Right of subrogation: derecho de subrogación
Right-to-work law: ley de libertad de trabajo
Robbery: robo
Rule 10b-5: Regla 10b-5

Sale: venta; contrato de compreventa
Sale on approval: venta a ensayo; venta sujeta a la aprobación del comprador
Sale or return: venta con derecho de devolución
Sales contract: contrato de compraventa; boleto de compraventa
Satisfaction: satisfacción; pago
Scienter: a sabiendas
S corporation: S corporación
Secured party: acreedor garantizado
Secured transaction: transacción garantizada
Securities: volares; titulos; seguridades
Security agreement: convenio de seguridad
Security interest: interés en un bien dado en garantía que permite a quien lo detenta venderlo en caso de incumplimiento
Service mark: marca de identificación de servicios
Shareholder's derivative suit: acción judicial entablada por un accionista en nombre de la sociedad

Signature: firma; rúbrica
Slander: difamación oral; calumnia
Sovereign immunity: immunidad soberana
Special indorsement: endoso especial; endoso a la orden de una person en particular
Specific performance: ejecución precisa, según los términos del contrato
Spendthrift trust: fideicomiso para pródigos
Stale check: cheque vencido
Stare decisis: acatar las decisiones, observar los precedentes
Statutory law: derecho estatutario; derecho legislado; derecho escrito
Stock: acciones
Stock warrant: certificado para la compra de acciones
Stop-payment order: orden de suspensión del pago de un cheque dada por el librador del mismo
Strict liability: responsabilidad uncondicional
Summary judgment: fallo sumario

Tangible property: bienes corpóreos
Tenancy at will: inguilino por tiempo indeterminado (según la voluntad del propietario)
Tenancy by sufferance: posesión por tolerancia
Tenancy by the entirety: locación conyugal conjunta
Tenancy for years: inguilino por un término fijo
Tenancy in common: specie de copropiedad indivisa
Tender: oferta de pago; oferta de ejecución
Testamentary trust: fideicomiso testamentario

Testator: testador (-a)

Third party beneficiary contract: contrato para el beneficio del tercero-beneficiario

Tort: agravio; cuasi-delito

Totten trust: fideicomiso creado por un depósito bancario

Trade acceptance: letra de cambio aceptada

Trademark: marca registrada

Trade name: nombre comercial; razón social

Traveler's check: cheque del viajero

Trespass to land: ingreso no authorizado a las tierras de otro

Trespass to personal property: violación de los derechos posesorios de un tercero con respecto a bienes muebles

Trust: fideicomiso; trust

Ultra vires: ultra vires; fuera de la facultad (de una sociedad anónima)

Unanimous opinion: opinión unámine

Unconscionable contract or clause: contrato leonino; cláusula leonino

Underwriter: subscriptor; asegurador

Unenforceable contract: contrato que no se puede hacer cumplir

Unilateral contract: contrato unilateral

Union shop: taller agremiado; empresa en la que todos los empleados son miembros del gremio o sindicato

Universal defenses: defensas legitimas o legales

Usage of trade: uso comercial

Usury: usura

Valid contract: contrato válido

Venue: lugar; sede del proceso

Vertical merger: fusión vertical de empresas

Voidable contract: contrato anulable

Void contract: contrato nulo; contrato inválido, sin fuerza legal

Voir dire: examen preliminar de un testigo a jurado por el tribunal para determinar su competencia

Voting trust: fideicomiso para ejercer el derecho de voto

Waiver: renuncia; abandono

Warranty of habitability: garantía de habitabilidad

Watered stock: acciones diluídos; capital inflado

White-collar crime: crimen administrativo

Writ of attachment: mandamiento de ejecución; mandamiento de embargo

Writ of *certiorari*: auto de avocación; auto de certiorari

Writ of execution: auto ejecutivo; mandamiento de ejecutión

Writ of mandamus: auto de mandamus; mandamiento; orden judicial

GLOSSARY

ABA-approved Program   A legal or paralegal educational program that satisfies the standards for paralegal training set forth by the American Bar Association.

Active Listening   The act of listening attentively to the speaker's verbal or nonverbal messages and responding to those messages by giving appropriate feedback.

Address Block   That part of a letter that indicates to whom the letter is addressed. The address block is placed in the upper left-hand portion of the letter, above the salutation (or reference line, if one is included).

Administrative Agency   A federal or state government agency established to perform a specific function. Administrative agencies are authorized by legislative acts to make and enforce rules relating to the purpose for which they were established.

Administrative Law   A body of law created by administrative agencies—such as the Securities and Exchange Commission and the Federal Trade Commission—in the form of rules, regulations, orders, and decisions in order to carry out their duties and responsibilities.

Adversarial System of Justice   A legal system in which the parties to a lawsuit are opponents, or adversaries, and present their cases in a light most favorable to themselves. The court arrives at a just solution based on the evidence presented by the parties, or contestants, and determines who wins and who loses.

Adverse (Hostile) Witness   A witness for the opposing side in a lawsuit or other legal proceeding.

Advocate   As a verb, to assist, defend, or plead (argue) a cause for another. As a noun, a person (such as an attorney) who assists, defends, or pleads (argues) for another (such as a client) before a court.

Affidavit   A written statement of facts, confirmed by the oath or affirmation of the party making it and made before a person having the authority to administer the oath or affirmation.

Affiliate   An entity that is connected (affiliated) with another entity. State and local branches of national or regional paralegal associations are often referred to as affiliates.

Affirmative Defense   A response to a plaintiff's claim that does not deny the plaintiff's facts but attacks the plaintiff's legal right to bring an action.

Aggressive Communication   Stating one's opinions without concern for the thoughts, feelings, or rights of the listener.

Allegation   A party's statement, claim, or assertion made in a pleading to the court. The allegation sets forth the claim that the party expects to prove.

Alternative Dispute Resolution (ADR)   The resolution of disputes in ways other than those involved in the traditional judicial process. Negotiation, mediation, and arbitration are forms of ADR.

American Arbitration Association (AAA)   The major organization offering arbitration services in the United States.

American Bar Association (ABA)   A voluntary national association of attorneys. The ABA plays an active role in developing educational and ethical standards for attorneys and in pursuing improvements in the administration of justice.

Annotation   A brief statement, comment, or explanation of a legal point, which is found in a case digest or other legal source.

Answer   A defendant's response to a plaintiff's complaint.

Appeal   The process of seeking a higher court's review of a lower court's decision for the purpose of correcting or changing the lower court's judgment or decision.

Appellate Court   A court that reviews decisions made by lower courts, such as trial courts; a court of appeals.

Appellate Jurisdiction   The power of a court to hear and decide an appeal; that is, the power and authority of a court to review cases that already have been tried in a lower court and the power to make decisions about them without actually holding a trial. This process is called appellate review.

Application software   Computer programs designed to instruct the central processing unit on the operation and performance of certain tasks.

Arbitration   The settling of a dispute by submitting it to a disinterested third party (other than a court), who renders a legally binding decision.

Arbitration clause   A clause in a contract that provides that, in case of a dispute, the parties will determine their rights by arbitration rather than through the judicial system.

Assertive Communication   Stating one's opinions confidently but tactfully and with concern for the thoughts, feelings, and rights of the listener.

Associate Attorney   An attorney who is hired by a law firm as an employee and who has no ownership rights in the firm.

Associate's Degree   An academic degree signifying the completion of a two-year course of study, normally at a community college.

Attorney-client Privilege   A rule of evidence requiring that confidential communications between a client and his or her attorney (relating to their professional relationship) be kept confidential, unless the client consents to disclosure.

Bachelor's Degree   An academic degree signifying the completion of a four-year course of study at a college or university.

Bankruptcy Court   A federal court of limited jurisdiction that hears only bankruptcy proceedings.

Bankruptcy Law   The body of federal law that governs bankrupcy proceedings. The twin goals of bankruptcy law are (1) to protect a debtor by giving him or her a fresh start, free from creditors' claims; and (2) to ensure that creditors who are competing for a debtor's assets are treated fairly.

Bill of Rights   The first ten amendments to the Constitution.

Billable Hours   Hours or increments of hours that are billed directly to a client for legal services performed on behalf of that client.

Boilerplate   Certain terms or clauses that are normally included in specific types of legal documents.

Bonus   An end-of-the-year payment to a salaried employee in appreciation for that employee's overtime work, work quality, diligence, or dedication to the firm.

Breach   To violate a legal duty by an act or a failure to act.

Briefing a Case   Summarizing a case. A typical case brief will indicate the case title and citation and then briefly state the factual background and procedural history of the case, the issue or issues raised in the case, the court's decision, the applicable rule of law and the legal reasoning upon which the decision is based, and conclusions or notes concerning the case made by the one who is briefing it.

Case Law   Rules of law announced in court decisions. Case law includes the aggregate of reported cases that interpret judicial precedents, statutes, regulations, and constitutional provisions.

Case on "All Fours"   A case in which all four elements of a case (the parties, the circumstances, the legal issues involved, and the remedies sought) are very similar.

Case on Point   A case involving factual circumstances and issues that are similar to the case at bar (before the court).

Central Processing Unit (CPU)   The part of a computer that controls the function of the other computer components, stores the information contained in software programs, and executes the operator's keyboard commands.

Certification   Formal recognition by a private group or state agency that an individual has satisfied the group's standards of proficiency, knowledge, and competence; ordinarily accomplished through the taking of an examination.

Certified Legal Assistant (CLA)   A legal assistant whose legal competency has been certified by the National Association of Legal Assistants (NALA) following an examination that tests the legal assistant's knowledge and skills.

Certified Legal Assistant Specialist (CLAS)   A legal assistant whose competency in a legal specialty has been certified by the National Association of Legal Assistants (NALA) following an examination of the legal assistant's knowledge and skills in the specialty area.

Challenge   An attorney's objection, during *voir dire*, to the inclusion of a particular person on the jury.

Challenge for cause   A *voir dire* challenge for which an attorney states the reason why a prospective juror should not be included in the jury.

Charge   The judge's instruction to the jury following the attorneys' closing arguments setting forth the rules of law that the jury must apply in reaching its decision, or verdict.

Citation   In case law, a reference to the volume number, name, and page number of the reporter in which a case can be found. In statutory and administrative law, a reference to the title number, name, and section of the code in which a statute or regulation can be found.

Citator   A book or on-line service that provides the subsequent history and interpretation of a court decision, statute, or regulation and a list of the cases, statutes, and regulations that have interpreted, applied, or modified a statute or regulation.

Civil Law   The branch of law dealing with the definition and enforcement of all private or public rights, as opposed to criminal matters.

Closed-ended Question   A question that is phrased in such a way that it elicits a simple "yes" or "no" answer.

Closing   A final comment to a letter that is placed above the signature, such as "Very truly yours."

Closing Argument   An argument made by each side's attorney after the cases for the plaintiff and defendant have been presented. Closing arguments are made prior to the jury charge.

Code   A systematic and logical presentation of laws, rules, or regulations.

Codify   To collect and organize systematically and logically a body of concepts, principles, decisions, or doctrines.

Common Law   A body of law developed from custom or judicial decisions in English and U.S. courts and not attributable to a legislature.

Communication Skills   All skills that assist in the communication process. Speaking, reading, writing, and listening skills are all communication skills.

Complaint   The pleading made by a plaintiff or a charge made by the state alleging wrongdoing on the part of the defendant.

Concurrent Jurisdiction   Jurisdiction that exists when two different courts have the power to hear a case. For example, some cases can be heard in a federal or state court.

Confirmation Letter   A letter that states the substance of a previously conducted verbal discussion to provide a permanent record of the oral conversation.

Conflict of Interest   A situation in which two or more duties or interests come into conflict, as when an attorney attempts to represent opposing parties in a legal dispute.

Conflicts Check   A procedure for determining whether an agreement to represent a potential client will result in a conflict of interest.

Contingency Fee   A legal fee that consists of a specified percentage (such as 30 percent) of the amount the plaintiff recovers in a civil lawsuit or if a settlement is reached in the plaintiff's favor. The fee must be paid only if the plaintiff prevails in the lawsuit (recovers damages) or receives money in an out-of-court settlement.

Corporate Law   Law that governs the formation, financing, merger and acquisition, and termination of corporations, as well as the rights and duties of those who own and run the corporation.

Criminal Law   The branch of law that governs and defines those actions that are crimes and that subjects persons convicted of crimes to punishment imposed by the government.

Cross-examination   The questioning of an opposing witness during the trial.

Damages   Money sought as a remedy for a civil wrong, such as a breach of contract or a tortious act.

Database Management System   Software that makes it possible to store information in fields, records, and files for easy retrieval and manipulation by the operator.

Default Judgment   A judgment entered by a clerk or court against a party who has failed to appear in court to answer or defend against a claim that has been brought against him or her by another party.

Defendant   A party against whom a lawsuit is brought.

Demand Letter   An adversarial letter that attempts to persuade the reader that he or she should accept a position that is favorable to the writer's client—that is, demanding that the reader do or not do a certain thing.

Deponent   A party or witness who testifies under oath during a deposition.

Deposition   A pretrial question-and-answer proceeding, usually conducted orally, in which an a party or witness answers an attorney's questions. The answers are given under oath, and the session is recorded.

Deposition Transcript   The official transcription of the recording taken during a deposition.

Digest   A compilation in which brief statements regarding court cases are arranged by subject and subdivided by jurisdiction and courts.

Direct Examination   The examination of a witness by the attorney who calls the witness to the stand to testify on behalf of the attorney's client.

Disbarment   A severe disciplinary sanction in which an attorney's license to practice law in the state is revoked because of unethical or illegal conduct.

Discovery   Formal investigation prior to trial. During discovery, opposing parties use various methods, such as interrogatories and depositions, to obtain information from each other to prepare for trial.

Diversity of Citizenship   Under Article III, Section 2, of the Constitution, a basis for federal court jurisdiction over a lawsuit between certain parties, such as citizens of different states.

Docket   The list of cases entered on a court's calendar and thus scheduled to be heard by the court.

Double Billing   Billing more than one client for the same billable time.

E-mail   An abbreviation for electronic mail; an electronic message sent over a computer network from one computer terminal to another or others.

Employment Policy Manual   A firm's handbook or written statement that specifies the policies and procedures that govern the firm's employees and employer-employee relationships.

Enabling Legislation   Statutes enacted by Congress that authorize the creation of an administrative agency and specify the name, purpose, composition, and powers of the agency being created.

Environmental Law   All state and federal laws or regulations enacted or issued to protect the environment and preserve environmental resources.

Estate Planning   Making arrangements, during a person's lifetime, for the transfer of that person's property or obligations to others on the person's death. Estate planning often involves executing a will, establishing a trust fund, or taking out a life-insurance policy to provide for others, such as a spouse or children, on one's death.

Ethics   Moral principles and values applied to social behavior.

Exclusive Jurisdiction   Jurisdiction that exists when a case can be heard only in a particular court or type of court.

Expense Slip   A slip of paper on which any expense, or cost, that is incurred on behalf of a client (such as the payment of court fees or long-distance telephone charges) is recorded.

Expert Witness   A witness with professional training or substantial experience qualifying him or her to testify on a particular subject.

Eyewitness   A witness who testifies about an event that he or she observed or has experienced.

Family Law   Law relating to family matters, such as marriage, divorce, child support, and child custody.

Federal Question   A question that pertains to the U.S. Constitution, acts of Congress, or treaties. A federal question provides jurisdiction for federal courts. This jurisdiction arises from Article III, Section 2, of the Constitution.

Federal Rules of Civil Procedure (FRCP)   The rules controlling all procedural matters in civil trials brought before the federal district courts.

Feedback   A response from the person to whom a message has been sent indicating whether the receiver received and understood the message.

Fixed Fee   A fee paid to the attorney by his or her client for having rendered a specified legal service, such as the creation of a simple will.

Forms File   A reference file containing copies of the firm's commonly used legal documents and informational forms. The documents in the forms file serve as models for drafting new documents.

Freelance Paralegal   A paralegal who operates his or her own business and provides services to attorneys on a contractual basis. A freelance paralegal works under the supervision of an attorney, who assumes responsibility for the paralegal's work product.

Friendly Witness   A witness who gives voluntary testimony at an attorney's request on behalf of the attorney's client; a witness who is prejudiced against the client's adversary.

General Licensing   A type of licensing in which all individuals within a specific profession or group (such as paralegals) must meet licensing requirements imposed by the state before they may legally practice their profession.

Hard Drive   A unit that enables a personal computer to store software programs and data files in permanent memory. The hard drive contains a hard disk.

Hardware   The physical components (mechanical, magnetic, electronic, and so on) of the computer, including the computer itself, the keyboard, the monitor, and other peripheral devices attached to the computer.

Headnote   A note near the beginning of a reported case summarizing the court's ruling on an issue.

Hypothetical Question   A question based on hypothesis, conjecture, or fiction.

Impeach   To call into question the credibility of a witness by challenging the truth or accuracy of his or her trial statement.

Independent Paralegal   A paralegal who offers services directly to the public, normally for a fee, without attorney supervision. Independent paralegals assist consumers by supplying them with forms and procedural knowledge relating to simple or routine legal procedures.

Informative Letter   A letter that conveys certain information to a client, a witness, an adversary's counsel, or other person regarding some legal matter (such as the date, time, place, and purpose of a meeting).

Intellectual Property   Property that consists of the products of individuals' minds—products that result from intellectual, creative processes. Copyrights, patents, and trademarks are examples of intellectual property.

Interrogatories   A series of written questions for which written answers are prepared and then signed under oath by a party to a lawsuit (the plaintiff or the defendant).

Interviewee   The person who is being interviewed.

Investigation Plan   A plan that lists each step involved in obtaining and verifying the facts and information that are relevant to the legal problem being investigated.

IRAC Method   IRAC is a mnemonic for issue, rule, application, and conclusion. The IRAC method helps legal researchers and writers focus on the four critical elements of a case.

Judgment   The court's final decision regarding the rights and claims of the parties to a lawsuit.

Jurisdiction The authority of a court to hear and decide a specific action.

Keyboard A computer input device with alpha-numeric characters (arranged similarly to the traditional type-writer) and function keys.

Law A body of rules of conduct with legal force and effect, prescribed by the controlling authority (the government) of a society.

Law Clerk In the context of law-office work, a law student who works as an apprentice, during the summer or part-time during the school year, with an attorney or law firm to gain practical legal experience.

Lay Witness A witness who can truthfully and accurately testify on a fact in question without having specialized training or knowledge; an ordinary witness.

Leading Question A question that suggests, or "leads to," a desired answer. Leading questions are used to elicit responses from witnesses who otherwise would not be forthcoming.

Legal Administrator An administrative employee of a law firm who manages the day-to-day operations of the firm. In smaller law firms, legal administrators are usually called office managers.

Legal Assistant A person sufficiently trained or experienced in the law and legal procedures to assist, under an attorney's supervision, in the performance of substantive legal work that would otherwise be performed by an attorney. Often referred to as a paralegal.

Legal Ethics The principles, values, and rules of conduct that govern legal professionals.

Legal-assistant Manager An employee who is responsible for overseeing the paralegal staff and paralegal professional development.

Licensing A government's official act of granting permission to an individual, such as an attorney, to do something that would be illegal in the absence of such permission.

Limited Licensing A type of licensing in which a limited number of individuals within a specific profession or group (such as independent paralegals within the paralegal profession) must meet licensing requirements imposed by the state before those individuals may legally practice their profession.

Litigation The process of working a lawsuit through the court system.

Litigation Paralegals Paralegals who specialize in assisting attorneys in the litigation process.

Local Area Network (LAN) A system of physically dispersed computers that are interconnected, via telecommunications, within a local area, such as an office building. Users at each connected computer can share information and software with other computers connected to the network.

Long-arm Statute A state statute that permits a state to obtain jurisdiction over nonresident individuals and corporations. Individuals or corporations, however, must have certain "minimum contacts" with that state for the statute to apply.

Mainframe Computer A large, centralized computer processing unit that can service multiple terminals simultaneously and that is capable of storing, handling, and retrieving vast amounts of data (used by large organizations, such as megafirms, government agencies, and universities).

Malpractice Professional misconduct or negligence—the failure to exercise due care—on the part of a professional, such as an attorney or a physician.

Managing Partner The partner in a law firm who makes decisions relating to the firm's policies and procedures and who generally oversees the business operations of the firm.

Mandatory Authority Any source of law that a court must follow when deciding a case. Mandatory authorities include constitutions, statutes, and regulations that govern the issue at bar and court decisions made by a superior court in the jurisdiction.

Mediation A method of settling disputes outside of court by using the services of a neutral third party, who acts as a communicating agent between the parties; a method of dispute settlement that is less formal than arbitration.

Memorandum of Law A document (known as a **brief** in some states) that delineates the legal theories, statutes, and cases on which a motion is based.

Mini-trial A private proceeding that assists disputing parties in determining whether to take their case to court. During the proceeding, each party's attorney briefly argues the party's case before the other party and (usually) a neutral third party, who acts as an adviser. If the parties fail to reach an agreement, the adviser renders an opinion as to how a court would likely decide the issue.

Minicomputer A computer with more power and capacity than a microcomputer but less than a mainframe computer. Like the mainframe, the minicomputer (server) can be connected to a number of terminals (clients) simultaneously.

Modem A device that converts the computer's digital signals into analog sound waves and vice versa so that messages can be transmitted and received over a telephone line. Using a modem and communications software, a user can transfer information from one computer to another via a phone line.

Monitor A black-and-white or multicolor display screen that displays the current activities of the computer.

Motion A procedural request or application presented by an attorney to the court on behalf of a client.

Motion for a Directed Verdict In a jury trial, a motion (also referred to as a motion for judgment as a matter of law in federal courts) for the judge to take the decision out of the hands of the jury and direct a verdict for the party making the motion on the ground that the other party has not produced sufficient evidence to support his or her claim.

Motion for a New Trial A motion asserting that the trial was so fundamentally flawed (because of error, newly discovered evidence, prejudice, or other reason) that a new trial is needed to prevent a miscarriage of justice.

Motion for Judgment as a Matter of Law A motion requesting that the court grant judgment in favor of the party making the motion on the ground that the other party has not produced sufficient evidence to support his or her claim.

Motion for Judgment Notwithstanding the Verdict A motion (also referred to as a motion for judgment as a matter of law in federal courts) requesting that the court grant judgment in favor of the party making the motion on the ground that the jury verdict against him or her was unreasonable and erroneous.

Motion for Judgment on the Pleadings A motion, which can be brought by either party to a lawsuit after the pleadings are closed, for the court to decide the issue without proceeding to trial. The motion will be granted only if no facts are in dispute and the only issue concerns how the law applies to a set of undisputed facts.

Motion for Summary Judgment A motion requesting the court to enter a judgment without proceeding to trial. The motion can be based on evidence outside the pleadings and will be granted only if no facts are in dispute and the only issue concerns how the law applies to a set of undisputed facts.

Motion to Dismiss A pleading in which a defendant admits the facts as alleged by the plaintiff but asserts that the plaintiff's claim fails to state a cause of action (that is, has no basis in law) or that there are other grounds on which a suit should be dismissed.

Mouse A device that lets a computer user move the cursor's position on the monitor and give commands to the computer without using a keyboard.

National Association of Legal Assistants (NALA) One of the two largest national paralegal associations in the United States; formed in 1975. NALA offers a certification program for paralegals and is actively involved in paralegal professional developments.

National Federation of Paralegal Associations (NFPA) One of the two largest national paralegal associations in the United States; formed in 1974. NFPA is actively involved in paralegal professional developments.

Negligence The failure to exercise the standard of care that a reasonable person would exercise in similar circumstances; in legal practice, the failure to fulfill professional duties.

Negotiation A method of alternative dispute resolution in which disputing parties, with or without the assistance of their attorneys, meet informally to resolve the dispute out of court.

Nonverbal Communication The sending and receiving of messages without using language. Nonverbal communication includes body language (such as facial gestures) and utterances or sounds that do not consist of words.

Office Manager An administrative employee who manages the day-to-day operations of a business firm. In larger law firms, office managers are usually called legal administrators.

Open-ended Question A question that is phrased in such a way that it elicits a relatively detailed discussion of an experience or event.

Opening Statement An attorney's statement to the jury at the beginning of the trial. The attorney briefly outlines the evidence that will be offered during the trial and the legal theory that will be pursued.

Operating-system Software A program allowing the computer to control the sequencing and processing of application software programs so that the computer responds correctly to the operator's commands.

Opinion A statement by the court expressing the reasons for its decision in a case.

Opinion (Advisory) Letter A letter from an attorney to a client that contains a legal opinion on an issue raised by the client's question or legal claim. The opinion is based on a detailed analysis of the law.

Ordinance An order, rule, or law enacted by a municipal or county government to govern a local matter unaddressed by state or federal legislation.

Original Jurisdiction The power of a court to take a case, try it, and decide it.

Out Card A large card inserted in a filing cabinet in the place of a temporarily removed file. The out card notifies others who may need the file of the name of the person who has the file and the time and date that the file was removed.

Overtime Wages Wages paid to workers who are paid an hourly wage rate to compensate them for overtime work (hours worked beyond forty hours per week). Under federal law, overtime wages are at least one and a half times the regular hourly wage rate.

Paralegal A person sufficiently trained or experienced in the law and legal procedures to assist, under an attorney's supervision, in the performance of substantive legal work that would otherwise be performed by an attorney. Often referred to as a legal assistant.

Paralegal Certificate A certificate awarded to an individual with a high school diploma or its equivalent who has successfully completed a paralegal program of study at a private, for-profit business school or trade school.

Parallel Citation   A second (or third) citation to another case reporter in which a case has been published. When a case is published in more than one reporter, each citation is a parallel citation to the other(s).

Partner   A person who has undertaken to operate a business jointly with one or more other persons. Each partner is a co-owner of the business firm.

Partnership   An association of two or more persons to carry on, as co-owners, a business for profit.

Peremptory Challenge   A *voir dire* challenge to exclude a potential juror from serving on the jury without any supporting reason or cause. Peremptory challenges based on racial or gender criteria are illegal.

Personal Computer (PC)   A desktop computer, or microcomputer, with its own central processing unit, which is ordinarily used for applications that are tailored to the user's employment, domestic, or educational needs.

Personal Liability   An individual's personal responsibility for debts or obligations. The owners of sole proprietorships and partnerships are personally liable for the debts and obligations incurred by their business firms. If their firms go bankrupt or cannot meet debts as they become due, the owners will be personally responsible for paying the debts.

Personal Time Diary   A journal or notebook used by paralegals and attorneys to record and track the hours (or fractions of hours) worked and the tasks completed on behalf of each client.

Persuasive Authority   Any legal authority, or source of law, that a court may look to for guidance but on which it need not rely in making its decision. Persuasive authorities include cases from other jurisdictions and secondary sources of law, such as scholarly treatises.

Plaintiff   A party who initiates a lawsuit.

Pleadings   Statements by the plaintiff and the defendant that detail the facts, charges, and defenses involved in the litigation.

Pocket Part   A separate pamphlet containing recent cases or changes in the law that is used to update hornbooks, legal encyclopedias, and other legal authorities. It is called a "pocket part" because it slips into a sleeve, or pocket, in the back binder of the volume.

Postbaccalaureate Certificate   A postgraduate certificate awarded by a college or university to an individual who, having already completed a bachelor's degree program, successfully completes a paralegal program of study.

Precedent   A court decision that furnishes an example or authority for deciding subsequent cases in which identical or similar facts are presented.

Pressure Question   A question intended to make the interviewee feel uncomfortable and respond emotionally.

Pressure questions are sometimes used by interviewers to elicit answers from interviewees who may otherwise be unresponsive.

Pretrial Conference   A conference prior to trial in which the judge and the attorneys litigating the suit discuss settlement possibilities, clarify the issues in dispute, and schedule forthcoming trial-related events.

Primary Source   In legal research, a document that establishes the law on a particular issue, such as a case decision, legislative act, administrative rule, or presidential order.

Privileged Information   Confidential communications between certain individuals, such as an attorney and his or her client, that are protected from disclosure except under court order.

Pro Bono Publico   Legal services provided for free or at a reduced fee by an attorney or paralegal to persons of limited financial means in need of legal assistance.

Probate   The process of "proving" the validity of a will and ensuring that the instructions in a valid will are carried out.

Probate Court   A court having jurisdiction over proceedings concerning the settlement of a deceased person's estate.

Procedural Law   Rules that define the manner in which the rights and duties of individuals may be enforced.

Profession   An occupation requiring knowledge of the arts or sciences and advanced study in a specialized field, such as the law.

Professional Corporation (P.C.)   A business form in which shareholders (those who purchase the corporation's stock, or shares) own the firm and share in the profits and losses of the firm in proportion to how many shares they own. Their personal liability, unlike that of partners, is limited to the amount of their investment.

Real Estate   Land and things permanently attached to the land, such as houses, buildings, and trees and foliage.

Recross-examination   The questioning of an opposing witness following the adverse party's redirect examination.

Redirect Examination   The questioning of a witness following the adverse party's cross-examination.

Reference Line   The portion of the letter that indicates the matter to be discussed in the letter, such as "RE: Summary of Cases Applying the Family and Medical Leave Act of 1993." The reference line is placed just below the address block and above the salutation.

Reporter   A publication in which court cases are published, or reported.

Reprimand   A disciplinary sanction in which an attorney is rebuked for his or her misbehavior. Although a reprimand is the mildest sanction for attorney misconduct, it is nonetheless a serious one and may significantly damage the attorney's reputation in the legal community.

Responsible Billing Partner   The partner in a law firm who is responsible for overseeing a particular client's case and the billing of that client.

Retainer   An advance payment made by a client to a law firm to cover part of the legal fee and/or costs that will need to be incurred on that client's behalf.

Retainer Agreement   A signed document stating that the attorney or the law firm has been hired by the client to provide certain legal services and that the client agrees to pay for those services in accordance with the terms set forth in the retainer agreement.

Retentive Listening   The act of listening attentively to what the speaker is saying for the purpose of remembering, or retaining, the information communicated.

Return-of-service Form   A document signed by a process server and submitted to the court to prove that a defendant received a summons.

Salutation   The formal greeting to the addressee of the letter. The salutation is placed just below the reference line.

Scheduling Conference   A meeting (conducted shortly after a plaintiff's complaint is filed) attended by the judge and the attorneys for both parties to the lawsuit. Following the conference, the judge issues a scheduling order for the pretrial events and the trial itself.

Secondary Source   In legal research, any publication that indexes, summarizes, or interprets the law, such as a legal encyclopedia, a treatise, or an article in a law review.

Security Code (Password)   A predetermined series of numbers and/or letter characters that an authorized user keys in to gain access to a computer system or data contained in computer files.

Self-regulation   The regulation of the conduct of a professional group by members of the group themselves. Self-regulation usually involves the establishment of ethical or professional standards of behavior with which members of the group must comply.

Service of Process   The delivery of and the summons and the complaint to a defendant.

Settlement   An out-of-court resolution to a legal dispute, which is agreed to by the parties in writing. A settlement agreement may be reached at any time prior to or during a trial.

Shareholder   One who purchases corporate stock, or shares, and who thus becomes an owner of the corporation.

Software   Computer programs that instruct and control the computer's hardware and operations.

Sole Proprietorship   The simplest form of business, in which the owner is the business. Anyone who does business without creating a formal business entity has a sole proprietorship.

Spreadsheet Program   A computer program that completes calculations, does numerical tracking, and allows the operator to manipulate numeric data for statistical and reporting purposes (such as budget reporting).

Stare Decisis   A flexible doctrine of the courts, recognizing the value of following prior decisions (precedents) in cases similar to the one before the court; the courts' practice of being consistent with prior decisions in cases involving similar facts.

State Bar Association   An association of attorneys within a state. Membership in the state bar association is mandatory in over two-thirds of the states—that is, before an attorney can practice law in a state, he or she must be admitted to that state's bar association.

Statute   A written law enacted by a legislature under its constitutional lawmaking authority.

Statute of Limitations   A statute setting the maximum time period within which certain actions can be brought or rights enforced. After the period set out in the applicable statute of limitations has run, normally no legal action can be brought.

Statutory Law   Laws enacted by a legislative body.

Subpoena   A document commanding a person to appear at a certain time and place to give testimony concerning a certain matter.

Substantive Law   Law that defines the rights and duties of individuals with respect to each other, as opposed to procedural law, which defines the manner in which these rights and duties may be enforced.

Summary Jury Trial (SJT)   A relatively recent method of settling disputes in which a trial is held but the jury's verdict is not binding. The verdict only acts as a guide to both sides in reaching an agreement during the mandatory negotiations that immediately follow the trial. If a settlement is not reached, both sides have the right to a full trial later.

Summons   A document served on a defendant in a lawsuit informing a defendant that a legal action has been commenced against the defendant and that the defendant must appear in court on a certain date to answer the plaintiff's complaint.

Support Personnel   Those employees who provide clerical, secretarial, or other support to the legal, paralegal, and administrative staff of a law firm.

Supportive Listening   The act of providing comments, utterances, or gestures that convey to the speaker an interest in what the speaker is saying and that encourage the speaker to continue speaking.

Suspension   A serious disciplinary sanction in which an attorney who has violated an ethical rule or a law is prohibited from the practice of law in the state for a specified or an indefinite period of time.

Syllabus   A brief summary of the holding and legal principles involved in a reported case, which is followed by the court's official opinion.

Third Party In the context of legal proceedings, a party who is not directly involved in the proceeding—that is, a party other than the plaintiff and defendant and their attorneys.

Time Slip A record documenting, for billing purposes, the hours (or fractions of hours) that an attorney or a paralegal worked for each client, the date on which the work was done, and the type of work that was undertaken.

Tort A civil wrong, other than a breach of contract; a breach of a legally imposed duty.

Treatise In legal research, a text, such as a hornbook, that provides a systematic, detailed, and scholarly review of a particular legal subject.

Trial Court A court in which most cases usually begin and in which questions of fact are examined.

Trial Notebook A binder that contains copies of all of the documents and information that an attorney will need to have at hand during the trial.

Trust An arrangement in which title to property is held by one person (a trustee) for the benefit of another (a beneficiary).

Trust Account A bank or escrow account in which one party (the trustee, such as an attorney) holds funds belonging to another person (such as a client); a bank account into which funds advanced to a law firm by a client are deposited.

Unauthorized Practice of Law (UPL) Engaging in actions defined by a legal authority, such as a state legislature, as constituting the "practice of law" without legal authorization to do so.

User Interface The computer connection, or link, between the software and the hardware that controls the image that an operator views on the monitor and the method of accomplishing a given task.

Venue The geographical district in which an action is tried and from which the jury is selected.

Verbal Communication The sending and receiving of messages using spoken or written words.

Verdict A formal decision made by a jury.

Voir Dire A French phrase meaning "to speak the truth." The phrase is used to describe the preliminary questions that attorneys for the plaintiff and the defendant ask prospective jurors to determine whether potential jury members are biased or have any connection with a party to the action or with a prospective witness.

Wide Area Network (WAN) A system of computers, physically dispersed over a large geographical area, in which the users are able to communicate directly with each other via computer.

Will A document directing what is to be done with the maker's property upon his or her death.

Witness A person who is asked to testify under oath at a trial.

Witness Statement The written transcription of a statement made by the witness during an interview and signed by the witness.

Word-processing Software Specialized application software that allows a computer user to create, edit, revise, save, and generally manipulate textual material and document formatting.

Work Product An attorney's mental impressions, conclusions, and legal theories regarding a case being prepared on behalf of a client. Work product normally is regarded as privileged information.

Workers' Compensation Statutes State laws establishing an administrative procedure for compensating workers for injuries that arise in the course of their employment.

Writ of Certiorari A writ from a higher court asking the lower court for the record of a case.

INDEX

PHOTO CREDITS AND ACKNOWLEDGMENTS

The publisher gratefully acknowledges the contributions provided by the many individuals who appear in the Paralegal Profiles and Featured Guests sections of the book—the cooperation they extended and the photographs they supplied are greatly appreciated.

Chapter Opening Images: 2 © Rommel, Masterfile; 28 © PBJ Pictures, Liason International; 58 © Larry Williams, Masterfile; 98 © Sam Sargent, Liaison International; 134 © J.A. Kraulis, Masterfile; 168 © John Chiasson, Gamma Liaison; 214 © Frank Fisher, Liaison International; 254 © Paul Figura, Liaison International; 292 © Ed Malitsky, Liaison International.

Exhibits 2.1 and 2.2 Copyright 1993, James Publishing, Inc. Reprinted with permission from *Legal Assistant Today*. For subscription information call 714–755–5450. **Exhibits 3.1, 3.2, and Appendix E** reprinted with permission from the American Bar Association. (Includes *Model Guidelines for the Utilization of Legal Assistant Services*, 9 Canons of Legal Ethics from *Model Code of Professional Responsibility and Code of Judicial Conduct*; Rule 1.6 and Headings from *Model Rules of Professional Conduct*. Copies of these publications are available from Member Services, American Bar Association, 541 North Fair Banks, Chicago, IL 60611.) **Exhibit 3.3 and Appendix D** reprinted with permission of NFPA. **Exhibit 3.4, Appendices B, C, and G** reprinted with permission from NALA. **Exhibit 8.1** photo courtesy of IBM; **Exhibit 8.2** photo courtesy of DEC Corporation; **Exhibit 8.3** photo courtesy of IBM; **Exhibit 8.4** photo courtesy of Microtech Corporation; **Exhibit 8.7** photo courtesy of 3M Corporation; **Exhibit 8.8** photo by Liane Enkelis; **Exhibit 8.13** courtesy of Micro Craft, Inc. Used with permission; **Exhibit 8.14** © Lotus Development Corporation. Used with permission; **Exhibit 9.12** reproduced by permission of Shepard's McGraw–Hill, Inc. Further reproduction is strictly prohibited.